Joy with Java

Understanding object-oriented programming is vital for a modern computer programmer, and the Java programming language has been one of the most powerful tools available to computer programmers since its inception in 1995. It has also consistently changed since then, making it a vast and powerful resource for object-oriented programming today, finding many applications like mobile programming, Internet programming and software development.

This lucid textbook introduces the student not only to the nuances of object-oriented programming, but also to the many syntaxes and semantics of the modern Java language. Each concept of programming is explained, and then illustrated with small but effective ready-to-run programs. Important points to be noted have been emphasized and hints have been given at the end of each discussion so that programmers are careful to avoid common pitfalls. Finally, a number of practice problems taken from real world scenarios encourage the student to think in terms of problem solving, consolidating the knowledge gained.

Some key features of the book include:

- A pedagogy-rich treatment of programming in the Java language.
- Complete coverage of all syntaxes, semantics and principles.
- Important points and typical pitfalls are highlighted in simple and succinct language.
- Frequently asked questions, over and above the normal discussions, are added at the end of every chapter.
- Short annotations alongside discussions help students understand the concepts better.
- Practice problems and a large variety of questions, including MCQs, help consolidate the knowledge gained.
- Includes an online supplements package comprising solutions to the practice problems and correct outputs of each programme for students and lecture slides for instructors.

Debasis Samanta is Professor, Department of Computer Science and Engineering, at the Indian Institute of Technology Kharagpur, India. His areas of interest include human computer interaction, biometric security and data analytics.

Monalisa Sarma is Assistant Professor, Subir Chowdhury School of Quality and Reliability, at the Indian Institute of Technology Kharagpur, India. Her areas of interest include big data analytics, software testing and verification, and human reliability analysis.

Joy with Java

Fundamentals of Object Oriented Programming

Debasis Samanta

Monalisa Sarma

CAMBRIDGE
UNIVERSITY PRESS

University Printing House, Cambridge CB2 8BS, United Kingdom

One Liberty Plaza, 20th Floor, New York, NY 10006, USA

477 Williamstown Road, Port Melbourne, VIC 3207, Australia

314–321, 3rd Floor, Plot 3, Splendor Forum, Jasola District Centre, New Delhi – 110025, India

103 Penang Road, #05–06/07, Visioncrest Commercial, Singapore 238467

Cambridge University Press is part of the University of Cambridge.

It furthers the University's mission by disseminating knowledge in the pursuit of education, learning and research at the highest international levels of excellence.

www.cambridge.org
Information on this title: www.cambridge.org/9781009211918

First published 2023

Printed in India

A catalogue record for this publication is available from the British Library

ISBN 978-1-009-21191-8 Paperback

To

Maa

The most admirable person in our life

Contents

Figures

Tables

Programs

SYMBOLS

Indicates that the adjoining discussion should be noted as important.

Indicates that the adjoining discussion should be noted carefully and the point(s) is(are) important while writing programs.

PREFACE

Welcome to the wonderful world of Java programming and thank you for your interest in this book. We would like to share some thoughts behind writing this book.

Background

With the growth of Information and Communication Technology (ICT), there is a need to develop large and complex software. To meet this requirement, object-oriented programming paradigms are popular among software professionals. The software is required to be platform independent, Internet enabled, easy to modify and update, secure, and robust. To cater to all these requirements, Java programming language appears to be the most suitable object-oriented programming language as it meets all these requirements. Java was developed by Sun Microsystems in 1995 and has emerged as the best programming environment according to the *Time* magazine. Today, Java is used for mobile programming, Internet programming, software development, and for numerous other applications in distributed systems and commercial hardware products. This book aims to cover the essential features of Java programming so that software professionals can improve their skills to cope with the current demands of the IT industry. In addition, this book can help students and faculty members to learn the programming language with the minimum effort and solve many problems in their fields.

Why This Book?

The need: Java is vast. Unlike other programming languages, Java is constantly evolving. The latest version, *Java 14* or *JDK 14*, was released on March 17, 2020. With every new release, many features are deprecated and many new features are added. Developers keep on adding new features so that the programming language can meet the changing needs of the software industry. Thus Java has become vast, with a large number of features. However, this is at the cost of increasing the difficulty in learning the language. It is not easy for programmers to grasp the numerous syntaxes and semantics that the language contains in its present form. As experienced teachers of Computer Science and Engineering, we know how to modulate a discussion so that learners can grasp the concepts with minimum cognitive load. The learners need to feel they have the competence to learn and start loving the language. In our opinion, existing books fail to do so. Hence the need of a new book like this.

Full Length coverage: Often, some (difficult) discussions are either ignored or covered superficially in books. This causes trouble to the readers for it involves extra effort to search for answers elsewhere; sometimes this defocuses their attention. We feel that each discussion should be complete at one go, without avoiding any major or critical insights into the language.

Balance approach for different learning capabilities: There is a need to take care the learners at all levels of learning capabilities. A thorough discussion is required for the students with lower learning capabilities, whereas a short discussion is enough for students with moderate to a higher level of learning capabilities. If the major points are emphasized, then students can skip or read the rest depending on their own level of understanding. This is particularly important to enable them to learn a vast programming language like Java. In our survey, the existing books failed to ensure this.

Learning with appropriate assignments: For effective learning, a student must solve problems. This requires a careful selection of problems. The problems should be relevant and pinpoint the important part of the discussion. Further, problems should be small so that unnecessary efforts can be avoided. This book includes many "Programs for Practice" in each chapter, to achieve this.

Companion guide: The authors of this book believe that reinforced learning is the best way to achieve confidence and competency in learning a procedure. In classroom teaching and in the laboratory, "teach and ask" has no alternative and is also a proven method in interactive teaching. This also enables *back-and-forth* reading, ensuring more maturity and confidence in the topics. While writing this book, we were highly influenced by this concept and planned its contents to give a feeling to the students that they were learning in the presence of their teacher. Indeed, this book is truly an alternative to a teacher-led teaching and works as a companion guide.

How is this book different from others?

Some unique features of the book are:

- *More pedagogical:* Each topic is discussed with easy-to-understand, simple, effective, and ready-to-run programs.
- *Complete coverage:* Full coverage of all syntaxes, semantics, and programming languages principles.
- *Discussion with comments:* Each discussion in the book is annotated with short comments which helps the learners to read according to their levels of understanding.
- *Highlights of the major points:* Important points that programmers should note while they are learning particular programming feature are highlighted in brief and in a to-the-point manner.

- *Smooth flow of discussions:* Sections (and subsections) are planned maintaining a smooth flow of discussions. Sufficient tables and figures are added making each discussion complete and suitable for both the beginners as well as the advanced readers.
- *FAQs:* There are some frequently asked questions, which may be beyond the normal discussions. All such FAQs are also important for students appearing for job interviews. The FAQs are added at the end of each chapter. This also helps to get a quick glimpse of the chapter.
- *Programs for practice:* Each chapter has a number of small yet effective programs for practice so that after learning a lesson, the readers can practice and hone their programming skills.
- *Comprehensive aptitude test questions:* A set of objective-type multiple choice questions (MCQs) are included at the end of each chapter. Such MCQs are a first-of-their-kind in programming books.
- *Writing with simple English:* Simple English is followed throughout which helps the reader to enjoy reading the book, in particular those whose first language is not English.
- *Novel presentation style:* Last but the least, a novel format and style is followed, giving an attractive look to the contents. Also, a sufficient space is provided so that the learners can annotate their own thoughts or important points they feel they need to note down while they read the book.

Who can be benefitted?

This book is suitable for the students of undergraduate and graduate studies from any discipline, including Computer Science and Engineering, Electrical Engineering, Electronics and Communication Engineering, Information Technology, and so on. Apart from the students, software engineers working in software development firms or those who wish to build their career in IT product development will be highly benefitted by reading this book. This book is useful to those who are keen to design and develop apps for personalized digital devices, mobile devices, systems software for appliances, etc. Many universities and engineering colleges around the globe add courses like Computer Programming, Object-Oriented Analysis and Design, Distributed Computing, Internet Programming, etc. This book can be considered as the textbook or reference book of such courses.

Organization of the book

This book covers the core Java programming features consisting of nine chapters:

Chapter 1: Getting Started

Chapter 2: Java Language Basics

Chapter 3: Encapsulation

Chapter 4: Inheritance

Chapter 5: Package and Interface

Chapter 6: Exception Handling

Chapter 7: Multithreading

Chapter 8: IO and File

Chapter 9: Generic Programming

Online support for this book

Associated with this book, a well-organized Internet repository is available at www.cambridge.org/9781009211918. The online material includes:

- Answers to FAQs.
- Hints and solutions to MCQs.
- Programs for practice.
- All programs used in discussions in different chapters with their output.
- Presentation slides for teachers as well as for students for quick comprehension.
- Live discussion forum, where questions can be posted and their answers received from the Java folks.

Have enormous joy with Java!

December 25, 2021

Acknowledgments

We found writing the acknowledgments section of the book the most difficult part. Difficult, because we are at a loss of words to express gratitude to the people who directly or indirectly helped us in giving shape to this book. Nevertheless, let us try.

First and foremost, our thanks go to the numerous students who enrolled in the MOOC's course "Programming in Java." From the first time the course was run, students constantly asked for some reference material containing the different concepts elucidated in the program, with real-world examples. This requirement sowed the seeds for writing this book. And like Alphonse Karr has rightly said, "I am thankful that thorns have roses," COVID 19 has given us ample amount of free time to work on projects which otherwise were just a distant dream.

The lockdown came, and lo, *Joy with Java* started getting shape! Many of our students, mainly from MOOC, put in a lot of effort to bring it to reality. We are indebted to all of them, too numerous to mention individually by name, for their penetrating questions and useful suggestions. In particular, our thanks go to Nilanjan Sinhababu, Deepak Mewada, Subhrasankar Chatterjee, Subrata Pain, Tutan Nama, and Priyabrata Dash who painstakingly verified all the programs used in this book, and worked out the examples and problems.

We would also like to record our appreciation and thanks to the many reviewers for their thoughtful suggestions which helped in improving the content and its presentation.

We often take for granted the people who deserve our gratitude the most. For us, this person is none other than our little darling, not so little anymore, Ananya. Due to our grueling working hours during the tiring COVID times, she suffered a lot, but she never complained. Her patient love enabled us to complete this work quickly. All our love goes to her.

Finally, we are indebted to the editorial team of Cambridge University Press (CUP) for their fine job in making the book error free. Working with Agnibesh Das, the acquisition editor at CUP, was a pleasant experience for us and no words are enough to express our gratitude.

December 25, 2021 Monalisa and Debasis

1

Getting Started

In the software industry across the globe, there is a need to develop large and complex software. This software should be platform independent, internet enabled, easy to modify, secure, and robust. To meet these requirements object-oriented paradigm has been advocated. Based on this paradigm, Java programming language emerges as the best programming environment. Java is used for mobile programming, internet programming, and many other applications compatible with distributed systems. This book aims to cover the essential components of Java programming so that the readers can improve their skills, cope with the demands of the IT industry and solve the problems in their own field of study.

1.0 Introduction

Necessity

IT industry operates in such a diverse environment that software programs should not be confined to a single PC. Rather, they should move from a single user environment to mainframes, to networks, to network of networks, and so on. A giant program can be developed which integrates numerous mini programs which were developed by geographically distributed programmers, and all of them can be connected online. Such a distributed programming techniques and environments are no longer a dream but a reality, and it is Java, the Internet programming language, which makes it possible.

Scope

Java was developed by Sun Microsystems Inc. with the intent to create a dynamic, object-oriented programming (OOP) language, suitable for using the same types of development tasks as C and C++, but without the difficulties and bugs common to those languages. This is why Java has been touted as "a better C++"; it contains all the essential OOP features, but with lower complexities than C++. Sun describes Java as a "simple, object-oriented, distributed, interpreted, robust, secure, architecture neutral, portable, high-performance, multithreaded, and dynamic language."

Your learning

In this chapter we shall briefly highlight the various features of Java programming, its superiority over other programming languages, and the tools available for its programming. At the end, you will be able to run your first program in Java.

1.1 Concept of Programming

Application systems

Computer programming is used to build a software system (e.g., Microsoft Word, Library Information System, Internet Explorer browser, mobile app, printer's driver software, to name a few). These software systems take an input and then produce an output (Figure 1.1). Note that input/output can be of any form like text, audio, video, handwritten character, and so on.

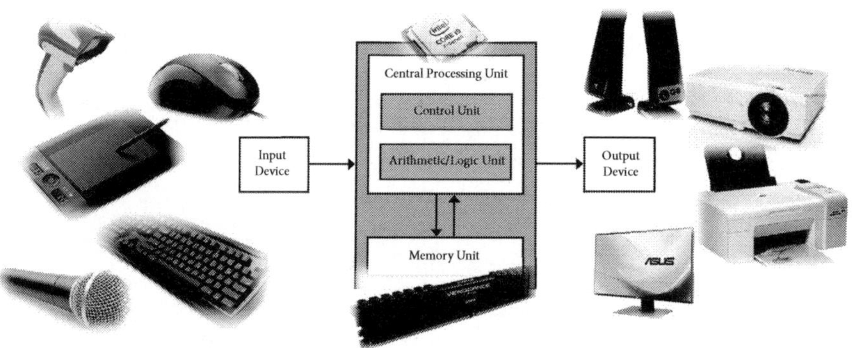

Figure 1.1 Computing system

1.1.1 Computer and Its Working

Programming

In order to process an input and produce an output, a program is required. A program contains of steps to transform input to a corresponding output. A computing system follows a basic architecture, popularly called Von Neumann architecture, to run programs. According to this architecture, a program is loaded into the memory of the computer. This program is then executed by the Central Processing Unit (CPU), which consists of a control unit, an arithmetic unit, and a logic unit.

Program translation

Thus, a program is a set of steps (or, instructions to the CPU). A program is written using a programming language. There are different kinds of programming languages, such as machine language (first generation language or 1GL), assembly language (second generation language or 2GL), high-level language (third generation language or 3GL), and so on. But a computer can understand instructions only in machine language. Hence, a program in 2GL or 3GL has to be translated into machine language. That is done by using a program translator, also called a compiler or interpreter (Figure 1.2). As shown in the figure, an assembler translates a program in assembly language to machine language and a compiler or interpreter translates a program in high-level language to machine language.

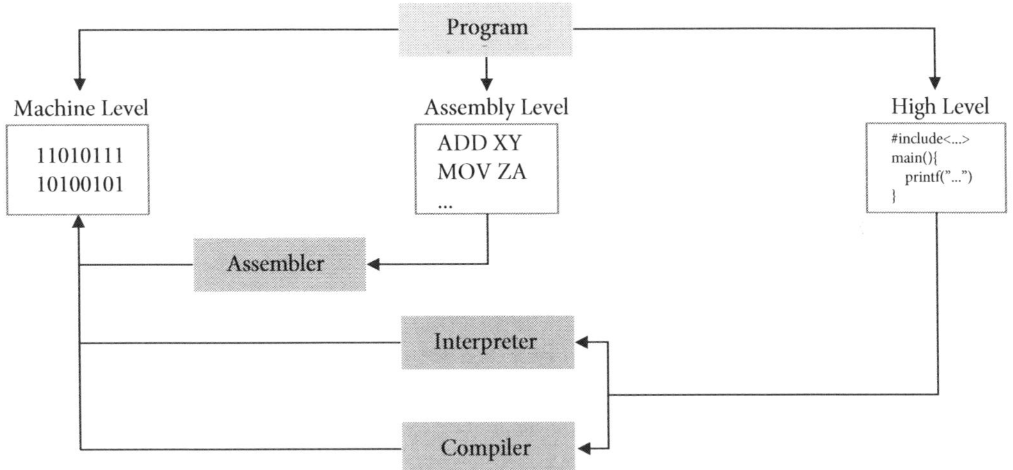

Figure 1.2 Program translation schemes

Java programming

Like different high-level languages (e.g., C, C++, Pascal, Python, Java), machine languages also vary from one CPU to another (e.g., Intel, Sun, IBM, Macintosh), and from one operating system (OS) to another (e.g., Windows, Solaris, MacOS, Android). Different assemblers, compliers or interpreters are required according to the different programming environments (CPU or OS). In contrast, the approach in Java is different. Here, a Java compiler translates a Java program into Java byte codes (according to a virtual machine, which is a hypothetical CPU). These byte codes are then interpreted by a Java interpreter to run the program. So, an application developed using Java is in the form of byte codes. This application, then, can be executed in any hardware or operating system and thus programming becomes architecture neutral or platform independent.

1.1.2 Programming Paradigms

Out of the numerous programming paradigms, two are followed more often in industries: function-oriented programming paradigms and object-oriented programming paradigms.

Concept of function

A function in its general sense is a mapping procedure from an input to an output. It takes one set of data as an input and produces another set of data as output. For example, $x = GCD(m,n)$ is a function which returns x as the greatest common divisor given two input numbers m and n. In another example, given an array of numbers, a sorting function on this data set will produce another array of numbers. A function in its simplest form can do one functional task. If a function is to complete more complex tasks, then it can be decomposed into a number of smaller functions (called sub functions, sub sub-functions, and so on). For example, there can be a function to find if a person's email address is available on the Internet repository. Here, the basic function is *search(…)*, which can be composed of *retrieve(…)* followed by *sort(…)* and then *check(…)*. Note that *sort(…)*, *check(…)* functions can be in terms of some other smaller functions, and so on.

Function-oriented programming

A programming principle which is based on concept of function is called function-oriented programming. To build a system, we have to build a set of functions. The system itself is a function, which can be composed as a set of functions. For example, in a bank ATM system, withdraw money, deposit money, balance enquiry, PIN change, and so on, are functions. The concept of function-oriented programming can be better understood through Figure 1.3. There are several functions in this figure which are centered around some data to be processed. Here, data is globally available to the functions. Thus, in function-oriented programming, a system is a collection of functions.

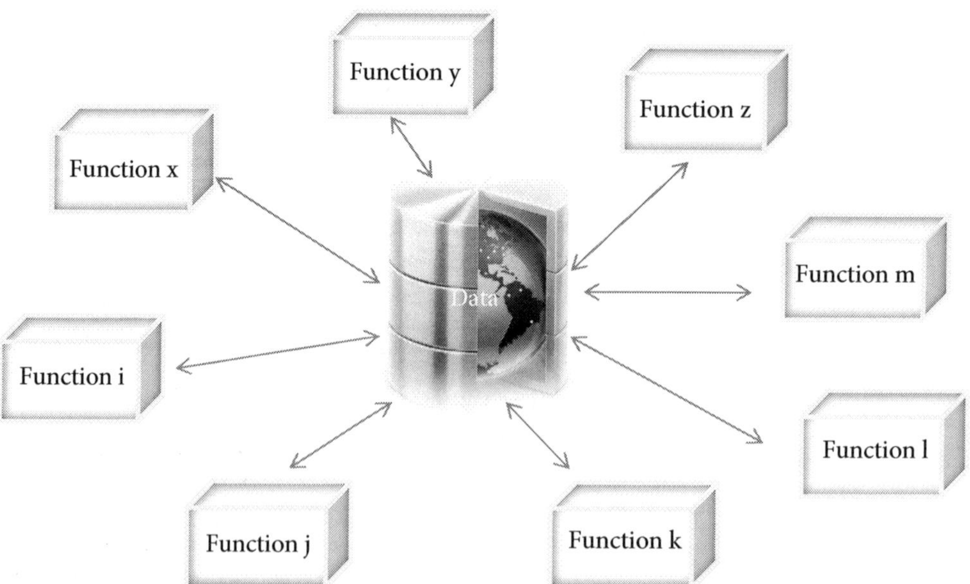

Figure 1.3 Function-oriented programming

Concept of object

Object-oriented programming, in contrast to function-oriented programming, is based on the concept of object. A function in function-oriented programming is a verb, whereas an object in object-oriented programming is a noun. In real world, a material thing that can be seen and touched, or a person or thing to which a specified action or feeling is directed, is called an object. A student, a car, and a book are some examples of objects. An object is defined by a set of attributes. For example, name, roll number, date of birth, and department are some attributes by which a student (object) can be defined. In real world, an object can send (or receive) message(s) to (or from) another object. For example, a student sends a message "issue" to a book and book can send a message "fine" to the student.

Object-oriented programming

Such a real-world scenario is modeled in object-oriented programming. A system's functionality is accomplished by means of communication of messages among the objects. On receiving a message, an object changes its state. States of an object are characterized by the change of value(s) of attribute(s). Each object has its data in it and also knows to how to process that data. Both data and operation on that data together define an object. A task is carried out by the invocation of operations by another object. Such a programming paradigm is illustrated in Figure 1.4.

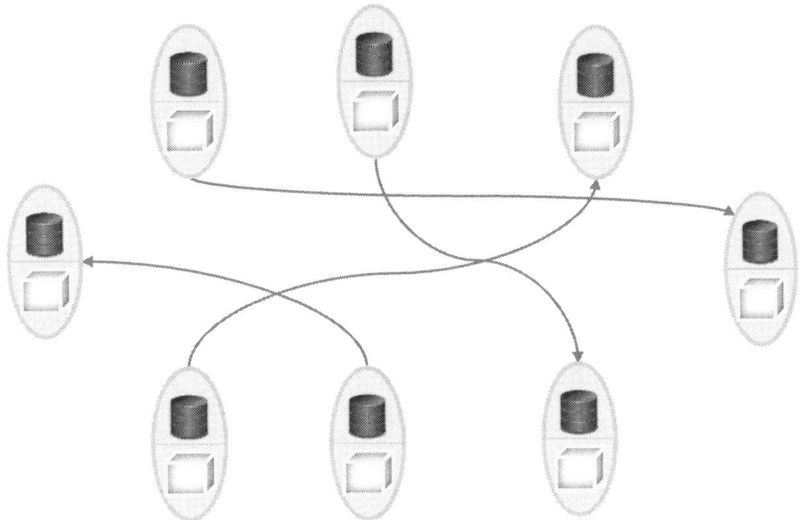

Figure 1.4 Object-oriented paradigm

In object-oriented programming, a system is a collection of objects. Unlike function-oriented programming, there is no global data here. Instead, the data is locally distributed among the objects.

Let us consider the system of getting an email address from the Internet. Here, a user "sends" a person's profile to a browser. The browser "retrieves" all email addresses "matching" the profile from the Internet. The browser then "sends" the list to the person. The person then "retrieves" the email address.

1.2 Object-Oriented Programming Paradigms

OOP paradigms

The programming principles followed in function-oriented programming include how to define a function, how a function can be decomposed to smaller functions, and how data can flow from one function to another. In contrast, object-oriented programming follows radically different programming paradigms. There are mainly four object-oriented programming paradigms: Encapsulation, Inheritance, information hiding and polymorphism. All these OOP paradigms are discussed in the following sections.

1.2.1 Encapsulation

Examples of objects

In object-oriented programming, the object is at the center of the stage. The object contains both data and the methods that operate the data. Encapsulation is the process of wrapping method and data together into a single unit. Figure 1.5 illustrates the encapsulations of two types of objects: a book and a borrower. The encapsulation procedure allows a programmer to define the type of object (such as books, borrowers). Such a type is called class. Thus, in Figure 1.5, *Book* and *Borrower* are two classes which define two types of objects. Notice that for simplicity, the body of the methods are not included in Figure 1.5.

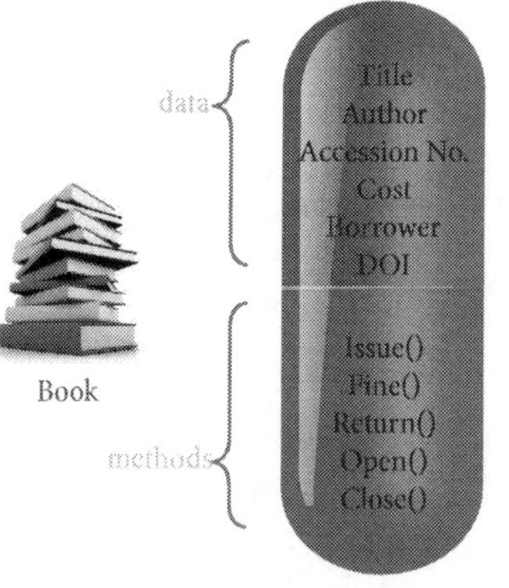

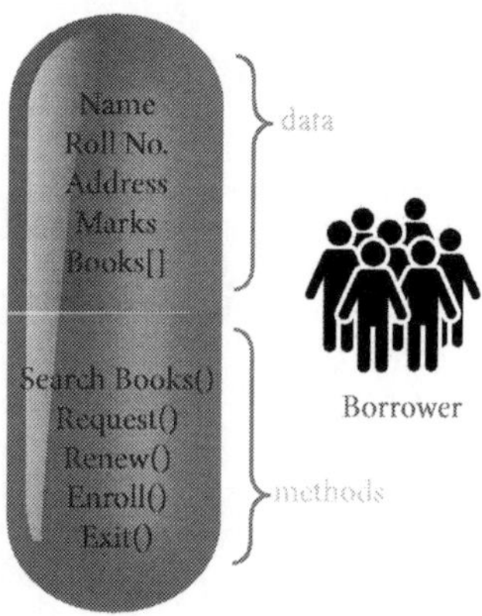

Figure 1.5 Encapsulation in OOP

1.2.2 Inheritance

Generalized to specialized object

Inheritance is a mechanism in which one object acquires all or some of the properties and behaviors of a parent object. This paradigm allows a programmer to extend a class into another. Such an extension is useful to update or modify the system without disturbing the existing system. It also allows code sharing.

Figure 1.6 illustrates the concept of inheritance. In this figure, *Book* is a class. Two child classes, namely *Text* and *Reference* are inherited from the parent class, *Book*. By this inheritance, the class *Text*, for example, inherits all the fields and methods in the class *Book*. In addition to these, the class *Text* has its own field and methods. The methods *Close()* and *Open()* are redefined in the class *Reference*.

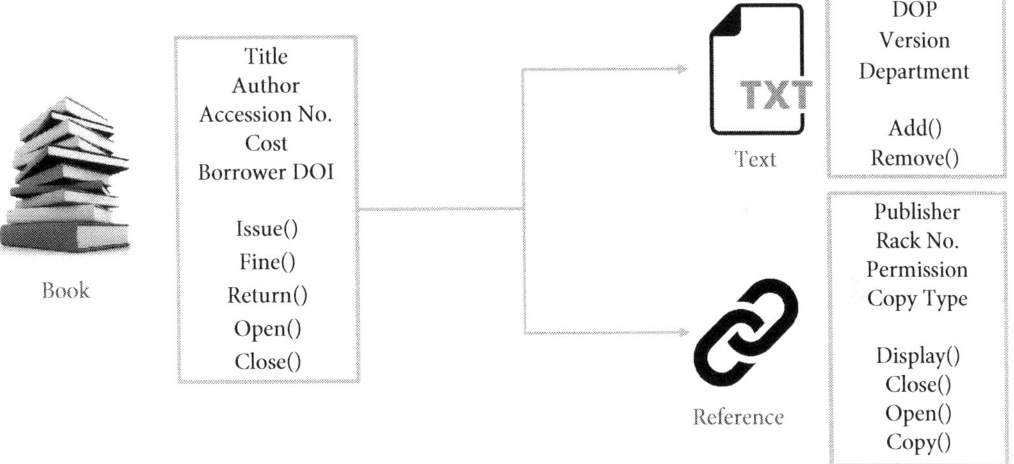

Figure 1.6 Inheritance in OOP

1.2.3 Information Hiding

This paradigm is allowed to limit the accessibility of fields and methods outside the class. This is particularly applicable when a class is inherited from another class. In such situations, the programmer may limit the access of some method and field to the methods in the child class. In object-oriented programming, such a mechanism is called information hiding.

Figure 1.7 illustrates the information hiding mechanism. In this case, we are talking about the class *Book*. It may be noted that there are access specifiers, namely *Public*, *Private*, and *Protected*. All fields and methods under *Public* access specifier are accessible to any methods belonging to any class. The field and methods which are under *Private* access specifier are accessible only to the methods inside the class *Book*, whereas the fields and methods under the *Protected* specifier are accessible to methods in the child class(es) of the class *Book*.

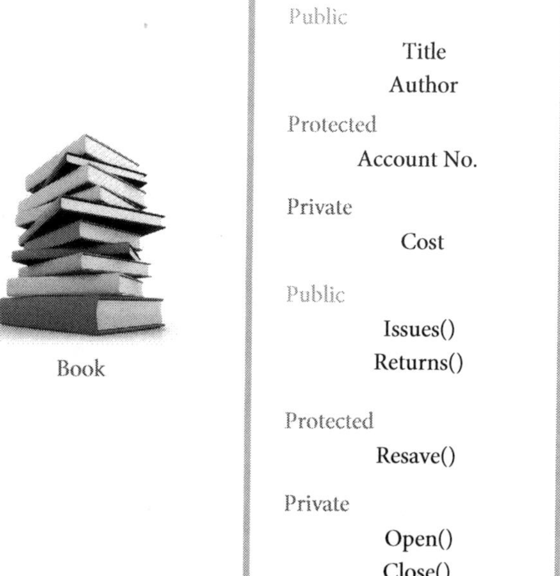

Figure 1.7 Information hiding in OOP

1.2.4 Polymorphism

Same name but different activity

In object-oriented programming, polymorphism (from Greek, meaning "having multiple forms") is the characteristic of being able to assign a different meaning or usage to the same thing but in different contexts, specifically, to allow an entity such as a variable, a method, or an object to have more than one form. The idea of polymorphism in an object-oriented paradigm can be better understood from Figure 1.8. The figure includes four polymorphic representations of the method `Add(...)`. Here, the method name `Add(...)` has polymorphic behavior. When `Add(...)` is called with `x`, `y`, two integer numbers, it will add the value and return the result. However, the same method, with two documents as input, will merge the two documents into a single document.

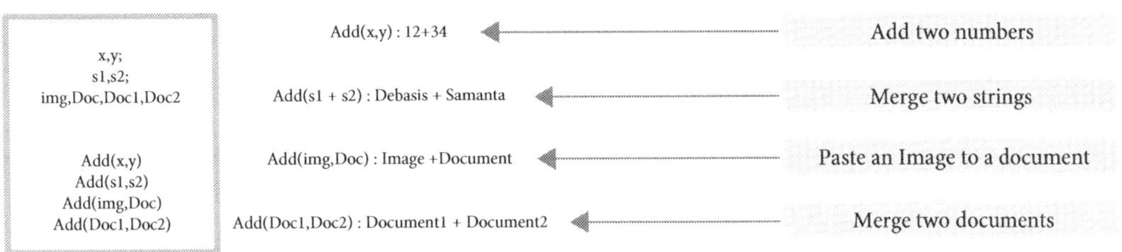

Figure 1.8 Polymorphism in OOP

1.3 About Java Programming

Origin of Java

James Gosling, Mike Sheridan, and Patrick Naughton initiated the Java language project in June 1991. This small team of Sun engineers is called the Green Team. The language was called "Greentalk" by James Gosling, and file extension of a program file was `.gt`.

Starting point

The language was originally designed for small, embedded systems in electronic appliances like set-top boxes, but it was a very advanced technology for the digital cable television industry at that time. Subsequently, the language was called "Oak" and was developed as a part of the Green project. The team members initiated this project to develop a language for digital devices. Later, this technology was used by Netscape as it was suitable for networking.

The name Java

The language was called "Oak" as oak is a symbol of strength and is the national tree of many countries like USA, France, Germany, and Romania. The team wanted something that reflected the essence of the technology: revolutionary, dynamic, lively, cool, unique, and easy to spell and fun to speak. In 1995, Oak was renamed as "Java." Java is an island in Indonesia where coffee was first produced (called java coffee).

Breakthrough

In 1995, *Time* magazine called Java one of the "Ten Best Products of 1995." JDK (Java Development Kit) 1.0 was released on January 23, 1996.

Figure 1.9 History of Java

1.3.1 Why Java?

Definition of Java

Java programming concept possesses all the advanced programming features of the recent programming languages. In addition, it has something special which makes it the first of its kind. The developer of Java described the Java language as: simple, portable, secure, high-performance, multithreaded, interpreted, platform independent, dynamic, architecture neutral, object-oriented, and robust. A few notable characteristics in Java programming language are summarized in Figure 1.10.

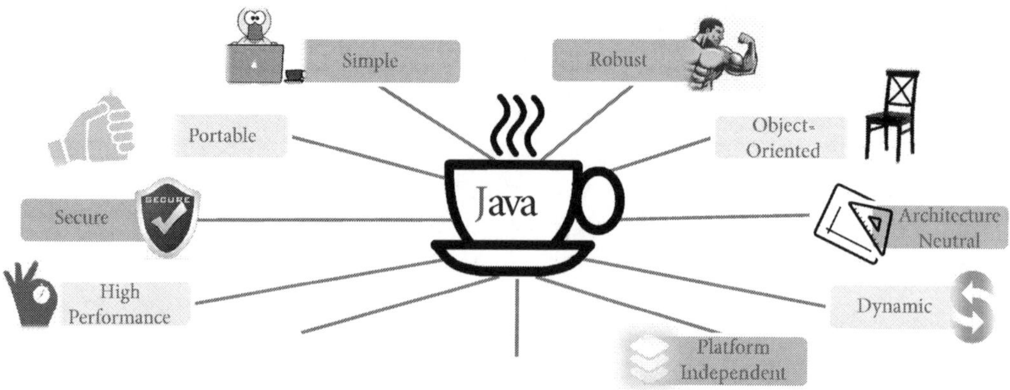

Figure 1.10 Characteristics of Java language

Object-oriented programming (e.g., C#, C++, Python, Smalltalk) has many advantages over other programming principles such as function-oriented programming (e.g., Ada, C, Pascal) and data-flow programming (e.g., ASCET, Joule, Orange). In general, object-oriented programming is preferable for developing large and complex software systems due to code reusability and better maintainability. Java is based on object-oriented programming (OOP) paradigm and incorporates almost every OOP feature. Object creation through object template (that is, class, data abstraction, and encapsulation), data and code sharing through inheritance, overloading concept through polymorphism, and data/process hiding, etc., are some basic OOP features in Java. Java is a bit like C++ but simpler than the aristocrat C++. It is an elegant language where the poorly understood, erratic, and redundant features of C++ have been eliminated. There are no pointers in Java – only lightly bounded heterogeneous collection of data/objects. Absence of any kind of pointers means it is free from huge bugs because pointers manipulation is one of the richest sources of bugs in almost all programs. Java is sophisticated enough to help programmers to express complex ideas in a simple manner. Global data and stand-alone function are not possible in Java, unlike C/C++. The basic programming components in Java are objects which are, directly or indirectly, decedents from the forefathers of classes. The class definition in Java permits both static and dynamic binding and therefore full reuse of code and data sharing. Java is truly object-oriented programming in the sense that many class definitions can be inherited dynamically. However, Java does not support multiple inheritance, whose semantic and usage has been quite controversial. Type casting or operator overloading is also not allowed in Java.

Object orientation

The microprocessor inside every computer can understand and execute only the machine language, that is, in terms of 0s and 1s. While using a high level programming language, programmers use source code (which resembles English). Then a translator converts the source code into the machine code relevant to the microprocessor. The machine code varies from microprocessor to microprocessor. So for the same source code, different translators are needed for different microprocessors. Hence, a program (source code) when converted into the machine code for an Intel chip, will vary from the version for a Motorola chip, which again will be different from the version for a Sun workstation. The same problem exists in case of computers having the same microprocessors but different operating systems.

Platform-independent programming

Java has overcome this problem of architecture and environment dependency. It solves this problem using a concept called the Java Virtual Machine (JVM). JVM specifies a dummy CPU and a detailed dummy instruction set that looks like standard assembly code. The Java compiler transforms the source programs into instructions of JVM. The compiled Java code is known as *byte code* (which is assembly code according to JVM). Next, the Java interpreter, which is specific to each environment (processor and OS), converts the byte code instructions into the native processor instructions before executing them. Thus, converting a program source into an object code is compiled halfway and interpreted halfway. Figure 1.11 illustrates this mechanism.

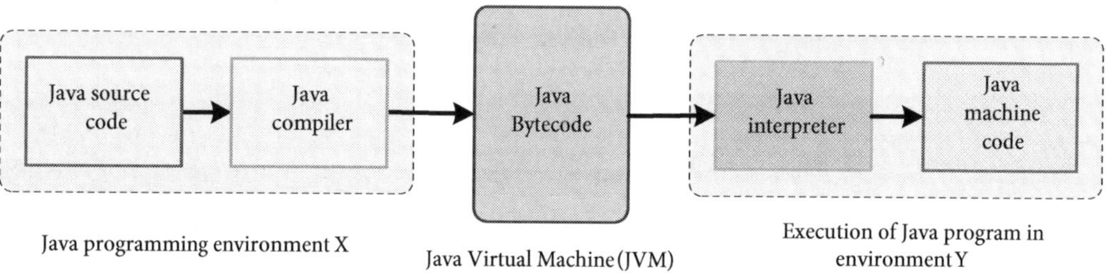

Figure 1.11 Platform independent mechanism

As the Java byte codes are architecture and operating system independent, they are highly portable and can be executed on any system without modification. This platform independence is illustrated in Figure 1.12.

Robust execution

Using the conventional programming languages like C or Pascal, if we need a slice of memory, we have to allocate it and then return it to the system once we are done with it. Thus, memory management is solely decided by the programmer. This overhead is eliminated in Java. In Java, a program does not need to be malicious and suck up memory and not release it. Java controls all of the memory using Java's run-time system called automatic garbage collectors-based memory management system. Every once in a while, it will scan through all of the objects in a process to see if any of them are not being used. The obsolete objects are reclaimed from the memory. As no explicit memory manipulation is required by the programmer, Java programs are highly robust.

Multi threading

Another important contribution of Java is its support of multithreading. Multithreading is the ability to run several tasks within the context of one large application. In a simple version, a program is a list of instructions, and the path through a list of instructions is called the thread of execution. In many cases, execution of a program through multiple threads makes more sense. For example, suppose a program needs to open a file, draw something on the screen, and print out something else. Each of these may require waiting for access to some resource. A multithreaded program can, in effect,

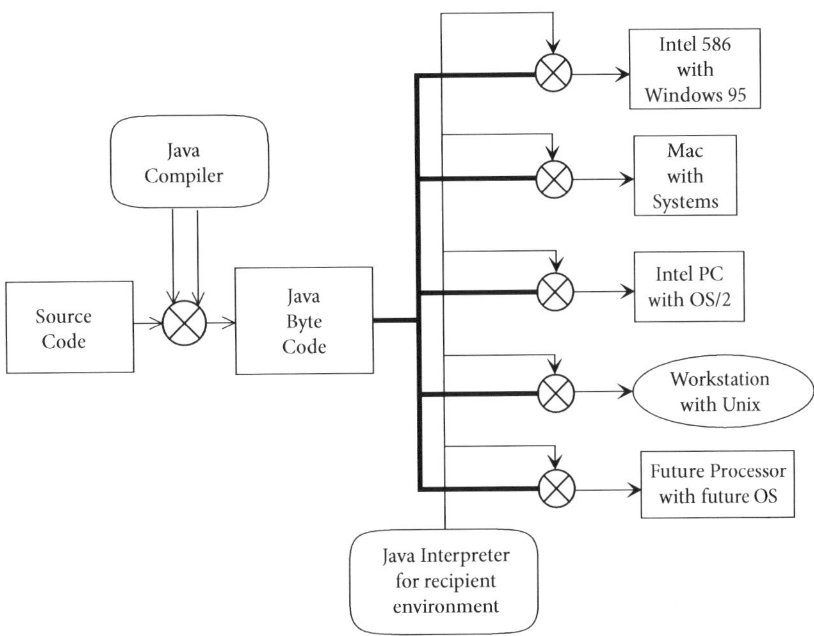

Figure 1.12 Platform independent execution

start up three different threads of executions for these tasks. If the printing thread is waiting for more paper to be loaded in the printer, then the file thread and drawing thread can continue operating. In Java multithreading, the interpreter can keep a track of all threads and it can switch among all of them, giving each a fair share of the processor's attention. For most applications, multithreading improves interactive performance and real time system development. Multithreading encourages Java to interface and support several features of modern operating systems and network protocols.

Secure programming

Java is based on client/server technology. After the translation of the source code into byte code, Java programs are downloaded from host machines and then run on one's client machine. Since Java programs are downloaded from several different places, some precautions are needed to prevent mala fide pieces of code (called computer viruses) embedded within the programs, which cause problems in the recipient system. This demands that distributed applications should exhibit the highest level of security concerns. A byte code verifier in the Java interpreter looks at the incoming byte codes and verifies whether the compiled code is strictly language compliant. In case it finds illegal code, the run-time system rejects the code and refuses to run it, thus trapping all mala fide codes. Once the strict verification is over, the application proceeds to run. In this manner, Java inhibits security holes, if any.

1.3.2 Java Is Unique!

Comparison with others

Java is a unique object-oriented programming language and comparable to the programming languages based on function-oriented programming (Table 1.1). Also, Tables 1.2 and 1.3 summarize the difference between Java and C++ and Java and Python, respectively.

Java versus C, Pascal

Table 1.1 Difference between C, Pascal, and Java

	C, Pascal	Java
Program organization	Program is divided into small parts called functions.	Program is divided into parts called classes.
Importance	Importance is not given to data but to functions.	Importance is given to the data rather than procedures.
Approach	They follow a top down approach.	It follows bottom up approach.
Access specifiers	Do not have any access specifier.	Has four access specifiers, namely default, public, private, protected.
Data moving	Data can move freely from one function to another function in the system.	Objects can move and communicate with each other.
Maintainability	To add new data and functions is not so easy.	Provides an easy way to add new data and operations.
Data access	Function uses global data for sharing that can be accessed freely from function to function in the system.	Object uses local data and can be accessed in a controlled manner.
Data hiding	No data hiding is possible; hence security is not possible.	Provides data hiding, hence secured programming is possible.
Overloading	Polymorphism is not possible.	Polymorphism is possible.

Table 1.2 Difference between C++ and Java

	C++	Java
Memory Management	Use of pointers, structures, union.	No use of pointers. Supports references, threads, and interfaces.
Libraries	Comparatively available with low level functionalities.	Wide range of classes for various high-level services.

Multiple Inheritance	Provide both single and multiple inheritance.	Multiple inheritance is partially done through interfaces.
Operator Overloading	Supports operator overloading.	Doesn't support this feature.
Documentation comment	C++ doesn't support documentation comment.	Java supports documentation comment (/* ... */) for source code.
Program Handling	Functions and variables can reside outside classes.	Functions and variables reside only in classes. Package is used to include classes.
Portability	Platform dependent, must be recompiled for a different platform.	Platform independent, byte code generated works on every OS.
Thread Support	No built-in support for threads, depends on libraries.	Has built-in thread support.

Java versus C++

1.3.3 Advantages of Java

Ease of development Object-oriented methodology in Java enables the software system developers to develop large complex applications with only a little effort. Experienced software developers understand that software systems are dynamic in nature and in continuous evolution. Keeping this in mind, the dynamic binding in Java can be utilized to provide a big advantage of code reusability. Here, unlike C++, a change of a base class need not require a recompile of derived classes. Applications can be embedded dynamically. Linkage manipulations are deferred until run-time. This concept allows easy modification and ability to upgrade the existing system.

Table 1.3 Difference between Python and Java

	Java	Python
Compilation process	Java is a compiled programming language.	Python is an interpreted programming language.
Code Length	Longer lines of code as compared to Python.	3–5 times shorter than equivalent Java programs.
Syntax Complexity	Define particular block by curly braces, end statements by semi colon.	No need of semi colons and curly braces, uses indentation.
Ease of typing	Strongly typed, need to define the exact data type of variables.	Dynamic, no need to define the exact data type of variables.

Java versus Python

Speed of execution	Java is much faster than Python in terms of speed.	Expected to run slower than Java programs.
Multiple inheritance	Multiple inheritance is partially done through interfaces.	Provides both single and multiple inheritance.

Easy development of large applications

Writing Java code is almost like writing English. Java is a "simple" programming language because complex programming features have been carefully avoided. It is easy to program and errors by programmers are minimized. For example, pointer concept in C and multiple inheritance in C++ are not included in Java.

Portable programming

Java programs are portable because they can be executed in any environment without needing any substantial change. Java byte codes are independent of any underlying architecture. Characters are based on Unicode for internationally portable applications. If one uses certain IO classes, one can render data portability on Java code. For example, `DataInputStream` and `DataOutputStream` are two classes in Java that utilize external data representation to normalize one's data to a network format. Data can be used by many different types of processors and machines. Currently, Java run-time environments that exist are Solaries™ 2.x, (SPARC and x86), Win32 (Windows 95 and Windows NT), OS/2, Macintosh Systems 7.5 for Power PCs, HP/Unix, etc.

Robust programming

Java programs are robust because there is no need of explicit memory manipulation. Memory address cannot be deferred nor can pointer arithmetic be used to access object contents. Array bounds are checked so that array indices are never out-of-bounds.

High performance programming

Execution of programs in Java is a two-step process: compile halfway and interpret halfway. But why an interpreter? An interpreter reads every line, converts it into the machine code of the system and then executes it. Every line of source code has to be converted to machine code every time it executes, making the application slow. The compiler compiles the entire source code into machine code before starting the execution and thus speeds up the overall process. The only drawback of the compiler is that an executable code can work only on one type of system, often specific to an operating system. You cannot compile code if you have no knowledge of the machine you are compiling it for. To make the same program suitable for different environments, the simplest solution is to look for an interpreter. But the interpreter is very slow and compiled code is quite fast, so the developer of Java decided to strike the middle ground in order to optimize the whole set. Most commands of the code of one CPU machine match with those of others. Instruction to load and move data, to add and subtract numbers, etc. form the basic building blocks of assembly programming and are often similar. Therefore, translating the source code into JVM code and then translating it for Pentium, for example, would not be as slow as conventional interpreting. By making a little compromise both ways, much has been achieved to get a high-performance computing environment.

Internet programming

It is well known that marriage of computer and communications gave birth to today's information society. After the successful maturity of ARPANET (Advanced Research Projects Agency Network), now Internet is a rapidly evolving network of networks, which essentially consists of very powerful computing systems with a variety of capabilities through high speed (at the speed of light!) and large bandwidth communication channels. Internet facilitates communication among the computers connected through it, and data or information can be conveniently transferred to and from any computer, anywhere in the world, at the click of a button. Through the Internet, a chunk of information can be simultaneously shared and read by people scattered around the globe. Information over the Internet is actually multimedia, which includes text, graphics, images, and sound. With Internet, there is Web (short for World Wide Web, often written as WWW). This is a wide area hypermedia (also called hypertext) information retrieval system, introduced by a group of physicists at the CERN European Laboratory for Particle Physics in Geneva, Switzerland, in 1991. Web facilitates online documentation to give universal access to a very large universe of documents. WWW on the Internet utilizes hyperlinks to make immediate network connection to any site anywhere in the world.

It was a challenge to create a document that looked like a simple document to a user on a computer system, but was actually spread across multiple systems in different parts of the world. But with the WWW and the Internet boom, the whole world is now a simple document page.

The Java programming concept changes the way Internet is used. Hypertext documents consist of multimedia, that is, a combination of text, data, audio, graphics, and pictures – still as well as video. Maintaining and retrieving such a multimedia-based hypertext is a technological challenge. For example, if web documents with features that include non-standard or incompatible extension to the html are made, most browsers may ignore them because the underlying computer systems (clients) are incapable of supporting them. In addition, the transmission of multimedia-based documents over the network involves a large channel bandwidth. As a consequence, such documents may not be transmitted in their complete form on most client systems. Moreover, documents may run into trouble because, the code marked in the text by the composer is specific to the local processor and operating system and hence may not be executed in the client systems.

Given these problems there was an obvious need to devise a programming language which could yield a sophisticated, system-independent hypertext so that users from different systems with different compatibilities could share information. Truly speaking, Java turned the Internet (or Net) and WWW (or Web) into one giant computer so that the Net and the Web became a common storehouse for billions of data and application units. One can download the required application from the Net into one's system, use it, and it will be automatically deleted from the system after use.

Distributed computing

Java is the first concrete example that moves to component and distributed computing. It envisages a new type of programming environment in which a program is truly task oriented and disposable. One can enjoy the benefits of the execution of ready-made compiled code as a single statement which can be dynamically downloaded from anywhere (maybe too remote) in the network of heterogeneous systems and executed transparently. This is the dream most software developers have had for years.

1.3.4 Popularity of Java

World Economic Forum Report

Java has popularity worldwide because of its elegant features. Java is used for mobile programming (Android mobile platform) and favored most because of its backward compatibility features. Java has consistently been more popular than any other computer language. Figure 1.13 is based on the report published by World Economic Forum in 2017.

1.4 Features of Java Programming

Potential of Java

Java facilitates development of many kinds of application software like word processor, system software like operating system, and embedded software like control system for instruments, digital gadgets, etc. Java solutions are suitable for many diversified settings like mobile applications, PC or laptop applications, distributed applications, and so on. It is indeed a mammoth facility that Java supports.

Programming in Java can be classified into three broad categories: (1) Core programming, (2) GUI programming, and (3) Advanced programming (Figure 1.14). Each of these is discussed in the following sections for a basic understanding of Java programming support.

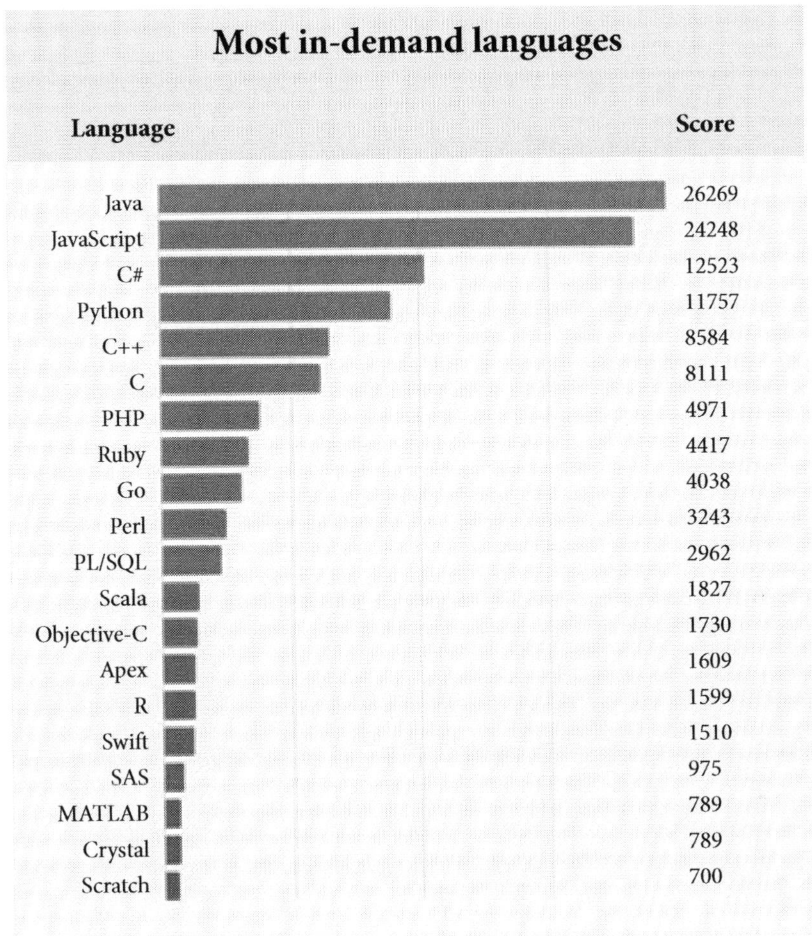

Figure 1.13 Popularity of Java

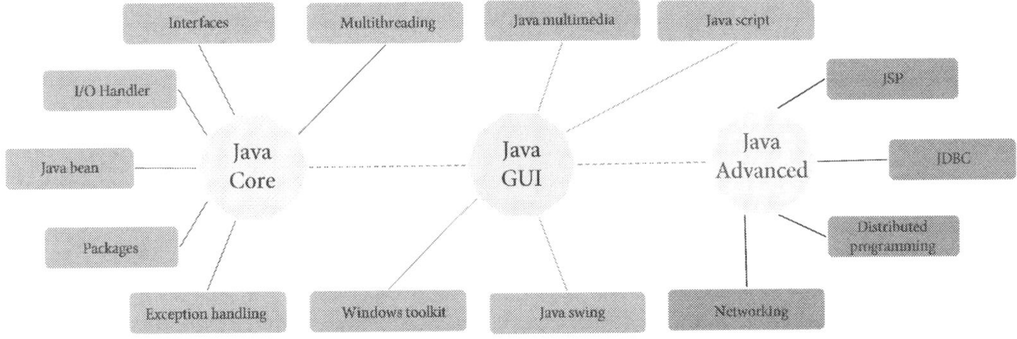

Figure 1.14 Programming in Java

1.4.1 Core Programming

Core programming and its advantages

The word "core" implies that this programming is at the center of all programming activities. Core programming is treated as the starting point for any programmer. This is the basic programming and further programming endeavors can be extended to other programming like GUI and network programming. All OOP paradigms, namely encapsulation, inheritance, information hiding, and polymorphism are used in this programming. In addition, it is necessary to learn some special paradigms in Java such as package (for developing large software with code reusability), interface (code sharing, maintenance), exception handling (robust and reliable software implementation), multithreading (for concurrent execution), and input-output streams (handling input and output with different types from different sources). If one is good in core programming, then he or she is also suitable for solving research problems in the field of numerical analysis, statistical analysis, data science, data mining, artificial intelligence, machine learning, natural language processing, signal processing, image processing, computer vision, computer security, and many more fields.

1.4.2 GUI Programming

What is GUI?

Core programming is mainly console based, that is, type command and then execute. In GUI programming, for each command, the programmer has to write a program. Thus console based programming focuses on keyboard as the standard input and display as the standard output to interact with the system. GUI (Graphical User Interface) allows WIMP (Windows, Icon, Menu, and Pointer) to interact with the system. There are many GUI elements, such as frame, button, checkbox, scrollbar, etc., which are used for the purpose. In contrast with Java core programming (where the programmer has to write detailed programs about how to perform an action), Java GUI programming is light weight (i.e., the programmer details what to do). In Java, the GUI programming is supported by many built-in packages. With GUI programming support of Java, a programmer can develop any user-friendly application software, system software, multimedia system, etc.

1.4.3 Advanced Programming

Programming for Internet, database, etc.

A software system is not confined to a single programming environment (like a desktop computer) but spreads over to remotely located distributed environment. To support distributed programming, Java supports excellent packages for networking and database management. With these two services, web programming (for developing web services, online systems, etc.), client-server programming (for distributed programming, remote database connectivity, etc.), intranet and internet programming (network protocol, secure transmission, data communication, etc.) are very simple and straightforward.

This book aims to cover the core programming concepts. The advanced topics in Java programming language will be covered in the next volume of this book.

1.5 Tools and Resources for Java Programming

Java programming supports

There are many tools and resources available; a majority of them are freely downloadable and compatible with many platforms. All tools and resources are broadly classified as: (1) Java program development environment, (2) Java integrated development environment, (3) Java browser, (4) Java program editor, and (5) Java tutorials. The following sections contain brief discussions of these tools and resources.

1.5.1 Java Program Development Environment

Free JDK download

Java developer supports the Java programmer with a complete support kit called JDK (Java Development Kit) to develop any software. JDK contains the basic tools and libraries necessary for creating, testing, documenting, and executing Java programs. There are many versions of JDK. The first version was released by JavaSoft, a division of Sun Microsystems Inc., in 1996. After that several versions have been released. JDK-17, which was released in September 2021. However, for beginners and for writing the basic programs, one should use JDK-8. This book will mainly cover the features according to JDK-8 version, unless specified otherwise. JDK-8 is versatile, matured and easy to use. This JDK can be downloaded from the official site of Oracle for Java™ 2 JDK, Standard Edition (SE):

https://www.java.com/en/download/index.jsp

You have to download the correct version of JDK according to the operating system (e.g., Windows, Linux, MacOS, etc.) and CPU (e.g., 32-bit, 64-bit processor, etc.).

Java Super Development Kit

In addition to the JDK software, a super development kit (SDK) is also available. Under SDK, a number of software are available: Java SE (Standard Edition), Java ME (Micro Edition), Java EE (Enterprise Edition), Java TV, Java Mobile, etc. Java SDK provides several platforms to develop software in different application settings. Details about SDK and the link to download SDK is:

https://www.oracle.com/technetwork/java/javase/downloads/index.html

We will not suggest you to download SDK, as it is for the advanced programmers only.

JDK bundle

The JDK is a bundle. It contains, mainly, seven programs.

- *javac:* the Java **compiler**.
- *java:* the Java **interpreter**.
- *javadoc:* generates **documentation** in HTML.
- *appletviewer:* the Java interpreter to **execute Java applets**.
- *jdb:* the Java **debugger** to find and fix bugs in Java programs.
- *javap:* the Java **disassembler** to display the accessible functions and data in a compiled class; it also displays the meaning of byte codes.
- *javah:* to **create interface** between Java and C routines.

In addition to this, JDK also includes API (Application Programming Interface) which is a packages of libraries. The following nine packages are present in JDK-8:

- *java.applet:* for applet programming.
- *java.awt:* the Abstract Windowing Toolkit for designing GUI-like *Button*, *Checkbox*, *Choice*, *Menu*, *Panel*, Window, etc.
- *java.io:* file input and output handling.
- *java.lang:* provides useful classes, for example, to handle *Object*, *Thread*, *Exception*, *String*, *System*, *Math*, *Float*, *Integer*, etc.
- *java.net:* classes for network programming.
- *java.util:* contains miscellaneous classes like *Vector*, *Stack*, *List*, *Date*, *Dictionary*, *Hash*, etc.
- *javax.swing:* for designing GUI-like AWT (Abstract Window Toolkit).
- *java.sql:* for database connectivity, SQL processing, etc.

1.5.2 Java Integrated Development Environment

Professional Java IDEs

In addition to free Java development environment, there are some sophisticated software development environments also available. They are called Java IDEs (Integrated Development Environments). The following IDEs are very popular among software practitioners:

1. Sun's Java Workshop from Sun's JavaSoft (powered with Visual Java).
2. Mojo from Penumbra Software (best visual environment for creating Java applets).
3. Jumba from Aimtech and IBM (graphical applet builder).
4. Semantic Café from Semantics (a de-facto standard for Java development on Windows systems).

Free Java IDEs

In addition to these four, there are a number of free Java IDEs available. Some of them are mentioned here.

Apache NetBeans IDE is a popular IDE. It is from Oracle and the latest is Apache NetBeans Release 12.6, which was released in November 2021 (with Java-8 support). This is available at:

NetBeans

https://netbeans.apache.org/download/index.html

Apache Tomcat 8.0 is downloadable from NetBeans from:

https://netbeans.org/downloads/8.0.1/

Eclipse Java IDE is available at:

Eclipse

http://www.eclipse.org/downloads/packages/release/kepler/sr1/eclipse-ide-java-developers

Android Studio from JavaWorld is for Android development. It is available for download on Windows, macOS and Linux based operating systems.

Android Studio

https://www.javaworld.com/blog/android-studio-for-beginners/

DrJava is a lightweight Java IDE designed primarily for students and beginners. It is actively developed and maintained by the JavaPLT group at Rice University. Its interface has been developed using Sun Microsystems Swing toolkit and therefore it has a consistent appearance on different platforms.

DrJava

http://www.drjava.org/

There are some online Java IDEs available for the beginners which support writing, compilation, execution, etc., of Java programs.

Online Java IDEs

https://www.jdoodle.com/online-java-compiler

https://www.tutorialspoint.com/compile_java_online.php

https://www.onlinegdb.com/online_java_compiler

https://www.codechef.com/ide

1.5.3 Java Browsers

Java supports web programming and to display a web page, a Java-enabled browser is required. Following are a few free Java-enabled browsers:

Java browsers

HotJava from JavaSoft web site (http://java.sun.com)

Netscape Navigator from Netscape home page http://home.netscape.com

Internet Explorer from Microsoft's web page (http://www.microsoft.com)

There are many browsers, such as Mozilla and Chrome, which can support Java provided a plug-in is installed.

1.5.4 Java Program Editor

There are several programs available (mostly free downloadable software) for writing Java programs. A few excellent editors are listed here.

Notepad

Notepad is a simple text editor for Microsoft Windows and a basic text-editing program which enables computer users to create documents. It was first released as a mouse-based MS-DOS program in 1983, and has been included in all versions of Microsoft Windows since Windows 1.0 in 1985.

Notepad++

This is a very advanced and handy Notepad, it has several built-in tools and functions for making program writing easy.

https://notepad-plus-plus.org/download/

jEdit

jEdit is a text editor for mature programmers available under the GNU General Public License version 2.0. It is written in Java and runs on any operating system with Java support, including BSD, Linux, macOS and Windows.

http://www.jedit.org/

jGRASP

jGRASP is a lightweight development environment created specifically to provide automatic generation of software visualizations to improve the comprehensibility of software. It produces static visualizations of source code structure and visualizations of data structures at run-time.

https://www.jgrasp.org/

1.5.5 Java Tutorials

There are many tutorials and documentation pages available on the Internet which programmers can consult, whether they are beginners or advanced Java programmers. A few links are given here.

Oracle Java tutorials

The Java™2 Tutorials: These are tutorials from Oracle itself and are a very trusted source.

https://java.sun.com/docs/books/tutorial/index.html

Official Java programming tutorial: This is from the developer of Java.

https://docs.oracle.com/javase/tutorial/java/

API Specification: Learning classes, interfaces, and methods are very important. A huge documentation of Java APIs can be found at the following links.

https://docs.oracle.com/javase/7/docs/api/

Core Java tutorial

Javatpoint: This is a core Java programming tutorial and is designed for students and working professionals.

https://www.javatpoint.com/java-tutorial

1.6 Writing Java Programs

This section describes how you can start your journey of Java programming. There are a few steps for beginners to take: (1) installation, (2) program editing, (3) compilation, and (4) execution. Let's try to understand each of these steps.

1.6.1 JDK Installation

This step is not required if you use a Java IDE or the Java software is already installed. In that case, go to Section 1.6.2.

In a non-IDE environment, you have to run the commands from the console. This is shown for Windows in Figure 1.15 and for Linux/Ubuntu in Figure 1.16.

Console in Windows

Figure 1.15 Command window in Windows

Console in Ubuntu

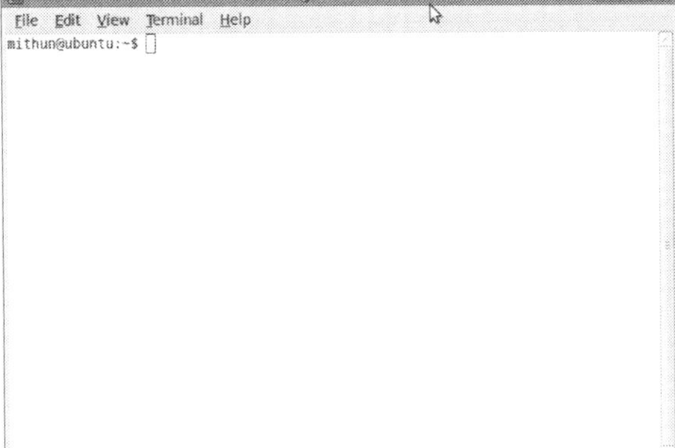

Figure 1.16 Terminal window in Ubuntu

JDK installation in Windows

The installation steps are pretty simple. You can find the installation guide from many sources and you are advised to follow the same from the site from where you download the Java software. Oracle being the official source of Java resource provides a native installer, which you can download from its website. In fact, it provides instructions about Java installation for all platforms. For an example, in case of Ubuntu, you can install Java 8 with the execution of the following commands on the command line. These commands might change over time, if they do not work, you are advised to search the Net for hints and tips of the installation.

JDK installation in Ubuntu

```
# Install Java from the OpenJDK project
  sudo apt-get install openjdk-8-jdk

# In case you prefer the Oracle Java distribution
# you can alternatively use the following commands
  sudo add-apt-repository ppa:webupd8team/java
  sudo apt-get update

sudo apt-get install oracle-java8-installer
```

You can test if the JDK is correctly installed in your computer. For this, type the following command.

```
java -version
```

If the JDK is correctly installed, this command prints information about your Java installation. On the other hand, if the command line returns the information that the "program could not be found", this means that you could not install Java successfully.

System setting

For successful completion of installation and to make the system ready for programming, you need to configure the system so that you can run your Java program from any directory. The procedure for setting a system is explained with reference to Windows and Ubuntu environment. General information for setting environment variable is as follows:

- The PATH is the system variable that your operating system uses to locate executables from the command line or terminal window.
- The PATH system variable can be set using "System Utility" in the control panel on Windows, or in your shell's startup file on Linux, Ubuntu, Solaris, etc.
- Making changes to the system PATH variable is typically not necessary for computers running Mac OS X.

Windows 10 and Windows 11

Environment variable setting in Windows 10, 11

- In "Search," search for and then select "System" (Control Panel)
- Click the "Advanced system settings" link.
- Click "Environment Variables." In the section "System Variables," find the "PATH" environment variable and select it. Click "Edit." If the PATH environment variable does not exist, click "New."
- In the "Edit System Variable" (or "New System Variable") window, specify the value of the PATH environment variable. Click "OK." Close all remaining windows by clicking "OK."
- Reopen the command prompt window and you will be able to compile and run your Java programs.

Windows 7

Environment variable setting in Windows 7

- From the desktop, right click the "Computer" icon.
- Choose "Properties" from the context menu.
- Click the "Advanced system settings" link.
- Click "Environment Variables." In the section "System Variables," find the PATH environment variable and select it. Click "Edit." If the PATH environment variable does not exist, click "New."
- In the "Edit System Variable" (or "New System Variable") window, specify the value of the PATH environment variable. Click "OK." Close all remaining windows by clicking "OK."
- Reopen the command prompt window and you will be able to compile and run your Java programs.

Windows Vista

Environment variable setting in Windows Vista

- From the desktop, right click the "My Computer" icon.
- Choose "Properties" from the context menu.
- Click the "Advanced" tab (Advanced system settings link in Vista).
- Click "Environment Variables." In the section "System Variables," find the PATH environment variable and select it. Click "Edit." If the PATH environment variable does not exist, click "New."
- In the "Edit System Variable" (or "New System Variable") window, specify the value of the PATH environment variable. Click "OK." Close all remaining windows by clicking "OK."
- Reopen the command prompt window and you will be able to compile and run your Java programs.

Windows XP

Environment variable setting in Windows XP

- Select "Start," select "Control Panel," double click "System," and select the "Advanced" tab.
- Click "Environment Variables." In the section, "System Variables," find the PATH environment variable and select it. Click "Edit." If the PATH environment variable does not exist, click "New."
- In the "Edit System Variable" (or "New System Variable") window, specify the value of the PATH environment variable. Click "OK." Close all remaining windows by clicking "OK."
- Reopen the command prompt window and you will be able to compile and run your Java programs.

Mac OS X

Mac OS

To specify the full path, or use the java_home tool:

```
% /usr/libexec/java_home -v 1.8.0_73 --exec javac -version
```

Solaris and Linux

Solaris and Linux

- To find out if the path is properly set:

In a terminal window, enter:

```
% java -version
```

This will print the version of the Java tool, if it can find it. If the version is old or you get the error "java: command not found" then you should set the path properly.

- Determine which java executable is the first one found in your PATH

In a terminal window, enter:

```
% which java
```

- Set the PATH permanently

To set the path permanently, set the path in your startup file.

Note: Instructions for two most-popular Shells on Linux and Solaris have been listed here. If you are using other shells, see the Path Setting Tutorial.

Bash Shell

- Edit the startup file (~/.bashrc)
- Modify PATH variable PATH=/usr/local/jdk1.8.0/bin:$PATH

export PATH

- Save and close the file
- Load the startup file

% . /.profile

- Verify that the path is set by repeating the java command

% java -version

C Shell (csh)

- Edit the startup file (~/.cshrc)
- Set Path

set path=(/usr/local/jdk1.8.0/bin $path)

- Save and close the file
- Load the startup file

% source ~/.cshrc

- Verify that the path is set by repeating the java command

% java -version

1.6.2 First Java Programming

Let us learn the step-by-step procedure to create, compile, and run your first Java program.

We will write a Java program, which will print `Hello World!` message on the display screen. The program will typically look as shown in Figure 1.17 and Figure 1.18 with different program editors. You should not be worried about the meaning of the different statements in the program (you shall learn these shortly).

Program 1.1 *(Your first Java program)*

```
/*
The FirstJavaProgram class implements an application that
simply prints "Hello World!" to the standard output, that
is, display screen.
*/
import java.lang.*;
class FirstJavaProgram
{
    public static void main(String args[]){
      System.out.println("Hello, World!");
    } // Print the message on the screen
}
```

Edit the Program

Any text editor can be used to write Java programs. For example, in Windows:

Notepad, Edit, MS-Word, etc.

In Unix:

vi, emacs, gedit, etc.

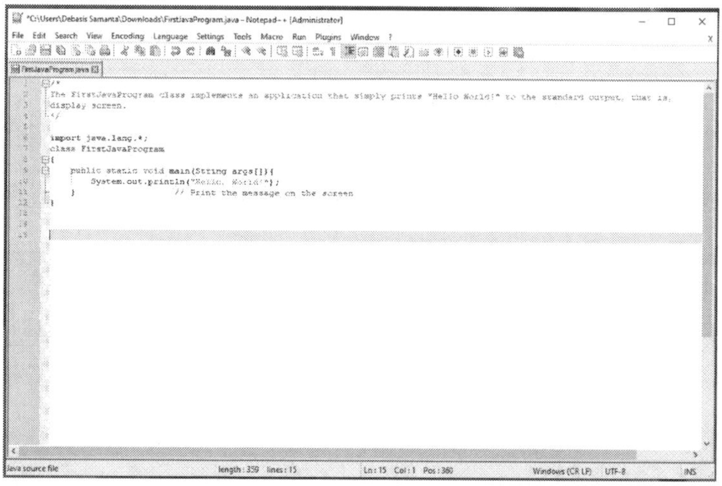

Figure 1.17 Editing the program with NotePad++

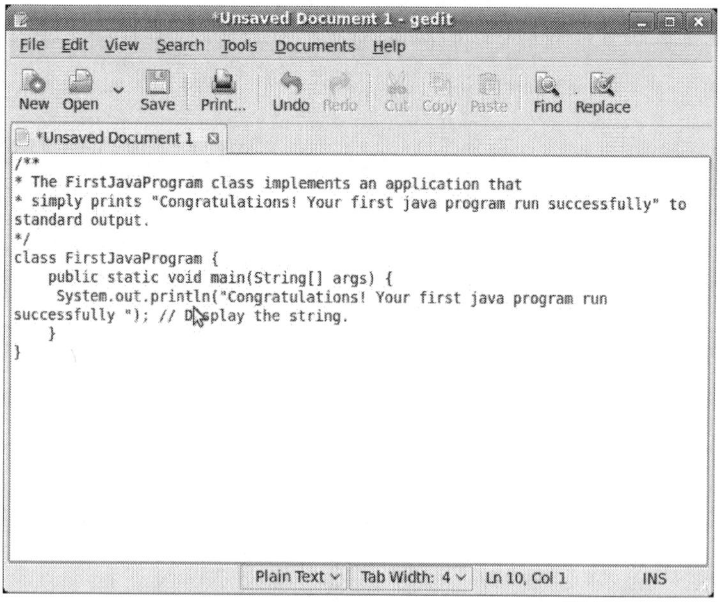

Figure 1.18 Editing the program with gedit program

Save the Program

You can create a directory where you should save the file you have created. Let the name of the directory be "Java."

Save the program in a file "precisely" with the name `FirstJavaProgram.java` in the directory `Java` (Figure 1.19).

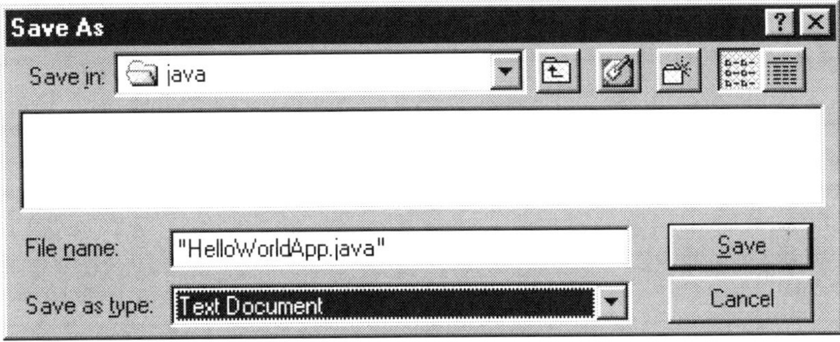

Figure 1.19 Saving the program in Windows

If you are working with Ubuntu, for example, then first choose the *File* > *Save As* menu item. Then, in the *Save As* dialog box:

1. Using the *Save* in combo box, specify the folder (directory) where you will save your file. In this example, the directory is /home/user/java on the hard drive.
2. In the *File name* text field, type "FirstJavaProgram.java" including the quotation marks (Figure 1.20).

From the *Save as type* combo box, choose *Text Documents*

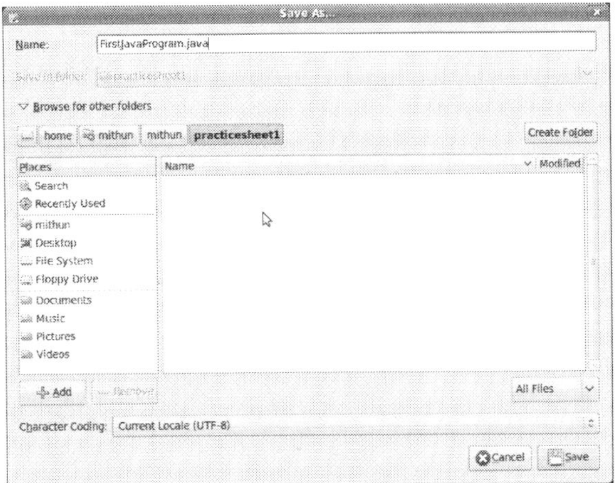

Figure 1.20 Saving the program in Ubuntu (with gedit)

Δ Type all codes, commands, and file names exactly as shown. The Java compiler (javac) and interpreter (java) are case-sensitive, so you must capitalize the letter(s) consistently. In this case, FirstJavaProgram.java ≠ firstjavaprogram.java

Δ Some OS may not distinguish between the upper and lowercase letters. In that case, give the name of the program file in all lowercase letters.

On successful saving, you can check the directory if the file is present (Figure 1.21).

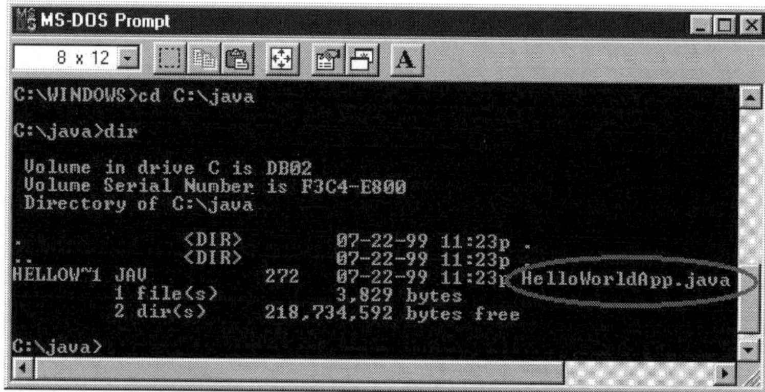

Figure 1.21 Saved file in Windows directory "java"

Compile the Program

To compile the code in the file, you should move to the directory "java" where your file is located (Figure 1.22). From that directory, run the following command:

```
javac FirstJavaProgram.java
```

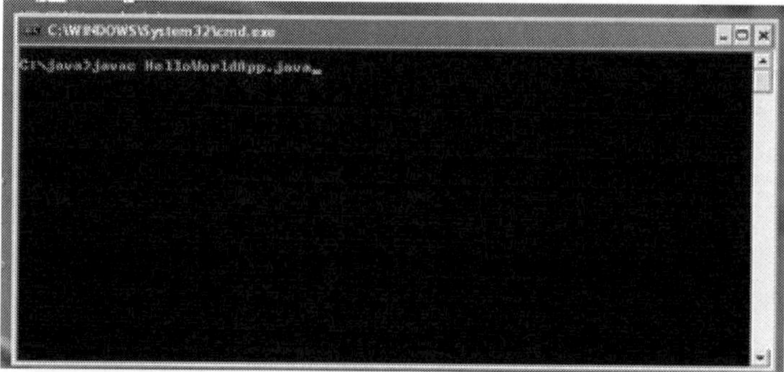

Figure 1.22 Compiling the program (in the directory "java") in Windows

After the compilation, the Java compiler (`javac`) takes your source file and translates its text into instructions that the Java virtual machine can understand. The instructions contained within this file are known as "byte codes." The byte code file is automatically saved by the `javac` in the same directory but with the name `FirstJavaProgram.class` (note the extension of the byte code file as .class. Hence, it is called "class file"). See Figure 1.23.

```
MS-DOS Prompt
C:\java>dir

 Volume in drive C is DB02
 Volume Serial Number is F3C4-E800
 Directory of C:\java

.              <DIR>        07-22-99 11:23p .
..             <DIR>        07-22-99 11:23p ..
HELLOW~1 JAV           272  07-23-99 12:39a HelloWorldApp.java
HELLOW~1 CLA           478  07-23-99 12:40a HelloWorldApp.class
         2 file(s)             750 bytes
         2 dir(s)      218,734,592 bytes free

C:\java>_
```

Figure 1.23 The compiled file (in the directory "java") in Windows

Execution of the Class File

Type the following command from the command prompt and then press enter to run the class file:

```
java FirstJavaProgram
```

o No need to type `.class` of the class file while you are executing.

The output of the program will be seen at the command window (Figure 1.24).

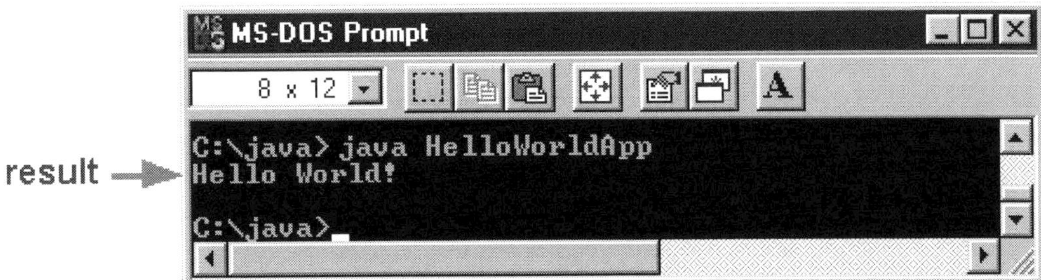

Figure 1.24 Output of the program in Windows

A Brief Explanation of Program 1.1

It is too early to understand the syntax in Java programming and hence the Program 1.1. However, it will be appropriate to mention few things which are not so difficult to understand at this stage.

```
1.  /*
2.  The FirstJavaProgram class implements an application
3.  that simply prints "Hello World!" to the standard
4.  output, that is, display screen.
5.  */
6.  import java.lang.*;
7.  class FirstJavaProgram
8.  {
9.      public static void main(String args[]){
10.       System.out.println("Hello, World!");
11.     } // Print the message on the screen
12. }
```

The content between the lines 1–5 is enclosed within `/*` and `*/` and is called the comments of the program. It is optional; however, it is a good programming habit to place reasonable comments in the program. Likewise, in line 11, the text followed by `//` is also a comment line. It is called short or inline comment, which should be confined to only a line. If you want to put a short comment, then you should put that after `//`. The statement in line 6 is to include the `java.lang` API into this program. This implies that if you refer to any class and method which are defined in `java.lang`, it is permitted. For example, we use a method (`System.out.println(...)`) in line 10, which is defined in `java.lang` package. In fact, `java.lang` is the default API, even if you don't import it, it will work. Codes in line 7–12 are the main program in this case. In Java, a program should be defined under a class with a name given by the programmer; in this case the class name is `FirstJavaProgram`. The codes under a class should be enclosed within "{" (in line 8) and "}" (in line 12), which are starting and ending curly brackets, respectively. In Java, the programmer can define methods to implement some operation. The `main(...)` method in line 9 is the only method in this program which contains code enclosed within "{" (in line 9) and "}" (in line 11). The `main(...)` in this case is very simple and contains only one statement (in line 10) to print a message on the screen. You may have many queries about `public`, `static`, `void`, and `String args[]` in line 9. We shall learn about these in later chapters. The statement in line 10 is the instruction to print any text (here it is `Hello World!` enclosed within "and") verbatim on the screen. This method is defined in class `System` which is in `java.lang` package.

- Δ A class is called as a main class if it contains the main(...) method. In this case, `class FirstJavaProgram` is the main class.
- Δ The name of the program should be same as the name of the "main class" with `.java` as the file extension.
- Δ You cannot run a java program without any main class.

1.6.3 First Java Applet Programming

There is another kind of programming known in Java called applet programming. Such a program is related to graphics on the screen and is primarily useful for developing a web page in HTML (hypertext mark-up language) which is an Internet programming language and is recognized by any browser.

Consider a simple program which will display the greeting "Hello World!" The following piece of code is an applet in this case:

Program 1.2
(Your first Java applet program)

```
// An applet to print a message
      import java.awt.Graphics;
      import java.applet.Applet;
      public class FirstAppletProgram extends Applet {
            public void paint (Graphics g) {
                g.drawString("Hello world!", 100, 50);
            }
      }
```

Editing the applet program

This procedure is same as what we have done in Program 1.1. Let the program be saved as `FirstAppletProgram.java` in a directory of your choice.

Compile the program

Compile the program with the following command:

```
javac FirstAppletProgram.java
```

After the successful compilation of the program, the byte code file will appear as `FirstAppletProgram.class` in the same directory as the `.java` file.

Running the applet

The program cannot be executed using the java command the way we have done in Program 1.1. To run an applet, we have to create an HTML file hosting the byte code file and then the HTML file can be run using any java-enabled browser or the `appletviewer` command in JDK. An HTML file in its simplest form hosting the `FirstAppletProgram.class` is given in Program 1.3.

Program 1.3

(An HTML file hosting an applet code)

```
< HTML >
    <HEAD>
      <TITLE > An HTML Containing HelloJavaApplet
      </TITLE>
    </ HEAD>
    <BODY>
      <HI> Very simple web page Demo </HI>
      <APPLET CODE="FirstAppletProgram.class" WIDTH=200
      HEIGHT = 100>
      </APPLET>
    </BODY>
<HTML>
```

The HTML file shown as Program 1.3 can be edited with any text editor and saved as a file with extension `.html` (or `.htm`). Let us save Program 1.3 as `applet1.html` (it should be saved in the same directory where the `.class` file is saved).

Finally, run the html file with following command:

```
appletviewer applet1.html
```

You will be able to see an output of the execution as shown in Figure 1.25.

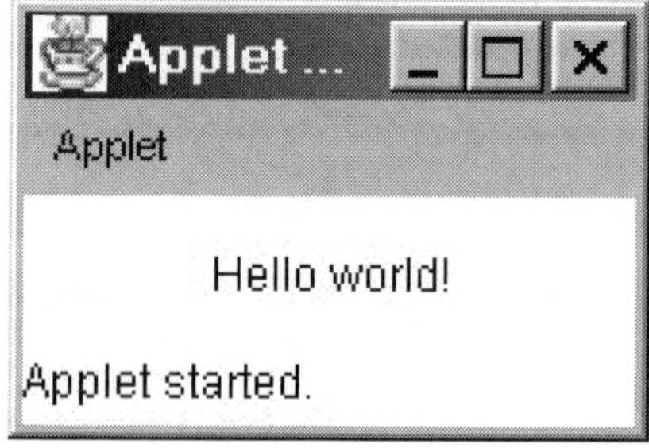

Figure 1.25 Applet on display

A brief explanation of Program 1.1, Program 1.2 and Program 1.3

You may notice a number of differences between Program 1.1 and Program 1.2. In Java, programs like Program 1.1 comes under "application" whereas Program 1.2 comes under "applet." Other than the actual usage of the two types of programming, there are several differences between the two which shall be discussed later in this book. Syntactically, for an applet program, there is no need to include any main method. Also, note the import section in Program 1.2 where two APIs, namely `java.awt` and `java.applet` packages are mentioned. Unlike, `System.out.println(...)` in Program 1.1, in Program 1.2, we use the method `g.drawString(...)` which is inside another method `paint(...)`.

In Program 1.3, the HTML tag `<Applet ... </Applet>` is to host the .class file. All other HTML tags are standard tags to write an HTML page.

- The name of the HTML file `hosting .class file` need not necessarily be the same as the name of the `.class` file.
- The `.class` file and `.html` file should be preferably in the same directory.
- The `.html` scripting is not case sensitive.

Summary

This chapter begins with the concept of computation, basic aspects of programming, and different programming paradigms. The concept of object-oriented programming is discussed in detail. A brief history of Java, its evolution and the advantages of Java programming over other programming languages are discussed. Java programming language is loaded with several features. The important points of each feature are discussed. For the beginners who are not very familiar with a computing environment, the tools for Java programming, setting, and installation guides in different platform are given. Finally, the chapter concludes with how programmers can write their first program in Java, compile it, and run it.

FAQs

1.1 What is a platform?

1.2 Why is Java platform independent?

1.3 What is JVM?

1.4 What is JRE?

1.5 What is JDK?

1.6 What is JIT compiler in Java?

1.7 What is object-oriented programming?

1.8 What are the main concepts of OOPs in Java?

1.9 Why is Java not a "pure" object-oriented programming language?

1.10 How does Java provide high performance?

1.11 What is the relationship between JavaScript and Java?

1.12 What is HotJava?

1.13 Which editor is good to type `.java` file?

The answers to these questions and other problems in this chapter are available at www.cambridge.org/9781009211918. You might have many questions like these. You can post your question in the discussion forum at https://cse.iitkgp.ac.in/~dsamanta/joywithjava/page8.php.

Programs for Practice

1.1 Write a program to print your name on the screen, preferably in the middle of the screen.

1.2 Type the following program and check the output:

```
/*
The following programs would print two message in one line.
*/
class HelloHi{
    public static void main(String args[]){
     System.out.print("Hello Java!");
    System.out.println(" Hi!");
    }
}
```

1.3 Type the following program and check the output:

```
/*
The following programs would print two messages in two lines.
*/
class HelloHiAgain{
    public static void main(String args[]){
    System.out.print("Hello Java! \n" + "Hi!");
    }
}
```

1.4 Write a Java program which will print 1, 2, ... 12 so that in each row there will be only four numbers.

1.5 Change the statement at line 6 in Program 1.2 with the following and notice the change in output:

```
g.drawString("My First Applet Program!",50,100 );
```

1.6 Change the statement at line 7 in Program 1.3 with the following and notice the change in output:

```
<APPLETCODE="FirstAppletProgram.class" WIDTH=300 HEIGHT=400>
```

MCQs

1.1 **Which of the following is true?**
- (a) Java uses only interpreter.
- (b) Java uses only compiler.
- (c) Java uses both interpreter and compiler.
- (d) None of these.

1.2 **A Java file with extension '.class' contains:**
- (a) Java source code.
- (b) HTML tags.
- (c) Java Byte code.
- (d) A program file written in Java programming language.

1.3 **Applet execution is:**
- (a) Server sided.
- (b) Client sided.
- (c) Both (a) and (b).
- (d) None of these.

1.4 **Which of the following is a "class" in Java?**
(a) int. (b) String. (c) short. (d) double.

1.5 **What is the length of the applet window made by the following program?**

```
import java.awt.*;
import java.applet.*;
public class myApplet extends Applet{
        Graphic g;
        g.drawString("A Simple Applet", 20, 30);
}
```
- (a) 20.
- (b) The same as the computer screen.
- (c) The program gives a compile-time error.
- (d) The program gives a run-time error.

1.6 **Which of the following is *not* an object-oriented programming paradigm?**
- (a) Encapsulation.
- (b) Inheritance.
- (c) Polymorphism.
- (d) Dynamic memory allocation.

1.7 **Which of the following features are not common in both Java and C++?**
(a) The class declaration.
(b) The access modifiers.
(c) The encapsulation of data and methods.
(d) Multiple inheritance from class.

1.8 **Choose the wrong statement:**
(a) Applets can read from or write to a file in the local computers.
(b) Applets cannot communicate with other servers in the networks.
(c) Applets can run any Java program.
(d) Applets can be viewed by a Java enabled browser.

1.9 **Java is a platform independent programming language because:**
(a) It compiles to an intermediate code targeting a virtual machine, which can be interpreted by an interpreter for a given OS.
(b) Java compiler translates the source code directly to the machine level language.
(c) It follows the concept of "write once and compile everywhere."
(d) It is written almost similar to English language.

1.10 **Which of the following is not a Language Processor?**
(a) Assembler. (b) Compiler. (c) Interpreter. (d) Fortran.

1.11 **A platform is the hardware or software environment in which a program runs. Which of the following is/are Java platform component(s)?**
(a) HTML.
(b) Java Virtual Machine.
(c) Java Application Programming Interface (API).
(d) HotJava.

2

Java Language Basics

Any language is characterized by two features: alphabets and grammar. To learn a language, it is necessary to learn these two features first. Once you have learned a language, you will be able to express a thought or idea, such as a poem, in the language. Language is used for communication and Java programming language is not an exception. Java language is used to express a programmer's instructions to solve a problem just like other programming languages, for example, C, C++, Python, etc. Java looks a lot similar to C++, and, by extension, like C. If you are an experienced C or C++ programmer, this chapter is mostly redundant for you. Java enables a programmer to write robust programs. This chapter aims to teach you all the basic features of Java that a programmer should know.

2.0 Introduction

Language elements

At this point, we are assuming that you have successfully installed Java and were able to run the sample programs given in Chapter 1. It is time now to start programming. As a Java programmer, it is necessary to have full understanding of the elements of the language like keywords, literals, data types, operators, loops, branches, etc.

Strongly typed language

Java programming language mostly follows syntax similar to that of C/ C++ to write statements and expressions. So if you are familiar with C/ C++, it will be easy for you to understand Java. As with all modern programming languages like C/ C++, Java is a strongly typed language, which means all data to be used should be defined their types in programs. Java supports several types of data, which are called primitive data types. In this chapter we will examine several data types, their structures, operations on them, and how they can be utilized to solve problems. Constants and variables are the two basic programming elements. It is necessary to learn how the variables of different data types can be defined. Java has a very good composition of defining arrays of elements of different types, which is also an interesting concept to learn. You may use different data types to declare variables and to create arrays of elements.

Control structures

Another feature in programming are the control structures. Java follows three control structures: sequence, iteration, and decision, similar to the function-oriented programming language like C, Pascal, etc. Like in C, Java allows different loop structures to iterate execution of some statements and branching mechanism to implement if-then-else rule.

Your learning

This chapter will help you to build robust and efficient programs. The Java compiler checks all programming elements strictly. Any type mismatches are errors which need to be resolved and hence a sound knowledge of Java language basics will help you to quickly fix the compilation errors.

2.1 Basic Elements of the Language

Java is a third-generation language (3GL), where programs are written using the English alphabet set. Besides, there are some specific features with which a program is usually composed of, such as comments, literals, reserved words, etc. This section attempts to familiarize you with them.

2.1.1 Comments

It is a good practice to include sufficient comments in each program. The comments are to improve the readability of the program and are neither compiled nor executed.

Java has three kinds of comments: two for regular comments and one for the special documentation system which is used by `javadoc` (the command `javadoc` is used to generate API documentation in HTML from code).

Multi-line comments

The symbols `/*` and `*/` surround multiline comments, as in C or C++. All text between the two delimiters is ignored while a program is compiled:

```
/* I don't know how I wrote this next part; I was working
really late one night and it just sort of appeared. I
suspect the code elves did it for me. It might be wise not
to try and change it.
*/
```

Single line comments

Double-slashes (`//`) can be used for a single line of comment. All the text up to the end of the line is ignored during program compilation:

```
System.out.println(""); // Print an empty string
```

Comments for document creation

The final type of comment begins with `/**` and ends with `*/`. The contents of these special comments are used by the `javadoc` system, but are otherwise used identically to the first type of comment.

These comments cannot be nested; you cannot have a comment inside a comment.

Avoid the following composition of comments:

```
/* This type of comment is bad.
// Earlier programming language this type is followed.
/* It is better to avoid such a style of commenting.*/
*/
// It is great! // Really!!
```

2.1.2 Java Lexical Elements

What is literal?

Literal is a programming language term that essentially means "what you type is what you get." For example, if you type "4" in a Java program, you automatically get an integer with the value 4. If you type "a", you get a character with the value a. Thus, literals are used to indicate simple values in your Java program. Text and numerals that are placed in program code are called literals, because the value is literally, rather than symbolically, in the program.

The program is typed using the computer keyboard (e.g., QWERTY keyboard). In this keyboard panel, you can see many keys; each is labelled with either an English alphabet (a–z, A–Z), numerals (0–9), or punctuation symbol, etc. in addition to some functional keys. Java language includes all the upper-case letters A to Z, lower case letters a to z and digits 0 to 9. In addition to these, it allows some special symbols which are listed in Table 2.1

Special character set

Table 2.1 Java special character set

<table>
<tr><td>,</td><td><</td><td>></td><td>.</td><td>_</td></tr>
<tr><td>(</td><td>)</td><td>;</td><td>$</td><td>:</td></tr>
<tr><td>%</td><td>[</td><td>]</td><td>#</td><td>?</td></tr>
<tr><td>'</td><td>&</td><td>{</td><td>}</td><td>"</td></tr>
<tr><td>^</td><td>!</td><td>*</td><td>/</td><td>|</td></tr>
<tr><td>-</td><td>\</td><td>~</td><td>+</td><td></td></tr>
</table>

ASCII codes

Note that each character that you can type is specified by an ASCII code (this is an 8-bit code). Sometime, in your program it is necessary to know the value of an ASCII code (it is in the range of 0 to 255) of a character. Table 2.2 lists all the symbols and their corresponding ASCII code values. Other 128 ASCII codes are called extended ASCII codes, which Java language does not recognize.

Table 2.2 First 128 ASCII code values

ASCII	Symbol	ASCII	Symbol	ASCII	Symbol	ASCII	Symbol
0	NUL (null)	32	SPACE	64	@	96	`
1	SOH (start of heading)	33	!	65	A	97	a
2	STX (start of text)	34	"	66	B	98	b
3	ETX (end of text)	35	#	67	C	99	c
4	EOT (end of transmission)	36	$	68	D	100	d
5	ENQ (enquiry)	37	%	69	E	101	e
6	ACK (acknowledge)	38	&	70	F	102	f
7	BEL (bell)	39	'	71	G	103	g
8	BS (backspace)	40	(	72	H	104	h
9	TAB (horizontal tab)	41	)	73	I	105	i
10	LF (NL line feed, new line)	42	*	74	J	106	j
11	VT (vertical tab)	43	+	75	K	107	k
12	FF (NP form feed, new page)	44	,	76	L	108	l
13	CR (carriage return)	45	-	77	M	109	m
14	SO (shift out)	46	.	78	N	110	n
15	SI (shift in)	47	/	79	O	111	o
16	DLE (data link escape)	48	0	80	P	112	p
17	DC1 (device control 1)	49	1	81	Q	113	q
18	DC2 (device control 2)	50	2	82	R	114	r
19	DC3 (device control 3)	51	3	83	S	115	s
20	DC4 (device control 4)	52	4	84	T	116	t
21	NAK (negative acknowledge)	53	5	85	U	117	u
22	SYN (synchronous idle)	54	6	86	V	118	v
23	ETB (end of trans. block)	55	7	87	W	119	w
24	CAN (cancel)	56	8	88	X	120	x
25	EM (end of medium)	57	9	89	Y	121	y
26	SUB (substitute)	58	:	90	Z	122	z
27	ESC (escape)	59	;	91	[	123	{
28	FS (file separator)	60	<	92	\	124	|
29	GS (group separator)	61	=	93	]	125	}
30	RS (record separator)	62	>	94	^	126	~
31	US (unit separator)	63	?	95	_	127	DEL

Unicode supports

As a more international application, Unicode is being planned to handle all characters in all written languages in the world. A Unicode is a 2-byte code. This allows 65,536 characters, of which about 35,000 are currently in use. This is far richer than the ASCII code set, which is a 1-byte code with 128 characters, or the commonly used ISO 8859-1 extension with 256 characters. This character set (which some programmers call the "Latin-1" character set) is a subset of Unicode. More precisely, it is the first 256 characters in the Unicode coding scheme. Thus, character codes like `a`, `1`, `[` and ä are valid Unicode characters with character codes < 256. Unicode characters have codes between 0 and 65535, but they are usually expressed as hexadecimal values that run from \u0000 to \uFFFF (with \u0000 to \u00FF being the ordinary ISO 8859-1 characters). The \u prefix indicates a Unicode value, and the four hexadecimal digits tell you what the Unicode character represents. For example, \u2122 is the trademark symbol (™). For more information on Unicode, you can check the website at http://www.unicode.org/.

Java source codes

Even though you may be entering your Java programs in an environment that stores ASCII characters, all Java source codes are in Unicode. The original source code that you create may be ASCII, but it is converted to Unicode characters internally before it is compiled. The reason that Java supports Unicode is to provide programmers an immense flexibility. In other words, the identifiers that you want to use in your program, you can define them using a national language character set that is defined within the Unicode character set. Thus, for examples, your programs can use Hindi, French, Greek, or Russian variable names, or even names in several different languages, provided that there is a mean to type them in the program. So, other than English, you can write your programs, say in Hindi!

Character combinations consisting of a backslash (\) followed by a letter or by a combination of digits are called "escape sequences." In Java, escape sequences are used to represent certain special characters within string literals and character literals. Few frequently used escape sequences which are used in Java programming are listed in Table 2.3. For example, \" to represent a double quotation mark, that is, if you want to print ".

Table 2.3 Escape sequences for special characters

Escape sequence	Name	Unicode value
\b	Back space	\u0008
\t	Tab	\u0009
\n	Line feed	\u000a
\r	Carriage return	\u000d
\"	Double quote	\u0022
\'	Single quote	\u0027
\\	Back slash	\u005c

Program 2.1 (String literals)

```
/*
The EscapeSequenceTest class illustrates the display of
      some escape sequences.
*/

import java.lang.*;
class EscpaeSequenceTest {
   public static void main(String args[]){
     System.out.println("Hi, I'm a string literal.");
                         // Print a string literal
     System.out.println("");
                         // Print an empty string
     System.out.println("A string with a \t tab in it");
     System.out.println("Nested strings are \"strings
                        inside of\" other strings");
     System.out.println("This string brought to
                              you by Java 2\u2122");
    }
}
```

In the last print statement in Program 2.1, the Unicode code sequence for \u2122 produces the trademark symbol (™).

C and C++ programmers should note that Java does not include character codes for \a (bell) or \v (vertical tab). Again, \0 which is frequently known in C and C++ as the delimiter of a string, is not used in Java.

Separators

There are a few characters in Java, which are used as separators. The most commonly used separators in Java are shown in Table 2.4.

Table 2.4 Separators in Java programming

Symbol	Name	Purpose
( )	Parentheses	Used to contain lists of parameters in method definition and invocation. Also used for defining precedence in expressions, containing expressions in control statements, and surrounding cast type.
{ }	Braces	Used to contain the values of automatically initialized arrays. Also used to define a block of code, for classes, methods, and local scopes.
[ ]	Brackets	Used to declare array types. Also used when dereferencing array values.
;	Semicolon	Terminates statements.
,	Comma	Separates consecutive identifiers in a variable declaration. Also used to chain statements together inside a for statement.
.	Period	Used to separate package names from sub-packages and classes. Also used to separate a variable or method from a reference variable.
::	Colons	Used to create a method or constructor reference.

- Just because you can represent a character using a Unicode escape does not mean that your computer can display that character; the computer or operating system where you are running your program may not support Unicode, or the font you are using may not have a glyph (picture) for that character. Unicode escapes in Java essentially provide a way to encode Unicode characters for systems that support Unicode.
- When you use a string literal in your Java program, Java automatically creates an instance of the `class String` for you with the value you give it. Strings are unusual in this respect; the other literals do not behave in this manner (none of the primitive data types are actual objects), and usually creating a new object involves explicitly creating a new instance of a class. You will learn more about strings, the `String` class, and the things you can do with strings later in this book.

Keywords

Java reserved words

Keywords are special reserved words in Java that you cannot use as identifiers (names) for classes, methods, or variables. Each keyword has its meaning to the compiler; the compiler uses them to figure out what your source code is trying to do. Table 2.5 contains all 49 keywords in Java language. Notice none of the reserved words have capital letters.

Table 2.5 Java keywords

`abstract`	`boolean`	`break`	`byte`	`case`	`catch`
`char`	`class`	`const`	`continue`	`default`	`do`
`double`	`else`	`extends`	`final`	`finally`	`float`
`for`	`goto`	`if`	`implements`	`import`	`instanceof`
`int`	`interface`	`long`	`native`	`new`	`package`
`private`	`protected`	`public`	`return`	`short`	`static`
`strictfp`	`super`	`switch`	`synchronized`	`this`	`throw`
`throws`	`transient`	`try`	`void`	`volatile`	`while`
`assert`					

As we learn the programming, we will learn about each keyword. There are some keywords we have just mentioned in Table 2.4 which rarely occur in programs. A brief discussion about these rare keywords is given here for your knowledge.

Rare keywords

`native`: Indicates a method is written in a platform-dependent language, such as C.

`strictfp`: Used in front of a method or class to indicate that floating-point numbers will follow FP-strict rules in all expressions.

`synchronized`: Indicates that a method can be accessed by only one thread at a time.

`transient`: Prevents fields from ever being serialized. Transient fields are always skipped when objects are serialized.

`volatile`: Indicates a variable may change out of sync because it is used in threads.

`instanceof`: Determines whether an object is an instance of a class, super class, or interface.

`assert`: Evaluates a conditional expression to verify the programmer's assumption.

- There are two keywords that are reserved in Java but are not used. Maybe they had been used in an earlier version but have now become obsolete. They are:

`const`: It is not used to declare a constant anymore; use `public`, `static`, `final` instead.

`goto`: Not implemented in Java now. It is considered harmful.

- If you try to use one of these keywords, the Java compiler will report a compile-time error.
- Further, `null`, `false`, `true` are not Java keywords; they are literals.

Program 2.2 *(Illegal use of keywords)*

```
/* A keyword cannot be used as name of a method or
     variable in a program */

class Foo {
     public void go() {      // Okay: go is not a keyword
              // Some code here
     }
     public int break(int b) {  // break cannot be used
              // Some more code here
     }
     public static void main (String [] args) {
              int true = 100;
                   //true: use of like this causes error
     }
}
```

2.1.3 Variables, Identifiers, and Constants

A program is used to process data. Such data should be stored in the memory. Data can be a constant or it can also be stored in the form of a variable. A variable should be identified uniquely by a name in the program. This is why a variable is synonymously called an identifier (because it identifies a program object). The following is an instruction in Java. Here, `int` is a keyword and this instruction says that `i` is a variable, which stores the value 100, where 100 is a constant.

A simple statement

```
int i = 100;
```

Variables are locations in memory in which values can be stored. Each variable has a name, a type, and a value. Before you can use a variable, you have to declare it. After it is declared, you can assign values to it (you can also declare and assign a value to a variable at the same time, as you will learn in this section). Thus a variable is a named piece of memory that you use to store information in your Java program. Each named piece of memory that you define in your program is able to store data in it. The name that you choose for a variable, or the name that you choose for anything in Java to store data, is alternatively called an identifier.

Naming an identifier

Of course, there are rules for choosing constant and variable names. You can't just type a bunch of characters on your keyboard and expect Java to accept them. First, every Java identifier must begin with one of these characters:

Rule 1

A–Z

a–z

_ (underscore)

$

The preceding characters are any uppercase letter from A through Z, any lowercase letter from a through z, an underscore, and the dollar sign.

Following the first character, the rest of the identifier can use any of these characters:

Rule 2

A–Z

a–z

_ (underscore)

$

0–9

As you may have noticed, this second set of characters is very similar to the first; the only difference is the addition of the digits from 0 through 9. It can include any characters except those used as operators in Java (such as +, –, / or *) and punctuation symbols, single and double quotes, etc.

Using the rules given so far, the following are valid identifiers in a Java program:

Some examples of valid identifiers

number

number2

amount_of_sale

$amount

The following identifiers are not valid in a Java program:

Some examples of invalid identifiers

```
1number         // First character should not be a digit
amount of sale  // Blanks space(s) is(are) not allowed
&amount         // & is not a valid character in naming
item#           // # is not a valid character in naming
switch          // A keyword cannot be used to name an identifier
```

- By carefully choosing variable names, you can make your programs self-documenting, which means that the program lines themselves tell, whoever might be reading the program, what the program does. If you strip away the comments from the preceding example, you can still see what calculations are being performed.

- Even though you may be entering your Java programs in an environment that stores ASCII characters, all Java source code is in Unicode. Although the original source code that you create may be ASCII, it is converted to Unicode characters internally, before it is compiled. Java supports Unicode providing you an immense flexibility. It means that the identifiers that you use in your source program can use any national language character set that is defined within the Unicode character set. This means that your programs can use variable names, in French, Greek, or Russian, for example, or even names in several different languages, as long as you have the means to enter them in your program through your program editor.
- Java is case-sensitive, so the names `item` and `Item` are two different identifiers and `Switch` is a valid identifier name.
- Blanks or tabs in the middle of a name are not allowed. For example, `roll number` is wrong; instead of you could say `roll_number`.
- It is customary to start an identifier with a lowercase letter and have uppercase letter(s) in the middle. For example, `rollNumber` is a good way to represent an identifier name.
- Although theoretically there is no limit in the length of an identifier, but a rule of thumb is to restrict the length to 10 characters.
- If you need more guidance in naming conventions (and coding conventions in general) have a look at http://www.javasoft.com/docs/codeconv/.

Constants

What is a constant?

In Java, a constant is nothing other than a value. In a program, a constant keeps a value unchanged throughout the program's execution. While the definition of a constant is fairly simple, constants themselves can come in many different forms. For example, the numeral 246, when it's used in a line of program code, is an integer constant. As another example, if you mention the word "Joy with Java" in a program, the characters that comprise the word is also a constant. In this example, such a constant, where characters are taken together is often referred to as a string constant. Such values as the numeral 246 and the string constant "Joy with Java" are sometimes called hard-coded values because the values that represent the constants are placed literally in the program code.

In the following, we see a statement with a constant (i.e., a floating point value .08) and three identifiers, namely `interest`, `principal` and `time`.

```
interest = principal * .08 * time;
```

Java allows declaring a constant in programs, they are often called symbolic constants, which are simply words that represent values in a program. For example, you could choose a word like RATE_OF_INTRESET whose value is, say .08. Then, at the beginning of your program, you set RATE_OF_INTRESET to be equal to the value. For an example, you can declare a constant as follows:

Constant declaration

```
final float RATE_OF_INTRESET = 0.08;
```

Carefully note the declaration in the example. Here, the word `final` tells Java that this data object is going to be a constant. The `float` is the data type, which, in this case, is a floating point value. (You'll learn more about data types later in this chapter.) The name `RATE_OF_INTRESET` is the symbolic constant. The equals sign tells Java that the word on the left should be equal to the value on the right, in this case, is 0.08. Now, if your application changes the rate of interest to 6 percent, you need only change the value you assign to the symbolic constant and the rest of the program automatically fixes itself. The change would look like this:

```
final float RATE_OF_INTEREST = 0.08;
```

In the preceding line, the word `final` tells Java that this data object is going to be a constant. The float is the data type, which in this case is a floating point. (You will learn more about data types later in this chapter.) The words `RATE_OF_INTEREST` is a symbolic constant. The equal to sign tells Java that the word on the left should be equal to the value on the right, which in this case is 0.08. Now, if your application changes the rate of interest to 6 percent, you need only change the value you assign to the symbolic constant and the rest of the program automatically fixes itself. The change would look like this:

```
final float RATE_OF_INTEREST = 0.06;
```

- In order to differentiate symbolic constants from other values in a program, programmers often use all uppercase letters when naming these constants.
- Unlike other languages, Java does not have global variables, that is, variables that are global to all parts of a program.

2.2 Primitive Data Types

Declaring a variable

Java is a strongly typed language. This means that to use any variable in a Java program, you must first declare it. Variable declarations consist of a type and a variable name. The following is a typical syntax in Java:

```
<type> <identifire_name>;
```

There are eight primitive types in Java to declare variables. They are called "primitive" because they are built by the language developer and you don't have to worry about how a variable with primitive data type is stored and manipulated in programs. Primitive data types are broadly categorized as integer types, floating-point types, character type, and Boolean types. In the following sections, we learn how to declare them, the range of values and operations on each data type.

2.2.1 Integer Data Types

Integer data type

Integer values are the most common values used in computer programs. Integer values represent whole numbers, such as 9, 1964, –214, etc. Note that integer values can be both positive and negative, or even the value 0. The size of the value that is allowed depends on the integer data type you choose. To facilitate the different sizes for integer values, Java supports four integer data types: `byte`, `short`, `int`, and `long` (Table 2.6). Note that all of Java's integers are signed, which means they can be positive or negative.

Table 2.6 The four integer types in Java

Integer data type	Description
`byte`	Variables of this type can have values from –128 to +127 and occupy **1 byte** (8 bits) in memory.
`short`	Variables of this type can have values from –32768 to 32767 and occupy **2 bytes** (16 bits) in memory.
`int`	Variables of this type can have values from –2147483648 to 2147483647 and occupy **4 bytes** (32 bits) in memory.
`long`	Variables of this type can have values from –9223372036854775808 to 9223372036854775807 and occupy **8 bytes** (64 bits) in memory.

`byte` data type

Declaring `byte` *variable*

In Java, you declare a `byte` value as follows:

```
byte count;
```

In the preceding line, `byte` is the data type for the value and count is the variable's name. You can also simultaneously declare and assign a value to a variable like this:

```
byte count = 100;
```

After Java executes the preceding line, your program will have a variable named `count` that currently holds the value of 100. Of course, you can change the contents of count at any time in your program. It only starts off holding the value 100.

`short` data type

Declaring `short` *variable*

The next bigger type of Java integer is `short`. A variable declared as short can hold a value from –32,768 to 32,767. You declare a short value like this:

```
short number;
```

or

```
short number = x;
```

In the preceding line, `x` (it is another number) can have any value from –32,768 to 32,767, as described previously. In Java, `short` values are as big as two bytes, or 16 bits in memory.

`int` data type

Next in the integer data types is `int`, which can hold a value from –2147483648 to 2147483647. Now you're getting into some big numbers! The `int` data type can hold such large numbers because it takes up 32 bits (four bytes) of computer memory. You declare `int` values like this:

Declaring `int` *variable*

```
int total;
```

or

```
int total = value;
```

`long` data type

The final integer data type in the Java language is `long`, which takes up a whopping 64 bits (eight bytes) of computer memory and can hold truly immense numbers. You may need such data type if you want to calculate the factorial value of a large number, for example. You declare a long value like this:

Declaring `long` *variable*

```
long identifier;
```

or

```
long identifier = value;
```

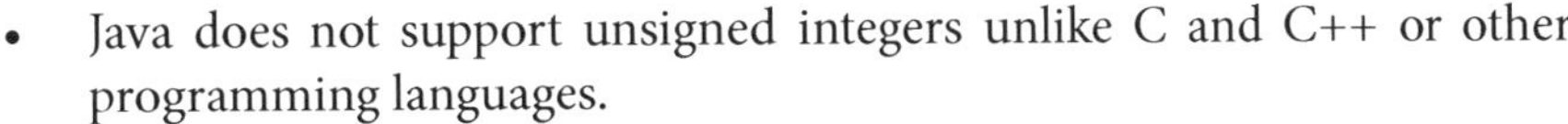

- Java does not support unsigned integers unlike C and C++ or other programming languages.
- In Java, the sizes of all numeric types are platform independent.
- In contrast, in C and C++, `int` denotes the integer type that depends on the target machine. On a 16-bit processor, like the 8086, integers are 2 bytes. On a 32-bit processor like the Sun SPARC, they are 4-bytes. On an Intel Pentium, the integer type of C and C++ depends on the operating system: for DOS and Windows 3.1, integers are 2 bytes. When using 32-bit mode for Windows programs, integers are 4 bytes.
- Under Java, the ranges of the integer types do not depend on the machine on which you will be running the Java code. This enables Java software to run from one platform to another, or even between operating systems on the same platform. In contrast, C and C++ programs that runs well on a 32-bit processor may exhibit integer overflow on a 16-bit system.
- Limiting the size of an integer value in Java has its own advantages. The smaller the data type, the faster the computer can manipulate it. For example, your computer can move a `byte` value, which consumes only eight bits of memory, much faster than an `int` value, which in Java is four times as large. So, if you know the range of values to be manipulated, then used that type only.
- When `int` and `short` values are used in an expression, they are promoted to `int` when the expression is evaluated. Suppose you have two integer values but of different type as in the following:

```
int x;
short y;
y = x;
```

If you put the value in x into y and if the value of x > y, then it is not true that a truncated value will be stored in y.

- Long integer numbers have a suffix (for example, 4000000000L). Hexadecimal numbers have a prefix 0x (for example, 0xCAFE). Octal numbers have a prefix 0. For example, 010 is 8.

Program 2.3 (Using integer data type)

```
/* Following program shows the use of integer data type */
public class FruitCount {
    public static void main(String[] args) {
       // Declare and initialize three variables
       byte numOranges = 5;     // Count of oranges
       short numApples = 10;    // Count of apples
       int numFruit = 0;        // Count of fruit
       numFruit = numOranges + numApples;
               // Calculate the total fruit count
       // Display the result
       System.out.println("A totally fruity program!");
       System.out.println("Total fruit count is " +
               numFruit);
    }
}
```

Integer literals

Integer literals

There are several integer literals. For example, 4 is a decimal integer literal of type `int` (although you can assign it to a variable of type `byte` or `short` because it is small enough to fit into those types). A decimal integer literal larger than an `int` is automatically of the type `long`. You also can force a smaller number to a `long` by appending an L or l to that number (for example, 4L is a long integer of value 4). Negative integers are preceded by a minus sign. For example, –45.

Integers can also be expressed as octal or hexadecimal: A leading 0 indicates that a number is octal. For example, 0777 or 0004. A leading 0x (or 0X) means that it is in hex (0xFF, 0XAf45). Hexadecimal numbers can contain regular digits (0–9) or upper or lowercase hex digits (a–f or A–F).

There are three ways to represent integer numbers in Java language: decimal (base 10), octal (base 8), and hexadecimal (base 16).

Decimal literals

Decimal integers are the simple way we are familiar with to express numbers. In Java,, they are represented as is, with no prefix of any kind, as follows:

```
int length = 343;
```

Octal literals

Octal integers use only the digits 0 to 7. In Java, you represent an integer in octal form by placing a zero in front of the numbers (Program 2.4).

Program 2.4
(Integers in octal form)

```
class OctalLiteralTest {
    public static void main(String [] args) {
        int six = 06;     // Equal to decimal 6
        int seven = 07;   // Equal to decimal 7
        int eight = 010; // Equal to decimal 8
        int nine = 011;   // Equal to decimal 9
        System.out.println("Octal 010 = " + eight);
    }
}
```

Note that we are only allowed the digits 0 through 7 for octal numbers; when we get past seven and are out of digits to use, we revert to zero, and the number 1 is added to the beginning of the number.

Hexadecimal literals

Hexadecimal (hex for short) numbers are constructed using 16 distinct symbols. Because we never invented single digit symbols for the numbers 10 through 15, we use alphabetic characters to represent these digits. Counting from 0 through 15 in hex looks like this:

0 1 2 3 4 5 6 7 8 9 a b c d e f

Java will accept capital or lowercase letters for the extra digits (one of the few places Java is not case-sensitive!). You are allowed up to 16 digits in a hexadecimal number, with the prefix 0x or 0X or the optional suffix extension L, which will be explained later.

Program 2.5
(Integers in hexadecimal form)

```
/* In the program given below, all of the following
            hexadecimal assignments are legal. */
class HexLiteralTest {
    public static void main (String [] args) {
        int x = 0X0001;

        int y = 0x7fffffff;
        int z = 0xDeadCafe;
        System.out.println("x = " + x + " y = " + y + " z
              = " + z);
    }
}
```

- For a hexadecimal digit with a declaration preceding with 0x or 0X, for example, 0XCAFE, 0xcafe, and 0xCafe are all legal representations.
- All three integer literals (octal, decimal, and hexadecimal) are defined as `int` by default, but they may also be specified as `long` by placing a suffix of L or l after the number. For example:

```
long jo = 110599L;   // Long integer in decimal

long so = 0xFFFFl;   // Note the lowercase 'l'
```

2.2.2 Floating Point Data Types

Numeric values that are not integral are termed as floating-point numbers (also called real numbers). A floating-point number can be with a fixed number of digits of accuracy but with a very wide range of values. With floating point values, you can manage a wide range of values, even though the number of digits is fixed, because the decimal point can "float." For example, the values 0.000005, 500.0, and 5000000000000.0 can be written as 5 × 10–6, 5 × e2, and 5 × E12, respectively. Here, you have just one digit 5 but you get three different values by moving the decimal point around.

There are two primitive floating-point types in Java which you can use: `float` and `double`. These types give you a choice about the level of precision to have your data values, and in the range of values that can be accommodated (Table 2.7).

Specification of real numbers in Java

Table 2.7 The two floating point date types in Java

Floating point data type	Description
float	Variables of this type can have values from –3.4E38 (–3.4 × 10^{38}) to +3.4E38 (+3.4 × 10^{38}) and occupy 4 bytes in memory. Values are represented with approximately 7 decimal digits accuracy.
double	Variables of this type can have values from –1.7E308 (–1.7 × 10^{308}) to +1.7E308 (+1.7 × 10^{308}) and occupy 8 bytes in memory. Values are represented with approximately 17 decimal digits accuracy. The smallest non-zero value that you can have is roughly 4.9 × 10^{-324}.

Let's us have a bit of insight into floating point types `float` and `double`. Each type allows a precision in calculations. What does this mean? Note that floating-point values can be very complex when they are used in calculations; particularly, in multiplication and division. For example, when you divide

3.9 by 2.7, you get 1.44444444. In actuality, though, the fractional portion of the number goes on forever. That is, if you were to continue the division calculation, you would observe that you keep getting more and more 4s in the fractional part of the answer. The answer to 3.9 divided by 2.7 is not really 1.44444444, but rather something more like 1.4444444444444444. But even that answer is not completely accurate. A more accurate answer would be 1.4 444444444444444444444444444444. The more 4s you add to the answer the more accurate the answer is, because the 4s extend on into infinity, you can never arrive at a completely accurate answer.

`float` data type

Dealing with floating-point values frequently means deciding how many decimal places in the answer are accurate enough for your purpose. That is where the difference between the `float` and `double` data types comes up. In Java, a value declared as `float` can hold a number in the range from around -3.402823×10^{38} to around 3.402823×10^{38}. These types of values are also known as single-precision floating-point values and take up 32 bits (4 bytes) of memory. You declare a single-precision floating-point number like this:

Declaring a `float` *variable*

```
float x;
```

or

```
float y = value;
```

In the second line, value must be in the range for `float` data type, followed by an upper or lowercase F. However, you can write floating-point numbers in a couple of ways, using regular digits and a decimal point or using scientific notation. For example, the following is a type of floating-point number:

356.552

Now, here is the same number written using Java rules. The number is in normal form and in the form of scientific notation:

356.552f

3.56552e2f

Value in floating-point format

Both of the preceding values are equivalent, and you can use either form in a Java program. The e2 in the second case is the equivalent of writing 10^2 and is a short form of scientific notation that is often used in programming.

`double` data type

The second type of floating-point data is called `double`. The name `double` refers to the fact that these numbers have twice the precision of the `float` type. A `double` precision value has a much more accurate representation than a (single-precision) floating-point number because it allows more decimal places. A `double` value can be in the range from $-1.79769313486232 \times 10^{308}$ to$1.79769313486232 \times 10^{308}$ and is declared like this:

```
double x;
```

or

```
double x = value;
```

Floating-point values of the `double` type are written exactly as their float counterparts, except you use an upper or lowercase D as the suffix, rather than an F. Here are a few examples:

3.14d

344.23456D

3.4423456e2d

- There are three special floating-point values to denote overflows and errors. These are:

  (a) positive infinity

  (b) negative infinity

  (c) NaN (not a number)

For example, the result of dividing a positive number by 0 is positive infinity. Computing 0/0 or the square root of a negative number yields NaN.

- All floating-point operations and the definitions for values of type `float` and type `double` conform to the IEEE 754 standard.
- Numbers of type `float` have a suffix F, for example, 3.402F. Floating-point numbers without an F suffix (such as 3.402) are always considered to be of type `double`. You can optionally supply a D suffix such as 3.402D.
- As with integer calculations, floating-point calculations in Java will produce the same results on any computer.

Program 2.6 (Use of floating point data type)

```
/* Following is a program to compute the area of a circle. */
   class CircleArea {
     public static void main(String args[]) {
        double pi, r, a;
        r = 10.8;          // Radius of circle
        pi = 22.0/7.0;     // Floating point value of 22/7
        a = pi * r * r;    // Compute area
        System.out.println("Area of circle is " + a);
     }
   }
```

Floating point literals

Floating-point literals usually have two parts, the integer part and the decimal part, for example, 5.77777. A floating point literal results in a floating-point number of type `double`, regardless of the precision of the number. You can force the number to the type `float` by appending the letter f (or F) to the number, for example, 2.56F.

You can use exponents in floating-point literals using the letter e or E followed by the exponent (which can be a negative number): 10e45 or .36E–2.

Floating-point numbers are defined as a number, a decimal symbol, and more digits representing the fraction.

```
double d = 11301874.9881024;
```

In the preceding example, the number 11301874.9881024 is the literal value. Floating-point literals are defined as double (64 bits) by default, so if you want to assign a floating-point literal to a variable of type `float` (32 bits), you must attach the suffix F or f to the number. If you don't, the compiler will complain about a possible loss of precision, because you are trying to fit a number into a (potentially) less precise "container." The F (or f) suffix tell the compiler to store it in precise form.

```
float f = 23.467890;
        // Compiler error, possible loss of precision
float g = 49837849.029847F; // OK; has the suffix "F"
```

You may also optionally attach a D or d to double literals, but it is not necessary because this is the default behavior.

```
double d = 110599.995011D; // Optional, not required
double g = 987.897;
                 // OK because the literal is a double
```

2.2.3 Character Data Type

Other than numeric values, often in your programs, you need to represent character values. A character is a symbol that is used to compose a text. The most obvious examples of characters are the letters of the English alphabet, in both upper- and lower case forms. Further, there are many other characters, such as spaces, exclamation points, commas, etc. Other than these, tabs, carriage returns, line feeds, etc. are also characters. Note that the symbols 0 through 9 are also characters when they are not being used in mathematical calculations; for example 12.05.1965 are characters representing a date of birth.

Size of `char` *data*

In order to provide storage for character values, Java provides a data type called `char`, which uses 16 bits to store. This means you can store 2^{16} different character values. However, the size of the `char` data type has little to do with the values it can hold. You can think of a `char` as being able to hold a single character.You declare a char value like this:

```
char c;
```

or

```
char c = 'A';
```

In the second example, you are not only declaring the variable `c` as a `char`, but also setting its value to an uppercase A. Note that the character being assigned is enclosed in single quotes.

Some characters cannot be written with only a single symbol. For example, the tab character is represented in Java as \t, which is a back slash followed by a lowercase t. There are several of these special characters, as shown in Table 2.3. Note that the special characters in Table 2.3 are represented by two symbols, the first of which is always a back slash, still they are considered as single characters. For example, to define a `char` variable as a back space character, you should write something like the following in your Java program:

```
char backspace = '\b';
```

When Java compiler sees the back slash, it knows that it is about to represent a special character. The symbol following the back slash tells the compiler which special character to use. There are several special characters that might confuse the compiler because they are used as a part of Java language. Because the back slash is used to signify a special character, when you want to specify the back slash character itself, you must use two back slashes together. Other special characters that might confuse the compiler are single and double quotes. When you want to use these characters in your program, you must also precede them with a back slash.

- `char` in Java is not the same as `char` in C/ C++. In C/C++, `char` is 8 bits. Here, a character is identified as the ASCII value, which is in the range of 0 to 127 and in the extended 8-bit character set, ISO-Latin-1, ranges from 0 to 255.
- Java uses Unicode to represent characters. In Java, the range of a character is 0 to 65,536. This allows representing any character in any human language around the globe (Table 2.8 gives some characters in different languages).
- There are no negative vlaues for any characters.
- Remember, characters are just 16-bit unsigned integers under the hood. That means you can assign a number literal, assuming it will fit into the unsigned 16-bit range (65535 or less).

Table 2.8 Some code point values as per the Unicode format

Character	Unicode code point	Glyph
Latin A	U+0041	A
Latin sharp S	U+00DF	ß
Han for East	U+6771	東
Deseret, LONG I	U+10400	𐐀

Program 2.7 *(Character data type)*

```
/* Here is a program that demonstrates char data type */

class CharDemo {
    public static void main(String args[]) {
    char ch1, ch2, ch3; // Three character type variables
    ch1 = 65;          // The ASCII code for A
    ch2 = 'c';        // 'c' is the ASCII code of c
    ch3 = '\u0074'   // The Unicode of English letter t
    System.out.print("ch1: "+ ch1 +  "ch2: " + ch2);
    System.out.print("ch3 :" + ch3 +"\uabcd");
                // t and Unicode of \uabcd are printed
    char a = 0x892;   // octal literal : legal
    char b = 982;    // int literal : legal
    char c = -29;   // Illegal
    char d = 70000 // Illegal
    char c = (char) 70000; // Casted to char : legal
    char d = (char) -98;  // Ridiculous, but legal
    }
}
```

2.2.4 Boolean Data Type

Declaration of Boolean variables

Often, in a program you need a way to determine if a specific condition has been met or not. For example, you might need to know whether a part of your program executed properly. In such cases, you can use Boolean values, which are represented in Java by the `boolean` data type. Boolean values are unique for they can take only one of two possible values: `true` or `false`. You declare a `boolean` value like this:

```
boolean b;
```

or

```
boolean d = value;
```

In the second example, value must be either `true` or `false`. In an actual program, you should write something like this:

```
boolean flag = true;
boolean f = 0;   // Compilation error, 0 does not mean false
```

- Boolean data type in Java represents 1 bit of information.
- In C and C++, Boolean variable `false` is 0 and a non-zero integer value is `true`.
- This is the type of value returned by all relational operators, as in the case of a < b where a and b are any primitive data type.

Program 2.8 *(Boolean data type)*

```
/* Demonstrate boolean values. */
class BooleanTest {
      public static void main(String args[]) {
      boolean b;
      b = false;
      System.out.println("b is " + b);
      b = true;
      System.out.println("b is " + b);
      // a boolean value can control the if statement
      if(b) System.out.println("This is executed.");
      b = false;

      if(b) System.out.println("This is not executed.");
      // outcome of a relational operator is a boolean
                                                // value
      System.out.println("10 > 9 is " + (10 > 9));
    }
}
```

2.3 Expressions and Operators

Assignment expression

Writing a program means you have to write a set of statements. The simplest form of statement in Java is called *expression.* An expression, when evaluated, returns a value. The simplest expression is an assignment statement. To store the result of a calculation in a variable, you should use an assignment statement. An assignment statement essentially consists of three parts: left part, the name of the variable where you want to store result; middle part, the assignment operator, =, which indicates that this is an assignment operation; right part, an arithmetic expression that defines the calculation you want to perform. Note, the whole thing should be terminated by a semicolon that marks the end of the assignment statement. Here is a simple example for your understanding:

```
int x, y;      // x and y are two integer variables
x = 10;        // 10 is stored in x
y = x;         // The value of x is copied into y;
               // Now both x and y hold the value 10
x = y = 50;    // This is also possible; both x and y
               // are assigned together the value 50
```

Operators in Java

Most of the expressions in Java use operators. Operators are special symbols for operations like arithmetic, various forms of assignment, increment and decrement, and logical operations. In Java, all the operators can be divided into four groups: arithmetic, bitwise, relational, and logical. Java also defines some additional operators that handle certain special situations. Let us now describe all the Java operators.

2.3.1 Arithmetic Operators

All the arithmetic operators can be classified into three categories: basic arithmetic operators, arithmetic compound assignment operators, and increment/decrement operators.

Basic arithmetic operators

Java has five operators for basic arithmetic operations, which are listed in Table 2.9.

Table 2.9 Basic arithmetic operators in Java

Operator	Operation
+	Addition (also unary plus)
–	Subtraction (also unary minus)
*	Multiplication
/	Division
%	Modulus

The basic arithmetic operations: addition, subtraction, multiplication, and division, are all applicable to numeric operands. All of them are binary operators in the sense that each operator takes two operands. However, the + and – also can be used for unary operation. The unary plus operator simply returns the value of its operand. The unary minus operator negates its single operand.

The following are a few examples:

```
x = -25;
x = y/2.0           // Floating-point division
```

Program 2.9 *(Arithmetic operations)*

```
/* Simple arithmetic test */
class ArithmeticTest {
    public static void main (String args[]) {
        short x = 6;
        int y = 4;
        float a = 12.5f;
        float b = 7f;

        System.out.println("x is " + x + ", y is " + y);
        System.out.println("x + y = " + (x + y));
        System.out.println("x - y = " + (x - y));
        System.out.println("x / y = " + (x / y));
        System.out.println("x % y = " + (x % y));

        System.out.println("a is " + a + ", b is " + b);
        System.out.println("a / b = " + (a / b));
    }
}
```

- Arithmetic operators are applicable to integer and floating point data types. They are not applicable to Boolean data.
- Integer division results in an integer. Because integers don't have decimal fractions, any remainder is ignored. The expression 31/9, for example, results in 3. On the other hand, 15.0/2, 15/2.0 or 15.0/2.0 will all result in 7.5.
- Note that integer division by 0 raises an exception, whereas floating-point division by 0 yields an infinite or `NaN` result.
- Modulus (%) gives the remainder once the operands have been evenly divided. For example, 31 % 9 results in 4 because 9 goes into 31 three times, with 4 left over.

Program 2.10
(% operation)

```
/* Demonstration of  % operator. */

class ModulusOpeartion {
    public static void main(String args[]) {
        int x = 25;
        double y = 25.3;

        float z = 4.5f;
        System.out.println("x mod 4 = " + x % 4);
              // Returns 1
        System.out.println("y mod 10 = " + y % 4);
              // Returns 1.3
        System.out.println("z mod 2.3 = " + z % 2.3);
              // Returns 2.2
    }
}
```

Character arithmetic

The basic arithmetic operators are also applicable to `char` types since the `char` type in Java is, essentially, a subset of `int`. When you use variables of type `char` in an arithmetic expression, their values will be converted to type `int` to carry out the calculation. The following are few examples for your understanding:

```
char myChar = 'X';

myChar = mu = yChar + 1;    // Now myChar is 'Y'.

char aChar = 0;

char bChar = '\u0028';

aChar = (char)(2*bChar + 8);

                    // holds the Unicode for 0x0058
```

Mixed arithmetic operations

Expressions with several operators as well as different type of operands are all allowed in Java. For example:

```
x = 20 - 3 * 3 - 9 / 3;
```

or

```
y = 12.34/2 +2*4-8643;
```

Such mixed arithmetic operations are governed by the rule of type promotion, operators' precedence and associativity rules (these topics are discussed in the later part of this section).

Program 2.11 (Arithmetic operation `char` *data)*

```
/* This example will demonstrate arithmetic operations
            with values of type char.   */

 class CharArithmetics {
  public static void main(String[] args){
   char letter1 = 'A';       // letter1 is 'A'
   char letter2 = (char)(letter1+1); // letter2 is 'B'
   char letter3 = letter2; // letter3 is also 'B'
   System.out.println("Here\'s a sequence of letters: "
     + letter1 + letter2 + (letter3+1));
           // letter3 is now 'C'
   System.out.println("Here are the decimal codes for
     the letters:\n"+ letter1 + ": " + (int)letter1
     + " " + letter2 + ": " + (int)letter2 + " " +
     letter3 + ": " + (int)letter3);
     }
 }
```

Java data type promotion

Concept of type promotion

If there is an expression containing variables of mixed data types, then the Java compiler will automatically convert from one numeric data type to the other. In Java this concept is called type promotion. Figure 2.1 shows the type promotion scheme.

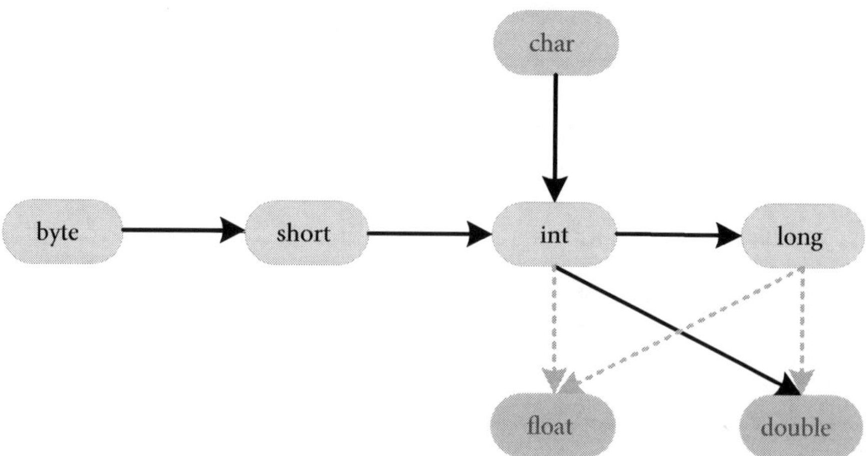

Figure 2.1 Type promotion rule

This scheme shows that, if in an expression data with `byte` and `int` are there, then the `byte` will be converted into `int`, and so on. Such a type promotion is alternatively called automatic type conversion or widening conversion. The type promotion rules are as follows:

Upward conversion

- If any of the operands is of type `double`, the other one will be converted to a `double`.
- Otherwise, if any of the operands is of type `float`, the other one will be converted to a `float`.
- Otherwise, if any of the operands is of type `long`, the other one will be converted to a `long`.
- Otherwise, both operands will be converted to an `int`.

There may be a loss of information in such a type promotion. The six black arrows (see Figure 2.1) show the type conversion without any information loss, whereas the grey and dotted arrows denote the conversion that may lose precision. For example, a large integer such as 123456789 has more digits than the float type can represent. When converting it to a float, the resulting value has the correct magnitude, but it loses some precision.

```
int n = 123456789;
float f = n;            // f is 1.23456792E8
```

Type casting in Java

Downward conversion

In the preceding section, you saw that `int` values are automatically converted to `double` values when necessary. However, there are times when you want to consider a `double` as an integer. Numeric conversions are possible in Java but, of course, information may be lost. Conversions where loss of information is possible are done by means of casts. Such a type conversion is also alternatively called forced conversion or narrowing conversion The syntax for casting is to give the target type in parentheses, followed by the variable name. For example:

```
double x = 9.997;
int nx = (int)x;
```

Then, the variable `nx` has the value 9, as casting a floating-point value to an integer is at the cost of discarding the fractional part.

Program 2.12 (Type conversion)

```
/* Type promotion and casting. */

class ConversionTest {
     public static void main(String args[]) {
          byte b;
          int i = 257;
          double d = 323.142;
          System.out.println("\nConversion of int to
               byte.");
          b = (byte) i;
          System.out.println("i and b " + i + " " + b);
          System.out.println("\nConversion of double to
               int.");
          i = (int) d;
          System.out.println("d and i " + d + " " + i);
          System.out.println("\nConversion of double to
               byte.");
          b = (byte) d;
          System.out.println("d and b " + d + " " + b);
     }
}
```

- `byte`, `short`, `int`, `long`, `char`, `float`, and `double` are compatible for type promotion and casting.
- There are no automatic conversions from the numeric types to `char` or `boolean`. Also, `char` and `boolean` are not compatible with each other.
- If you try to cast a number of one type to another that is out of the range for the target type, the result will be a truncated number that has a different value. For example, the value of 300 in byte is actually 44 in decimal. It is, therefore, a good idea to explicitly test that the value is in the correct range before you perform a cast. If the size of the whole number component is too large to fit into the target integer type, then that value will be reduced to modulo of the target type's range.
- When a floating-point value is assigned to an integer type, the fractional component is lost. For example, if the value 1.23 is assigned to an integer, the resulting value will simply be 1. The 0.23 will be truncated.

`OP=` operators

Java provides special operators that can be used to combine an arithmetic operation with an assignment. As you probably know, statements like the following are quite common in programming:

```
x = x + 5;
```

In Java, you can rewrite this statement as shown here:

```
x += 5;
```

Both statements perform the same action and they increase the value of x by 5. Here is another example,

```
i = i % 2;
```

Which can be expressed as:

```
i %= 2;
```

In this case, the %= obtains the remainder of i/2 and puts that result back into i. Alternatively, such a type of operation can be syntactically expressed as:

Syntax of op= operator

```
var op= expression;   // var = var op expression;
```

Such a shorthand operation is called op=, where op is any arithmetic operator and it is so common in programming that Java has several operators to do a shorthand version of this, borrowed from C and C++. Table 2.10 shows these shorthand assignment operators.

Table 2.10 op= operators

Expression	Meaning
x += y	x = x + y
x −= y	x = x − y
x *= y	x = x * y
x /= y	x = x / y

Program 2.13 *(op= operations)*

```
/* Demonstration arithmetic compound assignment
              operators. */

class OpEqualsOperation {
    public static void main(String args[]) {
       int a = 1;  int b = 2;   int c = 3

       a += 5;         // a = a + 5
       b *= 4;         // b = b*4
       c += a * b;     // c = c + a*b
       c %= 6;         // c = c%6

       System.out.println("a = " + a);
       System.out.println("b = " + b);
       System.out.println("c = " + c);
    }
}
```

Increment and decrement operators

One of the most common operations with a numeric variable is to add or subtract 1. Facilitating this and following in the footsteps of C and C++, Java provides increment and decrement operators (Table 2.11).

Table 2.11 Increment and decrement operators

Operator	Operation
++	Increases its operand by 1
--	Decreases its operand by 1

For example:

```
x++;          // Equivalent to x = x + 1
y--;          // Equivalent to y = y - 1
```

These two arithmetic operators are quite programmer friendly. They have some special properties that make them quite interesting. These are as follows:

- Both – – and ++ are unary operators.
- Because these operators change the value of a variable, they cannot be applied to numbers themselves. For example, 4++ is not a legal statement.
- There are actually two forms of these operators; you have seen the "postfix" form of the operator placed after the operand. There is also a prefix form, ++n. Both change the value of the variable by 1. The difference between the two only appears when they are used inside expressions. The prefix form does the increment (decrement) operation first; the postfix form first evaluates the old value of the variable and then does the increment (decrement). Let's look at the following examples:

```
int i = 4;
int j = 4;
int a = 2 * ++i;      // now a is 10, i is 5
int b = 2 * j++;     // now b is 8, j is 5
int x = 25;
int y = x++;          // y = 25, x = 26
int z = --y;         // z = 24, y = 24
```

- Nesting of both ++ and -- operator is not allowed. For example:

```
int a = 10;
int b = ++(++a); // Illegal : Compilation error
```

- The increment and decrement operators cannot be applied to final variables because of the simple reason that their value cannot be changed. For example:

```
final int X = 10;
X--;              // Illegal : Compilation error
```

- Increment and decrement operators can be applied to all primitive data types except boolean. This is unlike in C/C++, where increment/decrement operators are applicable to only integers data type. For example:

```
char c = 'x';
c++;             // c = 'y'
float y = 123.45;
y--;             // y = 122.45
boolean b = false;
b++;         // bad operand type boolean for ++
```

Program 2.14 (++ and – – operators)

```
/* Demonstration of prefix and postfix increment/
                decrement operators in Java. */

class PrefixPostfixTest {
    public static void main(String args[]) {
        int i = 1;
        int c;
        System.out.println("++i = " + ++i + "i++ = " +
            i++);
        c = 4 + i-- +(++i) + 5;
        System.out.println("c = " + c);
    }
}
```

2.3.2 Bitwise Operators

All integer variables that we have been talking about are represented internally as binary numbers. For example, a value of type int consists of 32 binary digits. You can operate on the bits that make up integer values using the bitwise operators. In Java, there are several bitwise operators that can be applied to the integer types: long, int, short, char, and byte. These operators act upon the individual bits of their operands. They are summarized in Table 2.12.

Table 2.12 Bitwise operators

Operator	Operation
~	Bitwise unary NOT
&	Bitwise AND
&=	Bitwise AND assignment
|	Bitwise OR
|=	Bitwise OR assignment
^	Bitwise exclusive OR
^=	Bitwise exclusive OR assignment
>>	Shift right
>>>	Shift right zero fill
>>=	Shift right assignment
>>>=	Shift right zero fill assignment
<<	Shift left
<<=	Shift left assignment

Memory representation of numbers

Since the bitwise operators manipulate the bits within an integer, it is necessary to understand how Java stores integer values and how it represents negative numbers in memory. So, before continuing, let's briefly review these two topics.

Representation of `byte` data

`byte` in memory

A `byte` data stores an 8-bit number. The bit at the left-most position is called MSB (most significant bit) whereas the bit at the right-most position is called LSB (least significant bit). Each bit has its own weight. The weights of different bits are shown in Figure 2.2. Figure 2.2 also shows how, for example, 41 is stored. Here, 41 is in decimal and 0010101001 is in its byte representation. Note that $0 \times 2^7 + 0 \times 2^6 + 1 \times 2^5 + 0 \times 2^4 + 1\times 2^3 + 0 \times 2^2 + 0 \times 2^1 + 1 \times 2^0 = 32 + 8 + 1 = 41$, the decimal value.

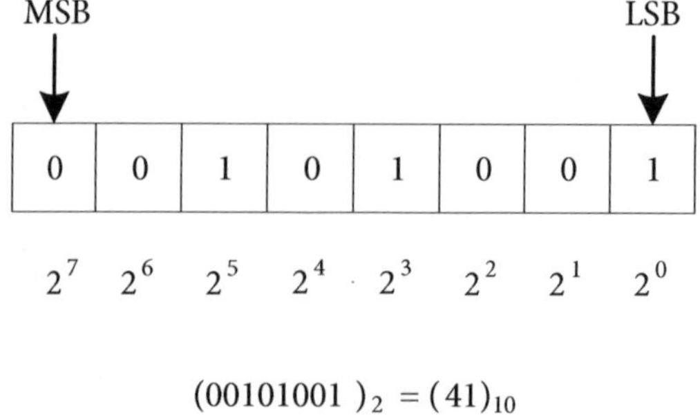

Figure 2.2 Representation of `byte` data

Representation of `char` data

`char` in memory

Similar storage is used in case of `char` data except that it has 16-bit representation instead of 8-bits. In Java, a 16-bit `char` data is encoded in hexadecimal as shown in Figure 2.3. Note that here, a 16–bit number is represented with the hexadecimal unit 0, 1, ... , 7, 8, 9, A, B, C, D, E, F (both lower and uppercase can be used). Thus, the `char` in Unicode looks like \u06CD. As another example, the Unicode \u6771 is "Han for East" character in Japan, whose glyph looks like 東.

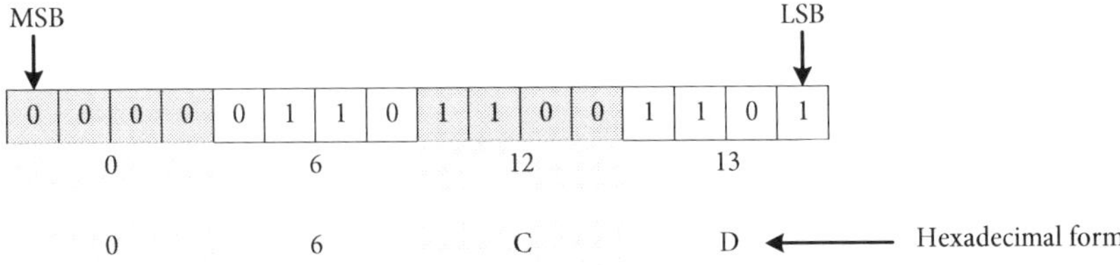

Figure 2.3 Representation of `char` data

Representation of `short`, `int`, and `long` data

All of the integer types (i.e., `byte`, `short`, `int`, and `long`) are represented by binary numbers of varying bit widths. All of the integer types are signed integers. This means that they can represent negative values as well as positive ones. Java uses an encoding known as "two's complement," which means that negative numbers are represented by inverting (changing 1s to 0s and vice versa) all of the bits in a value, then adding 1 to the result. For example, –42 is represented by inverting all of the bits in 42, or 00101010, which yields 11010101, then adding 1, which results in 11010110, or –42. To decode a negative number, first invert all of the bits, then add 1. For example, –42, or 11010110 inverted, yields 00101001, or 41, so when you add 1 you get 42. The Java (and most other computer languages such as C/C++) uses two's complement representation, where 0 (zero) is represented uniquely. For example, assuming a `byte` value, zero is represented by 00000000 and 10000000 (i.e., it is –0). This –0 problem is solved by using two's complement to represent negative values. When using two's complement, 1 is added to the complement, producing 100000000. This produces a 1 bit extra to fit a number and is discarded, resulting in the desired behavior, that is, –0 is the same as 0, and 11111111 is the encoding for –1, etc. Note that the range of integers in `byte` is –128, –127, … , –1, 0, 1, 2, … , 127. This basic principle applies to all of Java's integer types.

Bitwise logical operations: AND, OR, XOR, and NOT

Let us first discuss the basic bitwise logical operators, namely AND (&), OR (|), XOR (^) and NOT (~) operators. They are called bitwise because these operators work on the bits that make up the integers. If you are familiar with Boolean logic, you may recall how they work on bits (Table 2.13).

- & operator: The bitwise & operator combines the bits in its two operands in AND manner. For example, if both the first bit AND the second bit are 1, then the result is 1; otherwise, the result is 0.
- | operator: The bitwise | operator combines the bits in its two operands in OR manner. For example, if either or both bits are 1, then the result is 1. If both bits are 0, the result is 0.
- ^ operator: The bitwise ^ operator combines the bits in its two operands in XOR manner. For example, if both bits are the same the result is 0; otherwise, the result is 1.
- ~ operator: The ~ operator complements each bit in an operand, That is it takes a single operand and it toggles all the bits, so that each 1 bit becomes 0, and vice-versa.

The first three are binary operators and the last one is unary operator.

Table 2.13 Bitwise basic Boolean operations

A	B	A&B	A|B	A^B	~A
0	0	0	0	0	1
0	1	0	1	1	1
1	0	0	1	1	0
1	1	1	1	0	0

In the following, we explain the bitwise logical operations considering int data as the operands and they are expressed in hexadecimal format.

```
int a = 0x66CD ;      //Hexadecimal representation of a

int b = 0x000F;       //Hexadecimal representation of b
```

The different AND, OR, XOR and NOT logical operations are shown in Figure 2.4, which are self-explanatory.

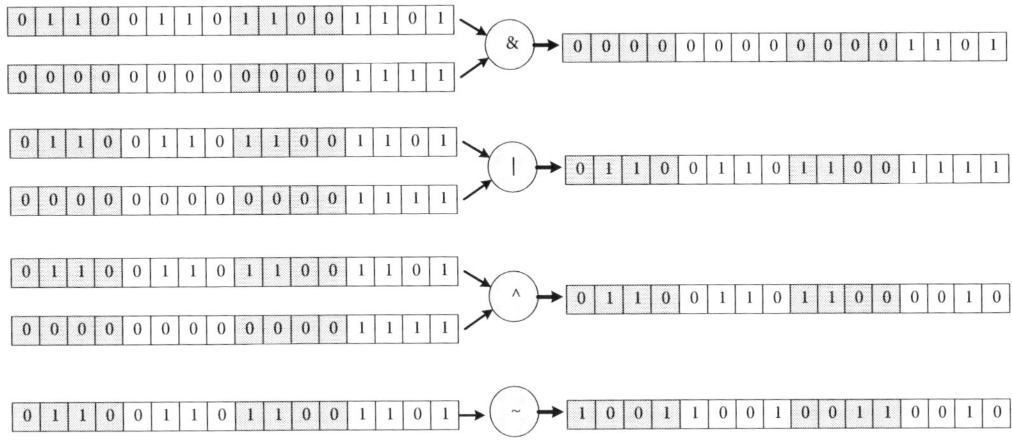

Figure 2.4 Illustration of AND (&), OR (|), XOR (^), and NOT (~) operations

The bitwise logical operators have many applications and their applications are mostly seen in hardware–software embedded system. In such applications, one operand is the system variable (an integer) and the other operand is used as the mask variable. The second operand is used to mask the first operand according to a logical operation. Program 2.15 attempts to show a usage of it.

Program 2.15 (Bitwise logical operations)

Printing a number in binary

```
/* Demonstration of bit-wise logical operations. */
class BitWiseLogicTest {
     public static void main(String args[]) {

          // To extract fourth bit in an integer
          int n = 0xABCD;    // n is an integer data
          int fourthBit = (n&8)/8;    //Here, 8 = 0x0008
                                                  //as mask
         System.out.println ("The 4th bit in "+ n + "is "
               +fourthBit);

          int a = 3;
          int b = 6;
          int c =  (~a&b)|(a&~b);    //XOR(a,b)
          System.out.println("c = " + Integer.
               toBinaryString(c));
          int d = ~a & 0x0F;
          System.out.println("d = " + Integer.
               toBinaryString(d));
     }
}
/* To print an integer data in its binary form, you
     can use the method toBinaryString(…), which is
     defined in java.lang.Integer class.*/
```

- Bitwise logical operators can be applied to `byte`, `char`, `short`, `int` and `long` data. Operations are the same; they are different only because the sizes are different.
- These operators should not be considered as returning an integer value from an expression with bitwise operators. For example, ~ operation to a positive integer produces a value which should not be interpreted as a negative number and vice-versa.
- Bitwise operators are not applicable to floating-point numbers and `boolean` data type.
- When you initialize an integer variable, you may do that with a hexadecimal value. For example:

```
short a = 0xFFFF;
```

Here, `a` is initialized with all its bits set to 1s. However, if you do the following, for example:

```
short a = 0xF;
```

Here, `a` will store 0000 0000 0000 1111. That is, if you don't mention the bit pattern, then it will automatically take 0s.

- Special care should be taken when initializing variables of the type `byte` and the type `short` with hexadecimal values to avoid surprised error. For example, if you initialize a variable of type `byte` with the following statement:

```
byte allBitsOne = 0xFF;
```

- It appears that the literal 0xFF is 1111 1111. Actually, 0xFF is not 1111 1111 at all. The literal 0xFF is type `int`, so it is the binary value 0000 0000 0000 0000 1111 1111. This happens to be equivalent to the decimal value 128, which is outside the range of type `byte`. The byte value you are looking for, 1111 1111, is equivalent to the decimal value –1, so the correct way to initialize `allBitsOne` to 1s is to write:

```
byte allBitsOne = 0xFFFFFFFF;
```

- In such a case, the high-order bits will be truncated to produce the result you are looking for.

Shift operations: shift left and shift right

In many logic circuit designs, shifting bits operations are frequent. Java supports bit shifting to help programmers to write system level programs. Java provides three basic shift operators to shift the bits in an integer to the right or the left (Table 2.14). For example, 0011 is a bit pattern, on shifting right and left by one bit becomes 0001 and 0110, respectively.

Table 2.14 Bit shift operators

Operator	Operation
>>	Shift right, propagating the sign bit from the left.
>>>	Shift right, filling with zeros from the left.
<<	Shift left, filling with zeros from the right.

The right shift operation

The right shift operator, >>, shifts all the bits in a value to the right a specified number of times. Its general form is shown here:

```
value >> num;
```

Here, `num` specifies the number of positions to right-shift the value in `value`. The >> moves all the bits in the specified value to the right by the number of bit positions specified by `num`.

The following code fragment shifts the value 32 to the right by two positions, resulting in `a` being set to 8:

```
int a = 32;  // a = 00100000

a = a >> 2; // a now contains 8 (00001000)
```

The shift right filling with zeros from the left are self-explanatory and its discussion is skipped for brevity.

- When a value has bits that are "shifted off," those bits are lost. For example, the next code fragment shifts the value 35 to the right by two positions, which causes the two low-order bits to be lost, resulting again in `a` being set to 8:

```
int a = 35;  // a = 00100011

a = a >> 2; // a contains 8 = 00001000
```

- When you are shifting right, the top (leftmost) bits exposed by the right shift are filled in with the previous contents of the top bit. This is called sign extension and serves to preserve the sign of negative numbers when you shift them right. For example, –8 >> 1 is –4, which, in binary, is:

```
int a = -8;  // a = 11111000

a = a >> 1; // a contains -4 = 11111100
```

- It is interesting to note that if you shift –1 right, the result always remains –1, since sign extension keeps bringing in more ones in the high-order bits.
- The process of shifting binary digits right is like dividing the number by two.

The left shift operation

The left shift operator, <<, shifts all the bits in a value to the left by a specified number of times. It has this general form:

```
value << num;
```

Here, `num` specifies the number of positions to left-shift the value in `value`. The << moves all the bits in the specified value to the left by the number of bit positions specified by `num`. For each shift left, the high-order bit is shifted out (and lost), and a zero is brought in on the right.

The following code fragment shifts the value 32 to the left by two positions, resulting in `a` being set to 8:

```
int a = 40;   // a = 00101000

a = a << 2; // a now contains 160 (10100000)
```

- The process of shifting binary digits left is like multiplying by power of two.
- When a left shift is applied to an `int` operand, bits are lost once they are shifted past the bit position 31. If the operand is a `long`, then bits are lost after bit position 63.

Java's automatic type promotions produce unexpected results when you are shifting `byte` and `short` values. As you know, `byte` and `short` values are promoted to `int` when an expression is evaluated. The result of such an expression is also an `int`. This means that the outcome of a left shift on a `byte` or `short` value will be an `int`, and the bits shifted left will not be lost until they shift past bit position 31. A negative `byte` or `short` value will be sign-extended when it is promoted to `int`. Thus, the high-order bits will be filled with 1s. For these reasons, to perform a left shift on a `byte` or `short` implies that you must discard the high-order bytes of the `int` result. For example, if you left-shift a `byte` value, that value will first be promoted to `int` and then shifted. This means that you must discard the top three bytes of the result if what you want is the result of a shifted `byte` value. The easiest way to do this is to simply cast the result back into a `byte`. The following program demonstrates this concept:

Program 2.16
(Left shift operation)

```
/* Left shifting a byte value. */
class ByteShiftLeftTest {
   public static void main(String args[]) {
      byte a = 64, b;
      int i;
      i = a << 2;  // Left shift bits by two pisitions
      b = (byte) (a << 2);
      System.out.println("Original value of a: " + a);
      System.out.println("After left shift: i and b "
               + i + "," + b);
   }
}
```

Logical operators with assignment

Similar to that of the algebraic operators, all the binary bitwise operators have a short-cut form which combines the assignment with bitwise operation (Table 2.15).

Table 2.15 Logical operators in the form op=

Operator	Operation
x &= y	AND= assignment (x = x & y)
x |= y	OR= assignment (x = x | y)
x ^= y	XOR= assignment (x = x ^ y)
>>=	Shift right, propagating the sign bit from the left.
>>>=	Shift right, filling with zeros from the left.
<<=	Shift left, filling with zeros from the right.

Following examples are given for your quick understanding:

```
a |= b;     // a = a | b;
a >>= 4;    // a = a >> 4;
```

Usefulness of bitwise logical operators

You may be curious about the practical applicability of the bitwise logical operators. In many operating systems, a single 32-bit value is sometimes used to store multiple values. For example, you could store two 16-bit screen coordinates in a single 32-bit word. Suppose, you want to store date in the form dd:mm:yy. If you consider two-digit numbers in each component (e.g., dd: 1–31, mm: 1–12, and yy: 00–99) of date and store each component with short data type, then it will take 3 short data, needing a total 3 × 16 = 48 bits. Now, let us see how the same can be stored only in 1 short data. Note that a value of dd lies within the range 1–31. This means that we need a maximum of 5 bits to store the value. With similar logic, we need 4 bits for mm and 7 bits for yy. Thus, we should use 5 + 4 + 7 = 16 bits. Figure 2.5 illustrates how a short variable can store dd:mm:yy and using some of the bitwise logical operators, how each component in it can be extracted. I leave it to you to write a program and test the program. Program 2.14 is given here, which packs 4 characters "J", "A", "V", "A" into a long data and then unpacks them to print on the screen.

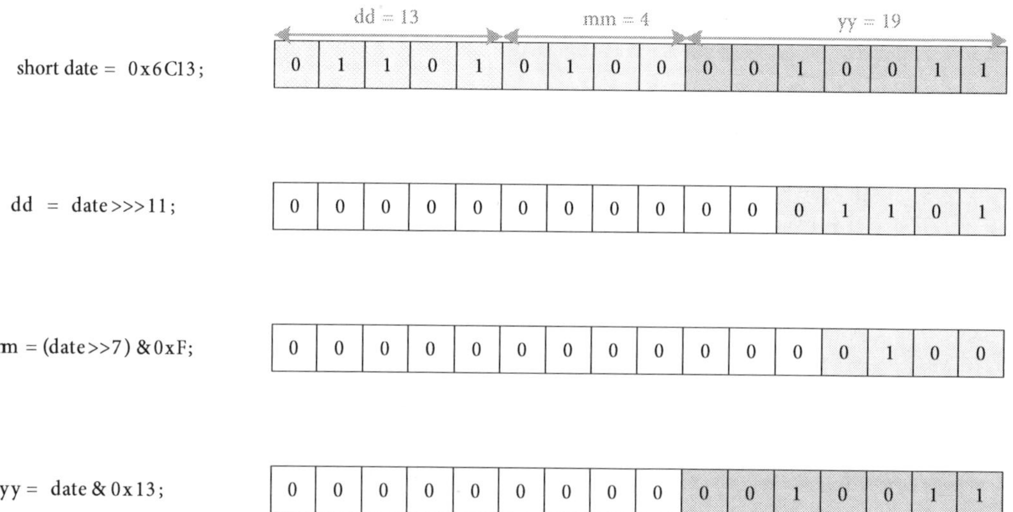

Figure 2.5 Extraction of multiple values from single data

Program 2.17 *(Application of bitwise operators)*

```
/* Packing multiple data into a single data and then
       unpacking them with bit-wise logical operators */

import java.lang.Long.Math;

public class BitWiseDataTest {
    public static void main(String[] args) {
    char a = 'J';
    char b = 'A';
    char c = 'V';
    char d = 'A';
    long string = 0L;
    string = d; // Store 'A'
```

```
        string = (string << 16) | c;
                        // Shift and add the next letter 'V'
        string = (string << 16) | b;
                        // Shift and add the next letter 'A'
        string = (string << 16) | a;
                        // Shift and add the next letter 'J'
        System.out.println("string contains 0x" + Long.
                    toHexString(string));

        // Now unpack the letters and output them
        long mask = 0xFFFF; // Rightmost 16 bits as 1
        char letter = (char)(string & mask);
                              //Extract the rightmost letter
        System.out.println("The letters in string are:");
        System.out.println(" " + letter + " 0x" + Long.
                    toHexString(letter));
        string >>= 16; // Shift out the rightmost letter
        letter = (char)( string & mask);
                              // Extract the rightmost letter
        System.out.println(" " + letter + " 0x" + Long.
                    toHexString(letter));
        string >>= 16; // Shift out the rightmost letter
        letter = (char)( string & mask);
                              // Extract the rightmost letter
        System.out.println(" " + letter + " 0x" + Long.
                    toHexString(letter));
        string >>= 16; // Shift out the rightmost letter
        letter = (char)( string & mask);
                              // Extract the rightmost letter
        System.out.println(" " + letter + " 0x" + Long.
                    toHexString(letter));
    }
}
```

2.3.3 Relational Operators

Java has several expressions for testing equality and magnitude. The relational operators (also called comparison operators) determine the relationship that one expression has with another. They determine equality and ordering. All these expressions return a `boolean` value (`true` or `false`). Table 2.16 shows the relational operators.

Table 2.16 Relational operators

Operator	Meaning	Example
==	Equal to	(x == y + 5)
!=	Not equal to	(x != y)
<	Less than	(a + b < c + d)
>	Greater than	(a – b > c – d)
<=	Less than or equal to	(a*b <= 100)
>=	Greater than or equal to	(0 >= a/b)

- An expression may be a constant, single operand, or any arithmetic expression.
- A relational operator always returns either `true` of `false`.

```
int a = 5;

int b = 10;

boolean c = a < b;      // c = true
```

- In Java, `false` and `true` are nonnumeric values that do not relate to zero or one (or any nonzero as in C/ C++). Therefore, to test for `true` or `false`, you must explicitly employ the relational operator(s).

2.3.4 Boolean Logical Operators

Expressions that result in `boolean` values (for example, the relational operators) can be combined by using logical operators that represent the logical combinations AND, OR, XOR, and logical NOT. Table 2.17 lists all the logical operators in Java. Here, e1, e2 denote expressions with relational operator(s). Program 2.18 includes a few examples of the Boolean logical operators.

Table 2.17 Boolean logical operator

Operator	Operation and meaning	Meaning
e1 & e2	Logical AND	Boolean AND of e1, e2
e1 | e2	Logical OR	Boolean OR of e1, e2
e1 ^ e2	Logical XOR	Boolean XOR of e1, e2
! e	Logical unary NOT	Boolean NOT of e
e1 && e2	Short-circuit AND	

e1 || e2	Short-circuit OR	
e1 &= e2	AND assignment	
e1 |= e2	OR assignment	
e1?e2:e3	Ternary operator	if e1 then e2 else e3

Program 2.18 *(Examples of Boolean logical operators)*

```
/* Examples of Boolean logical operators in Java */

class BooleanLogicalOperatorTest {
      public static void main(String args[]) {
            boolean a = true;
            boolean b = (5 < 3);
            boolean c = a & b;
            System.out.println(" a&b = " + c);
            boolean d = (a | b) & c;
            System.out.println(" (a | b) & c = " + d);
            boolean e = !d;
            System.out.println(" !d = " + e);
      }
}
```

- The Boolean logical operators shown here operate only on `boolean` operands. All the binary logical operators combine two `boolean` values to form a resultant `boolean` value.
- For AND combinations, use either the `&` or `&&` operators. The entire expression will be `true` only if both expressions on either side of the operator are `true`; if either expression is `false`, the entire expression is `false`. The difference between the two operators is in expression evaluation. Using `&`, both sides of the expression are evaluated regardless of the outcome. Using `&&`, if the left side of the expression is `false`, the entire expression is assumed to be `false` (the value of the right side doesn't matter), so the expression returns `false`, and the right side of the expression is never evaluated. (This is often called a "short-circuited" expression.) The AND (`&&`) operator requires all expressions to be true for the entire expression to be true. For example, the expression:

```
(3 + 2 == 5) && (6 + 2 == 8)
```

is `true` because the expressions on both sides of the `&&` are `true`. However, the expression:

```
(4 + 3 == 9) && (3 + 3 == 6)
```

is false because the expression on the left of the && is not true. Remember this when combining expressions with AND: If any expression is false, the entire expression is false.

- For OR expressions, use either | or ||. OR expressions result in true if either or both of the expressions on either side are also true; if both expression operands are false, the expression is false. As with & and &&, the single | evaluates both sides of the expression regardless of the outcome; and || is short-circuited: If the left expression is true, the expression returns true and the right side is never evaluated. The OR operator (||) requires only one expression to be true for the entire expression to be true. For example, the expressions:

```
(3 + 6 == 2) || (4 + 4 == 8)
```

and

```
(4 + 1 == 5) || (7 + 2 == 9)
```

Are both true because at least one of the expressions being compared is true. Notice that in the second case, both expressions being compared are true, which also makes an OR expression true.

- In addition, there is the XOR operator ^, which returns true only if its operands are different (one true and one false, or vice-versa) and false otherwise (i.e., if both are true). The exclusive OR operator (^) is used to determine if one and only one of the expressions being compared is true. Unlike a regular OR, with an exclusive OR, if both expressions are true, the result is false (weird, huh?). For example, the expression:

```
(5 + 7 == 12) ^ (4 + 3 == 8)
```

evaluates to true, whereas the following expressions evaluate to false:

```
(5 + 7 == 12) ^ (4 + 3 == 7)

(5 + 7 == 10) ^ (4 + 3 == 6)
```

- For NOT, use the ! operator with a single expression argument. The value of the NOT expression is the negation of the expression; if x is true, !x is false. The NOT (!) operator switches the value of (or negates) a logical expression. For example, the expression:

```
(4 + 3 == 5)
```

is false; however, the expression:

```
!(4 + 3 == 5)
```

is `true`.

- Note that similar to mathematical operators, there is no restriction on how you can combine the different comparison and logical operators. However, if you build a very complex expression, you may have trouble evaluating it yourself. For example, consider the following logical expression:

```
(3 < 5) && (2 == 2) || (9 > 6)
```

- Here five different logical operators and five comparisons are involved in the same expression. Because you are comparing the sub-expressions and because each of the sub-expressions is `true`, the result of this expression is `true`. Now, look at this expression:

```
((3 < 5) && (2 == 1)) || (7 == 7)
```

Is this expression `true` or `false`? (You can verify yourself that the expression will evaluate to `true`.)

- In general, only the `&&` and `||` are commonly used as actual logical combinations. The operators `&`, `|`, and `^` are more commonly used for bitwise logical operations.

The ? operator

Java includes a special ternary (three-way) operator that can replace certain types of if-then-else statements. This operator is represented as `?` and can seem somewhat confusing at first. But `?` can be used very effectively once mastered. The `?` has this general form:

```
expression1 ? expression2 : expression3
```

Here, `expression1` can be any expression that evaluates to a Boolean value. If `expression1` is true, then `expression2` is evaluated; otherwise, `expression3` is evaluated. The result of the `?` operation is thus the evaluation of an expression. Both `expression2` and `expression3` are required to return the same (or compatible) type, which should not be `void`. Here is an example of the way `?` is employed:

```
ratio = denom == 0 ? 0 : num / denom;
```

When Java evaluates this assignment expression, it first looks at the expression to the left of the question mark. If `denom` equals zero, then the expression *between* the question mark and the colon is evaluated and used as the value of the entire `?` expression. If `denom` does not equal zero, then the expression *after* the colon is evaluated and used for the value of the entire `?` expression. The result produced by the `?` operator is then assigned to `ratio`.

Program 2.19 demonstrates the `?` operator. It uses it to obtain the absolute value of a variable.

Program 2.19 *(Ternary operator example)*

```
/* Demonstrate ?: */

class TernaryOperatorTest {
    public static void main(String args[]) {
        int i, k;

        i = 10;
        k = i < 0 ? -i : i; // get absolute value of i
        System.out.print("Absolute value of ");
        System.out.println(i + " is " + k);
        i = -10;
        k = i < 0 ? -i : i; // get absolute value of i
        System.out.print("Absolute value of ");
        System.out.println(i + " is " + k);
    }
}
```

2.3.5 Precedence and Associativity of Operators

In any expression involving multiple operators, their execution is governed by two rules: precedence and associativity. A programmer should have clear understanding of these for each operator to be able to write the program logic correctly.

Operator precedence

Operator precedence determines the order in which expressions are evaluated. This, in some cases, can determine the overall value of the expression. For example, take the following expression:

```
y = 6 + 4 / 2;    // y = 5 or 8?
```

Depending on whether the `6 + 4` expression or the `4 / 2` expression is evaluated first, the value of `y` can end up being `5` or `8`. This ambiguity will be resolved if we fix a rule about which operator will be evaluated first. In this case, the correct answer is 8 as the / operator has higher precedence over the + operator.

Each operator in Java has a set priority or precedence in relation to the others, as shown in Table 2.18. Such a rule with arithmetic operators is known as the BODMAS rule. This stands for Bracket, Of, Division, Multiplication, Addition, and Subtraction. In certain regions, PEDMAS (Parentheses, Exponents, Division, Multiplication, Addition, and Subtraction) is the equivalent of BODMAS. These rules are taught to school children to solve arithmetic expressions. In the precedence is highest for operators in the top line in the table, down through to the operators in the bottom line, which have the lowest precedence. Operators that appear on the same line of the table have the same precedence.

Operator associativity

There is still another ambiguity. What will be the result if the same operator appears multiple times in an expression or operators having the same order of precedence appear together? Let us take the following example:

```
y = 22/7*3;        // y = 9 or 1?
```

To resolve this ambiguity, we need another rule called the rule of associativity. According to this rule, in an expression, if two operators with the same order of precedence occur, then they will evaluate from left-to-right or right-to-left rule according to their order of associativity. The operators * and / have the same order of precedence and they follow from left-to-right associativity. Thus, this expression will be evaluated as follows:

```
y = 22/7*3;     // y = 3 * 3 = 9
```

Associativity of all the operators in Java are listed in Table 2.18.

Table 2.18 Order of precedence and associativity of operators in Java

Operator	Associativity	Precedence
( )	Left to Right	1 (High)
- (unary)		2
–, ++	Right to Left	
!, ~		3
*, /, %	Left to Right	
+, -	Left to Right	4
<<, >>	Left to Right	5
<, <=, >, >=	Left to Right	6
== , !=	Left to Right	7
&	Left to Right	8
^	Left to Right	9
|	Left to Right	10
&&	Left to Right	11
||	Left to Right	12
?:	Right to Left	13
–>	Right to Left	14
=, op=	Right to Left	15 (Low)

- In binary operations, the order of evaluation is left to right (except for assignment, increment or decrement, and unary operators, which evaluate right to left).
- There are some separators, such as `[]`, `()`, and `.` (stop) can also act like operators. We shall discuss about them in a later chapter of this book. They have the highest precedence.
- JDK 8 has introduced an arrow operator (`->`). It is used in lambda expressions.
- Parentheses raise the precedence of the operations that are inside them. This is often necessary to obtain the result you desire. For example, consider the following expression:

```
y = a / b * c + d;
```

This expression first divides `a` by `b` and then multiplies the result with `c` and finally adds `d`. This expression can be rewritten using redundant parentheses like this:

```
y = (((a / b) * c) + d);
```

Here, the innermost parenthesis will be evaluated first (PEDMAS rule: Parenthesis, Exponents, Multiplication, Division, Addition, Subtraction). However, if you want to first add and then multiply followed by the division, then you can parenthesize the expression like this:

```
y = (a / (b * (c + d)));
```

- In addition to altering the normal precedence of an operator, parentheses can sometimes be used to help clarify the meaning of an expression. For anyone reading your code, a complicated expression can be difficult to understand. Adding redundant but clarifying parentheses to complex expressions can help to prevent confusion later. For example, which of the following expressions is easier to read?

```
y = a | 4 + c >> b & 7;

y = (a | (((4 + c) >> b) & 7));
```

2.3.6 Data Enumeration

You will often need variables that can have values only from a predefined fixed set. For example, suppose you want to define an integer variable with the name `Color`, which will store an integer value representing a color in a range of seven colors. A Java programmer can do this by an enumeration. For example, consider the following declaration:

```
enum Color {Violet, Indigo, Blue, Green, Yellow, Orange, Red}
```

This defines a new type, `Color`, for variables that can store only one or the other of the values specified between the braces. The names `Violet`, `Indigo`, and so on through to `Red` are called enumeration constants, and they identify the only values that are allowed for variables of type `Color`.

Once a data type is enumerated, you can use them to declare a variable. For example:

```
Color myColor; // myColor is a variable of type Color

myColor = Color.Yellow; // The value of myColor
```

- Note the absence of a semicolon at the end of the definition of the `enum` data type. Because you are defining a type here, no semicolon is required after the closing brace.
- These names will correspond to integer values by default, starting from 0.
- You can explicitly assign the values also. For example:

```
enum Switch {On = 1, Off = 0, OutOfOrder = 2}
```

The variable value of `enum` data type should not be treated as the same as integer variables because they exist only within the context of the enumeration.

Program 2.20 *(enum data type)*

```
/* Demonstration of enum data type */

public class EnumerationTest {
     enum Day {Monday, Tuesday, Wednesday, Thursday,
                    Friday, Saturday, Sunday }
                    //Define an enumeration type for
                                        //days of the week

     public static void main(String[] args) {
          // Define three variables of type Day
     Day today = Day.Sunday;
     Day yesterday = Day.Saturday;
     Day tomorrow = Day.Monday;

     // Output the values of the Day variables
     System.out.println("Today is " + today);
     System.out.println("Tomorrow will be " + tomorrow);
     System.out.println("Yesterday was " + yesterday);
   }
}
```

2.4 Arrays

Definition of array

Arrays in Java, as in other languages, are a way to store collections of items into a single unit. The array has some number of slots, each of which holds an individual item. An array is a finite ordered collection of homogeneous elements (i.e., all elements are of same type). Each element can store a primitive value (i.e., of built-in data type) or objects of any class. An array stores a finite number of elements, called the size of the array. All elements in an array are stored in an order in contiguous memory locations. The location of an array element is called index. Index starts from zero to size-1, where size is the maximum number of elements that an array can hold. An array can be of one dimensional or multi-dimensional (2, 3 dimension, etc.). Figure 2.6 shows 1-, 2- and 3-dimensional arrays. Each array is identified by a name, for example, in Figure 2.6, the 1D array is named `marks`. Note that in case of a 1D array, the ith element in `marks` is identified as `marks[i]`. A 2D array, on the other hand, is indexed by row and column numbers, a 3D array is row, column, and width numbers, and so on. As usual, each index starts from 0 to their respective sizes less one.

Examples of different types of arrays

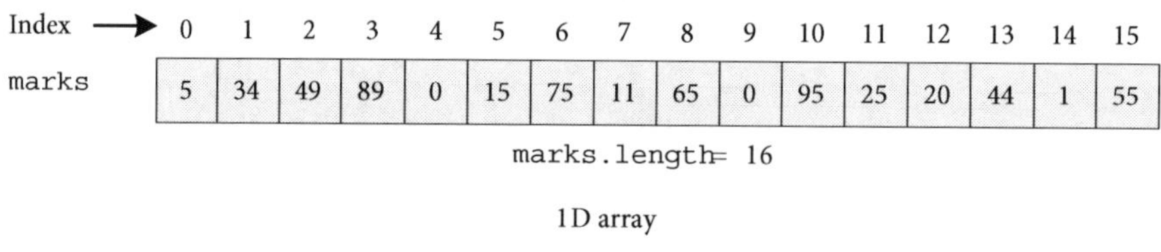

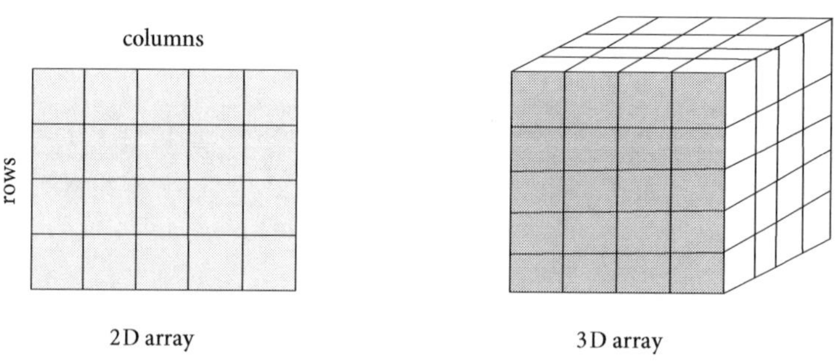

Figure 2.6 Different types of arrays

- Unlike in other languages, however, arrays in Java are actual objects that can be passed around and treated just like other objects.
- Arrays can contain any type of element (primitive types or objects), but you can't store different types in the same array.

- You can have an array of integers or an array of strings or an array of arrays, but you can't have an array that contains, for example, both integers and characters.
- A one-dimensional array is very similar to the concept of a set of elements or a list of elements. Like a set or a list, an array contains one or more occurrence(s) of same elements and the elements are not necessarily stored in a sorted order.

Procedure of making an array

To create an array in Java, you have to perform three basic steps:

Declaration: Each array should be declared with the type of elements it is supposed to store. This helps to make an array reference variable.

Construction: This step is necessary to allocate memory to store the array of the declared type.

Initialization: In the third step, you can store element in an array.

There are several different ways to perform each of these steps. We will discuss them in the subsequent sections.

2.4.1 One-Dimensional Arrays

A one-dimensional array is characterized by its name, type and size (Figure 2.6). Let us see how such an array can be created and then used.

Declaration of a one-dimensional array

A one-dimensional can be declared in any one of the following ways:

Way 1:

```
<type> <array_Name>[];
```

For example:

```
int ages[]; //Declares an array of type integers
Date dob[]; //Array of objects of class Date
```

Way 2:

```
<type> []<array_Name>[];
```

For examples

```
Float[] marks; //Declares an array of floats
Student[] name; //Array of objects of students
```

Construction of one-dimensional arrays

Once you have declared an array variable, you can decide its size and allocate the memory to store the elements. Following is the syntax to be followed:

```
<array_name> = new <type> [<size>];
```

For example,

```
ages = new int[10]; //Defines an array of size 10

name = new Student[100];
```

- Note the use of `new` in this definition. Here, `new` is a memory allocation operation, about which we shall learn more in a later chapter.
- Here, `<size>` should be an integer value or a variable of type integers.
- You can declare and define an array together.

```
<type> <arrayName> [ ] = new <type> [<size>];
```

For example:

```
int x[] = new int[100];
```

- Once you create an array, you can access its length with the following syntax:

```
<arrayName>.length;
```

For example:

```
y = x.length;    // y = 100
```

If an array is declared but not initialized, then each element in it will be with the default value of 0.

Initialization of an array

Now, you should populate the array you have declared with some elements. There are two ways to do this.

Way 1

```
<arrayName> [<subscript> ] = <value>;
```

For example:

```
x[0] = 55;
x[1] = 99;
x[2] = 66;            and so on.
```

Way 2:

```
<type> <arrayName> [ ] = { <list of values> };
```

For example:

```
int x [ ] = {12, 3, 9, 15};
```

Here declaration, definition, and initialization have all been done at one go!

If you declare a size which is not the same as the elements you have listed during initialization, then the initialization will discard the extras or initialize with default value if the size is more than the number of values in the list, whatever the case may be. For example:

```
int x[] = new int [5];
x = {1, 2, 3, 4, 5, 6};
// The last element will be discarded.
```

Or

```
x = {1, 2, 3};
//The last two elements will be set as 0.
```

Program 2.21 *(1D array example)*

```
/* Demonstrate a one-dimensional array */

class Array {
     public static void main(String args[]) {
       int month[];
         month = new int[12];
         month[0] = 31;
         month[1] = 28;
         month[2] = 31;
         month[3] = 30;
         month[4] = 31;
         month[5] = 30;
         month[6] = 31;
         month[7] = 31;
         month[8] = 30;
         month[9] = 31;
         month[10] = 30;
         month[11] = 31;
         System.out.println("April has " + month[3]
                + " days.");
     }
}
```

Accessing array elements

Once your array is fully initialized, you can access each element in it. A particular element can be accessed with the following syntax:

```
<arraName>[<subscript>]
```

Let's consider the following example:

```
int x [ ] = {12, 3, 9, 15};
System.out.println("The first element is " + x[0]);
System.out.print("The last element is " + x[x.
     length-1]);
float avg;
avg = (float) (x[0] +x[1]+x[2} +x[3])/4;
```

Java checks that the index value you use are valid. If you use an index value less than 0, or greater than or equal to the length of the array, then Java run-time will cause a run-time error and the program may be abnormally terminated.

2.4.2 Multi-dimensional Arrays

Example of multi-dimensional arrays are matrices with rows and columns, cuboid, etc. In Java, multi-dimensional arrays are actually arrays of arrays. For example, a 2D array with *m* rows and *n* columns is a collection of *m* 1D arrays, each with size *n*.

Creating 2D arrays

You can create a 2D array using any one of the following:

```
int twoDarray [ ] [ ];
myArray = new int [3] [4];
```

or

```
int row, column;
int twoDarray [ ] [ ] = new int [row] [column];
```

Initializing a 2D array

You can follow any one of the following methods, for example, to initialize a 2D array of size 2 × 3.

```
int myArray [2] [3] = {1, 2, 3, 4, 5, 6};
```

OR

```
int myArray [ ] [ ] = { {1, 2, 3}, {4, 5, 6} };
```

The 2D array will look like:

1 2 3

4 5 6

Creating 3D arrays

You can create a 3D array using any one of the following:

```
int threeDarray [ ] [ ][ ];
myArray = new int [3][4][5];
```

Or

```
int row = 3, column = 4, width = 5;
int threeDArray[][] = new int [row]
[column][width];
```

Variable length array

You can create a variable length multidimensional array, for example, the first row with two columns, the second row with four columns, and the third row with three columns (Figure 2.7).

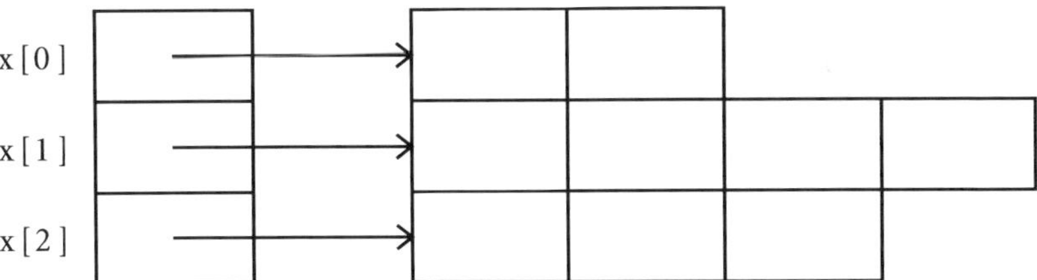

Figure 2.7 Multidimensional array with variable length

The following is a simple way to do this:

```
int x [] [] = new int [3][];
x[0] = new int [2];
x[1] = new int [4];
x[2] = new int [3];
```

Then you can initialize each array the way you have done it for a one-dimensional array.

2.5 Strings

A string is a collection of characters, where a character is any element from the language alphabet, or anything that you can type on the screen through your keyboard. If you are C/C++ programmer, then you may have used a string in many programs. For example, the following is a string literal:

```
"Java is the best programming language since 1999."
```

The concept of string in Java is much more significant as a lot of data in Java programs is treated as a string. To deal with such strings, Java includes a class `String`. The `String` class is a standard class that comes with Java, and it is specifically designed for creating and processing strings. The definition of the `String` class is in the `java.lang` package so it will be accessible in all your programs by default.

2.5.1 `String` Literals

You have already made extensive use of *String* literals in many of the programs discussed so far. Just about every time the `System.out.println("Hello Java!")` method was used in an example, you used a string literal as the argument. Note that a `String` literal is a sequence of characters between double quotes:

```
"Hello Java!"
```

This is actually a `String` literal with a capital S. A *String* literal in Java is a constant object of the class `String` that the compiler creates for use in your program.

As mentioned in Section 2.1.2, some characters cannot be entered explicitly from the keyboard so you cannot include them directly in a string literal. You cannot include a "newline" character by pressing the Enter key since this will move the cursor to a new line but not type the character itself. You also cannot include a double quote character as it is in a `String` literal because this is used to indicate where a string literal begins and ends. You can specify all these characters in a string in the same way as you did for `char` constant using an escape sequence. All the escape sequences you saw when you looked at `char` constants apply to strings. The statement:

```
System.out.println("This is \na string constant!");
```

will produce the output:

```
This is
a string constant!
```

since `\n` is interpreted as a newline character.

Like values of type `char`, strings are stored internally as Unicode characters. You can also include Unicode character codes in a string as escape sequences of the form `\uabcd` where `abcd` are the four hexadecimal digits of the Unicode coding for a particular character. For example, the Greek letter π is \u03C0.

2.5.2 Creating String Objects

As mentioned earlier, a `String` variable is simply a variable that stores a reference to an object of the class `String`. You declare a String variable in the same way as you define a variable of one of the basic types. You can also initialize it in the declaration, which is generally a good idea:

```
String myString = "It is a string in Java.";
```

In addition to this, you can declare a variable of type `String` in a method without initializing it. For example:

```
String anyString; // Uninitialized String variable
```

The `anyString` variable that you have declared here does not refer to anything. However, if you try to do the following:

```
String anyString = null;
// String variable that doesn't reference a string
```

Here, the literal `null` is an object reference value that does not refer to anything. The variable `anyString` will continue to be `null` until you use an assignment to make it reference a particular `String`. For example:

```
anyString="Hello";
```

Now, `anyString` refers to the string literal "Hello."

- Because an array is essentially an object, you can also use `null` as the value for an array variable that does not reference anything.
- Attempting to use a variable that has not been initialized is an error. It is a good practice to always initialize variables as you declare them.
- If you refer a string object, then at a later time you can make it `null`. For example:

```
String message = "Merry Christmas!";
```

Then the statement:

```
message = null;
```

or

```
message = "";
```

will replace the original reference stored. So the message now does not refer to anything.

- The *String* object itself is distinct from the variable you use to refer to it. In the same way as you saw with array objects, the variable `message` stores a reference to a `String` object, not the object itself (it is just like a pointer in C/C++). A `String` variable records where the `String` object is in memory. When you declare and initialize `message`, it references the object corresponding to the initializing string literal. When you execute the assignment statement, the original reference is overwritten by the reference to the new string and the old string is discarded. The variable `message` then contains a reference to the new string.
- String objects are said to be immutable and cannot be changed. This means that you cannot extend or otherwise modify the string that an object of type String represents.

Program 2.22 *(Dealing with* `String` *objects)*

```
/* The following program illustrates the use of strings
      in Java. */

public class StringTest {
     public static void main(String[] args) {
        String[] authors = {"Herbert Schildt",  "Ivor
              Horton", "Josuah Boch", "Debasis Samanta",
                                    "Gary Cornell"};

        System.out.println("The best author is "
              + authors[0]);
        System.out.print("\n" + authors[4]);
        System.out.println();
        System.out.println(authors[3]);
        System.out.println(authors[5]);
              //Run-time error!
    }
}
```

2.5.3 String Operations

It is not that a `String` object is only to reference a string literal. Many operations are possible to manipulate String object. Operations for manipulating `String` objects are defined as methods in class `String`, which is in `java.lang` package. In this subsection, you will learn some of the frequently used `String` methods operating on `String` object.

String concatenation

+ operator for string merging

There is + operator to merge two `String` objects to form a new single string. Consider the following example:

```
String message1 =  "Hi "
          // A string literal with three characters
String message2 =  "Java!"
          // Another string literal
String msg =  message1 + message2;
          // Merging of two strings
System.out.println("Merged string " + msg);
         //Printing the merged string on the screen
```

Let `msg` denote a reference to `String` object. Then all the following are valid `String` concatenation operations:

```
msg =  msg + 2019;
   // Merging of two strings and update

msg =  "Pi = " + 3.141;
   // 3.141 will be converted into string

msg =  "Pi = " + 22/7;
   //22/7 will be calculated first and then merged

msg = null;
msg +=  1 + 2 + 3;
   // It is 123 not 6!
```

Program 2.23 *(String merging)*

```
/* String merging and interesting result */

public class MergeStrings {
    public static void main(String[] args) {
        String string1 = "Happy ";
        String string2 = "New ";
        String string3 = "Year ";
        String string = null;
                // A string object is initially empty

        // Join three strings
        string = string1 + string2 + string3;
        System.out.println(string);
```

```
        // Convert an integer to String and join with
                                    //two other strings
        int year = 2019;
        string = string + year;
              //integer value is converted into string
        System.out.println(string);

        // Another example of combining numeric literal
                                       //into  a string
        string = "Ninety nine is " + 9 + 9;
        System.out.println(myString);

        // However, this result is interesting!
             //Could you explain it?
         string = 2 + 3 + " is 5";
         System.out.println(string);
    }
}
```

You have already used string concatenation as argument in many programs with `println()` method. For example:

```
System.out.println("The result is " + x);
```

Here, the value of x is concatenated with the string literal `"The result is "`.

- String is not an array of characters like:

```
char[] msg = {'H', 'I', ' '};
```

- Note that you can also use the += operator to concatenate strings.

String arithmetic

```
String string = "Hello ";
string += "Java!";     // string = string + "Java!"
System.out.println(string);
```

- The + operator is left associative. That is, `"Hi " + 5 + 5` is `"Hi 5" + 5` and hence `Hi 55`. Whereas, `5 + 5 + "Hi"` is `10 + "Hi"` which is `10Hi`

Testing `Strings` for equality

You should have a clear idea about a variable of type `String` class and the value it references (i.e., string literal). For example:

```
String name ="Albert Einstein";
```

Here, `name` is the object of type `String` which references to the string literal "Albert Einstein."

To compare values stored in variables of the primitive types for equality, you use the == operator. For example, `if (x == y)` where `x` and `y` are two variables of type, say, `int`. However, the same is not applicable to `String` objects. If `string1` and `string2` are two objects of type `String`, then:

```
if (string1 == string2)
```

is not valid in Java. To compare two `String` variables, that is, to decide whether the `String` they reference are equal or not, you must use the `equals()` method, which is defined for objects of type `String`. For example:

```
string1.equals(string2)
```

or

```
string2.equals(string1)
```

is as `if (string1 == string2)`

Here, if the two objects reference to the same string literal, then `equals()` method returns `true` else `false`. For example:

```
String string1 = "Hello";
String string2 = string1;
```

Note that `string 1` and `string 2` can be string variables or string constants. For example:

```
"Hello".equals("hello");
```

is valid, which returns `false`.

To test if two strings are identical except for the upper/lowercase letter distinction, use the `equalsIgnoreCase()` method. For example:

```
"Hello".equalsIgnoreCase("hello")
```

returns `true`.

Program 2.24 *(String equality)*

```
/* Two Strings are identical but not the same. */

public class StringEqualityTest {
    public static void main(String[] args) {
        String string1 = "Joy with";
        String string2 = "Java";
        String string3 = "Joy with Java";

        string1 += string2;
                    // Now, string 1 is "Joy with Java"
```

```
            // Test 1: Are string1 and string3 identical?
            if(string1 == string3) // Now test for identity
                  System.out.println("string1 == string3
                      is true.");
            else
                  System.out.println("string1 == string3
                      is false.");

            // Test 2: Are string1 and string3 the same?
            string3 = string1;    // Reference to the same
            if(string1 == string3) // Now test for identity
                  System.out.println("string1 == string3
                      is true.");
            else
                  System.out.println("string1 == string3
                      is false.");
    }
}
```

Ordering of strings

Consider three strings "abc," "bca," "cab" "a" and "A." If we order them in lexicographic order (i.e., dictionary order), then the ordering will be "A," "a," "abc," "bca," "def." If we say it is in sorted order according to collating sequence where you can say "A" < "a" or "def" > " abc," etc. That, is to sort strings you need to be able to determine whether one string is greater than or less than the other. For this reason, Java provides `compareTo()` method defined for `String` object in `java.lang` package. For example, to compare two strings, we can write:

```
string1.compareTo(string2)
```

or

```
string2.compareTo(string1)
```

or

```
"Hello".compareTo("hello")          etc.
```

Here, `compareTo()` method returns a negative value if `string1` comes before `string2` in dictionary order, a positive value if `string1` comes after `string2` in dictionary order, or 0 if the strings are equal.

Substring of a string

You can extract a substring from a given string with the `substring(...)` method of the `String` class. The there are two ways this can be used. The first way will extract a substring consisting of all the characters from a given index position up to the end of the string. Note that in Java the index portion starts from zero. The second way extracts a substring from a string by specifying the index positions of the first character in the substring and one beyond the last character of the substring as arguments to the method. For example:

Way 1:

```
String greeting = "Silver Spring";
String s = greeting.substring(7);
System.out.println(s); //it will print "Spring"
```

Way 2:

```
String greeting = "Hello";
String s = greeting.substring(0, 3);
System.out.println(s);  // it will print "Hell"
```

The method `substring(...)` will throw an exception (covered in Chapter 7)

`StringIndexOutOfBoundsException` if there is any illegal value in any index position.

String tokenizer

In a string (e.g., a in long text), there may be many substrings which are delimited with space and punctuation symbols like `, . ! ? " '` and so on. Such a substring is called a token. For example, "Joy with Java" has three tokens: "Joy" "with" and "Java." Here, the delimiter is space. Java provides the method `split(...)` to find all tokens in a string. Typically, the call of `split(...)` method is as follows:

```
String names = "Hope u r fine...?Me? Not good!"
String delimiters = "[, . ?]"; // Three delimiters
int block = 1;  //Two block
String[] tokens = text.split(delimiters, block);
```

Here, the `tokens` (which are an array of strings) contain the following:

```
Hope  u r  fine...  Me  Not  good!
```

Can you find all the tokens in "02/05/2019"? What is the delimiter here?

Some methods for `String` objects

Some frequently used methods to operate with `String` objects are listed in Table 2.19 in a concise form for ready reference. For a full list, you are advised to consult `java.lang.String` class in Java API.

Frequently used methods in `String`

Table 2.19 Some string methods

Method	Description
`char charAt(int index)`	Returns the character at `index` location.
`boolean endsWith(String suffix)`	Returns `true` if the string ends with `suffix`.
`boolean startsWith(String prefix)`	Returns `true` if the string begins with `prefix`.
`boolean equalsIgnore Case (String other)`	Returns `true` if the string equals the other, except for upper/lowercase distinction.
`int indexOf (String str)`	Return the start of the first substring equal to `str`, starting at index 0 or at `fromIndex`.
`int indexOf(String str, int fromIndex)`	
`int length()`	Returns the length of string.
`String replace(char oldChar, char newChar)`	Returns a new string that is obtained by replacing all characters `oldChar` in the string with `newChar`.
`String toLowerCase()`	Returns a new string containing all characters in the original string, with uppercase characters converted to lower case.
`String toUpperCase()`	Returns a new string containing all characters in the original string, with lowercase characters converted to uppercase.
`String trim()`	Returns a new string by eliminating all leading and trailing spaces in the original string.

Wrapper classes

You don't need to know about this at this point, but in case you were wondering, the conversion of values of the basic types to type `String` is actually accomplished by using a static method `toString()`, of a standard class that corresponds to the basic type. Each of the primitive types has an equivalent class called wrapper classes. Table 2.20 lists the wrapper classes.

Table 2.20 Wrapper classes

Basic type	Wrapper class
`byte`	`Byte`
`char`	`Character`
`short`	`Short`
`int`	`Integer`
`long`	`Long`
`float`	`Float`
`double`	`Double`
`boolean`	`Boolean`

The classes in Table 2.20 are called wrapper classes because objects of each of these class types "wrap" a value of the corresponding primitive type. Whenever a value of one of the basic types appears as the operand + and the other operand is a `String` object, the compiler arranges to pass the value of the basic type as the argument to the `toString()` method defined in the corresponding wrapper class. The `toString()` method returns the `String` equivalent of the value. All this happens automatically when you are concatenating strings using the + operator. As you will see, not only these classes have a `toString()` method, all classes do.

The `String` class also defines a method `valueOf()` that will create a `String` object from a value of any of the basic types. You just pass the value you want converted to a string as the argument to the method. For example:

```
String doubleString = String.valueOf(3.14159);
```

You call the `valueOf()` method using the name of the class `String`, as shown in the preceding line. This is because the method is a static member of the `String` class. You'll learn what static means in this context in Chapter 3. A literal or variable of any of the basic types can be passed to the `valueOf()` method, and it will return a `String` representation of the value.

2.5.4 Arrays of Strings

You can create arrays of strings. You declare an array of *String* objects with the same mechanism that you used to declare arrays of elements for the basic types. You just use the type `String` in the declaration. For example, to declare an array of five `String` objects, you could use the statement:

```
String[] cities = new String[5];
```

Then you can initialize the String arrays in the usual way of initializing an array. For example:

```
cities[0] = "Kolkata";
. . .
cities[4] = {'D', 'e', 'l', h', 'i'};
```

Or

```
String names[] = {"Joy", "Monalisa", "Lamport"};
```

These are all valid initialization attempts of strings.

2.6 Control Structures

Program flow is the order in which a program executes its statements. Most of the time the program flows in a sequential manner and the statements are executed one by one in the order in which they appear in the program. However, there are Java statements that make your program jump forward or backward, skipping over the program code that are not required at that moment. For these there are three basic constructs for controlling program execution, namely, sequence, decision, and loop. These are similar to what exists in many high-level programming languages. In this section, we shall learn about these three constructs.

2.6.1 Sequence

Sequence is the order in which the different statements in a program will be executed. As you know, a Java program can include one or more classes and there should be one class, called the main class, contacting the main method. The Java execution starts from this main() method. The statements in the method are executed in the same order as they appear in the method. Program 2.25 is a sample program to explain how this is executed. Numbers in the left are for reference. As we see, the first statement which will be executed is at line 2. And then the sequence is 3–4–5–6.

Program 2.25 *(Sequence of execution)*

```
0. /* Sequence of statements in Java program */

1. class  SequenceJavaTest {
2.  public void static main(String args[]) {
3.   int stmtNumber = 3;
4.   System.out.println("Executing ... " + ++stmtNumber);
5.   stmtNumber += 1;
6.   System.out.println("Executing ... " + stmtNumber++);
7.  }
8. }
```

Block statement

Java language allows its programmers to enclose some statements under a block; such a group of statement is called a block statement. A block statement is simply a group of Java statements surrounded by braces {}. You have seen a lot of blocks already; you have used a block statement to contain the variables and methods in a class definition, and inside that block you have also used blocks to hold the body of a method definition. The opening brace opens the block, and the closing brace closes the nearest closing block. You can use blocks even further, inside method definitions. The rule is that you can use a block any where a single statement can go. Each statement inside the block is then executed sequentially. Here is an example, for you. Note it is the same Program 2.25 but adding a method `blockTest()` in it. The method spans over lines 8–16. Also, note the group of statements enclosed within line 10–15.

Program 2.26 *(Block of statements)*

```
0.    /* Sequence of statements in Java program */

1.    class  SequenceBlockTest {
2.       public void static main(String args[]) {
3.            int stmtNumber = 3;
4.            System.out.println("Executing … " +
                   ++stmtNumber);
5.            stmtNumber += 1;
6.            System.out.println("Executing … " +
                   stmtNumber++);
7.       }

8.       void blockTest() {
9.         int x = 10;
10.        {                         // start of block
11.            int y = 50;
12.            System.out.println("inside the block:");
13.            System.out.println("x:" + x);
14.            System.out.println("y:" + y);
15.        }                         // end of block
16.      }
17.        y++; x++;      // Compilation error!
18.    }
```

So what's the difference between using a group of individual statements and using a block? The block creates a new local variable scope for the statements inside it. This means that you can declare and use local variables inside a block, and those variables will cease to exist after the block has finished executing. In Program 2.26, if you insert a statement, for example, at line 17, then you will find a compilation error. This is because the scope of `y` is only inside the blocks 10–16. Similarly, the scope of `x` is within 8–16.

- Blocks can be nested inside another. For example:

```
public static void main(String[] args)
{
        int n;
        . . .
        {
                int k;
                . . .
        } // k is only defined up to here
}
```

- It is not possible to declare identically named variables in two nested blocks. For example, the following is an error and will not compile:

```
public static void main(String[] args)
{
        int n;
        . . .
        {
                int k;
                int n; //Error: Can't redefine n  here
        . . .
        }
}
```

Program 2.26 is just for an illustration. You will learn about blocks when we discuss class and method definitions in a later chapter. There is another very common use of block statements, which is in the control flow constructs like decision and looping, which we shall learn next.

2.6.2 Decision

Most programs reach a point where a decision must be made about a piece of data. The program must then analyze the data, decide what to do about it, and jump to the appropriate section of the code. Virtually, no meaningful program can be written without this.

When the control of a program breaks a sequential flow and jumps to a new section of code, it is called branching. When this branching is based on a decision, then we call it as a conditional branching. When no decision-making is involved and the program always branches when it encounters a branching instruction, then we call it as unconditional branching. Unconditional branching is rarely used in modern programs. This book deals with only conditional branching. Besides, Java does not allow unconditional branching.

There are three basic constructs of conditional branching, namely `if`, `if... else` and `switch`, about which we will learn next.

`if` statement

Figure 2.8 shows the construct of if statement. A simple `if` statement includes the keyword `if` followed by a logical expression, which you have already learned is an expression that evaluates to either `true` or `false`. These expressions are surrounded by parentheses. You follow the parentheses with the statement that you want to execute if the logical expression is `true`. For example, look at this `if` statement:

```
int i, j;
.. .. ..
if(i<j)
{
        system.out.println(i + "is less than " + j);
        i++, j--; // Just some statelement
}
int k = 0;        // Next statement
```

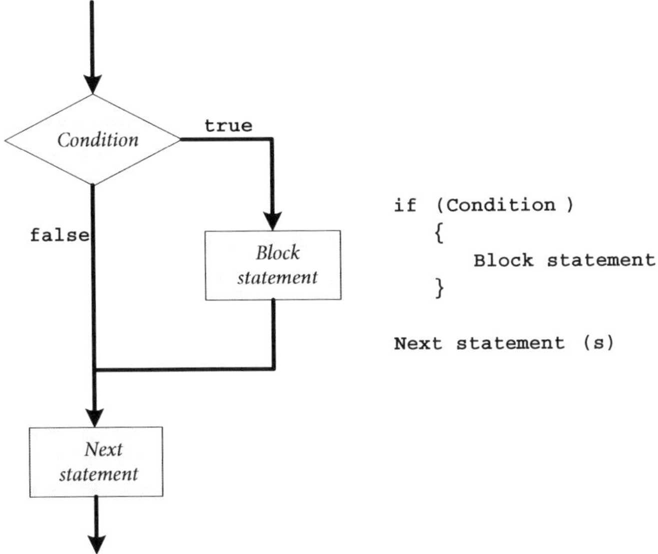

Figure 2.8 `if` statement

The `if` conditional statement is used when you want to execute different bits of code based on a simple test. `if` conditions are nearly identical to `if` statements in C/ C++. They contain the keyword `if`, followed by a `boolean` test, followed by either a single statement or a block statement to execute if the test is `true`.

Program 2.27 defines a class `BeeperTest` with a method `beepMe(int value)` where values are tested and then a message is printed. The `beepMe()` method starts by printing out the value that was passed to it. Then that argument is tested, using an `if` conditional to see if it is an even number, if so, then print the message.

Program 2.27 *(Simple `if` statement)*

```
/* Example of simple if statement */
class BeeperTest {

    void beepMe(int val) {
         System.out.println("Value is " + val + ". ");
         if (val % 2 == 0)
           System.out.println("Beep!");
    }

    public static void main (String args[]) {
          BeeperTest b = new BeeperTest();
                                    // Create an object

          b.beepMe(1); // Call the method for the object
          b.beepMe(2);
          b.beepMe(66);
          b.beepMe(99);
          b.beepMe(1000);
     }
  }
```

- The difference between `if` conditionals in Java and C/ C++ is that the test must return a `boolean` value (i.e., `true` or `false`). The "condition" in the `if` statement should be a `boolean` variable or a `boolean` expression (which returns a `boolean` value). In C/ C++, the condition can return an integer (where 0 implies false and any non-zero value implies true). For example, the following `if` statement is not valid in Java:

```
int i;
... ...
if (i/2) { ... }
```

However, the following is valid:

```
boolean i;
… …
if (i) { … }
```

- A block statement (sometimes called a compound statement) allows you to have more than one (simple) statement in any Java programming structure that might otherwise have a single (simple) statement.
- You may sometime write a simple `if` statement on a single line. That is, { } after `if` statement is not mandatory. For example:

```
if(i%2 != 0) ++i;   // If number is odd, make it even
```

`if-else` statement

Let's consider the following piece of code:

```
if (choice == 1)
{
     num = 1;
     num2 = 55;
}
if (choice != 1)
{
     num = -1;
     num2 = 99;
}
```

When Java gets to the first `if` statement, it compares the value of `choice` with the number 1. If this value does not match and the statement doesn't evaluate to `true`, Java skips over every line until it finds the next `if` statement. This brings Java to the second `if` statement. When Java evaluates the expression, it finds that it is not equal to 1, and it executes the second portion of the `if` statement.

You might think it is a waste of time to evaluate other `if` statements after it finds a match for the value of `choice`. You would be right, too. When you write programs, you should always look for ways to make them run faster; one way to make a program run faster is to avoid all unnecessary processing. But how? How do you avoid unnecessary processing when you have to compare a variable with more than one value?

One way to keep processing to a minimum is to use Java's `else` clause. The `else` keyword enables you to use a single `if` statement to choose between two outcomes. When the `if` statement evaluates to `true`, the `if` part of the statement is executed. When the `if` statement evaluates to `false`, the `else` portion is executed.

You can see the syntax of this statement, and how the program's control flow works in Figure 2.9.

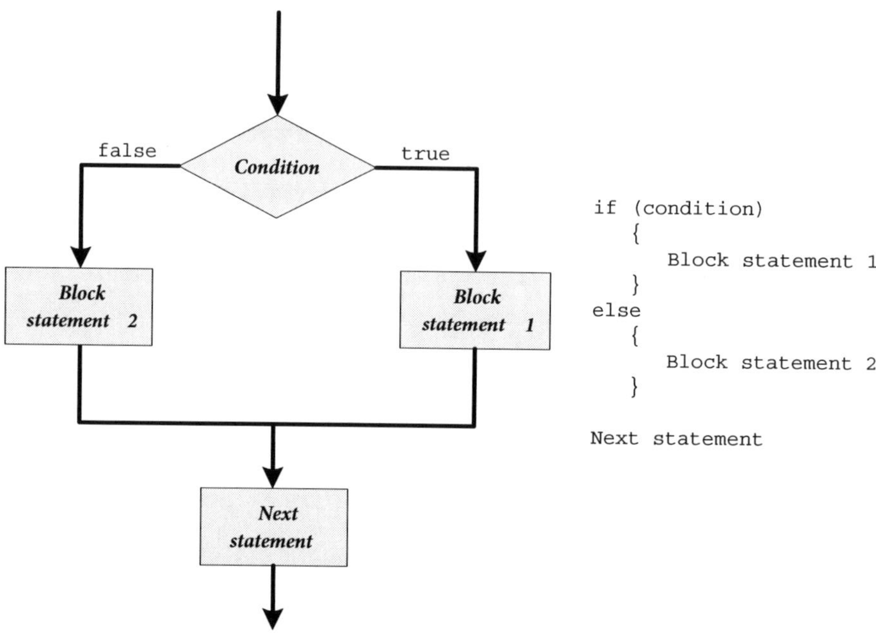

Figure 2.9 `if-else` statement

Thus, the listing of multiple `if` statement can be rewritten better with the following code:

```
if (choice == 1)
{
    num = 1;
    num2 = 55;
}
else
{
    num = -1;
    num2 = 99;
}
```

Nested `if` statement

A nested `if` is an `if` statement that is the target of another `if` or `else`. Nested `if` statements are very common in programming. For example, suppose you have to find the largest of any three given numbers. You can solve this problem using the nested `if-else` statement, which is shown in Figure 2.10 and the piece of code with `nested-if` statements is shown subsequently.

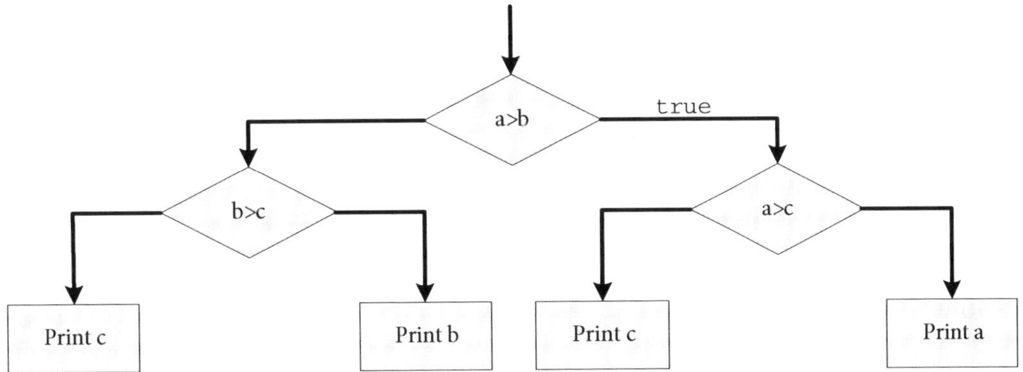

Figure 2.10 Program flowchart to find the largest of three numbers a, b, and c

```
int a, b, c;
… … …
if(a > b)
      if(a > c)
          System,.out.println("The largest is " + a);
      else
          System,.out.println("The largest is " + c);
else
      if(b > c)
          System,.out.println("The largest is " + b);
      else
          System,.out.println("The largest is " + c);
```

Dangling `else` in `if-else-if` ladder

Sometimes checking a program may become difficult for the programmer if there is an `if-then-else` ladder and there is(are) unmatched `if` statements(s). For example, consider the following code:

```
if (x <= 0) if (x == 0) sign = 0; else sign = -1;
```

Here, with which `if` should the `else` part be matched? Such an ambiguity can be resolved by the following rule: *An `else` always belongs to the nearest preceding `if` in the same block that is not already spoken for by another `else`.*

Thus, in this code, the `else` belongs to the second `if`.

Program 2.28 (Program for control flow graph)

```
/* This program figures out whether the character
      stored in the variable letter is an uppercase,
      a lowercase, or some other character. This
      program generates a random number in the range
      0...127, which becomes an ASCII code or a letter in
      English alphabet. */
public class LetterCheck {
    public static void main(String[] args) {
        char letter = 'A';
        // Generate a random character
        letter = (char)(128.0*Math.random());

        if(letter >= 'A')  // Is it A or greater?
           if(letter <= 'Z')   // Is it Z or less?
               System.out.println("It is capital
                                          letter " + letter);
           else       // It is not Z or less
               if(letter >= 'a') // Is it a or greater?
                  if(symbol <= 'z') // Is it z or less?
                     System.out.println("It is small
                         letter " + letter);
                  else   // It is not less than z
                   System.out.println("It's not a
                         letter");
                else
                  System.out.println("It's not a
                         letter");
         else
               System.out.println("It's not a letter");
    }
}
```

Hint: Draw a control flow graph of Program 2.28 to understand the logic better.

`switch` statement

The `if` statement (or `if-else` statement) is called conditional branching, where condition is in the form of a logical expression (which evaluates either `true` or `false`). Now, let us learn about another type of decision making in Java called `switch` statement. The `switch` statement is a multi-way branch statement. It provides an easy way to execute different parts of code based on the value of an expression. It provides a better alternative than a large series of `if-else-if` statements. The concept of multi-way branch is depicted in Figure 2.11.

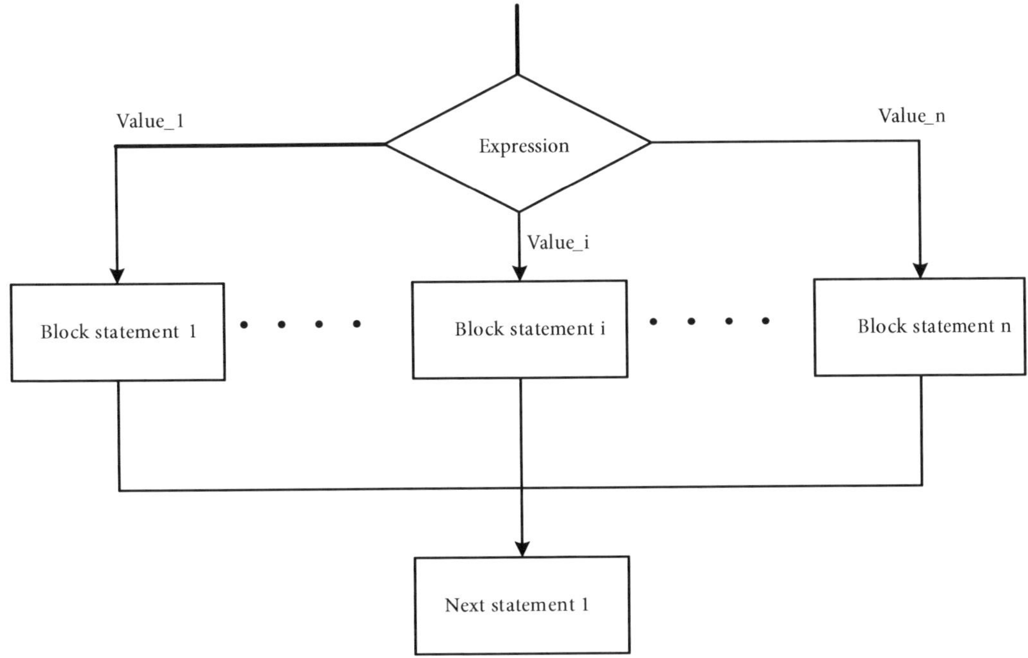

Figure 2.11 `Switch` construct

The general structure of the switch statement is as follows:

```
switch (expression) {
        case value1:
                // Block statement 1
                break;
        case value2:
                // Block statement 2
                break;
                .
                .
                .
        case valueN :
                // Block statement n
                break;
        default:
                // Default statement
    }
```

The `switch` statement works like this: The value of the `expression` is compared with each of the values in the `case` statements. If a match is found, the code sequence following that `case` statement is executed. If none of the cases match the value of the expression, then the `default` statement is executed. However, the default statement is optional. If no case matches and no default is present, then no further action is taken.

Program 2.29 illustrates the application of a `switch` statement.

Program 2.29 *(`switch` statement)*

```
/* This program read a key space from the keyboard and
      then print it if it is an arithmetic operator,
      otherwise a message. */

class SwitchTest {
      public static void main (String args[]) {
         int operator;
         operator = System.in.read();
              //Read a key from the keyboard

         switch (operator) {
           case '+':
                System.out.println("Addition : " +
                   operator);
                break;
           case '-':
                System.out.println("Subtraction : " +
                   operator);
                break;

           case '*':
                System.out.println("Multiplication : " +
                   operator);
                break;

           case '/':
                System.out.println("Division : " +
                   operator);
                break;

           default:
                System.out.println("Not a valid
                   arithmetic operator")
}
   }
}
```

Note the use of `break` statement under each case. The `break` statement is used inside the `switch` to terminate a statement sequence. When a `break` statement is encountered, execution branches to the first line of code that follows the entire `switch` statement. The `break` statement is optional. This has the effect of "jumping out" of the `switch`.

The Program 2.30 illustrates the impact of a `break` statement in a `switch` statement.

Program 2.30 *(`break` statement)*

```
/* This program explains how program is executed in
      presence and absence of break. */

class BreakTest {
      public static void main (String args[]) {
          int x; int y;
          x = System.in.read();
              // Read a digit from the keyboard

       switch(x) {
          case 1:
           y = 1;
          case 2:
           y = 2;
           break;
          case 3:
           y = 3;
           break;

          default:
            y = 0;
       }
   }
}
```

In Program 2.30, depending on whether the control variable `x` equals 1 or 2, it sets the value `y = 2`. This is so because if `x = 1`, it will execute `case 1` and then as there is no `break`, it will continue to `case 2` and hence `y = 2`. If you place a `break` under `case 1`, then you will get a different result.

Sometimes we don't want a `break` statement in a `switch`. Let's check the Program 2.31.

Program 2.31
(break statement again)

```
/* This program reads a letter pressed from the
      keyboard and then prints it if it is a vowel or
      consonant. */

class SwitchTest2 {
      public static void main (String args[]) {
          int letter;
          letter = System.in.read();
              //Read a character from keyboard

          switch (letter) {
            case 'a':
            case 'A':
            case 'e':
            case 'E':
            case 'i':
            case 'I':
            case 'o':
            case 'O':
            case 'u':
            case 'U':
               System.out.println("Vowel : " + letter);
               break;
            default:
               System.out.println("Not a vowel!")
          }
      }
}
```

- In the switch statement, the `expression` in `switch` is a variable or any arithmetic expression which must be evaluated as a `byte`, `char`, `short`, `int`, or `enumeration`. Note that the significant limitation of the `switch` in Java is that the expression and values can be only simple primitive types (and then only primitive types that are automatically castable to `int`). You cannot use larger primitive types (`long`, `float`).
- Expression can also be of type `String`. Program 2.32 is an example.
- Each value specified in the case statements must be a unique constant expression (such as a literal value).
- The type of each value must be compatible with the type of expression.
- Nested `if` can work for any kind of test on any type.
- Inside a case in a `switch`, any `if`, `if-else`, `switch`, or any other control statement such as `looping`, etc. are possible.

Program 2.32 *(String in switch statement)*

```
/* Use a string to control a switch statement. */

class StringSwitch {
   public static void main(String args[]) {
     String str = "apple";
     switch(str) {
         case "orange":
              System.out.println("Orange");
              break;
         case "apple":
              System.out.println("Apple");
              break;
         case "mango":
              System.out.println("Mango");
              break;
         default:
              System.out.println("no match");
     }
   }
}
```

Assertion statement

An assertion is a concept of testing the correctness of any assumptions that have been made in the program to test that some expected condition is met. Java assertion is a condition that should be `true` during the execution of a program. The Java developer has introduced a keyword called `assert` to implement assertion in a Java program.

The `assert` statement is used with a Boolean expression and can be written in two different ways.

Way 1:

```
assert condition;
```

Way 2:

```
assert condition : value;
```

Now, let us understand the working of these two forms of `assert` statements.

At the time of execution, when the program executes the `assert` statement, and if the `condition` is `false`, then the JVM throws up an error named `AssertionError` (we shall learn about Java's exception handling mechanism in Chapter 8). In the second form of assertion, if the `condition` is `false`, then `value` is passed to the `AssertionError` so that the error massage contains this `value`. Typically, `value` is a string literal.

Program 2.33 illustrates a simple application of assertion. The program expects that user should press a character key and then prompt accordingly. However, if a user presses any other key, then the program throws up an error at the time of execution.

Program 2.33
(`assert` statement)

```
/* This program demonstrates assertion (Way 1)
      statement. */

class AssertionTest1 {
  public static void main(String args[]) {
      int letter = System.in.read();
              // Read a key from keyboard
      switch(letter) {
          case "a":
             System.out.println("Vowel" + letter);
             break;
          case "A":
             System.out.println("Vowel" + letter);
             break;

             ... . . . . .
              // For all other vowels and consonant

          default:
              assert false; // Report that assertion is
                                                  //failed
      }
  }
}
```

Let us consider another simple example as shown in Program 2.34. This program assumes that the user will enter an age which is a positive number. If the user does that, the program will work fine. Otherwise, it will throw up an exception.

Program 2.34 *(another example of* `assert`*)*

```
/* This program demonstrates assertion (Way 2)
      statement. */

import java.util.Scanner;
             // For a new way to read data from keyboard

class AssertionTest2 {
  public static void main(String args[]) {
       Scanner scanner = new Scanner(System.in);
       System.out.print("Enter your age ");
       int age = scanner.nextInt();
              // Read any number from keyboard

       assert value <= 0: " Not valid";
              // Assertion is failed here

       System.out.println("Age is "+ value);
              // Assertion is true
   }
}
```

- The condition should be a Boolean expression.
- Assertion test can be included anywhere, for example, in `if-else`, `switch`, etc.
- In a program, a number of `assert` statements (with different conditions) are possible.
- Assertion is disabled by default. You should enable the assertion first, to make it work. Assume that your program file name is `ClasstEst.java`. It is compiled successfully with `javac` command. Then the syntax for enabling assertion statement in Java source code is:

```
java -ea ClassTest
```

or

```
java -enableassertions ClassTest
```

- Also, you can disable assertion. The syntax for disabling assertions in Java is:

```
java -da ClassTest
```

or

```
java -disableassertions ClassTest
```

Once it is disabled, JVM will not throw `AssertionError` object.

2.6.3 Looping

Varieties of loop constructs

In Java, as in all programming languages, there are control structures that let you repeat statements. There are two forms for repeating loops: determinate and indeterminate. In case of a determinate loop, you know how many times a loop should be rolled, whereas in case of an indeterminate loop, you do not know how many times a loop should be processed. The `for` construct is used to specify a determinate loop and `while` construct is used to specify indeterminate loop. There are two variations of `for` loop: numerical `for` loop and collection-based `for` loop (also called `for-each` loop). The `while` loop has two constructs: `while-do` and `do-while` loops. Let's learn about each type of loop construct, syntax, and usage to write programs in Java.

Determinate `for` loop

As we have mentioned, there are two forms of determinate loop: **n**umerical `for` loop and collection-based `for` loop.

Numerical `for` loop

The general structure of a numerical `for` loop and its syntax is shown in Figure 2.12. As you can see, the loop control mechanism has three parts, separated by semicolons. The first part, the initialization, executes once, before the loop starts. You typically use this expression to initialize a counter for the number of loop iterations, for example, `i = 0`. The second part gives the condition which will be tested before each new pass through the loop, for example, `i < 10`. The third part explains how to update the counter, for example, `i++`. Program 2.35 demonstrates a simple example of numerical `for` loop in a Java program. In this program, the variable `i` is the counter which is used to control the iteration.

- The condition should be a Boolean expression (i.e., a logical expression returning either `true` or `false`).
- The loop may not execute at all if the condition returns `false` at the very beginning of the loop.
- When a loop is controlled by a counter, the counter can be an integer or a floating-point variable.
- You can count up or down by whatever increment or decrement you want.
- When you declare a variable in the first part of the `for` statement, the scope of that variable extends until the end of the body of the `for` loop. Such a declaration is advisable if the loop variable is to control the loop only and not used elsewhere.

```
for (int i = 1; i <= 10; i++)
{
. . .
}
// i no longer defined here
```

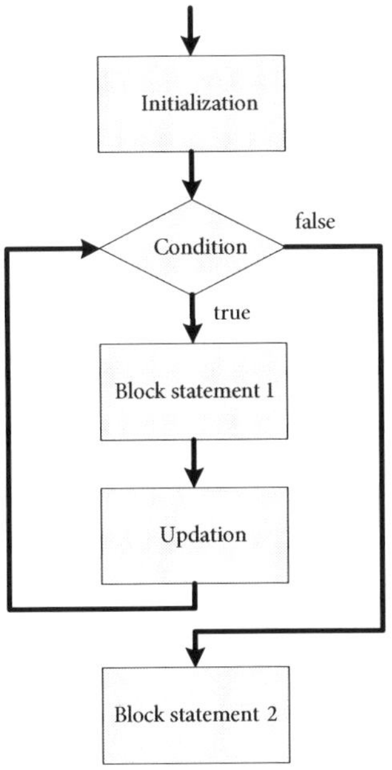

```
for(initialization; condition; updation) {
    . . .                    // Block statement 1
}
. . .                        // Block statement 2
```

Figure 2.12 Structure and syntax of numerical for-loop

Program 2.35 *(Numerical for-loop)*

```
/* This program demonstrates numerical for-loop.
      This program calculates the average of first n
      numbers. */

class NumericalForLoop {
  public static void main(String args[]) {
       int sum = 0; float avg;
       int n = 10;        // Let 10 be the limit here

       for(int i = 1; i <= 10;  i++) {
           sum += i;
       }

       avg = (float) sum/n;
       System.out.println("Average of first "+ n +
               " numbers is "+ avg);
    }
}
```

- If you define a variable inside a `for` statement, you cannot use the value of that variable outside the loop. Therefore, if you wish to use the final value of a loop counter outside the `for` loop, be sure to declare it outside the header for the loop!

```
int i;
for (i = 1; i <= 10; i++)
{
. . .
}
// i still defined here
```

- You can define variables with the same name in separate `for` loops:

```
for (int i = 1; i <= 10; i++)
{
. . .
}
. . .
for (int i = 11; i <= 20; i++) // ok to redefine i
{
. . .
}
```

- There will be times when you will want to include more than one statement in the initialization and iteration portions of the `for` loop. For example, consider the loop in the following program:

```
int a, b;
for(a=1, b=4; a<b; a++, b--) {
. . .
}
```

- The following is, however, a valid for-loop, which will never terminate:

```
for(  ;  ;  } { . . . }    //All parts are empty
```

or

```
for(  int i = 0;  i < 10;  i-- } { . . . }
```

- The body of the `for` (or any other of Java's loops) can be empty. This is because a *null statement* (one that consists only of a semicolon) is syntactically valid in Java. For example, consider the following program:

```
for(int i = 100; int j = 200; ++i < --j); );
// no body in this loop
System.out.println("Midpoint is " + i);
```

Be careful about testing for equality of floating-point numbers in loops. A `for` loop that looks like this:

```
for (double x = 0; x != 10; x += 0.1) {. . . }
```

may never end. Due to roundoff errors, the final value may not be reached exactly. For example, in the given loop, x jumps from 9.99999999999998 to 10.09999999999998, because there is no exact binary representation for 0.1.

Collection-based `for` loop

There is another type of `for` loop known in Java called collection-based for loop (also called as `for-each` loop). The construct of such a `for` loop and its syntax in Java is shown in Figure 2.13. Here, `type` specifies the type and `itemIdentifier` specifies the name variable that will iterate over the elements in a collection, one at a time, from the beginning to the end and `collection` refers to an array or a list defined by `enum`, etc. Note that the type should be same as (i.e., compatible with) the type of the elements stored in `collection`. Program 2.32 is an example to explain the collection-based `for` loop.

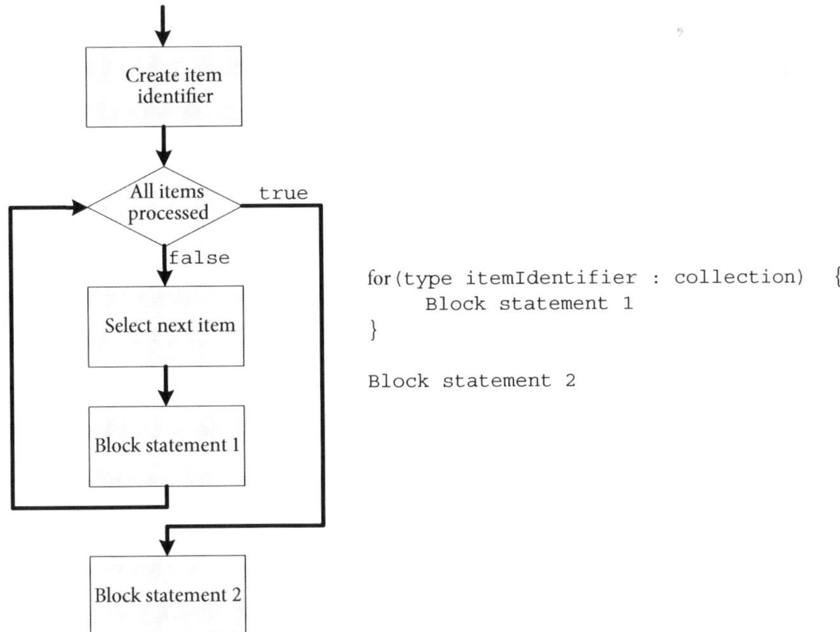

Figure 2.13 Structure and syntax of collection-based `for` loop

Program 2.36 (Collection-based `for` *loop)*

```
/* This program calculates the average of the number
      stored in an array using the collection-based
      for-loop. */

class CollectionForLoop {
    public static void main(String args[]) {
        float values[] = { 4.5, 6.7, 3.4, 8.9, 5.6,
              0.1, 9.0, 2.3, 1.2 };
        float sum = 0.0; int count = 0;

        for(float x : values) {
              // For each x in values do the following
           System.out.println("Current value from the
              collection: " + x);
           sum += x; count++;
        }
        System.out.println("Average: " + sum/count);
    }
}
```

- With each pass through the loop, `x` is automatically given a value equal to the next element in `value`. Thus, on the first iteration, `x` contains 4.5; on the second iteration, `x` contains 6.7; and so on. Also, note that `for` automatically cycles through an array in sequence from the lowest index to the highest.
- In the `for` part, `enum` type collection can also be used. Program 2.37 is an example of this.

Program 2.37 (Collection-based for-loop with enum)

```
/* This program illustrates the use of enum as
      collection in collection-based for-loop. */

public class CollectionForLoopEnum {
   enum Colors { Red, Blue, Green, White }
             //Enumeration type definition
   public static void main(String[] args) {
      for(Colors color : Colors.values()) {
             // Vary over all values
           System.out.println(" Color is " + color);
      }
   }
}
```

Indeterminate loop

The two `for` loop structures you have just learned are called determinate loop structures because from a close look of the loop statement, we can count the number of times the loop will iterate. As an alternative to this, there are other loop structures, called indeterminate loop, where the number of iterations varies with the input to the programs. There are two structures under this category: `while` and `do-while`.

`while` loop

The general structure of the `while` loop and its syntax are shown in Figure 2.14. The `condition` can be any Boolean expression. The body of the loop will be executed as long as the conditional expression is `true`. When the condition becomes `false`, the control passes to the next line of code immediately following the loop. There is no update part in the `while` statement; this is actually done inside the body of the loop. Program 2.38 includes a simple program using a `while` loop structure.

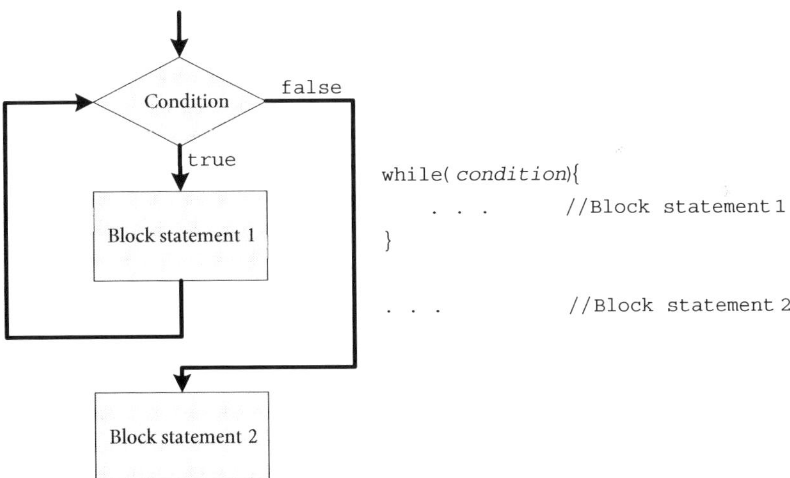

Figure 2.14 Structure and syntax of `while` loop

Program 2.38 (`while` loop)

```
/* This program shows the calculation of sum of odd
      numbers using while-loop. */

public class SumOfOddsWithWhileLoop {
    public static void main(String[] args) {
        int i = 1;
        int sum = 0;
        int n = 10;
```

```
        while(i < 10) {
            sum += i;
            i += 2;            // Move to next odd number
        }
        System.out.println(" Sum of odd numbers is " + sum);
    }
}
```

- Since the `while` loop evaluates its conditional expression at the top of the loop, the body of the loop will not execute even once if the condition is `false` to begin with. For example, in the following fragment, the call to `println()` is never executed:

```
int a = 10, b = 20;
while(a > b)
  System.out.print("No loop execution…");
```

- A `for` loop is equivalent to a `while` loop. The following statement:

```
for(initialization; condition; updation)
     statement;
```

is completely equivalent to:

```
initialization;
while (condition){
     statement;
     updation;
}
```

`do-while` loop

The `do-while` loop is the same as the `while` loop, except for the fact that the condition is checked at the end of the loop. The construct and syntax of this statement are shown in Figure 2.15. Each iteration of the `do-while` loop first executes the body of the loop and then evaluates the conditional expression. If this expression is `true`, the loop will repeat. Otherwise, the loop terminates. As with all of Java's loops, the condition must be a Boolean expression. Program 2.39 shows a program using `do-while` loop structure.

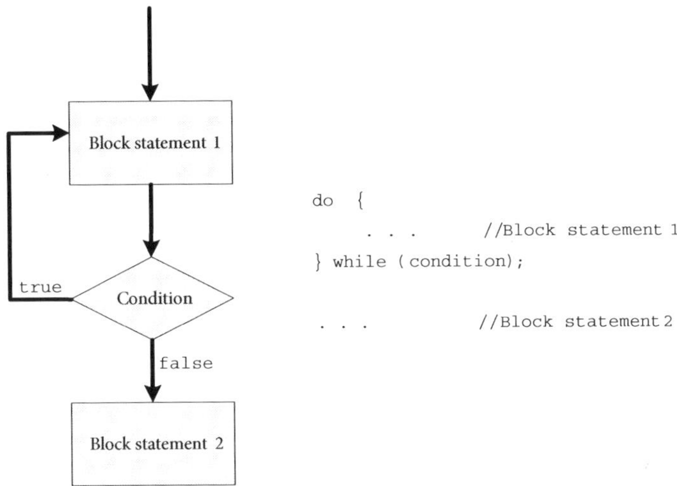

Figure 2.15 Structure and syntax of do-while loop

Program 2.39 *(do-while loop)*

```
/* This program shows the calculation of sum first even
      number using do-while loop. */

public class DoWhileLoop {
  public static void main(String[] args) {
   int limit = 10;     // Sum from 1 to this valuc
   int sum = 0;       // Accumulate sum in this variable
   int i = 0;        // Loop counter

   do {
       sum += i;    // Add the current value of i to sum
       i += 2;
   } while(i <= limit);
   System.out.println("sum = " + sum);
  }
}
```

- The do-while loop always executes its body at least once, because its conditional expression is at the bottom of the loop.

2.6.4 Nested Control Structures

The loop structures which you have learned can be nested. A for within a for (or while) a while within a while (or for), etc., are allowed. Such a nesting can be done up to any level. In Java, there is no restriction about this. Program 2.40 illustrates the multiplication of two 2-dimensional matrices.

Program 2.40
(Nested loop)

```
/* This program initialize a 3D array and then traverse
      the array to print each element in it. */
class a3DArrayTest {
      public static void main(String args[]) {
            int my3DArray [ ][ ][ ] = new int [3][4][5];
            int i, j, k;
            // Initializing the array
            for(i=0; i<3; i++)
             for(j=0; j<4; j++)
              for(k=0; k<5; k++)
                 my3DArray[i][j][k] = i * j * k;
                    //The value
            // Traversing the array
            for(i=0; i<3; i++) {
             for(j=0; j<4; j++) {
              for(k=0; k<5; k++){
                 System.out.print(my3DArray[i][j][k] +
                    " ");
                 System.out.println();
               }
               System.out.println();
            }
         }
     }
}
```

2.6.5 Jump Statements

Although the designers of Java kept `goto` as a reserved word, they decided not to include it in the language. In general, `goto` statements are considered poor style. Unrestricted use of `goto` is error-prone. However, there are some situations, when an occasional jump out of a loop is beneficial. Java supports two jump statements: `break` and `continue`. These are discussed in the following sections.

`break` statement

You have seen how to use the `break` statement in a `switch` block. Its effect is to exit the `switch` block and continue execution with the first statement after the `switch`. You can also use the `break` statement to break out from a loop. When `break` is executed within a loop, the loop ends immediately, and execution continues with the first statement following the loop.

Using **break** *to exit a loop*

Program 2.41 is an example how to do this. Consider the `while` loop that copied elements from an integer array into an array of floats until the end of the array or until a 0 is reached. You can instead test for the latter case inside the body of the `while` and then use `break` to exit the loop.

Program 2.41 *(break to exit a loop)*

```
/* This program is to test whether a number is prime
      number or not. This program uses break statement
      to exit loop. */

import jaba.util.Scanner;

public class PrimeTest {
    public static void main(String[] args) {
    boolean isPrime = false;
    Scanner scanner = new Scanner(System.in);
    System.out.print("Enter upto which number to be
              tested: ");
    int n = scanner.nextInt();
                        // Read a number from the keyboard

     for(int i = 2; i <= n; i++) {
      isPrime = true;
              // Assume the current number is prime
      // Try dividing by all integers from 2 to i-1
        for(int j = 2; j < i; j++) {
           if(i % j == 0) {
              // This is true if j divides exactly
           isPrime = false; // It is not a prime number
           System.out.println("Number: "+i+ "is NOT
              prime.");
           break;         // No more test, exit the loop
         }
      }
      if(isPrime) {     // So is it prime!
              System.out.println("Number: " + i + "is
                   prime.");
      }
     }
    }
}
```

`continue` statement

Sometimes it is useful to force an early iteration of a loop. You might want to continue running the loop but stop processing the remainder of the code in its body for that particular iteration. This is, in effect, a `goto` just past the body of the loop, to the loop's end. The `continue` statement performs such an action. In `while` and `do-while` loops, a `continue` statement causes control to be transferred directly to the conditional expression that controls the loop. In a `for` loop, control goes first to the iteration portion of the for statement and then to the conditional expression. For all three loops, any intermediate code is bypassed. Program 2.38 illustrates the application of `continue` statement in a loop.

Program 2.42 *(`continue` statement)*

```
/* This program will print only the odd number
      and skips printing even number. The program
      illustrates the use of continue statement in a
      while loop. */

public class ContinueTest {
    public static void main(String[] args) {

        for(int i = 1; i<10, i++) {
            if (i%2 == 0) continue;
              // Skip the next step
               System.out.print(i + " ");
        }
    }
}
```

Labelled loops

Both `break` and `continue` can have an optional label that tells Java where to break to. Without a label, `break` jumps outside the nearest loop (to an enclosing loop or to the next statement outside the loop), and continues (i.e., restarts) the enclosing loop. Using labelled `break` and `continue`, you can break to specific points outside nested loops or continue a loop outside the current loop.

To use a labelled loop, add the label before the initial part of the loop, with a colon between them. Then, when you use `break` or `continue`, add the name of the label after the keyword itself. Here is an example:

```
out:
    for (int i = 0; i <10; i++) {
        while (x < 50) {
            if (i * x == 400)
                break out;
            ...
        }
        ...
    }
```

In this snippet of code, the label `out` labels the outer loop. Then, inside both the `for` and `while` loops, when a particular condition is met, a `break` causes the execution to break out of both the loops and continue executing any code after both loops. Let's check another version of prime test program (Program 2.43).

Program 2.43 *(break with continue)*

```
/* This program is to print first n number of prime
      numbers rather than check if a given integer
      value is a prime or not. In this case, you
      don't know how many numbers you need to check to
      generate the required number of primes. This is
      a case where an indefinite loop is useful. This
      program uses break and continue statements to
      solve such a problem. */

import jaba.util.Scanner;

public class PrimeTest {
    public static void main(String[] args) {

      Scanner scanner = new Scanner(System.in);
      System.out.print("Enter how many prime numbers to
              be printed : ");
      int n = scanner.nextInt();
              // Read number from the keyboard

      Out:
      for(int i = 2; ; i++) {  Let's run forever
          // Try dividing by all integers from 2 to i-1
          for(int j = 2; j < i; j++) {
            if(i%j == 0) { // This is true if j divides
              exactly
              continue Out; // so exit the loop
              }
          }
```

```
            System.out.println(i); // Yes, it is prime
            if(--n == 0) {  // Decrement the prime count
                break;  // It is zero so we have them all
            }
        }
    }
}
```

Summary

Java programming language follows many of the basic elements from C/C++. So, if you are an experienced C/C++ programmer, this chapter will be a redundant for you. Otherwise, for a new programmer, this is a very important chapter. This chapter starts with a discussion about the basic elements of Java. It introduces Java keywords and syntax for writing statements, and declaring constants and variables. You get a complete idea of the different data types that Java allows to define in your program, followed by operations of each data type. How to write an expression and different operators in an expression, and associativity and precedence of different operators are discussed in detail. Two types of data, namely array and string, is frequent in Java programs. These two data types are discussed with illustrations. Learning a programming language will not be complete until you get acquainted with the control structures. All control structures in Java are introduced in this chapter.

FAQs

2.1 Why does Java include many features of the programming language C?

2.2 What is `final` keyword in Java?

2.3 What is a `break` statement?

2.4 What is a `continue` statement?

2.5 What is the precedence of an operator?

2.6 What is the associativity of an operator?

2.7 What is a "blank final" variable?

2.8 What is `super` keyword in java?

2.9 What is a `static` variable in Java?

2.10 Which features are there in C++ but not in Java?

The answers to these questions and other problems in this chapter are available at www.cambridge.org/9781009211918. You might have many questions like these. You can post your question in the discussion forum at https://cse.iitkgp.ac.in/~dsamanta/joywithjava/page8.php.

Programs for Practice

2.1 Following is a small program in C. Write an equivalent program using Java.

```
#include <stdio.h>
int main() {
     int x = 10, y = 3;
     int a, b;
     a = x + y;
     b = x - y;
     printf("x + y = %d\n", a); printf("x - y = %d\n", b);
     getch();
     return 0;
}
```

2.2 Write an equivalent program using Java for the following:

```
#include<stdio.h>

  main()
  {
     int i = 0;

     printf("Enter a value of i : ");
     scanf("%d", &i);

     printf("\n \n i = %d, i++ = %d, ++i = %d\n", i, ++i, i++);


     return;
  }
```

2.3 Evaluate the expression of T_p:

$$T_p = T_s\sqrt{\frac{R_s\sqrt{\frac{1-\alpha}{\sigma}}}{2D}}$$

where $\alpha = 0.306$, Ts = 6.96×10^8 m, $R_s = 6.96 \times 10^8$ m, D = 1.496×10^{11} m and $\alpha = 1.2$.

2.4 A ball is released from a height of h meters. Each time it bounces on the floor, its velocity becomes half. Write a program, which takes the value of h and then prints the total distance traversed by the ball when it touches the ground for the *n*th time. Assume that the value of acceleration due to gravity, g is 9.8 m/sec^2.

2.5 Acceleration due to gravity of a celestial object of mass M and radius R is given by:

$$g = G\frac{M}{R^2}$$

Calculate the values of g for the earth and moon, given that:

- Mass of the earth = 5.972×10^{24} kg
- Radius of the earth = 6361 km
- Mass of the moon = 7.35×10^{22} kg
- Radius of the moon = 1737 km
- Assume the value of Newton's constant G as 6.67408×10^{-11} $m^3 \cdot kg^{-1} \cdot s^{-2}$

You should define appropriate data types to store each value in your program.

2.6 Let the variables in the code be defined as: int a = 5; int b = –3; int c = 0.
Which of the following conditions evaluates to true in Java programming language?

(a) (a < b) || (c < b)
(b) (c < a) && (c < b)
(c) (a > b) && !c
(d) !(a + b > c)

2.7 Write a program to compute and print the taxi fare based on the following chart. Total number of kilometers travelled will be input by the user as a floating point number.

First 12 km: ₹100
Next 4 km: ₹8 / km
Next 4 km: ₹6 / km
Above km: ₹5 / km

2.8 There is a course with two components: Theory and Lab. Theory and Lab have a weightage of 70% and 30%, respectively, in evaluation. A grade has to be given based on the total marks, say X, which are the total marks obtained in Theory and Lab tests with the following breakup:

```
EX:    X ≥ 90
A:     80 ≤ X < 90
B:     70 ≤ X < 80
C:     60 ≤ X < 70
D:     50 ≤ X < 60
P:     40 ≤ X < 50
F:     X < 40
```

It is decided to award grace marks to some students based on their attendance, say Y, in the Theory and Lab classes, according to the following criteria:

- If Y ≥ 85% and marks in Theory are ≤ 70%, then add 15% of the obtained Theory marks to the Theory evaluation.
- If 75% ≥ Y > 85% and marks in Theory are ≤ 60%, then add 10% of the obtained theory marks to the Theory evaluation.
- If 60% ≥ Y > 75% and marks in Theory are ≤ 50%, then add 5% of the obtained theory marks to the Theory evaluation.

A total of 60 classes were held for Theory and Lab, together. Two tests, each, in Theory and Lab were conducted, each of 100 marks. Read the marks of a student in Theory and Lab evaluation, and attendance count of the student. Decide the grade that the student should get.

Write a program in Java for this. You should use only `switch-case` statements to implement condition and branching logic in your program.

2.9 Declare a variable to store an integer number. Initialize the variable with a number. Write a program to display all the factors of the number. For example, if the input number is 10, then it should print 1, 2, 5 and 10.

2.10 Read a sequence of integer numbers (terminated by 0) and write a program in Java to find the maximum, minimum, and average value of the numbers (excluding 0) that have been entered.

2.11 Declare and initialize any 4-digit-number. Print a number whose digits are in the reverse order to that of the input number. Print the difference between the new and the input numbers. For example, if the number entered is 1234, then it should print the result 4321 and 3087. Write a program in java to do this.

2.12 Write a program in java to find the sum of the following series for a given value of n. (Don't use a formula).

$$s = 1 - \frac{1}{3} + \frac{1}{3^2} - \frac{1}{3^3} + \cdots (-1)^n \frac{1}{3^n}$$

2.13 A number is called a perfect number if the number is equal to the sum of all its positive divisors except the number itself. For example, (6 = 1 + 2 + 3; 28 = 1 + 2+ 4 + 7 + 14). Write a program in Java to find and print all the perfect numbers less than or equal to 1000.

2.14 Write a Java program to find whether a number is prime or not.

2.15 Write a Java program to find whether a string or a number is palindrome or not.

2.16 An Armstrong number is a number which is the sum of the cubes of all its unit, tens and hundred digits, etc. For example, for a three-digit number, it is 153.

153 = 1*1*1 + 5*5*5 + 3*3*3 = 1 + 125 + 27 = 153

For a four-digit number, it is 1634

1634 = 1*1*1*1 + 6*6*6*6 + 3*3*3*3 + 4*4*4*4 = 1 + 1296 + 81 + 256 = 1634

Write a Java Program to check if a number is an Armstrong number.

2.17 Store a binary number in an array. Convert the binary number into its equivalent decimal value. For example, for 5 bits binary number 10101, the decimal value is 21. Write a program in Java to do this.

2.18 Store two sets of numbers into two arrays, say A and B. Find the sets C and D such that $C = A \cup B$ and $D = A \cap B$, where $\cup$ and $\cap$ denote the union and intersection operations on sets. Stores the results into two arrays say C and D. Print the arrays C and D. Write a program in Java to do this.

2.19 Store two matrices of integer numbers into two 2D arrays. Let the matrices be A and B. Find the 2D array C such that C = A × B, where × represents multiplication of two matrices. Write a program in java to do this.

2.20 A 3D vector X is represented as $X = ix + jy + kz$. The symbols bear the usual meanings. You should store such a vector in an array. Read two vectors say X and Y from the keyboard. Find their DOT and CROSS products. From their products values, check if the two vectors are orthogonal or parallel. Write a program in java to do this.

2.21 Write a Java program to check whether two given strings are an anagram or not. Two strings are said to be anagram if they contain the same set of characters but in different order. For example, "Listen"–"Silent" and "Debit Card"–"Bad Credit" are anagrams.

2.22 The saddle point of a matrix is an element in the matrix which is the smallest in its row and the largest in its column. For example, in the following matrix, 7 is the saddle point at (2,2).

$$\begin{matrix} 6 & 3 & 1 \\ 9 & 7 & 8 \\ 2 & 4 & 5 \end{matrix}$$

Write a program to find all the saddle point in a given matrix.

2.23 A number is called a Harshad number (also called as Niven number) if the number is divisible by the sum of its digits. For example, 210 is a Harshad number because 210 is divisible by the sum of its digits (2+1+0 = 3). Write a program which will print first 10 Harshad numbers with n digits. The number n will be known at the time of running your program.

2.24 A symmetric matrix is a square matrix which is equal to its transpose. If A[][] is a square matrix with (n x n) order, then this matrix is said to be symmetric if every element at i^{th} row and j^{th} column is equal to element at j^{th} row and i^{th} column, that is, A[i][j] == A[j][i]. Your program should take input matrix from the user, display it, and check whether the matrix is symmetric or not.

MCQs

2.1 **Which of the following is *not a correct* statement?**

(a) It is always necessary to use a *new* operator to initialize an array.
(b) An array can be initialized using comma separated expressions surrounded by curly braces.
(c) An array can be declared and memory can be allotted in one statement.
(d) An array can be declared in one statement and memory can be allocated in another statement.

2.2 Which of the following is an incorrect array declaration?

(a) `int [] a = new int[10];`
(b) `int [] a;`
(c) `int[][] a = new int[10];`
(d) `int[][] a = {{1, 2, 3}, {1, 2, 3}};`

2.3 Which of the following *cannot* be used for a variable name in Java?

(a) identifier. (b) final. (c) malloc. (d) calloc.

2.4 What is the output of this program?

```
class Increment {
    public static void main(String args[]) {
        int i = 3;
        System.out.print(++i * 8);
    }
}
```

(a) 24.
(b) 25.
(c) 32.
(d) Run-time error.

2.5 Consider the following piece of code:

```
public class Test {
  public static void main(String[] args){
      int[] x = {1, 2, 3, 4};
      char[] y = {'a', 'b', 'c', 'd'};
      for (int i = 0; i < x.length; i += 2)
          for (int j = y.length-1; j > 0; j--)
              if (((i+j) % 2) == 0)
                  System.out.print(x[i]);
              else
                  System.out.print(y[j]);
  }
}
```

Note: The value of k% 2 is 0 only when k is even.

Which of the following does this program print?

(a) d1bd3b (b) d1b1d3b3
(c) d12cd34c (d) d1b2c2d3b4c4

2.6 **Which of the following features are *not* common in both Java and C++?**
(a) The class declaration.
(b) The access modifiers.
(c) The encapsulation of data and methods.
(d) Multiple inheritance from class.

2.7 **What is the value returned by the method `f()` defined as follows?**

```
public static int f(int x, int y){return (x>y) ? y : x;}
```

(a) The sum of x and y, that is, x + y.
(b) The difference of x and y, that is, x – y.
(c) The maximum of x and y, that is, the larger value of x and y.
(d) The minimum of x and y that is, the smaller value of x and y.

2.8 **Why an array is called "a homogeneous collection of data"?**
(a) An array can store different types of data.
(b) Size of an array is limited (Figure 4.4).
(c) An array can store only one type of data.
(d) An array uses indices for addressing an item stored in it.

2.9 **In Java, which of the following data type groups are of the same size?**
(a) `int` and `long`
(b) `long` and `float`
(c) `float` and `double`
(d) `int` and `float`

2.10 **Consider the following program:**

```
public class Test {
   public static void main(String [ ] args) {
          Test t = new Test();
          t.start();
   }
   void start() {
         int a = 4;
         int b = 5;
         System.out.print("" + 8 + 3 + "");
         System.out.print(a + b);
         System.out.print(" " + a + b + "");
         System.out.print(foo() + a + b + " ");
         System.out.println(a + b + foo());
      }
      String foo(){
          return "foo";
      }
}
```

What is the output of the program?
(a) 839 45foo45 9foo
(b) 9 7 7 foo34 34foo
(c) 72 34 34 foo34 34foo
(d) 9 7 7 foo 7 7foo

2.11 What is the return type of a method that does not return any value?
(a) int. (b) float. (c) void. (d) double.

2.12 Consider the following program:

```
public class Question1{
      public static void main(String args[]){
            for(int a=1;a<3;a+=2){
                  System.out.print(--a);
            }
      }
}
```

What will be the output of the program if it is executed?
(a) 0 (b) 01 (c) 012 (d) 0123

2.13 Consider the following program:

```
public class Question2{
 public static void main(String args[]){
      if(true){
            System.out.print("Welcome");
      }
      if(1==1){
            System.out.print(" to ");
      }
      if(1){
            System.out.print("Java");
      }
 }
}
```

What will be the output of this code?
(a) Welcome. (b) Welcome to.
(c) Welcome to Java. (d) Compilation error.

2.14 Which of the following is an incorrect way of initializing a variable in Java?
(a) Different line declaration and initialization

```
int a,b;
 a=1;
 b=2;
```

(b) Single line declaration and initialization (One at each line)

```
int a = 1;

int b = 2;
```

(c) Single line declaration and initialization (One line multiple variable)
```
int a=1, b = 2;
```

(d) Single line declaration and initialization (One line multiple variable)
```
int a, b = 1, 2;
```

2.15 Consider the following program:

```
public class Question11{
        public static void main(String args[]){
                char a = '2', b='8';
                System.out.println(a+b);
        }
}
```

What will be the output of this program?

(a) 10. (b) 28. (c) 82. (d) 106.

2.16 Consider the following program:

```
public class Class1{
      int x=30;
      static int y=20;
      public static void main(String []args){
            Class1 t1=new Class1();
            t1.x=88;
            t1.y=99;
            int z1=t1.x+t1.y;
            Class1 t2=new Class1();
            System.out.println(t2.x+ " " +t2.y + " " +z1);
      }
}
```

What is the output of this program?

(a) 30 99 187 (b) 88 99 187 (c) 88 20 128 (d) 30 99 129

2.17 Consider the following program:

```
public class Operator3 {
     public static void main(String[] args) {
             String str1="NPTEL";
             String str2="java";
```

```
            System.out.println(str1+str2);     //Statement 1
            int a = 10;
            int b = 20;
            System.out.println(a+b);           //Statement 2
      }
}
```

Which of the following statement(s) is(are) correct?

(a) Except + (plus) operator all other operators are overloaded in Java.
(b) The output of the Statement 1 is
NPTELjava
(c) The output of the Statement 2 is
1020
(d) The output of the Statement 2 is
30

2.18 Which of the following is `true` about the `break` statement in Java?
(a) `Break` stops the execution of the entire program.
(b) `Break` halts the execution and forces the control out of the loop.
(c) `Break` forces the control out of the loop and starts the execution of the next iteration.
(d) `Break` halts the execution of the loop for a certain time frame.

2.19 Which of the following is possibly used with the `switch` statement?
(a) `continue` (b) `exit`
(c) `break` (d) `do`

2.20 Which of the following data structure is necessary to run a recursive method?
(a) Array. (b) Stack. (c) Queue. (d) Table.

3

ENCAPSULATION

Java is an object-oriented programming language. This means that a program is a collection of objects. Note that in the real world, everything is defined as an object and an object can interact with other objects. Java programming follows this philosophy. This means that writing a Java program means you need to create your objects and also mention how your objects interact with other objects which, thus, solves the problem. How an object can be created and the mechanism of object–object interaction, etc., are realized by means of one of the most important object-oriented programming paradigms called *encapsulation*. This chapter includes discussions related to this programming feature. Indeed, the concept of encapsulation is very important for any programmer to build their skill in Java programming.

3.0 Introduction

Object and its concept

Objects in this real world are physical entities, which can be seen and touched. For example, trees, tables, computers, fans, people, birds, and so on. Each object consists of several parts. For example, a tree consists of root, trunk, leaves, buds, flowers, fruits, seeds, and so on. Note that a part of the tree can again be another object, for example, a fruit. An object can be defined by its parts. Such a definition would make the object unique and distinguishable from other objects. In addition to the physical elements, objects are also characterized by behavioral parts. For example, a person is an object and has some behavior, such as climbing (a tree), plucking (a flower), cooking (food), and so on. Objects can be used to model our real world (which is also an object!) and then different activities in the world can be carried out.

Object-oriented approach

This is the philosophy of how we can build a system using the object-oriented concept. A system can be built on a bottom-up approach. Create the smallest objects. Use several small objects to build larger objects; larger objects are then assembled to build much larger objects, and so on, and then finally the target system is built. For example, if you want to make a computer, then build transistors, use transistors to build logic gates, use logic gates to build circuits, use circuits to build different functional units, use different functional units to build memory, CPU, Keyboard, display unit, and finally, all this makes up your computer.

Object-Oriented Programming (OOP) follows the same concept to build software (it is nothing but a system). As you see, if you know how to create an object, then you can also learn how to build your software. This chapter will help you to learn how an object can be created (in terms of structure, attributes, and behaviors) and how such objects can be managed to realize the functionality of a system.

3.1 Concept of Encapsulation

Your learning

Java provides the concept of class to create an object. Class is used to define the structure and functionality of an object. The class forms the basis of object-oriented programming in Java. It is the first and foremost object-oriented programming paradigm. Encapsulation is the concept of combining data and behavior into a unit called class.

3.1.1 Structure of Class

What is encapsulation?

A general structure of a class is shown in Figure 3.1. A class consists of two parts: fields and methods. In order to define a class, you have to declare the following three things:

Class name

A class should have a unique name. Following is the general syntax to declare the name of a class:

Syntax of declaring a class

```
[<Access specifier>]<ClassName>[[extends]| [implements]
<ClassName> [,<ClassName>, ...] ] [......}
```

The specifications in [ ] are optional specifications. The features of another two OOP paradigms, `extends` (for inheritance) and `implements` (for interfaces) will be discussed in Chapter 4 and Chapter 5, respectively. Here are some examples to declare classes:

Some examples

```
class Circle { ... }        // Declaring a class called Circle
public class Student { ... }// Declaring another class called
                                                    // Student
                               // Access specifier is public
public class Student extends Person{ ... }
            // Inherits an already existing class Person
public class Graphs extends Point, Line{ ... }
            // inherits from more than one classes
public class Employee implements Worker{ ... }
            // Implements an interface
```

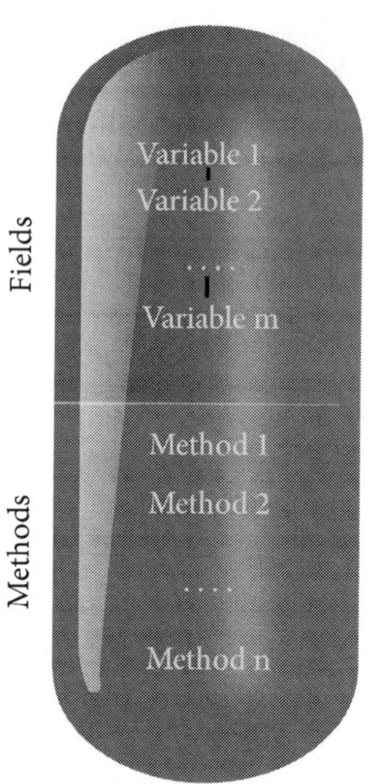

Figure 3.1 Concept of encapsulation

- Naming a class should follow the same rule as to declare an identifier in Java (Chapter 2). Except that, as customary, it should start with an uppercase letter (this is to distinguish from the name of a variable, which should start with lowercase letters).
- Access specifiers can be nothing, public, private, or protected (Chapter 4).
- Usually, the name of the class should be different from the names of the class defined in Java APIs.

Fields

Data in a class

These are variables that store data items that typically differentiate one object of the class from another. They are also referred to as data members of a class. The typical syntax to define a variable name is as follows:

```
<Access specifier> <type> <variableName>;
```

where `<type>` is a primitive data type or an already defined class type and `<Access specifier>` can be nothing (i.e., default), public, private, or protected.

Following are some examples of the declaring fields:

```
int x;              // Declaring a variable of type int
private long y;     // a private variable
String city[10];    // Declaring an array of type String
public static final void PI = 3.14159265358979323846;
                    // Declaring a constant named as PI
```

Methods

Operations on data

The first part of the class, that is, fields, should include all the attributes and data. The second part, that is, methods, should declare and define the operations you can perform for the class. These methods determine what you can do for objects of the class.

The typical syntax in Java to declare a method is as follows:

```
<Access specifier> <return type> <MethodName>(<Argument list>) { . . . }
```

Here, `<return type>` should be the type of data that the method should return to its caller, from which it is called for its operation. The list of arguments are the values to be passed to the method. It can also be empty.

- An attribute can be a variable of primitive data type, enumerated data, or an object of a class already defined.
- The scope of a variable is within or outside the class body depends on the access specification with which it has been declared.
- Methods typically operate on the fields that is, the variables of the class.
- A method is just like a function in C, and it should always return a value (it is the last statement in the method body). If a method does not need to return anything, then its return type should be declared as `void` and the last statement should be `return;` in the body.
- A method cannot run of its own until it is called through an object (this will be discussed in this chapter).
- You can declare a class without any field or method or both. The Java compiler will not report any error.
- The body of the method will include statements and expressions which are necessary to define a method. The Java compiler accepts a method without any statement in it.

Program 3.1 illustrates how you can define a class, for example, `Circle`. This class contains three fields, namely `x`, `y`, and `r`. All these are of type `double`. This class also contains two methods, `circumference()` and `area()`.

Program 3.1
(Simple class declaration)

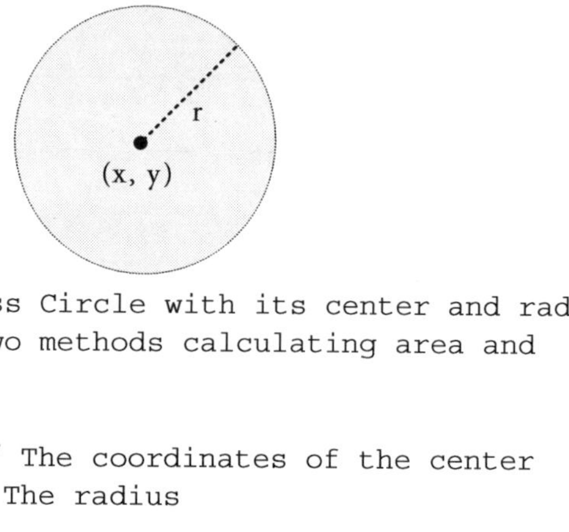


```
/* To declare a class Circle with its center and radius
as the fields and two methods calculating area and
circumference */
class Circle {
      double x,y; // The coordinates of the center
      double r;   // The radius

      // Method that calculates circumference
      double circumference(){
              return 2*3.14159*r;
      }
      // Method that calculates area
      double area(){
              return (22/7)*r*r;
      }
}
```

3.1.2 Creating Object

Instantiation

The class defines the template of a particular type of object. You define a new data type (just like `struct` in C programming). If you compile Program 3.1, there will be no compiler error. However, the program is not executable and it will not run to give any output. This means that you have only declared a class, which is a template of an object, but not the object. A single object or a group of objects of several classes play(s) the role of solving your problems. A Java program not only includes how to declare your class(es), it also stipulates how object(s) can be created and then the different operations on the objects can be executed. Now, let us learn how you can use this class definition to declare an object. Let us consider the case of creating objects for the class `Circle` (as defined in Program 3.1). Creating an object of a class is a two-step process.

Step 1: You must declare a variable of the class type. The step to do this is as follows:

```
class Circle c1;
```

Here, `c1` is the variable to name an object of type `Circle`. This variable does not create an object. Instead, it is simply a variable that can refer to an object.

Declaration of an object

Step 2: If you create an object, it should have a memory for existence. All the values of the variable (i.e., fields) in the object should be stored in a physical memory. You must acquire an actual, physical copy of the object and assign it to that variable. You can do this using the `new` operator. The syntax of this is as follows:

```
class Circle c1 = new Circle();
```

Memory reference

The `new` operator dynamically allocates (that is, allocates at run-time) memory for an object and returns a reference to it. This reference is the address of the object in the memory allocated by `new`. This reference is then stored in the variable.

- In Java, all class objects must be dynamically allocated.
- You can delete the object by assigning it to `null`. For example:

  ```
  c1 = null; //This will free the allocated space to memory
  ```
- There is no delete keyword in Java as in C++. This is because, Java follows the automatic garbage collector to free a memory space.

3.1.3 Structure of a Java Program

A class is a program

We are now in a position to create our Java program which will define a class, create an object of that class, and then run to give an output. A general structure of such a Java program is shown in Figure 3.2.

In general, a Java program can contain many things, which are not necessarily a must. These optional parts are shown within [ ] (Figure 3.2) and for the sake of simplicity, we will omit them for the time being. As you see in Figure 3.2, you can include more than one class in your Java program. We shall discuss about a Java program with multiple classes later. Right now we will discuss a single class, where a class can be defined and the same class is also responsible for creating an object and then the program is executable. Program 3.2, which is an extension of Program 3.1, is an example of this.

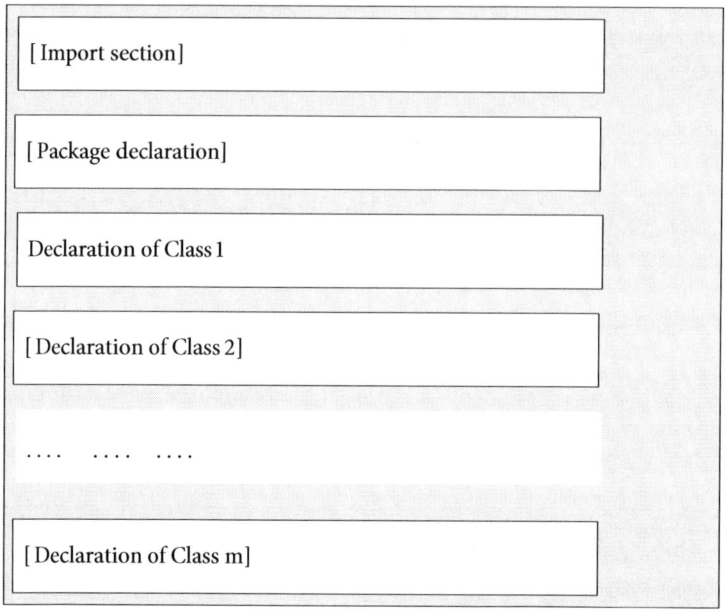

[Import section]

[Package declaration]

Declaration of Class 1

[Declaration of Class 2]

....

[Declaration of Class m]

Figure 3.2 General structure of a Java program

Program 3.2 *(Program with object)*

```
/* To declare a class Circle, create an object and then
print the result.*/

class Circle {
      double x,y;
      double r;

      double circumference(){
            return 2*3.14159*r;
      }

      double area(){
            return (22/7)*r*r;
      }
}
class CircleTest {
      // The main () below create and object and print
                                                  //the result
      public static void main(String args[]) {
            // Create an object
            class Circle c1 = new Circle();
```

```
                // Initialize the object so created
                c1.x = 1.0;
                c1.y = -4.5;
                c1.r = 12.36;

                // Calculate area and circumference of
                the circle object
                c1.area();
                c1.circumference();

                // Print the result
                System.out.println("Area = " + c1.area()
                 + "Circumference = " + c1.circumference());
        }
}
```

Running a program

After writing the program as mentioned, save the program as `CircleTest.java`. Compile the program and then run it with the following commands to see the output:

```
javac CircleTest.java
java CircleTest
```

It is pretty simple, isn't it?

It is important to note the following in this regard:

- To run a program, you should have a program (stored in `.java file`) with a class which includes the `main()`.
- To access the different members in an object, we use the dot (`.`) operator. For example, to assign the member variable `x` of `c1` the value 1.0, we use the following statement:

```
c1.x = 1.0;
```

- The dot operator is also used to call a method for `c1`. For example:

```
c1.area();
```

calls the method `area()` for the object `c1`.

Now, let us consider the case of a Java program with multiple classes. Suppose we want to add one more class, say, `Box` in addition to `Circle`. The class `Box` can be defined as shown in Program 3.3.

Program 3.3
(Declaration of class Box)

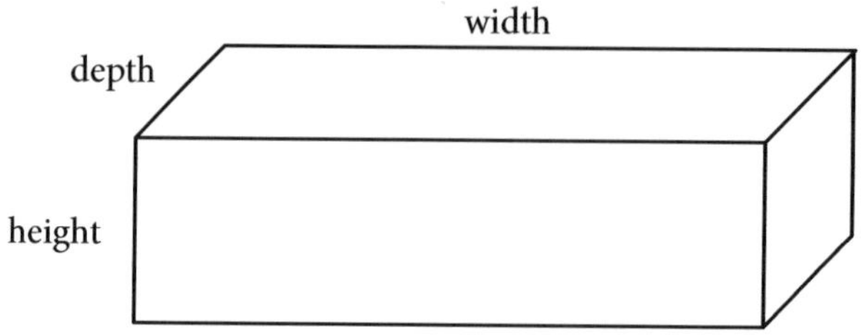

width
depth
height

```
/* To declare a class Box with its width, height and
depth as the fields and two methods calculating area
and volume of it. */

class Box{
   // Declaring the fields
   double width;
   double height;
   double depth;

   // Method that calculates area
   double area(){
      double a;
      a = (width*height + height*depth + width*depth) * 2;
      return a;
   }

   // Method that calculates volume
   double volume(){
      double v;
      v = width*height*depth;
      return v;
   }
}
```

- You may add as many classes as you wish; Java does not have any restriction. However, for better software engineering practice, it should not be like that. Maintaining a class in a separate file is a good practice (we shall learn about this in Chapter 5).
- In Java, a class is called main class if it contains the main method defined in it. For example, all the classes in Program 3.1 and 3.3 are not main classes, whereas the class `CircleTest` in Program 3.2 is.

- A main class is just like any other class; it can also include fields and methods in addition to `main()` method.
- A file can contain as many class you wish. Program 3.4 shows an example where a file contains multiple classes. Also see Program 3.2.
- There may not be a class with `main()` method when a file contains multiple classes.
- If there is a class with `main()`, then the name of the file should be the same as the name of the main class. For example, the name of the file of Program 3.2 should be *CircleTest.java*, and for Program 3.4 it should be *GeoObject.java*.

Program 3.4 *(Program with multiple classes)*

```
/* A Java program with multiple classes.*/

class Circle {
      double x,y;
      double r;

      double circumference(){
             return 2*3.14159*r;
      }
      double area(){
             return (22/7)*r*r;
      }
}
class Box{
      double width;
      double height;
      double depth;

      double area(){
         double a;
         a = (width*height + height*depth +
              width*depth) * 2;
         return a;
      }
```

```
        double volume(){
           double v;
           v = width*height*depth;
           return v;
        }
}

class GeoObjects { // Defining the main class
        public static void main(String args[]) {

           // Create object for the class Circle and
                                              //initialization
           class Circle c = new Circle();
           c.x = 1.0;
           c.y = -4.5;
           c.r = 12.36;

           // Create object for the class Box and
                                              //initialization
           class Box b = new Box();
           b.width = 2.0;
           b.height = 1.5;
           b.depth = 0.5;

           // Calculate area and circumference of the
                                              //circle object
           c.area();
           c.circumference();

           // Calculate area and volume of the box
                                                     //object
           b.area();
           b.volume();

           // Print the result
           System.out.println("Circle : Area = " +
                c.area() + "Circumference = " +
                     c.circumference());
           System.out.println("Box : Area = " +
                b.area() + "Volume = " + b.volume());
           }
}
```

3.1.4 Nested Class

It is possible to define a class within another class; such classes are known as nested classes. Program 3.5 illustrates the concept of nested class in Java.

Program 3.5 *(Nested class)*

```
/* The following program illustrates the use of nested
class in Java programs.*/

// Defining an outer class A.
class A {
   int x = 555;
   void test() {
      B b = new B();
      b.print();
   }
   // Following is the definition of nested class B
   class B {
     int y = 111;
     void print() {
        System.out.println("x = " + x + " and
              y = " + y);
     }
   }   // End of inner class B
}   // End of outer class A

class NestedClassDemo {
    public static void main(String args[]) {
        A a = new A();
        a.test();
    }
}
```

- The scope of a nested class is bounded by the scope of its enclosing class. Thus, if class `B` is defined within class `A`, then `B` does not exist independently of `A`. This means we cannot create an object of class `B` in the `main()`, for example.
- A nested class has access to the members of the class in which it is nested. However, the enclosing class does not have access to the members of the nested class. For example, you cannot print the value of `y` from the main class.

- A nested class declared directly within its enclosing class scope is a member of its enclosing class. It is also possible to declare a nested class that is local to a block.
- Logically, there is no restriction if another class is nested within a nested class, and so on.

3.1.5 Parameters Passing to Methods

Parameter passing

The method in a class can be defined with a list of arguments. A method is very similar to a function in C/ C++. Like a function, a method can take zero or more arguments to be passed when it is called (or accessed). However, unlike C/ C++, argument, if any, in Java is non-pointer type, as there is no pointer concept in Java. In Java, only the call-by-value principle for parameter passing is possible.

The methods discussed so far in this chapter do not have any arguments to be passed. In Java, you can pass a number of parameters of different types into a method. Program 3.6 gives an example of how values can be passed to a method, when it is called.

Program 3.6 *(Parameterized method)*

```
/* This program demonstrates a parameterized method */
class Circle {
    double x,y;
    double r;
    double circumference(){
       return 2*3.14159*r;
    }
    double area(){
       return (22/7)*r*r;
    }

    // Defining a parameterized method
    void setCircle(double a, double b, double c){
        x = a; // Set center x-coordinate
        y = b; // Set center y-coordinate
        r = c; // Set radius
    }
}

class ParameterizedMethodDemo {
   public static void main(String args[]){
      Circle c1 = new Circle();
      Circle c2 = new Circle();
      // Initialize the circles
```

```
        c1.setCircle(3.0,4.0,5.0);
        c2.setCircle(-4.0,8.0,10.0);
        System.out.println("Circumference Circle 1" +
                c1.circumference());
        System.out.println("Area of Circle 1" +
                c1.area());
        System.out.println("Circumference Circle 2" +
                c2.circumference());
        System.out.println("Area of Circle 2" +
                c2.area());
    }
}
```

- The number of maximum values that can be passed to a method is limited. This limit is defined in the JVM specification. The maximum number is 255 units. The total number of units is calculated by summing the contributions of the individual parameters. For example, a parameter of type `long` or `double` contributes two units to the length and a parameter of any other type contributes one unit.
- Object of any class can be passed as a parameter to a method. For example, an object of class `String` can be passed to a method.
- Note that the call-by-value method of parameter passing is applicable to all types of arguments. However, when you pass an object as argument, the effect is different from that for variables of the primitive types. The reason is that a variable of a class type implies a reference to an object, not the object itself. Therefore, when you use an object as an argument to a method, that is, a variable of a class type, a copy of a reference to that object is passed to the method, rather than a copy of the object itself. Because a copy of a reference refers to an object, the parameter name when used in the body of a method refers to the object which has passed as the argument.
- A method can take $0 \le n \le 255$ parameters, but it can return only one value. It can return an object.

3.1.6 Constructors

Automatic object initialization

You have learnt how to create an object and initialize it (e.g., Program 3.4). In Program 3.6, you learnt a better approach to initialize an object by means of a parameterized method. It is a tedious approach to initialize an object each time it is created. Because the requirement for initialization is so common, Java provides an elegant way to initialize objects whenever they are created and it is automatically, done, without any explicit call of a method. This automatic initialization is performed through the use of a constructor.

A constructor is like a method and it has the following properties that differentiate it from other class methods:

1. A constructor initializes an object immediately upon creation. Constructor initializes the internal state of an object.
2. Constructor in Java is a method.
3. This method has the same name as the class in which it resides.
4. Once defined, the constructor is automatically called immediately after the object is created.
5. Constructor is a method which has no return type. The implicit return type of a class constructor is the class type itself.

In our earlier class declarations, we have not defined any method like these. Once defined, the constructor is automatically called when the object is created, before the new operator completes. Program 3.7 is an extension of Program 3.2, where we define a constructor. Also, note the difference between Program 3.6 and Program 3.7.

Program 3.7 *(Class with constructor)*

```
/* This program defines the class Circle with a
constructor in it. */
class Circle {
    double x,y;
    double r;
    double circumference(){
       return 2*3.14159*r;
    }
    double area(){
       return (22/7)*r*r;
    }
    // Defining a constructor
    Circle(double a, double b, double c){
        x = a; // Set center x-coordinate
        y = b; // Set center y-coordinate
        r = c; // Set radius
    }
}
class ConstructorDemo {
   public static void main(String args[]){
      // Creating two objects with constructor
      Circle c1 = new Circle(3.0,4.0,5.0);
      Circle c2 = new Circle(-4.0,8.0,10.0);
```

```
        System.out.println("Circumference Circle 1" +
               c1.circumference());
        System.out.println("Area of Circle 1" +
               c1.area());
        System.out.println("Circumference Circle 2" +
               c2.circumference());
        System.out.println("Area of Circle 2" +
               c2.area());}
}
```

- You will notice that the constructor has the same name as the class and has no return type specified.
- A constructor can have any number of parameters like methods, including none.
- If you do not define any constructors for a class, the compiler will supply a default constructor that has no parameters and does nothing. Initializes that object's variables to a default (e.g., 0 for numbers, null for objects, false for Booleans, '\0' for characters) in that case.

3.2 Polymorphism

Meaning of polymorphism

Polymorphism in Java is a concept by which we can perform a single action in different ways. Polymorphism is derived from two Greek words: *poly* and *morph*. The word *poly* means many and *morph* means form. So polymorphism means many forms.

There are two types of polymorphism in Java: *compile-time polymorphism* and *run-time polymorphism*. In this chapter, we shall discuss the compile-time polymorphism. We will discuss run-time polymorphism in Chapter 4.

Types of polymorphism in Java

The concept of overloading in Java is an example of compile-time polymorphism. We will discuss two types of overloading here: constructor overloading and method overloading.

3.2.1 Constructor Overloading

In Java, it is possible to define two or more constructors within the same class which share the same name, as long as their parameter declarations are different. When this is the case, the constructors are said to be overloaded, and the process is called *constructor overloading*. Program 3.8 gives a simple example of constructor overloading.

Program 3.8 (Class with overloading constructor)

```
/* Example of Constructor overloading: This program
defines the class Circle with multiple constructors in
it. */

class Circle {
    double x,y;
    double r;
    double circumference(){
       return 2*3.14159*r;
    }
    double area(){
       return (22/7)*r*r;
    }
    // A constructor without any argument: Overloading 1
    Circle(){
        System.out.println("Initializing with default
        values...");
        x = 0.0; // Default value for x
        y = 0.0; // Default value for y
        r = 0.0; // Set radius with default value 0.0
    }

    // A constructor with arguments: Overloading 2
    Circle(double a, double b, double c){
        x = a; // Set center x-coordinate
        y = b; // Set center y-coordinate
        r = c; // Set radius
    }
}
class ConstructorDemo {
   public static void main(String args[]){
      // Creating two objects with constructor
      Circle c1 = new Circle();
              //Call Overloading 1 constructor
      Circle c2 = new Circle(-4.0,8.0,10.0);
              //Overloading 2
      System.out.println("Circumference Circle 1" +
              c1.circumference());
      System.out.println("Area of Circle 1" + c1.area());
      System.out.println("Circumference Circle 2" +
              c2.circumference());
      System.out.println("Area of Circle 2" + c2.area());}
}
```

- You can define as many as overloaded constructors.
- Which constructor will be invoked will be decided at the run-time; the compiler will try to match with the values of argument passed when object is instantiated with `new` operator.

3.2.2 Method Overloading

Another polymorphism feature in Java is the *method overloading*. Defining two or more methods with the same name in a class is called method overloading. With this feature, you can define several methods in a class with the same name, as long as each method has a unique set of parameters. The name of a method together with the types and sequence of the parameters form the *signature* of the method. If the two methods in the same class are with different signature, then they are overloaded. Let us look at Program 3.9, which shows method overloading in a class `Sum`.

Program 3.9 *(Method overloading)*

```
/* Java program to demonstrate method overloading in
Java. */
public class Sum {
      // Overloaded sum(). This sum takes two int
                                                //parameters
    public int sum(int x, int y)
    {
        return (x + y);
    }
    // Overloaded sum(. This sum takes three int
                                                //parameters
    public int sum(int x, int y, int z)
    {
        return (x + y + z);
    }
    // Overloaded sum(). This sum takes two double
                                                //parameters
    public double sum(double x, double y)
    {
        return (x + y);
    }
```

```
    public static void main(String args[])
    {
        Sum s = new Sum();
        System.out.println(s.sum(10, 20));
        System.out.println(s.sum(10, 20, 30));
        System.out.println(s.sum(10.5, 20.5));
    }
}
```

- The signature of each method in a class must be distinct to allow the compiler to determine exactly which method you are calling at any particular point. Program 3.10 illustrates this.
- If the exact prototype does not match with the arguments, then the compiler resolves the issue with the policy of *type promotion*. According to this compile-time resolution policy, one type is promoted to its higher type implicitly if no matching type is found. Priority wise, the compiler takes these steps:
    - Type conversion but to higher type (in terms of range) in the same family.
    - Type conversion to the next higher family (e.g., if there is no `long` data type available for an `int` data type, then it will search for `float` data type).
- Refer to Figure 2.1 (in Chapter 2) regarding the type promotion rule. According to this rule, `byte` can be promoted to `short`, `int`, `long`, `float`, or `double`. The `short` data type can be promoted to `int`, `long`, `float`, or `double`. The `char` data type can be promoted to `int`, `long`, `float`, or `double`, and so on. Program 3.11 is an example for clarifying the concept.
- The return type has no effect on the signature. You cannot differentiate between two methods just by the return type. This is because the return type is not necessarily apparent when you call a method. Program 3.12 illustrates this.
- A method declared with static keywords can be overloaded. We can have two or more static methods with same name, but differences in input parameters. For example, consider Program 3.13.
- The `main()` method can be overloaded too. Program 3.14 is an example.

Program 3.10
(Different signature in method overloading)

```
/* This program illustrates how signature of the method
should be different so that the method overloading is
successful. */
  class Sum{
    void sum(int a,int b){          //Overloading I
       System.out.println(a+b);
    }
    void sum(int a,long b){        //Overloading II
       System.out.println(a+b);
   }
    void sum(int a,int b,int c){ //Overloading III
       System.out.println(a+b+c);
   }
 class OverloadingTest1 {
    public static void main(String args[]){
      Sum obj = new Sum();
      obj.sum(20,20);              //Overloading I
      obj.sum(20,123456789L);  //Overloading II
      obj.sum(20,30,40);        //Overloading III
   }
 }
```

Program 3.11
(Type promotion policy resolving ambiguity)

```
/* This program illustrates how the ambiguity in type
will be resolved during method overloading in Java. */
class TypePromo {
    public void show(int x)    // Overloading I
    {
        System.out.println("In int" + x);
    }
    public void show(String s) // Overloading II
    {
        System.out.println("In String" + s);
    }
    public void show(byte b) // Overloading III
    {
        System.out.println("In byte" + b);
    }
}
class OverloadingTest2 {
    public static void main(String[] args)
    {
       byte a = 25;
       TypePromo obj = new TypePromo();
       obj.show(a);      // Matches Overloading III
```

```
        obj.show("Hello"); // Matches Overloading II

        obj.show(250);    // Matches Overloading I

        obj.show('A');
        /* char is  not available, however, the data
              type higher than char is int and thus
              matched with Overloading I. */
        obj.show(7.5);
        /* Since float data type is not available
              and no type promotion is applicable,
              so this call will be an error. */
    }
}
```

Program 3.12 *(Only a different return type is not method overloading!)*

```
/* This program shows if difference in return type is
sufficient for method overloading. */

class Sum{
   int sum(int a,int b){      //Overloading I
      return a+b;
   }
   double sum(int a,int b){
      return a+b;}
   }
class OverloadingTest3{
     public static void main(String[] args){
       Sum obj = new Sum();
       System.out.println(obj.sum(11,11));
              //Compile-time error
   }
 }
```

Program 3.13 *(Static methods can be overloaded)*

```
/* Methods declared with static keyword can be
overloaded as usual */

class Foo {
   public static void foo() {
             // Overloading I
        System.out.println("Test.foo() called ");
    }
    public static void foo(int a) {
             // Overloading II
```

```
            System.out.println("Test.foo(int) called ");
    }
}

class OverloadingTest4 {

     Foo obj  = new Foo();
     public static void main(String args[])
    {
        obj.foo();      //Refer to Overloading I
        obj.foo(10);   //Refer to Overloading II
    }
}
```

Program 3.14 *(main() can be overloaded)*

```
/* This program demonstrates how the main() can be
overloaded. */

class Foo {
     public static void main(String[] args)
    {
        System.out.println("I am from normal main... ");
        Foo.main("Overloading I");
              //It will call main-I
    }

    // Overloaded main methods
    public static void main(String arg1)
              //Overloading main-I
    {
        System.out.println("I am from main-I() " +
              arg1);
        Foo.main("God is good", "Joy with Java");
              //It will call main-II
    }
    public static void main(String a1, String a2)
              //Overloading main-II
    {
        System.out.println("Hi, " + a1 + ", " + a2);
    }
}
```

3.3 Frequently Used Keywords

There are a few keywords such as `static`, `this`, `final`, etc., which appear frequently in Java programs.

3.3.1 `static` Keyword

Referencing objects

You have learnt how to declare a class using the concept of *fields* and *methods* in it. Once a class is declared, you can use it to create objects. Creating an object is a two-step process: declaration and instantiation. Let's consider the case of the class `Circle`. Two steps to create an object of the class `Circle` are stated as follows:

Step 1: Declaration

```
Circle c; // Declare that c is an object of type class Circle
```

Step 2: Instantiation

```
c = new Circle(); //Memory is allocated for the object c
```

In our previous discussions, we have done these two steps together as:

```
Circle c1 = new Circle();
```

or

```
Circle c2 = new Circle(3.0, 4.0. 5.0);
```

The operator `new` does a lot for us. It allocates memory to the object to store the values of all the fields in them. Here `c1` and `c2` are the reference variables and they refer to the memory locations of the physical copies (in memory) of `c1` and `c2`. The following is also a valid declaration for another object, say `c3`:

```
Circle c3 = c2;
```

Here, `c2` and `c3` refer to the same object and hence the same physical copy (Figure 3.3 illustrates this). If you do the following:

```
c3 = null;
```

then it will not free the memory, as the same memory is also referred to by `c2`. In other words, `c1`, `c2`, `c3`, etc. are the logical names of the objects. Alternatively, an object of a class is referred to as an *instance* of that class. When you create an object, the object will contain all the fields that were included in the class definition. Note that object name is just like a pointer as in C++.

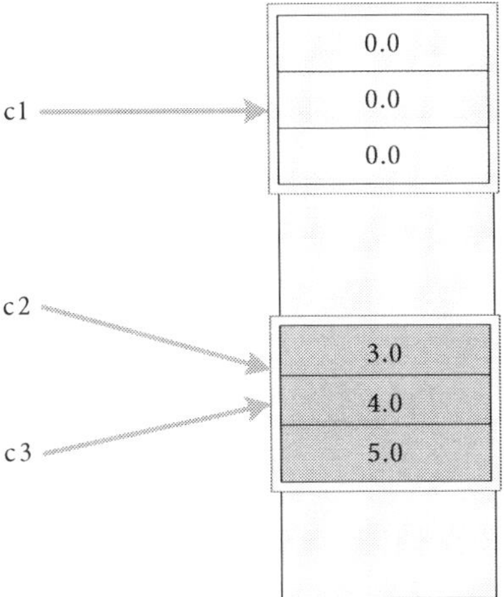

Figure 3.3 Assigning references to objects

However, the fields in a class definition are not all the same. There are two kinds of fields: non-static fields and static fields.

Non-static field

Instance variable

This is also called *instance variable.* This type of variable in a class is associated with each object uniquely. Each instance of the class has its own copy of each of the non-static fields, that is, each with its own value assigned. The name *instance variable* came from the fact that an object is an instance, that is, an occurrence of a class, and the values stored in the instance variables for the object differentiate the object from others of the same class type. Note that an instance variable is declared within the class definition in the usual way, with a type name and a variable name, and can have an initial value specified.

Static field

This is also called *class variable.* This type of variable is shared by all objects of the class. In other words, there is only one copy of each of these type of fields no matter how many class objects are created; in fact, they exist even if no objects of the class have been created. This type of variable is called as a *class variable* because the variable belongs to the class and not to any particular object.

Class variable

A static field must be declared using the keyword `static` preceding the type name (that is why they are referred to as static fields).

Program 3.15 and Program 3.16 illustrate the declarations of instance class variables and a class variable. Figure 3.4 illustrates the memory map of the two declarations of objects.

Program 3.15
(Class and instance variables)

```
/* To declare a class variable and instance variable in
a class declaration. */

class Circle {
    double x, y, r;  // Declaration of instance variables
    static double PI = 3.1432;
              // Declaration of class variable
    double circumference(){
              return 2*PI*r;
    }
    double area(){
              return PI*r*r;
    }
}

class StaticVariableTest {
    public static void main(String args[]) {

        // Create two objects
         class Circle c1 = new Circle();
         class Circle 21 = new Circle();
        // Initialize the object so created
         c1.x = 1.0;        c2.x = 3.4;
         c1.y = -4.5;       c2.y = 2.6;
         c1.r = 12.36;      c3.r = 4.9;

        // Calculate areas and circumferences of two
                                                //circles
         c1.area();                c2.area();
         c1.circumference();    c2.circumference();

        // Print the results
        System.out.println("Areas: c1 = " + c1.area() +
              "c2 = " + c2.area();)
        System.out.println("Circumferences: c1 = " +
              c1.circumference() + "c2 = " +
              c2.circumference();)
    }
}
```

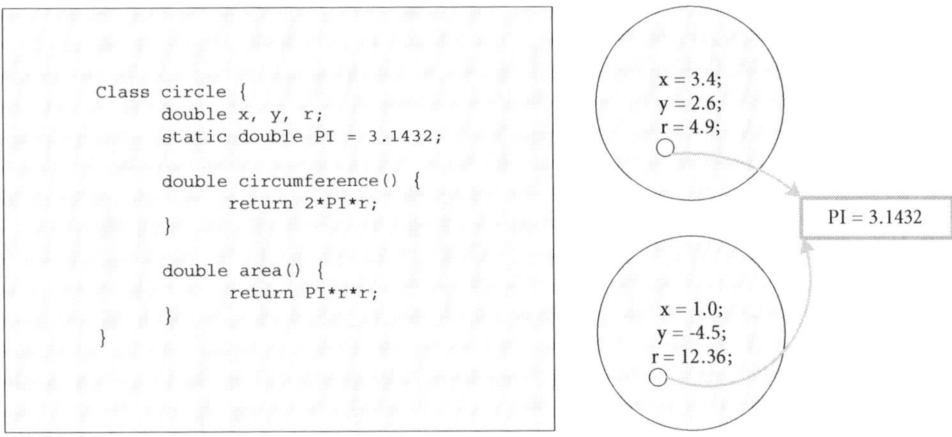

Figure 3.4 Class and instance variables

Program 3.16 *(Another example of class and instance variables)*

```
/* This program illustrates  the use of static variable
in a program. */

public class Circle{
    static int circlecount = 0;  // class variable
    static double PI = 3.1432;  // class variable
    public double x,y,r;        // instance variables
    public Circle(double a, double b, double c){
       x = a; y = b; r = c;
       circlecount++;
    }
    public Circle(double d){
       x = 0; y = 0; r = c;
       circlecount++;
    }
    public Circle(Circle c){
       x = c.x; y = c.y; r = c.r;
       circlecount++;
    }
    public Circle(){
       x = 0; y = 0; r = 0;
       circlecount++;
    }
    public double circumference(){
       return (2*PI*r);
    }
    public double area(){
        return(PI*r*r);
    }
```

```
    public static void main(String args[ ]){
        Circle c1 = new Circle();
        Circle c2 = new Circle(5.0);
        Circle c3 = new Circle(c1);
        System.out.println("c1#" + c1.circlecount +
                "c2#" + c2.circlecount + "c3#" +
                    c3.circlecount);
    }
}
```

- A static variable works like a global variable (as in C/ C++) for all the objects belonging to a class.
- The value of a static variable remains even if all the objects are deleted.
- If the value is changed, then it will be reflected in all objects having this variable.

Instance method and class method

Analogous to the variables in a class definition, there are two varieties of methods: *instance methods* and *class methods*. If a method is a class method, then you can execute the method even when no objects of a class exist. Instance methods can be executed only in relation to a particular object, so if no objects exist, you have no way to execute any of the instance methods defined in the class. Like class variables, class methods are declared using the keyword `static`, that is why they are sometimes referred to as *static methods*. Program 3.17 includes an example of static method in a program.

Program 3.17 *(Example of instance and class methods)*

```
/* This program illustrates class and instance methods.
*/

public class CircleMethods{
     public double x,y,r;
     // All constructors in Program 3.15 are here.
     // An instance method. Return the bigger of two
                                              //circles.
     public Circle bigger(Circle c){
        if(c.r>r) return c;
        else return this;
     }
     // A class method: Return the bigger of two
                                              //classes.
     public static Circle bigger (Circle a, Circle b) {
         if (a.r > b.r) return a;
         else return b;
     }
```

```
public static void main(String args[]){
     Circle a = new Circle (2.0);
     Circle b = new Circle (3.0);
     Circle c = a.bigger (b);
              //Call of the instance method
     Circle d = Circle.bigger (a,b);
              //Call of the class method
    }
}
```

- A static method can directly call other static methods.
- A static method can directly access static data.
- If you need to do computation in order to initialize your static variables, you can declare a static block that gets executed exactly once, when the class is first loaded. Program 3.18 shows a class that uses a static initialization block.

Program 3.18
(Static block)

```
/* Demonstrates static block in a program. */
   class StaticBlockDemo {
       static int i;   //If not initialized, then its
                                             //value is 0
       static int b = 555;
       static void myMethod(int x) {  // A class method
           System.out.println("x = " + x);
           System.out.println("a = " + a);
           System.out.println("b = " + b);
       }
       static {          // Declaration of static block
           System.out.println("Static block
              initialized.");
           a = b - 444;
       }
       public static void main(String args[]) {
           myMethod(96);       // No object is needed
           myMethod(69);      // Here static block is
                                          //not executed
     }
 }
```

3.3.2 `this` Keyword

Concept of `this` keyword

Another frequently used keyword is `this`. The keyword `this` is used to reduce name-space collisions. Sometimes a method will need to refer to the object that invoked it. To allow this, Java defines `this` keyword. The keyword `this` refers to the current object for which the method is being called. The compiler uses this implicitly when your method refers to an instance variable of the class. That is, `this` is always a reference to the object on which the method was invoked. The following are some common uses of `this` keyword in Java programs:

1. To refer to current class instance variables (Program 3.19).
2. To invoke current class constructor (Program 3.20).
3. To return the current class instance (Program 3.21).
4. To use as method parameter (Program 3.22).
5. To invoke current class method (Program 3.23).
6. To use as an argument in the constructor call (Program 3.24).

Program 3.19 *(`this` for name-space resolution)*

```
/* Illustrating the use of this keyword to resolve the
name space. */
 class Circle {
    double x,y;
    double r;
    static double PI = 3.1432;
    double circumference(){
        return 2*PI*r;
    }
    double area(){
        return PI*r*r;
    }
    void setCircle(double a, double b, double c){
         x = a; // Set center x-coordinate
         y = b; // Set center y-coordinate
         r = c; // Set radius
    }
    Circle (double x, double y, double r){
       this.x = x; // Set center x-coordinate
       this.y = y; // Set center y-coordinate
       this.r = r; // Set radius
   }
 }
```

```
class ThisDemo1 {
   public static void main(String args[]){
       Circle c1 = new Circle();
             // Default constructor
       c1.setCircle(3.0,4.0,5.0);
             // Instance method
       Circle c2 = new Circle (-4.0,8.0,10.0);
             // Constructor
       // Here write code to print results for c1
                                                //and c2
   }
}
```

Program 3.20 *(Calling current class constructor)*

```
/* Using this to invoke current class constructor in
multi-constructors */

class Circle {
    double x, y;
    double r;
    Circle (double x, double y, double r){
       this.x = x; this.y = y; this.r = r;
    }
   Circle (double r){
       this(0.0, 0.0, r);
    }
    Circle (Circle c){
       this(c.x, c.y. c.r);
    }
    Circle (){
       this(0.0, 0.0, 1.0);
    }
    double circumference(){
       return 2*3.14159*r;
    }
    double area(){
       return (22/7)*r*r;
    }
}
```

Program 3.21 (Returning current class instance)

```
/* Using this to return the current class instance. */

class Foo
{
    int i;
    int j;

    Foo() {         //Default constructor
        i = 66;
        j = 99;
    }
    Foo get()   //Method that returns current class
                                                //instance
    {
        return this;
    }
    void print() {  //Displaying value of variables i
                                                //and j
         System.out.println("i = " + i + "  j = " + j);
    }

    public static void main(String[] args) {
        Foo obj = new  Foo();
        obj.get().print();
    }
}
```

Program 3.22 (`this` as a method parameter)

```
/* Using 'this' keyword as method parameter.*/

  class Foo
  {
    int i;
    int j;

    Foo()  {    //Default constructor
        i = 99;
        j = 66;
   }

   void print(Foo f) {  // Method that receives
                             //'this' keyword as parameter
        System.out.println("i = " + f.i + "  j = " +
              f.j);
   }
```

```
    void get() {    // Method that returns current
                                    //class instance
        print(this);
    }

    public static void main(String[] args) {
        Foo obj = new Foo();
        obj.get();
    }
}
```

Program 3.23 *(Invoking current class method)*

```
/* Using this to invoke current class method */

class Foo {
      void print()      {
        this.show();  // Calling function show() of
                                   //the current object
        System.out.println("From print
              function . . .");
      }

      void show() {
        System.out.println("From show function . . .");
      }

      public static void main(String args[]) {
        Foo f = new Foo();
        f.print();
    }
}
```

Program 3.24 *(Argument in a constructor)*

```
/* Using this as an argument in constructor  call.*/

class A  { // Class with object of Class B as its data
                                              //member
    B obj;
    A(B obj){// Parameterized constructor with object
                                  //of B  as a parameter
        this.obj = obj;
        obj.print();// Calling print method of class B
    }
}
```

```
class B {
    int x = 5;
    B()  {
         A obj = new A(this); //Pass the object of B
    }

    void print()    {
        System.out.println("Value of x in Class B : "
              + x);
    }

    public static void main(String[] args) {
        B obj = new B();
    }
}
```

3.3.3 `final` Keyword

This `final` keyword in Java is used in a different context. Here, we shall discuss its application in the context of field. A field can be declared as `final`. When a field is declared with `final` keyword, its value can't be modified and the field becomes a constant. This means that declaring a field `final` prevents its contents from being modified. Program 3.25 shows the different ways that a `final` variable can be declared and initialized in programs.

Program 3.25 *(Initializations of `final` variables)*

```
/* This program demonstrates different ways of
initializing final variables. */

class Final {
    final int ALPHA = 5;  // Direct initialization
    final String PASS;
    final float LIMIT;
              //A blank final variable: No initialization

    static final double PI = 3.141592653589793;
                 // A final variable can be declared as
                                           //static also

    static final double N; // A  blank final static
                                              //variable
```

```
    // An instance initializer block for initialization
    {
        LIMIT = 2.5;
    }
    // A static initializer block for initialization
    static {
        N = 6.023e23;
    }

    // Constructor for initializing
    public Final()  {
        PASS = "Joy with Java";
    }

        public static void main(String[] args) {
              int array[] = {1, 2, 3};
              for (final int i : array)
                   // for-each statement is legal
                System.out.print(i + " ");
     }
}
```

- It is a common coding convention to choose all uppercase letters as identifiers for `final` fields.
- You must initialize a `final` variable; otherwise the compiler will throw compile-time error.
- A final variable can only be initialized once. Re-initialization will throw a compile-time error.
- If you initialize through a constructor, and there is more than one constructor, then you must initialize in each of them.
- In addition to fields, both method parameters and local variables can be declared `final`.
    - Declaring a parameter `final` prevents it from being changed within the method.
    - Declaring a local variable `final` prevents it from being assigned a value more than once.
- The keyword `final` can also be applied to methods and classes. This aspect will be discussed in the Chapter 4, when inheritance is described.

3.3.4 A Close Look at a Java Program

Now you are in a position to understand many features in a Java program (we discussed the program structure in Section 3.1.3). Let us consider a program as shown in Program 3.26. Annotations are self-explanatory.

Program 3.26 *(Analyzing a program)*

```
import java.lang.*;   <-- Import statement,as this package is needed for this program

class Calculator{   <-- Declaration of a class
    double i;
    double x = Math.sqrt(i);   <-- This class is in..lang package and sqrt() is a static method
}
class Example{
    public static void main(String args[]){
        Calculator a= new Calculator();
        a.i = 20;
        System.out.println("Square root of "+a.i+" is "+a.x);
    }
}
```

Now, here is a question. From, which line does Java start its execution? It starts from the `main()` method! The `main()` method is the starting point of the execution of the *main thread*. If there are multiple classes, then ambiguity is resolved by incorporating a `main()` method into only one special class called *main class*. This is why a Java program should be named after this class so that *Java interpreter* invariably chooses this class to start its execution.

Now, let us discuss the `main()` in the program. You see that the main method (Figure 3.5) is defined with many keywords, some of which we are already familiar. Let us understand their meanings.

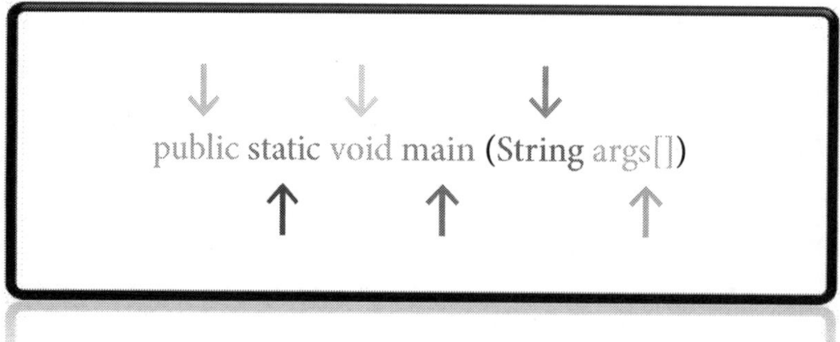

Figure 3.5 Close look at `main()`

Public

- It is an access specifier, which allows the programmer to control the visibility of class members. The `public` member may be accessed by code outside the class in which it is declared. The `main()` must be declared as `public`, since it must be called by code outside of its class when the program is started. There are some other access specifiers which we shall discuss in Chapter 5.

static

- The keyword `static` allows `main()` to be called without having to instantiate a particular instance of the class. This is necessary since `main()` is called by Java interpreter before any objects are made.

void

- In Java, each method should return a value; if it does not return anything, then the return type should be `void`. The keyword `void` simply tells the compiler that `main()` does not return any value after its execution.

main

- In Java, `main` is the name of a method in a class. This method is searched by JVM as a starting point for an application with a particular signature only.

String args[]

- Here, `String` is a class defied in `java.lang API` and `args[]` is an array to store objects of class `String`. You could write anything, say `String x[]` instead of `String args[]`. Here `args[]` is a common practice that every programmer uses. It is a customary to do so.
- Java stores anything as `String` objects, that is why this argument is mentioned in `main()`. This helps to read an input and then store into the array `args[]` as `String` objects. We shall learn in the next section about the use of this array.

`println()` method

Let us come to the last statement in the `main()`, which is a print statement of the form:

```
System.out.println("Square root of " +a.i+ " is " +a.x);
```

Here,

`System` is a final class from the `java.lang` package;

`out` is a class variable of type `PrintStream` declared in the `System` class;

`println` is a method of the `PrintStream` class;

`a.i` and `a.x` represent the names of variables to be printed;

+ is a concatenation operator, it is used to concatenate the string values.

`print()` method

The `println()` takes an argument a `String` object. It prints a `String` object and then moves the cursor to the next line. Why is it `println` and not just *print*, for example? Actually, *ln* is to stress that the cursor should move to the next line. The println("...") method prints the string "..." and moves the cursor to a new line. There is `print()` method defined in `PrintStream` class also. The `print("...")` method instead prints just the string "..." but does not move the cursor to a new line. Hence, subsequent printing instructions will print on the same line. Consider the following lines to be printed as output:

Debasis
Samanta

This can be done using both `println()` and `print()` functions, which is as follows:

```
System.out.println("Debasis");
System.out.println("Samanta");
```

or

```
System.out.print("Debasis");
Syste.out.print("\n");
System.out.print("Samanta");
```

Note: The use of `\n` in the program: This is a newline character defined in Java character set. Alternatively, `println()` method can also be used without any parameter to position the cursor on the next line.

Formatting output using `System.out.printf()`

`printf()` in Java

Java also allows formatted output to print in a given specified format as the `printf()` function in C programming language. Program 3.27 gives an example of formatted output printing in Java.

Program 3.27 *(Formatted print)*

```
/* A Java program to demonstrate working of printf() in
Java program. */

class FormattedPrint {
  public static void main(String args[]) {
    int x = 100;
    System.out.printf("Printing simple integer:
             x = %d\n", x);

    // This next will print x upto 2 decimal places
    System.out.printf("Formatted with precison:
             PI = %.2f\n", Math.PI);

    float n = 5.2f;

    // Automatically appends zero to the rightmost part
                                         //of decimal
    System.out.printf("Formatted to specific width:
             n = %.4f\n", n);

    n = 2324435.3f;

    // Another formatted: before decimal upto maximum
                                          //20 digits
    System.out.printf("Formatted to right margin:
             n = %20.4f\n", n);
  }
}
```

- `main()` method in helper class

In a Java program, there may be one or more classes. There should be at least one class containing `main()`. The name of the program should be same as the name of the class containing `main()` method. Java run-time environment will use this `main()` method as the main thread of execution. Other classes are termed as the helper classes.

- Helper classes may be included in the same `.java` file as the main class in or in different `.java` files (in the same directory of main class, different directories, or in distanced locations). Chapter 5 has a detailed discussion on this topic.

3.4 Java Run-Time Input

Mostly the programs we have described so far don't take input while the programs are in execution. But, for practical utility, there should be some mechanism by which a program can take input from the external sources, such as a user (via a keyboard), file, network, etc. We shall limit our discussion in this section to learn how a program can take input from a user while the program is running. Following are the well-known ways to do this:

Several ways to give input to a running program

1. Command line input
2. Using `System.in.read()`
3. Using `Scanner` class
4. Using console object
5. Using `BufferedRedaer` class
6. Using `DataInputStream` class

3.4.1 Command Line Input

Command line argument

In DOS/ Unix command, we usually type command followed by a number of arguments. For example, the `cat` command in Unix will take zero or more arguments. There is a similar concept in Java also. In this case, command is the program which you have written and compiled successfully. In Java, the command line argument is a mechanism of passing information to the program when you run the program. The information is passed as arguments in the `main()` and is stored as an array of `String` objects. Later, you can use the command line arguments in your program. Let's consider the execution of Program 3.28.

Program 3.28 *(Command line argument: Example 1)*

```
/* This program will take input through command line
arguments and the print the values on the screen. */
class Echo{
    public static void main(String args[]){
        for(int i=0;i<args.length;i++){
            System.out.print(args[i]+ " ");
            System.out.print("\n");
        }
        System.exit(0);  // It is customary, not
                                                //mandatory
    }
}
```

First compile the program using `javac` command:

```
javac echo.java
```

Then run the program with following two input:

```
java echo Hi Debasis Samanta   // Run 1
java echo 1 2 3 4 5 6 7 8 9 0 // Run 2
```

In Run 2, as you see, the results are stored in the array `args` as `{1, 2,3 4, 5, 6, 7, 8, 9, 0}` being 1 in `args[0]` and 0 in `args[9]`.

Program 3.29 is another example to explain the same concept.

Program 3.29 *(Command line argument: Example 2)*

```
/* To understand how input are stored in arguments
array args. */

class CommandLineInput1{
    public static void main(String args[]){
        System.out.print("Hi ");
        System.out.print(args[0]);
        System.out.print(", How are you?");
    }
}
```

Run this program as:

```
java CommandlineInput1 Debasis Samanta
```

We have discussed how to pass the data to your program. Here, you give the data not by writing it in the program (e.g., assigning values to some variables), rather, keep your data ready till you are just about to run. Also, we have seen that data is stored as an array of `String` objects. Does it imply that only string data can be passed? The answer is yes and no. Actually, you can pass data of any type, but all of them will be stored as `String` objects. In your program, you can convert a `String` object to your required data type. Program, 3.30 illustrates how such a conversion can be done. Consider the statement in Program 3.29:

```
a.i = Integer.parseInt(args[0]);
```

The class `Integer` is wrapper class and the `parseInt()` method in that class can convert a string to an integer. In this manner, using the appropriate wrapper class, you can convert data to any numeric type.

Program 3.30 (Command line argument: Example 3)

```
/* This program demonstrates how a string object can be
converted to an integer value. */
     class Calculator{
       double i, x;
       double sqrtCal(){
           x = Math.sqrt(i);
           return x;
       }
     }
     class IntExample{
       public static void main(String args[]){
       Calculator a = new Calculator();
       a.i = Integer.parseInt(args[0]);
       System.out.println("Square root of" +a.i+ " is "
              +a.sqrtCal());
     }
   }
```

Let us run Program 3.30 with the following two instances:

```
java IntExample 56        // Okay: It will give result
java IntExample Debasis // Error: The wrapper class fails here
```

- There is no restriction on the number of java command line arguments. You can specify any number of arguments.
- `args.length` will tell you how many values you have passed.
- Mixed type of data can be passed to a program.

3.4.2 Using `System.in.read()`

There are two classes in Java to deal with a *standard input* (i.e., keyboard) and a *standard output* (i.e., display screen): `InputStream` and `PrintStream` (we have mentioned about `PrintStream` class while we were discussing about printing results on the screen. Under `InputStream` class, `System` is a `final` class and `in` is a class variable of type `InputStream`. This stream is already open and ready to supply input data. Typically, `System.in` is an input stream object that corresponds to keyboard input (or another input source specified by the host environment or user). There is a method named `read()` in the `InputStream` class. The `read()` method reads the next byte of data from the input stream. The value byte is returned as an `int` in the range 0 to 255. If no byte is available because of the end of the stream has been reached, then the value –1 is returned. Program 3.31 illustrates the use of `System.in.read()` to read input from the keyboard.

Program 3.31 (Reading standard input)

```
/* The following program will take two values from the
keyboard and pass the same to a method to calculate a
result. */

   class ReadInput {
      static int anyFunction (int x, int y ){
            int a = x/y;
            return a;
      }
      public static void main (String args[]) {
          int a,b, result;
          a = 0; b = 0;
          a = System.in.read();
                         // Read a number from keyboard
          b = System.in.read();
                   // Read another number from keyboard
          result  = anyFunction (a, b);
          System.out.println ( "\nResult : " + result);
      }
   }
```

- If you enter 0 for `b`, then it will return 48; this is the ASCII value of 0.
- If you enter 123, for example, then `read()` function will return 49, which is the ASCII value of 1 and it only reads the first byte in the keyboard buffer.
- You can use `read(byte b[])` method to read data from keyboard and store the data in the byte array `b`.

3.4.3 Using `Scanner` Class

`Scanner` is one of the predefined classes, which is used for reading the data dynamically from the keyboard. The class `Scanner` is defined in `java.util` package. This is probably the most preferred method to take input. Program 3.32 explains the working of the class to read input from the keyboard. For the `Scanner` class object, there are predefined methods to read a long string (`nextLine()`) and parsing primitives (`nextXXX()`). The `nextXXX()` methods are `nextInt()`, `nextFloat()`, `nextByte()`, `nextShort()`, `nextDouble()`, `nextLong()`, `next()`.

Program 3.32 *(Reading using* `Scanner` *class)*

```
/* Java program to demonstrate working of Scanner in
Java program. */

   import java.util.Scanner;
              // To access the Scanner class

   class ScannerInput {
     public static void main(String args[])
     {
         // Create Scanner class object ready to read
                                    //from the keyboard
         Scanner scn = new Scanner(System.in);

        System.out.print("\nEnter your name : ")
        String s = scn.nextLine();
              //To read a string data
        System.out.println("\n Hi! " +s);

        System.out.print("\nEnter your luck number : ")
        int n = scn.nextInt();
              //To read an integer data
        System.out.println("\n Is it " + n + "!");

        System.out.print("\nWhat is the G value of
              gravity?");
        double g = scn.nextDouble();
              //To read a double value
        System.out.println("God! " +g);
     }
}
```

Program 3.33 also illustrates the use of `Scanner` class to read input from the keyboard.

Program 3.33 *(Example with* `Scanner` *class)*

```
/* The program reads a set of numbers, stores them in
an array and then calculates the average value. This
program uses ArrayList class defined in java.util
package. */

   import java.util.*;

   class AverageOfNumbers{
      public static void main(String args[]){
         int sum = 0;
```

```
            float avg = 0;
            ArrayList <Integer> list = new
                 ArrayList<Integer>();
            System.out.println("Enter numbers :
                 Press Ctrl+Z to stop entering");
            Scanner input = new Scanner(System.in);
            while (input.hasNextInt()) {
               list.add(input.nextInt());
            }
            for (int i = 0; i < list.size(); i++) {
               sum += list.get(i);
            }
            avg = sum/(list.size());
            System.out.println("Average : " + avg);
      }
   }
```

3.4.4 Using `Console` Object

It has become a preferred way for reading user's input from the command line. In addition, it can be used for reading password-like input without echoing the characters entered by the user. Program 3.34 illustrates the use of console object to read data from the keyboard. You can read a string object and then parse it to your desirable primitive types using the wrapper class methods.

Program 3.34 *(Reading data using* `Console` *class)*

```
/* Java program to demonstrate working of System.
console(). This program may not run in IDE, e.g.,
NetBean. */

public class ConsoleInput {
    public static void main(String[] args)   {
        // Using Console to input data from user
        String name = System.console().readLine();
        System.out.println(name);
    }
}
```

3.4.5 Using `BufferedReader` Class

`BufferedReader` class is defined in `java.io` package. Like `Scanner` class, `BufferedReader` class reads text from a character-input stream, buffering characters so as to provide for the efficient reading of the sequence of characters. Program 3.35 is a simple example to illustrate the use of `BufferedReader` class in a Java program.

Program 3.35 *(Reading data using* `Buffered Reader` *class)*

```
/* Code using BufferedReader Class for input. */

import java.io.*;

class BufferInput {
    public static void main(String args[])
                throws IOException
    {
        BufferedReader br = new BufferedReader
                (new InputStreamReader(System.in));
        System.out.println("Enter an integer");
        int n = Integer.parseInt(br.readLine());
        System.out.println("Enter a String");
        String s = br.readLine();
        System.out.printf("You have entered: "
                + n + " and " + s);
    }
}
```

It appears that both the `Scanner` class and the `BufferedReader` class work in the same manner. However, there is a difference between the two. Using `Scanner` class, if we call `nextLine()` method after any one of the seven `nextXXX()` method, then the `nextLine()` does not read values from the keyboard and the cursor will not come into the console; it will skip that step. This is due to `nextXXX()` methods, which ignore newline character and `nextLine()` only reads till the first newline character. But in `BufferedReader` class there is no such type of a problem. With `BufferedReader` class, if we use one more call of `nextLine()` method between `nextXXX()` and `nextLine()`, then this problem will not occur because `nextLine()` will consume the newline character. This is a similar type of problem faced when you use `scanf()` followed by `gets()` in C/C++.

In addition to this, there are a few more differences between the `Scanner` and `BufferedReader` classes:

- `BufferedReader` is synchronous while `Scanner` is not. `BufferedReader` should be used if we are working with multiple threads (discussed in Chapter 7).
- `BufferedReader` has significantly larger buffer memory than `Scanner` class.
- The `Scanner` has a little buffer (1KB `char` buffer) as opposed to the `BufferedReader` (8KB `byte` buffer), but it's more than enough.
- `BufferedReader` is a little faster as compared to `Scanner` because `Scanner` does parsing of input data and `BufferedReader` simply reads the sequence of characters.

3.4.6 Using `DataInputStream` Class

`DataInputStream` class is another class defined `in java.io` package. It is also useful for reading data from a keyboard, file, network channel, etc. We shall learn about its detailed use in Chapter 8. Here, as a limited discussion, let us see how such a class can be used in Java programs to take input from a keyboard and use the data in some calculations.

Look at Program 3.36. This program will read three values: principal amount, rate of interest, and year. Use these values to calculate the simple interest and print the result. Note that `DataInputStream` object reads anything from the keyboard as a `String` object. Also, note the use of `System.out.flush()` methods. Actually, when a user enters some data, it is stored in the keyboard buffer. From the keyboard buffer, the `DataInputStream` object gets the value as a line, that is, the content of the whole buffer. It is better to flush the buffer to avoid any interference of the current data with the previous data. Reading using `DataInputStream` should take place under try-catch block as a procedure of dealing with any error while reading the keyboard (for more details, see Chapter 8).

Program 3.36 (Reading data using `DataInput Stream` *class)*

```
/* This program demonstrates data entry with
DataInputStream class */
import java.io.*;     // The package where the class
                                             //is defined

   class InterestCalculator{
     public static void main(String args[ ] ) {
       Float principalAmount = new Float(0);
             //Create a Float object
       Float rateOfInterest = new Float(0);
             //Create another Float object
       int numberOfYears = 0;
       try {
           //Creating a stream object to read data
                                             //from keyboard
           DataInputStream in = new DataInputStream
              (System.in);

           //Reading the value of principal amount
           String tempString;
           System.out.println("Enter Principal
              Amount: ");
           System.out.flush();
           tempString = in.readLine();
              //Read the keyboard buffer
           principalAmount = Float.valueOf(tempString);

           //Reading the value of interest rate
           System.out.println("Enter Rate of Interest:");
           System.out.flush();
           tempString = in.readLine();
              //Read the keyboard buffer
           rateOfInterest = Float.valueOf(tempString);
           //Reading number of years
           System.out.println("Enter number of years:");
           System.out.flush();
           tempString = in.readLine();
           numberOfYears = Integer.parseInt
              (tempString);
   catch(Exception e) {}   //Whole code is kept in
                                           //try-catch block
```

```
            // Input is over: calculate the interest
            Float interest = principalAmount*
                  rateOfInterest*numberOfYears;
            System.out.println("Total Interest = "
                  + interest);
      }
}
```

3.5 Recursion in Java

The methods we have discussed so far in Java classes are simple methods. In contrast with simple methods, Java also allows a programmer to define recursive methods like C/C++. A method that calls itself is said to be recursive. A recursive method follows the principle of recursion, which is shown in Figure 3.6.

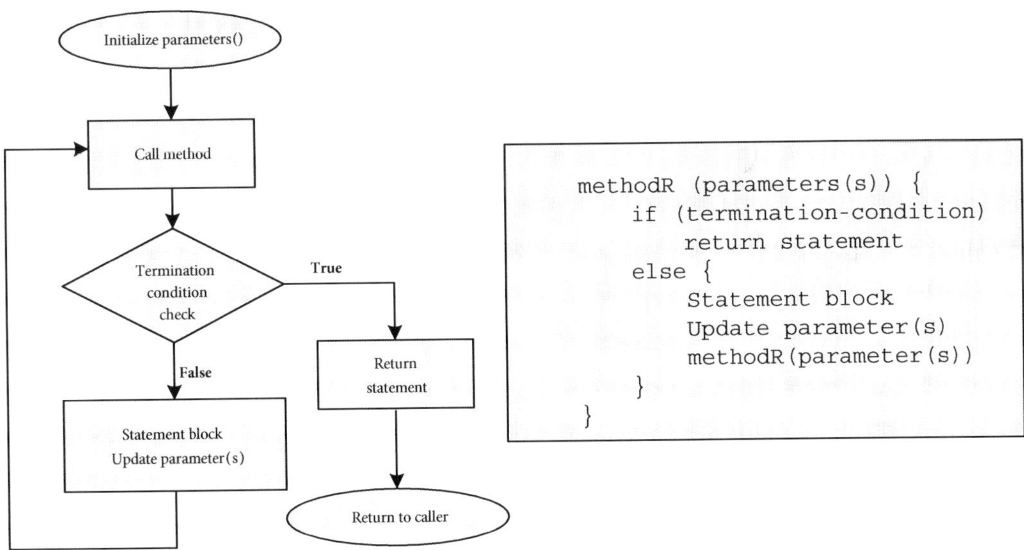

Figure 3.6 Recursion concept

Let us explain this with an example. Consider the calculation of factorial of *n*, an integer value. The calculation is defined as follows:

Factorial definition

$$n! = n \times (n - 1) \times (n - 2) \times \ldots 3 \times 2 \times 1$$
$$= 1 \times 2 \times 3 \times \ldots (n - 2) \times (n - 1) \times n$$

It can be noted that `0!` = 1. We can use a simple `for` (or `while` loop) to calculate the factorial of an integer value `n (n ≥ 0)`. Such a method is shown in Program 3.37. Let us see how the same can be defined using recursion. We can define the factorial calculation recursively, which is as follows.

$$n! = n \times (n - 1) \times (n - 2) \times \ldots 3 \times 2 \times 1$$
$$= n \times (n - 1)! \text{ with } 0! = 1$$

The same recursive definition can be followed to write the recursive method for factorial calculation, which is shown in Program 3.38.

Here are a few more problems. The recursive implementations have been given. You have to write programs giving their equivalent simple methods.

Program 3.37 *(Factorial calculation with simple method)*

```
/* Factorial calculation using simple method. */

  public class SimpleFactorial{
    static int n;

    static int factorial(int n) {      // Simple method
       int facto = 1;
       for(int i = 1; i <= n, i++)
           facto = facto * i;
       return (facto);
    }

    public static void main(String[] args) {
        n = Integer.parseInt(args[0]);
              // Read command line argument
      System.out.println("Factorial of " + n + ": " +
              factorial(n));
      return;
    }
 }
```

Program 3.38 *(Factorial calculation with recursive method)*

```
/* Factorial calculation using recursive method. */

public class RecursiveFactorial{
   static int n;
   static int factorial(int n) {
      if (n == 0)
          return(1);
      else
          return(n*factorial(n-1));
   }
```

```
  public static void main(String[] args) {
     n = Integer.parseInt(args[0]);
            // Read command line argument
     System.out.println("Factorial of " + n + ": " +
            this.factorial(n));
  }
}
```

Calculation of Fibonacci sequence

Following is a series of numbers called the Fibonacci sequence:

0 1 1 2 3 5 8 13 21

Let us denote F_n as the nth Fibonacci sequence, where $F_0 = 0$ and $F_1 = 1$, $F_2 = 1$, $F_3 = 2$, etc. The sequence can be defined recursively for any nth Fibonacci number as follows:

$$F_n = F_{n-1} + F_{n-2} \text{ with } F_0 = F_1 = 1$$

Program 3.39 demonstrates the Java program with recursive implementation of Fibonacci sequence.

Program 3.39 *(Fibonacci sequence with recursive method)*

```
/* Fibonacci sequence calculation using recursive
method. */

class Fibonacci {
    static int n;
    static int fibonacci(int n){
       if (n == 0)
           return 0;
       else if (n == 1)
          return 1;
            else
               return(fibonacci(n-1) + fibonacci(n-2));
     }
       public static void main(String args[]){
         n = Integer.parseInt(args[0]);
         for(int i = 0; i <= n; i++){
              System.out.println(this.fibonacci (i));
         }
       }
  }
```

Calculation of greatest common divisor of two integers

The greatest common divisor (GCD) of two integer numbers, say m and n is denoted as GCD(m, n). For example:

```
GCD(35, 15) = 5
GCD(10, 50) = 10
GCD(11, 0) = 11
GCD(8, 8) = 8
GCD(1, 13) = 1
```

For any two integers *m* and *n* (such that $m < n$), the *GCD (m, n)* calculation can be defined recursively as follows:

```
GCD(m, n) = GCD(n, m) if m>n;
GCD(m, n) = m, if m = 0;
GCD(m, n) = 1, if m = 1;
GCD(m, n) = m, if m = n;
GCD(m, n) = GCD(m, n%m);
```

Program 3.40 demonstrates the Java program with recursive implementation of the greatest common divisor calculation.

Program 3.40 *(GCD calculation with recursive method)*

```
/* Calculation of GCD with recursive method. */
public class RecursiveGCD {
    int m, n;
    int gcd(int m, int n){
        if(m>n) return gcd(n,m);
        if(m==n)return m;
        if(m==0)return n;
        if(m==1)return 1;
        return gcd(m,n%m);
    }

    public static void main(String[] args) {
        RecursiveGCD g = new RecursiveGCD();
        g.m = Integer.ParseInt(args[0]);
        g.n = Integer.ParseInt(args[1]);
        System.out.printf("GCD of %d and %d is %d.",
                g.m, g.n, g.gcd(g.m, g.n));
    }
}
```

Tower of Hanoi puzzle

The *Tower of Hanoi* (also called the *Tower of Brahma* or *Lucas' Tower*) is a mathematical game or puzzle. It consists of three pegs and a number of disks of different sizes, which can slide on to any peg. The puzzle begins with the disks in a stack and all the disks are in ascending order of size on one peg, with the smallest disk at the top, thus making a conical shape. The objective of the puzzle is to move the entire stack to another peg, obeying the following rules:

1. Only one disk can be moved at a time.
2. Each move consists of taking the upper disk from one of the stacks and placing it on top of another stack or on an empty peg.
3. No larger disk may be placed on top of a smaller disk.

With 3 disks, the puzzle can be solved in 7 moves, moving all disks from Peg A to Peg B through Peg C as an auxiliary peg (Figure 3.7). The minimum number of moves required to solve a Tower of Hanoi puzzle is 2n – 1, where `n` is the number of disks. The recursive definition of the puzzle is given as follows:

```
Move n disks from A to C
        = move (n-1) disks from A to B
        + move the disk from A to C
        + move (n-1) disk from B to C
```

The Java program solving the problem with a recursive implementation is shown in Program 3.41. The method to be defined recursively is `move (int n, from, to, aux)`.

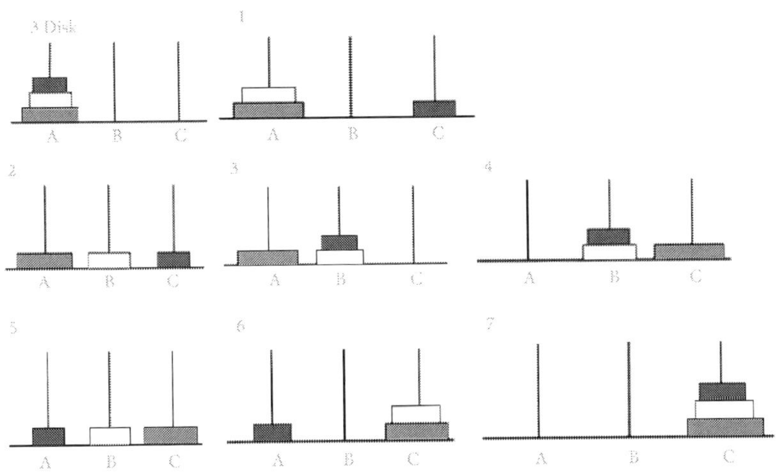

Figure 3.7 Illustration of Tower of Hanoi puzzle

Program 3.41 (Tower of Hanoi puzzle)

```
/* This Java program demonstrates the recursive method
to solve Tower of Hanoi puzzle. */

class TowerOfHanoi {
    static void move(int n, char a, char c, char b){
        if (n == 1) {
            System.out.println("Move disk 1 from Peg "
              + a + " C " + c);
            return;
        }
        move(n-1, a, b, c);
        System.out.println("Move disk " + n + " from "
              + a + " to " + c);
        move(n-1, b, c, a);
    }
    public static void main(String args[]) {
        int n = Integer.ParseInt(args[0]]);
        move(n, 'A', 'C', 'B');  // A, B and C are
                                        //names of pegs
    }
}
```

- For all iterative methods, there is an equivalent recursive method.
- If you can define a task recursively, you have done enough for writing the recursive method.
- A recursion may go to an infinite call or abrupt termination if the termination condition is not defined properly.

Summary

Encapsulation is one of the most crucial object-oriented programming features. This chapter is devoted to discuss encapsulation in Java. This chapter discusses using the concept of encapsulation and the way a class can be defined. How a class includes data and methods as members is illustrated with a number of simple examples. Constructor being a special type of method, its usefulness and different forms are discussed. Method overloading is an important aspect of encapsulation, which is also included in this chapter. There are some keywords which are common while a programmer defines the class. These frequently used keywords have been explained. A class is essentially a program and how input can be passed to a program while the program is running is an important concept to learn. The run-time input mechanisms are discussed to facilitate the new learners in Java. Finally, this chapter discusses the recursion concept and its use to solve many problems elegantly.

FAQs

3.1 What is a class in Java?

3.2 What is an object? How it can be created?

3.3 Why is the syntax "public static void main(String args[])"?

3.4 Can a program contain two (or more) classes with `main()` in each of them?

3.5 Can a class define multiple `main()` methods?

3.6 What are wrapper classes in Java?

3.7 What are constructors in Java?

3.8 What is a singleton class in Java? How can you make a class singleton?

3.9 How can the encapsulation mechanism hide data?

3.10 What is `final` keyword used for?

3.11 Why is method overloading not possible by changing the return type?

The answers to these questions and other problems in this chapter are available at www.cambridge.org/9781009211918. You might have many questions like these. You can post your question in the discussion forum at https://cse.iitkgp.ac.in/~dsamanta/joywithjava/page8.php.

Programs for Practice

3.1 Define a class which will generate a random number in between the range `low` and `high`. Here, `low` and `high` are the two fields of the class and `randGen(low, high)` is the method in the class to generate random number.

3.2 Define a class `Matrix2D` which will include `row`, `column` and a 2D array of integer numbers of size `row` × `column` as `data`. Define the methods for matrix addition, subtraction, and multiplication, where each method takes an argument as another matrix to do the operation with the current matrix and return the resultant matrix. Also, define another method `print()` to print the matrix it stores.

Write a main class, where you create three matrix objects `a`, `b` and `c` of type `Matrix2D` and obtain result `c = a.add(b)` for addition of two matrix, that is, `c = a + b`, etc.

3.3 The nth ($n \geq 2$) Fibonacci number is defined as follows:

$F_n = F(n-1) + F(n-2)$ w with $F_1 = F_0 = 1$

Define a class which will solve the following:

Read any integer number `x` from the keyboard and write a method `int checkFibonacci(int x)`, if it is an *n*th Fibonacci number, and if so, then the value of *n*.

Call the method from the `main()` method.

3.4 Binomial coefficient written as `C(n,r)` is the coefficient of the x^r term in the polynomial expansion of $(1 + x)^n$. Binomial coefficient can be recursively computed as:

`C(n,r) = C(n - 1, r) + C(n - 1, r - 1)`

where and `C(n,r) = 1` if `r = 0`. Define a method `int ncr(int n, int r)`, which would calculate the value of `C(n,r)` recursively.

[Hint: You should verify the calculation that] $C(n,r) = \dfrac{n!}{r!(n-r)!}$

3.5 The nth harmonic number is defined as $H_n = 1 + \frac{1}{2} + \frac{1}{3} + \cdots + \frac{1}{n}$. Write a recursive function to calculate H_n, for any integer $n > 0$.

[Hint: You should verify your calculation using the calculation of the sum of the series iteratively and write another function for that.]

3.6 Two numbers are said to be co-prime if the greatest common divisor of the numbers is one. For examples, 13 and 14 are co-prime but 14 and 21 are not. Write a method void CoPrime(int a, int b) to test whether the pair of numbers `a` and `b` are co-prime. In the main program, read five numbers and use this function to test how many pairs of them are co-prime.

[Hint: you should define gcd(...) to find the greatest common divisor of two numbers and pair(...) to find all the pairs from a given set of numbers.]

3.7 Read a set of *n* numbers and store them in an array. Write the following methods recursively:

`int min(...)` : to return the smallest value in the array.

`int max(...)` : to return the largest value in the array.

`int sum(...)` : to return the sum of the values in the array.

3.8 Write a class which would store a list of values, say floating point values. Define a constructor to read values, methods which recursively reverse the ordering of values and print the values.

3.9 Read any string of characters from the keyboard. Write a recursive function to check if it is a palindrome or not. For example, MALAYALAM is palindrome and PUPPY is not.

Now, extend the same thing to check if a sentence (i.e., a collection of words) is a palindrome or not. For example, MADAM TOP POT MADAM is a palindrome sequence.

3.10 An encoding mechanism is decided as follows:

It is a two-step method to convert a word into another word of the same length.

(1) The first and the last letters are swapped, then the second letter and the last but one letter, and so on.
(2) The word obtained after swapping the letters then undergo the following conversions:
   (a) Convert lower case to upper case and vice-versa.
   (b) Change a character to another with the following rule:

   A → D or a → d

   B → E or b → e

   C → F or c → f

   ...

W → Z or w → z

X → a or x → a

Y → B or y → b

Z → C or z → c

Write a method void `encode()` to encode a text read from the keyboard. The function should print the displayed character before its termination.

Write another function void `decode()` to get back the original text which has been converted by void `encode()`.

MCQs

3.1 Consider the following program:

```
public class ArgumenTest {
        public static void main(String [ ] args) {
                Test t = new Test();
                t.start();
        }
        void start() {
                int a = 4;
                int b = 5;
                System.out.print("" + 8 + 3 + "");
                System.out.print(a + b);
                System.out.print(" " + a + b + "");
                System.out.print(foo() + a + b + " ");
                System.out.println(a + b + foo());
        }
        String foo(){
                return "foo";
        }
}
```

What will be the output of this program?

(a) 839 45foo45 9foo
(b) 9 7 7 foo34 34foo
(c) 72 34 34 foo34 34foo
(d) 9 7 7 foo 7 7foo

3.2 Consider the following program:

```
public class VarPrint{
        int x = 30;
        static int y = 20;

        public static void main(String []args){
                VarPrint t1 = new VarPrint();
                t1.x = 88;
```

```
                t1.y = 99;
                int z1 = t1.x + t1.y;
                VarPrint t2 = new VarPrint();
                System.out.println(t2.x+ " " +t2.y + " " +z1);
        }
}
```

What will be the output of this program?

(a) 30 99 187 (b) 88 99 187
(c) 88 20 128 (d) 30 99 129

3.3 Consider the following object declaration statement:

```
Scanner in = new Scanner(System.in);
```

What does `System.in` stand for in this declaration?

(a) Any file storing data.
(b) Reference to standard input device, that is, keyboard.
(c) Reference to a scanner as an input device.
(d) Reference to a mouse as an input device.

3.4 Which of the following is *not* a valid declaration of an object of class `Box`?

(a) `Box obj = new Box();` (b) `Box obj = new Box;`
(c) `Box obj; obj = new Box();` (d) `Box obj;`

3.5 Which of the following is a class in Java?

(a) `int` (b) `boolean` (c) `double` (d) `Double`

3.6 Which of the following statements is(are) *incorrect*?

(a) Every class must contain a `main()` method.
(b) Applets do not require a `main()` method at all.
(c) There can be only one `main()` method in a program.
(d) The `main()` method must be made public.

3.7 What should be the return type of a method which need not return any value?

(a) `int` (b) `null` (c) `void` (d) `false`

3.8 What is the process of defining more than one method in a class having the same name but differentiated by method signature?

(a) Method overriding. (b) Method overloading.
(c) Encapsulation. (d) Inheritance.

3.9 Which of the following is called when a method having the same name as the name of the class where it is defined?

(a) abstract. (b) this.
(c) final. (d) constructor.

3.10 Consider the following piece of code:

```
public class ScopeTest {
        public static void main(String args[]){
                int x = 9;
                if (x == 9) {
                        int x = 8;
                        System.out.print(x + " ");
                }
                System.out.println(x);
        }
}
```

Which of the following will be the output of the above program?

(a) 8 9
(b) 8 8
(c) 9 8
(d) Compilation error.

3.11 Which of the following statements is(are) *incorrect*?

(a) Two or more methods with the same name can be differentiated on the basis of their parameters data type.
(b) Two or more method having the same name can be differentiated on the basis of number of parameters.
(c) Any already defined method in Java library can be defined again in the program with different data type of parameters.
(d) No method can call another method without creating an object of the class to which it is defined.

3.12 Consider the following program:

```
class Box {
  int width;
  int height;
  int length;
  }

class Test {
  public static void main(String args[]) {
  Box b1 = new Box();
  Box b2 = new Box();
  b1.height = 1;
  b1.length = 2; b1.width = 3;
  b2 = b1;
  System.out.println(b2.height);
  }
}
```

What will be the output of this program?

(a) 1.
(b) 2.
(c) 3.
(d) Compile-time error.

3.13 What is the limit on number of arguments that can be passed to a method in Java?

(a) 16.
(b) 255.
(c) Any number of arguments.
(d) Varies from one compiler to another.

3.14 Which of the following is *not* a use of `this` keyword in Java?

(a) Passing itself to another method.
(b) Calling another constructor in constructor chaining.
(c) Referring to the instance variable when local variable has the same name.
(d) Passing itself to a method of the same class.

3.15 During constructor overloading, which of the following should be used in a parameterized constructor to call the default constructor?

(a) The parameterized constructor should be declared `final` in order for it to call the default constructor.
(b) The `this()` reference should be used as the first statement inside the parameterized constructor.
(c) The `this()` reference should be used anywhere inside the parameterized constructor.
(d) It is not possible to implicitly call the default constructor from the parameterized constructor.

3.16 Which of the following is an *invalid* method overloading?

(a)
```
static double add(int a, double b){return a*b;}
static double add(double a, int b){return a*b;}
```
(b)
```
static int add(int a, int b){return a*b;}
static int add(int a, int b, int c){return a*b*c;}
```
(c)
```
static int add(int a, int b){return a*b;}
static double add(int a, int b, double c){return a*b*c;}
```
(d)
```
static int add(int a,int b){return a*b;}
static double add(int a,int b){return a*b;}
```

3.17 Which of the following is(are) *true* regarding the string array provided as a parameter to the main method in Java?

(a) It can be used to get command line arguments from the user.
(b) It is mandatory to name the string array as `args`.
(c) Accessibility of the values provided as command line argument is restricted only to the main method.
(d) Only one command line argument input is allowed at a time.

3.18 Which of the following can be used to take input from the user during the execution of a program?

(a) Using the `String` array provided as a parameter to the `main()` method.
(b) Defining `getText()` method to get user input from the command line.
(c) Using `Scanner` class bypassing the predefined object `System.in`.
(d) Once the execution starts, there is no way to provide user input.

3.19 **Which of the following is *not* true about a method in a class?**

(a) A method can be defined recursively.
(b) A method can be defined without any statement in it.
(c) A constructor is a special kind of a method which can be defined recursively.
(d) A method can be defined with a variable number of arguments passed into it.

3.20 **Which of the following is an incorrect way of initializing a variable in Java?**

(a) Different line declaration and initialization:
```
int a,b;
a = 1;
b = 2;
```
(b) Single line declaration and initialization (one in each line):
```
int a = 1;
int b = 2;
```
(c) Single line declaration and initialization (one line multiple variable):
```
int a = 1,b = 2;
```
(d) Single line declaration and initialization (one line multiple variable):
```
int a, b = 1, 2;
```

3.21 **Consider the following piece of code:**

```
public class CommnadLineInput {
        public static void main(String args[]){
                System.out.println(args[5]);
        }
}
```

Consider the following input on command line.
Input:
(a) A: Indian Institute of Technology
(b) B: 1 2 3 4 5 6
(c) C: Indian Institute of Technology Kharagpur
(d) D: 1 2 3 4 5

What will happen during the execution of the code for the command line input?
(a) Only A executes successfully.
(b) Only B executes successfully.
(c) Only C executes successfully.
(d) Only D executes successfully.

3.22 **Consider the following program:**

```
public class HelloWorld {
        HelloWorld() {
                this();
        }
        public static void main(String []args){
                HelloWorld obj = new HelloWorld();
        }
}
```

Which of the following statement is true?
(a) The program will execute infinite loop.
(b) The program will run successfully.
(c) The code will give an error at the time of compilation.
(d) It will produce a run-time exception.

3.23 Consider the following program:

```
public class HelloWorld{
        HelloWorld() {
                HelloWorld obj1 = new HelloWorld();
        }
        public static void main(String []args) {
                HelloWorld obj = new HelloWorld();
        }
}
```

Which of the following statements is(are) true?
(a) The program will execute an infinite loop.
(b) The program will run successfully.
(c) The code will give an error at the time of compilation.
(d) The program will produce a run-time exception.

3.24 Carefully check the following piece of code written in Java:

```
class A {
        static int x = 100;
        A() {
                x++;
                System.out.println(x);
        }
}
class B {
        public static void main(String[] args)
                A a1 = new A();
                A a2 = new A();
        }
}
```

What will be the correct output from this program?

(a) 100 101	(b) 101 102
(c) 100 100	(d) 100 103

3.25 Which of the following is *not* true about a method in a class?
(a) A method can be defined recursively.
(b) A method can be defined without any statement in it.
(c) A constructor is a special kind of method, which can be defined recursively.
(d) A method can be defined with variable number of arguments.

4

INHERITANCE

Java developer aims at Java programming suitable for fast, large, complex, and safety-critical software development. One important requirement towards this is to code reusability. Code reusability helps a programmer to use code which is already developed by someone else. For this reason, Java developer introduces one of the most magnificent object-oriented programming features called *inheritance*. This feature allows a programmer to access fields and methods of an existing class to their new class under development. Inheritance thus facilitates inheriting some of the characteristics in a child class from its parent class. It is just like a ladder from the child class to the parent class. In addition to code sharing, access privilege is also taken into consideration in the inheritance mechanism. This enables protection of data and code from unauthorized access.

4.0 Introduction

Why inheritance?

Class is the basic element of any software in object-oriented system design approach. In the last chapter, you have learned about how to write classes in Java programs. In software development, a software is under constant updation, for example, extension (from one version to the next or from one release to another, etc.), or modification (correction of some faults or to make it compatible with new technology, hardware, etc.). The requirement is that all the development should take place without disturbing the existing system and, of course, with minimum effort and time.

Your learning

Inheritance in Java is a clever mechanism to support these requirements. It allows an efficient and secure way to share code, modify it, and reuse it. With the help of inheritance, you will learn how to extend a given class and thus access its fields and methods. You will also learn how to hide some fields and methods from a parent class to the extended class.

4.1 Concept of Inheritance

Basic concept

The inheritance concept is related to taxonomy or classification. For example, Figure 4.1 shows taxonomy (in partial form) of animals. It looks like a tree (this is why it is also called and inheritance tree). This tree bears the information that lion and hyena, for example, have some common characteristics. In addition, they have their own characteristics. Alternatively, you can say that Lion and Hyena are two classes that inherit from the class Carnivore. In this manner, the inheritance concept is a mimic of a real-life situation.

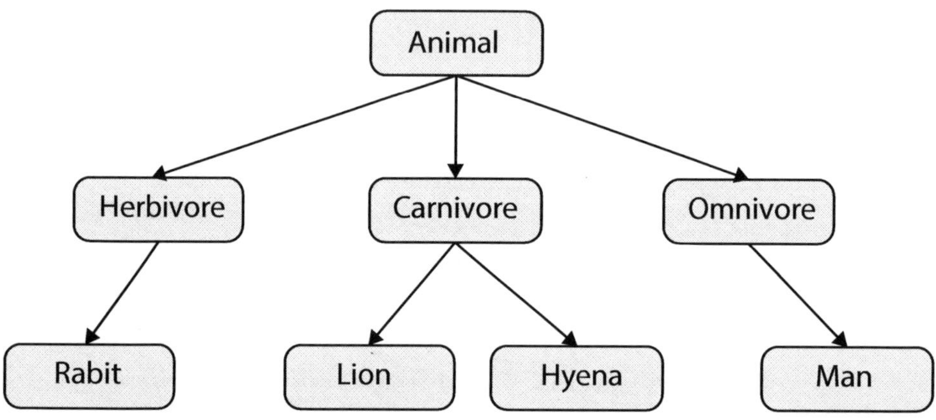

Figure 4.1 Taxonomy of animals

Types of inheritances

There are three different basic types of inheritance: single inheritance, multiple inheritance, and multi-level inheritance. In case of single inheritance, a class is derived from a single class as shown in Figure 4.2(a). If a class is derived from two or more classes, then it is called multiple inheritance as shown in Figure 4.2(b). Figure 4.2(c) shows the case of multi-level inheritance, where there is a chain of single inheritances. The class at the higher level is called super class (or parent class). A class which is extended from a super class is called derived class (or child class). In the case of multi-level inheritance, a derived class becomes a super class. In the case of multiple inheritance, there are more than one super classes. Java supports only single and multi-level inheritances.

4.1.1 Syntax of Declaring Single Inheritance

The extends keyword is used to define a new class that derives from an existing class. Following is the general syntax:

```
class <DerivedClass> extends <Super class>  {

        //Fields and methods in this derived class

}
```

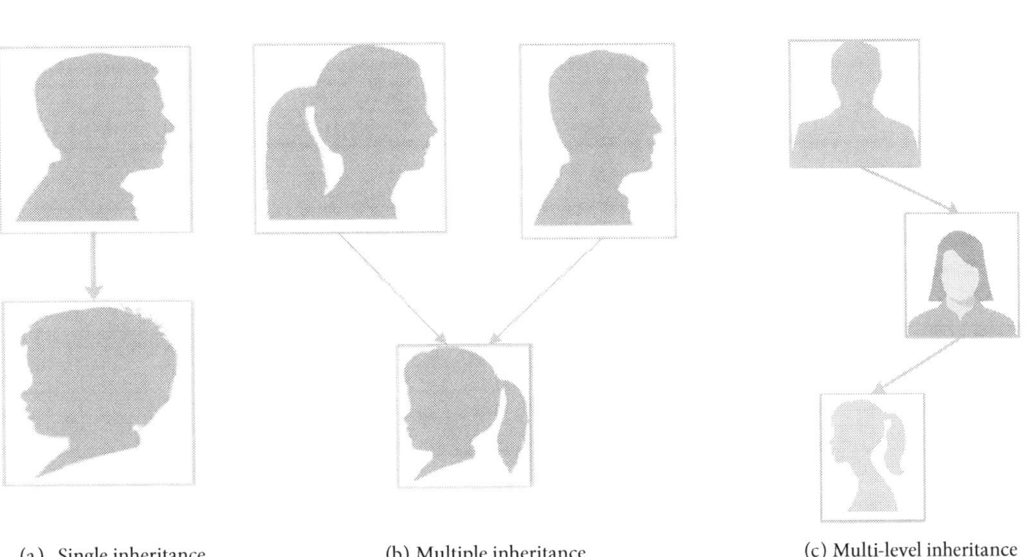

(a) Single inheritance (b) Multiple inheritance (c) Multi-level inheritance

Figure 4.2 Types of inheritances

Program 4.1 illustrates a simple example of a single inheritance.

Program 4.1 *(Single inheritance)*

```
/* Example of Single inheritance. */
class Point2D{            // Super class declaration
      int x;
      int y;
      void display2D(){
           System.out.println ("x :" + x + "y :" + y);
      }
}

class Point3D extends Point2D{
                          // Derived class definition
      int z;              // A new field in derived class
      void display3D(){
          System.out.println("x :" + x + "y :" + y +
                "z :" + z);
      }
}
```

```
// Driver class declaration
class SingleInheritance{
   public static void main(String arge[]){
      Point2D p1 = new Point2D();
          //Declaration of super object
      Point3D p2 = new Point3D ();
          // Declaration of derived object
      p1.x = 10;
      p1.y = 20;
      System.out.print("2D Point P1 is:");
          p1.display2D());
      // Initializing Point3D
      p2.x = 5;
      p2.y = 6;
      p2.z = 15;
      System.out.println("3D Point P2 is:");
          p2.display3D());
      }
}
```

- The class `Point2D` is a super class, but not because it is superior to its derived class or it contains more functionality. The opposite is true: derived class has more functionality than the super class. For example, the `Point3D` class has three fields and two methods (one of its own and the other is derived from its super class) in it.
- Super class cannot access any field/method which is/are defined in the derived class.
- Java does not support multiple inheritance. This is to avoid ambiguity. For example, the following syntax is not valid in Java:

```
class D extends A, B  {
...
}
```

The reason of ambiguity can be understood from the following piece of code:

```
class A {
      int x:
      . . .
}
```

```
class B {
        int x;
        . . .
}
class D extends A, B {  // Assume that it is allowed...
        int i;
        . . .
        x = 5:  // Ambiguity. Which x? The x from
                A or B?
}
```

- From a super class any number of classes can be extended. Logically, there is no limit on this.

Program 4.2 is another example of extending more than one derived class from a super class. Also refer to Figure 4.3 where the fields and methods in each class are shown.

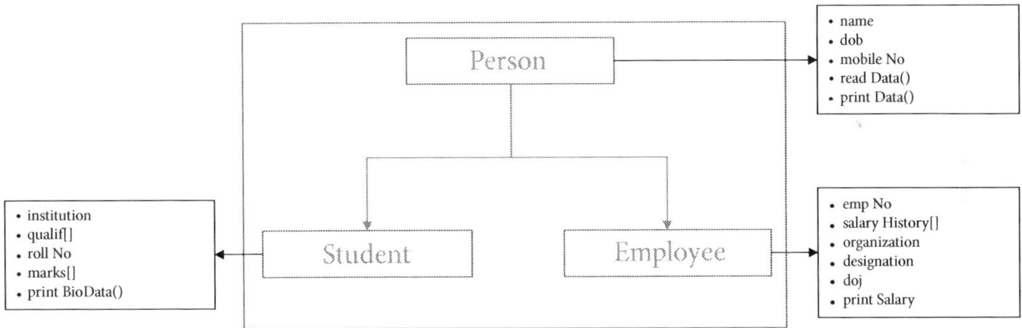

Figure 4.3 Multiple single inheritance

Program 4.2 *(Multiple single inheritance)*

```
/* Another illustration of single inheritance: deriving
more than one child class from a parent class. */
import java.util.Date;
class DOB {       // This is a helper class
    int dd;
    int mm;
    int yy;
}
class Person{     // Thc parent class
      String name;
      Date dob;
```

```
    long mobileNo;
    void readData(String n, Date d, int m){
        name = n;
        dob = d;
        mobileNo = m;
    }
    void printData(){
        System.out.println("Name : "+ name);
        dob.printDate();
         //Define a method in class DOB to print date
        System.out.println("Mobile : "+ mobileNo);
    }
}
class Student extends Person{   // First child class
    String institution;
    int[] qualif = new int[20];
    int rollNo;
    int[] marks = new int[5];

    void printBioData(){
          printData();
              // This method is from super class
         System.out.println("Institution :" +
              institution);
         System.out.println("Roll :" + rollNo);
         for(int q=0; q<qualif.length;q++){
            System.out.println("Marks" +q+ ":" +
                  qualif[q]);
         }
         for(int m=0; m<marks.length; m++){
             System.out.print("Result" +m+ ":"
                  +marks[m]);
         }
     }
}
class Employee extends Person{    // Second child class
    int empNo;
    int[] salaryHistory = new int[12];
    String organization;
    String designation;
    Date doj;
    void printSalary(){
        for(int s=0; s<salaryHistory.length;s++){
           System.out.println("Salary" +s+ ":"
               +salaryHistory[s]);
```

```
            }
        }
}

//Finally, the driver class is as follows.

class SimpleIheritance2{
     public static void main(String args[]){
                Person p = new Person();
                //Code with the object p:To read and
                                           //print data
                Student s = new Student [10];
                //Code with the objects s….:To read and
                                           //print data
                Employee e = new Employee[5];
                //Code with the objects e….:To read and
                                           //print data
          // You are advised to compete code and run….
     }
}
```

4.1.2 Syntax of Declaring Multi-level Inheritance

The same idea of single inheritance can be applied to have child class derivation. Here is an example:

```
class B {       // Super class
   . . .
}
class C extends  B {  // Level 1 inheritance
   . . .
}
class D extend C {    // Level 2 inheritance
   . . .
}
...
```

Theoretically, there is no restriction on the number of levels of inheritance; the inheritance tree can be of any depth in Java programming.

4.2 Method Overriding

Method overriding is another polymorphism mechanism in Java. You can define a method in a derived class having the same name and signature as a method in its super class. If you do so, then the method in the derived class is said to override the method in the super class. Method overriding is used to provide the specific implementation of a method which is already provided by its super class. The following are the basic rules for method overriding in Java programming:

- The method must have the same name as in the parent class.
- The method must have the same return type and parameter(s) as in the parent class.

Let us learn the method overriding with a simple example (Program 4.3).

Program 4.3 *(Method overriding)*

```
/* The following program illustrates the method
overriding in Java. */

class Point2D{          // Super class
      int x = 0;
      int y = 0;
      Point2D(int a, int b){
          x = a;
          y = b;
      }
      void display(){    // Method in a super class
            System.out.println("x :" + x + "y :" + y);
      }
}

class Point3D extends Point3D{      // Derived class
      int z;
      Point3D(int c){
          z = c;
      }
      void display(){    // Overridden method in derived
                                                //class
          System.out.println("x :" + x + "y :" + y +
           "z:" + z);
      }
}
```

```
//Driver class
class MethodOverridingTest{
      public static void main(String args[]){
     Point2D p = new Point2D(3, -4);
     p.display();  // Refers to the method in Point2D

     Point3D q = new Point3D(0);
     q.display();  // Refers to the method in Point3D
     }
}
```

- When an overridden method is called through an object of the child class, it will always refer to the version of that method defined in the child class.
- In a chain of inheritance, if you call a method for an object, and if the method is defined in the class of that object, it will be resolved from there; otherwise, it will be resolved in the nearest class in the chain where it is defined (provided that the method is accessible; we shall discuss about the access restriction of a method later in this chapter).
- A child class object can reference a super class method if it is not overridden.
- A super class object cannot reference a variable or a method in child class; they are explicit to the child class object.

4.2.1 Method Overriding versus Method Overloading

In Chapter 3, you have learned about the method overloading as a polymorphism mechanism in Java. Method overriding is another form of polymorphism; however, there are many differences between method overloading and method overriding. Comparisons and differences between method overloading and method overriding are given in Figure 4.4 and Table 4.1.

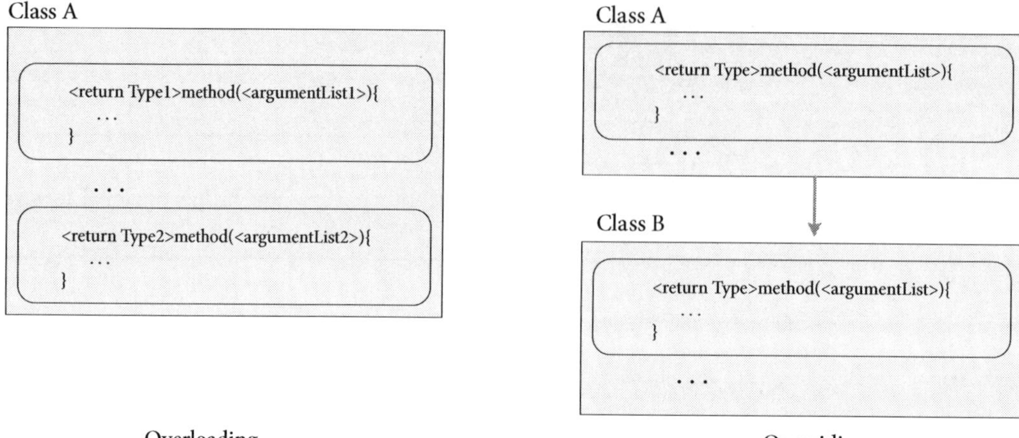

Figure 4.4 Comparison between method overloading and method overriding

Table 4.1 Differences between method overloading and method overriding

Method Overloading	Method Overriding
Method overloading is used to increase the flexibility of the program.	Method overriding is used to provide the specific implementation of the method already provided by its super class.
Method overloading is performed within class.	Method overriding occurs in two classes that are under inheritance relationship.
In case of method overloading, the parameter must be different.	In case of method overriding, the parameter must be the same.
Method overloading is the example of compile-time polymorphism.	Method overriding is the example of run-time polymorphism.
Method overloading can't be performed by only changing return type of the method. Return type can be the same or different in method overloading. But you must change the parameter.	Return type must be the same or covariant in method overriding.
Static methods can be overloaded, which means a class can have more than one static method of the same name.	Static methods cannot be overridden, even if you declare the same static method in child class, it has nothing to do with the same method of parent class.
Static binding is used for overloaded methods.	Dynamic binding is used for overridden/overriding methods

4.2.2 Constructors in Inheritance

In each class, you can define constructors with or without overloading feature. However, while you plan the derived class constructor(s), you have to take special care. This is because the derived class constructor should initialize all the fields (including static) which are defined in super class as well derived class. This can be done in three ways: (a) using proper initialization steps in the derived class constructor, (b) passing an object as the parameter to a derived class constructor, and (c) explicitly invoking the super class constructor from the derived class constructor. Program 4.4 illustrates these techniques in Java.

Program 4.4 *(Constructors in derived class)*

```
/* The following program illustrates how to define
constructors in a derived class. */


class Point2D{          // Super class
      int x;
      int y;
      Point2D(int a, int b){
          x = a;
          y = b;
      }
      void display(){    // Method in a super class
            System.out.println("x : " + x + "y : " + y);
      }
}

class Point3D extends Point3D{      // Derived class
      int z;
      Point3D(int a,int b,int c){
                                 //I: Explicit initialization
          x = a;
                  // Initialize the parent class member x
           y = b;
                  // Initialize the parent class member y
           z = c;
                  // Initialize the parent class member z
      }
       Point3D(Point2D p,int c){
                   // II. Through object passing
          x = p.x;
            // Initialize the parent class member x
```

```
            y = p.y;
             // Initialize the parent class member y
            z = c;
             // Initialize the child class member z
       }
        Point3D(int c){
             // III. Calling super class constructor
           super(0,0);
             // Initialize the parent's members with
                                                   //values
           z = c;
             // Initialize the child class member z
       }
       void display(){
                     // Overridden method in derived class
           System.out.println("x :" + x + "y :" + y +
             "z : " + z);
       }
}
//Driver class
class ConstructorOverridingTest{
       public static void main(String args[]){
           Point2D p = new Point2D(3, -4);
           p.display();
                        // Refers to the method in Point2D

           Point3D q = new Point3D(p, 0);
                  // Constructor II
           q.display();
                  // Refers to the method in Point3D

     Point3D r = new Point3D(5);
                  // Constructor III
           r.display();
                  // Refers to the method in Point3D
       }
}
```

- Whenever a child class object is declared, its constructor calls the default constructor of its parent automatically.
- The `super(...)` is a Java standard which refers to the super class constructor.
- To call the default constructor of a parent class, you can user `super()`.

- The `super(...)`, if used, must be the first statement executed in a derived class constructor.
- In a multilevel inheritance, when a child class object is created, it is interesting to note the order in which the constructors will be called. For example, given a child class D and a parent class A, is A's constructor executed before D's, or vice-versa? The answer is that in a class hierarchy, constructors complete their execution in the order of derivation, from super class to derived class. Program 4.5 illustrates the order of invocation of constructors in an inheritance chain.

Program 4.5 *(Order of constructors call)*

```
/* Illustrates the order of execution of constructors
in inheritance chain. */

 class A {    // Super class.
    A() {
        System.out.println("I am from class A ...");
    }
 }

 class B extends A {    // Level-I derived class
     B() {
         System.out.println("I am from class B ...");
     }
 }

 class C extends B {  // Level-II derived class
     C() {
         System.out.println("I am from class C ...");
     }
 }

 class OrderingOfConstructors {
     public static void main(String args[]) {
         C c = new C();
     }
 }
```

4.3 Access Specification

Information hiding

You have just learned how a class (i.e., data and methods) can be accessed by an extended class. Sometimes you may want to share some data/method(s), but not the whole class. To ensure this, Java developer provides an elegant access control mechanism. With the access control mechanism, you will be able to hide information in several ways. For example, you can control what parts of a program can access the members of a class. By controlling access, you can prevent misuse. For example, allowing access to data only through a set of privileged methods, you can prevent the unauthorized use of that data. Java's access control mechanism allows a software engineer to create a class as a "black box" which may be used, but the inner workings of which are not open to tampering. In this section we will learn about the information hiding feature in Java.

Java has the concept of access modifier to control the access to different parts of a program (Figure 4.5). The following are the four different access modifiers:

```
default

public

private

protected
```

These access specifiers are mostly related to inheritance and package (a package is essentially a group of classes kept together, the concept of which will be covered in details in Chapter 5). Let's learn about these four access modifiers.

4.3.1 Access Specifier `default`

If you don't use any modifier, it is treated as `default` automatically. Such an access specifier can be applied to a class, field, and method. Any item with `default` access modifier is accessible within the package. In Program 4.6, We have defined two classes. class `A` and class `B`.

Case 1

Two classes are in the same file

The two classes are defined in the same file, say `B.java`. As there is no specifier used, then both the classes are `default` as well as all methods in class `A` and class `B` are `default`. If you compile the `B.java` file and run the program, then you will see that the program is running successfully.

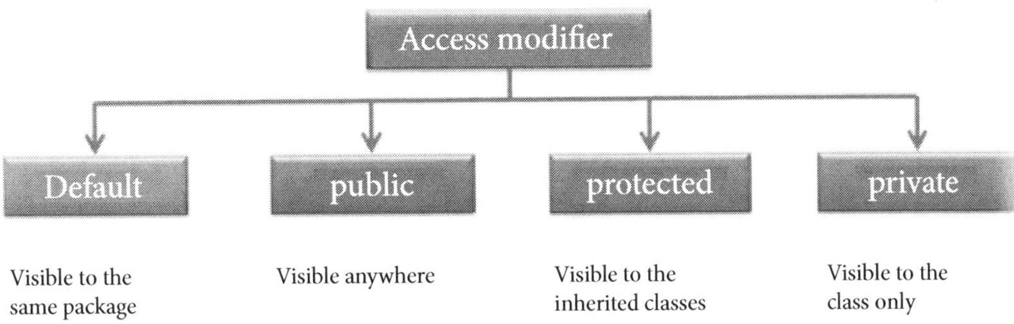

Visible to the same package

Visible anywhere

Visible to the inherited classes

Visible to the class only

Figure 4.5 Access modifiers in Java

Program 4.6 (Case 1 of program execution)

```
/* This program demonstrates the use of default access
specifier.
Case 1: All classes are in one file.
*/
   class A {            // Default class
      void msg(){       // Default method
         System.out.println("Hi! I am in Class A");
      }
   }
   class B{
        public static void main(String args[]){
           A obj = new A();   //Okay. It is accessible.
           obj.msg();         //It is also accessible.
        }
    }
```

Case 2

Two classes are in different files

Now, let us do the thing in a different manner. This time you store class A and class B in two different files, say A.java and B.java, but in the same directory. Compile both the files and then run B.java program. This time also you will not face any problem.

Case 3

Two classes are in a different directory

Next, let's store the two files A.java and B.java in two different files and keep them in two different directories, say temp1 and temp2. Now, try to compile them. You will see that A.java file is compiled successfully; however, B.java file will not. This is because class A is with default access specifier and hence any method in class B (which is outside of the directory that of class A) cannot access class A.

Program 4.7 (Case 3 of program execution)

```
/* This program demonstrates the use of default access
specifier.
Case 3: Save class A in temp1 directory and class B in
temp2 directory. */
//-----------------------------------------------------
   class A {
      void msg(){
         System.out.println("Hi! I am in Class A");
      }
   }
//-----------------------------------------------------
   class B{
        public static void main(String args[]){
             A obj = new A();
                //Compilation Error!  class A is default
             obj.msg();
                  //Compilation Error!  msg() is default
        }
    }
```

- Any class, field, method, or constructor that has no declared access modifier is accessible only by classes in the same package.
- The default modifier is not used for fields and methods within an interface (Chapter 5).

4.3.2 Access Specifier `public`

The public access modifier is specified using the keyword `public`. Classes, methods, or data members, which are declared as `public` are accessible from everywhere in the program. There is no restriction on the scope of public data members. Program 4.8 is the modified version of Program 4.7, where we make class as `public`.

Program 4.8 (public access specifier)

```
/* This program demonstrates the use of public access
specifier.
   Save class A in temp1 directory and class B in temp2
directory. */

//-----------------------------------------------------
   public class A {
      void msg(){
```

```
        System.out.println("Hi! I am in Class A");
      }
    }
//-----------------------------------------------------

    class B{
        public static void main(String args[]){
             A obj = new A();
                   //Perfect!  class A is public
             obj.msg();
               //Perfect!  msg() is public as A is publc
        }
    }
```

- If we make a class as `public`, then all its default members are also public.
- The `public` access modifier has the widest scope among all other access modifiers.
- You cannot use `public` keyword in a class among other class(es), when all are defined in the same file.

4.3.3 Access Specifier `private`

The `private` access specifier can be applied to fields and methods. Any method within the class can access any `private` member. Program 4.9 illustrates the use of `private` access specifier.

Program 4.9 *(private access specifier)*

```
/* This program demonstrates the use of private access
specifier.
   Save class A in temp1 directory and class B in temp2
directory. */

//-----------------------------------------------------
   public class A {
      int i;            // public by default
      private int x;    // private member
      void accessA(){   // public method by default
         System.out.println("i :" + i + "x = :" + x);
                                                //Okay
      }
   }
//-----------------------------------------------------
```

```
public class B{
    public static void main(String args[]){
         A obj = new A();
                            //Perfect! class A is public
         obj.i = 555;
                        // Okay: Both A and i are public
         obj.x = 999;      // Error! x is private
    }
}
```

- In a class, if a data is declared as `private` and a method is `public`, then you can note an interesting situation. We know that the `private` member is not accessible outside the class; however, through the `public` method, it can be accessed from an outside class. Program 4.10 illustrates this.

Program 4.10 *(Accessing* `private` *member via public method)*

```
/* This program demonstrates how a private member
indirectly can be accessed from an outside class.
Save class A in temp1 directory and class B in temp2
directory. */

//-------------------------------------------------------
  public class A{
     private int data = 40;
     public void accessA(){
     System.out.println("Hello Java!" + data);
     }
  }
//-------------------------------------------------------

   public class AccessTest1{
      public static void main(String args[]){
         A obj = new A();
           // Okay : Class A is public
         System.out.println(obj.data);
           // Error : data is private
         obj.accessA();
           // No error!
      }
   }
```

- The `private` members in a super class are not accessible to the derived class. In a class hierarchy, `private` members remain private to their classes. Program 4.11 illustrates this type of accessing.

Program 4.11 *(Accessing* `private` *member via inheritance)*

```
/* A private member in a super class cannot be accessed
in its derived class. This program illustrates the
access protection of private members.  */

   class A {            // Default super class
      int i;            // public by default
      private int j;    // private to A

      void accessA(int a, int b) {
            // This can accesses all members
         i = a;
         j = b;
     }
     private void foo() {};
   }
   class B extends A {
      int k;           // B's default member
      void add() {
          k = i + j; // Error! "private" j is not
                                        //accessible here
      }
  }
  class AccessTest2 {
       public static void main(String args[]) {
           B  b = new B();
           b.accessA(55, 99);
                // accessA is publicly inherited here
           b.add();
           b.foo();      // Error! foo() is private in A
           System.out.println("k is : " +  b.k);
      }
   }
```

- A constructor in a class can be made `private`. The use of `private` constructor is to create singleton classes. A singleton class is one that can have only one object (i.e., instance of the class) at a time. Using `private` constructor, you can ensure that no more than one object can be created at a time.

- By providing a `private` constructor you prevent class instances from being created in any place, other than this very class. Program 4.12 illustrates the use of private constructor to create a singleton class.

Program 4.12 *(`private` constructor and singleton class)*

```
/* This program demonstrates the idea of creating a
singleton class. Also, it shows if you make any class
constructor private, you cannot create an instance of
that class from outside the class. */

//---------------------------------------------------------
   public class Singleton {
       private static Singleton s = null;
          // Create a static reference
       public String x;
       private A(){                    // Private constructor
          x = "Joy with Java";
       }

       //The following method ensures to create one
                                       //object at a time
       public static Singleton createS() {
          if (s == null)
             s = new Singleton();   // Create the object
          return s;

       public static void main(String args[]){
           // Creating three instances ...
           Singleton a = Singleton.createS();
           Singleton b = Singleton.createS();
           Singleton c = Singleton.createS();

           // Changing the data of instance x
           a.x = (a.x).toUpperCase();

           // Printing the result ...
           System.out.println("From a : " + a.x);
           System.out.println("From b : " + b.x);
           System.out.println("From c : " + c.x);

           // Changing the data of instance c
           c.x = (c.x).toLowerCase();
```

```
            // Printing the result ...
             System.out.println("From a : " + a.x);
             System.out.println("From b : " + b.x);
             System.out.println("From c : " + c.x);
        }
   }
//-----------------------------------------------------

//-----------------------------------------------------
   public class B {
      Singleton a = new Singleton();
            // Compile time error!
   }
//-----------------------------------------------------
```

4.3.4 Access Specifier `protected`

The `protected` access specifier is used to limit the access of data and methods of a class and to its extended classes. This implies that if a member is declared as `protected` in a class, then the same member can be accessible to any method in any class declared in the same package or from any derived class of the class. If you want to allow a member to be accessible outside your current package, but only to classes that extend your class, then declare the member `protected`. The `protected` access can be specified to fields, methods and constructor. Let us consider Program 4.13 to understand the accessing of `protected` members.

Program 4.13 *(Accessing `protected` member in the classes in different directories)*

```
/* This program demonstrates the accessing of protected
members.
   Keep all the classes in separate directories. */

//-----------------------------------------------------
public class A{
        int d = 0;
        public int i = 1;
        private int j = 22;
        protected int k = 333;
        public void msg(){
           System.out.println("Class A:
                 Default!" + d);     //OK
        }
```

```
    public void msg1(){
       System.out.println("Class A:
              Public!" + i);      //OK
    }
    private void msg2(){
       System.out.println("Class A:
              Private!" + j);     //OK
    }
    protected void msg3(){
       System.out.println("Class A:
              Protected!" + k);   //OK
    }
  }
//---------------------------------------------------

//---------------------------------------------------
class B {
     public static void main(String args[]){
         A a = new A();    // A is a public class
         a.msg();          // OK  : msg() is public
         a.msg1();        // OK : msg1() is public
         a.msg2();       // Error : Private members!
         a.msg3();     // Error : Protected members!
     }
}
//---------------------------------------------------

//---------------------------------------------------
class C extends A {
      public static void main(String args[]){
         A a = new A(); // A is a public class
         a.msg();          // OK  : msg() is public
         a.msg1();         // OK  : msg1() is public
         a.msg2();         // Error : Private members!
         a.msg3();         // OK : Protected member is
                                              //fine here
      }
}
//---------------------------------------------------
```

- A `protected` member can be accessed from any class which belongs to the same package. There is no need to hide any information of any member as all members are in the same package. A package is under the discretion of the owner. Program 4.14 illustrates this aspect of protected access specifier. Test the same program, while you keep the file for class `A` and class `B` in the two different directories. Note that a `protected` member in the same package behaves like a `public` member.

Program 4.14 *(Accessing* `protected` *member in the same directory)*

```
/* This program explains the access specification of
a protected member in the same package. Keep all the
classes in different files but in the same directory.
*/

//----------------------------------------------------
class A {
    public int pubA = 10;
    protected int proA = 20;
}
//----------------------------------------------------

//----------------------------------------------------
class B {
    void foo() {
        System.out.println("In B : " + pubA + proA);
    }
}
//----------------------------------------------------
```

- A `protected` member in a super class remains protected in its derived class. This is true for all derived classes in a chain of inheritance relationship. Program 4.15 is a quick example. It has inheritance up to three levels and can be extended to any number of levels.

Program 4.15 *(*`Protected` *member in inheritance chain)*

```
/* This program explains the access specification of a
protected member in an inheritance chain. */

class A {
    private int priA = 10;
    protected int proA = 20;
}
```

```
class B extends A {
    System.out.println("In B : " +proA);
            //Protected member is accessible
}

class C extends B {
    System.out.println("In C : " + proA);
            // Here is also accessible
}

class ProtectedTest {
    public static void main(String[] args){
        A a = new A();
        B b = new B();
        C c = new C();
        System.out.println(a.priA);
           // Error! PriA is not accessible
        System.out.println(b.priA);
           // Error! PriA is not accessible
        System.out.println(b.proA);
           // Okay : Output is 20
        System.out.println(c.priA);
           // Error! PriA is not accessible
        System.out.println(c.proA);
           // Okay : Output is 20
    }
  }
```

- If a member is declared as `protected` (or `public`), then you can not only access the member in the derived class, but you can also override the method. However, the same is not true for a `private` method. A `private` method cannot be overwritten in its derived class. Program 4.16 will make your understanding clear.

Program 4.16 *(Overriding* `private` *and* `protected` *members)*

```
/* This program demonstrates, if private and protected
members can be overridden in derived class. */

class A {
 private testPrivate() {
   System.out.println("I am private in super class");
   }
```

```
 protected testPrivate() {
   System.out.println("I am protected in super class");
   }
}
class B extends A {
    private testPrivate() {
       System.out.println("I am private in derived
          class");  //ERROR!
    }
    protected testPrivate() {
        System.out.println("I am protected in
          derived class"); // Okay
    }
}
```

4.3.5 Summary of Access Specifiers

Table 4.2 gives a quick summary of all the access specifiers we have learned in this section. As we can see, the `private` access modifier has the strictest access. The `public` is the weakest access specifier.

Table 4.2 Summary of access specifiers

		Default	Private	Protected	Public
	Same class	Yes	Yes	Yes	Yes
Same package	Derived class	Yes	No	Yes	Yes
	Non-derived class	Yes	No	Yes	Yes
Different packages	Derived class	No	No	Yes	Yes
	Non-derived class	No	No	No	Yes

- The Java access modifiers `private` and `protected` cannot be assigned to a class. They can be assigned only to constructors, methods, and fields which are present inside classes.
- Classes can only have the `default` (package) and `public` access modifier assigned to them.
- `public`, `private` and `protected` are reserved keywords in Java.
- If other programmers use your class, try to use the most restrictive access level that makes sense for a particular member. In that case, use `private` unless you have a good reason not to.
- Avoid `public` fields except for constants.

4.4 Java Special Keywords Related to Inheritance

There are a few keywords in Java which help programmers to write their programs. We need a complete understanding of some of the frequently used keywords. This section has detailed discussions on the following keywords in Java:

`super`

`this`

`abstract`

`final`

4.4.1 `super` Keyword

The `super` keyword in Java is a reference variable which is used to resolve the ambiguity when you refer to class members which are present in both super and derived classes. Following are the three main uses of `super` keyword:

(a) `super` can be used to refer to immediate parent class instance variable.
(b) `super` can be used to invoke immediate parent class method.
(c) `super()` can be used to invoke immediate parent class constructor.

Use of `super` to refer to immediate parent class instance variable

There may be a situation when both the derived class and super class have the same field declared in them. In that case, there is a possibility of ambiguity for the JVM to resolve the reference. Such an ambiguity can be resolved by specifying the `super` keyword. Program 4.17 gives an example of the use of super keyword with variables.

Program 4.17 *(Use of `super` with a variable)*

```
/* In this program, both super class and derived class
have a member color. We refer to color of super class
in derived class using super keyword. */

class Flower{
   String color="white";
}
class Rose extends Flower{
   String color = "red";
   void printColor(){
```

```
        System.out.println(color);
             // This refers to the field of Rose
        System.out.println(super.color);
             //Refers to the field of parent class
    }
}
class TestSuper1{
    public static void main(String args[]){
        Rose r = new Rose();
        r.printColor();
    }
}
```

Use of `super` to invoke immediate parent class method

The `super` keyword can be used to invoke an immediate parent class method. It should be used to resolve the ambiguity in method referencing if a derived class contains the same method as its parent class (i.e., overridden method). Program 4.18 will help you to understand the usage of `super` keyword.

Program 4.18 *(Use of* `super` *with method)*

```
/* This program explains the use of super keyword to
refer to the method of a super class. */
class Animal{
    void eat(){
        System.out.println("I can eat you!");
    }
}
class Dog extends Animal{
    void eat(){    // Overridden method
        System.out.println("Eating my bread...");
    }
    void bark(){
        System.out.println("Vowww...Vooke ...");
    }
    void work(){
        super.eat();
                // It refers to the eat() in Animal class
        eat(); // This will call the eat() in Dog class
        bark();
    }
}
```

```
class TestSuper2 {
    public static void main(String args[]){
        Dog d = new Dog();
        d.work();
    }
}
```

Use of `super` to invoke parent class constructor

We can also use `super` keyword to invoke the overloaded parent class constructor; if arguments are there, then they should be specified accordingly. Program 4.19 demonstrates the use of `super` to call a specific constructor in a parent class.

Program 4.19 *(Use of* `super` *with constructor)*

```
/* This program demonstrates the call of a super class
constructor using super() */

class Animal{
      String color = "White";
      Animal(){         // Constructor 1
          System.out.println(" Bommm Bomm !");
      }

      Animal(String skin) {     // Constructor 2
          color = skin;
      }
}
class Dog extends Animal{
      Dog(){
           super();
              // Call the first constructor in Animal
           System.out.println("I am " + color +
              "dog!");
      }
}

class TestSuper3{
       public static void main(String args[]){
          Dog d = new Dog();
      }
}
```

If there are a number of overloading constructors in the `super` class, then you should define the derived class constructors matching with each constructor. Program 4.20 illustrates this.

Program 4.20 *(`super` with overloaded constructor)*

```
/* Calling an overloaded super class constructor from a
derived class constructor. */

class Point2D{
     double x, y;
     Point2D(){                    // Constructor I
        x = 0.0; y = 0.0  //Default initialization
     }
     Point2D(double a, double b){    // Constructor II
         x = a;  y = b;
     }
  }
  class Point3D extends Point2D {
     double z;
     Point3D(){
       super(); // Call super class constructor I
       z = 0.0  //Default initialization
     }
     Point3D(double x, double y, double z){
     super(x, y);  // Call super class constructor II
     this.z = z; }
  }
  class TestSuper4{
     public static void main(String args[]){
         Point3D p = new Point3D(2.0, 3.0, 4.0);
     }
  }
```

- A constructor in derived class can call a `super` class constructor. In Program 4.19, a constructor in child class calls a constructor of `super` class.
- Call to `super()` must be the first statement in a derived class constructor.
- If a constructor does not explicitly invoke a `super` class constructor, the Java compiler automatically inserts a call to the default constructor (no-argument constructor) of the super class.

- If a child class constructor invokes a constructor of its `super` class, either explicitly or implicitly, you might think that a whole chain of constructors called all the way back to the constructor of `Object` (this is a universal super class of any class, which we shall learn shortly in this chapter). This is called constructor chaining.
- Note the difference between `super ()` and `this()` (discussed in Chapter 3). In Java, `super()` as well as `this()` are both used to make constructor calls; `super()` is used to call `super` class's constructor while `this()` is used to call current class's constructor. Program 4.21 is an illustration.

Program 4.21 *(super() versus this())*

```
/* This program illustrates the difference between
super() and this()*/

class Parent {
   String expt;
    Parent() {
        System.out.println("Calling parent class's
           constructor.");
    }
}

class Child extends Parent {
    Child() {       // Constructor 1
        super();    // Calls the parent's constructor
        System.out.println("Child class's first
           constructor");
    }

    Child (String s) {  // Constructor 2
        expt = s;
        System.out.println("Child class's second
           constructor");
    }
    Child (int n) // Constructor 3
    {
        this("Java experiment");
                    // Calls the child's constructor 2
        System.out.println("Child class's third
           constructor");
    }
```

```
    public static void main(String[] args)
    {
        new Child();      // Child object is created
                                  // with constructor 1
        System.out.println("Inside Main");
    }
}
```

4.4.2 `final` Keyword

The `final` keyword in Java is used to restrict the access of an item from its `super` class to a derived class. The Java `final` keyword can be used in the following context:

Variable: If a variable is declared as `final`, it cannot be modified in a derived class.

Method: If a method is declared as `final`, it cannot be modified in a derived class.

Class: If a class is declared as `final`, it cannot be sub classed and you cannot. extend it.

Let us discuss the use of `final` keyword in these cases.

Case 1: `final` keyword to declare a variable as a constant

The following is the syntax to declare a variable as `final`.

```
final [static] <type><varName> [= <initialization Value>];
```

Program 4.22 illustrates a program using some variable declaration with `final` keywords.

Program 4.22 *(Use of* `final` *variable)*

```
/* This program illustrates the different  ways of
declaring  variables as final and restrictions of final
variables. */

class FinalFields  {

    final int ALPHA = 5; //Final variable declaration
                                  // with initialization
    final int BETA; // Blank final variable declaration

    static final double PI = 3.141592653589793;
          // A final static variable
```

```
    static final double GAMMA;
          // A  blank final static  variable

    public FinalFields()  {                  // Constructor
        BETA = -1;
    }

    public FinalFields( int const)  {
     // Another constructor
        BETA = const;
    }

    static {
        //Another way of initializing in a static block
        GAMMA = 2.3e-10;
    }

    public void demoMethod() {
          ALPHA = 10;  // ERROR: Final variable value
                                  // cannot be modified
          System.out.println("G value is " +
                4.2345*GAMMA);
          System.out.println("A-B value is " +
                ALPHA-BETA);
    }

    public static void main(String args[]){
         FinalFields x = new  FinalFields (123);
         x.demoMethod();
    }
}
```

- It is Java programming standard to declare a `final` variable with all uppercase letters.
- A `final` variable without declaration is called blank `final` variable.
- The following are the ways to initialize a `final` variable:
  (a) You can initialize a `final` variable when it is declared. This approach is the most common.
  (b) A blank `final` variable can be initialized inside instance-initializer block.
  (c) A blank `final static` variable can be initialized inside `static` block.
  (d) A `final` variable can be initialized inside a constructor.

- Other access modifiers are applicable to `final` variable declaration.
- Many programmers call `final` keyword under access modifiers.
- We must initialize a `final` variable. Otherwise, the compiler will throw compile-time error.
- A `final` variable can only be initialized once. More than one attempt to initialize a `final` variable leads to a compile-time error.
- If you have more than one constructor in your class, then the `final` variable must be initialized in all of them, otherwise a compile-time error will be thrown.

Case 2: `final` keyword to prevent method overriding

When a method is declared with `final` keyword, it is called a `final` method. Following is the syntax to declare a method as `final`:

```
final [static] <returnType><methodName> (<argList>) { ... };
```

You declare methods with `final` keyword when it is required to follow the same implementation throughout all the derived classes. Program 4.23 illustrates `final` keyword with a method.

Program 4.23 *(Use of* `final` *method)*

```
/* This program illustrates a final method declaration
in a class. */

class A {
    final void methodA() {
        System.out.println("This is a final method.");
    }
}

class B extends A {
    void methodA() {
              // ERROR! Cannot override a final method.
        System.out.println("Illegal!");
    }
    public static void main(String args[]){
         A a = new  A ();
         B b = new  B ();
         a.methodA();
         b.methodA();
    }
}
```

- A `final` method cannot be overridden.
- Normally, Java resolves calls to methods dynamically, at run-time. This is called late or dynamic binding. However, since `final` methods cannot be overridden, a call to one can be resolved at compile-time. This is called early or static binding.

Case 3: `final` keyword to prevent class inheritance

When a class is declared with `final` keyword, it is called a `final` class. A `final` class cannot be extended (inherited). Program 4.24 illustrates the situation if you want to extend a `final` class.

Program 4.24
(Use of `final` class)

```
/* Program illustrating the use of final class. */

final class Car{    // Declaring a class as final
   int i = 234;
   run(iny k){
      final int speed = k;
   }
}

class Honda extends Car{
     // ERROR: You cannot extend a class!
    void run(){
      System.out.println("Running safely with
           100kmph");
    }

    public static void main(String args[]){
        Car ford = new Car();
        Ford.run();
        Honda honda = new Honda();
        honda.run();
     }
}
```

- If a class is declared as `final` then all the methods present in that class are automatically `final` but variables are not.
- There are two uses of a `final` class:
  (a) As final classes cannot be extended, declaring a class final, you can prevent inheritance. For example, all wrapper classes like `Integer`, `Float`, etc. are final classes. You cannot extend them.

(b) The other use of declaring a class as `final` is to create an immutable class. For example, the predefined class `String`. For such a class, once an object is created, you cannot change its content.

- When a final variable is a reference to an object, then this final variable is called reference final variable. A final variable cannot be re-assigned. But in case of a reference final variable, internal state of the object pointed by that reference variable can be changed. This is not re-assigning. This property of `final` is called *non-transitivity*. Program 4.25 illustrates this property.

Program 4.25 *(Reference* `final` *variable)*

```
/* Java program to demonstrate reference final
variable. */

class RefFinalVar {
    public static void main(String[] args)  {
        final String s = new String("Java");
        System.out.println(s);
        s.append(" is interesting!");
           //Changing internal state of object
        System.out.println(s);
    }
}
```

- Like `final`, there are two more Java reserved keywords called `finally`, and `finalize`. These two will be discussed in the context of exception handling in Chapter 6.

4.4.3 `abstract` Keyword

The keyword `abstract` is used to modify the access like `final` in Java. This modifier can be applied to classes and methods but not variables. It is used to achieve abstraction, which is one of the pillars of object-oriented programming (OOP). Abstraction is a process of hiding the implementation details and showing only functionality to the user. Abstraction lets you focus on what the object does instead of how it does. Following are the different contexts where `abstract` keyword can be used in Java programs:

(a) To partially implement a class. To declare a class abstract, use this general form:

```
abstract class <className> {
       /* body of this class is here. */
}
```

(b) To partially implement a method. To declare an abstract method, use this general form:

```
abstract <type> <methodName>(<argumentList>);
```

Program 4.26 illustrates the use of `abstract` keyword with classes and methods.

Program 4.26 *(`Abstract` class and method)*

```
/* A java program to demonstrate  the use of abstract
keyword. */

abstract class A  {  // Declaring an abstract class
    abstract void m1();    // An abstract method
                                  // declaration: No body
    void m2() { // Regular method also can be
                            // declared in abstract class
        System.out.println("This is a fully
             defined method.");
    }
}
class B extends A  {      // Declaring a class
    void m1() {           // Abstract method must be
                                         // defined here
        System.out.println("B's implementation of
             m1 ...");
    }
     void m2() {          // Regular method also can
                                        // be overridden
        System.out.println("This is overridden in B.");
    }
}
class AbstractDemo  {
    public static void main(String args[])  {
        A a = new A();//ERROR: Object can't be
                            // defined for abstract class
        B b = new B();
        b.m1();
        b.m2();
    }
}
```

- A class which is declared with the `abstract` keyword can have `abstract` and `non-abstract` methods (i.e., method with the body only without its definition).
- Due to the partial implementation, you cannot create object of an abstract class. Any derived class of an abstract class must either implement all of the abstract methods in the super class, or be declared itself `abstract`.
- There are several predefined classes in Java are abstract. For example, `java.lang.Number` is an abstract class. They depend on their sub classes to provide complete implementation.
- The abstract methods are referred to as *sub classer responsibility* because they have no implementation specified in the super class. Hence, a derived class must override them to provide method definition.
- Any class that contains one or more `abstract` methods must also be declared `abstract`.
- If an `abstract` method in a super class is not defined in a derived class, then the derived class is also `abstract` by default.
- An abstract class cannot be used to instantiate object. However, an abstract class can be used to create object reference. This enables Java's approach to run-time polymorphism. Using this approach, it is possible to create a reference to an abstract class, so that it can be used to point to an object of a derived class object.
- The following are illegal combinations of other modifiers for methods with respect to `abstract` modifier:

```
final

abstract synchronized

abstract static

abstract private
```

- In Java, you will never see a class or method declared with both `final` and `abstract` keywords. For classes, `final` is used to prevent inheritance whereas `abstract` classes should have their child classes for complete implementation. In cases of methods, `final` is used to prevent overriding, whereas `abstract` methods need to be overridden in derived classes.

4.5 Run-Time Polymorphism

Concept of polymorphism

At the beginning of this chapter, we said that class inheritance supports code reusability. Class inheritance is not just about reusing classes. It also adds enormous flexibility to the way in which you can program your applications. This is possible with a mechanism called *polymorphism*. The word polymorphism means the ability to assume different forms or shapes. We have learned Java polymorphism mechanism earlier in the form of method overloading and method overriding. We shall learn more about Java polymorphism in this section.

The third type of polymorphism is called run-time polymorphism. This is also termed as *dynamic method dispatch* or *dynamic binding*. In programming terms, run-time polymorphism implies the ability of a single variable of a given type to be used to reference objects of different types and to automatically calls the method specific to the type of object that the variable references.

Dynamic method dispatch or dynamic binding

Let us clarify this with a few more statements. The inheritance concept is to establish "`is-a`" relationship. This means that that every object of the derived class is an object of the super class. For example, say, `Person` is a super class and `Student` is a derived class. Thus, a `Student` "`is-a`" person. Note that the reverse is not true. A person "`is-a`" student is not always true. The "`is-a`" rule provides the *substitution principle*. The principle states that you can use a derived class object whenever the program expects a super class object. And this is exactly the basis of run-time polymorphism concept in Java.

`is-a` relationship

Dynamic binding enables a single method call to behave differently, depending on the type of the object to which the call applies. Let us see how this is possible. Let us consider the multiple single class inheritance as shown in Figure 4.6. Here, `Dog` is the super class and it has three child classes, namely `Dobermann`, `Labrador`, and `Spaniel`. Each class has a method called `bark()`. Thus, `bark()` in child classes are overridden methods.

Now, having these classes, let us create the object instances, which are as follows:

```
Dog aDog = new Dog();

Dobermann dDog = new Dobermann();

Labrador lDog = new Labrador();

Spaniel sDog = new Spaniel();
```

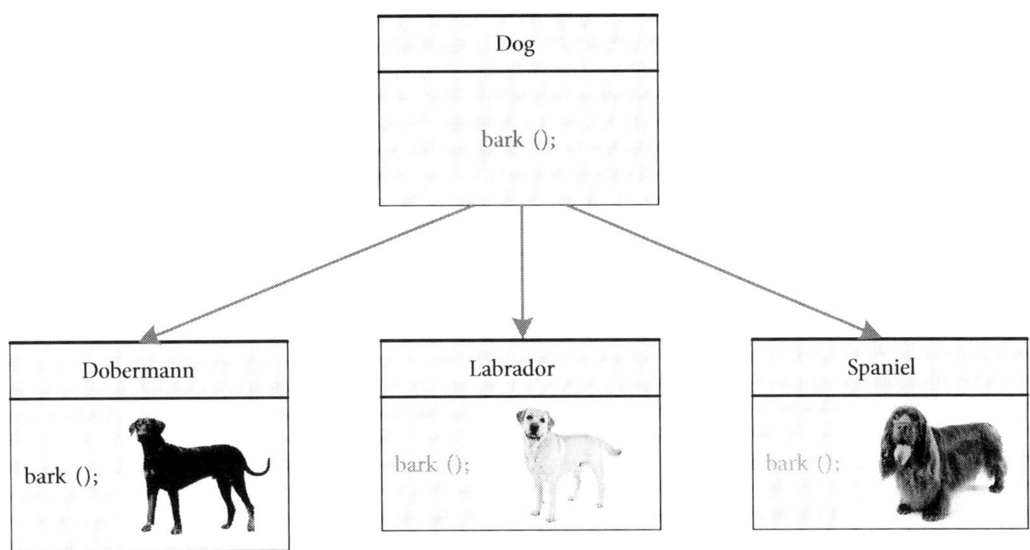

Figure 4.6 Multiple single class inheritance

All these object creations are as usual. The call of the methods for each object is without any more surprise. All thc following calls are acceptable:

```
dDog.bark();        // A Dobermann is barking

lDog.bark();        // A Labrador is barking

sDog.bark;          // A spaniel is barking
```

You know that Java supports `upcasting (i.e., casting)`. The following are also quite acceptable in Java:

```
Dog d;

d = new Dog();            // This is expected

d = new Dobermann();     // It is also absolutely fine

d.bark();               // Who will bark? Yes, Dobermann!

d = new  Labrador();    // Okay, Labrador as well

d.bark();              //  Here, Labrador will bark
```

Thus, in Java, object variables are polymorphic. A variable of type `Dog` can refer to an object of type `Dobermann` or an object of any derived class of the `Dog` class.

We can do the same thing but in a little different manner. Let us consider the following code snippet:

```
Dog aDog[] = new Dog[3];    // An array of objects

// Create three dogs and store them in the array

Dobermann dDog = new Dobermann();

aDog[0] = dDog;    // Upcasting is possible for Labrador

lDog = new Labrador();

aDog[1] = lDog;

Spaniel sDog = new Spaniel();

aDog[2] = sDog;


for (Dog d : aDog)

d.bark();        // All dogs will bark the way they do
```

Here, `aDog[i]` refers to a child class object. And the method will be called accordingly.

- You cannot assign a super class reference to a derived class variable. For example, it is not legal to make the following assignment:

```
Dobermann d = aDog[i];        // ERROR!
```

The reason is clear: not all dogs are Dobermans.

You can try Program 4.27 to test your understanding.

Program 4.27
(Run-time polymorphism)

```
/* The following program illustrates the dynamic method
dispatch in Java. */
class A {
     void callMe() {
       System.out.println("I am from A");
    }
}
class B extends A {
    void callMe() {    // Override callMe() method
         System.out.println("I am from B");
    }
}
```

```
class C extends B {
    void callme() {  // Override callMe() method
        System.out.println("I am from C");
    }
}
class WhoAmI {
     public void static main (String args [  ] ) {
         A  a[] = new A[3];
         A x = new A (); a[0] = x;
         B y = new B (); a[1] = y;
         C z = new C (); a[2] = z;
         for (A r: a)
           // For each object in the collection a
           r.callMe();
           // Bind the method dynamically
     }
}
```

If a super class contains a method overridden by a derived class, then when different types of objects are referred through a super class reference variable, different versions of the method are executed.

- Dynamic method dispatch is the mechanism using which a call to an overridden method is resolved at run-time, instead of at compile-time.
- When an overridden method is called through the reference of a super class, Java determines which version (super/derived class) of that method is to be executed based on the type of the object being referred to at the time the call occurs. Thus, this determination is done at run-time.
- At run-time, which version of an overridden method will be executed depends on the type of the object being referred to rather than the type of the reference variable.
- Note that a super class reference variable can refer to a derived class object. This is known as upcasting. But, the reverse is not true. Java uses the fact of upcasting to resolve calls to overridden methods at run-time.
- When the program runs and uses dynamic binding to call a method, then the Java Virtual Machine (JVM) must call the version of the method that is appropriate for the actual type of the object to which it refers. Suppose, there is an inheritance chain: `A`→`B`→`C`→`D`. If the class `D` defines a method `m()`, that method is called. If not, then `D`'s super class is searched for a method `m()`, and so on.

- You can override only methods, not the variables (i.e., data members), so run-time polymorphism cannot be achieved by data members. See Program 4.28. In this program, both the class `A` (super class) and `B` (derived class) have a common variable `x`. Now, we make object of class `B` referred by `a` is of type of class `A`. Since variables are not overridden, so the reference `a.x` will always refer to data member of super class.

Program 4.28
(Binding with data member)

```
/* This Java program illustrates the fact that dynamic
binding is not applicable to data members. */

class A  {
    int x = 55;
}
class B extends A {
    int x = -99;
}

class BindingTest {
    public static void main(String args[]) {
        A a = new B(); // Object of type B is created
        System.out.println(a.x);
        // Data member of class A will be referred to here
    }
}
```

Static binding versus dynamic binding

Following are the key differences between the static binding and dynamic binding:

Static binding and dynamic binding

- If the method is `private`, `static`, `final`, or a constructor, then the compiler knows exactly which method to call. This is called *static binding*.
- Static binding is done during compile-time while dynamic binding is done during run-time.

4.6 Universal Super Class

Default super class of any class

One important tenet of OOP is that classes can be built on other classes (Figure 4.7). A program will usually contain many classes including their "`is-a`" relations, that is, inheritances. We say that a class that builds on another class extends it. All the classes that you define are sub classes by default. Java defines a class called `Object`, which acts as a *universal super class*. If you define a class, then automatically this new class extends the universal super class `Object`. This universal super class is defined in `java.lang.Object` in Java API.

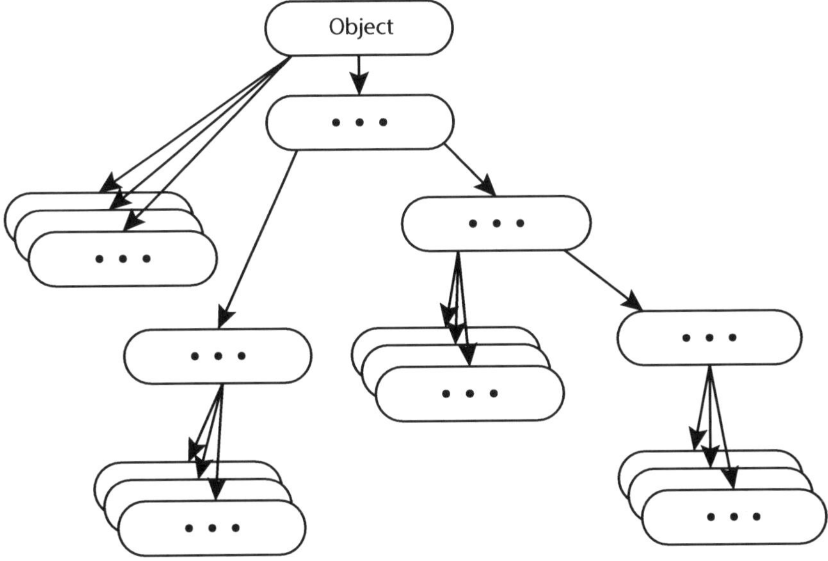

Figure 4.7 Class hierarchy in a Java application program

Why universal super class?

Because every class in Java extends `Object`, it is important to be familiar with the services provided by the `Object` class. Some of the important usages of this universal super class are listed here and will be discussed in subsequent subsections.

1. Casting objects
2. Object management activities
3. Generic programming
4. Method with variable list of arguments
5. Wrapper classes

4.6.1 Casting Object

Since the `Object` is a super class of all other classes, this implies that a reference variable of type `Object` can refer to an object of any other class. For example, if `Person` is a class, then we can write the following:

```
Object obj = new Person(); // Object is the super class
```

Notice that parent class reference variable can refer to the child class object, known as *upcasting*. Program 4.29 is an example which explains the upcasting of `Object` type variable reference can help you to store several objects into a single array.

Program 4.29 *(Arrays with different types of objects)*

```
/* This program illustrates how upcasting can help to
maintain an array with heterogeneous object types. */

class Person { }     // A user defined helper class
class Point { }     // Another user defined helper class

class HeterogeneousArray { // Driver class
    public static void main(String args[]) {
        Object obj[] = new Object[3];
          // An array of size 3
        Object x = new Person();
          // Create an object of type Person
        Object y = new Point();
          // Create an object of type Point
        Object z = new Person();
          // Create another object of type Person

        // Loading the array with object elements
        Obj[0] = x;  // Stores the reference of the
                              // object x (type Person)
        Obj[1] = y;  // Stores the reference of the
                               // object y (type Point)
        Obj[2] = x;  // Stores the reference of the
                              // object z (type Person)
    }
}
```

A variable of type `Object` is only useful as a generic holder for arbitrary values. To do anything specific with the value, you need to have some knowledge about the original type and then apply a cast. For example:

```
Person p = (Person) obj; // Casting an object
                                  // to a type
```

- All values of any class type can be held in variables of type `Object`. For example, the following are all legal:

```
class Student { }
     // Assume Student class is defined
     // with its field and methods
Student s = new Student();
class Date { }
     // Assume Date class is defined
     // with its field and methods
Date d = new Date();
class Employee { }
     //Assume Employee class is defined
     //with its field and methods
Employee e = new Employee();

// Following are all okay initialization
Object obj = s;
Object obj = d;
Object obj = e;
```

- A type `Object` can reference a string literal. This is because in Java a string is an object of class `String`. Thus, the following is legal:

```
Object obj = "Joy with Java";
```

- The following initializations, however, are not legal. This is because numbers, characters, and Boolean values are not objects.

```
Object obj = 555;   // An integer is not an object
Object obj = false;// A Boolean literal is also not
```

- All array types, no matter whether they are arrays of objects or arrays of primitive types, are class types that derive from `Object`. For example, the following statements are acceptable in Java:

```
Student[] s = new Student[10];
Object a = s;          // OK
a = new int[10];       // Array of integers also object
```

4.6.2 Object Management Activities

Since `Object` is a class, like other class it has many methods. There are seven public methods and two protected methods in it. Table 4.3 lists the methods in `Object` class. Since any class inherits the `Object` class, it means that all these methods are available in every object.

Table 4.3 The methods in `Object` class

Method	Description
`public String toString()`	Returns the `String` object that describes the current object.
`public boolean equals(Object)`	Compares the object passed as an argument with the reference to the current object and returns true if they are equal.
`public final Class getClass()`	Returns an object of type `Class` that identifies the class of the current object. We will discuss a little more about this later in this chapter.
`public int hashCode()`	Calculates a hash code value for an object and returns it as type `int`. The `hashcode` values are used in classes defined in the package `java.util` for storing objects in hash tables.
`public final void notify()`	This is used to wake up a thread associated with the current object. This will be discussed in Chapter 7.
`public final void notifyAll()`	This is used to wake up all threads associated with the current object. This will also be discussed in Chapter 7.
`public final void wait()`	Causes a thread to wait for a change in the current object. This will also be discussed in Chapter 7.
`protected Object clone()`	Creates and returns the exact copy (clone) of this object.
`protected void finalize()`	This method is called to clean up when an object is destroyed.

`getClass()`, `notify()`, `notifyAll()`, and `wait()` cannot be overridden in your own class definitions; they are fixed with the keyword `final` in the class definition for `Object`.

Some of the methods listed in Table 4.3 are discussed in brief in the following:

toString() method

The `toString()` method provides string representation of an object and is used to convert an object to string. The default `toString()` method for class `Object` returns a string consisting of the name of the class of which the object is an instance, the at-sign character @, and the unsigned hexadecimal representation of the hash code of the object. Following is an example:

```
Student s = new Student();
// Below two statements are equivalent
System.out.println(s);
System.out.println(s.toString());
```

You may note that whenever you try to print any object reference, then internally `toString()` method is called. It is always recommended to override `toString()` method to get your own string representation of object. For an example, here is an implementation of the `toString()` method for the `Person` class. Assume that the class has defined with three fields: `name`, `address`, `dob`:

```
public String toString()  {
     return "Person[Name=" + name
          + ",Address=" + address
          + ",DoB=" + dob
          + "]";
}
```

getClass() method

This method is used to identify the class of an object. If this method is called for an object, it returns `Class` object giving the name of the class to which the object belongs. In the class `Class` (we shall discuss about the class `Class` in this chapter later), `getName()` is there, which returns the name of the class. For example, let us refer to Program 4.30.

Program 4.30 *(Use of getClass() method)*

```
/* This program demonstrates the working of getClass()
method. */

public class GetClassTest {
    public static void  main(String[] args) {
        Object obj  = new String("Joy with Java");
        Class c = obj.getClass();  // Getting the class
        System.out.println("Class of Object obj is : "
                        + c.getName());
                          // Getting the name of the class
    }
}
```

As another example, refer to Program 4.29, where an array stores a variety of objects. You can easily guess the purpose of the following statements:

```
Class c = obj[i].getClass();

System.out.println(c.getName());
```

Alternatively,

```
System.out.println(obj[i].getClass().getName());
```

will produce the same result.

`hashCode()` method

For every object, JVM generates a unique number which is a hash code. It returns distinct integers for distinct objects. It converts the internal address of an object to an integer by using a hash algorithm. The `hashCode()` method is native because in Java it is impossible to find address of an object, so it uses native languages like C/C++ to find address of the object. Such a method is used to search an object in a collection of objects. It is recommended to override the `hashCode()` such that for every object we generate a unique number. Program 4.31 illustrates a use of the `hashCode()` method.

Program 4.31 *(Use of `hashCode()` method)*

```
/* Java program to demonstrate working of  hashCode()
method. */

public class Student {
    int rollNo;

    public static void main(String args[]) {
            Student s = new Student();
           System.out.println(s.toString());
           System.out.println(s.hashCode());
    }
}
```

`clone()` method

The `clone ()` method returns a new object that is exactly the same as the object. For example, consider the following code:

```
Person q =(Person) p.clone();
```

Here, `p` and `q` are two objects, identical to each other.

- Note that `p` and `q` are not the same object. It is not true that `p` and `q` are the two reference variables and point to an instance of an object.
- If objects are to be cloned, the class must implement the `Cloneable` interface. We will discuss interfaces in Chapter 5.

`finalize()` method

This method is called just before an object is garbage collected. It is called by the Java automatic garbage collector mechanism on an object when the garbage collector determines that there are no more references to that object. You should override `finalize()` method to dispose system resources, perform clean-up activities and minimize memory leaks. Program 4.32 shows how `finalize()` method can be used in your class.

Program 4.32 *(Use of* `finalize()` *method)*

```
/* The following program demonstrates the working of
finalize() method. */

public class FinalizeTest {
    public static void main(String[] args) {
        FinalizeTest t = new FinalizeTest ();
        System.out.println(t.hashCode());

        t = null;  // Object is no more exist, but
                              // still it occupies space

        System.gc();
                // Explicitly calling garbage collector
        System.out.println("Space is freed up by Java's
          automatic GC");
    }
    protected void finalize() {
                // This method will be called implicitly
        System.out.println("finalize method is
          called");
    }
}
```

4.6.3 Generic Method and Class

It will be a great achievement if you can write a method, which will work for every type of data! That is, make a method generic. If you are experienced with C++, you may recall the *concept of template* in C++ for generic programming. Java is in no way behind C++. It also facilitates a programmer to have generic programming. In Java, you can define a method as generic; a class also can be made generic. Let us learn how you can do that.

Generic method

Here, the key concept is that an array of objects of a class type can be converted to an array of `Object`. For example, a `Student[]` array can be passed to a method that expects an `Object[]` array. That conversion is useful for generic programming.

A simple example illustrates the concept of writing a method using generic programming. Suppose, you want to find the index of an element in an array. You may try this method and include any class.

```
static int find(Object[] a, Object key)  {
    for (int i = 0; i < a.length; i++)
        if (a[i].equals(key)) return i;
    return -1;      // Otherwise, not found
}
```

This is a generic situation, and by writing the code for objects, you can reuse it (the `find()`) for any type of class, for example, `Student`, `Date`, or whatever).

Generic class

A generic class is a class whose method can deal with any type of object in it. Like C++, you use <> to specify parameter types in generic class creation.

Following is the general syntax to declare a generic class:

```
[Access] class <ClassName> <<Type1> [, <Type2>, ...]>    {
    ... body of the class
}
```

Following is the syntax in Java to create objects of a generic class:

```
<ClassName>  <Type><<Type1>  [,  <Type2>,  ...]>  obj  =  new
<ClassName>  ><<Type1> [, <Type2>, ...]> (<Values>)
```

Program 4.33 gives a simple example to define a generic class with one type and its use in main class.

Program 4.33 *(Simple generic class)*

```
/* A Simple Java program to show working of user
defined generic class. */
class GenericClass<Type>  {
                        // Use < > to specify class type
    Type obj;     // An object of type Type is declared
    GenericClass(Type obj) {
                     // Constructor of the generic class
        this.obj = obj;
    }
    public Type getObject()  {    // Method in a class
        return this.obj;
    }
}

class GenericClassTest  {
                       // Driver class to test the above
    public static void main (String[] args) {
        GenericClass <Integer> iObj = new GenericClass
           <Integer>(15);    // A class with Integer type
        System.out.println(iObj.getObject());

        GenericClass <String> sObj = new GenericClass
           <String>("Java");
                       // Another class with String type
        System.out.println(sObj.getObject());
    }
}
```

- You cannot use primitive data types, namely `int`, `short`, `long`, `float`, `double`, `boolean`, `char` in case of type specification in < >. Instead, you can use the wrapper class to tackle such type of values.
- You can also pass multiple parameters in type specification to design your generic classes. Program 4.34 illustrates a generic class with specification of two types of class.

Program 4.34 (Generic class with multiple types)

```
/* This program illustrates multiple  type parameters
in generic class. */

class GC2<T1, T2>  {
    T1 obj1;      // An object of type T1
    T2 obj2;      // An object of type T2

    GC2(T1 obj1, T2 obj2)      {    // Constructor
        this.obj1 = obj1;
        this.obj2 = obj2;
    }
}
   public void print()     {     // A local method in GC2
        System.out.println(obj1);
        System.out.println(obj2);
    }
}

class GC2Test {         // Main class using generic class
    public static void main (String[] args)  {
        GC2 <String, Integer> obj = new GC2<String,
          Integer>("GC", 9);
        obj.print();
    }
}
```

4.6.4 Methods with Variable List of Arguments

In C, there are some standard methods like `printf(...)`, `scanf(...)`, etc. which take variable number of arguments. In C program you can also define a method with a variable number of arguments to be passed. It is interesting to see if you can do similar jobs in Java.

One solution can be to write as many overloading methods. But this is inefficient. There are some elegant ideas that Java developer provides you to write a method that will accept an arbitrary number of arguments when it is called. This feature in Java is called *varargs method* also called *variable-arity method*. There are three ways to do this:

(a) Using an array
(b) Using ellipsis (three dots)
(c) Using Object class

Let us examine each idea in the following discussions.

Varargs method using array

This is the simplest method. Here, you can define a varargs method with an array (of any type) as its argument. Store the values which you want to pass to a method in an array and then pass the array to the method. That's all! This approach is illustrated in Program 4.35.

Program 4.35 *(Varargs method using array)*

```
/* This program demonstrates a varargs method using
an array to pass a variable number of arguments to a
method.  */
class VarargsMethod1 {
     static void varargsMethod1(int v[])  {
         System.out.print("Number of args: " + v.length
           +" Elements: ");
         for(int x : v)
             System.out.print(x + " ");
         System.out.println();
    }
    public static void main(String args[])  {
        // Following arrays are created for test...
          int x[] = { 1, 3, 5, 7 };
          int y[] = { 2, 4};
          int z[] = { };
          varargsMethod1 (x);
                      // Passed 4 values to the method
          varargsMethod1 (y);
                      // Passed 2 values to the method
          varargsMethod1 (y); // Passed no value to
                      // Passed no value to the method
    }
}
```

Varargs method using ellipsis

The second method is similar but with a different syntax which is special in Java. The syntax to define varargs method with this approach is as follows:

```
<AccessSpec><ReturnType><MethodName>(<Type>...
<arrayName>) {  . . . // Method body

}
```

Program 4.36 illustrates the approach.

Program 4.36 *(Varargs method using ellipsis)*

```
/* This program demonstrates varargs method with
ellipses. */

class VarargsMethod2 {
    //Defining a varargs method
    static void varargsMethod2(int ...v) {
       System.out.println("Number of arguments: " +
          v.length);
        for (int i: v) // For each item i in array v
            System.out.print(i + " ");
        System.out.println();
    }

    public static void main(String args[])     {
      // Calling the varargs method with variable
                                            // arguments
      varargsMethod2 (9);               // One parameter
      varargsMethod2 (1, -2, 3, -4); // Four parameters
        varargsMethod2 ();             // No parameter
    }
}
```

- The two approaches need values to be packed into an array prior to calling.
- Command line argument is also varargs method for the `main()` in your Java program.
- As it is an array to be passed, all values that can be passed are of the same type.
- A method can have "normal" parameters along with a variable-length parameter. However, the variable-length parameter must be the last parameter declared by the method. For example, the following is a valid varargs method declaration:

```
int varMethod(int a, int b, double c, float ... v) {  }
```

In this case, the first three arguments used in a call to `varMethod ( )` are matched with the first three parameters. Then, any remaining arguments are assumed to belong to `v`.

- You can overload a method that takes a variable-length argument. Program 4.37 demonstrates how a varargs method can be overloaded.

Program 4.37 *(Overloading varargs)*

```
/* This program demonstrates the overloading of a
varargs method. */

class OverloadingVarargs {
      static void varTest(int ... v) {
                                   //Overloading method 1
           System.out.print("Arg(int ...):" + "Number
                of args: " + v.length + " Contents: ");
           for(int x : v)
               System.out.print(x + " ");
           System.out.println();
       }
     static void varTest(boolean ... v) {
          //Overloading method 2
           System.out.print("Arg(boolean ...) " +
                "Number of args: " + v.length +
                                         " Contents: ");
           for(boolean x : v)
               System.out.print(x + " ");
           System.out.println();
      }

       static void varTest(String msg, int ... v) {
           //Overloading method 3
           System.out.print("Arg(String, int ...): "
                + msg + v.length + " Contents: ");
           for(int x : v)
               System.out.print(x + " ");
           System.out.println();
       }

      public static void main(String args[])  {
           varTest(1, 2, 3);
           varTest("Testing: ", 10, 20);
           varTest(true, false, false);
      }
}
```

- The varargs parameter must be the last. For example, the following declaration is incorrect:

```
int varMethod(int a, float ... v, double c) {  }
```

- There is one more restriction to be aware of: there must be only one varargs parameter. For example, the following declaration is also invalid:

```
int varMethod (int ...a, double ...b) { }
```

The attempt to declare the second varargs parameter is illegal.

- Sometimes, unexpected errors can result when overloading a method that takes a variable length argument. These errors involve ambiguity because it is possible to create an ambiguous call to an overloaded varargs method. For example, if you exclude overloading method 3 and change the `main()` method as follows, then there will be a compilation error.

```
public static void main(String args[])  {
    varTest(1, 2, 3);  // Okay
    varTest();  // Compile-time error
                // as it does not match with anyone
    varTest(true, false, false); // Okay

}
```

Varargs method using Object class

This is possibly the most elegant approach to implement the varargs method in your Java program. It uses the ellipsis and, in addition, also uses the `Object` type. For example, to define a varargs method, your method declaration may take the following form:

```
public static void methodName(Object ... obj)  {

// Body of the method

 }
```

You may note the restriction that the method can have zero or more parameters preceding this, but this must be the last for reasons you have already learned. Let's consider Program 4.38 to demonstrate the process. This program defines a varargs method which takes any type of values with any count.

Program 4.38 *(Varargs method with Object)*

```
/* This program demonstrates the varargs method taking
any type of arguments as well as any number. */

class VarargsMethod3  {
       public static void varargsMethod3(Object ...
           obj) {
           for(Object o : obj)
              System.out.print(" "+o);
           System.out.println();
      }
      public static void main(String[] args) {
           varargsMethod3( 1, "String", 2.3, true);
                // Four arguments
           varargsMethod3 ();
                // No arguments
           varargsMethod3 (15, 25, 35, 45, 55);
                // Five arguments
      }
}
```

4.6.5 Wrapper Classes

All values of any class type can be held in variables of type `Object`. For example, if `Student` is a class already defined, then:

```
Object obj = new Student();
```

`String` values are objects. Hence, the following is also valid:

```
Object obj = "Hello";
```

However, any data of primitive type such as numbers, characters, and boolean values cannot be assigned as object reference. This is because all the values of such type of data are not objects. Hence, the following statements in a class will report compilation error:

```
Object obj1 = 5;

Object obj2 = false;
```

Now, let us learn how the primitive type of data can be converted into wrapper classes and then we can convert them into objects.

In Chapter 2 (Section 2.5.3), you have learned basic forms of the wrapper classes, namely `Byte`, `Character`, `Integer`, `Long`, `Short`, `Double`, `Float`, `Boolean`, etc. They are also called as *object wrappers*. An object wrapper wraps a primitive value to an object. We shall learn how a primitive value can be converted to an object and how a wrapper object can return a primitive value, which it stores. Finally, we will see an interesting application of wrapper objects. Table 4.4 lists some methods related to wrapper classes.

Table 4.4 Methods for to-and-from transformation

Wrapper class	Constructor	Unwrap method
`Character`	`Character(char c)`	`char charValue()`
`Boolean`	`Boolean (boolean b)` `Boolean(String s)`	`boolean booleanValue()`
`Byte`	`Byte (byte b)` `Byte (String s)`	`byte byteValue()`
`Short`	`Short (short i)` `Short (String s)`	`short shortValue()`
`Integer`	`Integer (int i)` `Integer (String s)`	`int intValue()`
`Long`	`Long (long l)` `Long (String s)`	`long longValue()`
`Double`	`Double (double d)` `Double (String s)`	`double doubleValue()`

Converting primitive value to wrapper object

Each wrapper class has constructors (column 2, Table 4.4). You can use the constructor to wrap a primitive value to an object. Following are two examples for converting `float` value to corresponding wrapper objects:

```
Float fObj = new Float(12.345);

Float fObj = new Float ("4.6E-4");
                                  // 4.6x10^-4  in string form
```

- String to number exception error may result if you don't include a number. For example, see the following:

```
Integer i = new Integer(123);      // Okay

Integer j = new Integer("123");    // Okay

Integer k = new Integer("Java");   // Error
```

Getting primitive value from wrapper object

For each wrapper class, there are methods (column 3, Table 4.4). You can use these methods for wrapper objects to unwrap primitive values from objects. Following are two examples for getting `float` value from corresponding wrapper objects:

```
float f = fObj.floatValue();
```

- All the wrapper classes are `final`. This means that you cannot override the `toString()` method in these classes or change the value in them.
- All of the numeric type wrappers inherit the abstract class `Number`. `Number` declares methods that return the value of an object in each of the different number formats.
- Each wrapper class is defined in `java.lang` package with a number of methods. Table 4.5 contains the list for `Integer` class. For other classes, they are equivalent.

Table 4.5 `java.lang.Integer` class

Method	Description
`int intValue()`	Returns the value of this `Integer` object as an `int` (overrides the `intValue` method in the `Number` class).
`static String toString(int i)`	Returns a new `String` object representing the specified integer in base 10.
`static String toString(int i, int radix)`	Lets you return a representation of the number `i` in the base specified by the radix parameter.
`static int parseInt(String s)`	Returns the `Integer`'s value, assuming the specified `String` represents an integer in base 10.
`static int parseInt(String s, int radix)`	Returns the `Integer`'s value, assuming the specified `String` represents an integer in the base specified by the radix parameter.
`static Integer valueOf(String s)`	Returns a new `Integer` object initialized to the integer's value, assuming the specified `String` represents an integer in base 10.
`static Integer valueOf(String s, int radix)`	Returns a new `Integer` object initialized to the integer's value, assuming the specified `String` represents an integer in the base specified by the radix parameter.
`Number parse(String s)`	Returns the numeric value, assuming the specified `String` represents a number.

Some applications of wrapper objects

There are many applications and it is not possible to cover all of them. Some of the interesting applications are discussed in the following:

Storing a primitive value as an object

We started our discussion with wrapper class that a numeric value cannot be assigned to an object of class `Object`. Following piece of code illustrates how this can be done:

```
Integer iObj = new Integer(123);

            // Wrap an integer value to a wrapper object

Object obj = new Object[5];  // Create an array of object

Obj[0] = iObj;    // Store the integer in the array
```

Conversion from one primitive value to another

You can change an integer value, for example, to `String` or to a `float`. Program 4.39 illustrates how you can convert a `byte` value to `string` and `float` types.

Program 4.39 *(Type conversion with wrapper classes)*

```
/* The following program demonstrates the conversion of
a primitive type to another. */

class TypeConversionTest {
   public static void main(String[] args)   {
       Byte bObj = new Byte("10");
           // Create a byte object
       String s = bObj.toString();    // Byte to String
       System.out.println("Byte in string " + s);
       float f = bObj.floatValue();  // Byte to float
       System.out.println("Byte to float " + f);
   }
}
```

Call by reference parameter passing

It is impossible to write a Java method that increments an integer inside the method and then the results get affected to the value passed to it. This is because parameters in Java methods are always passed by values (this is unlike in C/ C++, where you can pass values by references). Let us consider Program 4.40.

Program 4.40
(Call-by-value example)

```
/* The following program demonstrates the call by value
passing in Java. */

class CallByValuePass {
     int i = 456;
     public static int increment(int x) {
                         // It is a pass by value method
         return(x++);    // Work on copy only
     }

     public static void main(String[] args) {
        int a = 3;       // Value under test
        System.out.println("Value of a before call "
           + a);
        increment(a);  // Call method to increment a
        System.out.println("Value of a after call "
           + a);
     }
}
```

Maths wrapper classes are immutable

Let us see if we can use the wrapper classes to implement methods that can modify a numeric parameter. A wrapper class based implementation of the program 4.40 is shown in Program 4.41. If you run the program, you will see that it also does not have any effect. This can be explained as follows: Now `a` and `x` are references to the same object. It seems that if you update `x`, then `a` would also be updated. However, `Integer` objects are *immutable*: the information contained inside the wrapper can't be changed. The statement `x++` is also not applicable to `Integer` objects. Thus, you cannot use these wrapper classes to create methods that modify numeric parameters.

Program 4.41
(Wrapper class approach)

```
/* The following program investigates the feasibility
of call by reference passing using wrapper class. */

class CallByReferencePass {
     int i = 456;
     public static int increment(Integer x) {
        return(x++);    // Not applicable for Integer x
     }

     public static void main(String[] args) {
        int a = 3;      // Value under test
```

```
        Integer i = new Integer(a);
                    // Wrap the value as wrapper object
        System.out.println("Value of a before call "
            + i.intValue());
        increment(i);  // Call method by passing object
        System.out.println("Value of i after call "
            + i.intValue());
    }
}
```

So, this didn't work for you. Can you think any other solution? You can try if Program 4.42 works for you.

Program 4.42 *(Call by reference in Java)*

```
/* The following program demonstrates the call by
reference using wrapper class. */

class IntegerWrapper {      // Create a wrapper class
     int i;
     IntegerWrapper(i) {  // Constructor initializing i
        this.i = i;
      }
}

class CallByReferenceTest {
     public static IntegerWrapper increment
           (IntegerWrapper x) {
         x.i = x.i + 1;
                    // Increment the member of object x
         return((x);       // Return the object
     }

     public static void main(String[] args) {
        int i = 456;          // Value under test
        // Create wrapper object for i
        IntegerWrapper x = new IntegerWrapper(i);
        System.out.println("Value of i before call "
           + x.i);
        x = increment(x);    // Increment the value of i
           via x
        System.out.println("Incremented value of i "
           + x.i);
    }
}
```

I hope you have understood why this works for you. Here, we pass the object (and this is a reference variable, just like a pointer in C/ C++). `IntegerWrapper` is not immutable as the wrapper class `Integer`. Since this is a tricky business in Java, I would like to clarify the concept with three more examples. For the first example, consider the `swap(a, b)` function that will interchange the value between `a` and `b`. This function interchanges two integer values whose code is given as follows:

```
void swap (int a, int b) {
    int temp;    // Declare a temporary variable
    temp = a;    // Copy a into temp
    a  = b;      // Copy b to a
    b = temp;    // Copy temp (that is old a) to b
}
```

You can easily try the same with Java class and then test print the values of `a` and `b` before and after the call of `swap(a, b)` method. Obviously, it did not work for you. We shall see how we can apply our methods for two other objects.

Program 4.43 defines a class `Student` and creates two objects `s1` and `s2` and then swaps the two objects (that is, the value of `s1` becomes the value of `s2` and vice-versa).

Program 4.43 *(Swap test 1: a working case)*

```
/* This program demonstrates the working of swap
function in Java. */

class Student {
        int rollNo;
        Student(int rollNo) {
                this.rollNo = rollNo;
        }
}

class SwapTest1 {
    public static void swap(Student s1, Student s2) {
        int temp = s1.rollNo;
        s1.rollNo = s2.rollNo;
        s2.rollNo = temp;
    }
```

```
    public static void main (String[] args) {
        Student s1 = new Student(101);
                                        // s1 with RollNo 101
        Student s2 = new Student(202);
                                        // s2 with RollNo 202
        swap(s1, s2);   // Call interchange of s1 and s2
        System.out.println("Roll No. of s1 " +
            s1.rollNo);
        System.out.println("Roll No. of s2 " +
            s2.rollNo);
    }
}
```

You will see that this program works fine. Java provides call-by-value only. But when you change an object member here, it will be referred to object, which has the single instance only. This is why it works.

Now, let us see another situation. I have changed the `Student` class definition a little and `swap(...)` function itself. See Program 4.44.

Program 4.44 *(Swap test 2: a failed case)*

```
/* This program demonstrates the working of swap method
in Java. */

class Student {
        int rollNo;
        float marks;
        Student(int rollNo, float marks) {
                this.rollNo = rollNo;
                this.marks = marks;
        }
}
class SwapTest2 {
      public static void swap(Student s1, Student s2) {
        Student temp = s1;     // Copy object s1 to temp
        s1 = s2;               // Copy s2 to s1
        s2 = temp;             // Copy temp to s2
    }
    public static void main (String[] args) {
        Student s1 = new Student(101, 99.96);
        Student s2 = new Student(202, 71.45);
        swap(s1, s2);   // Call interchange of s1 and s2
```

```
        System.out.println("Student1 : " + s1.rollNo +
          "  " + s1.marks);
         System.out.println("Student2 : " + s2.rollNo +
          "  " + s2.marks);
    }
}
```

You might be surprised to see the result that this did not work. It should not work for obvious reasons: because of the call-by-value effect. In this swap function, the values, `s1` and `s2`, are passed to the method only as values, not their references. Hence, whatever are the changes are inside the swap method, all copies are local to only the method.

Here is the solution to the failed case: Yes, we should use wrapper class as we did in Program 4.42. Let us see Program 4.45.

Program 4.45 *(Swap test 3: object wrapping method)*

```
/* This program demonstrates the working of swap method
in Java. */

class Student {
       int rollNo;
       float marks;
       Student(int rollNo, float marks) {
             this.rollNo = rollNo;
             this.marks = marks;
       }
}
// A Wrapper over class that is used for swapping
class WrapperObject {
   Student s;
   WrapperObject(Student s)   {this.s = s;}
}

class SwapTest3 {
  public static void swap(WrapperObject ws1,
         WrapperObject ws2) {
    Student temp = ws1.s;    // Copy s of ws1 to temp
    ws1.s = ws2.s;          // Copy s of ws2 to s of ws1
    ws2.s = temp;          // Copy temp to s of ws2
    }
```

```
    public static void main (String[] args) {
          Student s1 = new Student(101, 99.96f);
          Student s2 = new Student(202, 71.45f);
          WrapperObject ws1 = new WrapperObject(s1);
                // Wrap s1
          WrapperObject ws2 = new WrapperObject(s2);
                // Wrap s2
          swap(ws1, ws2);
                      // Call interchange of ws1 ans ws2
          System.out.println("Student1 : " +
                ws1.s.rollNo + " " + ws1.s.marks);
          System.out.println("Student2 : " +
                ws2.s.rollNo + " " + ws2.s.marks);
    }
}
```

- The method as discussed in Program 4.45 works even if you do not know the class composition. You need not have any access to members of the classes whose objects are to be swapped.
- You can define a universal swap method which will work for any type of object. To do that, you can define a swap method with arguments of type `Object` class and then upcast your objects to be swapped to class `Object`.

Summary

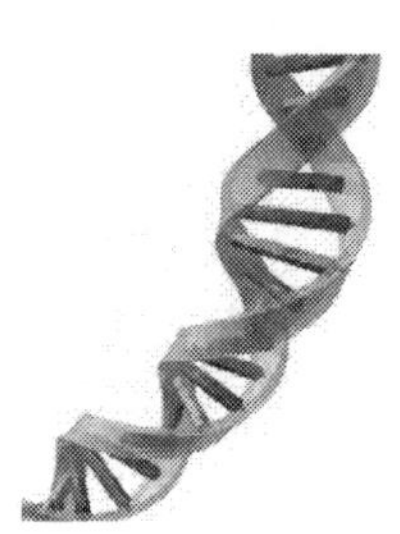

This chapter covers all the aspects of the inheritance feature in Java. It starts with a basic discussion on the concept of inheritance and different types of inheritance that a programmer can think in the program. The class hierarchy, constructor chaining, and method overriding mechanisms are illustrated in depth. The four access specifications regarding information access/ hiding are then discussed in detail. Special Java keywords related to inheritance and their uses are illustrated. Run-time polymorphism and dynamic binding concepts are then discussed. Universal super class and object management activities are keys to many advanced level coding, and are included in this chapter. Brief discussions on generic method and polymorphic method with a variable list of arguments are also included. Finally, the chapter concludes with a highlight of wrapper classes in Java.

FAQs

4.1 What is inheritance?

4.2 What are the different types of inheritance in Java?

4.3 What is method overriding?

4.4 What are the differences between method overloading ad method overriding?

4.5 Can you override a private or static method in Java?

4.6 What are the different access specifiers known in Java?

4.7 What is the difference between `this` and `super` keywords in Java?

4.8 What is the difference between `this()` and `super()` in Java?

4.9 What is run-time polymorphism or dynamic method dispatch?

4.10 Why does Java not support multiple inheritance from classes?

4.11 What is object cloning in Java?

4.12 Can a top level class be private or protected?

4.13 What is an abstract class? Can it be a super class?

4.14 How can you prevent a method from overriding it in its derived class?

4.15 Can the scope of an overridden method in a sub class be changed in its super class?

The answers to these questions and other problems in this chapter are available at www.cambridge.org/9781009211918. You might have many questions like these. You can post your questions in the discussion forum at https://cse.iitkgp.ac.in/~dsamanta/joywithjava/page8.php.

Programs for Practice

4.1 Define a class "Person" with "name," "age," and "cellNo" as the fields in it. Declare the filed "cellNo" as final. Define an appropriate parametrized constructor to initialize an object of this class. Also, define a method `print()` to print the state of an object.

Derive a class "Student" from the class "Person" with fields "regnNo" and an array to store marks in four examinations the individual has qualified. You should have an overridden constructor and `print()` method in this class.

Derive another class "Employee" from the class "Person." Add two fields: "employer" as `String` and "salary" as double. You should have an overridden constructor and `print()` method in this class as well.

Define the main class which will store 10 objects of different classes. Traverse the array of objects to print each object.

4.2 Define a class, say "Array1D," to maintain a 1D array of numbers of a length, initialize the array and print the array.

Define another class, say "Array2D," derived from the class "Array1D" as its super class. The "Array2D" class is an array of arrays and it maintains an array of 1D array objects. Define appropriate constructor(s) to initialize and print an object of this type.

Define another class, say "Array3D," derived from the class "Array2D" as its parent class. The "Array3D" class is an array of arrays and it maintains an array of "2DArray" objects. Define appropriate constructor(s) to initialize and print an object of this type.

Write a main class to create objects of the different class and test the working of objects.

4.3 This program shows how code can be shared from on class to another.

Consider a class to read a text from keyboard and store the text in an array. Name this class as Input.

Write another class Output which extends the class Input and it counts the number of characters, words, and sentences in the text entered.

Next extend the class Output to Special, which will compare two texts and find out the count of common words in them.

4.4 This program is to test if you can override public, private, and protected methods. Also, the program examines if a sub class can access default, public, private, and protected data.

```
class Parent {
  int i = 555;
  public String = "Parent";
  private  double x = 1.213
  protected int j = 100;
  public void mPublic() {
        System.out.println("I am from public method of Super");
  }
  private void mPrivate() {
        System.out.println("I am from private method of Super");
  }
  protected void mProtected() {
        System.out.println("I am from protected method of Super");
  }
}

class Child extends Parent {
  public void mPublic() {
        System.out.println("I am from public method of Child");
  }
  private void mPrivate() {
        System.out.println("I am from private method of Child");
  }
  protected void mProtected() {
        System.out.println("I am from protected method of Child");
  }
```

```
    public void print() {
            System.out.println{"i = " + i);
            System.out.println{"j = " + j);
            System.out.println{"x = " + x);
            System.out.println{"Name = " + name);
    }
    public static void main(String[] args) {
            Parent obj = new Child();
            obj.mPublic();
            obj.mPrivate();
            obj.mProtected();
            ojb.print();
    }
}
```

4.5 An inner class can access private members of its outer class. This program shows what will happen if you extend an inner class and override a method in the outer class in it.

```
class Outer {
    private String me = "Joy with Java";
    private void print() {
          System.out.println("Outer: " + me);
    }

    class Inner extends Outer {
          private void print()  {
                  System.out.println("Inner: " + me);
    }
    }

    public static void main(String args[])  {
          Outer out = new Outer();
          Inner in   = o.new Inner();

          out.print();
          in.print();

          out = in;
          out.print();
    }
}
```

Note:

In order to create instance of Inner class, you need an Outer class instance.

4.6 Run this program to check the order of call of constructors in constructor chaining:

```
class  A {
      A() {
        System.out.println(" A ");
      }
}

class  B extends A {
      B () {
              super();
              System.out.println(" B ");
      }
}

class  C extends B {
      C () {
              super();
              System.out.println(" C ");
      }
}

class ConstructorChainTest {
       C c = new C();
       System.out.println("C extends B and B extends A");
}
```

4.7 Run this program to test how the values to be passed to initialize data in different classes in inheritance chain:

```
class  A {
      int a;
      A(int a) {
             This.a = a;
       }
}

class  B extends A {
      float b;
      B (int a, float b) {
              super(a);
              this.b = b;
      }
}
```

```
class  C extends B {
      String c;
      C (int a, float b, String c) {
             super(a, b);
             this.c = c;
      }
}

class InheritanceChainTest {
      C c = new C(123, 4.567, "Jai Ho!");
      System.out.println(c.a + " " + c.b + "  " + c.c);
}
```

MCQs

4.1 Which of the following statement(s) is(are) incorrect?
(a) Public members of a class can be accessed by any code in the program.
(b) Private members of class can only be accessed by any members in the same class.
(c) Private members of a class can be inherited by a sub class, and become protected members in that sub class.
(d) Protected members of a class can be inherited by a sub class, and become private members of that sub class.

4.2 Which of the following access specifier must be used for class so that a sub class can inherit it?
(a) Public. (b) Private. (c) Protected. (d) Default.

4.3 Which of these inheritance in Java programming is not supported?
(a) Multiple inheritance using classes. (b) Multiple inheritance using interfaces.
(c) Multilevel inheritance. (d) Single inheritance.

4.4 How can a protected member be accessed?
(a) Accessible only within the class.
(b) Accessible only within the package.
(c) Accessible within the package as well as outside the package but through inheritance only.
(d) Accessible everywhere.

4.5 Advantage(s) of inheritance in Java programming is(are):
(a) Code sharing. (b) Code maintainability.
(c) Code reusability. (d) All of these.

4.6 For each description on the left, find the best matching modifier on the right. You may use a choice more than once or not at all.

(1) Hides the instance variable from code in other files. A. Private
(2) Hides the method from code in other files. B. Public
(3) Hides the sub class from code in other files. C. Final
(4) Exposes the API method to code in other files. D. Static
(5) Prevents the value of the instance variable from being changed once initialized. E. None matches

(a) 1-A, 2-A, 3-C ,4-D, 5-E. (b) 1-A, 2-A, 3-A, 4-B, 5-C.
(c) 1-C, 2-B, 3-A, 4-A, 5-D. (d) None of these.

4.7 Suppose the class Graduate extends the class `Student` which extends the class `Person`. Given the following variable declaration:

```
Person p = new Person();
Student s = new Student();
Graduate g = new Graduate();
```

Following are some assignments made:

(1) `p = ug;`
(2) `p = new Graduate;`
 (1) `g = new Student();`
 (2) `g = p;`
 (3) `s = new Person();`

Which of the following assignments are legal?

(a) 1 and 4.
(b) 3, 2, and 4.
(c) 1 and 2.
(d) 3 and 4.

4.8 If there is an abstract method in a class, then which of the following is(are) *not* true?

(a) The class should be declared abstract.
(b) No object of the class can be created.
(c) Any sub class of the class may or may not be abstract class.
(d) A final class can have abstract method(s) and an abstract class can be declared final.

4.9 Which of the following statement is true regarding the order of execution of constructors in an inheritance hierarchy?

(a) Base class constructor will be called followed by the derived class constructor (s) from top to bottom.
(b) Derived class constructor(s) from bottom to top will be called followed by the base class constructor.
(c) Only the base class constructor will be called.
(d) Only the derived class constructor for which object s created will be called.

4.10 What is the process of defining more than one method in a class having the same name but differentiated by method signature?
(a) Method overriding. (b) Method overloading.
(c) Encapsulation. (d) Inheritance.

4.11 Consider the following class definition:

```
class Student extends String {

}
```

Which of the following statement(s) is/ are *true*?
(a) Code will not compile because the body is not defined.
(b) Code will not compile because the class is not declared as public.
(c) Code will not compile because the class String cannot be a super class.
(d) Code will compile successfully.

4.12 Consider the following piece of code in Java:

```
class A {
  protected int aMethod (int a, int b){
    return a+b;
  }
}
```

Which of the following are valid in a class that extends class A?

(a)
```
public int aMethod (int a, int b) {
        return a+b;
    }
```
(b)
```
private int aMethod(int a, int b) {
        return a+b;
    }
```
(c)
```
protected int aMethod(int a, int b) {
        return a+b;
    }
```
(d)
```
public short aMethod(int a, int b) {
        return a+b;
    }
```

4.13 Carefully read the two code segments given:

Program 1

```
class P1 {
        void a1() {
```

```
            System.out.println("Tom Hanks");
        }
}
public class C1 extends P1 {
        void a1() {
            System.out.println("Colin Hanks");
        }
        public static void main(String[] args) {
            C1 c = new C1();
            c.a1();
        }
}
```

Program 2

```
class P2 {
        final void a2() {
            System.out.println("Tom Hanks");
        }
}
public class C2 extends P2 {
        void a2() {
            System.out.println("Colin Hanks");
        }
        public static void main(String[] args) {
            C2 c = new C2();
            c.a2();
        }
}
```

Which of the following statement(s) is(are) correct with respect to these programs?

(a) Program 1: overriding the method `a1()` is possible.
(b) Program 2, overriding the method `a2()` is possible.
(c) The output of Program 2 is Tom Hanks.
(d) The output of Program 2 is Colin Hanks.

4.14 Carefully review the following program:

```
class P {
        private void m() {
            System.out.println("Victoria");
        }
}
```

```
public class C extends P {
        private void m() {
                System.out.println("Elizabeth");
        }
        public static void main(String[] args) {
                P c = new C();
                c.m();
        }
}
```

Which of the following statement(s) is(are) correct with respect to this program?

(a) Overriding the method `m()` is possible.
(b) The program will give compile-time error.
(c) The output of the program is Victoria.
(d) The output of the program is Elizabeth.

4.15 Consider the following program:

```
class P {
        public static void m() {
                System.out.println("C++");
        }
}
public class C extends P {
        public static void m() {
                System.out.println("Java");
        }
        public static void main(String[] args) {
                P c = new C();
                c.m();
        }
}
```

Which of the following statement(s) is(are) correct with respect to this program?

(a) Overriding the method `m()` is possible.
(b) The program will give compile-time error.
(c) The output of the program is C++.
(d) The output of the program is Java.

4.16 Consider the following program:

```
abstract class Base {
        abstract void foo();
}
```

```
class Derived extends Base {
        void foo() {
                System.out.println("Fooooooooooo!"); }
}
class AbstractClassTest {
        public static void main(String args[]) {
                Base c = new Derived();
                c.foo();
        }
}
```

With reference to this program, which of the following statement(s) is(are) true?

(a) You cannot create an instance of an abstract class.
(b) The program will give compile-time error.
(c) The program will compile but give run-time error.
(d) The program will run successfully with the output.

4.17 Which of the following is *not* true?

(a) The static method cannot use non-static data member or call the non-static method directly.
(b) `this` and `super` can be used in static context as they are non-static.
(c) A static method defined in a super class cannot be redefined in any of its sub class.
(d) A sub class extending an abstract super class also may be abstract.

4.18 Consider the following program:

```
abstract class Test
{
        static int i = 123;
        static void testMethod()  {
                System.out.print("Welcome : ");
        }
}

public class TestClass extends Test  {
        public static void main (String args[])   {
                i++;
                Test.testMethod();
                System.out.println(Test.i);
        }
}
```

What output will this program produce?
(a) The program will not compile.
(b) It will compile but give run-time error.
(c) It will give output: Welcome : 123.
(d) It will give output: Welcome : 124.

4.19 Consider the following program:

```
class Person  {
    int a = 1;
    int b = 0;
    public Person()     {
        System.out.println(a + b + " Java " + a + b);
    }
}

public class Employee extends Person  {
    int a = 0;
    int b = 1;
    public Employee()    {
        System.out.println(a*b + " Java " + a*b);
    }

Public class Question {
    public static void main (String args[])  {
        Person p = new Employee();
    }
}
```

What output will the following Java program display?
(a) `10 Java 1`
`0 Java 0`
(b) `0 Java 0`
`10 Java 1`
(c) `0 Java 0`
(d) `10 Java 10`

4.20 Consider the following piece of code:

```
public class A{
    static int a;
    A(int a)  {
        this();
```

```
            this.a = a;
        }
}
class B extends A {
        static int b;
        B(int a, int b) {
            this();
            super(a);
            this.b = b;
        }
}
Class C {
        public static void main(String []args){
        A a = new A(11);
        A b = new B(69, 96);
}
```

What will happen if you attempt to compile and run the program?

(a) Program will not compile successfully.
(b) Program will compile with a warning message.
(c) Program will run without any error.
(d) Program will give a run-time error.

4.21 Consider the following program:

```
class Base    {
    protected void print()   {
        System.out.println("Base class...");
    }
}

class Derived extends Base    {
    public void print()   {
        System.out.println("Derived class...");
    }
}

public class Question    {
    public void main (String args[])   {
```

```
        Base b = new Derived();
        b.print();
    }
    private static void main (String args[])  {
        Base b = new Base();
        b.print();
        Derived d = new Derived();
        D.print();
    }
}
```

How many errors does this program have?

(a) 0. (b) 1. (c) 2. (d) 3.

4.22 Consider the following program:

```
class Car{
  final int speed;
  final void run() {
      speed = 40;
  }
}
Class Audi extends Car {
    Audi(int speed) {
        super.speed = speed;
    }
    void run() {
        System.out.println("Audi's speed: " + speed);
    }
}
class SpeedTest {
    public static void main(String args[]){
        Car bmw = new  Audi();
        bmw.run();
    }
}
```

How many errors does this program have?

(a) 0. (b) 1. (c) 2. (d) 3.

4.23 Consider the following program:

```
1.  class Parent   {
2.    protected final void print()    {
3.        System.out.println("I am from Prent...");
4.    }
5.  }

6.  public class Child extends Parent  {
7.    protected final void print()    {
8.        System.out.println("I am from family...");
9.    }
10.    public static void main(String[] args)    {
11.        Child c = new Parent();
12.        c.print();
13.    }
14.  }
```

Which of the line number(s) are erroneous in this program?

(a) 2. (b) 7. (c) 11. (d) 12.

5

Package and Interface

Package and interface are two incredible concepts in Java programming language. These features make Java programming suitable for developing large software in any application domain. The concept of package and interface allows the programmers to organize classes and hence methods and fields or constants for developing a large software program. This concept is called *programming in large*. It also helps the programmers to write code in their own styles, which is called *programming in small*. With this you will feel Java is like C when programming in small and like Smalltalk (a pure object-oriented programming language) when programming in large. This means that Java is powerful like any function-oriented programming language while you are coding individual lines, and has the extensibility and expressive power of a pure object-oriented programming language while you're designing.

5.0 Introduction

From design to coding

The separation of "designing" from "coding" was one of the most fundamental advances in programming style in the recent past, and object-oriented languages are capable of implementing a strong form of this separation. According to this programming paradigm, you design the classes first and decide the relationships between these classes, and then you implement the Java code needed for each of the methods in your class design. The advantages with this style is that, you can change your mind about aspects of the design without affecting anything but small, local pieces of your programs; vice-versa, you can change the implementation of any method without affecting the design.

To achieve this, the Java developer includes two very innovative features: package and interface. Packages provide class repositories, grouping them together, and controlling their access to the outside world. Interfaces provide a way of grouping abstract method definitions and sharing them among classes.

Your learning

This chapter plans to discuss the package and interface concepts in Java. You will learn how to design, use, and create your own packages and interfaces. The specific topics which you will learn include: a detailed discussion of designing classes and coding classes; what are packages and why they are useful for designing classes; using other available packages in your own classes; how you can create your own packages; what interfaces you can utilize in terms of code reuse and design; designing and working with interfaces; and many more.

5.1 Concept of Package

Why package?

You have gone through many programs so far (i.e., many classes). Have you noticed where you have stored all these programs? If you are meticulous, possibly you have created directories such as `Chapter1`, `Chapter2`, etc. and stored them there. This is fine, but not an excellent idea. The more Java programming you do, the more classes you will have. If you want to use some classes which are distributed over different sub directories, then what you should do? Copy all those in your current directory? Or, if you want to share your project implementation, should you make a copy of the whole stuff? You will be happy to know that Java gives you a very nice way, called package, to help you in all these activities.

What is a package?

Package is a way of organizing groups of classes. A package contains any number of classes that are related in purpose, in scope, or by inheritance. Packages are useful for many reasons:

Benefits of packages

- They allow you to organize your classes into units. Just as you have folders or directories on your hard disk to organize your files and applications, packages allow you to organize (group) your classes so that you use only what you need for a particular application.
- Packages reduce problems with conflicts in names. As the number of Java classes grow, so does the likelihood that you use the same class name present somewhere else, and thus open up the possibility of naming clashes and errors. Packages allow you to "hide" classes so that conflicts can be avoided.
- Packages allow you to protect classes, variables, and methods in a number of ways than on a class-by-class basis. In fact, packages provide information hiding capability in a better way.
- Packages can be used to identify your classes better. For example, suppose you have implemented a set of classes to perform some purpose. You can name a package of those classes with a unique identifier that identifies you, your organization, or anyone else permitted.

As far as Java programming environment is concerned, all packages can be broadly classified into two categories:

- Built-in packages
- User defined package

Let's first discuss the Java built-in packages.

5.1.1 Built-in Java Packages

In reality, you have already benefitted from the concept of packages. You may remember that in some programs, you have started with the `import` statement. For example:

```
import java.lang.*;
```

This statement, allows you to access all the classes (e.g., `System`, `Math`, `Integer`, `Object`, etc.) in the package called `lang`. This package, which is already developed by the Java developer and bundled with JDK (Java Development Kit), is the software you have already installed in your machine for Java programming. This is why such a package is called a built-in package. Also, it is called a Java API (Application Programming Interface). Java API includes all the Java packages which, in turn, include all classes, interfaces, along with their methods, fields, and constructors. These prewritten classes provide a tremendous amount of functionality to a programmer.

Java API is a rich source of many packages to cover different application domains. The different packages in API are listed in Table 5.1 and Figure 5.1. For more details about each package and elements in them, you can consult the following link:

https://docs.oracle.com/javase/7/docs/api/

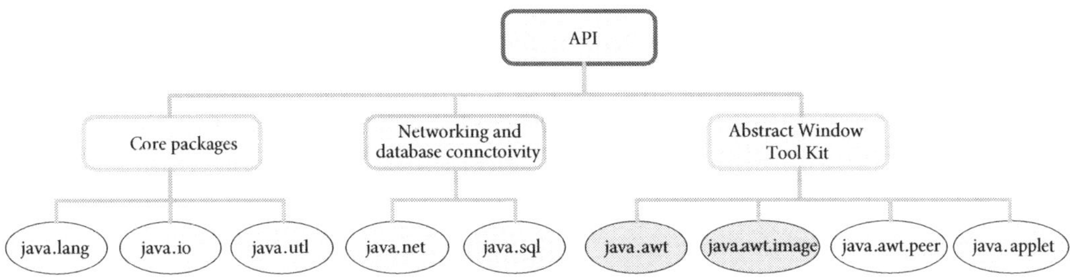

Figure 5.1 Java APIs

Table 5.1 Built-in Java packages

Package	Description
`java.applet`	Provides the classes necessary to create an applet and the classes an applet uses to communicate with its applet context.
`java.awt`	Contains all of the classes for creating user interfaces and for painting graphics and images.
`java.io`	Provides for system input and output through data streams, serialization, and the file system.
`java.lang`	Provides classes that are fundamental to the design of the Java programming language.
`java.net`	Provides the classes for implementing networking applications.
`java.sql`	Provides the classes and interfaces for accessing and processing data stored in a data source (usually a relational database).
`java.util`	Contains the collections framework, legacy collection classes, event model, date and time facilities, and miscellaneous utility classes.

- To include a class belonging to a package, you should use the `import` statement. You can include all the classes and interfaces by specifying `.*;` and you can include a specific class by explicitly mentioning that class only. For example

```
import java.awt.*;
    // All classes and interfaces in the package

import java.util.Scanner;
    // To include the Scanner class
```

- The package `java.lang` is automatically imported in any program.
- Essentially, a package is a collection of classes. Also, a package may contain other package(s), forming yet another level of organization analogous to the inheritance hierarchy. In such an organization, a "level" usually represents a smaller, more specific grouping of classes. The Java class library itself is organized in the same way. Here, the top level is called `java`; the next level includes packages, such as `lang`, `io`, `net`, `util`, and `awt`. The last of these has an even lower level, which includes the package `image`.
- There are also some packages under `javax`. Originally, everything that was a part of the standard API was a part of the `java` package, whereas everything that was not a part of the standard API was released under the package name `javax`. Hence, packages essential to the API were `java`, while `javax` contained the extensions to the API. It can even be said that `javax` is just `java` with an `x`, which stands for extension. For example, `javax.crypto` provides the classes and interfaces for

cryptographic operations `javax.swing`, which is built on the top of AWT (Abstract Windowing Toolkit) and provides lightweight and platform independent components.

- Java also supports `org.omgCORBA` and others to provide the mapping of the OMG CORBA APIs to Java programming language, including the class `ORB`, which is implemented so that a programmer can use it as a fully-functional Object Request Broker (ORB).

5.1.2 User-Defined Package

A programmer can create his or her own package. There are three steps to be followed for this:

1. Choose a package name.
2. Create the directory structure.
3. Add classes to the package.

These three steps are discussed in the following:

Choose a package name

Package naming convention

The first step is to decide what the name of your package is going to be. The name you choose for your package depends on how you are going to use the classes. Suppose, you are in the process of building an application system called Human Computer Interaction. So, you can name your package as `hci`.

The dot convention as in the Internet domain name can also be used. For example, you are working for a company called `abc` and the software product to be packaged is `xyz.com`. Then you can name the package as `com.xyz.abc`. You might add another package name, say `bci` (brain computer interface, a sub package) to refer to another product or extended version of the product; then you can add it to the end as `hci.bci` or `com.xyz.abc.bci`. Whatever system you follow, the idea is to make sure your package name is unique.

- By convention, package names should begin with a lowercase letter to distinguish them from class names. For example, in the full name of the built-in `String` class, `java.lang.String`, it's easier to identify the package name from the class name. This convention helps to reduce name conflicts.

- There is no way to make sure your package won't be in conflict with someone else's package if you both use the same package name.
- You should not choose the name of your package the same as the a name in Java API. Java compiler will not mind it, but it will invite unnecessary conflict in your programming.

Creating the directory structure

A directory is the place where all classes under a package name are maintained. Name of the directory structure on your disk should match the package name. For example, if your package has just one name (say `hci`), you'll only have to create a directory with the same name. If the package name has several parts, then you will have to create directory within directory. For example, for the package name `hci.bci`, you will need to create a `hci` directory and then create a `bci` directory inside `hci`. Your classes and compiled files can then go inside the `bci` directory.

Adding classes to a package using `package` command

The final step to putting your class inside packages is to add the `package` command to your source files. For example, to add the class `<ClassName>` in the package `hci`, you should write as follows:

```
package hci;

public class <ClassName> {

      ... // Body of the class

}
```

- All the `.java` files under a package should be pre-compiled and their corresponding `.class` files should be stored in the same directory as that of the `.java` file.
- If the compiled version of the file is not found, then the program will give run-time error.
- The compiler does not check directories when it compiles source files. For example, suppose you have a source file that starts with a directive:

```
package hci.bci;
```

You can compile the file even if there is no sub-directory `hci/bci`. The source file will compile without errors, but the virtual machine will not find the resulting classes when you try to run the program. Therefore, you should use the same hierarchy for source files as for class files.

- The `package` command, if any, must be the first line of code in your source file, after any comments or blank lines and before any import commands.
- If you put a file into a sub-directory, then it should match the full package name properly. For example, if the name of your package is `hci.bci`, when `java` is your working directory, then you should store the file in `java/hci/bci` or `java\hci\bci` or, `java:hci:bci` on Unix, Windows or Macintosh file system, respectively. That is:

```
package hci.bci;
java              // Your working directory
   /hci           // Your package directory
       /bci       // Your package sub-directory
public class <ClassName> {      // Your class file
     ... // Body of the class
}
```

- To compile the `.java` file in the package `hci.bci`, simply change to the directory containing `<ClassName>.java` and run the command:

```
javac <ClassName>.java
```

- More than one file can include the same package statement. A package can contain zero or more files.
- You should add one class at a time into a package. And its compiled file should be with the same name as the class name. If you include two or more classes into a single `.java` file in a package then it is not proper, because this will lead to an ambiguity in naming the `.class` file. So, if two classes, for example class `A` and class `B`, are to be included in a package `P`, then add class `A` in package `P` and class `B` into package `P` one after another.
- If you do not put a package statement in the source file, then the classes in that source file belong to the *default package*. The default package has no package name. Up to now, all our example classes were located in the default package.
- Any class in any package can access the classes in the default package.

5.2 Accessing Packages

Thus far we have learned how a package can be created and classes can be added into it. Now we shall learn how a class belonging to a package can be accessed.

In Java, there is *import statement*, which can be used to reference a package and to be included in a program. The syntax of an import statement is as follows:

```
import <PackageName>;
```

However, instead of importing the whole package, it is possible to import a class in order to instantiate an object. For example, if `P` is a package and class `A`, `B`, `C`, etc. are in `P`, then you can access a particular class, say `A`, in the following manner:

```
java.P.A  a = new java.P.A ( ); // Explicit reference
```

Program 5.1 is an example of creating a package and accessing it in another class.

Program 5.1 *(Creating a package)*

```
/* This program illustrates how to create a package,
add a class into the package. */

package hci;                  // Tell that this file is
in hci directory
public class MyClass {        // Add the file
    public void test ( ) {
         System.out.println ("Welcome to My Class in
           package \"hci\" !");
    }
}

/* Note: Create a directory under your working
directory named as hci. Save the MyClass.java file
there. Compile successfully the MyClass.java file and
ensure that MyClass.class file is available in the hci
directory. */
```

Program 5.2 *(Accessing a class of a package)*

```
/*This program illustrates importing a package into a
class which is not in the same directory as the package
directory. */

import hci;       // Accessing the class

class PackageTest {
   public static void main ( String args [ ] ) {
        MyClass theClass = new MyClass ( );
           // Create an object
         theClass.test ( );         // Access the member
   }
}
```

- In order to make a class of a package accessible, the class should be declared as `public`.
- A class with default access specification is not accessible to a class outside the package. You can try this with the default access specification of `MyClass` in Program 5.1.

- If there is a class in a default package with the `public` access specifier, accessing it from any class in the same package (i.e., the same directory) leads to a compilation error. You can try this by copying both the classes in Program 5.1 and 5.2 (i.e., `MyClass.java` and `PackageTest.java`) into a directory, say `temp`.
- Note that in all programs until Chapter 3 having multiple classes are without the `public` access specifier.
- Static import is a feature introduced in Java (versions 5 and above) that allows members (fields and methods) defined in a class as `public static` to be used in Java code without specifying the class in which the field is defined. Program 5.3 demonstrates the use of `static import` in a Java program.

Program 5.3 *(Static import)*

```
/* This program demonstrates the use of static import
statement in Java.*/

import static java.lang.System.*;

class StaticImportDemo {
   public static void main(String args[]) {
        out.println("Joy with Java");
             // We don't need to use System.out
                                    // as imported using static.
   }
}
```

The package concept in Java is both a name and visibility control mechanism. Let's discuss how Java does these two jobs.

5.2.1 Name Control Mechanism

The package is a matter of organizing many files in the file system. Let us see how Java knows where to look for packages that you create and refer to in your program. Following are the ways Java run-time manager resolves the location of a class in a program:

1. Location tracking by default.
2. Setting of CLASSPATH
3. Using JAR utility

Location tracking by default

This is the simplest one, when no specific location is available to the Java system. This is considered as the default situation. In this situation, the Java system uses the current working directory as its starting point. Thus, if your package is in a sub-directory of the current directory, it will be resolved. Otherwise, it will report an error. Such an error will be reported at the time of compilation. You can test this by executing Program 5.4. Program 5.4 defines a package in a sub-directory `bci` which is under the directory `hci`. The package contains one class, namely, `DefaultPacakageTest`.

Program 5.4 *(Package location checking)*

```
/* This program illustrates default location checking
of package by Java run-time system. */

package hci.bci;
  // Tell that it is a package and in hci\bci directory
public class DefaultPacakageTest {       // Add the file
    public static void main (String args[] ) {
     System.out.println ("I am in hci\\bci directory");
    }
}
```

Suppose, your working directory is `C:\java` under which there is `hci\bci`. The file is successfully compiled and the `.class` file is stored in `bci` directory. Following are the cases you can try one after another and check whether your program runs or not.

Case 1: Run the program from `java` directory // Okay

Case 2: Run the program from `java\hci` directory // Okay

Case 3: Run the program from `java\hci\bci` directory // Okay

Case 4: Run the program from `java\temp` directory, `temp` is a sub-directory under `java` directory // Run-time error

BE CAREFUL

- To run the program, the program file name should be qualified with the package name. That is:

```
java   defaultPackageTest            // Will not work
java   hci.bci.defaultPackageTest // It will work
```

Setting CLASSPATH

The approach we have stated is not flexible and is also tedious. There is a better approach to sharing packages among programs: by setting the CLASSPATH variable of the system. CLASSPATH is the collection of all base directories whose sub-directories can contain class files. There are two ways to set the CLASSPATH of a system:

1. Setting CLASSPATH environment variable in operating system.
2. Using Java commands.

Setting CLASSPATH environment variable

A class path states the directories where the system should look for a file to resolve its location. In the class path setting, we should mention those paths only. The setting procedure depends on your operating system. Here are some tips for setting the CLASSPATH environment variable in UNIX/Linux and Windows:

Unix/Linux system

In a Unix/Linux system, the class paths are separated by colon (:). For example:

```
/home/user/java:.:/homc/user/archives/archive.jar
```

This class path states three directories:

The working directory	`/home/user/java`
The current directory	`.`
The JAR file	`/home/user/archives/archive.jar`

To set the class path, edit your shell's start-up file.

If you use the C shell, add a line such as the following to the `.cshrc` file in your home directory.

```
setenv CLASSPATH /home/user/java:.
```

If you use the Bourne Again shell or bash, add the following line to the `.bashrc` or bash_profile file in your home directory:

```
export CLASSPATH=/home/user/java:.
```

Windows systems

On Windows, the class paths are separated by semicolons (;). For example:

```
c:\programs\java;.;c:\archives\archive.jar
```

Like Unix/ Linux, in Windows also, . (dot) represents the current directory. To set the class path, you can do the following:

Choose `Control Panel` `System` `Advanced system settings` `Environment Variables` Choose `System Variables` (for all the users) or `User Variables` (only the currently login user) choose `Edit` (if CLASSPATH already exists) or `New` Enter "CLASSPATH" as the variable name Enter the required directories, JAR files , etc. (separated by semicolons) as the values.

Using Java commands

Instead of using the CLASSPATH environment variable, you can also use the command line option `-classpath` or `-cp` of the `javac` and `java` commands. For example, using Java JDK/SDK, a programmer can set the class path variable easily, which is as follows (in Unix/ Linux):

To set the class path for the compiler for a file `archive.jar` is as follows:

```
javac  -classpath  /home/user/java:.:/home/user/archives/
  archive.jar
```

To set the class path for the byte code interpreter:

```
java -cp /home/user/java:.:/home/user/archives/archive.jar
```

On Windows, use \ instead of /.

Using JAR utility

JAR (Java Archive). You can also use the JAR utility to add class files to an archive. An archive contains multiple class files and sub-directories inside a single file, saving space and reducing access time. For example, the thousands of classes of the run-time library are all contained in the run-time library file `rt.jar`. You can find this file in the `jre/lib` sub-directory of the Java SDK.

The basic format of the command for creating a JAR file is:

```
jar cf jar-file input-file(s)
```

The options and arguments used in this command are:

- The `c` option indicates that you want to create a JAR file.
- The `f` option indicates that you want the output to go to a file rather than to `stdout`.
- `jar-file` is the name that you want the resulting JAR file to have. You can use any filename for a JAR file. By convention, JAR filenames are given a `.jar` extension, though this is not required.

- The `input-file(s)` argument is a space-separated list of one or more files that you want to include in your JAR file. The `input-file(s)` argument can contain the wildcard `*` symbol. If any of the "input-files" are directories, the contents of those directories are added to the JAR archive recursively.

The `c` and `f` options can appear in either order, but there must not be any space between them. This command will generate a compressed JAR file and place it in the current directory.

There is a possibility of getting into a naming conflict. This is particularly possible when you import many packages from many sources. For example, both `java.util` and `java.sql` packages have a class named `Date`. So if you import both packages in a program, then it will report a compile-time error. For example:

```
import java.util.*;

import java.sql.*;

Date today ;  //ERROR-- java.util.Date or java.sql.Date?
```

The compiler will not be able to figure out which `Date` class you want. This problem can be solved by using specific import statement. For example:

```
java.util.Date dob = new java.util.Date();

java.sql.Date today = new java.sql.Date();
```

5.2.2 Visibility Control Mechanism

In Chapter 3, we learned about three access specifiers: `public`, `private`, and `protected` and, in addition, the default access specification. Packages add another dimension to access control. Java provides many levels of protection to allow fine-grained control over the visibility of variables and methods within classes, derived classes, and packages, which need to be discussed in detail and with illustrations.

Classes and packages are both means of encapsulating and containing the name, space, and scope of variables and methods. Classes are the containers for data and code, whereas packages are the containers for classes and sub-packages. The class is Java's smallest unit of abstraction; on the other hand, packages are of unlimited capacity. Since there are an inter- and intra-relationships among classes and packages, Java addresses four categories of visibility for class members which are as follows:

- Inherited classes in the same package.
- Non-inherited classes in the same package.
- Inherited classes in different packages.
- Classes that are neither in the same package nor inherited.

Figure 5.2 illustrates these four categorizations. Table 5.2 summarizes the visibility control mechanism

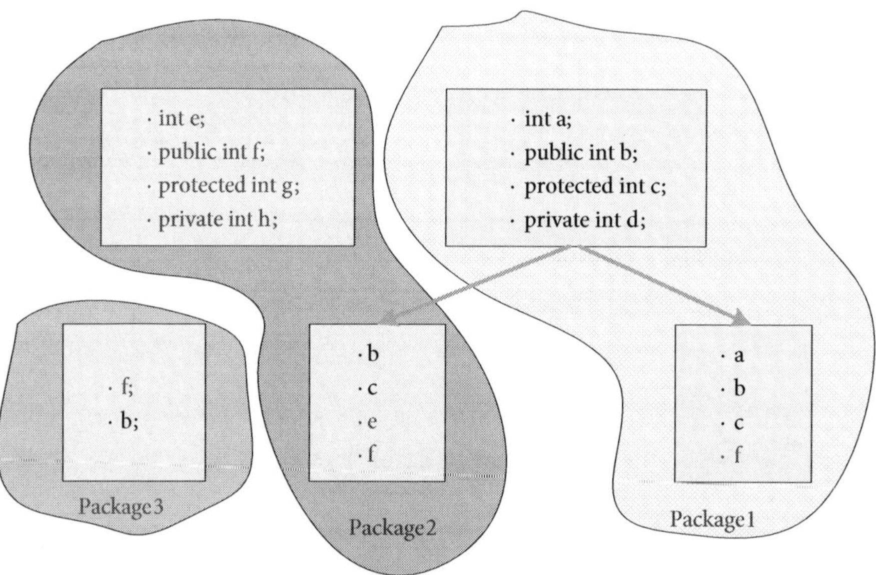

Figure 5.2 Intra- and inter-visibility of elements across classes in packages

Table 5.2 Visibility control in classes and packages

Code	Private	Default	Protected	Public
Same class	Yes	Yes	Yes	Yes
Same package inherited class	No	Yes	Yes	Yes
Same package non-inherited class	No	Yes	Yes	Yes
Different package inherited class	No	No	Yes	Yes
Different package non-inherited class	No	No	No	Yes

As you can see from Figure 5.2 and Table 5.2, a derived class that you define in the same package as its super class inherits everything except for private data members of the super. If you define a derived class outside the package containing the super class, then the private data members are not inherited, and neither are any data members in the super class that you have declared without access attributes. Members defined as private in the super class are never inherited under any circumstances. The super class must be declared as public in Package 1, otherwise it would not be accessible from Package 2 as the super class for derived class in Package 2.

Also, see how the explicit access specifiers are related to one another. The `public` specifier is the least restrictive on class members since a `public` member is accessible from everywhere. Next comes `protected`. This specifier prevents access from classes outside of a package except the inherited classes. Note that putting no access specifier (i.e. default) on a class member limits its access from classes outside the same package and also prevents inheritance in sub classes that are defined in a different package. The most restrictive is `private` since access is limited to the same class.

- The access specification rule is applicable to static members as well.
- Rules in Table 5.2 apply only to members of classes. A non-nested class has only two possible access levels: `default` and `public`. When a class is declared as `public`, it is accessible by any other code. If a class has default access, then it can only be accessed by other code within the same package. When a class is `public`, it must be the only `public` class declared in a file, and the file must have the same name as the class name.

5.2.3 Package Sealing

You can use a mechanism called package sealing to address the issue of indiscriminate package access. If you seal a package, no further classes can be added to it. Sealing protects the features while allowing package visibility. In the following, a method is discussed with which you can produce a JAR file that contains sealed packages.

You put all classes of the package into a JAR file. By default, packages in a JAR file are not sealed. You can change that global default by placing the line

```
Sealed: true
```

into the main section of the manifest (which is automatically generated when you jar file using the Java jar command). For each individual package, you can specify whether you want the package sealed or not, by adding another section to the JAR file, like this:

```
Name: com/mycompany/mypackage/
Sealed: true
Name: com/hal/util/
Sealed: false
```

To seal a package, make a text file with the manifest instructions. Then run the jar command:

```
jar cvfm MyPackage.jar sealed.mf
```

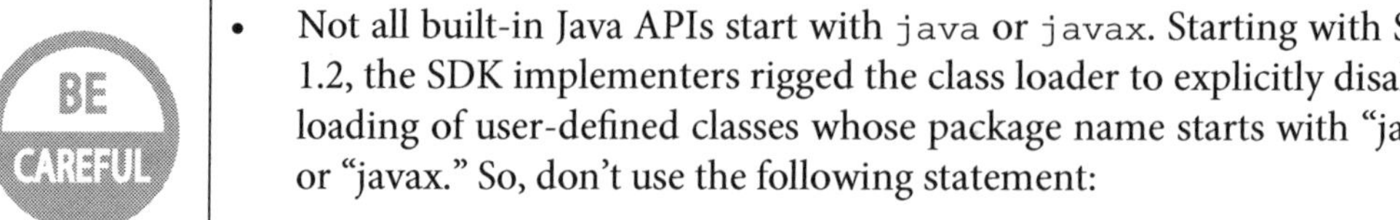

- Not all built-in Java APIs start with `java` or `javax`. Starting with SDK 1.2, the SDK implementers rigged the class loader to explicitly disallow loading of user-defined classes whose package name starts with "java." or "javax." So, don't use the following statement:

```
package java.hci;
```

5.3 Interfaces

Packages are fairly easy to understand, being little more than a way to organize related classes, whether supplied with Java or created by a programmer like you. Interfaces are a concept that is a bit harder to grasp. To really understand Java's interfaces, you have to know about something called multiple inheritance, which is not allowed in Java but which is often used in other object-oriented languages like C++.

Now, let's begin with an example (Program 5.5). In the program, two classes, `Taxi` and `Zeep`, are defined.

Program 5.5 *(Problem with multiple inheritance)*

```
class Taxi {
    String carNo;
    public void start() {
        System.out.println("Engine started ...");
    }

    public void Stop() {
        System.out.println("...Stopping engine!");
    }
    public void horn() {
        System.out.println("peep, peeeep");
    }
}

class Zeep {
    String modelNo;
    public void start() {
        System.out.println("Turbo started ...");
    }
```

```
    public void Stop() {
        System.out.println("...Stopping turbo!");
    }

    public void horn() {
        System.out.println("poonk, pooonk");
    }
}

class Vehicle extends Taxi, Zeep {
    String ownerName;

    public void vHorn() {
        this.horn();            //Ambiguity: Which horn()??
    }
}
```

This would be an example of multiple inheritance if Java allowed such a thing. You will notice that the Java compiler will not support you to compile the class `Vehicle` as stated in the program. There are several reasons for this. One simple reason is that there is a name conflict. By virtue of the inheritance property, `start()`, `stop()`, and `horn()` methods from both the classes `Taxi` and `Zeep` are the members of the class `Vehicle`. For example, if you call the `horn()` method in the class `Vehicle`, then which method it will refer to? The problem with multiple inheritance is that it makes a programming language more complex to learn, to use, and to implement. With multiple inheritance, questions of method invocation and how the class hierarchy is organized become far more complicated. Multiple inheritance leads to more confusion and ambiguity. Because one of the goals of Java programming is that it should be simple, multiple inheritance is not considered in Java. Rather, it favours the simpler single inheritance.

However, Java's designers still liked the idea, though, of being able to declare a set of behaviors that can be inherited by one or more classes. So they came up with interfaces.

An interface is like a class, but with one important difference. The name indicates its primary use, specifying a set of methods that represent a particular class interface, which can then be implemented appropriately in a number of different classes. None of the methods declared in an interface are implemented in the interface itself. Instead, these methods must be implemented in any class that uses the interface. Thus, interfaces describe behaviors but do not detail how these behaviors will be carried out. A Java interface is a collection of abstract behavior that can be mixed into any class to add to that class behavior not supplied by its super classes. A Java interface contains nothing but abstract method definitions and constants; there are no instance variables and no method implementations.

5.3.1 Defining an Interface

The keyword `interface` is used to define an interface. The following is a general syntax in Java to declare and define an interface:

```
<access specifier> interface <name> {
     <type> final <name_1> = <value 1>;
     <type> final <name_2> = <value 2>;
     // ...
     <type> final <name_m> = <value m>;
     <return type> <method name_1>(<parameter-list>);
     <return type> <method name_2>(<parameter-list>);
     //...
     <return type> <method name_n>(<parameter-list>);
}
```

Program 5.6 is an example which shows how you can define an interface. You can store this program as `.java` file (the name should be the same as the name of the interface and may be in a package of your own) and then compile the interface into `.class` file. Note that you will not be able to execute this `.class` file.

Program 5.6 *(Interface declaration)*

```
/* This program illustrates a declaration of an
interface. This can be considered as a skeleton of a
class. */

interface Converter {
    final double PI = 3.14159;
      // Declaration of a constant
    double converter(double inputValue);
      //An abstract method declaration
}
```

- All methods in an interface are automatically `public`, fields are always `public static final`. An interface may contain only method(s) or only filed(s) or both method(s) and field(s).
- Interfaces are syntactically similar to classes, but they lack instance variables and, as a general rule, their methods are declared without any body.
- An interface is essentially a collection of related constants and/or abstract methods, and in most cases it will contain just methods. An interface doesn't define what a method does. It just defines its form: its name, its parameters, and its return type. So by definition, the methods in an interface are abstract.
- You can define an interface without any access specifier. When no access specifier is included, then `default` access specification will be implied. The interface is only available to other members of the package in which it is declared.
- When an interface is declared as `public`, the interface can be used by any other program. In this case, the interface must be the only public interface declared in the file and the file must have the same name as the name of the interface.
- You can declare an interface without any members in it. In this case, the program will compile without any warning or error. An interface with no methods in it is referred to as a *tagging interface*. Tagging interface is used to create a common parent. For example, in Java, there is an interface called `EventListener` interface which is extended by dozens of other interfaces in Java API. When an interface extends `EventListener`, the JVM knows that this particular interface is going to be used in an event delegation scenario. As another use, you can add a data type to a class. This situation is where the term tagging comes from. A class that implements a tagging interface does not need to define any methods (since the interface does not have any), but the class becomes an interface type through polymorphism.
- From Java 9 onwards, interfaces can contain following also:

```
Static methods
Private methods
Private static methods
```

So far you have learnt how you can define an interface. There are many more aspects to learn about interfaces. Let us mention briefly what we are going to learn in the following subsections:

- How to implement an interface once it is defined.
- How to use an interface in a user's program.
- Difference between an interface and an abstract class.
- Partial implementation of an interface.

- Inheritance of interfaces.
- Mixing of "extends" and "implements" while defining a new class.
- Overloading and overriding with interface (overloading + overriding).
- Multiple inheritance concept in Java using interface.

5.3.2 Implementing Interface

Once it is defined, any number of classes can implement an interface. This allows you to fully utilize the "one interface, multiple methods" aspect of polymorphism. To implement an interface, the keyword `implements` is used in a class definition and then the methods required by the interface in the class are defined. The general syntax to implement an interface is as follows:

```
class <classname> [extends super class]
            [implements interface [,interface...]] {
/* class-body including the definition of method(s)
   in the interface(s) */
}
```

Program 5.7 is an illustration how an interface can be implemented.

Program 5.7 *(Implementing an interface)*

```
/* This program demonstrates the implementation of an
interface. */

/* Store all the programs, that is, interface and
classes in separate files but in the same working
directory. */

// Edit the following interface definition and save as
                                        // Converter.java

interface Converter {
    final double PI = 3.14159;
            // Declaration of a constant
    double converter(double inputValue);
            //An abstract method declaration
}
// Edit the following class and save it as
                          // CentigradeToFahrenheit.java

class CentigradeToFahrenheit implements Converter {
         double aTemp;
```

```
   CentigradeToFahrenheit (double cTemp) {
        this.aTemp = cTemp;
   }

    public double converter(double aTemp){
     // Method implementation
        double fTemp;
        fTemp = (9.0/5.0)*aTemp + 32.0;
        return(fTemp);
    }
}

/* Another class implementing the interface Converter.
Save this class as FahrenheitToCentigrade.java */

class FahrenheitToCentigrade implements Converter {
        double aTemp;

   FahrenheitToCentigrade (double fTemp) {
        this.aTemp = fTemp;
   }

    public double converter(double aTemp) {
     // Another implementation
        double cTemp;
        cTemp = (5.0/9.0)*(fTemp - 32.0);
        return(cTemp);
    }
}
/* Here is the main class definition, say TempToTemp.
java */

class TempToTemp {
   static double aTemp;
   static double temp;
   public static void main ( String args [ ] ) {
        class FahrenheitToCentigrade fc=new
           FahrenheitToCentigrade(0.0);
        class CentigradeToFahrenheit cf=new
           FahrenheitToCentigrade(0.0);
        aTemp = 35.6;
           // A temperature in Centigrade scale
        temp = fc.converter (aTemp);
```

```
            System.out.println(aTemp + "C = " + temp +
               "F");

            aTemp = 101.5;
               // A temperature in Fahrenheit scale
            temp = cf.converter (aTemp);
            temp = FahrenheitToCentigrade (aTemp);
            System.out.println(aTemp + "F = " + temp +
               "C");
    }
}
```

- Since the methods in an interface are, by definition, `public`, you must use the `public` keyword when you define them in your class; otherwise, your code will lead to compile time error.
- The implementation of an interface method in a class must not have an access specifier that is more restrictive than that of the abstract method declaration. However, you can implement a method as `private/protected` as well.
- You must implement in your new class all the methods declared in the interface you implement. If a class implements an interface but does not fully implement the method(s) required by that interface, then that class must be declared as `abstract`. Program 5.8 illustrates how to partially implements an interface.

Program 5.8 *Partial implementation of an interface)*

```
/* This program illustrates a partial implementation of
an interface by an abstract class. */

interface Animal {
     void miu();
     void vow();
}
abstract Pet implements Animal {
      String name;
      public void miu(){
           System.out.println(name + " Miaoooo!");
      }
}
```

- Any class can inherit the class `Pet` and if so, then it must implement other method, otherwise the class should be declared `abstract`.

One class can also implement any number of interfaces as it needs to. To implement multiple interfaces by a single class, just list the interfaces after the `implements` keyword, separating each interface name from the others with a comma. Remember to implement all methods in the interface, otherwise declare the class `abstract`. Program 5.9 explains this. In Program 5.9, the interface `Converter` defines two methods, whereas in another interface `Factor`, 4 fields (constants) are defined.

Program 5.9 *Multiple implementation)*

```
/* This program demonstrates the implementation of
multiple interfaces by a single class. */
package myPackage;
      // Define an interface in a package myPackage

public interface Converter {
    double converter(double inputValue, double factor);
    double geoArea(double r, double h);
      // Another abstract method
}
package myPackage;
     //Define another interface in the same package, say

public interface Factors {
    final double PI = 3.14159;
    double POUND_TO_GRAM = 453.5924;
    double INCH_TO_MM = 25.4;
    double USD_TO_INR = 69.74;
}
import myPackage.*;
      //Now, interfaces are accessible to this class

/* A class implementing the interface Converter and
Factor. Save this class as MyClass.java (in any
directory). */

class MyClass implements Converter, Factor {
   double aInput;
   double theResult;

   public double converter (double aInput,
     double aFactor) {
        return(aFactor * aInput);
   }
```

```
    public static void main (String args [ ] ) {

        aInput = 50.5;  // A length in inch
        theResult = this.converter (aInput, INCH_TO_MM);
        System.out.println(aInput + "inch = " +
            theResult + "mm");

        aInput = 25000;  // A currency in Indian Rupees
        theResult = this.converter
            (aInput, (1.0/USD_TO_INR));
        System.out.println(aInput + "INR = " + theResult
            + "USD");

        aInput = 2500;  // A currency in USD
        theResult = this.converter (aInput, USD_TO_INR);
        System.out.println(aInput + "USD = " + theResult
            + "INR");
    }
}
```

Before proceeding further, let us summarize what we have learnt so far.

Similarities between class and interface

- Classes and interfaces, despite their different definitions, have a lot in common. Like classes, interfaces should be stored in a file and the files can also be compiled using the Java compiler into `.class` files.
- Like classes, we can define multiple interfaces along with declaration(s) of class(es) in a single program file or in different `.java` files spread over in different packages or directories.
- Almost everywhere this book has a class name (i.e., declared with `class`) in any of its examples, you can substitute an interface name (i.e., declared with `interface`). This means you say "class" when they actually mean "class or interface." On the other hand, interfaces complement and extend the power of classes, and the two can be treated almost exactly the same way.
- In most cases, anywhere you can use a class (as a data type for a variable, as the result of a cast, and so on), you can also use an interface.

Difference between class and interface

- An interface is the concept of "programming in the large," which means it states "what" to do. It specifies a structure to be followed by another programmer. A class is a concept of "programming in the small" and implements "how" to do a task.
- Interface should not have any constructor method in it.
- Interfaces are not classes. You can never use the new operator to instantiate an interface. For example:
```
Converter x = new Converter();     // ERROR
```
- However, even though you can't construct interface objects, you can still declare interface variables. For example (Program 5.7):
```
Converter x;          // OK
```
- An interface variable must refer to an object of a class that implements the interface. For example (Program 5.7):
```
Converter x;
x = new CentigradeToFahrenheit();
```
- It is legal to tag interface methods as `public`, and fields as `public static final`. You can do this for greater clarity. However, the Java language specification recommends not to supply redundant keywords.
- Some interfaces define just constants and no methods (Program 5.9). Any class that chooses to implement such an interface automatically inherits these constants.

5.3.3 Inheritance Hierarchy with Interfaces and Classes

You have already learnt that Java supports only single inheritance with classes. You can derive a sub class from a super class and this chain can be extended to any depth (sub class becoming a super class to other sub class and so on). However, the following statement for creating a class `C` is invalid given that `A` and `B` are two classes already known:

```
class C extend A, B {…}             // Not VALID in Java
```

In contrast, if `A` and `B` are two interfaces, then the following statement is legal:

```
class C implements A, B {…}             // Okay
```

Also, the following is valid given that `A` is a class and `B` is an interface:

```
class C extends A implements B {…}             // Okay
```

In fact, Java facilitates a hierarchy of classes and interfaces of any breadth and depth, which is illustrated in the following few illustrative programs (see Program 5.10 to Program 5.16).

Single inheritance with interface

Program 5.10 *(An interface inherits another interface)*

```
/* This program demonstrates how an interface can
inherit from another interface. */

interface A {
    int a = 111;
    void methodA();
}

interface B extends A {      // B inherits A
    int b = 555;
    void methodB();
} // The interface B has two constants a and b and
    two methods,
  // that is, methodA and methodB

/* A class, say C can be defined to implement B. If
so, C should implement all of A's and B's methods in
addition to its own. */

class C implements B {
    int c = 999;    // C's own field as instance
     variable
    public void methodA() {
         System.out.println("I am for A");
    }

    public void methodB() {
         System.out.println("I am for B");
    }

    public void methodC() {
         System.out.println("I am C's native with
           asset:" + a + b + c);
    }
}

class MainClass {
     public static void main(String arg[]) {
          C x = new C();
          x.methodA();
          x.methodB();
          x.methodC();
     }
}
```

Class inheriting another class and interface

Program 5.11 *(A class inherits a class and interface)*

```
/* This program demonstrates how a class can inherit
from another class and interface. */

class A {
    int a = 111;        // A's variable
    public void methodA() {
         System.out.println("I am from A");
    }
}

interface B {
    int b = 555;       // B's constant
    void methodB();
}

/* A class, say C inherits both A and B. */

class C extends A implements B {
    int c = 999;     // C's variable

public void methodB() {
     // Implementation of B's method
         System.out.println("I am for B");
    }

    public void methodC() {
         System.out.println("I am from C with fields :
          " + a + b + c);
    }
}

class MainClass {
     public static void main(String arg[]) {
          C x = new C();
           // Creating an object of class C
          x.methodA();
          x.methodB();
          x.methodC();
     }
}
```

It is quite possible that out of the multiple interfaces under implementation by a single class, there is a method name which is common (i.e., the same method name and argument list) in two or more interfaces. In that case, you need to implement only one occurrence. Consider Program 5.12 to appreciate this. The same is applicable, for example, if an interface `C` extends an interface `B` which in turn extends another interface `A` and both the interfaces `A` and `B` contain methods in them with identical signature. If the method is declared identically in all the interfaces that declare it, then a single definition in the class will satisfy all the interfaces.

Program 5.12 *(Interfaces with same method name)*

```
/* This program illustrates if a class inherits two
interfaces, when they are having same method name. */

interface A {
    int a = 111;        // A's variable
    void method();
}

interface B {
    int b = 555;        // B's constants
    void method();
}

/* A class, say C inherits both A and B. */

class C implements A, B {
    public void methodC() {     // C's own method
        System.out.println("I am from C with data :
        " + a + " " + b);
    }

    public void method() {
    // Implementation of inherited method
        System.out.println("I am a common method!");
    }
}

class MainClass {
    public static void main(String arg[]) {
        C x = new C();
        // Creating an object of class C
```

```
            x.method();
            x.methodC();
        }
}
```

You should take care when you use this feature. If two or more super interfaces declare a method with the same signature (i.e., with same names and parameters) then the method should have the same return type in all the interfaces where you declare it. Violation of this leads to the compile-time error. Error is reported because it is impossible for a class to implement both methods having the same signature. Program 5.13 can help you understand this better.

Program 5.13 *(Interfaces with same method name)*

```
/* This program illustrates if a class implements two
interfaces which have methods having common method name
in each but different return type. */

interface A {
   public void aaa();
}

inLerface B {
   public int aaa();
}

class C implements A,B {
   public void aaa() {          // Eror
        // Some code here....
   }
   public int aaa() {           // Error
        // Some code here....
   }
   public static void main(String args[])  {
        // Some code here....
   }
}
```

Suppose that there are two interfaces, say `A` and `B`, both of which contain the same variable name and of same type, and a class `C` is planned to implement the interfaces. In that case, the program will not be compiled successfully. Program 5.14 is an example of this.

Program 5.14 (Interfaces with same variable name)

```
/* This program illustrates if a class implements two
interfaces which have a common constant declaration in
each. */

interface A {
   int CONST = 123;
   void aaa();
}

interface B {
   int CONST = 234;
   int bbb();
}

class C implements A,B {
   public void aaa() {
        // Some code here....
   }
   public int bbb() {
        // Some code here....
   }
   public static void main(String args[])  {
        // Some code here....
   }
}
```

However, variable names conflict can be resolved by explicit references of the names of the interfaces. Program 5.15 is an example.

Program 5.15 (Explicit reference of variables)

```
/* This program illustrates how variable name conflicts
can be resolved by interface name. */

interface A {
    int i = 111;
}
interface B {
    int i = 555;
}

class C implements A, B {
    public static void main(String args[])      {
        /* Reference to i is ambiguous as both
           variables are i.
```

```
            You should use interface name to
                resolve the
            variables' references        */
        System.out.println(i);     // ERROR!
        System.out.println(A.i);  // Okay
        System.out.println(B.i);  // Okay
    }
}
```

What will happen: class `C` extends a class `A` and implements an interface `B` and both have a common method with same signature? Program 5.16 illustrates such a case. In this case, the program will override the method in class `A`.

Program 5.16 *(Method overriding with interface)*

```
/* This program illustrates if a class extends a class
and implements an interfaces where both of them have a
common method declaration. */

class A {
   void aaa() {
      System.out.println("I am a method in class A");
   }
}

interface B {
   int CONST = 123;
   void aaa();       // An interface method: Same method
}

class C extends A implements B {
   public void aaa() {
         System.out.println("Okay:The method is
            overwritten here!");
   }

   public static void main(String args[])  {
         // Some code here....
   }
}
```

Interface with multiple inheritance

An interface can extend any number of interfaces, whereas a class can extend only one other class. You specify the names of the interfaces separated by commas following the keyword `extends` to define an interface that inherits the members of several other interfaces. For example:

```
public interface I extends IX, IY {
   // Constants and abstract methods to be defined here.
}
```

Here, the interface `I` inherits all the methods and constants which are the members of `IX` and `IY`. This is called as multiple inheritance. In Java, classes do not support multiple inheritance, but interfaces do.

When you use this feature you should take some necessary precautions. Usually, there should not be any method having the same signature, that is, having the same method name and the same list of parameters in the super-interfaces. If so, the method should be distinguishable with respect to the return type in all the interfaces where it has declaration. If it does not, you will not be able to compile your program. Note that for a class, all methods are unique and you cannot define two methods having the same signature. Further, if a method is declared identically in all the interfaces that declare it, then a single definition in the class implementing the interfaces will match. Note that every method in a class being unique must have a unique signature; however, the return type is not a part of it.

5.3.4 Static Method in Interface

Another feature that was added in JDK 9 onward is that you can define `static` methods in interfaces which can be called independently without an object. Program 5.17 is an example.

Program 5.17 *(`Static` method in interface)*

```
/* An example to show that interfaces can have a static
method. */

interface I {
    final int A = 10;
    static int cube( int x) {
        return x*x*x;
    }
}
```

```
// A class that implements interface.
class C implements I {
    public static void main (String[] args)  {
        System.out.println(I.cube(5));
    }
}
```

5.3.5 Explicitly Accessing an Interface Member without Inheritance

A constant member in an interface can be accessed in a class without implementing the interface in that class. Program 5.18 demonstrates how it can be done.

Program 5.18 *(Explicit reference of an interface's member)*

```
/* This program demonstrates how an interface's
constant can be accessed without its implementation. */

package myPacakge;
     // An interface is defined in a package

public interface Factors {
    final double PI = 3.14159;
    double POUND_TO_GRAM = 453.5924;
    double INCH_TO_MM = 25.4;
    double USD_TO_INR = 69.74;
}

import myPackage;

class ImplicitAccess {
    public static void main(String args[]) {
        double pi = myPackage.Factor.PI
           // Explicit access of PI
        System.out.println("PI is " + pi);
     }
}
```

5.3.6 Default Method in an Interface

Prior to JDK 8, interface could not define implementation. This meant that all the methods specified by an interface were `abstract`, containing no body. We can now add `default` implementation for interface methods. This `default` implementation has special use and does not affect the intention behind interfaces. A default method lets you define a `default` implementation for an interface method. By use of a default method, it is now possible for an interface method to provide a body, rather than being `abstract`.

A `default` method in an interface is defined in the same way a method is defined in a class. However, to define a method `default` you should use the keyword `default`. For example, consider Program 5.19.

Program 5.19 *(Default method in interface)*

```
/* This program illustrates the occurrence of a normal
method as well as a default method in an interface. */

interface I {
    int a = 10;                 // public, static and final
    void display();             // Normal abstract method
    default void draw() {       // Default method
        System.out.println(" A simple statement it
          is!");
    }
}
class C implements I {
     // Implementation of the interface I
     public void display(){
         System.out.println("Implementing the abstract
          method...");
    }
}

class TestInterfaceDefault {
     public static void main(String args[]) {
          C c = new C();
          c.display();  // Implemented method is called
          c.draw();     // Default method is called
     }
}
```

5.3.7 Nested Interface

An interface can be declared a member of a class or another interface. Such an interface is called a nested interface (also called member interface). A nested interface can be declared as `public`, `private`, or `protected`. This differs from a top-level interface, which must either be declared as `public` or use the default access level, as previously described. When a nested interface is used outside of its enclosing scope, it must be qualified by the name of the class or interface of which it is a member. Thus, outside of the class or interface in which a nested interface is declared, its name must be fully qualified. Program 5.20 is an example that demonstrates a nested interface.

Program 5.20 *(Nested Interface)*

```
/* This program illustrates the concept of nested
interface in Java. */

// The following class A contains an interface as a
member.
class A {
    public interface NestedIF {
            // This is a nested interface
       boolean inPositive(int x);
    }
}
// The class B implements the nested interface.
class B implements A.NestedIF {
     public boolean isNotNegative(int x) {
           return (x > 0 ? true: false);
     }
}
class NestedIFDemo {
     public static void main(String args[]) {
          A.NestedIF nif = new B();
                                   //Create a reference
          if(nif.ispositive(10))
              System.out.println("10 is postive");
           if(nif.ispositive(-12))
              System.out.println("-12 is not
                positive");
     }
}
```

- Note that A defines a member interface called NestedIF and that it is declared public.
- Next, B implements the nested interface by specifying implements A.NestedIF
- Note that the name is fully qualified by the enclosing class' name. Inside the main() method, an A.NestedIF reference called nif is created, and it is assigned a reference to a B object. Because B implements A.NestedIF, this is legal.

5.3.8 Nested Class

You can put the definition of a class inside the definition of an interface. The class will be an inner class of the interface. An inner class of an interface will be `static` and `public` by default. The code structure would be like this:

```
interface I {
      // Methods & constants in the interface...
     class InterI {
          // Definition of the class...
    }
}
```

This declares the interface `I` with an inner class `InterI`. Objects of the inner class would be of type `I.InterI`. You may create one with a statement like this:

```
I.InterI i = new I.InterI ();
```

- The inner class should not have the default constructor inside the class definition. You may define a class as an inner class to an interface, in case when objects of the inner class type have a strong logical association with the interface.
- A class which implements the interface would have no direct connection with the inner class to the interface. The class would just need to implement the methods declared by the interface. Nevertheless, it is highly likely that it would make use of objects of the inner class type.

5.3.9 Difference between an Abstract Class and Interface

Both abstract class and interface are used for abstraction. The salient differences between the two are summarized in Table 5.3.

When to use what?

Usefulness

In Java applications, there are some related classes that need to share some lines of code. In that case, you can put these lines of code within abstract class and this abstract class should be extended by all these related classes.

Table 5.3 Difference between abstract class and interface

Feature	Abstract class	Interface
Declaration	The keyword `abstract` is used to declare an abstract class.	The keyword `interface` is used to declare an interface.
Type of methods	Can have abstract and non-abstract methods.	Can have only abstract methods. Versions from Java 8 onwards can have default and static methods also.
Variables	Can have final, non-final, static, and non-static variables.	Has only static and final variables.
Access specification	Can have class members like public, private, protected, etc.	In general, members are public. Since JDK 9 and onward, methods are public or default.
Abstraction	An abstract class achieves partial abstraction (0 to 100%).	An interface achieves full abstraction (100%).
Single inheritance	Can extend another Java class and implement multiple Java interfaces. Can be extended using keyword `extends`. Once an abstract class is extended, its method(s) can be overwritten in the sub classes.	Can extend another Java interface only. An interface can be implemented using keyword `implements`. A class can be defined to implement interface(s).
Multiple inheritance	Does not support multiple inheritance.	Supports multiple inheritance.

5.3.10 Some Examples of User Defined Interfaces in User's Programs

By this time you have learned the concept of interface in Java programming. In summary, you have learnt the following:

- An interface declaration can contain method signatures, default methods, static methods, and constant definitions. If an interface contains a method with implementation, then it should be declared as default and static method.
- A class that implements an interface must implement all the methods declared in the interface.
- An interface name can be used anywhere a type can be used.

With some simple and yet effective programs, we shall try to learn how we can utilize the interface concept in your programs. In summary, you can use an interface for the following main reasons:

1. Constants in programs
2. Dynamic binding/ run-time polymorphism
3. Multiple inheritance
4. Proxies

Let's discuss the use of each of these usefulness in the following cases:

Constants in Java Programs

In C/C++, there is a provision to maintain some constants which can be used globally among many functions or programs. This is not possible in Java. You will often find that a program makes use of a set of constant values that you really want to define only once. You might have values that your program uses in calculations such as conversion factors from one set of units to another. In Java, a common approach is to define a set of related constants in an interface and then implement the interface in any class that uses any of the constants. Program 5.21 explains this concept.

In Program 5.21, an interface is defined that contains variables that are initialized to the desired values. This program makes use of one of Java's standard classes: `Random`, which provides pseudorandom numbers. Note that the class `Random` is imported into this program where the defined method `nextDouble()` is used to return random numbers in the range 0.0 to 1.0.

Program 5.21 *(Constants in Java programs)*

```
import java.util.Random;
interface MyConstants {
        int NO = 0;
        int YES = 1;
        int MAYBE = 2;
        int LATER = 3;
        int SOON = 4;
        int NEVER = 5;
}

/*The following class Question is defined to implement
the interface MyConstants; thus, all constants are now
a part of the class Question.*/

class Question implements MyConstants {
     Random rand = new Random();
      int ask() {
          int prob = (int) (100 * rand.nextDouble());
           if (prob < 30)
              return NO;                       // 30%
           else if (prob < 60)
                   return YES;                 // 30%
               else if (prob < 75)
                        return LATER;          // 15%
                   else if (prob < 98)
                             return SOON;      // 13%
                        else
                             return NEVER;     // 02%
```

```
        }
}

/*The next program defines another class which use some
other constants defined in the interface MyConstants.
*/

class AskMe implements MyConstants {
    static void answer(int result) {
        switch(result) {
            case NO:
                  System.out.println("No");
                  break;
            case YES:
                  System.out.println("Yes");
                  break;
            case MAYBE:
                 System.out.println("Maybe");
                 break;
            case LATER:
                 System.out.println("Later");
                 break;
            case SOON:
                  System.out.println("Soon");
                  break;
            case NEVER:
                  System.out.println("Never");
                  break;
            }
        }

      //The drive class to create an object of class
            Question and use it.
       public static void main(String args[]) {
            Question q = new Question();
            answer(q.ask());
            answer(q.ask());
            answer(q.ask());
            answer(q.ask());
       }
}
```

It gives a flexible solution indeed. For example, you can add few more features (i.e., more constants, or methods, or modify the initial values, etc.). This can be done without any effect on the existing classes which shares the constants in the interface.

Dynamic binding/run-time polymorphism

You know a number of classes can implement (according to their defined way) an interface. If so, all objects of such classes can be utilized in a uniform manner. For example, consider an interface `GeoAnalyzer` (Figure 5.3). Three classes namely, `Circle`, `Ellipse`, and `Rectangle` are planned to implement the interface `GeoAnalyzer`. The interface, its several implementations, and subsequent creation of different objects of the different class, are illustrated in Program 5.22. In this program, you can see how interface type objects can be declared and then the same objects can store the references of the objects which implement the interface. This typecasting is possible. An interface variable can refer to any class variable which implements the interface. Next, run-time polymorphism, that is, a reference to a method call, will be dynamically resolved depending on the type of the object the interface object is referring to.

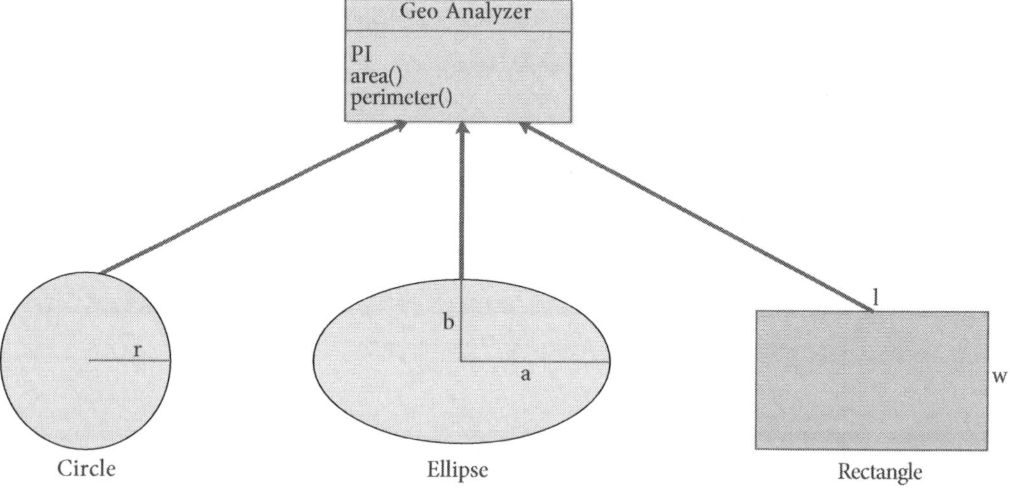

Figure 5.3 Implementation of an interface by classes

Program 5.22 *(Implementation of an interface and dynamic binding)*

```
/* This program demonstrates how an interface can be
implemented by a number of classes and then utility
of interface type object to support dynamic binding.
Assume that all parts of the program are stored in the
same directory. */


interface GeoAnalyzer    {      // Interface declaration
     final static float PI = 3.142F;
```

```
      float area( );
      float perimeter( );
}

class Circle implements GeoAnalyzer {
      // Implementation 1
         float radius;
         Circle(float r) {
            radius = r;
         }
         public float area( ) {
                return (PI*radius*radius);
         }
           public float perimeter( ) {
                 return (2*PI*radius);
         }
 }
class Ellipse implements GeoAnalyzer {
      // Implementation 2
         float major;
         float minor;
         Ellipse(float a, float b) {
                major = a;
               minor = b;
         }
         public float area( ) {
              return(PI*major*minor);
         }
         public float perimeter( ) {
               return(PI*(major+minor);
         }
 }

class Rectangle implements GeoAnalyzer
      // Implementation 3
 {
         float length;
         float width;
         Rectangle(float l, float w) {
              length = l;
             width = w;
         }
         public float area() {
              return(length*width);
         }
```

```
        public float perimeter( ) {
            return(2*(length+width));
        }
}

/* The following is the main class, which declare a
number of objects of the types as declared above. */

class Geometry  {
    static void display(float x, float y) {
        System.out.println("Area = " + x +
           "Perimeter = " + y);
    }
    public static void main(String args[ ]) {
        Circle c = new Circle(5.2f);
        Ellipse e = new Ellipse(4.5f, 3.6f);
        Rectangle r = new Rectangle(6.5f, 4.3f);
        //An array of references to interface
        GeoAnalyzer[] geoItems = new geoItems[3];

  /* Last three initializations  store all objects into
     the array of interface GeoAnalyzer */

        geoItems[0]  = c;
        geoItems[1]  = e;
        geoItems[2]  = r;

/* The call of the methods dynamically bind into the
object of respective types. */

        for(int i = 0; i < 3; i++)
           display(geoItems[i].area(), geoItems[i].
           perimeter());
     }
 }
```

You can declare variables as object references that use an interface rather than a class. Note that an instance of any class which implements a declared interface can be referred to by such a variable. Further, note that when you call a method through one of these references, the correct version will be called based on the actual instance of the interface being referred to. In fact, this is one of the key features of interfaces. Also, note that the method to be executed is looked up dynamically, that is, at run-time, allowing classes to be created later than the code which calls methods on them. More precisely, the "caller" can dispatch through an interface without any knowledge about the "callee". This process is similar to using a super class reference to access a sub class object as discussed in Chapter 4.

Multiple inheritance

With the class definitions, you are well familiar with the single inheritance (i.e., inheriting class attributes) from a super class to its sub class. Multiple inheritance inherits the class attributes from two or more out of which one can be a class, other(s) is(are) interface(s). Figure 5.4 shows the three situations of multiple inheritances that programmers can plan in their program. In Figure 5.4, a circle symbolizes a class and a rectangle symbolizes an interface. In the following, three instances are showing with three programs. In the programs (Program 5.23 to Program 5.25), two instances imply multiple instances.

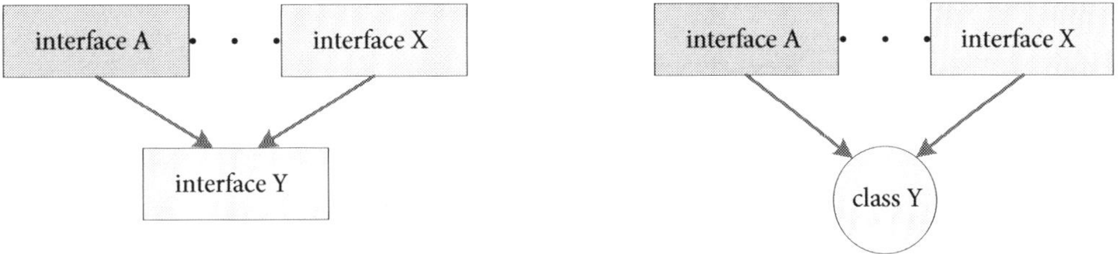

Case 1: Interface `extends` multiple interfaces

Case 2: Class `implements` multiple interfaces

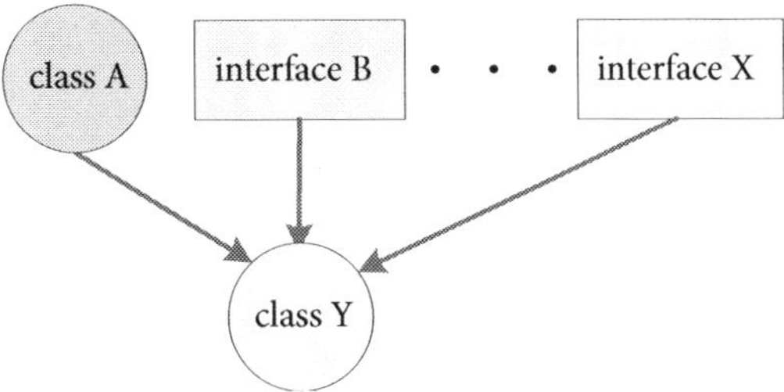

Case 3: Class `extends` a class and `implements` multiple interfaces

Figure 5.4 Different ways of multiple inheritances

Case 1: An interface inherits (extends) from two (or more) interfaces

Program 5.23 *(Inheritance from two interfaces)*

```
/* Case 1:  Example of interface which "extends"
two interfaces. This is an example of the multiple
inheritance when an interface inherits from multiple
interfaces.  */

interface A {
    void methodA();
}
interface X {
    void methodX();
}

interface Y extends A, X {
     // Interface inherits by extends
    int y = 55;
    void methodY();
}

class Z implements Y {
     // A class must implements an interface to use
    public void methodA()      {
        System.out.println("Defining A's method..."
          + y);
    }

    public void methodX() {
     System.out.println("X's method is defined here.");
    }

     public void methodY() {
        System.out.println("C's method is called " + );
    }
}
public class TestCase1 {
    public static void main(String[] args) {
        Z z = new Z();
          // An object of class Z is created
        z.methodA();
        z.methodX();
        z.methodY();
    }
}
```

- A class should implement an interface to be used in programs.
- An interface cannot implement an interface. Thus, the following declaration is not valid:

```
interface A {…}    // A is declared as an interface
interface B implements A {…}  // Not possible
```

- An interface can extend any number of interfaces (Program 5.24).

Case 2: A class implements any number of interfaces

Program 5.24 *(Class implements two interfaces)*

```
/* Case 2:  Example of a class which "implements" two
interfaces.
This is an example of multiple inheritance when a class
inherits from multiple interfaces.  */

interface A {
    int i = 123;
    void printA();
}
interface X {
    public static int j = 555;
    void printX();
}

class Y implements A, X{
     public int aValue = 999;

     public void printA() {
          System.out.println("I am from A " + i);
     }
     public void printX() {
         System.out.println("I am from X " + j);
    }
    public void printY() {
         System.out.println("I am from Y " +
           (aValue = i+j));
    }
}
class TestCase2 {
      public static void main (String[] args)     {
           Y y = new Y();
           y.printY();
          y.printA();
          y.printX();
    }
}
```

- An interface cannot have any constructor.
- When a method of an interface is implemented in a class, that method should be declared as `public`.
- A reference to an interface type can be declared. However, no object can be created for an interface. For example, check the following:

```
      interface I {...}     // I is an interface
    i x;     // It is valid: reference to type interface
    i y = new I(); // Not valid: object can't be created
```

- An implemented method can be accessed through an interface reference. For example, the following code is valid:

```
interface I {
    i();    // i() is an abstract method declared
}
class C implements I {
    public i() {  ... }  // The method is defined here
}
class Test {
     public static void main(String args[]) {
          I  a = new C();
          /* Here, a is the reference and it refers
             to object of its implementing class */
          a.i();
          /* It is valid: An implementation can be
             accessed through interface reference */
     }
}
```

Case 3: A class extends another class and implements interface(s)

Program 5.25 *(Class extends a class and implements interfaces)*

```
/* This is an example of a class which "extends" a
class and "implements" two interfaces. */

class A {
    protected int i = 1000;
    public void print() {
            System.out.println("I am from A "+i);
    }
}
interface B {
     public static int j = 555;
     void printB();
}
```

```
interface X {
     public static int k = 666;
     void printX();
}

class Y extends A implements B, X  {
     public int aValue = 999;
     public void printB() {
      System.out.println("I am from interface B " + j);
  }
     public void printX() {
      System.out.println("I am from interface X " + k);
   }
     public void printY() {
           super.print();
           printB();
           printX();
    }
}

class Z implements B {
     // Another implementation of interface B
      public void printB() {
         System.out.println("I am another form of B ");
     }
}
class TestCase3 {
     public static void main (String[] args)     {
          Y y = new Y();
          y.printY();
     Z z = new Z();
     z.printB();
   }
}
```

Although interfaces are usually used to mix in behavior to classes (method signatures in the interface give guideline to methods in classes and those to be implemented there), interfaces can also be used to mix in useful constants in classes. For example, if an interface defined a set of constants, and then multiple classes used those constants, the values of the constants could be globally changed without having to modify multiple classes. This is yet another example of where the use of interfaces to separate design from implementation can make your code more general and easier to maintain.

5.3.11 Some Frequently Used Built-in Java Interfaces

There are many interfaces defined in Java APIs. Some of the frequently used interfaces with a brief description about them is stated in Table 5.4 for the sake of simplicity of understanding. These interfaces and many more will be learned when we shall discuss advanced topics on Java programming in the coming chapters.

Table 5.4 Some frequently used interfaces in Java APIs

Interface	Description
`Iterator`	To run through a collection of objects without knowing how the objects are stored, for example, in array, list, bag, or set.
`Cloneable`	To make a copy of an existing object via the `clone()` method on the class `Object`.
`Serializable`	To make a total order of objects, for example, 3, 56, 67, 879, 3422, 34234.
`Comparable`	Pack a web of objects such that it can be sent over a network or stored in a disk. Such a web of objects is of type `Comparable`.

Iterator interface

The `Iterator` interface in the package `java.util` is a basic iterator (it is a concept of traversing) that works on collections. A simple program (Program 5.26) illustrates the usefulness of this interface.

Program 5.26 *(`Iterator` interface)*

```
/* This program illustrates the use of Iterator
interface in a program. This program assumes a class
Shape storing a collection of objects. */

import java.util.*;

public interface Iterator {
     public abstract boolean hasNext();
                              // Check if the list has more
     Object next();        // Return the next element
     void remove();        // optional throws exception
 }
 // use an iterator
 Shape myShapes = new Shape(); // Has a set of objects
 Iterator iter = myShapes.iterator();
     while (iter.hasNext()) {
           Shape s = (Shape)iter.next(); // downcast
           s.draw();
      }
}
```

`Cloneable` interface

A class `X` that implements the `Cloneable` interface tells clients that the objects of class `X` can be replicated. The interface is empty and has no method. It returns an identical copy of the object. Program 5.27 is an example of this interface.

Program 5.27 *(`Cloneable` interface)*

```
/* This program illustrates the use of Cloneable interface
in a user's Java program. */

public class Car implements Cloneable{
      private String make;
      private String model;
      private double price;
      public Car() {.                    // default constructor
             this("", "", 0.0f);
       }
      // give reasonable values to instance variables
      public Car(String make, String model, double price){
            this.make = make;
            this.model = model;
            this.price = price;
       }
     public Object clone(){      // the Cloneable interface
       return new Car(this.make, this.model, this.price);
     }
 }
```

`Serializable` interface

A class X that implements the `Serializable` interface tells clients that X objects can be stored on a file or other persistent media. The interface is empty and has no methods. Program 5.28 shows an example of this interface.

Program 5.28 *(`Serializable` interface)*

```
/* This program illustrates the use of Serializable
interface in a user's Java program. */

public class Car implements Serializable {
       // rest of class unaltered

}
      // write to and read from disk
```

```
import java.io.*;
public class SerializeDemo{
    Car myToyota, anotherToyota;
    myToyota = new Car("Toyota", "Carina", 42312);
    ObjectOutputStream out = getOutput();
    out.writeObject(myToyota);
    ObjectInputStream in = getInput();
    anotherToyota = (Car)in.readObject();
}
```

Comparable interface

This interface is defined in the package `java.lang`. It returns a negative integer, zero, or a positive integer depending on whether this object is less than, equal to, or greater than the specified object. Program 5.29 as an example of this interface.

Program 5.29 *(`Serializable` interface)*

```
/* This program illustrates the use of Comparable
interface in a user's Java program. */

package java.lang.*;
public interface Comparable {
      int compareTo(Object o);
}

public class IPAddress implements Comparable{
     private int[] n;
             // here IP stored, e.g., 125.255.231.123
     /** The Comparable interface */
     public int compareTo(Object o){
         IPAddress other = (IPAddress) o; // downcast
         int result = 0;
         for(int i = 0; i < n.length; i++){
               if (this.getNum(i) < other.getNum(i)){
               result = -1;
               break;
          }
          if (this.getNum(i) > other.getNum(i)){
               result = 1;
               break;
          }
         }
         return result;
     }
}
```

Summary

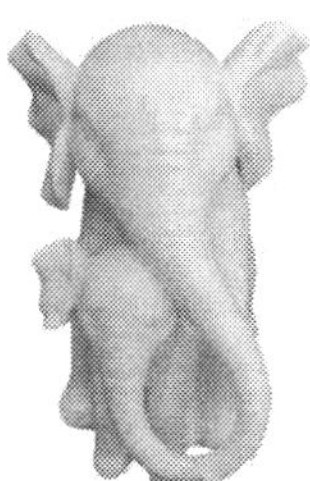

Package and interface are two important concepts which all Java programmers and software practitioners working with large software, must follow. This chapter provides precise information on the package and interface features in Java. A basic discussion has been included giving a clear view of packages in programming. Java has a number of built-in packages to help programmers. These are highlighted, with a link to all the packages in Java that have been covered. Programmers can organize their programs in the form of packages, for which Java gives efficient mechanisms. How the user can define their own packages is discussed in detail. Code sharing, information hiding, and code maintainability are some of the challenging tasks which every programmer has to deal with while using packages. Concise discussions with illustrations on accessibility of code and access control mechanisms are included in this chapter. The next part of chapter includes a detailed coverage of the concept of interfaces. Why an interface is used, how it can be defined, and how multiple inheritance can be handled with the help of interfaces are discussed in detail in this chapter. The built-in interfaces and how users can define their own interfaces and implement them are also discussed. Finally, the chapter concludes with demonstration of some frequently used interfaces in Java programs.

FAQs

5.1 What is a package in Java? List down various advantages of packages.

5.2 What is abstraction in Java? How can it be achieved?

5.3 What is an interface in Java?

5.4 What are the key differences between abstract classes and interfaces?

5.5 What is a marker interface? Give some example of marker interfaces in Java.

5.6 Can you use `import abc.xyz.B*;` to import all the classes in a package in the path `abc.xyz` that begin with `B`?

5.7 What does `.*` imply in import statement?

5.8 Why is full multiple inheritance so complex that Java has abandoned it?

5.9 Abstract classes do not have to implement all the methods in an interface themselves; if so, then where should the methods be implemented?

The answers to these questions and other problems in this chapter are available at www.cambridge.org/9781009211918. You might have many questions like these. You can post your question in the discussion forum at https://cse.iitkgp.ac.in/~dsamanta/joywithjava/page8.php.

Programs for Practice

5.1 Consider the given Java program.

Underline the statement(s), which are not correct. Assume that all the classes are stored in their respective directories. The main class is stored in current working directory and CLASSPATH environment variable is set which includes the current working directory.

```
package myPacakage1;
public class A {
    public void methodA() {
        System.out.println("Hello I am Class A");
    }
}
package myPackage2;
import myPacakage1;
public class B {
    public void methodB(){
        System.out.println("Hello I am Class B");
    }
}
import myPacakage2.*;
public class Testing {
    public static void main(String[] args){
        A a = new A();
        myPackage1.A a2 = new myPacakage1.A();
        B b = new B();
        myPackage2.B b2 = new myPacakage2.B();
        C c = new C();
        a1.methodA();
        b1.methodB();
        c.methodC();
    }
}
class C extends A{
    public void methodC(){
        System.out.println("Hello I am Class C");
    }
    }
```

5.2 Practice the following program to learn how you can access a class from a package without importing the class explicitly:

```
public class DirectImportTest {
     public static void main(String arg[])   {
          java.util.ArrayList list<String> =
                              new java.util.ArrayList<String>();

           // java.util.ArrayList is not imported, hence we
           // referring to it using the complete  package.

            list.add("C");
            list.add("C++");
```

```
            list.add("Java");
            list.add("Python");

            System.out.println(list);
        }
    }
```

5.3 Practice the following program to learn how you can create your own package and use the same package in your program:

```
/* Save the following code as myClass1.java in a sub-directory,
say myPackage. Compile the .java file and save the .class file in
the same sub-directory */

package myPackage;

public class myClass1 {
    public void msg(){
        System.out.println("muClass1: Hello! ");
    }
}

/*Further, add one more class in the same package. Save the
following code as myClass2.java in the same sub-directory
myPackage. Compile the .java file and save the .class file in
the same sub-directory */

package myPackage;

public class myClass2 {
     public void msg(){
          System.out.println("myClass2: Hello! ");
     }
}

/* You can run the following program from any directory, you
wish. */

import myPackage.*;

class OwnPacakgeTest{
     public static void main(String args[]){
          myClass1 obj1 = new myClass1();
          obj1.msg();
```

```
            myClass2 obj2 = new myClass1();
            obj2.msg();
        }
    }
```

5.4 You should be careful about the declaration of classes. You should use the access specifier public to access the package from anywhere. No other access specifier (private or protected) is allowed. However, you can use default access specifier. In that case, you can run your test program in the same directory as in the package directory. Practice the following program:

```
/*Save the following code as myClass1.java in a sub-directory
myPackage. Compile the .java file and save the .class file in
the same sub-directory */

package myPackage;

class myClass1 {
    public void msg(){
        System.out.println("muClass1: Hello! ");
    }
}

/*Further, add one more class in the same package. Save the
following code as myClass2.java in the same sub-directory
myPackage. Compile the .java file and save the .class file in
the same sub-directory */

package myPackage;

class myClass2 {
     public void msg(){
          System.out.println("myClass2: Hello! ");
     }
}


//-----------------------------------------------------------
/* Case 1: You can run the following program: from any directory,
you wish, and Case 2: from the same as package directory. */
import myPackage.*;
class OwnPacakgeTest{
     public static void main(String args[]){
          myClass1 obj1 = new myClass1();
          obj1.msg();
```

```
            myClass2 obj2 = new myClass1();
            obj2.msg();
        }
    }
    //--------------------------------------------------------------
    /* Case 2: You can run the following program: from the same as
    package directory. */

    class OwnPacakgeTest{
        public static void main(String args[]){
            myClass1 obj1 = new myClass1();
            obj1.msg();
            myClass2 obj2 = new myClass1();
            obj2.msg();
        }
    }
```

5.5 Practice the following program to see how you can use two classes having the same name, but belonging to two different packages:

```
package myPackage1;   // Creating a package myPackage1
public class myClass {
    public void msg1() {
        System.out.println("Hello! It is myPackage1 Class!! ");
    }
}
package myPackage2;   // Creating a package myPackage2
public class myClass {
    public void msg2() {
        System.out.println("Hello! It is myPackage2 Class!! ");
    }
}

/* Run the following program to test the packages. */
import myPackage1.myClass;
import myPackage2.myClass;
public class DuplicateClassTest{
    public static void main(String[] args){
        myPackage1.myClass a = new myPackage1.myClass();
        myPackage2.myClass b = new myPackage2.myClass ();
        a.msg1();
        b.msg2();
    }
}
```

5.6 Practice the following program to learn how you can derive a sub class from a class defined in a package:

```
package myPackage;      // A class in a myPackage

public class Balance {
        String name;
        double bal;
        Balance(String n, double b) {
              name = n;
              bal = b;
        }
        void show() {
              if (bal < 0) {
                    System.out.print("Sorry! Negative balance ");
              }
                    System.out.println(name + ": $" + bal);
        }
}
/* Derive a sub-class in a program to be run from Demonstration-
        VIII directory */
import myPackage.Balance;
public class Savings extends Balance{
     String branch;
     Int customerID;
     Savings(String n, double bal, String br, int id) {
         Balance(n, bal);
         Branch = br;
         customerID = id;
     }
  void show() {
     if (bal < 0) {
         System.out.print("Sorry! Negative balance ");
     }
     System.out.println(name + ": $" + bal + " "+ branch + " "+id);
}
class Demonstration_810{
     public static void main(String args[]) {
     Savings current[] = new Savings[3];
     current[0] = new Balance("Debasis", 123.23, "Kolkata", 555);
     current[1] = new Balance("Monalisa", 157.02, "Chennai", 420);
     current[2] = new Balance("Ananya", -12.33, "Mumbai" + 999);

     for (int i = 0; i < 3; i++) {
        current[i].show();
        }
     }
}
```

5.7 Consider the following piece of code:

```
// Encapsulation of data by accessor methods and mutators
class Point {
    private double x;
    private double y;
    public Point(double x, double y) {
       this.x = x;
       this.y = y;
    }
    public double getX() { return x; }        // Accessor method
    public double getY() { return y; }
                                        // Another accessor method
    public void setX(double x) {this.x = x; } // Mutator method
    public void setY(double y) {this.y = y;}
                                         // Another mutator method
    }
```

Analyze this program with reference to the following points:

(a) Create an object of the class `Point` (say in a main class, defined in the same package) and call the accessor methods getX, setX, etc.

(b) Maintain the class `Point` in a package. Use the class in another class defined in some other package.

(c) Repeat the problem (b) but with private modifier of the class `Point`.

(d) Create another class which would inherit the class `Point`. Consider the cases when two classes (parent and child) are in the same directory or in different directories (i.e., in two different packages).

5.8 How can you make a class immutable? Following are some points to consider:

(a) Don't provide methods that modify the object's state (i.e., mutators).

(b) Ensure that the class can't be extended.

(c) Make all fields `final`.

(d) Make all fields `private`.

(e) Ensure exclusive access to any mutable components.

Cite illustration for each of these.

5.9 Check, if the following class is immutable or not:

```
// Immutable complex number class
public final class Complex {
            private final double re;
            private final double im;
            public Complex(double re, double im) {
                      this.re = re;
                      this.im = im;
            }
            public double realPart() { return re; }
                    public double imaginaryPart() { return im; }
```

```
            public Complex plus(Complex c) {
                    return new Complex(re + c.re, im + c.im);
             }
    public Complex minus(Complex c) {
        return new Complex(re - c.re, im - c.im);
    }
    public Complex times(Complex c) {
        return new Complex(re * c.re - im * c.im, re * c.im + im
             * c.re);
    }
    public Complex dividedBy(Complex c) {
        double tmp = c.re * c.re + c.im * c.im;
        return new Complex((re * c.re + im * c.im) / tmp, (im * c.re - re
             * c.im) /
    tmp);
}
```

Note:

- An immutable object can be exactly in one state only.
- Immutable objects are inherently thread-safe; they require no synchronization (i.e., they cannot be corrupted by multiple threads accessing them concurrently).
- Immutable objects can be shared freely.

5.10 Check, if the following class is immutable:

Recall that to guarantee immutability, a class must not permit itself to be sub classed. This can be done by making the class `final`, but there is another, more flexible alternative. Instead of making an immutable class `final`, you can make all its constructors `private` or `package-private` and add `public static` factories (i.e., methods) in place of the public constructors (as in Question 5.9). To make this concrete, here's how `Complex` would look if you took this approach:

```
// Immutable class with static factories instead of constructors
public class Complex {
       private final double re;
       private final double im;

       private Complex(double re, double im) {
           this.re = re;
           this.im = im;
       }

       public static Complex valueOf(double re, double im) {
           return new Complex(re, im);
       }
       ... // Remainder unchanged
}
```

5.11 Regarding the member and methods in an interface are concerned, there are some restrictions. For example, all members should be declared as `public static` and `final`. Practice the following program to see the outcome, if the rule is violated:

```
interface I1 {
     public static final double PI = 3.1413434567;    //OK
     static final double lambda = 0.04; //OK: public is implicit

     int x;  //Declaration of any instance variable is NOT allowed.
     private static final p = 444;
                    //ERROR: private/ protected is NOT allowed.
     abstract public static void methodI1(); // OK: with explicit
     void methodI2(); //public static by default
}
class A1 implements I1 {
       public void int a1 = 555;
       public void methodI1(){
           System.out.println("From I1 …" + PI);
       }
       public void methodI2(){
          System.out.println("Again from I1 …" + lambda);
      }
}
// Here, is the main class….
public class InterfaceTest {
        public static void main(String[] args) {
              A1 a = new A1();
          a.methodI1();
          a.methodI2();
      }
}
```

5.12 An interface acts like a class. We can do everything as we do with class except object instantiation. Here is an example of single inheritance with interface:

```
interface I1 {
     double x = 4.444;
        void methodI1(); //public static by default
}
interface I2 extends I1 {
     double y = 5.555;
        void methodI2(); //public static by default
}
class A1 implements I2 {
       public void int a1 = 555;
       public void methodI1(){
           System.out.println("From I1 …");
       }
```

```
        public void methodI2(){
           System.out.println("From I2 ...");
        }
}
public class SingleInheritanceInterface {
        public static void main(String[] args) {
             A1 a = new A1();
           a.methodI1();
           a.methodI2();
      }
}
```

5.13 An interface is a significant feature in Java in the sense that it enables multiple inheritance. Follow the program and check if it can enable the **multiple inheritance** or not.

```
/* Case 1:  Example of class which "implements" two interfaces */

interface I1 {
    int i = 123;
    void printI1();
    }

interface I2 {
    public static void int j = 555;
    void printI2();
}

class A implements I1, I2{
     public int aValue = 999;

     public void printI1() {
          System.out.println("I am from I1 " + i);
     }
     public void printI2() {
         System.out.println("I am from I2 " + j);
    }
    public void printA() {
         System.out.println("I am from A " + (aValue = i+j));
    }
}

class MuktileInheritance1 {
        public static void main (String[] args)      {
          A a = new A();
          a.printA();
            a.printI2();
            a.printI1();
    }
}
```

5.14 Practice the following program to see how multiple inheritance with class and interface is possible:

```
/* Case 2:  Example of "extends" with "implements" */

class A {
    protected int i = 1000;
    void print() { System.out.println("I am from A "+i);
    }
}

interface C {
    public static void int i = 555;
    void printInterface();
}

class B extends A implements C{
     public int aValue = 999;

     void printInterface() {
          System.out.println("I am from C " + i);
     }
     Public void printB() {
         super.print();
         printInterface()
    }
}
//Driver code in main class
class MultipelInheritance2 {
        public static void main (String[] args)      {
              B b = new B();
        b.printB();
    }
}
```

5.15 Practice the following program to see how multiple inheritance with class and multiple interfaces are possible:

```
/* Case 3:  Example of "extends" with "implements" two or more
interfaces*/

class A {
    protected int i = 1000;
    void print() { System.out.println("I am from A "+i);
    }
}

interface C {
    public static void int i = 555;
    void printInterfaceC();
}
```

```
interface D {
    public static void int j = 666;
    void printInterfaceD();
}

class B extends A implements C, D{
     public int aValue = 999;
     super.print();
     void printInterfaceC() {
          System.out.println("I am from C " + i);
     }
     void printInterfaceD() {
          System.out.println("I am from D " + j);
     }
     public void printB() {
         super.print();
         printInterfaceC();
          printInterfaceD();
    }
}

class Demonstration_910 {
     public static void main (String[] args)     {
          B b = new B();
          b.printB();
     }
}
```

5.16 Practice the following program to understand practical usefulness of interface in Java programming. This program shows how an interface helps a programmer to share variables like a library.

```
package myInterface;

 interface SharedConstants {
    int NO = 0;
    int YES = 1;
    int MAYBE = 2;
    int LATER = 3;
    int SOON = 4;
    int NEVER = 5;
 }

import myInterface.*:
import java.util.Random;

class Question implements SharedConstants {
 Random rand = new Random();
  int ask() {
      int prob = (int) (100 * rand.nextDouble());
```

```
          if (prob < 30)
                  return NO;
          else if (prob < 60)
                  return YES;
              else if (prob < 75)
                  return LATER;
                  else if (prob < 98)
                       return SOON;
                     else
                       return NEVER;
    }
  }
  class AskMe implements SharedConstants {
     static void answer(int result) {
        switch(result) {
           case NO:
              System.out.println("No");
              break;
           case YES:
              System.out.println("Yes");
              break;
           case MAYBE:
              System.out.println("Maybe");
              break;
           case LATER:
              System.out.println("Later");
              break;
           case SOON:
              System.out.println("Soon");
              break;
           case NEVER:
              System.out.println("Never");
              break;
        }
      }
    }

    public static void main(String args[]) {
        Question q = new Question();
        answer(q.ask());
        answer(q.ask());
        answer(q.ask());
        answer(q.ask());
    }
  }
```

5.17 Practice the following program to understand run-time polymorphism with interface:

```
/* Run-time polymorphism with interface objects GeoAnalyzer
program implementation using interface */

package myInterface;

interface GeoAnalyzer {
        final static float pi = 3.142F;
        float area();
        float perimeter();
}

class Circle implements GeoAnalyzer {
        float radius;

        Circle(float r) {
              radius = r;
        }

        public float area() {
              return (pi * radius * radius);
        }
        public float perimeter() {
              return (2 * pi * radius);
        }
}

class Ellipse implements GeoAnalyzer {
        float major;
        float minor;

        Ellipse(float m, float n) {
              major = m;
              minor = n;
        }

        public float area() {
              return (pi * major * minor);
        }

public float perimeter() {
              return (pi * (major + minor));
        }
}

class Rectangle implements GeoAnalyzer {
        float length;
        float width;
```

```
        Rectangle(float l, float w) {
              length = l;
              width = w;
        }


        public float area() {
              return (length * width);
        }

        public float perimeter() {
              return (2 * (length + width));
        }
}

class Run-timePolymorphism1 {
        static void display(float x, float y) {
              System.out.println("Area = " + x + "Perimeter = " + y);
        }

public static void main(String args[]) {
              Circle c = new Circle(5.2f);
              Ellipse e = new Ellipse(4.5f, 3.6f);
              Rectangle r = new Rectangle(6.5f, 4.3f);
              GeoAnalyzer geoItem;
              geoItem = c;
              display(geoItem.area(), geoItem.perimeter());
              geoItem = e;
              display(geoItem.area(), geoItem.perimeter());
              geoItem = r;
              display(geoItem.area(), geoItem.perimeter());
              }
}
```

5.18 Practice the following program to understand run-time polymorphism with abstract class. This is an alternate approach to Program 5.17.

```
/* Run-time polymorphism with abstract class
   GeoObjects program implementation using abstract class */

//An abstract class  and its sub class

package myInterface;

public abstract class Geometry {
  public abstract double area ();
  public abstract double circumference();
}

package myInterface;
import myInterface.*;
```

```
// Extending Geometry for Circle
class Circle extends Geometry {
        public double r;
        protected static final double PI = 3.14159265358979323846;
        public Circle (){
                r=1.0
        }
        public Circle (double r){
                this.r=r;
        }
        public double area() {
                return PI*r*r;
        }
        public double circumference() {
                return 2*PI*r;
        }
        public double getRadius() {
                return r;
        }
}
class Rectangle extends Geometry {
        protected double l,w;
        public Rectangle() {
                l = 0.0;
                w = 0.0;
        }
        public Rectangle(double l, double w) {
                this.l = l;
                this.w = w;
        }
        public double area() {
                return l*w;
        }
        public double circumference() {
                return 2*(l+w);
        }
        public double getwidth() {
                return w;
        }
        public doub;le getlength() {
                return l;
        }
}
```

```
package myInterface;
import myInterface.*;

class Ellipse extends Geometry {
      protected double a,b;
      public Ellipse() {
                  a = 0.0;
                  b = 0.0;
      }

      public Ellipse(double a, double b) {
                  this.a = a;
                  this.b = b;
      }

      public double area() {
                  return PI * a*b;
      }

      public double circumference() {
                  return PI*(a+b);
      }

      public double getMinorAxis() {
                  return a;
      }

      public double getMajorAxis() {
                  return b;
      }
}
package myInterface;
import myInterface.*;

public class Run-timePolymorphism2 {
      public static void main(String args[]) {

            // use the above class definition
            Geometry [] geoObjects = new Geometry[3]
            // create an array to hold Geometry objects
            geoObjects [0] = new Circle (2.0);
            geoObjects [1] = new Rectangle (1.0,3.0);
            geoObjects [2] = new Ellipse (4.0,2.0);

            double totalArea = 0;

            for (int i = 0; i < 3; i++) {
            totalArea = totalArea + geoObjects[i].area();
            }
      Sytem.out.println("Total area of the geo-objects is "
             + totalArea);
}
```

5.19 Consider the following piece of code:

```
interface MyInterface {
}

class MyClass implements MyInterface {
      public static void main(String args[]) {
            System.ou.println("Am I okay?");
      }
}
```

Suppose, you save the interface's source code in a file with the `.java` extension. The class `MyClass` should be saved in the same directory as the interface `MyInterface`. Which of the following statement(s) is(are) true?

(a) You should compile an interface exactly the same way you compile a class.
(b) Just like a normal class, the byte-code file will have the `.class` extension.
(c) The preceding example is a complete interface, meaning that it can be compiled, after which other Java programs can reference it.
(d) The program will compile and execute successfully if the interface is declared as public.

5.20 Which of the following statements is(are) not true?

(a) We can't create instance of interface but we can make reference of it that refers to the object of its implementing class.
(b) A class can implement more than one interface.
(c) An interface can extend another interface or interfaces.
(d) A class that implements an interface must implement all the methods in that interface.
(e) All the methods are public and abstract. And all the fields are public, static, and final.
(f) Interface is used to achieve multiple inheritance.
(g) While providing implementation in a class of any method of an interface, it needs to be mentioned as public.
(h) Interface cannot be declared as private, protected.
(i) Interface variables must be initialized at the time of declaration otherwise compiler will throw an error.
(j) Inside any implementation class, you cannot change the variables declared in an interface because by default they are public, static, and final. Here we are implementing the interface `Try` which has a variable `x`. When we tried to set the value for variable `x`, we got compilation error as the variable `x` is public static final by default and final variables cannot be re-initialized.
(k) If two or more methods are the same in two interfaces and a class implements both interfaces, implementation of the method once is enough.
(l) A class cannot implement two interfaces that have methods with the same name but different return type.
(m) Two interfaces can have a common variable (same name and type) when they are implemented by a class or multiply inherited into an interface.

MCQs

5.1 If there are two packages, both containing the same class name in them, and both the packages are included, then what will happen?
  (a) Compile-time error.
  (b) Run-time error.
  (c) This is a case of run-time polymorphism and the output is unpredictable.
  (d) Erroneous output will be obtained.

5.2 Which of the following is(are) *not* true in the following statements?
  (a) A package may contain zero or more files.
  (b) A package must contain at least one file.
  (c) A package contains class with inheritance.
  (d) A package contains a class which inherits a class belonging to another package.

5.3 Which of the following is(are) true in the following statements?
  (a) In order to make a class of a package accessible, the class should be declared as public.
  (b) A class with default access specification is not accessible to a class outside the package.
  (c) A class in a default package and with the public access specifier is not accessible to any class in the same package (i.e., the same directory).
  (d) A class with default access specification is accessible to any class belonging to any directory.

5.4 Which of the following is(are) true in the following statements? Assume that there is no import statement at the beginning of the program.
  (a)
```
java.util.Date toDay = new java.util.Date ( );
System.out.println(toDay);
```
  (b)
```
import java.util.Date;
Date today = new Date( );
```
  (c)
```
import java.lang.*;
Date today = new Date( );
```
  (d)
```
import java.lang.Date;
Date today = new Date( );
```

5.5 Suppose two user-defined packages **p1** and **p2** are there in your system. Both the packages contain a number of classes, out of which one class named as class **A**. The two classes are declared as **public**, however, with different implementations. A programmer uses the following codes in his program:

```
import p1.*;
import p2.*;
...
A a = new A();
...
```

Which of the following statements is true?
(a) The object a will be created successfully.
(b) The object a will be created with a warning message.
(c) The program will produce compile-time error
(d) The program will be compiled successfully, but there will be a run-time error.

5.6 **Suppose two user-defined packages `p1` and `p2` are there in your system. Both the packages contain a number of classes, out of which one class is named as class `A`. In one package `A` is declared as `public`, and in other without any access specification. Both the class are with different implementations. A programmer uses the following codes in his program.**

```
import p1.*;
import p2.*;
...
A a = new A();
...
```

Then which of the following statements is true according to you.
(a) The object a will be created successfully.
(b) The object a will be created with a warning message.
(c) The program will produce compile-time error.
(d) The program will be compiled successfully, but there will be a run-time error.

5.7 **If two interfaces I and J are defined with a constant name, say `int PI` in each. A class, say `C` implements the interfaces like**

```
class C implements I, J { ... }
```

Which of the following is true in this regard?
(a) The program will compile successfully.
(b) The program will compile successfully but not execute.
(c) The program will compile successfully if both are initialized with the same value.
(d) The program will show an error while compiling it.

5.8 **For which purpose are packages used in Java?**
(a) Categorize data.
(b) Organizing Java classes into name spaces (i.e., across different storage locations).
(c) For faster compilation.
(d) For debugging programs.

5.9 **Which of the following keywords is used to define a package in Java?**
(a) class (b) implements (c) extends (d) package

5.10 **Which of the following is an incorrect statement about packages?**
(a) Package defines a name space in which classes are stored.
(b) A package can contain another package within it.
(c) Java uses file system directories to store packages.
(d) A package can be renamed without renaming the directory in which the classes are stored.

5.11 **Which of these access specifiers can be used for an interface?**
(a) public (b) private (c) protected (d) All of these

5.12 **Which of the following is an incorrect statement about packages?**
(a) Interfaces specify what class must do but not how it does it.
(b) Interfaces are specified public if they are to be accessed by any code in the program.
(c) All variables in an interface are implicitly final and static.
(d) All variables are static and methods are public if the interface is defined public.

5.13 **Which one is a correct declaration for implementing two interfaces?**
(a) `class C implements A, B { }`
(b) `class C implements A, implements B { }`
(c) `class C implements A extends B { }`
(d) `class C extend A, B { }`

5.14 **The fields in an interface are implicitly specified as:**
(a) public (b) protected
(c) private (d) static and final

5.15 **Let us consider the following piece of code in Java:**

```
interface  A  {
     int  i = 111;
 }
class B implements A  {
    void  methodB() {
         i  = 222;
         System.out.printl(i);
    }
}
```

What will be the result of this code?
(a) There is no `main ()` method so the program will not compile successfully.
(b) The value of `i` will be printed as `111`, as it is static and final by default.
(c) The value of `i` will be printed as `222`, as it is initialized in class `B`.
(d) Compile-time error.

5.16 **Review the following statements:**
(a) Every class is a part of some package.
(b) All classes in a file are a part of the same package.
(c) If no package is specified, the classes in the file go into a special unnamed package.
(d) If no package is specified, a new package is created with the folder name of the class and the class is put in this package.

The correct statements(s) are:
(a) Only a, b, and c (b) Only c and d
(c) Only a and c (d) Only c

5.17 **Which of the following access specifiers can be used for a class so that its members can be accessed by a different class in the same package?**
(a) public (b) protected (c) private (d) default

5.18 **Which of the following is(are) *not* correct regarding packages in Java?**
(a) Java supports both pre-defined and user-defined packages.
(b) Packages are used to organize a set of related classes and interfaces.
(c) Pre-defined packages help to develop programs easily by providing thousands of classes.
(d) Packages are used to organize only a set of related classes and not interfaces.

5.19 **Which of the following access specifier(s) should you choose if you need access restricted to only the sub class in the same package or different package?**
(a) default (b) public (c) protected (d) private

5.20 **What is the significance of the * in the following line, where `package` denotes the name of a package?**

```
import package.*;
```

Select the correct statement in the following:
(a) Only the classes of this package will be imported.
(b) Only the interfaces of this package will be imported.
(c) All the classes and interfaces of this package will be imported.
(d) All the classes, interfaces, and sub-packages of this package will be imported.

5.21 **Which of the following statement(s) is(are) correct regarding an interface in Java?**
(a) An interface can contain only abstract methods and standard methods but no static methods are allowed.
(b) Method bodies in an interface do not exist for default methods and abstract methods.
(c) An interface cannot be instantiated but can be implemented by classes.
(d) An interface cannot be instantiated but can be extended by other interfaces.

5.22 **How does Java Run-time Environment (JRE) know where to look for a package that you create?**
(a) It searches in the current directory.
(b) It searches in the location set in the `CLASSPATH` environment variable.
(c) A user can set the path during run-time using the `-classpath` option.
(d) Using the `-path` option, a user can set the path.

5.23 Which of the following statement(s) is (are) ***not*** true?
   (a) The default package in the Java language is `java.lang`.
   (b) `String` is a final class and it is present in `java.lang` package.
   (c) `FileWriter` is a class present in `java.util` package.
   (d) `Thread` is a class present in `java.lang` package.

5.24 All interface methods are implicitly
   (a) public and final
   (b) public and abstract
   (c) protected and abstract
   (d) private and abstract

5.25 Which of the following is not true as far as inheritance with interfaces is concerned?
   (a) An interface can extend one or more other interfaces.
   (b) An interface cannot implement another interface or class.
   (c) A class can inherit from multiple interfaces at the same level.
   (d) An interface can inherit from multiple interfaces at the same level.

6

Exception Handling

There is a need for software developers to build reliable and robust software. To make such a software, the 80:20 rule has to be followed, that is, 80 percent of the effort should go into checking and handling errors, and only 20 percent in writing the software. Error detection and error handling remain an important issue in software development. Java arms developers with an elegant mechanism for handling errors that produces efficient and organized error-handling code. This mechanism is a unique feature in Java and called *exception handling*. Exception handling allows developers to detect errors easily without writing special code to test return values. Even better, it lets the programmer keep exception-handling code cleanly separated from the exception-generating code. It also lets the programmer use the same exception-handling code to deal with a range of possible exceptions.
This chapter devotes to cover the fascinating concept of exception handling in Java.

6.0 Introduction

What is the issue?

Programmers in any language endeavor to write bug-free programs, programs that never crash, programs that can handle any situation efficiently, and that can recover from unusual situations without causing the users any undue inconvenience. Good intentions aside, programs that cover all these points don't exist. In real life, errors occur, either because the programmer didn't anticipate every situation the code would get into (or did not have the time to test the programs enough), or because of situations outside the programmer's control like bad data from users, corrupt files that do not have the right data in them, network connections that do not connect, hardware devices that do not respond, to name a few.

Requirement

In Java, unusual events that may cause a program to fail are called exceptions. The dictionary meaning of "exception" is "an abnormal situation." What will happen to the program if an abnormal situation occurs? For example, what result will your calculations return when divide `x` by `y` when `y = 0`? Or, if you want to store a value in the array in its 100th location while the size of the array is 50? In practice, in such a situation, your execution will be suspended immediately, for which you are not really prepared. Alternatively, it would be good if you can handle such a situation well (e.g., save data, intimation of the situation to user, etc.). It will be good if you can avoid abnormal termination, that is, if an exception occurs at the `i`th statement, then the `(i+1)`th statement onward should be executed, of course, if they are without any exception.

Remedy

For all these reasons, Java has exceptions to deal with managing, creating, and expecting errors and other unusual situations. Through a combination of special features, consistency checking at compile-time and a set of extensible exception classes, errors, and other unusual conditions in Java programs can be relatively easily managed. Given these features, you can now add a whole new dimension to the behavior and design of your classes, of your class hierarchy, and of your overall system. Your class and interface definitions describe how your program is supposed to behave given the best circumstances. By integrating exception handling into your program design, you can consistently describe how the program will behave when circumstances are not quite as good, and allow people who use your classes to know what to expect in those cases.

Your learning

This chapter covers exception handling mechanism in Java in detail. You will learn the concept of errors, exceptions, and the different types of exceptions which are possible in a Java program. Specific topics include the different constructs of handling exceptions and built-in classes in Java JDK. Java allows users to build their own exception classes and you will learn how to do that. Finally, we will discuss when to use and when not to use exception handling and some bad practices of dealing with exceptions.

6.1 Concept of Error and Exception

Error vs. exception

Error and exception are two things which software developers face while developing software. We should clear our understanding about these two before proceeding to the core discussion.

Errors

Concept of error

If you do something which is not exactly what it should be, it is called an error. For example, you write `z = x + y` instead of the intended `z = x - y`. This is an error made by you as it will not give the right output as desired. In this case, your program will complete its execution, but with an error in output. Such an error is called *semantic error*. An error is a serious problem that no one is there to *try* to *catch*. An error is tedious to detect and to do that you have to follow a software testing methodology.

Now, let us turn into another form of error. Suppose, you write a statement `z = x + y` for which you have not declared the identifier `z`. This is also an error. Such an error is called *syntax error.* A syntax error occurs if a statement is not written as per the rule of the programming language. Another example of syntax error is writing a statement, say,

```
system.out.print();
```

Since, you are an experienced Java programmer, you are thinking correctly that such type of errors can be detected while you compile the program. This is why syntax errors are also called *compile-time errors.* In contrast to semantic errors, the compiler is there to catch syntax error and as a programmer you have to fix the errors. A program with compilation error(s) cannot be executed. Study Program 6.1 and see how many compilation errors you can locate.

Program 6.1 *(Compilation errors)*

```
/* This program will not compile successfully. Fix all
the errors and then run it. */

class Error {
     Public static void main (string args [ ]) {
         System.out.print("Can you find errors in it?")
    }

Class AnotherError {
    public void insert( ){
         System.out.println(To insert a text);
    }

    abstract void delete( ){
          System.out.printx("To delete a text");
     }
}
```

There are several sources of compile-time errors. In the following, some common compile-time errors are listed, which a Java programmer often faces:

- Missing semicolons.
- Missing (or mismatch of brackets) in classes and methods.
- Misspelling of identifiers or keywords.
- Missing double quotes in strings.
- Use of undeclared variables.
- Incomplete types in assignment/initialization.
- Bad references to objects.

Exceptions

Concept of exception

A program is written correctly and there is no syntax or semantic errors. Your program, may work for many inputs but can fail to run for some inputs. For example, the equation `z = x/y;` for all valid identifier declarations works well, except `y = 0`. Such an instance is called an "abnormal situation." As an illustration, consider Program 6.2. This program will not give any error during compilation. But the program will still give run-time error on some occasions.

Program 6.2 *(Run-time error)*

```
/* This program can produce run-time error whenever the
second input value is zero (0). */
class Exception {
      public static void main (String args [ ]) {
            int a = Integer.parseInt(args[0]};
            int b = Integer.parseInt(args[1]};
            int c = a/b;
            System.out.println("Value of c =" + c);
      }
}
```

Here are some input with which you can run Program 6.2. You will observe the corresponding outcome.

`javac Error.java`	→	Error.class	// Compiled successfully
`java Error 1 2`	→	Value of `c = 0`	
`java Error -10 -2`	→	Value of `c = 5`	
`java Error 0 5`	→	Value of `c = 0`	
`java Error 1 0`	→	Run-time error occurs	
`java Error 2.5 1.5`	→	Here also, run-time error occurs	

As you have noticed, an abnormal situation occurs during the run-time of the program, mainly due to "erroneous" input. Examples of such input is when you want to open a file which does not exist, want to store something when memory is insufficient, when you want to read an array element whose index is beyond the boundary, etc. An abnormal situation while executing a statement is called an *exception*.

- If an exception occurs, unlike an error, the program execution halts at that point of execution.
- Of course, all the errors we are discussing occur at run-time.

Like compile-time errors, there are several reasons for which one can face run-time errors. A few common ones for your quick reference are:

- A user has entered invalid data.
- Dividing an integer by zero.
- Accessing an element that is out of the bounds of an array.
- Trying to store a value into an array of an incomplete class or type.
- Trying to cast an instance of a class to one of its sub classes.
- Trying to illegally change the state of a thread.
- Attempting use a negative size for an array.
- Null object reference.
- A file that needs to be opened cannot be found.
- A network connection has been lost in the middle of communication, or the JVM has run out of memory.

Run-time errors are due to users, when they give some illegal input. A good programmer can take a precaution to debar wrong inputs while writing a program. For this, the programmer will need to check every possible kind of input and then avoid exceptions from occurring. This is indeed a tedious and even infeasible task.

Compile-time errors versus run-time errors

Types of errors

It appears confusing to distinguish between errors and exceptions, as both occur at the time of execution of programs. The errors occur mainly due to incorrect semantics or mistaken logic. Figure 6.1 highlights some salient points about these two types of errors.

Handling exceptions

Java's solution to exceptions

Here is the magic that Java does for you. Java allows every method an alternate exit path if it is unable to complete its task in the normal way. In this situation, the Java Run-Time Environment (its JVM) *throws* an object that encapsulates the error information. Depending on the type of exception, it will throw different objects. All objects are of class `Exception` or its child class (defined in `java.lang` package). For example, JVM throws an object called `IllegalArumentType` when a method, say `m(int x, int y)` is called as `m(1.5, 4)`; it throws an object called `ArithmeticException` when `a = x/(b - c)`; and `b = c`.

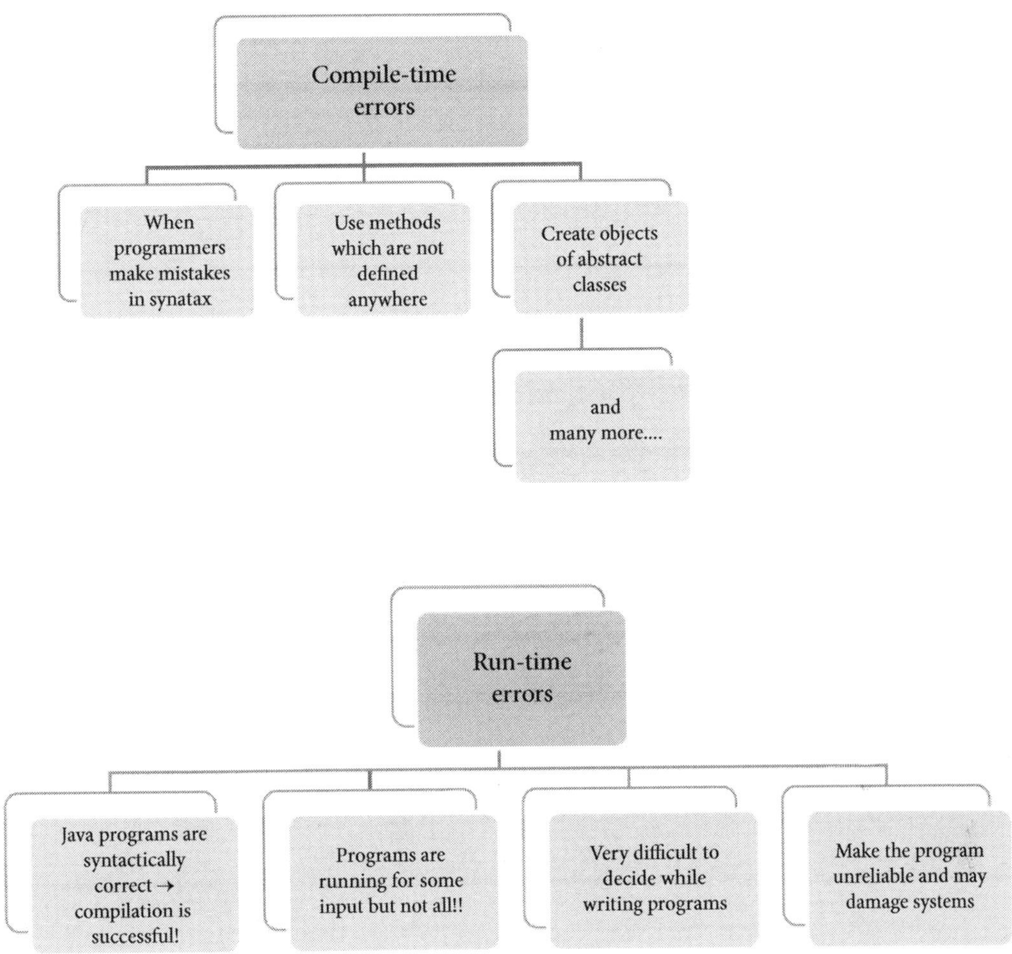

Figure 6.1 Compile-time versus run-time errors

Note that whenever an exception occurs in a method, the method exits immediately; it does not return its normal (or any) value and hands it over to the JVM.

Java's exception objects

The exception object contains the name and description of the exception, and the current state of the program where the exception has occurred. Program 6.3 illustrates this. Here the exception is generated when this program is executed:

```
java.lang.ArithmeticException: / by zero
at ExceptionThrow.main(ExceptionThrow.java:5)
```

Program 6.3 (Exception throwing)

```
/* This program illustrates how JVM throws Exception
object when an exception occurs. */

class ExceptionThrow {
     public static void main(String args[]) {
          double x; int d = 2;
          x = 22/d; System.out.println(x);
          x = 22/(d-2); System.out.println(x);
          x = 22/(d+2); System.out.println(x);
     }
}
```

Thus, an exception object is created automatically whenever an exception occurs. A programmer can take an appropriate exception managing activity (i.e., exception handling routine) on the occurrence of such an object. The different types of exception objects and how to manage exceptions with the exception objects are discussed in the following sections.

- On occurrence of the exception, execution throws the exception object and it is then terminated at line 5.
- If this object is caught, then the premature termination can be avoided.

6.2 Types of Exceptions

All exception types are sub classes of the built-in class `Throwable`. This means that an exception is always an object of some sub class of the standard class `Throwable`. The class `Throwable` is defined in `java.lang` package. Two direct sub classes of the class `Throwable`: the class `Error` and the class `Exception`, cover all the standard exceptions. Both these classes themselves have sub classes that identify specific exception conditions. Figure 6.2 shows the hierarchy of Java exception classes. The `java.lang.Throwable` class is the root class of Java exception hierarchy which is inherited by two sub classes: `Exception` and `Error`.

In the following, a brief discussion of different categories of exception handling classes is discussed. A detailed discussion of all the sub classes of `Throwable class` can be checked at: https://docs.oracle.com/javase/7/docs/api/index.html.

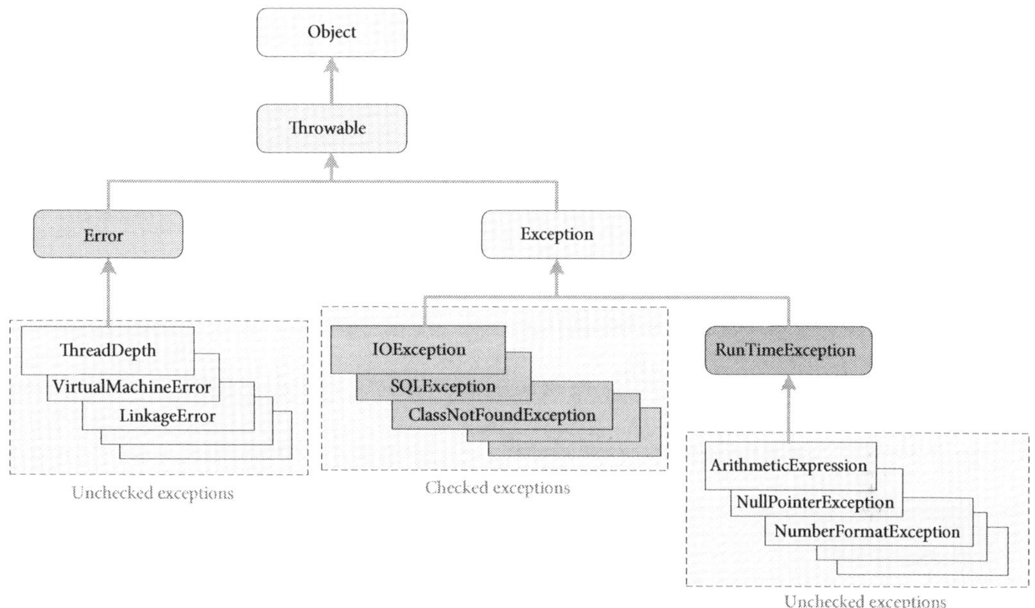

Figure 6.2 Hierarchy of Java exception classes

6.2.1 Error Exceptions

An `Error` is a sub class of `Throwable` that indicates serious problems that an application should not try to get affected with. Most of such errors are abnormal conditions. The `ThreadDeath` error, though a "normal" condition, is also a sub class of `Error` because most applications should try not to catch it. `Error` has the following sub classes:

```
AnnotationFormatError, AssertionError, AWTError,
CoderMalfunctionError, FactoryConfigurationError,
FactoryConfigurationError, IOError, LinkageError,
ServiceConfigurationError, ThreadDeath,
TransformerFactoryConfigurationError,
VirtualMachineErrorthree
```

Out of all these, we will discuss three sub classes, namely, `ThreadDeath`, `LinkageError`, and `VirtualMachineError`.

- `ThreadDeath`

  A `ThreadDeath` exception is thrown whenever an executing thread is deliberately stopped. You should not catch this exception for the thread to be destroyed properly. However, in some situations you may want to catch it. For example, for clean-up operations, where you must be sure to rethrow the exception to allow the thread to die properly. Note that when a `ThreadDeath` exception is thrown and not caught, it is the thread that ends, not the program. We shall discuss about this in detail in Chapter 7.

- `LinkageError`

  The `LinkageError` exception class has sub classes that throw exceptions whenever there are errors with the classes in your program. For example, incompatibilities between classes, attempting to create an object of a non-existent class type, etc. are some cases that cause these exceptions to be thrown.

- `VirtualMachineError`

  When a serious failure of the Java Virtual Machine occurs, exceptions of class `VirtualMachineError` will be thrown. This class has four sub classes specifying the different exceptions. A programmer may write code dealing with these exceptions. There is little scope in attempting to catch them.

The exceptions objects of type `LinkageError` and `VirtualMachineError` are all the results of catastrophic failure conditions. Once such failure occurs, there will be little or nothing to recover from them during the execution of the program. In such a situation, usually a programmer can read the error message that is generated by the exception being thrown. Particularly, in the case of a `LinkageError` exception, the programmer tries to figure out what might be wrong with the code to cause the failure.

6.2.2 Checked Exceptions

In Java, there are two categories of sub classes under the sub class `Exception`: checked and unchecked exceptions (Figure 6.2). Checked exceptions are the exceptions that are checked at compile-time. The checked exceptions which are defined in `java.lang` package are listed in Table 6.1.

Compile-time exception

The compiler checks that you have either handled the exception in a method where the exception may be thrown or that you have indicated that the method can throw such an exception. If you do neither, your code will not compile. If some code within a method throws a checked exception, then the method must either handle the exception or it must specify the exception using `throws` keyword (discussed in Section 6.4). For example, consider Program 6.4 that opens a file at location, say, `C:\test\aFile.txt` and prints the first three lines of it (readers can skip this discussion if they are new to `java.io` API).

Table 6.1 Java's checked exceptions

Exception Class Name	Exceptional Condition
`ClassNotFoundException`	Class not found.
`CloneNotSupportedException`	Attempt to clone an object that does not implement the Cloneable interface.
`IllegalAccessException`	Access to a class is denied.
`IOException`	Exception dealing with inout–output stream classes.
`InstantiationException`	Attempt to create an object of an abstract class or interface.
`InterruptedException`	One thread has been interrupted by another thread.
`NoSuchFieldException`	A requested field does not exist.
`NoSuchMethodException`	A requested method does not exist.
`ReflectiveOperationException`	Super class of reflection-related exceptions.
`SQLException`	Exception dealing with database connectivity

Program 6.4 *(Checked exception)*

```
/* This program demonstrates that the program will not
compile due to the checked exception. */

import java.io.*;

class CheckedExceptionDemo {
    public static void main(String[] args) {
        FileReader file = new FileReader
           ("C:\\test\\aFile.txt");
        BufferedReader fileInput =
           new BufferedReader(file);

        // Print first 3 lines of file "C:\test\aFile.txt"
        for (int i = 0; i < 3; i++)
          System.out.println(fileInput.readLine());

        fileInput.close();
    }
}
```

Program 6.4 doesn't compile because the function `main()` uses `File Reader()` and `FileReader()` throws a checked exception `FileNotFound Exception`. It also uses `readLine()` and `close()` methods, and these methods also throw checked exception `IOException`. An attempt to compile the program will produce the following output:

```
Exception in thread "main" java.lang.Exception:
Uncompilable source code - unreported exception java.
io.FileNotFoundException; must be caught or declared to be
thrown
at CheckedExceptionDemo.main(CheckedExceptionDemo.java:5)
```

To fix this program, you either need to specify a list of exceptions using the keyword `throws`, or you need to use `try-catch` block (we shall learn about these in detail later in this chapter). A remedial program using the keyword `throws` is shown in Program 6.5. The program specifies `throws IOException` in the `main()` method line. We do so because `FileNotFoundException` is a sub class of `IOException`, and hence we can just specify `IOException` in the list of throws and make the program compiler-error-free.

Program 6.5 *(Remedy for checked exception)*

```
/* This program demonstrates that the program will
compile as it has been fixed with throws keyword in the
main method line. */

import java.io.*;

class CheckedExceptionDemo {
    public static void main(String[] args) throws
      IOException {
        FileReader file = new FileReader("C:\\test\\a.
          txt");
        BufferedReader fileInput = new BufferedReader
          (file);

        // Print first 3 lines of file "C:\test\a.txt"
        for (int i = 0; i < 3; i++)
            System.out.println(fileInput.readLine());

        fileInput.close();
    }
}
```

If a method in a program has the provision to generate an exception of a type that has `Exception` as a super class, you must either handle the exception within the method or your method may throw such an exception. Your program will not compile successfully if you do not follow this.

When a method in a class declares that it throws an exception that is an instance of a particular class, then it may throw an exception of that class or of any of its sub classes.

6.2.3 Unchecked Exceptions

Unchecked are the exceptions that are not checked at compiled time. In Java, exceptions under `Error` and `RuntimeException` classes are unchecked exceptions, everything else under `Throwable` is checked. One group of sub classes of `Exception` that is exempted from a check at compile-time consists of those derived from `RuntimeException`. The fact is that `RuntimeException` exceptions are to be treated differently, and that the compiler allows you to ignore them, is that they generally arise because of serious errors in your code. Consider Program 6.6. It compiles fine, but it throws `ArithmeticException` when run. The compiler allows it to compile, because `ArithmeticException` is an unchecked exception.

Program 6.6 *(Unchecked exception)*

```
/* This program will compile successfully, but has run-
time error.*/

class UncheckedExceptionDemo {
   public static void main(String args[]) {
       int a = 1;
       int b = 0;
       int c = a/b;
   }
}
```

The exception classes under `RuntimeException` as a parent class listed in Table 6.2. A brief description for each is given for quick reference.

For almost all the exceptions that are represented by sub classes of the `Exception` class, you must include a code in your program to deal with them if your code is causing them to be thrown.

Your code may run into a problem that is not adequately described by any of the standard exception classes. In that case, it is easy enough to create your own exception class. Just derive it from `Exception` or from a child class of `Exception`.

Table 6.2 Java's unchecked exceptions under `RuntimeException` class

Exception class name	Exceptional condition
`ArithmeticException`	When an invalid arithmetic condition has arisen, such as an attempt to divide an integer value by zero.
`ArrayIndexOutOfBoundsException`	When the array index is out-of-bounds.
`ArrayStoreException`	When an attempt to store an object in an array that is not permitted for the array type.
`ClassCastException`	When you try to cast an object to an invalid type, the object is not of the class specified, nor is it a sub class or a super class of the class specified.
`EnumConstantNotPresentException`	When an attempt is made to use an undefined enumeration value.
`IllegalArgumentException`	When you pass an argument to a method that doesn't correspond with the parameter type.
`IllegalMonitorStateException`	When a thread has tried to wait on the monitor for an object that the thread does not own (threads are discussed in Chapter 7).
`IllegalStateException`	When you try to call a method at a time when it was not legal to do so.
`IllegalThreadStateException`	Requested operation is not compatible with current thread state.
`IndexOutOfBoundsException`	When an attempt to use an index that is outside the bounds of the object it is applied. This may be an array, a String object, or a Vector object.
`NegativeArraySizeException`	When an array is defined with a negative dimension.
`NullPointerException`	If an object variable contains null and there is a reference to a field for that object, for example, calling a method or accessing a data member.
`NumberFormatException`	Invalid conversion of a string to a numeric format.
`SecurityException`	When a program has performed an illegal operation that is a security violation. For example, trying to read a file on the local machine from an applet.
`StringIndexOutOfBounds`	Attempt to index outside the bounds of a string.
`TypeNotPresentException`	Type not found.
`UnsupportedOperationException`	This is thrown if you request an operation to be carried out that is not supported.

6.3 Exception Handling Mechanisms

If an exception occurs, Java Run-time Environment throws the corresponding exception object. This object is very important for the programmer to handle the exception so that the program can be made robust and does not terminate abnormally. In this section, you will learn a number of mechanisms to catch the exception objects and handle them.

Exception handling constructs

In a very basic sense, during the execution of a program, when an exceptional condition arises, an object of the respective exception class is created and thrown in the method which caused the exception. That method may choose to catch the exception (can be called as the *exception handler*) and then can guard against premature exit or may have a block of code to execute. To realize this basic idea of exception handling, Java developer introduces five basic constructs.

```
try { ...  }
catch(){ ...  }
finally { ... }
throw
throws
```

Marking blocks

The `try` keyword is used to mark a block of code in which exceptions may occur. This block of code is called a *guarded region* (which really means "risky code goes here"). If an exception occurs, then there should be a way to tell the JVM what code to execute when the exception happens. This is accomplished by a block of code (i.e., the *exception handler code*) which is preceded by the keyword `catch`. A simple structural representation is shown in Figure 6.3.

Java allows a programmer to handle exceptions with many constructs. All such constructs can be classified as follows:

Four constructs

1. Simple try-catch: One try block followed by one catch block.
2. Single try multiple catch blocks: One try block followed by a number of catch blocks.
3. Try-catch-finally block: The code for final exit, if an exception occurs.
4. Nested try-catch block: Try-catch inside another try-catch.

In the following subsections, these constructs are discussed in detail.

```
methodM {

    /* Part of code in the method body. */

    try {
                /* This is the first line of the "guarded region"
                   that is governed by the try keyword.
                   Put code here that might cause some kind of exception.
                   We may have many code lines here or just one. */
    }

    catch (ExceptionType e ) {
                /* Put code here that handles this exception object e.
                   This is the next line of the exception handler.
                   ...
                   This is the last line of the exception handler.
    }

    /* The rest part of the method body, if any. */
}
```

Figure 6.3 Basic construct of try-catch block

6.3.1 Simple `try-catch` Block

This is the simplest exception handling construct in Java. This construct is suitable if you want to handle one exception at a time. The construct is shown in Figure 6.3. As an example, let us consider Program 6.7. You can check that the statement at line 3 has an exception issue. When `y = 0`, it will throw an exception object of type `ArithmeticException`.

Program 6.7 *(Program with exception)*

```
/* This program has an abnormal situation issue. */

1.    class DivideByZero {
2.        static int methodM ( int x, int y ) {
3.            int a = x/y;
                // Exception occurs here, if y = 0
4.            return (a);
5.        }

6.        public  static void main (String args [ ] ) {
7.            int i = 5, j = 0;
8.            int result = methodM (i, j);
9.            System.out.println ( " Result : "
                + result );
10.       }
11.   }
```

The following is what the output will look like.

```
Exception in thread "main" java.lang.ArithmeticException:
/ by zero
        at DivideByZero.methodM(DivideByZero.java:5)
        at DivideByZero.main(DivideByZero.java:11)
```

To handle the exception, you should guard the code using `try-catch` block. The revised program with try-catch block is shown in Program 6.8.

Program 6.8 *(Program with exception handling mechanism)*

```
/* The program illustrates the use of simple try-catch
block to handle an exception. */

class DivideZero {
    static int methodM (int x, int y ){
       try {
           int a = x/y;
           return(a);
        }
        catch (ArithmeticException e) {
              System.out.println ( "Divide by zero
               occurs..." );
       }
    }
    public static void main (String args[ ] {
        int a,b, result;
        system.out.print("Enter any two integers : ");
        a = System.in.read( );   b = System.in.read( );
        result  = methodM (a, b);
        System.out.println ( "Result : " + result);
    }
}
```

- The catch blocks immediately follow the try block. This is a requirement.
- If the type of exception object that occurs in the try block does not match the exception type mentioned in the catch block, then the code in the `catch` block will not be in effect. For example, in Program 6.8, `catch (ArrayIndexOutOfBoundException e)` instead of `catch (ArithmeticException e)` will not work.
- Since, `Exception` class is the super class of any `RuntimeException` sub class, it will work if you mention `catch(Exception e){...}`.

- If the exception object thrown in the `try` block is not handled by a `catch` block, then the program will be terminated abruptly. Figure 6.4 illustrates this.
- You can put try-catch block in the caller method where the buggy method is called. This concept is discussed in the following.

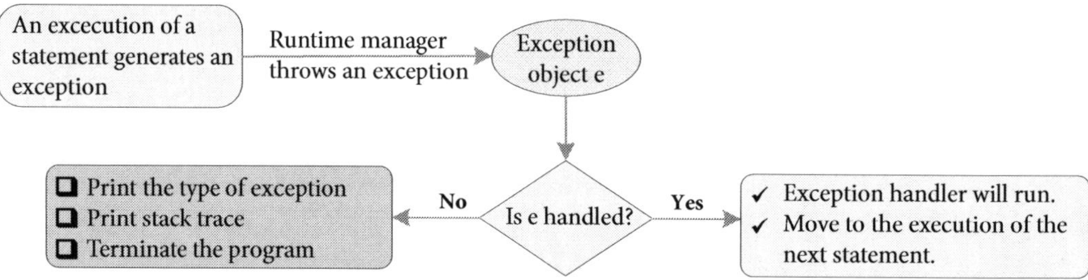

Figure 6.4 Control flow in exception handling

Stack trace in exception handling

You may have noticed the output generated by the JVM when an exception occurs and it is not handled. For example, see the outputs of Program 6.3 and Program 6.8. They clearly, show the type of exception and its complete trace (also called *call trace*). JVM uses a stack called *call stack*, to keep a trace of calling sequence of methods. To understand the call stack better, let us consider the execution of Program 6.9.

Program 6.9 *(Call stack in JVM)*

```
/* This program illustrates call stack concept used in
JVM. */

    class RealCalculator {
        static int mul ( int x, int y ) {
            int a = x * y;
            return (a);
        }

        static int div ( int x, int y ) {
            int b = x / y;
            return (b);
        }

        static double realVal ( int x, int y ) {
            int a  = mul(x,y);  int b = div(x,y);
            return (a/b);
        }
```

```
14.     public  static void main (String args [ ] ) {
15.         int i = 5, j = 10;
16.         double result1 = realVal (j, i);
17.         double result2 = realVal (i, j);
18.         System.out.println ( result1  + " | "
              + result2 );
19.         }
20.     }
```

The program starts its execution with the call of `main()`. The method `main()` calls `realVal()`, which in turn calls two methods `mul()` and `div()`. JVM keeps a track of which method calls which method(s), so that after the end of the execution of the current method, the control returns to its caller method. This is the stack of calls or simple known as *call stack*. Figure 7 illustrates the call stack of Program 6.9.

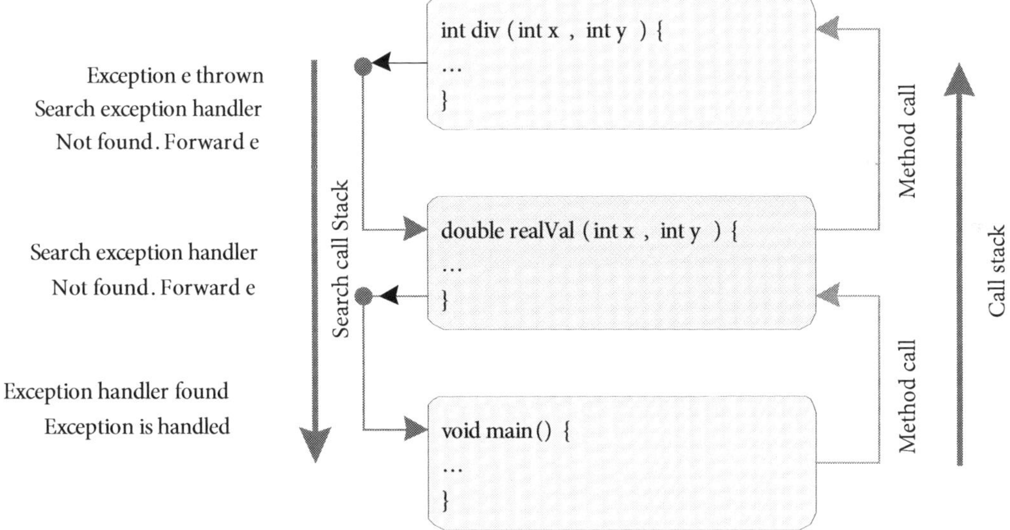

Figure 6.5 Call stack and searching call stack for the exception handler

Now, let us come to the execution of the program. Consider three situations of input values:

Case 1: In `main()`, you assign `i = 5` and `j = 5` (line 15). In this case, there is no exception in any methods and the program will execute successfully.

Case 2: Input `i = 5` and `j = 10` (as in line 15), the method call `realVal(10,5)` is successful with the `result1` = 5.0. However, the method call `realVal(5,10)` at line 17 faces the divide-by-zero arithmetic exception. As there is no exception handler, the program execution will be terminated with a report of exception.

Case 3: If `i = 5` and `j = 0`, then it will throw `ArithmeticException` object at line 7 and as there is no exception handler program, it will be abnormally terminated.

Handling exceptions with `try-catch` construct

In Program 6.9, there are two sources of exceptions, both are the same type of exception namely, `ArithmeticException`. To avoid, abnormal termination, you can plan two exception handler routines (at `div(...)` and `realVal(...)`). In this case, you can use only one exception handler, which is at the `main()` only. A remedial program is shown in Program 6.10.

How does it work?

See Figure 6.5, which shows the call stack and then searches the call stack for the right exception handler.

- JVM starts searching from the method in which exception occurred, proceeds through call stack in the reverse order in which methods were called.
- If it finds the appropriate handler, then it passes the occurred exception to it. If it does not find, then forward it to its caller method, and so on.

If JVM searches all the methods on call stack and does not find the right handler, then JVM will hand over the `Exception` object to the default exception handler, which is a part of run-time system. This handler finally prints the exception information and terminates the program abnormally at the location of occurrence of exception.

Program 6.10 *(Call stack searching by JVM)*

```
/* This program illustrates call stack search to find
the appropriate exception handler in a program. */

    class RealCalculator {
        static int mul ( int x, int y ) {
            int a = x * y;
            return (a);
        }

        static int div ( int x, int y ) {
```

```
            int b = x / y;
            return (b);
        }

        static double realVal ( int x, int y ) {
            int a  = mul(x,y);  int b = div(x, y);
            return (a/b);
        }

        public  static void main (String args [ ] ) {
            int i = 5, j = 10;
            try {
               double result1 = realVal (j, i);
               double result2 = realVal (i, j);
            }
            catch(ArithmeticException e) {
                 System.out.println ( "Execution is
                      successful!" );
            }
        }
    }
```

Robust programming

Let us consider how you can use the exception handler and make the program robust. Program 6.11 is designed to read a number of integer values as input from command line input. The `parseInt()` method returns `NumberFormatException` exception object whenever it encounters a non-integer entry. Accordingly, the exception handler used is in the form of simple try-catch block. Note how the exception handler code written is to take account of invalid input. You can run the program with the following input for your understanding:

```
java CommandLineInput 10 22.34  55  Java   K  69  2012
```

Program 6.11 *(Robust program with exception handler)*

```
/* The program given below illustrates the continuation
of the program even if in presence of exceptions
provided that exceptions are handled. */

class CommandLineInput {
   public static void main (String args[ ] {
      int number, invalidCount = 0; validCount = 0;
      for (int i = 0; i < args.length; i++)  {
         try {
            number = Integer.parseInt(args[i]);
```

```
            } catch (NumberFormatException e)  {
                inavlidCount++;
                System.out.println("Invalid number at" +
                  i + args.[i]);
            }
            validCount++;
            System.out.println ( "Valid number at " + i +
             args.[i]);
        }
            System.out.println ( "Invalid entries: " +
             inValidCount);
            System.out.println ( "Valid entries: " +
             validCount);
    }
}
```

Similar exception but multiple times in the try block

It is quite possible that a similar exception occurs in a try block, but at several locations. In that case, the single catch is sufficient to catch the exception. This is because exceptions will be thrown one after the other and hence one `catch` block will catch them. Program 6.12 illustrates this fact. You are advised to run the program with initializations of `a = 0, b = 2, c = 5` and `a = 5, b = 15, c = 0.`

Program 6.12 *(Multiple occurrences of same exception)*

```
/* This program illustrates that a single catch block
is sufficient to handle multiple exceptions of similar
type. */

class SingleCatchTest {
    public static void main(String args[]) {
        int a, b, c;
        try {
            a = b/c;
            b = 12 / a;
        } catch (ArithmeticException e) {
            System.out.println("Division by zero.");
            a = 1; c = 2; // Say, set the values and
                                                // continue
        }
        System.out.println("a: " + a + "b: " + b + "c: "
          + c);
    }
}
```

Different type of exceptions but with a single try-catch block

Let us examine how you can utilize the simple try-catch block constructs to handle multiple exceptions that may be thrown in a single `try` block. Program 6.13 illustrates this. Note how exception information can be displayed using `println()` statement.

Program 6.13 *(Multiple occurrences of multiple exceptions)*

```
/* This program illustrates how a single catch block
can handle multiple exceptions of different types */

class ExceptionTest {
    static void main (String   args[ ] ) {
      int j;
      for (int i = 0; i < 4; i++ ) {
         try {
           switch (i) {
              case 0 :
                  int zero = 0;
                  j = 999/ zero; // Divide by zero
                break;
              case 1:
                int b[ ] = null;
                j = b[0] ; // Null pointer error
                break;
              case 2:
                  int c = new int [2] ;
                  j = c[10];
                          // Array index is out-of-bound
                  break;
               case 3:
                  char ch = "Java".charAt(9) ;
                        // String index is out-of-bound
                  break;
             }
      }
       catch (Exception e) {
        System.out.println("In Test case#"+i+ "\n" + e);
            // Alternatively,  System.out.println
                  (e.getMessage() );
       }
      }
    }
}
```

When adding a try block to an existing code, you should take some care. Note that a try block is no way different from any other block (i.e., code between braces) when it comes to the consideration of scope of a variable. All variables declared in a try block are available only within the block. It is easy to include a declaration of a variable in a try block. If you do so, you inadvertently limit the scope of the variable and need to be careful about its limit. Program 6.14 illustrates the scope of variables in the context of a try–catch construct.

Program 6.14 *(Scope of variables declared inside a try block)*

```
/* This program illustrates scope of variables if a
variable is declared inside a try block. */

class TryBlockScope {
     public static void main(String args[]) {
          int a = 50, b = 0, c = 50;
          try {
              int x = b/c;
              int y = 12 / a;
          } catch (ArithmeticException e) {
              System.out.println("Division by zero.");
              x = 0; y = 0;
                          // Set the values and continue
                  // x and y have out of scope here
          }
         System.out.println("x: " + x + "x: " + y);
            // Here, also x and y have out of scope
     }
}
```

6.3.2 Single `try` Multiple `catch` Blocks

The concept

In the previous sections, you have learned how a simple try-catch block construct can handle even multiple exceptions which occur in the try block. However, you may need to handle different exceptions differently. To handle this type of a situation, you can specify two or more catch clauses, so that each clause catches a different type of exception. When an exception is thrown, each catch statement is inspected in order, and the *first one whose type matches* that of the exception is executed. After the execution of the catch statement, others are clauses are bypassed, and the execution continues. Figure 6.6 illustrates the basic construct of single try multiple catch blocks.

```
methodM {
    /* Part of code in the method body. */

    try {
            /* This is the first line of the "guarded region"
               that is governed by the try keyword.
               Put code here that might cause some kind of exception.
               We may have many code lines here or just one. */
    }

    catch (Except i on Type 1 e1) {
            /* Put code here that handles this exception object e1.
               This is the next line of the exception handler.
               ...
               This is the last line of the exception handler.
    }

    catch (Except i on Type 2 e2) {
            /* Put code here that handles this exception object e2.
               This is the next line of the exception handler.
               ...
               This is the last line of the exception handler.
    }

    • • •

    catch (Except i on Type n en) {
            /* Put code here that handles this exception object en.
               This is the next line of the exception handler.
               ...
               This is the last line of the exception handler.
    }

    /* The rest part of the method body, if any. */
}
```

Figure 6.6 Single try multiple catch block constructs

Let us consider Program 6.15, which may throw multiple exceptions. Run this program for the following input combinations, in order to enable a number of exceptions to occur:

```
java MultiCatch Java Welcome
java MultiCatch Welcome to Java World !
java MultiCatch
```

The exceptions which may occur during the execution of codes are highlighted as the comments for your understanding.

Program 6.15 (Multiple exceptions in a program)

```
class MultiCatch  {
 public static void main (String args[ ]) {
   int i = args.length;
             // Number of arguments in the command line
   String myString = new String [i];
       //#1: If i = 0 then  myString null pointer error
   if(args[0].equals("Java"))
         System.out.println("First word is Java !");
   System.out.println( " Number of arguments = " + i );
           int x = 18/ i;
                // #2: Arithmetic exception, if i = 0
           int y[ ] = {555, 999};
              // The size is 2 and indices are 0,1
           y[ i ] = x;
                // #3: Index is out-of-range if i > 1
   }
}
```

Program 6.16 is written with an objective to handle all the exceptions in Program 6.15.

Program 6.16 (Handling multiple exceptions in Program 6.15)

```
class MultiCatchTest  {
    public static void main (String args[ ]) {
     int i = args.length;
       try {
        String myString = new String [i]; //#1
        if(args[0].equals("Java"))
           System.out.println("First word is Java !");
         System.out.println( " Number of arguments = "
              + i )
         int x = 18/ i;            //#2
         int y[ ] = {555, 999};
         y[ i ] = x;                //#3
      }
      catch (NullPointerException  e ) {
          // To catch exception at #1
        System.out.println (" A null pointer exception
          : " + e );
      }
      catch (ArithmeticException  e ) {
          // To catch exception at #2
           System.out.println ( " Divide by 0 : "+ e );
      }
```

```
        catch (ArrayIndexOutofBoundsException e ) {
            // To catch at  #3
          System.out.println ("Array Index OoB : " + e);
        }
    }
}
```

- If you have multiple catch blocks, they must immediately follow the try block. Additionally, the catch blocks must all follow each other, without any other statements or blocks in between.
- No code can sneak in between try and, as well as between, two catch blocks.
- The ordering of catch blocks in a single try multiple catch block construct matters a lot. The catch blocks must be in sequence with the most derived type first and the most basic type last. Otherwise, your code will not compile. This is because a catch statement related to a super class will catch exceptions of that type plus its sub classes, if any. Thus, a sub class would never be reached if it comes after its super class. Further, in Java, unreachable code treats as an error and the compiler will detect that this is the case and then report error. Program 6.16 illustrates this aspect.

Program 6.17 *(Ordering of exception hierarchy in multiple catch blocks)*

```
/* This program illustrates the ordering of exception
hierarchy. If not in order, then it will not compile.
*/
class ExceptionHirearchyMultipleCatch {
    public static void main(String args[]) {
         try {
              int i = 0;
              int [] x = new int [3];
              x[3] = 99 / i;
          }
          catch(Exception e) {
               System.out.println("Generic Exception
                catch.");
          }
          catch(ArithmeticException e) {
                // ERROR - unreachable
               System.out.println("This will never
                reach!");
          }
     }
}
```

6.3.3 The `finally` Block

Suppose, there is an action in your code that you must perform, no matter what happens, and even if an exception is thrown. Usually, this is to free some external resource after acquiring it, to close a file after opening it, or something similar. While you could put that action both inside a catch and outside it, that would amount to duplicating the same code in two different places. Instead, put one copy of that code inside a special optional part of the try-catch construct called `finally`. The `try-catch-finally` construct looks as shown in Figure 6.7.

```
methodM {
    /*Part of code  in the method body. */

    try{
          /*This is the first line of the "guarded region"
            that is governed by the. try keyword
            Put code here that might cause some kind of exception.
            We may have many code lines here or just one
    }

    catch (Exception Type1 e1)  {
          /* Put code here that handles this exception object e1.
            This is the next line of the exception handler.
            . . .
            This is the last line of the exception handler. */
    }

    catch (Exception Type2 e2)  {
          /* Put code here that handles this exception object e2.
            This is the next line of the exception handler.
            . . .
            This is the last line of the exception handler. */
    }
      • • •
    catch (Exception Typen en)  {
          /* Put code here that  handles this exception object en.
            This is the next line of the exception handler.
            . . .
            This is the last line of the exception handler.
    }

    finally {
          /* Put the code which are always to be executed
            . . .
            Whether there is an exception or not.
            Catch blocks(s) are not mandatory. */
    }

    /*The rest part of the method body,if any. */
}
```

Figure 6.7 `try-catch-finally` construct

Program 6.18 illustrates the use of `try-catch-finally` construct in a program. In this program, the `while` loop correctly executes for `i = 0, 1, 2`. When `i = 3`, it throws an `IndexOutOfBoundEception` exception, which is caught by the associated `catch` block. Then, the code in `finally` block is executed.

- It is illegal to use a `try` clause without either a `catch` clause or a `finally` clause. A `try` clause by itself will result in a compile-time error.
- It is legal to omit either the `catch` clause or the `finally` clause, but not both.
- Any `catch` clauses must immediately follow the `try` block. Any `finally` clauses must immediately follow the last `catch` clause.
- Like in `try-catch` block construct, no code can be included in between `catch-finally` or `try-finally`. This is why the following will not compile:

```
try {
        // Some code under the try block ...}
System.out.print("below the try block"); //Illegal!
finally {
// Some code under the try block ...}
```

Program 6.18 (`try-catch-finally` *construct)*

```
/* This program illustrates the use of finally block.
*/

class FinallyDemo1 {
   public static void main (String [ ] args ) {
      int i = 0;
      String greetings [ ] = { "Joy", "with", "Java! "};
      while ( i < 4) {
         try {
            System.out.println (greetings [i++]);
         }catch (Exception e ) {
              System.out.println (e.toString() );
         }
         finally {
           System.out.println("Make array index < 3 :");
      }
    }
  }
}
```

- If you use a `finally` block, then `catch` block is not mandatory. Program 6.19 illustrates this fact.
- If there is no `catch` block, and if any exception occurs, then that exception will not be handled.

Program 6.19 *(`try-finally` construct)*

```
/* This program illustrates the use of finally block
without any catch. */
class FinallyDemo2 {
   public static void main (String [ ] args ) {
      int i = 0;
      String greetings [ ] = { "Joy", "with", "Java! "};
      while ( i < 4) {
         try {
            System.out.println (greetings [i++]);
         }
         finally {
            System.out.println("Make array index < 3 :");
      }
    }
  }
}
```

- The `finally` clause is executed on the way out. If there is a return statement inside a `try` block in a method, then the `finally` clause is executed before the method returns. Program 6.20 is an example.
- Program 6.20 illustrates the fact that if a method exited normally or with exception, whatever be the case, the `finally` block is always executed.

Program 6.20 *(Execution of `finally` block is a must)*

```
/* This program illustrates that finally block will
always be executed before a method returns. */
class FinallyDemo3 {
   static int methodM(int a, int b) {
      try {
           System.out.println("I am from methodM");
           int c = a/b;     // Exception may occur
           return(c);
      } finally {
            System.out.println("Good bye M!");
      }
   }
```

```
    public static void main (String [ ] args ) {
       try{
         System.out.println("I am from Main()");
         int a = Integer.parseInt(args[0]);
           // Exception may occur
         int b = Integer.parseInt(args[1]);
           // Exception may occur
         methodM(a,b);
       }
       catch (Exception e) {
           System.out.println(e.getMessage());
      }
    }
}
```

The `finally` clause is actually useful outside exceptions; you can also use it to execute code after a `return`, a `break`, or a `continue` inside loops. For the latter cases, you can use a `try` clause with a `finally` but without a `catch` clause. Program 6.21 is an illustration of this.

Program 6.21 *(Execution of `finally` block with loop elements)*

```
/* This program illustrates the execution of finally
block, even if return, break or break or continue
inside a loop. */

class MysteriousFinally {
   public static void main(String args[]) {
    try {
      int  mysteriousState = Integer.parseInt(args[0]);
      while (true) {
            System.out.print("Who ");
            try {
                System.out.print("is ");
                if (mysteriousState == 1)
                    return;
                System.out.print("that ");
                if (mysteriousState == 2)
                    break;
                System.out.print("strange ");
                if (mysteriousState == 3)
                    continue;
                System.out.print("but kindly ");
                if (mysteriousState == 4)
                    throw new Exception();
```

```
                    System.out.print("not at all ");
                } finally {
                    System.out.print("amusing man?\n");
                }
                System.out.print("I'd like to meet the man");
            }
            System.out.print("Please tell me.\n");
        } catch (Exception e){
            System.out.println("Enter any one digit
                command line...");
        }
    }
}
```

6.3.4 Nested `try` Construct

A `try` construct (i.e., `tri-catch`, `try-finally` or `try-catch-finally`) can be nested. A `try` construct can be inside the block of another `try` construct, and so on. Figure 6.8 shows a scenario of nested `try` construct.

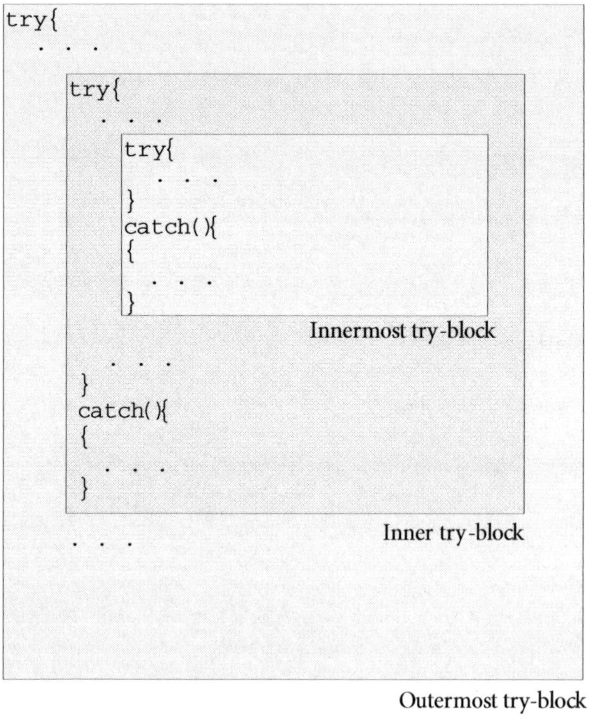

```
try{
  . . .
    try{
      . . .
        try{
          . . .
        }
        catch(){
        {
          . . .
        }
                        Innermost try-block
      . . .
    }
    catch(){
    {
      . . .
    }
                        Inner try-block
  . . .

                        Outermost try-block
```

Figure 6.8 Nested `try` construct

Program 6.22 has multiple exceptions. Let us see how it can be made robust against any sort of exceptions.

Program 6.22 *(A simple program with multiple exceptions)*

```
/* This program should take any number of command line
input. */

class NestedTry {
    public static void main(String args[]) {
        int n = args.length;
          // Number of inputs entered
        int a = 11 / n;
          // Divide by zero, if no input
        System.out.println("n = " + n);
        if(n==1)
           n = n/(n-n);
                // Divide by zero, if only one input
        if(n==2) {
           int c[ ] = {1, 2};
           c[n] = 99;
                // If n = 2, array-index-out-of-bound
        }
    }
}
```

Program 6.23 illustrates a solution with the nested `try` construct.

Program 6.23 *(Solution with nested `try` blocks)*

```
/* Solution of problems in Program 6.22 with nested try
construct. */

class NestedTry {
      public static void main(String args[]) {
          try {   // Outermost try to catch divide-by-
                                          // zero exceptions
             int n = args.length;
             int a = 11 / n;
             System.out.println("a = " + a);
             if(n==1)
                 n = n/(n-n);
          try {  // Innermost try for index out-of-
                                          // bound exception
                if(n==2) {
                   int c[ ] = { 1, 2 };
                   c[n] = 99;
                }
```

```
                } catch(ArrayIndexOutOfBoundsException e) {
                    System.out.println("Exception: " +
                        e.getMessage());
                }
            } catch(ArithmeticException e) {
             System.out.println("Exception:"+e.toString());
        }
    }
}
```

If there is an exception in an innermost try block for which there is no exception handler, then it will search for a match in the next outer. This continues until one of the catch statements succeeds, or until all the nested try statements are exhausted. If no catch statement matches, then the JVM will print the exception report and the program will be terminated abnormally.

6.4 Explicit Exceptions Throwing

So far you have learned how Java run-time environment (JVM) automatically throws an exception and that it can be handled by the exception handler routine defined either in a `catch` or `finally` block or both. In addition to this, you can define your own set of conditions or rules and throw an exception explicitly using `throw` keyword. For example, you can throw `ArithmeticException` when a number is divided by 5, or any other number you specify.

There are two ways of throwing an exception explicitly: using `throw` and `throws`. These two ways are discussed in the following:

6.4.1 The `throw`

The syntax of throwing an exception explicitly is as follows:

```
throw  <ExceptionObject>;
```

or

```
throw new <ExceptionName>(<StringMessage>);
```

In the first form, `<ExceptionObject>` is a throwable object `e`, such as `Exception e`. In the second form, `<ExceptionName>` is any child class of the super class `Throwable` and `<StringMessage>` is a string of characters. Program 6.24 is a simple example showing how a programmer can throw an exception explicitly.

Program 6.24 *(`throw` statement for explicit throwing)*

```
/* This program checks if the student's marks < 60
and age >30. If it breaks this rule, then the program
throws an exception with a message. */

public class ThrowDemo {
   static void checkEligibilty(int marks, int age){
     try {
        if(marks < 60 || age > 30){
            throw new ArithmeticException("Student is
                disqualified");
        }
      else {
         System.out.println("Student is eligible");
           }
      }catch (ArithmeticException e){
         System.out.println("Rule violation occurs");
         throw e;    //Rethown the exception
     }
   }

   public static void main(String args[]){
     System.out.println("Welcome to the Registration
          process!!");
     try {
         checkEligibilty(79, 31);
         checkEligibilty(95, 25);
         checkEligibilty(56, 39);
         checkEligibilty(45, 27);
     }
     catch(ArithmeticException e) {
         System.out.println(e.getMessage());
     }
  }
}
```

- In Java, you can throw only objects of child classes of `Throwable`. Primitive types, such as `int` or `char`, as well as non-`Throwable` classes, such as `String` and `Object`, cannot be used as exceptions.
- Note the Java syntax for creating a new `Throwable` object using `new` operator. In Program 6.24, `new` operator is used to construct an instance of `ArithmeticException`. Many of Java's built-in run-time exceptions have at least two constructors: one with no parameter and the other that takes a parameter of type `String`. When the second form is used, the argument specifies a string that describes the exception. This string is displayed when the object is used as an argument to `print()` or `println()`. It can also be obtained by a call to `getMessage()`, which is defined by `Throwable`.

- `throw` keyword can also be used for throwing custom exceptions which we shall discuss in the next subsection.
- The flow of execution stops immediately after the `throw` statement and hence any subsequent statements will not be executed. The nearest enclosing `try` block is inspected to see if it has a `catch` statement that matches the type of exception. If it finds a match, control is transferred to that statement. If not, then the next enclosing `try` statement is inspected, and so on. If no matching `catch` is found, then the default exception handler halts the program and prints the stack trace accordingly.

6.4.2 The `throws`

During the discussion of checked exception (Section 6.2.2), we have mentioned the use of `throws` keyword. If a method is capable of causing an exception that it does not handle, it must specify this behavior so that callers of the method can guard themselves against that exception. You do this by including a `throws` clause in the method's declaration. A `throws` clause lists the types of exceptions that a method might throw. The syntax of doing so is as follows:

```
<methodDeclaration> throws <Exc1 [, Exc 2, …, Exce_n] {
          // Body of the method
}
```

Program 6.25 is an illustration. In this program, the method `aMethod()` when it is executed, an exception of type checked exception (here, thrown explicitly for an illustration) is thrown and it does not catch. Because the program does not specify a `throws` clause to declare this fact, the program will not compile.

Program 6.25 *(Usefulness of* `throws`*)*

```
/* This program will not compile, because it is not
able to catch a checked exception. */

class ThrowsDemo {
   static void aMethod() {
        System.out.println("I am from aMethod...");
        throw new IllegalAccessException("Exception is
            not handled");
   }

   public static void main(String args[]) {
        aMethod();
   }
}
```

When the method `aMethod()` is defined with `throws` keyword, it will compile and run successfully. Program 6.26 is an example.

Program 6.26 *(Remedy with* `throws`*)*

```
/* This program will now compile and run as exceptions
are handled. */

class ThrowsDemo {
  static void aMethod() throws IllegalAccessException {
      System.out.println("I am from aMethod...");
      throw new IllegalAccessException("An exception
           occurs");
   }

   public static void main(String args[]) {
       try {
          aMethod();
       } catch(IllegalAccessException e) {
          System.out.println (e + " and handled now.");
       }
   }
}
```

- A `throws` clause lists the types of exceptions that a method might throw. This list includes any exception which belongs to the checked class; it cannot include exceptions types of `Error` or `RuntimeException`, or any of their sub classes.
- All other exceptions that a method can throw must be declared in the `throws` clause. If they are not declared, a compile-time error will result.
- `Throws` can include a list of exception classes and can check for a number of exceptions. If you are not sure about a specific type, to be on the safer side, you can throws `Exception`, because `Exception` class is a super class of any checked exception. Program 6.27 is an illustration. In this program, an `IOException` may occur due to the `DataInputStream` class.

Program 6.27 *(*`throws` *with multiple exceptions)*

```
/* This program illustrates a default inclusion as
checked exception. You can check that if you remove
"throws Exception" in the main() definition, it will
not compile, although the program is syntactically
correct. */

class InterestCalculator{
   public static void main(String args[ ] ) throws
      Exception {
```

```
        Float principalAmount = new Float(0);
        Float rateOfInterest = new Float(0);
        int numberOfYears = 0;
    try {
        DataInputStream in = new DataInputStream(System.in);
        String tempString;
        System.out.println("Enter Principal Amount: ");
        System.out.flush();
        tempString = in.readLine();
        principalAmount = Float.valueOf(tempString);
        System.out.println("Enter Rate of Interest: ");
        System.out.flush();
        tempString = in.readLine();
        rateOfInterest = Float.valueOf(tempString);
        System.out.println("Enter Number of Years: ");
        System.out.flush();
        tempString = in.readLine();
        numberOfYears = Integer.parseInt(tempString);
      }
      catch (Exception e) {}
         float interestTotal = principalAmount *
            rateOfInterest * numberOfYears;
        System.out.println("Total Interest = " +
            interestTotal);
    }
}
```

6.4.3 Difference between throw and throws

Some salient difference between throw and throws are summarized in Table 6.3.

Table 6.3 throw versus throws in Java

throw	throws
throw keyword is used to explicitly throw an exception.	throws keyword is used to declare an exception.
Checked exception cannot be propagated using throw.	Checked exception can be propagated with throws.
throw is used within a method.	throws is used with a method signature.
throw is followed by an object name.	throws is followed by class(es).
You cannot throw multiple exceptions.	You can declare multiple exceptions.

6.5 User Defined Exception

You now understand how to put `try` block(s) together with `catch` block(s) and `finally` block and nested structure in your methods to handle exceptions. The exceptions are Java's built-in exceptions defined in `java.lang` package. The most general of these exceptions are sub classes of the standard type `RuntimeException`. In Java these are called *unchecked exceptions* (Table 6.2) because the compiler does not check to see if a method handles or throws these exceptions. These exceptions are set to trigger different events. For example, when we divide a number by zero, this triggers `ArithmeticException`, when we try to access the array element out of its bounds then we get `ArrayIndexOutOfBoundsException`, and so on.

Besides the built-in exceptions which handle most of the common exceptions, Java provides facility to users to create their own exception types to handle situations specific to their applications. This is quite easy to do: just define a sub class of `Exception` (which is a sub class of `Throwable`). Your sub classes don't need to actually implement anything: it is their existence in the type system that allows you to use them as exceptions. The general syntax for defining your own exceptions is as follows:

```
class <NewExceptionName> extends Exception {
      // User defined body of the class
}
```

Note that `Exception` class does not define any methods of its own. It does, of course, inherit those methods provided by `Throwable`. Thus, all exceptions, including those that you create, have the methods defined by `Throwable` available to them. The methods in `Throwable` class are shown in Table 6.4. You may override any of these methods in exception classes that you create. `Exception` class defines the following two constructers:

```
Exception( );
Exception(String msg);
```

The first form is a default one and the second form allows a programmer to specify a description of the exception. Alternatively, an exception can be specified by overriding the `toString()` method defined in `Throwable` class.

Table 6.4 The methods defined in `Throwable` class in `java.lang`

Method	Description
`final void addSuppressed(Throwable e)`	Adds `e` to the list of suppressed exceptions associated with the invoking exception. It is mainly used in `try-with-resources` statement.
`Throwable fillInStackTrace( )`	Returns a `Throwable` object that contains a full stack trace. This object can be rethrown.
`Throwable getCause( )`	Returns the exception that underlies the current exception. If there is no underlying exception, `null` is returned.
`String getLocalizedMessage( )`	Returns a localized description of the exception.
`String getMessage( )`	Returns a description of the exception.
`StackTraceElement[ ] getStackTrace( )`	Returns an array that contains the stack trace, one element at a time of the array of `StackTraceElement`.
`final Throwable[ ] getSuppressed( )`	Obtains the suppressed exceptions associated with the invoking exception and returns an array that contains the result. Suppressed exceptions are primarily generated by `try-with-resources` statement.
`Throwable initCause(Throwable e)`	Associates `e` with the invoking exception as a cause of the invoking exception.
`void printStackTrace( )`	Displays the stack trace.
`void printStackTrace(PrintStream stream)`	Sends the stack trace to the specified stream.
`void printStackTrace(PrintWriter stream)`	Sends the stack trace to the specified stream.
`void setStackTrace(StackTraceElement elements[ ])`	Sets the stack trace to the elements passed in `elements`. This method is for specialized applications, not normal use.
`String toString( )`	Returns a `String` object containing a description of the exception. This method is called by `println( )` when outputting a `Throwable` object.

Program 6.28 is a simple example showing how a programmer can define his or her own exception and utilize it in their program.

Program 6.28
(User-defined exception)

```
/* This program demonstrates the use of user-defined
exception in a Java program. */

// Defining a user defied Exception class

class MyException extends Exception {
       MyException (String message) {
             super(message);
       }
}

class TestMyException {
      public static void main (String args[ ]) {
      int x = 5,  y = 1000;
      try {
       float z = (float) x / (float) y;
           if (z < 0.01)  throw new MyException
                ("Given data are not proper");
       }
       catch (MyException e) {
             System.out.println(e.getMessage());       }
       finally {
             System.out.println ("It prints always!");
      }
  }
}
```

Another example of custom exception is shown in Program 6.29. This example shows how a custom defined exception can be thrown with `throws` keyword.

Program 6.29
(Another user-defined exception)

```
/* Another example of custom exception. */

class InvalidException extends Exception {
    public InvalidException(String s){
        // Call constructor of parent Exception
        super(s);
    }
}

public class CustomDemo {
   void productCheck(int weight) throws InvalidException{
      if(weight<100){
```

```
            throw new InvalidException("Product is
                invalid");
        }
    }
    public static void main(String args[])      {
      CustomDemo obj = new CustomDemo ();
        try {
            obj.productCheck(60);
        }
        catch (InvalidException e)
        {
            System.out.println("Caught the exception");
            System.out.println(e.getMessage());
        }
    }
}
```

Program 6.30 is an application for your better understanding of exception handling in Java. Check it carefully.

Program 6.30 *(An application program)*

```
/* A practical example dealing with exception
handling in Java. Let the file is saved as
InsufficientFundsException.java */

public class InsufficientFundsException extends
     Exception {
   private double amount;
   public InsufficientFundsException(double amount) {
      this.amount = amount;
   }
   public double getAmount(){
      return amount;
   }
}

/* This is the another part of the program. Let the
file is named as CheckingAccount.java */

public class CheckingAccount {
   private double balance;
   private int number;
   public CheckingAccount(int number) {
     this.number = number;
   }
```

```
    public void deposit(double amount)    {
      balance += amount;
    }
     public void withdraw(double amount) throws
            InsufficientFundsException {
       if(amount <= balance){
          balance -= amount;
       }
       else {
          double needs = amount - balance;
         throw new InsufficientFundsException(needs);
      }
    }
    public double getBalance() {
        return balance;
    }
    public int getNumber(){
        return number;
    }
}

/* The following is the main class. Save the file as
BankDemo.java */
public class BankDemo {
    public static void main(String [] args)    {
       CheckingAccount c = new CheckingAccount(101);
       System.out.println("Depositing $500...");
       c.deposit(500.00);
       try {
          System.out.println("\n Withdrawing $100...");
           c.withdraw(100.00);
           System.out.println("\n Withdrawing $600...");
           c.withdraw(600.00);
       } catch(InsufficientFundsException e){
          System.out.println("Fund insufficient!
            $"+ e.getAmount());
            e.printStackTrace();
       }
   }
}
```

6.6 Some More Features of Exception Handling

Exception handling in Java is characterized with some unique features which are discussed in the following subsections:

6.6.1 Chained Exception

Many times it happens that an exception occurs due to another exception. For example, consider a situation in which a method throws an `ArithmeticException` because of an attempt to divide by zero but the actual cause of exception was an IO error which caused the divisor to become zero. The concept of chained exceptions (the features beginning with Java 1.4) allows the programmer to relate one exception with another exception. The chained exception throws the actual exception when it occurs in a method and at the same time allows the calling code to know the underlying cause of the exception.

`Throwable` class has two constructors and two methods to support chained exceptions. First, let's look at the constructors.

```
Throwable(Throwable cause);
Throwable(String desc, Throwable cause);
```

The first form has a single parameter which specifies the actual cause of an *Exception.* Here, `cause` is the exception that causes the current exception. That is, `cause` is the underlying reason why an exception occurred. The second form accepts an exception description with the actual cause of the exception as well. This constructor allows you to specify a description at the same time that you specify a cause of exception.

Second, the methods that the `Throwable` class provides to handle chained exceptions are (Table 6.4):

```
Throwable getCause( );
Throwable initCause(Throwable cause);
```

The `getCause( )` method returns the actual cause associated with the current exception. If there is no underlying exception, `null` is returned.

The `initCause( )` method associates `cause` with the invoking exception and returns a reference to the exception.

Thus, you can associate a cause with an exception after the occurrence of an exception. Program 6.31 gives an example illustrating the mechanism of handling chained exceptions. The output from Program 6.31 will appear as follows:

```
Caught: java.lang. ArithmeticException: Top Level Exception
Original cause: java.lang.ArithmeticException: IO Cause
```

In this example, the top-level exception is `ArithmeticException`. It is actually due to an `IOException`. When an exception is thrown out of `createException()`, it is caught by `main()`, the top-level exception is displayed, followed by the underlying exception, which is obtained by calling `getCause()`.

- Chained exceptions can be carried on to whatever depth is necessary. Thus, the cause exception can itself have a cause.
- An overly long chain of exceptions indicates a poor design. Chained exceptions are not something that every program should have. However, in cases where knowledge of an underlying cause is useful, their inclusions offer an elegant solution.

Program 6.31 *(Chained exception)*

```
/* This program demonstrates the mechanism of chained
exception. */

class ChainedExceptionDemo {
     static void createException() {
     // Create an exception
          ArithmeticException ae = new Arithmetic
                Exception("Top Level Exception.");
           ae.initCause(new ArithmeticException
                ("IO Cause"));
                 // Add a cause
           throw ae;
     }

     public static void main(String[] args) {
        try {
            createException();
        } catch(ArithmeticException ae) {
            System.out.println("Caught : " + ae);
            System.out.println("Original cause:"+
                ae.getCause());
        }
     }
}
```

Let's discuss the utility of chained exception handling with an example. We need to chain the exceptions to make logs readable. Let's consider Program 6.32. Check the log of the exceptions thrown on the execution of the program.

Program 6.32
(Chained exception application)

```
/* Program without chaining exceptions. */
class NoSalaryException extends Exception {
    public NoSalaryException(String message,
     Throwable cause) {
        super(message, cause);
    }
    public NoSalaryException(String message) {
        super(message);
    }
}
class BadPerformanceException extends Exception {
    public BadPerformanceException (String message,
     Throwable cause) {
        super(message, cause);
    }
    public NoSalaryException(String message) {
        super(message);
    }
}
public class ExceptionDemo1 {
    static void paySalary() throws NoSalaryException {
        try {
            performance();
        } catch (BadPerformanceException e) {
            e.printStackTrace();
            throw new NoSalaryException("No salary");
        }
    }

    void performance() throws BadPerformanceException {
        throw new BadPerformanceException
           ("Poor performance");
    }
     public static void main(String[] args) throws
          Exception {
        paySalary();
    }
}
```

6.6.2 Multiple Exceptions by a Single Catch

In the current version of JDK, three interesting and useful features related to the exception handling mechanism are available. The first feature is about an automatic procedure of releasing a resource, such as a file, when it is no longer needed. This is based on an expanded form of the `try` statement called `try-`

`with-resources`. This feature will be discussed in Chapter 8. The second feature is called `multiple exception by a single catch`, and the third is referred to as `rethrow`. These two features are briefly mentioned here.

You have studied multiple catch blocks associated with a single `try` block in Section 6.3.2 to catch multiple exceptions generated in a single try block. This multi-exceptions catch feature allows two or more exceptions to be caught by the same `catch` clause. In many situations, it is common for two or more exception handlers to use the same code sequence even though they respond to different exceptions. Instead of having to catch each exception type individually, you can use a single catch clause to handle all of the exceptions without code duplication. To use a `multi-catch`, separate each exception type in the catch clause with the logical-OR operator. Each multi-catch parameter is implicitly final. However, you can explicitly specify final.

Program 6.33 illustrates a catch statement that uses the `multi-catch` feature to catch both `ArithmeticException` and `ArrayIndexOutOfBounds Exception` exception, for example. In this program, an `ArithmeticException` occurs when there is a division by zero, and also an `ArraIndexOutOfBoundsException` is generated in the `try` block. Both exceptions are caught by the single `catch` statement succeeding the `try` block.

Program 6.33 *(Multiple exceptions caught by a single catch block)*

```
/* This program illustrates the catch of multiple
exceptions by a single catch block. */

class MultiExceptionSingleCatch {
    public static void main(String args[]) {
      int a = 99, b = 0;
      int x[] = { 1, 2, 3 };
      try {
         int result = a / b; // An ArithmeticException
         x[10] = 11; // An ArrayIndexOutOfBoundsException
     }
     catch(ArithmeticException | ArrayIndexOutOfBounds
           Exception e) {
            System.out.println("Exception caught: "
                + e);
     }
     System.out.println("Execution is successful.");
  }
}
```

6.6.3 The `rethrow` of Exception Handling

Sometimes we may need to rethrow an exception in Java. If a `catch` block cannot handle the particular exception it has caught, we can rethrow the exception. The `rethrow` keyword causes the originally thrown object to be rethrown. Let us illustrate this concept with an example (Program 6.34).

Program 6.34 *(Rethrow feature)*

```
/* This program illustrates the rethrow feature
introduced in JDK 7. */

public class RethrowExceptionsDemo {
        //User defined exception-1
        static class Exception1 extends Exception{
            public Exception1 (String msg) {
                super(msg);
        }
        //User defined exception-1
       static class Exception2 extends Exception {
          public Exception2 (String msg) {
                super(msg);
          }
       }
        //User defined exception-3
       static class Exception3 extends Exception {
          public Exception3(String msg) {
                super(msg);
          }
     }

     // Defining rethrow method
      static void myRethrow(String s) throws
                  Exception1, Exception2, Exception3 {
          try {
             if (s.equals("First"))
               throw new Exception1("First Exception");
             else if (s.equals("Second"))
               throw new Exception2("Second Exception");
             else
               throw new Exception3("Third Exception");
          } catch (Exception e) {
                 throw e;
          }
     }
```

```
        public static void main(String[] args) {
             try{
                  myRethrow("abc");
             }catch(Exception1 | Exception2 | Exception3
                  e){
                  //e = new Exception();
                  System.out.println(e.getMessage());
             }
        }
}
```

As you can see that in `myRethrow()` method, `catch` block is catching exception but it's not part of `throws` clause. Java 7 compiler analyzes the complete `try` block to check what types of exceptions are thrown and then rethrown from the `catch` block.

- Java rethrow exception feature allows you to stipulate more specific exception types in the `throws` clause of a method declaration.
- The more precise `rethrow` feature restricts the type of exceptions that can be rethrown to only those checked exceptions that the associated try block throws that are not handled by a preceding catch clause, and which are a sub type or supertype of the parameter. For the more precise `rethrow` feature to be in force, the catch parameter must be either effectively final, which means that it must not be assigned a new value inside the catch block, or explicitly declared final.
- Because the exception has already been caught at the scope in which the rethrow expression occurs, it is rethrown out to the next enclosing try block. Therefore, it cannot be handled by `catch` blocks at the scope in which the rethrow expression occurred. Any `catch` blocks for the enclosing `try` block have an opportunity to catch the exception.

6.6.4 Exception Handling with `try-catch` Resource

This discussion is related to working with input and output streams (it is discussed in detail in Chapter 8). Consider a situation where a file is used as an input stream from where you can read data; it is also used as an output stream to which you can write data. The `java.io` package defines two classes, `FileInputStream` and `FileOutputStream`, for reading and writing data from and to a file, respectively. Prior to read/write, you have to open a file. To do this you have to create an object of one of these classes specifying the name of the file as an argument to the constructor. For example:

```
FileInputStream(String fileName);
                              // To open a file for reading
FileOutputStream(String fileName);
                              // To open a file for writing
```

Here, `String fileName` denotes the name of the file, for example, `abc.txt`. These two constructors throw `FileNotFoundException` in case of any errors, such as file is not present, or it does not have permission to open for reading, writing, etc. `FileNotFoundException` is a sub class of `IOException` class. When you are done with a file, you must close it. It is necessary to close a file always. Closing a file releases the system resources allocated to the file, allowing them to be used by another file. Failure to close a file can result in "memory leaks" because of unused resources remaining allocated. The file closing is done by calling the `close()` method, which is implemented by both `FileInputStream` and `FileOutputStream` class. In case, if a file is not closed successfully, then `close()` method throws `IOException`.

Note that there are two standard approaches which you can use to close a file when you are done with it. The first is the traditional approach, in which `close()` is called explicitly when the file is no longer needed. Program 6.35 illustrates how opening and closing a file in the process of copying the content of a file *input.txt* to a file *output.txt*. In the program, notice the try–catch blocks that handle the IO errors which may occur. Each IO operation is monitored for exceptions, and if an exception occurs, it is handled.

Program 6.35 *(File handling)*

```
/* This program illustrates opening and closing a file
in the process of copying the content of a file input.
txt to a file output.txt. Notice the try-catch blocks
that handle the I/O errors that might occur. This
program will be better understandable after reading
Chapter 8. */

import java.io.DataInputStream;
import java.io.DataOutputStream;
import java.io.FileInputStream;
import java.io.FileOutputStream;
import java.io.IOException;
import java.io.InputStream;
import java.io.FileNotFoundException;

class FileHandling {
    public static void main(String args[]) {
         // Declaring I/O files...
```

```
        FileInputStream fin=null;     // Input file
        FileOutputStream fout=null;   // Output file
        int i;
        // Opening the files...
           try {
               FileInputStream fin = new FileInputStrem
                  ("input.txt");
               FileOutputStream fout = new FileOutputStrem
                  ("Output.txt");
           } catch(FileNotFoundException e) {
               System.out.println("Cannot Open File...");
           }

           // At this point, the files are open and can
                                          // be read and write.
           // The following reads characters until EOF is
           // encountered and copy the content into
                                              // another file.
           try {
               do {
                  i = fin.read();
                       // Read a byte
                  if(i != -1). fout.write(i);
                       // Write the byte
               } while(i != -1);
           } catch(IOException e) {
                 System.out.println("File error(s)");
           } finally {
             try {
                 fin.close();     fout.close();
             } catch(IOException e) {
                 System.out.println("Error closing
                       file(s)");
          }
      }
  }
```

The second approach is to close a file automatically using the feature added in JDK-7. The feature is called automatic resource management or ARM for short. ARM is based on an expanded form of the `try` statement and it has the following syntax:

```
try (all-resources) {
    // Code to use the resource(s)
}
```

Here, `all-resources` is a statement that declares and initializes all resources under management. Program 6.36 illustrates the use of this feature and is an alternate program to Program 6.35.

Program 6.36 (*`try-with-resources`* *in file handling*)

```
/* This program illustrates automatic closing files. */

import java.io.DataInputStream;
import java.io.DataOutputStream;
import java.io.FileInputStream;
import java.io.FileOutputStream;

class FileHandlingARM {
    public static void main(String args[]) {
         // Opening the file...
         try (FileInputStream fin = new FileInputStrem
           ("input.txt");
             FileOutputStream fout = new FileOutputStrem
                ("Output.txt")){
             //At this point, the files are open and
                                          //ready read & write.
             //The following reads characters until EOF
                //is encountered and copy the content
                                           //into another file.
             try {
                 do {
                    int i = fin.read();
                     // Read a byte
                    if(i != -1). fout.write(i);
                     // Write the byte
                 } while(i != -1);
             } catch(IOException e) {
                System.out.println("File error(s)");
             }
         } catch(FileNotFoundException e) {
             System.out.println("Cannot Open File");
         }
    }
}
```

- This new form of `try` is called the *try-with-resources* statement.
- When the `try` block ends, the resource is automatically released. In this case the files are automatically closed. Thus, there is no need to call `close()` explicitly.
- In this form of try-with-resource, you can also include `catch` and `finally` clauses.

The try-with-resources statement can be used only with those resources that implement the `AutoCloseable` interface defined by `java.lang`. This interface defines the `close()` method. `AutoCloseable` is inherited by the `Closeable` interface in `java.io`. Both interfaces are implemented by the stream classes, for example, `FileInputStream` and `FileOutputStream`.

Summary

In this chapter, the exception handling mechanism is discussed in detail. The chapter starts with a basic introduction to errors and exceptions of which every programmer should be aware. Since exceptions have to be managed to make robust programs, the topic of exceptions and categorization of all exceptions are discussed in detail. Java provides elegant features of handling all sorts of exceptions. The syntaxes of different exception handling features are elaborated, which include try, try-catch, try-catch-finally, nested try, and multiple try constructs. How the user can define their own exceptions is also covered in this chapter. All exceptions are automatically raised when they occur. In many applications it is necessary to raise exception. How explicitly exception can be thrown is also discussed. This chapter concludes with a brief discussion of advanced exception handling features such as chained exceptions, rethrow exceptions, multiple exceptions, catch with a single try, and try with resources.

FAQs

6.1 What do you mean by errors and exceptions? How are they different?
6.2 What are the basic keywords for handling exceptions in Java programs?
6.3 When is an exception called a checked exception?
6.4 What is an unchecked exception?
6.5 What do the Java keywords `final`, `finally`, and `finalize()` stand for?
6.6 Is there a situation when `finally` will not execute?
6.7 List the salient points of `throw` in exception handling.
6.8 List the salient points of `throw` in exception handling.
6.9 How can you create your own exception?
6.10 What is a `Throwable` class?

The answers to these questions and other problems in this chapter are available at www.cambridge.org/9781009211918. You might have many questions like these You can post your question in the discussion forum at https://cse.iitkgp.ac.in/~dsamanta/joywithjava/page8.php.

Programs for Practice

6.1 Consider the following program. What are the different exceptions possible? Use `try-catch` block to catch all the exception that it throws.

```
/* This program illustrates how JVM throws Exception object when
an exception occurs. */

class ExceptionThrow {
     public static double divide(int a, int b) {
         return(a/b);
     }
     public static void main(String args[]) {
          double x; int d = 0;
          x = divide(4,5); System.out.println(x);
          x = divide (5, d); System.out.println(x);
          x = divide (5, d+1); System.out.println(x);
      }
   }
```

6.2 Is the following program robust, that is, can it handle all the exceptions it may throw? If not, apply the exception handling routine to make it robust.

```
Class TestException {
    public static void main (String args[ ] {
        int a, b, c;
         int x, y;
        try {
            x = a / (b-c);
        }
        catch (ArithmeticException e) {
            System.out.println(" b=c: Divide-by-zero error!");
        }
        y = a / (b + c);
        System.out.println ( "y = " + y);
    }
  }
```

6.3 What are the vulnerabilities in this program?

```
class CommandLineInputTest {
    public static void main (String args[ ] {
        int number, count;
        for (int i = 0; i < args.length; i++)  {
            number = Integer.parseInt(args[i]);
            System.out.println ( "Number at " + i + args.[i]);
```

```
            }
        }
    }
```

Hint: try with the following test input:

```
java CommandLineInputTest  1    2  3
java CommandLineInputTest  1   -2  3
java CommandLineInputTest  1.5  2  3.9
java CommandLineInputTest  1  Java -0.5
```

6.4 Following is a program to test how many valid inputs a user enters into the program. Note that the program reads input as command line input and the inputs are to be passed as integer value.

```
class CommandLineInput {
  public static void main (String args[ ] {
     try {
         int number, InvalidCount = 0; validCount = 0;
         for (int i = 0; i < args.length; i++)  {
            number = Integer.parseInt(args[i]);
     } catch (NumberFormatException e)  {
           inavlidCount++;
           System.out.println("Invalid number at " +i+args[i]);
     }
     validCount++;
     System.out.println ("Valid number at " +i + args[i]);
     System.out.println ( "Invalid entries: " + inValidCount);
     System.out.println ( "Valid entries: " + validCount);
  }
}
```

6.5 Run the following program and check how JVM searches the call stack and in which order.

```
class TestEx {
      public static void main (String [] args) {
          doStuff();
     }
     static void doStuff() {
         doMoreStuff();
     }
     static void doMoreStuff() {
        int x = 5/0; // Can't divide by zero!
     }
}
```

6.6 Why will the following program not compile successfully? What should you do to run?

```
// This program doesn't compile

class test
{
    public static void main(String[] args)       {
       Thread.sleep(10000);
        System.out.println("Hello Geeks");
    }
}
```

Hint: In `main()` use `throws InterruptedException` as the method may face `InterruptedExcpetion` when the `sleep()` method of the Thread class is executed. Compiler checks this and hence demands an exception should be thrown explicitly.

6.7 What remedy should you do to run the following program?

```
class ThrowsExecp
{
    static void fun()
    {
        System.out.println("Inside fun(). ");
        throw new IllegalAccessException("demo");
    }
    public static void main(String args[])
    {
        try
        {
            fun();
        }
        catch(IllegalAccessException e)
        {
            System.out.println("caught in main.");
        }
    }
}
```

Hint: The method `fun()` should be defined with `throws IllegalAccessException`.

6.8 The following program is not robust. You have to make it robust using Java's exceptional handling mechanism. Critically locate the vulnerabilities and insert the exception handler routine in it.

```
import java.util.Scanner;
    public class MaximumCalculator {
        public static void main(String args[]) {
        Scanner scnr = new Scanner(System.in);
```

```
        // Calculating the maximum two numbers in Java
        System.out.println("Please enter two numbers to find
              maximum of two");
        int a = scnr.nextInt();
        int b = scnr.nextInt();
        if (a > b) {
              System.out.printf("Between %d and %d, maximum is
                     %d \n", a, b, a);
        }
        else {
                System.out.printf("Between %d and %d, maximum
                     number is %d \n", a, b, b);
        }
    }
}
```

6.9 The Following program is not robust. You have to make it robust using Java's exceptional handling mechanism. Critically locate the vulnerabilities and insert the exception handler routine in it.

```
import java.util.*;
     class SimpleArrayList{
     public static void main(String args[]){
         int sum = 0;
         float avg = 0;
         ArrayList <Integer> l = new ArrayList<Integer>();
         System.out.println("Enter the input ");
                    Scanner input = new Scanner(System.in);
     while (input.hasNextInt()) {
           l.add(input.nextInt());
     }
     for (int i = 0; i < l.size(); i++) {
           sum = sum+l.get(i);
     }
     avg = sum/(l.size());
     System.out.println("Average : " + avg);
  }
}
```

6.10 Modify the following program to catch all the exceptions that may occur with a single `try` and multiple `catch` blocks.

```
// Case : try with multiple catch block......

public class SingleTryMultiCatch  {
   public static void main (String args[ ]) {
        int i = args.length;
```

```
            String myString[] = new String[i];
            if(myString[0].equals("Java")){
               System.out.println("First word is Java !");
            }
             System.out.println( " Number of arguments = " + i );
             int x = 12/ i;          /
             int y[ ] = {555, 999};
             y[ i ] = x;
        }
    }
```

6.11 Modify the following program to catch all the exceptions that may occur with a single `catch` block.

```
class Demonstration_108   {
    public int j;
    static void main (String   args[ ] ) {
        for (int i = 0; i < 4; i++ ) {
              switch (i) {
                    case 0 :
                          int zero = 0;
                          j = 999/ zero; // Divide by zero
                          break;
                    case 1:
                          int b[ ] = null;
                          j = b[0] ; // Null pointer error
                          break;
                    case 2:
                          int c = new int [2] ;
                          j = c[10]; // Array index is out-of-
                                bound
                          break;
                    case 3:
                          char ch = "Java".charAt(9) ;
                                // Index is out-of-bound
                          break;
                    }
              }
        }
}
```

6.12 Modify the following program to catch all the exceptions with nested `try-catch` construct.

```
class NestedTry {
      public static void main(String args[]) {
            int a = args.length;
```

```
                int b = 42 / a;
                System.out.println("a = " + a);
                if(a==1)
                   a = a/(a-a);
                if(a==2) {
                   int c[ ] = { 1 };
                   c[2] = 99;
                }
          }
    }
```

MCQs

6.1 **When does an exception occur?**

(a) During the time of compilation of a Java program.
(b) During the time of execution of a Java program.
(c) Any time during compilation and execution of a program.
(d) At the end of execution of a Java program, if there is an exception.

6.2 **Consider the following piece of code:**

```
try {
      System.out.println{};
}
      Systcm.out.print("Below the try");
catch(Exception ex) { }
```

What error will this give?

(a) Compile-time error.
(b) Run-time error.
(c) A `println` without any argument is illegal.
(d) A `catch` block without any code I it is illegal.

6.3 **If there is a `try` block, then:**

(a) There should be a `catch` block.
(b) There may not be any `catch` block.
(c) There should be a `finally` block.
(d) There may be multiple `catch` blocks.

6.4 **Which of the following is true?**

(a) The multiple `catch` blocks should be listed in the order from general exception classes to more specialized ones.
(b) If there is no exception, the `finally` block will not be executed.
(c) If there are multiple `catch` blocks, only the first one matching the exception will be executed.
(d) If there are multiple `catch` blocks, all blocks that match the exceptions will be executed.

6.5 Consider the following part of a program:

```
try {
    int num = Integer.parseInt("Two thousand nineteen");
} catch (NumberFormatException e) {
    System.out.println("You don't have a number.");
} catch (Exception e) {
      System.out.println("Something went terribly wrong!");
} finally {
       System.out.println("Program is in execution…");
}
                        }
```

What is the output of the code? Select the appropriate choice as your answer.

(a) You don't have a number.
Program is in execution ...
(b) Something went terribly wrong!
Program is in execution ...
(c) Program is in execution ...
(d) You don't have a number.
Something went terribly wrong!
Program is in execution ...

6.6 Consider the following program:

```
  class ExceptionHandling        {
        public static void main(String args[ ])    {
            try  {
                int a, b;
                b = 0;
                a = 5 / b;
                System.out.print("A");
            } catch(ArithmeticException e)    {
                    System.out.print("B");
            }
            finally  {             {
                System.out.print("C");
            }
        }
     }
  }
```

What is the output of this program?

(a) A (b) B (c) AC (d) BC

6.7 In which of the following Java package is the `Exception` class defined?

(a) `java.awt` (b) `java.io`
(c) `java.lang` (d) `java.util`

6.8 Consider the following piece of code:

```
public class TryCatchFinally {
     public static void main(String []args) {
        try {
              System.out.println("try");
              System.exit(0);
        }
        catch(ArithmeticException e){
              System.out.println("catch");
        }
        finally {
              System.out.println("finally");
        }
     }
}
```

Which of the following statement(s) is(are) correct?

(a) The output of the code is:

```
try
catch
finally
```

(b) The output of the code is:

```
try
```

(c) The output of the code is:

```
try
finally
```

(d) The output of the code is:

```
catch
finally
```

6.9 Which sub class of **`Throwable`** is checked at compile-time?

(a) `NullPointerException`
(b) `ArithmeticException`
(c) `IOException`
(d) `ArrayIndexOutOfBoundsException`

6.10 Which of the following is true about **`try-catch`** construct in Java?

(1) A `try-catch` block must have a finally block.
(2) A `try` block is limited to maximum two `catch` blocks.
(3) Barring the Java Virtual Machine from exiting, the `finally` block will always be executed.

Select the correct answer from the following.

(a) 1 and 3 (b) 1 only (c) 3 only (d) 1 and 2

6.11 Consider the following two lists containing some statements in each:

LIST1:

(a) `int [] b;`
    `b[0] = 0;`

(b) `ArrayIndexOutOfBoundException`

LIST2:

(1) Compile-time exception
(2) Compilation error
(3) Run-time exception

Match each item in the first list with an item in the second list. Select the correct matching from the following options:

(a) a→2 b→1
(b) a→2 b→3
(c) a→1 b→2
(d) a→3 b→3

6.12 Consider the following code:

```
public class B1{
  public static void main(String[] args) {
        try  {
                int a=100;
                System.out.println(a);
                int b=a/0;
                a=a+1;
                System.out.println(a);
        }
        catch(ArithmeticException e)  {
                System.out.println("Exception thrown:
                                        cannot divide by zero");
        }
  }
}
```

Which of the following will be printed if the program is executed?

(a) 100

Exception thrown: cannot divide by zero

(b) 101

Exception thrown: cannot divide by zero

(c) 100

101

(d) 101

100

6.13 Consider the following piece of code in Java:

```
public class Test{
  public static void main(String args[]){
     class Foo{
          public int i = 3;
     }
     Object o = (Object)new Foo();
     Foo foo = (Foo)o;
     System.out.println("i = " + foo.i);
  }
}
```

Which of the following is the result?

(a) i = 3.
(b) The program will not be able to compile successfully.
(c) A `ClassCastException` is thrown at line 6.
(d) A `ClassCastException` is thrown at line 7.

6.14 Consider the following piece of code in Java:

```
public class Test {
  public static void aMethod() throws Exception {
   try {
     throw new Exception();
   }
   finally {
       System.out.print("finally ");
   }
}
public static void main(String args[]){
   try {
       aMethod();
   }
   catch (Exception e) {
       System.out.print("exception ");
   }
   System.out.print("finished ");
   }
}
```

What the result will be if this program is executed?

(a) finally.
(b) exception finished.
(c) finally exception finished.
(d) Program will not compile successfully.

6.15 Consider the following program:

```
public class Question4{
        public static void main(String args[]){
                int arr[]={0,1,2,3,4,5,6,7,8,9};
                int index=0;
                while(arr[index]==index){
                        System.out.print(arr[index]);
                        index++;
                }
        }
}
```

If the program is executed, then what will be the output from the execution?

(a) 0123456789
(b) 0123456789 with ArrayIndexOutOfBoundsException
(c) ArrayIndexOutOfBoundsException
(d) Compilation error

6.16 Consider the following program:

```
public class Question8{
        static public void method1(){
                System.out.println("This");
        }
        public static void method2(){
                System.out.println("is");
        }
        static public int method3(){
                System.out.println("Java");
                return 0;
        }
        public static void main(String args[]){
                try{
                        method1();
                }catch(Exception e){
                        System.out.println("1:"+e);
                }
                try{
                        method2();
                }catch(Exception e){
                        System.out.println("2:"+e);
                }
                try{
                        method3();
```

```
            }catch(Exception e){
                  System.out.println("3:"+e);
            }
      }
}
```

What will be the output of this program?

(a) This is Java
(b) Exception at method 1
(c) Exception at method 2
(d) Exception at method 3

6.17 Consider the following program structure:

```
statement 1
statement 2
try {
        statement 3
        try {
              statement 4
              statement 5
        }
        catch () {
              statement 6
              statement 7
        }
}
        catch () {
              statement 8
              statement 9
        try {
              statement 10
              statement 11
        }
        catch () {
              statement 12
              statement 13
        }
}
statement 14
statement 15
```

Which of the following statement(s) is(are) *not* true for this program?

(a) If there is no exception in the program, then statement 1, 2, 3, 4, 5, 14, 15 will be executed and lead to a normal termination.
(b) If the exception is raised only in statement 2, then the program execution will terminate normally.
(c) If the exception raised only in statement 14, then statement 1, 2, 3, 4, 5 will be executed and there will be an abnormal termination.
(d) If the exception is raised in statement 3, then statement 1, 2, 8, 9,10, 11, 14, 15 will be executed and lead to a normal termination.

6.18 Consider the following program fragment:

```
import java.util.*;

public class TestException {
   public static void main(String[] args) {
        Scanner s=new Scanner(System.in);
        System.out.println("Enter the value of n ");

        int n=s.nextInt();
        try {
              System.out.println(10/n);
              String str=null;

              System.out.println("Course  name is :"+str);
        }
        catch (Exception ae) {                  //block 1
              System.out.println("Exception"+ae);
        }
        catch (ArithmeticException ne) {        //block 2
              System.out.println("Exception"+ne);
        }
        System.out.println("Rest of the code");
  }
}
```

Which of the following statement(s) is (are) *not* true for this program fragment?

(a) Compilation error: exception `ArithmeticException` has already been caught.
(b) If block 1 and block 2 are swapped and `n` is non-zero value, then there exists `ArithmeticException`: /by zero in the program.
(c) If block 1 and block 2 are swapped and `n` is a non-zero value, then there is no exception in the program.
(d) If block 1 and block 2 are swapped and `n` is zero, then there exists `Arithmetic Exception` /by zero.

7

MULTITHREADING

Java is the most suitably programming language for developing application software for a distributed environment with concurrent execution. To enable this, Java has been designed as a multithreaded programming language. This means that a program can be executed with one or more threads to solve a problem while utilizing the computing resources in the most efficient manner. Since the inception of Java, an elegant feature called "multithreading" has been introduced. With this unique feature, a programmer can write a program with multiple flows of executions along with robust control in the executions. More significantly, Java is a lightweight programming language that is designed to have a very small memory footprint, it has minimalist syntax and features, and it is easy to port an implementation to different systems.

7.0 Introduction

Why multi-threading?

Multitasking is a very common features in today's computation environment. Java supports thread-based approach to multi-tasking, which is more precisely called *multithreading*. Multithreading means multiple flow of control. Multithreading programming is a conceptual paradigm for programming where one can divide a program into two or more processes which can be run in parallel. There are two main advantages of multithreading: First, a program with multiple threads will, in general, result in better utilization of system resources, including the CPU, because another line of execution can use the CPU when one line of execution is idle or blocked. Second, there are several problems which are solved better by multiple threads. For example, we can easily write a multithreaded program to show animation, play music, display documents, and download files from the network, etc., all of them at the same time.

Heavyweight versus lightweight programming

Multitasking involves complex processing that an execution environment has to perform while it executes the program. If processes are heavyweight tasks, they require their own separate address spaces. The inter-process communication becomes expensive and reduces the advantages of the concurrent execution. Context switching from one process to another is also costly. Java follows the concept of threads and thus the concept of thread-based multitasking. All the threads are lightweights, which share the same address space. Hence interthread communication remains inexpensive and context switching from one thread to the next is at a lower cost. This is called multithreaded multitasking.

How is multi-threading done?

To create and run threads in a program, Java provides an elegant solution in the API package `java.lang`. The `Runnable` interface and classes namely `Thread`, `ThreadGroup`, and `ThreadLocal`, are there with built-in implementation, which are simple in syntax and easy to use in programs. Many issues in multithreading such as controlling the execution of threads, interthread communication, and execution of threads in a safe condition can be addressed elegantly.

Your learning

This chapter offers basic concepts of multitasking and the essential features of multithread programming. The programming features and their syntaxes to be followed in these programs are discussed and illustrated. A thread can be in a number of states. How a thread can change its state is important to be learned. Threads can be maintained with their own priorities so that a better control in program execution can be achieved. Thread-safe execution is a concern to avoid erroneous results, which is also an important topic to be learned in this chapter.

7.1 Concept of Concurrent Programming

A complex task can be decomposed into a number of sub tasks, such a sub task again can be divided into a number of sub sub-tasks, and so on. Figure 7.1 shows a simple two-level task composition as an example. Note that a program is a set of instructions to solve each task and hence the complex tasks itself.

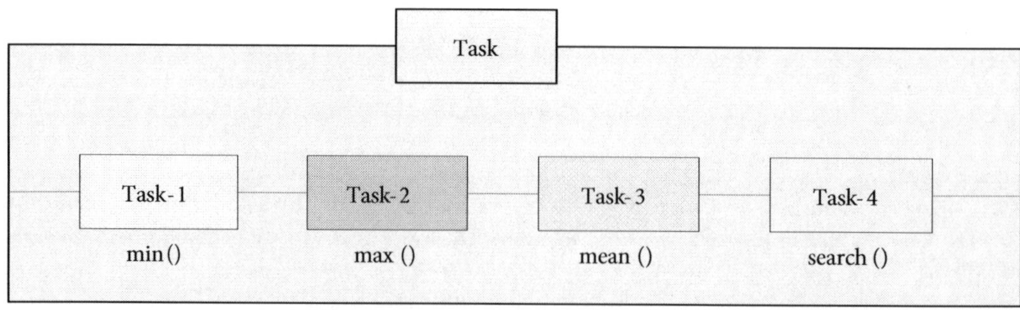

Figure 7.1 Composition of a task

Single-CPU execution

Case 1: *Single-CPU execution of the task*

Here, the batch of sub tasks are given to the CPU. A scheduler (e.g., operating system), assigns a sub task to the CPU, wait until the CPU finishes it and then assign the next sub task, and so on. Figure 7.2 shows how CPU executes sub tasks of a task.

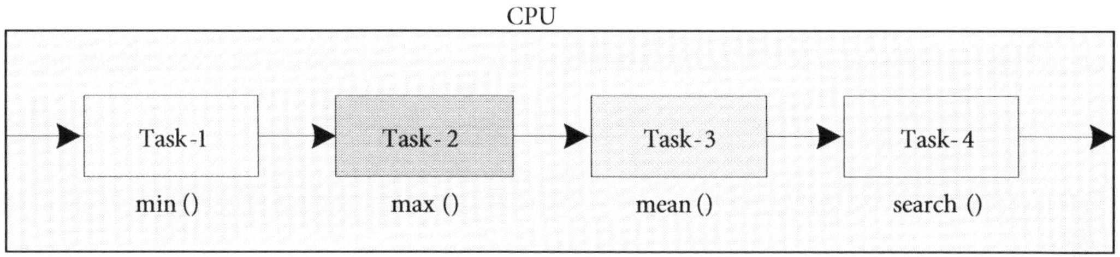

Figure 7.2 Single-CPU execution

Multi-processor processing

Case 2: *Multi-processor execution of the task*

Suppose, there are four processors which are available to execute a task. The scheduler assigns sub task to the four processors at the same time. Figure 7.3 shows how multiple processors execute sub tasks of a task.

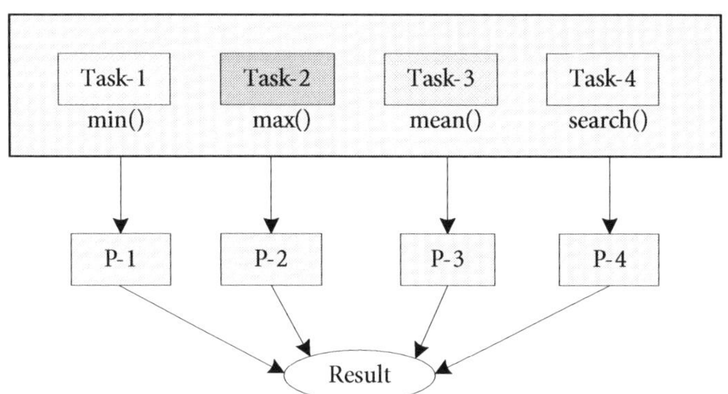

Figure 7.3 Concurrent execution with multiple processing

Multi-user programming

Case 3: *One server to serve multiple users concurrently*

Here, a server with a single processor serves requests from multiple users. The requests from multiple users can come to the server at any instant. The server should serve each client with a time slice, for example, in a round-robin manner so that each user feels that the server is serving him or her. Figure 7.4 depicts a multi-user programming environment. This is also called multi-tasking programming.

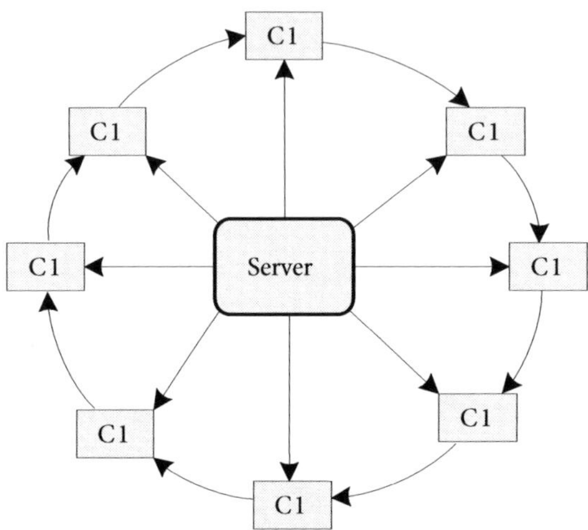

Figure 7.4 Multi-user programming

Case 4: *Multiple programs execution using a single CPU*

Multi-programming

This is the most common case we come across. With your operating system, say Windows, you can run more than one application concurrently. For example, as shown in Figure 7.5, you can run Word to edit a document, save a file or copy a file from the Internet to your machine, print a document on your printer connected to your machine, play your favorite songs, and so on. The operating system (it is a program) assigns the applications to the CPU, which in turn runs all the applications concurrently. We can say that there are threads corresponding to the main program as well as programs related to individual applications. This multi-programming concept is also known as multithreading.

Multi-threaded programming

Definition of a thread

We have learned three different ways of doing concurrent executions: multi-processing, multi-tasking, and multithreading. In each case, the CPU executes multiple programs in parallel. Each program execution is called a *thread*. In each case, the CPU controls one or more threads and runs them simultaneously. A thread can be defined as *a single independent sequential flow of control within a program.* A multithreaded program execution is a concurrent execution of multiple threads. Figure 7.6 shows single-threaded versus multithreaded program execution.

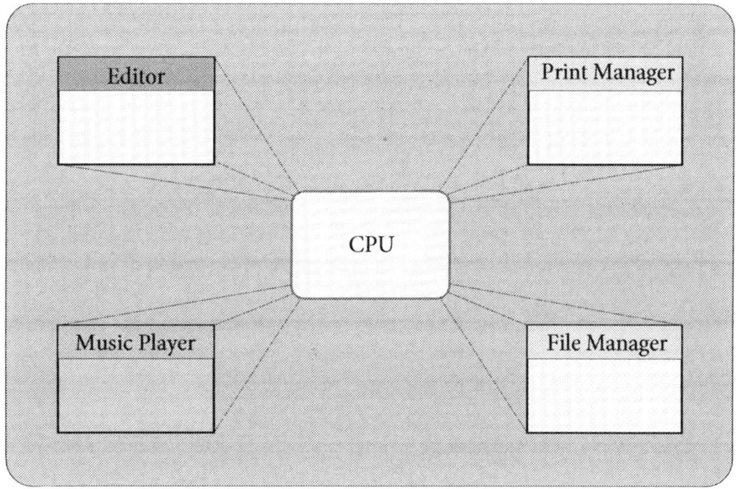

Figure 7.5 Multi-programming execution

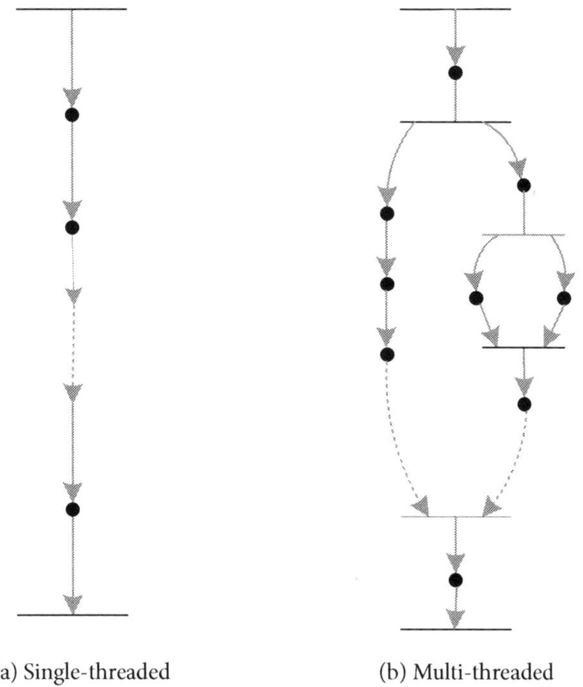

Figure 7.6 Single-threaded versus multithreaded executions

A brief comparison among multi-processing, multi-tasking, and multithreading is given in Table 7.1.

Comparison of different approaches to multi-threading

Table 7.1 Comparison among multiprocessing, multi-tasking, and multithreading executions

	Multi-processing	Multi-tasking	Multithreading
Concept	The availability of more than one processor per system, which can execute several sets of instructions in parallel is called multiprocessing.	The execution of more than one task simultaneously is called multitasking.	A process is divided into several different sub-processes called as threads, which have their own path of executions.
Number of CPU	More than one.	One.	One or more.
Processing time	Fast.	Slow.	Moderate.
Number of processes	More than one process can be executed at a time.	CPU time is shared among multiple processes during execution.	Various sub-processes of the same process are being executed at a time.
Number of users	One or more.	More than one.	Usually one.
Economical	Expensive.	Moderate.	Economic.

Java supports multithreaded programming. Program 7.1 is a simple Java program as an illustration.

Program 7.1 *(A simple Java program and its thread)*

```
1.    /* A simple program to print a message.*/

2.    class ProgramThreadDemo {
3.        public static void main(String args[]) {
4.                System.out.println("Message from
                        ProgramThreadDemo");
5.        }
6.    }
```

After successful compilation, this program can be executed with the command:

```
java ProgramThreadDemo
```

Java run-time manager creates a thread (in this case only one thread and is called as the "main thread") whose control starts at line number 3. The main thread in this case is the default thread of the execution of the program.

- Your program always has at least one thread: the one created when the program begins execution.
- In a normal Java application program, this thread starts at the beginning of `main()`.

7.2 Java API for Multithreaded Programming

Major facility in Java for multi-threading

Java allows you to write a program where more than one task can be executed concurrently within a single program. In this section, you will learn how to create multiple threads relevant to different tasks in a program.

In `java.lang` API package, three classes and one interface are defined, which you can use to create a thread and perform many other operations on the threads.

- `class Thread`
- `class ThreadGroup`
- `class ThreadLocal`
- `interface Runnable`

Let us first learn about these classes and interface.

7.2.1 Thread Class

The class `Thread` is defined in `java.lang` package. It has the class hierarchy depicted in Figure 7.7. In this figure, the class `Object` is the supper class of the class `Thread`. The class `Thread` implements the `Runnable` interface. Two more classes are also related to multithreading: `ThreadGroup` and `ThreadLocal`.

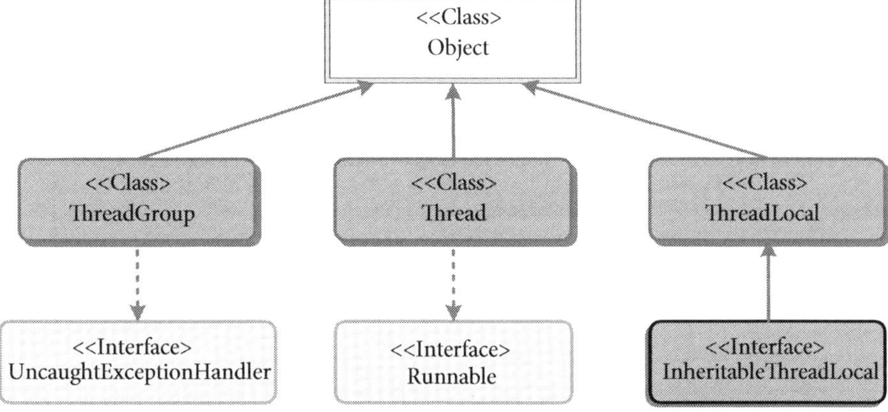

Figure 7.7 The declaration of java.lang.Thread class

Fields defined in the class Thread

Every thread runs with a priority. The priority of a thread is assigned with three constant field values which are shown in Table 7.2.

Table 7.2 Fields in the class Thread

Field	Description
`static int` MIN_PRIORITY	The minimum priority that a thread can have. The value of this constant is 1.
`static int` MAX_PRIORITY	The maximum priority that a thread can have. The value of this constant is 10.
`static int` NORM_PRIORITY	The default priority assigned to a thread. The value of this constant is 5.

Constructors defined in the class Thread

Several constructors are defined by `java.lang.Thread` class to create thread objects in different manner. The constructors in the class are listed in Table 7.3.

Table 7.3 Constructors in the class Thread

Constructor	Description
`Thread()`	Allocates a new thread object.
`Thread(Runnable target)`	Allocates a new thread object. Here, `target` is the object whose run method is invoked when this thread is started.
`Thread(String name)`	Allocates a new thread object with the given name `name`.
`Thread(Runnable target, String name)`	Allocates a new thread object with the name `name` when `target` is the object whose run method is invoked.
`Thread(ThreadGroup group, Runnable target)`	Allocates a new thread object under the thread group `group` to run the object `target`.
`Thread(ThreadGroup group, String name)`	Allocates a new thread object under the thread group `group` with a given name `name`.
`Thread(ThreadGroup group, Runnable target, String name)`	Allocates a new thread object under the thread group `group` with the given name `name` to run the object `target`.
`Thread(ThreadGroup group, Runnable target, String name, long stackSize)`	Allocates a new thread object so that it has `target` as its run object, has the specified `name` as its name, and belongs to the thread group referred to by `group`, and has the specified stack size.

Methods defined in the class Thread

The `java.lang.Thread` class defines several methods that help to manage threads. All the methods defined for this class are listed in Table 7.4.

Table 7.4 Methods defined for the class java.lang.Thread

Methods	Description
`static int activeCount()`	Returns the number of active threads in the current thread's thread group.
`void checkAccess()`	Determines if the currently running thread has permission to modify this thread.
`protected Object clone()`	Returns a clone if the class of this object is `Cloneable`.
`static Thread currentThread()`	Returns a reference to the currently executing thread object.
`static void dumpStack()`	Prints a stack trace of the current thread to the standard error stream.
`static int enumerate(Thread[] tarray)`	Copies into the specified array every active thread in the current thread's thread group and its sub groups.
`static Map<Thread. StackTraceElement[]> getAllStackTraces()`	Returns a map of stack traces for all live threads.
`ClassLoader getContextClassLoader()`	Returns the context `ClassLoader` for this thread.
`static Thread. UncaughtExceptionHandler getDefaultUncaughtException Handler()`	Returns the default handler invoked when a thread abruptly terminates due to an uncaught exception.
`long getId()`	Returns the identifier of this thread.
`String getName()`	Returns this thread's name.
`int getPriority()`	Returns this thread's priority.
`StackTraceElement[] getStackTrace()`	Returns an array of stack trace elements representing the stack dump of this thread.
`Thread.State getState()`	Returns the state of this thread.
`ThreadGroup getThreadGroup()`	Returns the thread group to which this thread belongs.
`Thread. UncaughtExceptionHandlerget UncaughtExceptionHandler()`	Returns the handler invoked when this thread abruptly terminates due to an uncaught exception.
`static boolean holdsLock(Object obj)`	Returns true if and only if the current thread holds the monitor lock on the specified object.

Methods	Description
`void interrupt()`	Interrupts this thread.
`static boolean interrupted()`	Tests whether the current thread has been interrupted.
`boolean isAlive()`	Tests if this thread is alive.
`boolean isDaemon()`	Tests if this thread is a daemon thread.
`boolean isInterrupted()`	Tests whether this thread has been interrupted.
`void join()`	Waits for this thread to terminate its execution.
`void join(long millis)`	Waits at most `millis` milliseconds for this thread to terminate.
`void join(long millis, int nanos)`	Waits at most `millis` milliseconds plus `nanos` nanoseconds for this thread to terminate.
`void run()`	If this thread was constructed using a separate `Runnable`'s run object, then that `Runnable` object's run method is called; otherwise, this method does nothing and returns.
`void setContextClassLoader(ClassLoader cl)`	Sets the context `ClassLoader` for this thread.
`void setDaemon(boolean on)`	Marks this thread as either a daemon thread or a user thread.
`static void setDefaultUncaughtException Handler (Thread. UncaughtExceptionHandler eh)`	Sets the default handler invoked when a thread abruptly terminates due to an uncaught exception, and no other handler has been defined for that thread.
`void setName(String name)`	Changes the name of this thread with the given name.
`void setPriority(int newPriority)`	Changes the priority of this thread.
`void setUncaughtExceptionHandler (Thread.Uncaught ExceptionHandler eh)`	Sets the handler invoked when this thread abruptly terminates due to an uncaught exception.
`static void sleep(long millis)`	Causes the currently executing thread to sleep (temporarily cease execution) for the specified `millis` number of milliseconds.
`static void sleep(long millis, int nanos)`	Causes the currently executing thread to sleep for the specified number of milliseconds plus the specified number of nanoseconds.
`void start()`	Causes this thread to begin execution; the Java Virtual Machine calls the `run()` method of this thread.

Methods	Description
`String toString()`	Returns a string representation of this thread, including the thread's name, priority, and thread group.
`static void yield()`	Causes the currently executing thread object to temporarily pause and allow other threads to execute.

- Some methods like `stop()`, `destroy`, `resume()`, `suspend()`, etc. have been deprecated since Java 1.4 version.
- Since `java.lang.Thread` class is the sub class of the super class `Object`, all the methods such as `equals`, `finalize`, `getClass`, `notify`, `notifyAll`, `wait`, etc. are inherited into this class.

7.2.2 Runnable Interface

This interface is designed to provide a common protocol for objects that wish to execute code while they are active. Being active simply means that a thread has been started and has not yet been stopped. In addition, `Runnable` provides the means for a class to be active while not sub classing `Thread`.

Only one method `public void run()` is declared in the `Runnable` interface.

- `Runnable` is implemented by class `Thread`.
- The `Runnable` interface should be implemented by any class whose instances are intended to be executed by a thread. The class must define a method of no arguments called `run()`.
- When an object implementing interface `Runnable` is used to create a thread, starting the thread causes the object's `run()` method to be called as a separately executing thread.
- A class that implements `Runnable` can run without sub classing `Thread` by instantiating a `Thread` instance and passing itself as the target.
- The `Runnable` interface should be used if you are only planning to override the `run()` method and no other Thread methods. This is important because classes should not be sub classed unless the programmer intends to modify or enhance the fundamental behavior of the class.

7.2.3 ThreadGroup Class

Sometime a group of threads are to be managed coherently. To create a group of threads, the class `java.lang.ThreadGroup` can be considered. Here, a `ThreadGroup` object represents a set of threads. The thread groups form a tree in which every thread group except the initial thread group has a parent.

Constructors defined in the class ThreadGroup

Two constructors are defined for `java.lang.ThreadGroup` which are mentioned in Table 7.5.

Table 7.5 Constructors defined for the class java.lang.ThreadGroup

Constructor	Description
`ThreadGroup(String name)`	Constructs a new thread group with a given name `name`. The parent of this new group is the thread group of the currently running thread.
`ThreadGroup(ThreadGroup group, String name)`	Creates a new thread group with the name `name`. The parent of this new group is the specified thread group.

Methods defined for the class ThreadGroup

A number of methods are defined for `java.lang.ThreadGroup` which are mentioned in Table 7.6.

Table 7.6 Methods defined for the class java.lang.ThreadGroup

Methods	Description
`int activeCount()`	Returns an estimate of the number of active threads in this thread group.
`int activeGroupCount()`	Returns an estimate of the number of active groups in this thread group.
`void checkAccess()`	Determines if the currently running thread has permission to modify this thread group.
`void destroy()`	Destroys this thread group and all of its sub groups.
`int enumerate(Thread[] list)`	Copies into the specified array every active thread in this thread group and its sub groups.
`int enumerate(Thread[] list, boolean recurse)`	Copies into the specified array every active thread in this thread group.
`int enumerate(ThreadGroup[] list)`	Copies into the specified array references to every active sub group in this thread group.
`int enumerate(ThreadGroup[] list, boolean recurse)`	Copies into the specified array references to every active sub group in this thread group.
`int getMaxPriority()`	Returns the maximum priority of this thread group.
`String getName()`	Returns the name of this thread group.
`ThreadGroup getParent()`	Returns the parent of this thread group.
`void interrupt()`	Interrupts all threads in this thread group.

`boolean isDaemon()`	Tests if this thread group is a daemon thread group.
`boolean isDestroyed()`	Tests if this thread group has been destroyed.
`void list()`	Prints information about this thread group to the standard output.
`boolean parentOf(ThreadGroup g)`	Tests if this thread group is either the thread group argument or one of its ancestor thread groups.
`void setDaemon(boolean daemon)`	Changes the daemon status of this thread group.
`void setMaxPriority(int pri)`	Sets the maximum priority of the group.
`String toString()`	Returns a string representation of this Thread group.
`void uncaughtException(Thread t, Throwable e)`	This method called by the Java Virtual Machine when a thread in this thread group stops because of an uncaught exception, and the thread does not have a specific `Thread.UncaughtExceptionHandler` installed.

- A thread group represents a set of threads. In addition, a thread group can also include other thread groups. A thread is allowed to access information about its own thread group, but not to access information about its thread group's parent thread group or any other thread groups.
- The `java.lang.ThreadGroup` class inherits the methods defined in its super class `Object` such as `equals`, `finalize`, `getClass`, `hashCode`, `notify`, `notifyAll`, `wait`, etc.

7.2.4 ThreadLocal Class

The `java.lang.ThreadLocal` class provides thread-local variables. These variables differ from their normal counterparts in that each thread that accesses one (via its `get` or `set` method) has its own, independently initialized copy of the variable. `ThreadLocal` instances are typically private static fields in classes that wish to associate state with a thread. It has the following constructor:

`ThreadLocal(): This creates an instance of a thread local.`

The methods defined for this class are summarized in Table 7.7.

Table 7.7 Methods defined for the class java.lang.ThreadLocal

Methods	Description
`T get()`	This method returns the value in the current thread's copy of this thread-local variable.
`protected T initialValue()`	This method returns the current thread's "initial value" for this thread-local variable.
`void remove()`	This method removes the current thread's value for this thread-local variable.
`void set(T value)`	This method sets the current thread's copy of this thread-local variable to the specified value.

- Each thread holds an implicit reference to its copy of a thread-local variable as long as the thread is alive and the `ThreadLocal` instance is accessible.
- After a thread goes away, all its copies of thread-local instances are subject to garbage collection (unless other references to these copies exist).

7.3 Creating Threads

Main thread in a program

All programs in this book so far are single-threaded programs. Such a thread begins its execution from `main()` method and is called main thread. The main thread has the following characteristics:

- This thread starts its execution automatically.
- From the program execution point of view, this is the starting thread as well as the ending thread (of course, if there is no abnormal termination in the program execution).
- Other threads, if any, start from this thread.
- The main thread remains active with default priority value as 5.
- If you do not set its name, then its default name is `main`.

Program 7.2 illustrates many insights about the main thread.

Program 7.2 *(Creating the main thread)*

```
/* This program illustrates about the main thread and
some operations in it. */

class MainThreadDemo {
  public static void main(String args[]) {
        // Let's know which is the current thread at
                                            // this point
        Thread t = Thread.currentThread();
```

```
        // Printing information about the current thread
        System.out.println("Current thread: " + t);

        // You can update the thread's name
        t.setName("My Thread");
        System.out.println("After update: " + t);
        // Do some tasks as the execution of this thread
        try {
             for(int x = 1; x < 5; x++) {
                  System.out.println("f(x) = " + 2*x*x
                       - 3*x - 5);
                  Thread.sleep(1000);
                       // Stay idle for 1000 milliseconds
             }
         }
         catch (InterruptedException e) {
              System.out.println("Main thread is
                interrupted");
         }
    }
}
```

- Any thread is characterized by three main information: Name, Priority, and Thread group.
- The `System.out.println()` statements with thread object `t` as an argument print such information about the thread `t`. In this case, only thread, namely main thread, is running and the default name of the thread is `main`. By default, its priority is 5, and the thread is under the group `main` thread itself. When a thread runs, it is called an active thread.
- A thread can be suspended for many reasons: interrupted by other thread, error occurs during the execution, etc.
- `java.lang.*` package includes all classes and `Runnable` interface, and is imported by default in all your programs. There is no need to explicitly import it.
- Starting with the main thread as the parent thread, any other thread(s) can be initiated as child thread(s), which can initiate other thread(s), and so on. Thus, a chain of threads can be executed concurrently.
- The main thread does not have any parent thread. A thread may not have any child thread.

- Execution of many thread methods usually throw exception object and to make the program robust, it is customary to include the code under `try-catch` block.
- This is why, in all subsequent programs in this chapter, all thread related codes are enclosed within `try-catch` block.

Procedure for creating threads

Multithread programming is all about running multiple threads and controlling the executions of threads. In the beginning, it is necessary to learn how a thread can be defined in a Java program and its execution can be initiated. There are two ways to define a thread:

1. Defining a sub class of the class `Thread`.
2. Defining a class which implements the `Runnable` interface.

The above two ways are discussed in the following sub sections.

7.3.1 Creating Thread with Sub Classing of the Class Thread

Composition of a thread class

With this method, you have to define a class as a sub class of the `Thread` class. This sub class should contain a body which will be defined by a method `run()`. This `run()` method contains the actual task that the thread should perform. An instance of this sub class is then to be created by a new statement, followed by a call to the thread's `start()` method to have the `run()` method executed.

Let us consider Program 7.3 which includes a program to create a thread to print the message "Hello World !".

***Program 7.3** (Creating a thread and its execution)*

```
/* This program demonstrates how a thread can be
defined and  the same can be executed. */

// Creating a thread with sub classing of the class
                                                //Thread
class MyThread extends Thread{
     public void run( ) {
          System.out.println("Hello World!");
     }
}

class ThreadRunDemo {
     public static void main(String args[]) {
          System.out.println("Main thread is
          started...");
          MyThread t = new MyThread();
                // Instantiate a thread object
```

```
            t.start();
                  // Start the execution of the thread
            System.out.println("End of the concurrent
                  execution.");
      }
}
```

- When you run the program `ThreadRunDemo`, two threads, main thread and `t`, run in parallel.
- You may get the output (the string messages) in different sequences if you run the same program in different sessions.
- The two threads are with the same default priority 5.

Same thread, multiple executions

You can run several instances of the same thread sub class. Program 7.4 illustrates the multiple execution of threads.

Program 7.4 *(Execution of multiple threads)*

```
/* This program demonstrates how multiple threads of a
given implementation can be executed. */

// Creating a thread with sub classing of the class
                                                //Thread
class MultiThread extends Thread{
      String name;
      long life;
      MultiThread(String name, long life) {
            // Constructor
            this.name = name;
            this.life = life;
      }

      public void run( ) {
            // The task and entry point of the thread
            try {
                 sleep(life);        // Let's live idle
                 System.out.println("I am " + name + "!");
            } catch (InterruptedException e) {
                 System.out.println("The thread execution
                   is interrupted");
            }
      }
}
```

```
class MultiThreadDemo {
     public static void main(String args[]) {
          System.out.println("Main thread is
                started...");

          // Creating three instances of threads
          MultiThread t1 = new MultiThread("Google",
                300L);
          MultiThread t2 = new MultiThread("Yahoo",
                500L);
          MultiThread t3 = new MultiThread("Bingo",
                100L);

          // Start the execution of the threads
          t2.start();  // Print and sleep for 500 ms
          t1.start();  // Print and sleep for 300 ms
          t3.start();  // Print and sleep for 100 ms

          try {
              Thread.sleep(1000);
                // Let's make wait main thread
          } catch (InterruptedException e) {
              System.out.println("Main thread is
                interrupted.");
          }
          System.out.println("End of the multi-thread
                execution.");
     }
}
```

Execution of multiple threads

You can define a number of threads (that is, different tasks) by sub classing the class `Thread` and then running them concurrently. Program 7.5 illustrates the parallel execution of three different tasks.

Program 7.5 *(Execution of multiple threads of different tasks)*

```
/* Creating three threads using the class Thread and
then running them concurrently. */

class ThreadA extends Thread{
     public void run( ) {
        for(int i = 1; i <= 5; i++) {
           System.out.println("From Thread A with
                i = "+ -1*i);
        }
```

```
        System.out.println("Exiting from Thread A
          ...");
     }
}
class ThreadB extends Thread {
    public void run( ) {
       for(int j = 1; j <= 5; j++) {
         System.out.println("From Thread B with j= "+2*
           j);
       }
       System.out.println("Exiting from Thread B ...");
     }
}

class ThreadC extends Thread{
     public void run( ) {
         for(int k = 1; k <= 5; k++) {
             System.out.println("From Thread C with
                k = "+ (2*k-1));
         }
         System.out.println("Exiting from Thread C ...");
     }
}
public class MultiThreadingDemo {
    public static void main(String args[]) {
         // Create the instances of three threads
         ThreadA a = new ThreadA();
         ThreadB b = new ThreadB();
         ThreadC c = new ThreadC();

         // Start execution of the threads
         a.start();
         b.start();
         c.start();

         /* Threads a, b, c and main are running
           concurrently... */

         System.out.println("... Multithreading is
           over! ");
    }
}
```

Run the program at least three times and check if you get the same or different output.

- In Program 7.5, the threads `a`, `b`, and `c` are the child threads and the main is their parent thread.
- Priority values of all the threads is the default value 5.
- You can print the threads' information using `System.out.println()` statement (as in Program 7.2).
- In Program 7.3, 7.4, and 7.5, you overrode the `run()` methods in each of the sub classes of the class `Thread`. When you start a thread, it runs the corresponding `run()`. If you do not write any code for the `run()`, and do not override the `run()` method, then the default `run()` method of the class `Thread` will be executed. In this case, it will do nothing and return.

7.3.2 Creating Thread with Implementation of the Runnable interface

The interface `Runnable` is defined in the system package `java.lang` with a single method `run()` as follows:

About the `Runnable` interface

```
public interface Runnable {
      public abstract void run( );
}
```

The second way to create a thread is to create a new class that implements `Runnable` interface. The implementing class must define the `run()` method. An instance of that class can then be created. Let this instance be `target`. A thread object can be created with any one of the following constructors defined in the class `Thread` (Table 7.2):

Running the run() of `Runnable` interface

```
Thread(Runnable target);
Thread(Runnable target, String name);
Thread(ThreadGroup group, Runnable target);
Thread(ThreadGroup group, Runnable target, String name);
Thread(ThreadGroup group, Runnable target, String name,
   long stackSize);
```

Program 7.6 illustrates how a thread class can be defined, created, and executed using the `Runnable` interface.

Program 7.6 (Creating a thread using Runnable interface)

```
/* This program demonstrates how a thread can be
defined and  the same can be executed using Runnable
interface. */

// Defining a class implementing the Runnable interface
class RunnableThread implements Runnable {
     public void run( ) {
          System.out.println("Hello World!");
     }
}

class ThreadRunnableDemo {
     public static void main(String args[]) {
          System.out.println("Main thread is
               started...");
          // Create an instance of the class MyThread
          RunableThread x = new RunnableThread();

          // Create a thread object to run the run()of x
          Thread t = new Thread(x);

          // Start the execution of the thread
          t.start();
          System.out.println("End of the concurrent
               execution.");
     }
}
```

- Program 7.6 is an alternate implementation of what you have done in Program 7.3.
- `Thread` class has many methods (as mentioned in Table 7.3) and also implements the `Runnable` interface. This implies that all methods in the class `Thread` can also be invoked for the object, for example, in this case, the object `x`.

Let us repeat the Program 7.5 using the implementation of `Runnable` interface as illustrated in Program 7.7.

Program 7.7 *(Execution of multiple threads using Runnable interface)*

```
/* Creating three threads using the Runnable interface
and then running them concurrently. */

class ThreadX implements Runnable {
     public void run( ) {
        for(int i = 1; i <= 5; i++) {
           System.out.println("From Thread A with
                i = "+ -1*i);
        }
        System.out.println("Exiting from Thread X ...");
     }
}

class ThreadY implements Runnable {
    public void run( ) {
       for(int j = 1; j <= 5; j++) {
         System.out.println("From Thread B with j= "+2*
j);
       }
       System.out.println("Exiting from Thread B ...");
     }
}

class ThreadZ implements Runnable {
     public void run( ) {
         for(int k = 1; k <= 5; k++) {
             System.out.println("From Thread C with
                k = "+ (2*k-1));
         }
         System.out.println("Exiting from Thread C
           ...");
     }
}

public class MultiThreadingRunnableDemo {
    public static void main(String args[]) {
         // Create the instances of three threads
         ThreadX x = new ThreadX();
         Thread t1 = new Thread(x);

         ThreadY y = new ThreadY();
         Thread t2 = new Thread(y,"Second child");

         Thread t3 = new Thread(new ThreadZ());
```

```
        // Start execution of the threads
        t1.start();
        t2.start();
        t3.start();

        /* Threads t1, t2, t3 and main are running
              concurrently... */

        System.out.println("... Multithreading is
              over! ");
    }
}
```

- In Program 7.7, after implementing objects, how their threads are created and then execution started is shown. For illustration, different constructors of the `Thread` class are considered.
- Also note that a class instance with the `run()` method defined within must be passed as an argument in creating the thread instance so that when the `start()` method of this `Thread` instance is called, Java run-time knows which `run()` method to execute.
- In the same program, thread objects of classes defined by both the sub class of `Thread` and implementation of `Runnable` interface can be used.

- If you do not extend the `Thread` class or define a class implementing the `Runnable` interface, your class object would not be treated as a thread object.
- In a multithreaded program, the main thread must be the last thread to finish running. If the main thread finishes before a child thread has completed, then the Java run-time system may "hang."
- For example, Program 7.8 may encounter this problem because the main thread is likely to finish its execution before the child thread finishes. To avoid this, you can make the main thread wait for sufficiently long time so that the child thread can finish its execution first.
- There is a better approach to control the thread operation, which is discussed in Section 7.4.2.

Program 7.8 (Anomaly in multithread programming)

```
/* This program illustrates an erroneous execution of a
multi-threaded program. */

class ThreadX implements Runnable {
    Thread t;
    ThreadX() {
     // Constructor which creates and run a thread
         t = new Thread(this, "Child thread");
         System.out.println("Child thread: " + t);
         t.start();
                // Start the thread with its run method
    }
    // Defining the method for the class TheadX
    public void run() {
         try {
             for(int i = 1; i < 5; i++) {
                 System.out.println(i + "-th run of the
                     child thread");
                 Thread.sleep(100);
                          // Sleep for 100 milliseconds
             }
         } catch (InterruptedException e) {
              System.out.println("Thread execution is
                interrupted");
         }
         System.out.println("Exiting child thread...");
    }
}
class ThreadAnomalyDemo {
     public static void main(String args[ ] ) {
          System.out.println("Main thread is running
               ... ");
          new ThreadX();
               // Create and run the child thread

          /* Add the following code to force waiting
             the main thread longer time than the
             execution time of the child thread. */
          /* try {          // If not uncommented ERROR!
                 Thread.sleep(1000);
             } catch (InterruptedException e) {
                   System.out.println("Main thread is
                     interrupted.");
             } */
```

```
            System.out.println("Main thread is
                exiting...");
        }
}
```

7.3.3 Thread versus Runnable Interface

`Thread` versus `Runnable` has always been a confusing decision for beginners. `Thread` in Java seems easy in comparison to `Runnable` because you just deal with one class `java.lang.Thread` while in case of using `Runnable` to implement `Thread` you need to deal with both `Thread` and `Runnable`. The decision of using `Runnable` or `Thread` should be taken considering differences between `Runnable` and `Thread` and the pros and cons of both approaches.

Differences between `Runnable` *and* `Thread`

1) Java doesn't support multiple inheritance, which means you can only extend one class in Java. So once you extended the `Thread` class you lose your chance and cannot extend or inherit another class in Java.
2) Inheriting all `Thread` methods are additional overhead just for representing a task which can be done easily with `Runnable`.
3) In object-oriented programming, extending a class generally means adding new functionality, modifying or improving behaviors. If we are not making any modification on `Thread` then use `Runnable` interface instead.
4) `Runnable` interface represents tasks which can be executed by either plain `Thread` or any other means. So logical separation of task as `Runnable` from `Thread` is good design decision.
5) Separating task as `Runnable` means we can reuse the task and also have liberty to execute it by different means. Comparing `Runnable` versus `Thread` for tasks, `Runnable` is the winner.

Throughout the rest of this chapter, in most of the programs we will create threads by sub classing the class `Thread`.

7.4 Managing Execution of Threads

In a single-thread execution, instructions (statements) to solve a problem are executed in a sequential manner. Here, control is implicit. With multithreaded execution, implicit control may not lead to a desirable execution. It is necessary to manage the executions of threads. Java provides many facilities to do this. The following topics are included in this section:

Different mechanisms to control multithreading

- Thread priority
- Ordering of threads
- Synchronization of threads

7.4.1 Thread Priority

We mentioned earlier that threads run concurrently. While conceptually this is true, in practice it is usually not so. Most computer configurations have a single CPU, so threads actually run one at a time in such a way as to provide an illusion of concurrency. Execution of multiple threads on a single CPU, in some order, is called *scheduling*. The Java run-time supports a very simple, deterministic scheduling policy known as *fixed priority scheduling*. This policy schedules threads based on their *priority* **relative to other runnable threads.**

When a Java thread is created, it is created with a default priority value NORM_PRIORITY or it inherits its priority from the thread that created it. The programmer can explicitly assign priority to a thread with integer values ranging between MIN_PRIORITY and MAX_PRIORITY. These constants are defined in the `Thread` class (Table 7.1). Two methods defined in class `Thread` (Table 7.3) can be used to get the priority and set the priority:

```
public final int getPriority();
public final void setPriority(int newPriority);
```

The `getPriority()` method returns the priority of a thread and `setPriority()` method changes the priority of thread to the value `newPriority`. The `setPriority()` method throws `IllegalArgument Exception` if the value of the parameter `newPriority` goes beyond minimum 1 and maximum 10. Program 7.9 illustrates how a programmer can assign priority to a thread.

Program 7.9 *(Setting priority to threads)*

```
/* This program demonstrates how the priority
information of threads can be accessed and modified. */

public class ThreadPriorityDemo extends Thread {
     public void run() {
          System.out.println("Running...");
     }

     public static void main(String[] args) {
          Thread t = Thread.currentThread();
            // Get the current thread
```

```
        // Creating two threads
        ThreadPriorityDemo t1 = new ThreadPriorityDemo();
        ThreadPriorityDemo t2 = new ThreadPriorityDemo();

        // Getting the default priority values of all
              the threads
        System.out.println("Priority of t1: " +
              t1.getPriority());
        System.out.println("Priority of t1: " +
              t1.getPriority());
        System.out.println("Priority of t2: " +
              t2.getPriority());

        // Modifying the priority values
        t1.setPriority(MAX_PRIORITY);
        t2.setPriority(MIN_PRIORITY);

        // Modifying the priority values
        t1.setPriority(MAX_PRIORITY);
        t2.setPriority(MIN_PRIORITY);

        // Printing the updated information
        System.out.println("Thread t is: " +
              t.getName());
        System.out.println("Thread t1 is: " + t1);
        System.out.println("Thread t2 is: " +
              t2.getPriority());

        // Running the threads
        t1.start();
        t2.start();
        t2.setPriority(6);
          // Priority can be changed during execution

        // Printing the current priority values
        System.out.println("Thread t is: " +
              t.getPriority());
        System.out.println("Thread t1 is: " +
              t1.getPriority());
        System.out.println("Thread t2 is: " +
              t2.getPriority());
    }
}
```

- A thread can run with any priority value in the range 1 to 10, both inclusive.
- The priority of a thread can be reassigned once a thread is created and at any time during its execution.
- Thread priorities are integers that specify the relative priority of one thread over another.
- A higher-priority thread doesn't imply that it runs faster than a lower-priority thread.

Execution of threads with different priorities

At any given time, when multiple threads are ready to be executed, the run-time system chooses the thread with the highest priority for execution. Only when that thread stops, yields, or becomes not runnable for some reason, will a lower priority thread start executing. If two threads of the same priority are waiting for the CPU, the scheduler chooses one of them to run on a round-robin basis.

The Java run-time system's thread scheduling algorithm is also *preemptive*. If at any time a thread with a higher priority compared to all other runnable threads becomes runnable, the run-time system chooses the new higher priority thread for execution. The new higher priority thread is said to *preempt* the other threads.

You should assign specific priority to a thread depending primarily upon the nature of the function performed by the thread. For example, a thread should be assigned low priority if it performs some kind of non-critical background task, particularly one that takes a long time to complete. If a thread spends most of its time working for input and performs a task that must complete quickly, then it should usually be assigned a high priority.

Now let us consider Program 7.10. Three threads are defined and allowed to run with different priorities.

Program 7.10 *(Execution of threads with different priorities)*

```
/* This program demonstrates the execution of different
threads with different priorities. */

class Man extends Thread {
     public void run() {
          System.out.println("Hi...! I am super
               man!!");
          for(int i=0; i<5; i++) {
             System.out.println("\t Printing natural
                number: " + i);
          }
          System.out.println("\t \t Bye super man! ");
     }
}
```

```
class Pet extends Thread {
      public void run() {
           System.out.println("Miaoo...! I am your
                pussy!!");
           for(int i=0; i<5; i++) {
                System.out.println("\t Printing odd
                     number:: " + 2*i+1);
            }
            System.out.println("\t \t Let's take a nap
                now!");
      }
}

class Wild implements Runnable {
      public void run() {
           System.out.println("Thread Z started");
           for(int i=0; i<5; i++) {
               System.out.println("\t Garrrrer! I am
                hungry tiger!!");
           }
           System.out.println("\t \t See you in the
                zoo!");
      }
}

class ThreadPriorityDemo {
      public static void main(String[] args) {
           System.out.println("Main thread started
                ...");

           // Creating threads
           Man joy = new Man();
           Pet jim = new Pet ();
           Thread tom = new Thread (new Wild());
           // Setting priorities
           joy.setPriority(Thread.MAX_PRIORITY);
                // Priority = 10
           jim.setPriority(jim.getPriority()+1);
                // Priority = 6
           tom.setPriority(Thread.MIN_PRIORITY);
                // priority = 1

           // Run the threads
           tom.start(); jim.start(); joy.start();
```

```
            // Wait for all threads to finish
             try {
                tom.join(); jim.join(); joy.join();
             } catch (InterruptedException e) {
                     System.out.println("Main thread is
                       interrupted.");
             }
             System.out.println("...Main thread is
                       finished.");
       }
}
```

Run Program 7.10 assigning different priority values and note the output. You may try the following:

Case 1: All threads are of different priorities

```
joy.setPriority(Thread.MIN_PRIORITY);
jim.setPriority(Thread.NORM_PRIORITY);
om.setPriority(Thread.MAX_PRIORITY);
```

Case 2: All threads are with equal priority

```
joy.setPriority(6);
jim.setPriority(6);
tom.setPriority(6);
```

Preemptive and time-slicing in thread execution

The following points are pertinent when you run two or more threads with different priority values:

- Threads with higher priority are executed in preference to threads with lower priority.
- A thread's priority is used to decide when to switch from one running thread to another.
- When two threads with the same priority compete for the CPU, it is the operating system which decides whom to allow first. You will get different results in different run of the same program.

Program 7.11 will illustrate these points better.

Program 7.11 *(Pre-empting and time-slicing in thread executions)*

```
/* This program demonstrates how a high priority thread
preempts  a lower priority thread and execution of two
equal priority threads in the time-slice manner. */

class Runner1 extends Thread {
     public int tick = 0;
     public void run() {
        while (tick < 400000) {
            tick++;
            if ((tick % 50000) == 0) {
                System.out.println
                     ("Runner 1: " + " tick = " + tick);
        }
    }
}

class Runner2 extends Thread {
     public int tick = 0;
     public void run() {
        while (tick < 400000) {
            tick++;
            if ((tick % 50000) == 0) {
                System.out.println
                     ("Runner 2: " + " tick = " + tick);
        }
    }
}

class ThreadSchedulingDemo {
      public static void main(String[] args) {
           Thread t;
           t = Thread.currenhtTread();
                // t is the main thread
           Runner1 t11 = new Runner1();
           Runner2 t12 = new Runner2();

/*****************************************************/
           /* Preemptive thread execution: Run Runner 1
                with higher priority than Runner 2. */

           System.out.println("Preemptive thread
                execution...");
           t.setPriority(Thread.MIN_PRIORITY);
           t11.setPriority(Thread.MAX_PRIORITY);
           t12.setPriority(Thread.NORM_PRIORITY);
```

```
            t11.start();
            t12.start();
             // t, t11, and t12  are running concurrently

/************************************************/
            /* Thread execution with time-slicing:
                 Run both Runner 1 and
            Runner 2 with same priority. */

            System.out.println("Time-sliced thread
                 execution...");
            Runner1 t21 = new Runner1();
            Runner2 t22 = new Runner2();

            t21.setPriority(Thread.NORM_PRIORITY);
            t22.setPriority(Thread.NORM_PRIORITY);

            t21.start();
            t22.start();
             // t, t21, and t22  are running concurrently
      }
}
```

- In each thread class `Runner1` and `Runner2`, the `while` *loop in the run methods is in a tight loop. Each* `run()` *contains a* `while` loop that increments the integer tick and every 50,000 ticks prints out the thread's identifier and its tick count.
- Once the scheduler chooses the `run()` method for execution as a single-threaded execution, the thread continues to run until the while loop terminates naturally or until the thread is interrupted.
- In case of preemptive scheduling, when threads compete for the CPU, JVM schedules the thread with higher priority to run first and then the next lower priority and so on. In this case, three threads `t`, `t11`, and `t12` with their priorities 1, 10, and 5, respectively started executions in parallel. Since `t11` has higher priority than `t` and `t12`, it will preempt the execution of others and get the full control of the CPU until it finishes its execution; next `t12` will get control. This is why you will see that the program prints the count of ticks from `Runner 1` first and then from `Runner 2`. After that the control goes to `t` and `t` starts the next part of the execution (time-slice scheduling).

- When running the second part of the program, three threads are in the running list: `t`, `t21`, and `t22` with their thread priorities 1, 5, and 5, respectively. Threads `t21` and `t22` will run on a time-sliced based; you will see messages from both threads intermingled with one another. Such output is produced because a time-sliced system divides the CPU into time slots and alternatively gives each of the equal-and-highest priority threads a time slot in which to run.
- Finally, in this program, after the termination of the executions of `t21` and `t22`, the main thread `t` will be executed and the program will finish its execution.

7.4.2 Ordering of Threads

Concurrent precedence graph (CPG) is a concept common in operating system design. A CPG gives fork–join construct in parallel computation. For example, Figure 7.8 shows a CPG of a hypothetical program where double horizontal lines are the fork (i.e., splitting of threads) nodes and thick horizontal lines join (i.e., merging of threads after completion of tasks) nodes. In this example, the main thread (`t0`) begins its execution and calls two threads `t1` and `t2` (at Fork 1). The thread `t2` calls three threads `t21`, `t22`, and `t23` (Fork 2). The controls of the executions `t21`, `t22`, and `t23` merge on their completions (Join 2). Next, `t1` and `t2` merge (Join 1) on their terminations, and finally `t0` ends its execution.

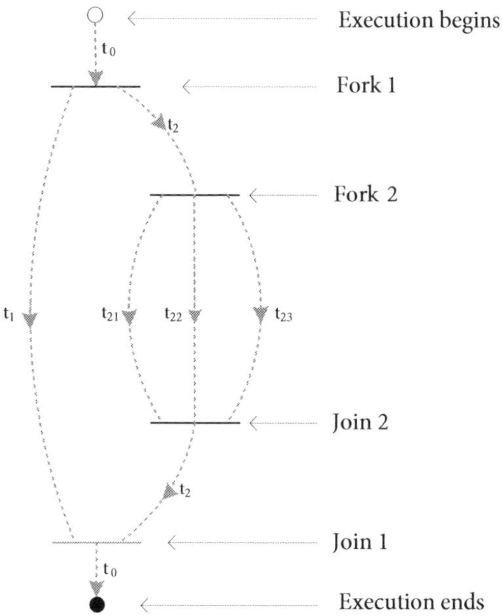

Figure 7.8 A sample CPG

As shown in the CPG, multithreaded programming in Java also supports nested concurrent execution, that is, multithreading inside a multithreading and it can go up to any depth.

It is obvious that in an actual multithreading application, there is a need to make a sequence in the execution of threads in addition to the (nested) concurrent execution. Let's discuss how the CPG of a program can be implemented in Java. Figure 7.9 gives an example of a simple CPG for a concurrent program.

The fork in the CPG can be implemented explicitly by calling the `start()` methods of the threads to begin their executions. The join in CPG can be accomplished by `join()` method defined in the class `Thread` (Table 7.4).

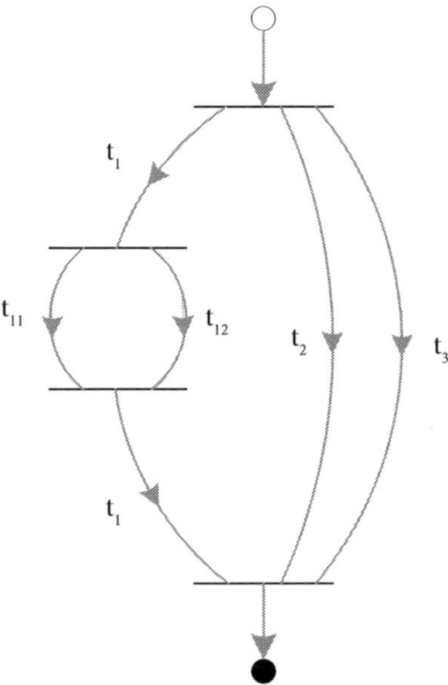

Figure 7.9 A simple CPG of an application program

Program 7.12 (in its two-part representation as Program 7.12a and 7.12b) illustrates the implementation of the simple CPG shown in Figure 7.8. Given an array of integers, the program calculates the normalized values of the numbers, variance of the input numbers, and sorts the input numbers in ascending order. In this program, `main()` has to run three tasks: `normalization()`, `variance()`, and `sort()`, in parallel. Normalization task calculates `min()` and `max()` concurrently. The calculation of normalized value $\left(a\left[\hat{\imath}\right]\right)$ of a number, say `a[i]`, in the input array `a` and variance (σ) of an array of `n` numbers with their mean $\bar{a}$ are shown as follows:

$$a\left[\hat{\imath}\right] = \frac{a[i]}{\max(a) - \min(a)}$$

$$\sigma = \frac{1}{n-1}\sum_{i=0}^{n}\left(a[i] - \bar{a}\right)^2$$

Program 7.12a includes all the unit tasks: `min()`, `max()`, `normalization()`, `mean()`, `variance()`, and `sort()` operations as sub classes of the class `Thread`. Program 7.12b is the main class which utilizes all the threads solving the problems.

Program 7.12a *(Definitions of threads for the CPG)*

```
/* This part of the program includes all the necessary
threads to implement the simple CPG shown in Fig. 7.8.
*/

// This thread is to find the minimum value in an array.

class Min extends Thread {
     public int a[];    // To store the array
     int x;             // To store the result
     Min(int a[]) {     // Constructor to copy the array
         this.a = a;
     }

     public void run() {
        x = a[0];
        for (int i = 1; i < a.length; i++) {
            if ((a[i] < x)
                x = a[i];
        }
    }
}

// This thread is to find the maximum value in an array.

class Max extends Thread {
     public int a[];    // To store the array
     int x;             // To store the result
     Max(int a[]) {     // Constructor to copy the array
         this.a = a;
     }
```

```
    public void run() {
       x = a[0];
       for (int i = 1; i < a.length; i++) {
           if ((a[i] > x)
               x = a[i];
       }
    }
}

// This thread calculates the normalized values for an
                                        // array of numbers

class Normalize extends Thread {
     public int a[];    // The array as input
     double b[];        // The array as output
     Normalize(int a[]) {
          // Constructor to copy the input array
        this.a = a;
     }

     public void run() {
          // The entry into the task of normalization
          // Fork 2 : Start the tasks for min() and
               max() calculations
        Min t11 = new Min(a);
          // Create the thread for min calculation
        Max t12 = new Max(a);
          // Create the thread for max calculation
        t21.start();
        t22.start();


          // Join 2: Wait till min() and max()finish
                                          // their jobs
          try {
              t11.join();
              t12.join();
          } catch (InterruptedException e) {
              System.out.println("Thread execution is
                    interrupted.");
          }

          // Consolidation of result
          double b[] new double[a.length];
              //Allocate memory for output
```

```
            for(int i = 0; i < a.length; i ++) {
                b[i] = a[i]/(t12.x - t11.x);
            }
        }
}

// This thread is to find the arithmetic mean of an
                                                    // array.

class Mean extends Thread {
     public int a[];      // To store the array
     double x;            // To store the result
     Mean(int a[]) {      // Constructor to copy the array
         this.a = a;
     }
     public void run() {
        int sum = a[0];
        for (int i = 1; i < a.length; i++) {
            sum += a[i];
        }
        x = sum/a.length;
    }
}

// This thread calculates the variance  of an array of
                                                   // numbers

class Variance extends Thread {
     public int a[];          // To store the array
     double x;                // To store the result
     Variance(int a[]) {
                          // Constructor to copy the array
         this.a = a;
     }

     public void run() {
        // Calculate the mean
        Mean  t21 = new Mean(a);
        t21.start();
            // Start the thread to calculate mean of a[]

        try {
            t21.join();
                //Wait till the thread finishes its task
```

```
        } catch (InterruptedException e) {
            System.out.println("Thread execution error
                occurs.");
        }

        double sum = 0;
        for (int i = 0; i < a.length; i++) {
            sum += (a[i]-mean.x)* (a[i]-mean.x);
                // Sum of the squares
        }
        x = sum/(a.length-1);
    }
}

// This thread sorts an array of numbers in ascending
                                                // order
class Sort extends Thread {
    int a[]:           // To store the array of numbers
    Sort( int a[]) {
        this.a = a;    // Copy the input
    }

    public void run() {     // Bubble sort technique
        for(int i = 0; i < a.length-1; i++)
            for(int j = 0; a.length-i-1, j++)
                if(a[j] > a[j+1]) {    // Swap
                    int temp = a[j];
                    a[j] = a[j+1];
                    a[j+1] = temp;
                }
        }
    }
}
```

Program 7.12b
(Main program for the CPG)

```
/* This part of the program is the main program for the
CPG shown in Fig. 7.9 */

class CPGDemo {
    public static void main(String args[]) {

        // Create an input array reading data from
                                        // command line
        try {
```

```
            int a[args.length];
            for(int i = 0; i < args.length; i++)
                a[i] = Integer.parseInt(args[i]);
        } catch{Exception e) {
             System.out.println(e);
        }

       // Create three thread instances for the
             // tasks to be executed in parallel
        Normalize t1 = new Normalize(a);
             // For normalization of a[]
        Variance t2 = new Variance(a);
             // For variance calculation
        Sort t3 = new Sort(a);
             // Sorting the array a[]

        // Fork 1: Start executions of the three
                                        // threads
        t1.start();  t2.start();   t3.start();

        // Join 1: Wait till all threads finish
                                    // their tasks
        try {
            t1.join(); t2.join(); t3.join();
        } catch(InterruptedException) {
             System.out.println("Thread exception
                  error occurs.");
        }
        System.out.println("CPG program is
             terminated...");
    }
}
```

- You should note how a thread can store the result(s) of computation so that the caller thread can utilize the results. A simple idea is to store the result(s) as field value(s) of the thread class.
- The result of a thread object remains available to the caller thread until the callee thread is active; and a callee thread remains active until it is not stopped, destroyed, or caller is dead. The `isAlive()` methods defined in the class `Thread` (Table 7.4) can be called to check whether a thread is active or not.

7.4.3 Synchronization of Threads

An issue with multithreading

Multithreading is an elegant feature in Java to write programs for distributed systems, client–server applications, etc. Thus far you have learnt about the basic approaches to write programs using multithreading features in Java. There is an issue which every programmer should be aware about and accordingly write reliable code.

We mentioned earlier that threads in Java are running in the same memory space. Because all the threads of a program share the same memory space, it is possible for two threads to access the same variables and methods in object. Problems may occur when two or more threads are accessing the same data concurrently, for example, one thread stores data into the shared object and the other thread reads data. There can be synchronization problem if the first thread has not finished storing the data before the second one goes to read it. So we need to take care that only one thread process accesses the data at a time.

Let's elaborate the problem with an example. In Figure 7.10, `x` is the data and two methods `add(...)` and `sub(...)` work on the data. That is, `x` is the shared data for the operations `add(...)` and `sub(...)`. If the two operations occur one after another as shown in Figure 7.10 (Scenario 1) and (Scenario 2), then there is no issue. However, there is a chance that the two operations read the data simultaneously, perform the operations, and produce the result, but the final result may be incorrect. The problem occurs here because the two threads `add(...)` and `sub(...)` run on common data at the same time instead of one at a time.

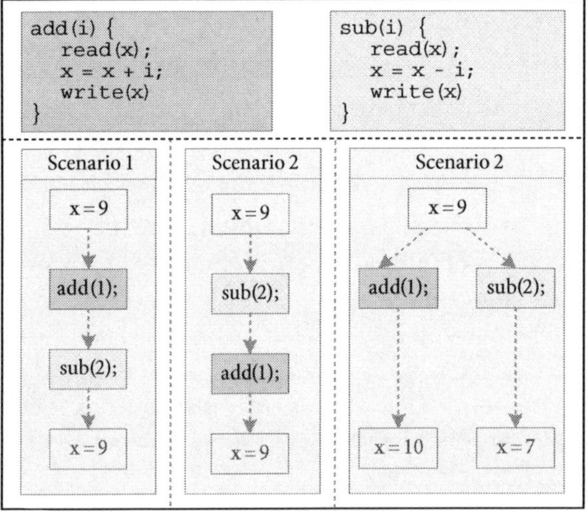

Figure 7.10 Issue in a multithreading program with shared data

Program 7.13 demonstrates how a concurrent program suffers from non-serialization (non-synchronization) problem.

Program 7.13 *(Execution of program with non-serialization issue)*

```
/* This program demonstrates concurrent execution
of threads with shared data and erroneous behaviour
thereafter. */
// This class defines a critical storage
class CriticalResource {
     int x;         // This is a shared data

     CriticalResource(int a) {
          // Constructor to initialize the data
         x = a;
     }
     void print( ) {
          System.out.print(" x = " + x);
     }
     void add(int z) {
          x += z;      // x = x + z;
     }
     void sub(int z) {
          x -= z;      // x = x-z;
     }
}

// This class defines a thread to perform addition to
                                            // the shared data
class Add implements Runnable {
     CriticalResource r;
     int z;    // This value is to be added to r's data
     Thread t;
     Add (CriticalResource a, int z) {
          // Constructor for initialization
         r = a;
         this.z = z;
         t = new Thread(this, "Adder");
          // Create a thread to add z to r
         t.start();
          // Start the thread to run the body
     }
     public void run() {
          // Define the body of the thread
         r.add(z);          // Add z to r's x
         System.out.println("Adder : ");
```

```
            r.print();
        }
}

// The main program for concurrent execution of add()
                                                // and sub()
class NonSynchronizationDemo {
      public static void main(String args[]) {
            CriticalResource r = new CriticalResource(9);
                  // r.x = 9

            // Start running the threads for concurrent
                                                // operations
            Add t1 = new Add(r, 1);
                  // add(1): r.x = r.x + 1
            Sub t2 = new Sub(r, 2);
                  // sub(2): r.x = r.x - 2

            try {
                  t1.t.join(); t2.t.join();
                  // Wait threads to finish
             } catch(InterruptedException e) {
                  System.out.println("Thread exception
                        error occurs.");
             }
             System.out.println("Program execution is
                  over...");
      }
}
```

The execution of Program 7.13 involves a situation when the two methods access the data at the same time, but this situation is infrequent. This is why you may not see the erroneous output unless you run the program several times.

Critical section problem

This problem is known as the *critical section problem*. To solve the critical section problem, one often used concept is called *monitor.* A monitor is an object which is used as a mutually exclusive lock (called *mutex*). Only one thread may own a monitor at a given time. When a thread acquires a lock, it is said to have entered the monitor. All other threads attempting to enter the locked monitor will be suspended until the owner-thread exits the monitor. So, to address the critical section problem, when multiple threads are accessing a shared resource, we need a monitor. In Java, each object has its own implicit monitor associated with it.

Concept of synchronization

The process by which the concept of monitor is implemented is called *synchronization*. Multithreading and synchronization are two very important subjects for any Java programmer. Good knowledge of multithreading, synchronization, and thread-safety can put you ahead of other programmers. Let us learn how synchronization in multithreading program can be accomplished.

How synchronization is done

Java language supports a keyword called `synchronize` for the purpose. There are two approaches to ensure synchronization in the execution of threads:

- Using synchronized methods
- Using synchronized blocks

Using synchronized method

This approach allows you to synchronize the methods and execute methods of threads in synchronized manner.

The following is the syntax to declare a method synchronized:

```
synchronize method(…) {
    // Body of the method
}
```

Let us illustrate the mechanism with an example. Consider the case of an online transaction in a banking system. The system maintains a database of all the customers of the bank. The system can be subjected into many transactions, such as balance enquiry, deposit, withdraw from a given account, and so on, concurrently. This may suffer from the synchronization problem when two or more transactions are executed in a customer's account.

Program 7.14 gives a simple implementation of a basic version of such a system.

Program 7.14 *(Synchronization of methods)*

```
/* The following class defines a class for an account
of a bank's customer. */

class Account {
     int balance;
     int accountNo;

     Account(int a, int b) {
          accontNo = a;
          balance = b;
     }
```

```
    void displayBalance() {
        System.out.println("Account#:" +accountNo
          +"Balance:"+balance);
    }

    synchronized void deposit(int amount){
      balance = balance + amount;
      System.out.println( amount + " is deposited");
      displayBalance();
    }

    synchronized void withdraw(int amount){
      balance = balance - amount;
      System.out.println( amount + " is withdrawn");
      displayBalance();
    }
}

// The following class defines a thread class for
                                    // deposit operation

class TransactionDeposit implements Runnable{
    int amount;
    Account accountX;
         // Transaction to the target account
    TransactionDeposit(Account x, int amount){
      accountX = x;
      this.amount = amount;
      Thread t = new Thread(this);
      t.start();   // Start run()
    }
public void run(){
      accountX.deposit(amount);
         // Perform deposit to the account
    }
}

// The following class defines a thread class for
                                   // withdraw operation

class TransactionWithdraw implements Runnable{
    int amount;
    Account accountY;
         // Transaction to the target account
```

```
    TransactionWithdraw(Account y, int amount) {
      accountY = y;
      this.amount = amount;
      Thread t = new Thread(this);
      t.start();       // Start run()
    }

    public void run(){
        if (accountY.balance < amount)
            System.out.println("Fund is
               insufficient...withdraw failed!");
        else
         accountY.withdraw(amount);
               // Perform withdraw from account
    }
}

/* The main class to perform two transactions in
parallel. */

class BankTransactionsDemo{
    public static void main(String args[]) {
        // A customer of the system
      Account aCustomer = new Account(123, 10000);

        // Perform two transactions to be executed in
                                            // parallel
      TransactionDeposit t1= new TransactionDeposit
          (aCustomer, 500);
      TransactionWithdraw t2 = new TransactionWithdraw
          (aCustomer,1000);
        // One more concurrent withdraw request
      TransactionWithdraw t3 = new TransactionWithdraw
          (aCustomer,10000);
    }
}
```

The working of Program 7.14 can be explained as follows.

- In the class definition of `Account`, two methods, `withdraw()` and `deposit()`, are declared with `synchronize` modifier. This ensures that the method for an object will be executed one at a time, if called in parallel.

- In Java, all objects have their own implicit monitor associated with them. In this case, the object is of class `Account`.
- While a thread executes a synchronized method, it enters the monitor, and all other threads that try to call it (or any other synchronized method) on the same instance have to wait.
- When a `synchronize` method finishes its execution, it exits the monitor and relinquishes control of the object to the next waiting thread.

- In the main class, you can practice adding some more customers, and for a particular customer, calling any transaction any number of times. For example, two or more deposits on the same account, etc.
- You can run Program 7.14, without `synchronize` modifier of the methods in the class `Account` and see the differences in results. Of course, in both experiments, you have to run the programs several times.
- Refer to Program 7.13, which suffers from the synchronization problem. Modify the program using the concept of synchronized methods to make the program serializable.

- Constructors cannot be synchronized in Java. Using the keyword `synchronize` with a constructor is a syntax error. The JVM by default ensures that only one thread can invoke a constructor call at a particular time. This is why there is no need to declare a constructor as synchronized.
- Like instance methods, static methods also can be declared with `synchronize` modifier. If the static synchronized methods are located in different classes (i.e., multiple definitions), then for a call of a static method, codes of all static methods will be executed as one thread at a time for all the classes regardless of which static synchronized method it calls.

Using synchronized block

You have learnt how a method can be declared with synchronize modifier so that such a method defined in an object can be executed in a non-overlapping manner when two or more threads run in parallel and access the data of the same object.

There is another approach to run two or more threads with a more powerful control of synchronization in their execution. This alternate approach is to use the synchronize keyword for a block of code. This approach takes the following syntax in Java:

Syntax

```
// Non-synchronized part of the code
synchronize(objRef) {
    // Block of code
}
// Non-synchronized part of the code
```

Applications

Use of synchronize keyword for a block of code can be done to achieve two objectives:

- Partial synchronization
- Synchronization of third party code

Partial synchronization

If you need to execute only a part of the code in a non-overlapping manner instead of all lines (instructions) of code within a method, then you should synchronize only that block of the code instead of the entire method. For example, suppose, there is a method that contains 100 lines of code, but there is a block containing only 10 lines of code which is the critical section (that is, needing synchronization). In that case, you should synchronize only the critical section of the code to be executed in a strict serialization allowing the rest of the code in parallel execution.

Let's illustrate the approach with an example. Program 7.15 includes three parts:

(a) Definition of a class `DataHouse` with data `city[]` and `code[]` and two methods `printCity()` and `printCode()`,

(b) Definition of two classes for threads `ThreadCity` and `ThreadCode`, and

(c) A driver class running threads in parallel.

Program 7.15 *(Partial synchronization)*

```
/* This program defines a class to be used in
multithreaded programming. */
class DataHouse {
   String city[] = {"London", "Montreal", "New Delhi",
     "New York", "Oslo", "Perth"};
   int code[] = {11, 22, 33, 44, 55, 66, 77, 88, 99};

   static void printCity() {
       // Printing odd numbers...
       for(int i = 0; i < 5; i++)
           System.out.println("Odd: " + 2*i+1);
```

```
        // Printing cities ...
        synchronize(this){
            // Synchronizing a block of code
            int j = 0;
            for(String x: city)     // For each x in city
                System.out.println("City " + ++j +
                 " : " + x);
        }

        // Printing even numbers...
        int k = 0;
        while(k < 5) {
            System.out.println("Odd: " + 2*k);
            k++;
        }
    }
    static void printCode() {
        // Printing small numbers...
        for(int i = 1; i < 6; i++)
            System.out.println("Small : " + i);

        // Printing codes ...
        synchronize(this){
            // Synchronizing a block of code
            int j = 0;
            for(int x: code)     // For each x in city
                System.out.println("Code " + ++j +
                 " : " + x);
        }
        // Printing large numbers...
        int k = 999;
        while(k > 994) {
            System.out.println("Large: " + k);
            k--;
        }
    }
}

// Defining Thread1
class Thread1 implements Runnable {
    Thread t;
    Thread1() {
        t = new Thread(this);
        t.start();
    }
```

```
    public void run() {
         DataHouse a = new DataHouse();
         a.printCity();
    }
}

// Defining Thread2
class Thread2 implements Runnable {
    Thread t;
    Thread2() {
        t = new Thread(this);
        t.start();
    }
    void run() {
         DataHouse a = new DataHouse();
         a.printCode();
    }
}

// The main class running the threads in multithreaded
                                                   // manner
class PartialSynchronizationDemo {
     public static void main(String args[]) {
        // Ctearting two threads and running...
        Thread1 t1 = new Thread1();
        Thread2 t2 = new Thread2();

        try {
            t1.t.join(); t2.t.join();
        } catch(InterruptedException e) {
              System.out.prinyln(e);
        }
    }
}
```

Working of Program 7.15

- In Program 7.15, no method is synchronized. However, inside the methods `printCity()` and `printCode()`, the `synchronize` keyword is used to mark the two blocks as synchronized.
- Notice how the Java synchronized block construct takes an object in parentheses. In the example, `this` is used, which is the instance the methods are called on. It is mandatory for any synchronized block that it should be synchronized on some object.

- The object taken in the parentheses by the synchronized construct is called a monitor object. The code is said to be synchronized on the monitor object.
- In Program 7.15, two threads running in parallel call the methods `printCity()` and `printCode()` to be executed concurrently.
- There are three loops in each method. All the loops, except the two `for` loops (these are the code under synchronized blocks) can enter the monitor and execute in intermingled manner.
- The synchronized blocks synchronized on the same object can only have one thread executing inside them at one time. The other thread attempting to enter the synchronized block will be blocked until the thread inside the synchronized block exits the block.

You are advised to experiment how the program behaves in the following three scenarios:

1. Case 1: Run Program 7.15 as it is.
2. Case 2: Remove the synchronize keyword for each block; modify the program to make it without any synchronization and then run.
3. Case 3: Remove the synchronize keyword for each block, make both the methods synchronized, and then run the modified program.

You will notice, the program behaves differently in the three cases.

As another experiment, you can modify Program 7.11 making use of the synchronize block construct in the `run()` of each thread and compare the results from Program 7.11 and its modified version.

Synchronization of third party code

You may have to work with a situation when you want to synchronize a multithreaded program with a given class definition (e.g., a library program or a third party program), which is originally not designed for synchronized access. Let us consider the case of writing a synchronized multithreaded program for the bank system which we have implemented in Program 7.14 using synchronized method construct. Program 7.16 solves the same problem but uses the synchronized block construct. Note that Program 7.16 includes the same class definition (`class Account`) as in Program 7.14, except no method is modified with the `synchronize` keyword. You can consider this class as a third party code without any synchronized access capability.

The next part of the program includes the definitions of two thread classes. Note how the blocks in the `run()` are synchronized. The main program is reproduced exactly as in Program 7.14. You will see the same output from both Program 7.14 and Program 7.16.

Program 7.16
(Modification of Program 7.15 with the synchronized block construct)

```
/* The following class definition is reproduced
from the  class definition in Program 7.14. Here,
neither any method nor block is with the synchronized
keyword.*/

class Account {
     int balance;
     int accountNo;

     Account(int a, int b) {
         accountNo = a;
         balance = b;
     }

     void displayBalance() {
         System.out.println("Account#:" +accountNo
           +"Balance:"+balance);
     }

     void deposit(int amount){
       balance = balance + amount;
       System.out.println( amount + " is deposited");
       displayBalance();
     }

     void withdraw(int amount){
       balance = balance - amount;
       System.out.println( amount + " is withdrawn");
       displayBalance();
     }
}

/* The following class defines a thread class for
deposit operation. This definition is modified with
synchronized block construct in the run(). */

class TransactionDeposit implements Runnable{
     int amount;
     Account accountX;
          // Transaction to the target account
     TransactionDeposit(Account x, int amount){
       accountX = x;
       this.amount = amount;
       Thread t = new Thread(this);
       t.start();   // Start run()
     }
```

```
     public void run(){
          synchronized (accountX) {
            accountX.deposit(amount);
                //Perform deposit to the account
          }
     }
}


/* The following class defines a thread class for
withdraw operation. This definition is modified with
synchronized block construct in the run(). */


class TransactionWithdraw implements Runnable{
     int amount;
     Account accountY;
          // Transaction to the target account

     TransactionWithdraw(Account y, int amount) {
       accountY = y;
       this.amount = amount;
       Thread t = new Thread(this);
          t.start();        // Start run()
     }

     public void run(){
         if (accountY.balance < amount)
             System.out.println("Fund is
                insufficient...withdraw failed!");
         else
             synchronized (accountY) {
              accountY.withdraw(amount);
                    //Perform withdraw from account
             }
     }
}

/* The main class to perform two transactions in
parallel. This part remains same as in Program 7.14. */

class BankTransactionsDemo{
     public static void main(String args[]) {
         // A customer of the system
       Account aCustomer = new Account(123, 10000);
```

```
            // Perform two transactions to be executed
                                                // in parallel
        TransactionDeposit t1 = new TransactionDeposit
            (aCustomer, 500);
        TransactionWithdraw t2 = new TransactionWithdraw
            (aCustomer,1000);
            // One more concurrent withdraw request
        TransactionWithdraw t3 = new TransactionWithdraw
            (aCustomer,10000);
    }
}
```

Synchronizing block construct is more powerful than the synchronized method construct. This statement can be justified by the following points:

- You can achieve the same results using synchronized block as the synchronized method construct (e.g., Program 7.14 and 7.16).
- The code which is not under any critical section can be kept outside the synchronized operation, thus allowing non-synchronized code to be executed concurrently and giving better utilization of CPU. This produces better throughput in execution (e.g., Program 7.15).
- The code without synchronized access can be brought under synchronized execution (e.g., Program 7.16).

BE CAREFUL

Be careful to avoid a deadlock situation when you are working with synchronized keywords in multithreading programming.

Deadlock situtation

Let's first learn about deadlock. Let us assume there are two resources A and B, both have critical data, and only one thread can enter the critical section at one time. There are two threads T1 and T2 running concurrently and both are competing for the resources A and B. T1 and T2 cannot end their tasks until both finish with A and B. Consider a situation where T1 enters the critical section of A and locks the object A; at the same time T2 enters the critical section of B and locks the object of B. Now, T1 is waiting for T2 to unlock B and T2 is waiting for T1 to unlock A. Since no one can unlock the objects, both are in a waiting state without any result. Such a situation is called deadlock. Figure 7.11 illustrates a deadlock situation with two threads T1 and T2 and two resources A and B.

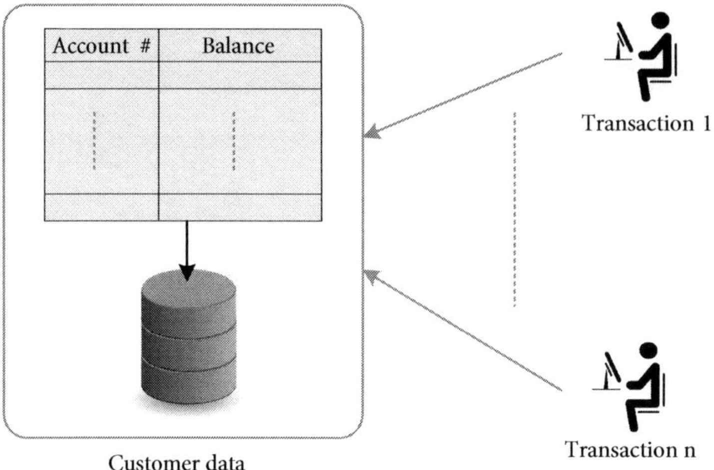

Figure 7.11 Deadlock situation in multithreading

A Java multithreaded program may suffer from a deadlock situation because the `synchronize` keyword causes the executing of threads to block while waiting for the locks from the monitors associated with the objects managing critical resources. Program 7.17 can be tested to see how deadlock occurs in the program.

Program 7.17 *(Multithreading program with deadlock situation)*

```
/* This program exhibits deadlock situation of a
multithreading program. */
// Defining two classes representing resources A and B

// Resource A
class A {
     private int a;

     public int get() {
         return a;
     }

     public void put(int i) {
         a = i;
     }
}
```

```
// Resource B
class B {
     private int b;

     public int get() {
         return b;
     }

     public void put(int i) {
         b = i;
     }
}

// Defining the program for thread  T1
class T1 extends Thread {
    A a;
    B b;

    T1 (A a, B b) {
        this.a = a; this.b = b;
    }

     public void run() {
          synchronized (a) {
              a.put(111); System.out.println
                (" From a : " + a.get());
              try {
                  Thread.sleep(10000);
              } catch (InterruptedException e) {}

              System.out.println("T1: Requesting for
                B ...");
              synchronized (b) {
                  b.put(555); System.out.println
                     (" From b : " + b.get());
              }
          }
     }
}

// Defining the program for thread  T2
class T2 extends Thread {
    A a;
    B b;
```

```
    T2 (A a, B b) {
        this.a = a; this.b = b;
    }

     public void run() {
          synchronized (b) {
              b.put(222); System.out.println
                (" From b : " + b.get());
              try {
                  Thread.sleep(10000);
              } catch (InterruptedException e) {}

              System.out.println
                ("T1: Requesting for A ...");
              synchronized (a) {
                  a.put(999); System.out.println
                     (" From a : " + a.get());
              }
          }
     }
}

// The main program running the threads in parallel

public class DeadlockDemo {
    public static void main(String args[]) {
        // Creating two resources
        A a = new A();
        B b = new B();

        // Creating two threads
        T1 t1 = new T1(a, b);
        T2 t2 = new T2(a, b);

        // Concurrent execution of the threads
        t1.start();
        t2.start();

        System.out.println("Program execution is
successful...");
    }
}
```

Working of Program 7.17

The execution of the program will be as follows:

Both `t1` and `t2` start simultaneously. As the two threads `t1` and `t2` starts executing, `t1` requests the lock of the object `a`, the first synchronized block of `t1`'s `run()` and `t2` requests lock of the object `b`, the first synchronized block of `t2`'s `run()`. Receiving the two simultaneous requests, JVM allows lock of `a` to `t1` and lock of `b` to `t2`. Both `t1` and `t2` then wait for 10 seconds by going to sleep. On awaking, `t1` requests the lock of the object `b`, the innermost synchronized block of `t1`'s `run()`, and at the same time `t2` also requests the lock of the object `a`, the innermost synchronized block of `t2`'s `run()`. Since at this point `t1` has the lock of `a` but not of `b` and `t2` has the lock of `b` but not of `a`, and they cannot unlock the locks unless they finish their respective `run()` methods, they will be waiting for ever!

A solution for avoiding the deadlock situation is shown in Program 7.18.

Program 7.18 *(Multithreading program without deadlock situation)*

```
/* This program exhibits deadlock situation of a
multithreading program. */
// Defining two classes representing resource A and B
// Resource A
class A {
     private int a;

     public int get() {
         return a;
     }

     public void put(int i) {
         a = i;
     }
}
// Resource B
class B {
     private int b;

     public int get() {
         return b;
     }

     public void put(int i) {
         b = i;
     }
}
```

```
// Defining the program for thread  T1
class T1 extends Thread {
    A a;
    B b;

    T1 (A a, B b) {
        this.a = a; this.b = b;
    }

     public void run() {
          synchronized (a) {
              a.put(111); System.out.println
                (" From a : " + a.get());
              try {
                  Thread.sleep(10000);
              } catch (InterruptedException e) {}

              System.out.println
                ("T1: Requesting for B ...");
              synchronized (b) {
                  b.put(555); System.out.println
                     (" From b : " + b.get());
              }
          }
     }
}

// Defining the program for thread  T2
class T2 extends Thread {
    A a;
    B b;

    T2 (A a, B b) {
        this.a = a; this.b = b;
    }

     public void run() {
          synchronized (a) {
              b.put(222); System.out.println
                (" From b : " + b.get());
              try {
                  Thread.sleep(10000);
              } catch (InterruptedException e) {}

              System.out.println
                ("T1: Requesting for A ...");
```

```
                synchronized (b) {
                    a.put(999); System.out.println
                       (" From a : " + a.get());
                }
            }
        }
}

public class DeadlockDemo {
    public static void main(String args[]) {
        // Creating two resources
        A a = new A();
        B b = new B();

        // Creating two threads
        T1 t1 = new T1(a, b);
        T2 t2 = new T2(a, b);

        // Concurrent execution of the threads
        t1.start();
        t2.start();

        System.out.println("Program execution is
           successful...");
    }
}
```

Working of Program 7.17

A simple solution involves a small modification of Program 7.17, which you can see in the two `run()` methods of `T1` and `T2` classes. In the modified program, locking of objects in the same order: `T1` and `T2` first approach for lock of `A` (it will be granted to any one) keeping the other waiting. Thus, entering into the monitors takes place in a mutually exclusive manner. This is the necessary condition to avoid the occurrence of a deadlock situation.

7.5 Other Aspects of Threads

A few important aspects of threads which are worth learning for writing better multithreaded programs are as follows:

- Life cycle of threads
- Interthread communication
- Thread group and daemon thread

We will discuss the concepts, Java language supports, utilities, and illustration of each of these.

7.5.1 Life Cycle of a Thread

A thread can be any one of the five states at any time: new, runnable, running, blocked, and terminated.

1. New

When a thread is created (by the `new` statement) but is not yet ready to run (i.e., `start()` is not called for the thread), it is called in *New* state. In this state, the memory space for local data members, if any, is allocated and initialized.

2. Runnable

The *Runnable* state means that a thread is ready to run and is awaiting the control of the processor; the thread in this state is in a queue and waiting for its turn to be executed.

3. Running

Running means that the thread has control of the processor, its code is currently being executed, and the thread will continue in this state until it gets preempted by a higher priority thread, finishes its execution, or relinquishes control.

4. Blocked

A thread is *Blocked* means that it is being prevented from the *Runnable* or *Running* state and is waiting for some event to occur for it to re-enter the scheduling queue.

5. Terminated

A thread is *Terminated* when it finishes its execution, or is stopped, or is killed by another thread.

Each thread can transit from one state to the other. This life cycle of threads is depicted in Figure 7.11.

You can obtain the current state of a thread by calling the `getState()` method defined by `Thread` (Table 7.3). It returns a value of type `Thread.State` that indicates the state of the thread at the time at which the call was made. `State` is an enumeration defined by `Thread` and it has the elements Blocked, New, Runnable, Terminated, Waiting.

Program 7.19 is a simple program showing threads in a few basic states.

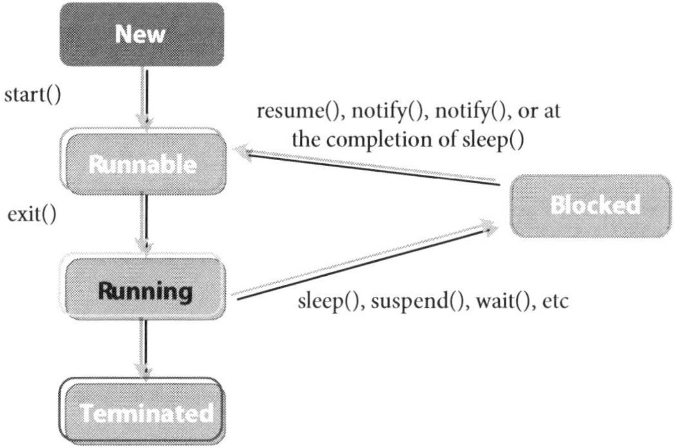

Figure 7.12 Thread state transition diagram

Program 7.19
(Different states of a thread)

```
/* This program demonstrates how a thread  is in New,
Running, Blocked, Runnable and Terminated states. */

// Define a thread class
class ThreadX extends Thread {
    public void run()  {
       try {
         // Displaying the thread that is running
         System.out.println("Running: "+Thread.
           currentThread().getId());
       }
       catch (Exception e)  {
            // Throwing an exception
            System.out.println ("Exception occurred.");
       }
    }
}

public class ThreadStatesDemo{
    public static void main(String[] args) {
        // Main thread by default starts running as
                                    // program is executed
        Thread t;
        t = Thread.currentThread();
          // t refers to the main thread now
        System.out.println("Starting thread:
          " + t + t.getState());
```

```
        // The following thread is in newborn state
        System.out.println("Thread t1 is just
          created...");
        ThreadX t1 = new ThreadX();
        t1.setPriority(Thread.MAX_PRIORITY);
        System.out.println("A newborn thread: " + t1
          +t1.getState());

        t1.start();   // Thread t1 is running thread...
        System.out.println("Thread: " + t1 +
          t1.getState());

        t1.sleep(200L);
       // Thread t1 is suspended and is in blocked state
        System.out.println("Sleeped thread:
          " + t1 + t1.getState());

        t.setPriority(Thread.MIN_PRIORITY);
        System.out.println("Main thread enters into
          runnable state...");

       try {
           t1.join();
             // Control wait until t1 ends its execution
       } catch (Exception e) {
           System.out.println(e);
       }
       // Here, thread t1 is  in terminated state...
       System.out.println("Thread: " + t1 +
          t1.getState());
       System.out.println("Finally main thread is
          terminated.");
   }
}
```

- In Program 7.19, if the priority of `t1` is set as `MIN_PRIORITY`, then the program may hang. This is because out of thread `t1` and `main`, `main` will finish its execution before `t1` ends. So, if main is dead, then JVM returns the control to the run-time manger and the pending `t1` comes to its end.
- State of a thread changes and hence its state value as its execution progresses.

Threads move from one state to another via a variety of means. The common methods for controlling a thread's state are shown in Figure 7.11. The methods are summarized here for a quick reference (Table 7.3 has some additional information).

`start()`: With this method, a newborn thread enters into Runnable state, Java run-time creates a system thread context and starts it running. This method for a thread object can be called only once.

`stop()`: This method causes a thread to stop immediately. This is often an abrupt way to end a thread.

`suspend()`: This method is different from `stop()` method. It takes the thread and causes it to stop running but later it can be restored by calling it again.

`resume()`: This method is used to revive a suspended thread. There is no guarantee that the thread will start running right way, since there might be a higher priority thread running already; `resume()` only makes the thread to become eligible for running.

`sleep(long n)`: This method causes the run-time to put the current thread to sleep for n milliseconds. After n milliseconds, this thread will be eligible to run again.

`yield()`: This method causes the run-time to switch the context from the current thread to the next available runnable thread. This is one way to ensure that the threads of lower priority may get a chance to start their execution.

Program 7.20 illustrates how a thread can switch from one state to another with these methods.

Program 7.20
(State transition of threads)

```
/* This program illustrates the use of yield(), stop()
and sleep() methods for changing the states of a
thread. */

// This thread relinquishes its control to a waiting
                                                // thread
class ThreadA extends Thread{
   public void run() {
       System.out.println("Running Thread A ....");
       for(int i = 1; i <= 5; i++) {
         if (i==1) yield();
              // Allow a runnable thread, if any
            System.out.println("From Thread A:
              i = " + i);
       }
       System.out.println("... Exiting Thread A");
   }
}
```

```
// This thread will end abruptly half way
class ThreadB extends Thread{
    public void run() {
     System.out.println("Start Thread B ....");
     for(int j = 1; j <= 5; j++) {
         System.out.println("From Thread B: j = "+ j);
          if (j==2) stop();
                // Moves to terminated state on 2nd run
     }
     System.out.println("... Exiting Thread B");
    }
}

// This thread runs, sleeps for a while and then awakens
class ThreadC extends Thread{
    public void run() {
     System.out.println("Start Thread C ....");
     for(int k = 1; k <= 5; k++) {
        System.out.println("From Thread C: k = "+ k);
        if (k==3){
            try{
             Thread.sleep(1000);
               // Move to runnable for 1 second
            }catch(Exception e){}
        }
     }
     System.out.println("... Exiting Thread C");
    }
}

// The main program, which runs the different threads
public class StateTransitionDemo {
     public static void main (String args[]) {
       // Three threads with different priority
       ThreadA t1 = new ThreadA(); t1.setPriority(10);
       ThreadB t2 = new ThreadB(); t2.setPriority(5);
       ThreadC t3 = new ThreadC(); t3.setPriority(1);

       t1.start(); t2.start(); t3.start();

          try {
              System.out.println("Is t1 alive?
                " + t1.isAlive());
              t1.sleep(5000L);
                // Main thread is suspended for 500ms
              System.out.println("Is t2 alive?
                " + t2.isAlive());
```

```
                // Let's know the states of the threads
                                                // running
                t1.getState();t2.getState();t3.
                  getState();

                t1.join(); t3.join();
                  // Wait until t1 and t3 finish

            } catch (InterruptedException e) {
                System.out.println(e);
            }
            System.out.println("... End of execution. ");
    }
}
```

- Literally, to "yield" means to let go, to give up, to surrender. A yielding thread tells the virtual machine that it's willing to let other threads be scheduled in its place. This indicates that it is not doing something critical. Note that *this is only a hint*, and not guaranteed to have any effect at all.
- Yield is a `static` method and native, too.
- Yield tells the currently executing thread to give a chance to the threads that have equal priority in the queue of threads.
- There is no guarantee that yield will make the currently executing thread to runnable state immediately.
- It can only make a thread go from running state to runnable state, not from waiting or blocked state.

7.5.2 Interthread Communication

In Java programming, a thread can communicate with other threads. There are three ways for threads to communicate with each other:

1. Through commonly shared data

All the threads in the same program share the same memory space. If an object is accessible to various threads then these threads share access to that object's data members and thus communicate with each other. Since a thread is an object of a class, this is the usual method by which one object communicates with another object.

2. Using thread control methods

There are three such methods by which threads communicate for each other.

`suspend()`: A thread can suspend itself and wait till some other thread resumes it.

`resume()`: A thread can wake up another waiting thread, which is waiting using `suspend()`, through its `resume()` method and then it can run concurrently.

`join()`: This method can be used for the caller thread to wait for the completion of the called thread.

3. Using three specialized methods

There are three methods, namely `wait()`, `notify()`, and `notifyAll()` *defined in class* `Object` of package `java.lang`.

`wait()`: This method tells the calling thread to give up the monitor and makes the calling thread wait until either a time-out occurs or another thread calls the same threads `notify()` or `notifyAll()` method.

`Notify()`: This method wakes up only one (first) waiting thread that called wait() on the same object.

`notifyAll()`: This method will wake up all the threads that have called wait() on the same object.

Interthread communication is very useful in many applications. Some applications which you should learn in this book are:

- Controlling the execution of threads.
- Producer–Consumer problem.

Controlling the execution of threads

Let us solve a problem using multithread programming. Consider two threads, say `PrintN` and `PrintA`. First, `PrintN` would print 10 numbers 1, 2, 3, … , 10 and then allow `PrintA` to print 10 odd numbers 1, 3, 5, … , 19. Next, `PrintN` would print 11, 12, … , 20 and then `PrintA` would print 10 even numbers 0, 2, 4, … , 20. This problem can be solved using two thread controlling methods in `java.lang.Thread` class, namely `suspend()` and `resume()`.

Program 7.21 gives an implementation showing how two threads can communicate with each other using `suspend()` and `resume()` methods.

Program 7.21 *(Controlling threads' execution using suspend() and resume()*

```
/* This program demonstrates the interthread
communication using thread control methods   suspend()
and resume().*/

class PrintN extends Thread {
    public void run( ) {
     try{
        System.out.println("Phase 1 printing of 1 to
          10..." );
        for(int i = 1; i< 11, i++)
             System.out.println(i + "\t");
          suspend( );     // Suspended its execution
          System.out.println("Phase 2 printing of 11
               to 20..." );
          for(int i = 11; i< 21, i++)
             System.out.println(i + "\t");

     } catch(Exception e){      }
    }
}

class PrintA extends Thread {
    public void run( ) {
     try{
         System.out.println("Printing of 10 odd numbers
          up to 20..." );
         for(int i = 0; i< 10; i++)
             System.out.println(2*i+1 + "\t");
         suspend( );     // Suspended its execution
         System.out.println("Printing of 10 even
          numbers up to 20..." );
         for(int i = 0; i< 11; i++)
             System.out.println(2*i + "\t");
     } catch(Exception e){      }
    }
}

class ThreadControlDemo{
    public static void main (String args[ ] ){
        //Creating the threads
        PrintN t1 = new PrintN ( );
        PrintA t2 = new PrintA ( );

     t1.start( );
       //t1 is scheduled  for running for printing 1..10
```

```
        // t1 is now in suspended state
      t2.start( );
      // t2 is scheduled for running for printing 1,3,5..
        // t2 is now in suspended state

      try {
            // Resume t1 for printing 11..20
            t1.resume( );
            // t1 is now finishes its execution
            // Resume t2 for printing 0,2,..20
            t2.resume( );

            t2.join();
           // Wait t2 to finish before main thread to end
            // t2 is now finishes its execution
      }  catch(Exception e){      }
      System.out.println("Multithreading program is
            over.");
    }
}
```

- The `resume()` *method is used only with* `suspend()` method. You cannot resume a thread unless the thread has been suspended earlier.
- The two methods are deprecated and hence you may receive warning message during compilation.

Producer–Consumer problem

Java includes an elegant inter-process communication mechanism via the `wait()`, `notify()`, and `notifyAll()` methods. These methods are implemented as `final` methods in the class `Object`, so the methods are accessible to any class. All three methods should be called only from within a synchronized context.

Let's consider a very popular program in the field of Computer Science dealing with the critical section problem. This problem is called *Producer-Consumer* problem (this is also known as *Reader–Writer* problem). There is a shared buffer (let's call it *QBuffer*), where an agent called *Producer* writes data. There is another agent called *Consumer*, who reads data from QBuffer. Reading data should be in a first-in-first-out (FIFO) manner and Consumer reads in the same order as the Producer writes. This QBuffer being a shared resource, only one agent is allowed to access it at a time. In other words, `read()` by Consumer and `write()` by Producer are mutually exclusive. The situation is represented in Figure 7.12. The problem is to develop a program which would adhere to the following:

1. *Producer* writes in *QBuffer* **then only** the Consumer can read it.
2. The system **runs** in an **infinite loop** until it is stopped deliberately.
3. **Speeds** of the *Producer and Consumer* are **different**. *Consumer* **waits** *until the Producer writes.*
4. *Producer and Consumer* work in **parallel**.

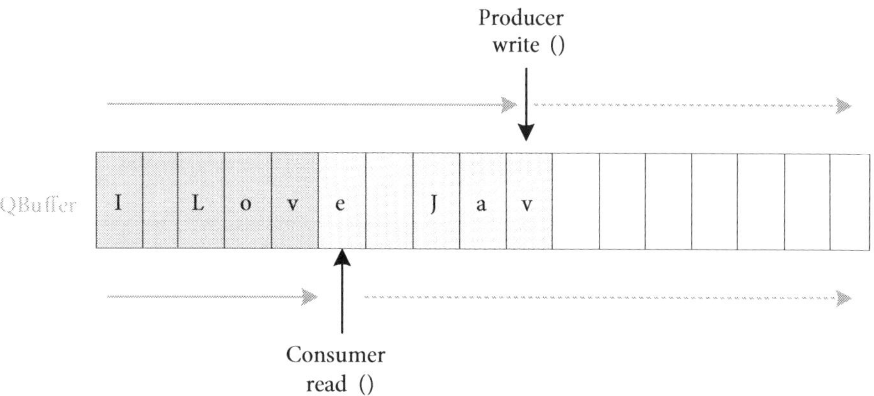

Figure 7.13 Producer-Consumer problem

The Producer–Consumer problem can be solved using Java's multithreading features. Program 7.22 is an implementation of the Producer–Consumer problem.

Program 7.22 *(Producer-Consumer problem)*

```
/* The following class defines the QBuffer, which is
the shared resource. This buffer stores maximum one
item at a time. Suppose, it stores any integer number
in it. */

class QBuffer {
    int item;             // The data to be stored here
    boolean flag = false;
     // Indicates that buffer is free for writing

    // Producer call this method to write a data into
                                             // the buffer
    synchronized void write( int data) {
     // Produces a data
```

```
      if(flag)
      // Check if buffer is free for writing
         try { wait( );}  // Producer sends signal to
                                    // consumer for wait
         catch(InterruptedException e){}

         item = data;      // Write data into buffer
         System.out.println( "Produce : " + data);
         flag = true;
          // Producer makes the buffer ready for consumer
         notify( );
              // Producer sends ready signal to consumer
     }

     // Consumer call this method to read data from the
                                                // buffer
     synchronized void read( ) {
      if(!flag)        // If buffer is ready for reading
         try { wait( );}
           // Consumer sends signal to producer for wait
         catch(InterruptedException e){}

         System.out.println( "Consume : " + item);
         flag = false;
           // Now, buffer is free for writing
         notify( );
              // Consumer sends ready signal to producer
     }
}

// The following class defines a thread for Producer
class Producer implements Runnable  {
     QBuffer  q;
     Producer ( QBuffer q ) {
      // Producer to access the buffer object
         this.q = q;
         Thread t = new Thread(this, "Producer");
         t.start  ( );
           // Start running the Producer thread
     }
    // Producer produces 1, 2, 3, ... and write them
                                      // into the buffer
     public void run( ) {
          int item = 1;
           // Otherwise, you can generate a random number
```

```
        while (true )     // Go on producing ...
         q.write ( item++ );
    }
}

// The following class defines a thread for Consumer
class Consumer implements Runnable  {
    QBuffer  q;
    Consumer ( QBuffer q ) {
          // Consumer to access the buffer object
         this.q = q;
         Thread t = new Thread(this, "Consumer");
         t.start ( );
          // Start running the Producer thread
    }

    // Consumer read from buffer one after another as
          producer produces
    public void run( ) {
      while (true)
         q.read ( );  // Go on consuming ...

    }
}

// The main program running the threads
class ProducerConsumerDemo   {
    public static void main( String args[ ] ) {
     QBuffer q = new QBuffer( );
          // Create a buffer instance
     new Producer(q) ;
          // Run the thread for producer
     new Consumer (q);
          // Run the thread for consumer
    }
}
```

Working of Program 7.22 is explained as follows:

- The methods `read()` and `write()` of `QBuffer` are modified with `synchronized` keyword to ensure that only one thread calling them can enter into the monitor object (in this case an object of the class `QBuffer`).

- The Boolean variable flag is used to maintain the state of the buffer. The value `true` implies the buffer is ready for reading and then Consumer can read the `item` from `QBuffer`; otherwise, Producer writes data into it.
- Interthread communication is made in this program using `wait()` and `notify()` methods, which are self-explanatory from the comments in the program.
- Both the `run()` methods defined in the two thread class run with infinite loop. So, the program will run until user presses *Control–C* or some program execution causes interruption from the console.

- The same program can be easily modified to two or more producers and consumers (this is just adding threads for each!). In that case, you should use the method `notifyAll()` instead of `notify()`.
- Oracle recommends to use `wait()` inside a condition check to avoid spurious awakens, which may occur accidently in Java program execution.

7.6 Thread Group and Daemon

There are two other variations in thread class: `ThreadGroup` and `Daemon`.

7.6.1 Thread Group

`ThreadGroup`, as its name implies, is a group of threads. A thread group can have both threads and other thread groups as its member elements. In Java, there is a default thread group called `SystemThreadGroup` which is nothing but the Java run-time program (JVM) itself. When a Java program starts its execution, the JVM creates the main thread group as a member of the system thread group. The main thread is created in the main thread group to run the `main()` method of the program. Every thread instance is a member of exactly one thread group. By default, all user created threads and other thread groups, if any, will become members of the main thread group. All the threads in a program form a tree where there are several thread groups. All thread groups have their parents (except the system thread group) and in the tree, the system thread group as the root.

The concept of thread group offers a convenient way to manage groups of threads as a unit. This is particularly useful in situations where you want to issue some controls, such as suspend, resume, destroy, interrupt, etc., to a number of related threads. To facilitate the creation of thread groups and different operations managing thread groups, the class `ThreadGroup` is defined in `java.lang` package. The different constructors and methods defined by `java.lang.ThreadGroup` class are listed in Table 7.5 and Table 7.6, respectively.

A new thread group can be created by instantiating the thread group class. For example:

```
Threadgroup tg1 = new ThreadGroup (String name1 ) ;
```

or

```
ThreadGroup tg2 = new ThreadGroup(ThreadGroup tg1,
String name2);
```

In the first case, a new thread group `tg1` is created with the name `name1`. In this case, by default, `SystemThreatGroup` is its parent. In the second case, a new thread group is created with the name `name2` whose parent is the thread group `tg1`.

You can add a thread to a thread group with the following:

```
Thread T = new Thread (tg2) ;
```

This creates a new thread under the thread group `tg2` which contains the thread `t` as the only member.

Program 7.23 illustrates how a thread group can be created, three threads can be added as members of that thread group, and then how they can be executed together.

Program 7.23 *(Thread group with threads)*

```
/* This program demonstrates how a thread group can be
created with three threads as members of it. */

// Define three thread classes
class T1 implements Runnable {
     public void run() {
          System.out.println("From thread T1...");
     }
}
class T2 implements Runnable {
     public void run() {
          System.out.println("From thread T2...");
     }
}
/* This program demonstrates how a thread group can be
created with three threads as members of it. */

// Define three thread classes
class T1 implements Runnable {
     public void run() {
```

```
            System.out.println("From thread T1...");
        }
}
class T2 implements Runnable {
        public void run() {
            System.out.println("From thread T2...");
        }
}
class T3 implements Runnable {
        public void run() {
            System.out.println("From thread T3...");
        }
}

// Define the  main program
public class ThreadGroupDemo {
    public static void main(String[] args) {
          // Create a thread group
          ThreadGroup tg = new ThreadGroup("ParentTG");

          // Create threads as a member of tg and start
                                                   // execution
          T1 x = new T1();
          Thread t1 = new Thread(tg, x, "T1");
          t1.start();

          T2 y = new T2();
          Thread t2 = new Thread(tg, y,"T2");
          t2.start();

          T3 z = new T3();
          Thread t3 = new Thread(tg, z,"T3");
          t3.start();

          System.out.println("Thread Group: "+tg.
               getName());
          System.out.println("Active count: "+tg.
               activeCount());
          System.out.println("Printing the thread list... ");
          tg.list();
        }
}
```

You can run a common program, for example, the same `run()` method for all and execute it as a routine. Program 7.24 demonstrates this. Note how you can assign priority to a thread group.

Program 7.24 *(Thread group with threads and common run())*

```
/* This program demonstrates how a tree of threads can
be formed and running task for all threads belong to
each thread group. */

public class ThreadGroupsDemo implements Runnable
      throws Exception {
   public void batch() throws Exception{
          // create a parent thread group
          ThreadGroup ptg = new ThreadGroup
            ("Parent Thread Group");
          // set maximum priority as 8 for the parent
                                          // thread group
          ptg.setMaxPriority(Thread.MAX_PRIORITY - 2);

          // Create a child ThreadGroup for parent
                                           // ThreadGroup
          ThreadGroup ctg = new ThreadGroup(ptg,
            "Child Thread Group");
          // set maximum priority as 5 for child
          ctg.setMaxPriority(Thread.NORM_PRIORITY);

         // Create a thread under ptg with priority as MAX
          Thread t1= new Thread(ptg, this);
            //run() defined in this class
          t1.setPriority(Thread.MAX_PRIORITY);
          System.out.println("Starting " + t1.getName()
            + "...");
          t1.start();

          // Create another thread under ctg with
                                       // priority as MIN
          Thread t2 = new Thread(ctg, this);
            // Run run() of this class
          t1.setPriority(Thread.MIN_PRIORITY);
          System.out.println("Starting " + t2.getName()
            + "...");
          t2.start();
```

```
// display the number of active threads with actual
                                              // priority
        System.out.println("Active threads in \"" +
          ptg.getName()
            + "\" = " + ptg.activeGroupCount());

        // Wait until the other threads finish
        t1.join();
        t2.join(500L);
    }

    // Define the run() methods for the thread
    public void run() {
        System.out.println(Thread.currentThread().
          getName() + " [priority = " + Thread.
          currentThread(). getPriority() + "] finished
          executing.");
    }

    public static void main(String[] args) throws
      Exception {
       ThreadGroupsDemo tg = new ThreadGroupsDemo();
       tg.batch();
    }
}
```

- You can define any thread class (you should define the class using `Runnable` interface) anywhere, add them as a member in a thread group, and run them passing its object as a runnable target.
- You can interrupt all threads by the following statement:

```
Thread.currentThread().getThreadGroup().interrupt();
```

7.6.2 Daemon Thread

Daemon threads are service threads. They exist to provide services to other threads. They normally run in an infinite loop and attend the client threads that request services. When no other threads exist, daemon thread is automatically ceased to exist. There are certain properties which makes Daemon threads special as compared to the normal threads listed below.

- Daemon threads are utmost low priority threads.
- Daemon thread cannot prevent the JVM from exiting when all the user threads finish their execution.
- JVM terminates itself when all user threads finish their execution. If JVM finds a running daemon thread, it terminates the thread and shuts down itself after that.
- A Daemon thread mostly runs in background to perform tasks such as garbage collection, releasing memory of unused objects and removing unwanted entries from the cache. Most of the JVM threads are daemon threads.

To create a daemon thread, the method `setDaemon()` can be called just after the creation of a thread and before the execution is started. For example, the following two statements are used to make a thread as demon thread.

```
Thread t = new Thread ( ) ;
t.setDaemon (true);
```

The constructor of the thread is a good candidate for making this method call. Also, by default, all the threads created by a daemon thread are also daemon threads. Some commonly used methods defined in class `java.lang.ThreadGroup` (Table 7.5 has some additional information) for handling daemon are as follows:

`getName()`	:	Returns the name of the thread group.
`setName()`	:	Sets the name of the thread group.
`getParent()`	:	Returns the parent thread group of the thread group.
`getPriority()`	:	Returns the current maximum priority of the thread group.
`activeCount()`	:	Returns the number of active threads in the thread group.
`isDaemon()`	:	Returns true if the thread is a daemon thread.
`setDaemon()`	:	Set the thread as a daemon thread prior to its starting execution.

Program 7.25 *(Running a daemon thread)*

```
/* This program demonstrates how daemon thread can be
created and run in addition to the normal thread. */

class DaemonThread implements Runnable {
    public void run() {
        while(true){
            doTask();     // Do some background task
        }
    }
```

```
    private void doTask() {
        // Checking about the thread's status
        Thread t;
        t = Thread.currentThread();

        System.out.println("Is Daemon? " +
           t.isDaemon());
        System.out.println("Name :" + t.getName());
        System.out.println("Priority : " +
           t.getPriority());
        System.out.println("Parent : " + t.getParent().
           getName());

        // Doing some task...
       for (int i = 0; i < 10; i++)
            System.out.println("Daemon counts ..." + i);

        try {
            System.out.println("Daemon thread is
                idle...");
            Thread.sleep(5000);
        } catch (InterruptedException e) {
            e.printStackTrace();
        }
    }
}

class UserThreads implements Runnable {
     public void run() {
        // Checking about the thread's status
        Thread t;
        t = Thread.currentThread();

        System.out.println("Is Daemon? " + t.isDaemon());
        System.out.println("Name :" + t.getName());
        System.out.println("Priority : " +
           t.getPriority());
        System.out.println("Parent : " +
           t.getParent());

        // Doing some task...
        for (int i = 0; i < 10; i++)
            System.out.println("User Thread counts ..."
                + i);
    }
}
```

```
// The driver class running the threads
public class DaemonThreadDemo {
    public static void main(String[] args) throws
      InterruptedException {
        Thread dt = new Thread(new DaemonThread(),
          "Daemon Thread");
        Thread ut = new Thread(new DaemonThread(),
          "User Thread");
        ut.start();
          // Start running the normal thread
        dt.setDaemon(true);
          // Set that this becomes a daemon thread
        dt.start();
          // Start running the daemon thread

        Thread.sleep(30000);
        System.out.println("Exiting program...");
    }
}
```

From the execution of Program 7.25, you can note the following:

1. A newly created thread inherits the daemon status of its parent. That's the reason all threads created inside main method (child threads of main thread) are non-daemon by default, because main thread is non-daemon. However you can make a user thread as daemon by using `setDaemon()` method of thread class.
2. When the JVM starts, it creates a thread called `Main`. Your program will run on this thread, unless you create additional threads yourself. The first thing the main thread does is to look for your `static void main (String args[])` method and invokes it. That is the entry-point to your program. If you create additional threads in the main method, those threads would be the child threads of the main thread.
3. The `public void setDaemon(Boolean)` method is used for making a user thread to daemon thread or vice-versa. For example, if you have a user thread `ut` then `ut.setDaemon(true)` would make it daemon thread. If you have a daemon thread `dt` then by calling `dt.setDaemon(false)` would make it normal thread (i.e., user thread/non-daemon thread).
4. The `public boolean isDaemon()` method is used for checking the status of a thread. It returns `true` if the thread is daemon, otherwise it returns `false`.

5. The `setDaemon()` method can only be called before starting the thread. This method would throw `IllegalThreadStateException` if you call it after the thread's `start()` method (Program 7.26).
6. User threads are high-priority threads. The JVM will wait for any user thread to complete its task before terminating it. Daemon threads are low-priority threads which will run when the execution of all high-priority threads is over.

- If you call the `setDaemon()` method after starting the thread, it would throw `IllegalThreadStateException`.
- Program 7.26 illustrates what happens when you set a thread as daemon thread after its execution has started.

Program 7.26 *Incorrect setting of a thread as daemon thread*

```
/* This program illustrates that you cannot set a
thread as a daemon thread after it is started. */

class DaemonThread extends Thread {
    public void run() {
       Thread t;
        t = Thread.currentThread();
        System.out.println("Thread : " + t.getName());
        System.out.println("Is Daemon?  " +
           t.isDaemon());
    }
    public static void main(String[] args) {
        DaemonThread t1 = new DaemonThread();
        DaemonThread t2 = new DaemonThread();

        t1.start();
        t2.start()

        t1.setDaemon(true); // Run-time exception!
    }
}
```

Some suggestions and tips on daemon thread usage:

1. Since daemon threads are meant to serve user threads and are only needed while user threads are running, they won't prevent the JVM from exiting once all the user threads have finished their execution.
2. That is why infinite loops, which typically exist in daemon threads, will not cause problems, because any code, including the `finally` blocks, won›t be executed once all the user threads

have finished their execution. For this reason, daemon threads are not recommended for IO tasks.

3. However, there are exceptions to this rule. Poorly designed code in daemon threads can prevent the JVM from exiting. For example, calling `Thread.join()` on a running daemon thread can block the shutdown of the application.
4. Usually we create a daemon thread for functionalities that are not critical to the system. For example, logging thread or monitoring thread to capture the system resource details and their state. If you are not okay with a thread being terminated, do not create it as a daemon thread.
5. Also it's better to avoid daemon threads for IO operations because it can cause resource leak when the program just terminates and resources are not closed properly.

Summary

This chapter begins with an introduction to concurrent programming and its applications. Multithreading is a highly acclaimed feature of Java, and Java API to support multithreading is discussed thoroughly. Two approaches to create threads using Runnable interface and sub classing of the class Thread followed the execution of threads, are discussed next. Management of execution of threads is a critical task which every programmer should be thorough about. The aspects of threads priority, ordering of threads, and synchronization of threads are discussed with illustration to each. Other aspects of threads, namely life cycle of a thread and inter thread communication is than included in this chapter. Finally chapter offers a concise discussions on grouping of threads, daemon threads and their application in multithreaded programming.

FAQs

7.1 What is a thread?
7.2 What is multithreading?
7.3 What are the advantages of multithreading?
7.4 What are the two ways to create a thread?
7.5 What are the difference between the two ways of creating threads?
7.6 What is the usefulness of join() method?
7.7 What is the application of wait() method?
7.8 What are the purpose of sleep() method?
7.9 What are the difference between `wait()` and `sleep()` methods?
7.10 What is synchronization?
7.11 What do you mean by interthread communication?
7.12 What is the purpose of a synchronized block?

7.13 What is static synchronization?
7.14 What is deadlock?
7.15 What is race-condition?
7.16 How is the safety of a thread achieved?
7.17 What is the volatile keyword in Java?

The answers to these questions and other problems in this chapter are available at www.cambridge.org/9781009211918. You might have many questions like these. You can post your question in the discussion forum at https://cse.iitkgp.ac.in/~dsamanta/joywithjava/page8.php.

Programs for Practice

7.1 Define two threads which produce an output as follows:

`Producer`: This thread will generate any random number, say `N`
`Consumer`: This thread will write `N` in words. For example, if `N` = 2468, then it will print Two Thousand Four Hundred Sixty Eight.
Write a multithreaded program so that if the `Producer` thread produces `N`, then `Consumer` thread will print `N` in words.

7.2 What will the following program most likely produce as output?

```
// Defining a class for a thread
class ThreadX extends Thread {
    public void run()  {
        System.out.println("Welcome to Java!);
    }
}

class ThreadY extends Thread {
    public void run()  {
        System.out.println("Joy with Java!);
    }
}

public class RunThreads{
    public static void main(String[] args) {
        ThreadX t1 = new ThreadX();
        ThreadY t2 = new ThreadY();
        t1.start();
        t2.start();
        System.out.println("Bye Fox!!);
    }
}
```

7.3 Write a multithreaded program running with a minimum number of threads such that for some integer `n` given by the programmer, first it will print `n` natural numbers, followed by first `n` even number, and finally the first `n` odd numbers.

7.4 Consider the following program:

```
// Defining a class for a thread
class ThreadX extends Thread {
    public void run()  {
        try {
            // Displaying the thread that is running
            System.out.println
                   ("Running " + Thread.currentThread().getId());
        } catch (Exception e)  {
            System.out.println ("Exception occurred.");
        }
    }
}

public class RunThreads{
    public static void main(String[] args) {
        int n = 8; // Number of runs
        for (int i=0; i<8; i++) {
            ThreadX t = new ThreadX();
            x.start();
        }
    }
}
```

How many threads are running when the loop variable i takes its value 0, 4, and 8?

7.5 Using a multithreaded program define a thread which will print `n` natural numbers 1, 2, 3, … , n for any integer n = 1, 2, 3, … , 26. Define another thread which will print any letter A, B, C, … , Z. Use the two threads write a program to print a sequence of output as follows:

```
1       A
1
2       B
1
2
3       C
1
2
3
4       D
...
…
24
25      Y
1
2
3
```

```
...
...
25
26      Z
```

7.6 What will following program produce most likely as output?

```
// Defining a class for a thread
class ThreadX extends Thread {
    public void run()  {
        System.out.println("Welcome to Java!);
    }
}

class ThreadY extends Thread {
    public void run()  {
        System.out.println("Joy with Java!);
    }
}

public class RunThreads{
    public static void main(String[] args) {
        Thread t;
        t = Thread.currentThreda();
        t.setPriority(MIN_PRIORITY);
        ThreadX x = new ThreadX();x.setPriority(NORM_PRIORITY);
        ThreadY y = new ThreadX();y.setPriority(MAX_PRIORITY);
        x.start();
        y.start();
        System.out.println("Bye Fox!!);
    }
}
```

7.7 Read any three long integers, say `x`, `y`, and `z` from a user. There will be three threads: `T1`, `T2`, and `Main` thread. The three threads will run concurrently so that `Main` thread will print "`Sleeping for x milliseconds`" and then will sleep for `x` milliseconds. The other two threads will do a similar task for `y` and `z` as input. The three threads should run in the order: `Main` thread, `T1`, `T2`.

7.8 Consider the following multithreading program:

```
public class YieldExample {
   public static void main(String[] args) {
      Thread producer = new Producer();
      Thread consumer = new Consumer();

      producer.setPriority(Thread.MIN_PRIORITY); //Min Priority
      consumer.setPriority(Thread.MAX_PRIORITY); //Max Priority
```

```
        producer.start();
        consumer.start();
    }
}

class Producer extends Thread {
    public void run() {
        for (int i = 0; i < 5; i++) {
            System.out.println("I am Producer : Produced Item " + i);
            Thread.yield();
        }
    }
}

class Consumer extends Thread {
    public void run() {
        for (int i = 0; i < 5; i++) {
            System.out.println("I am Consumer : Consumed Item " + i);
            Thread.yield();
        }
    }
}
```

What output will these program produce? If you remove all method calls `Thread.yield()`, then what will be the output?

7.9 The following is a naïve implementation of the Producer–Consumer problem. Identify if it works or not. If not, state why it does not work.

```
class QBuffer {
        int item;
        synchronized void read() {
            System.out.println("Consumer : " + item );
        }

        synchronized void put(int data) {
            item = data;
            System.out.println("Producer : " + item);
        }
    }

class Producer extends Thread {
        QBuffer q;
        Producer(QBuffer q) {
            this.q = q;
            Thread t = new Thread("Producer"));
            t.start();
        }
```

```
            public void run() {
                int item = 1;
                while( )
                    q.read(item++);
            }
        }

class Consumer implements Runnable {
        QBuffer q;
        Consumer(QBuffer q) {
             this.q = q;
             Thread t = new Thread("Consumer");
             t.start();
}

public void run() {
    while( )
        q.write();
}
        }

class ProducerConsumer {
     public static void main(String args[]) {
          QBuffer q = new QBuffer();
          new Producer(q);
          new Consumer(q);
     }
}
```

7.10 Modify the Producer–Consumer problem to implement the following:

- `Producer` to write into `QBuffer` *then only* `Consumer` can read it.
- The `Producer` writes into `QBuffer` in a *sequential* manner. Assume the size of the *`QBuffer`* is finite, of size n > 1 and it follows a cyclic queue.
- The system `runs` in an *infinite loop*.
- *Speed* of the `Producer` and `Consumer` are different. `Consumer` `waits` until `Producer` produces.
- `Producer` and `Consumer` work in *parallel*.

7.11 Modify the Producer–Consumer problem as stated in Question 7.10 so that it works with `p` number of producers and `q` number of consumers (`p` > 0 and `q` > 1).

7.12 What will the following program do? Justify the reason of the output.

```
/* Data race e. */

public class DataRaceDemo extends Thread {
    public static int x;
    public void run() {
        for (int i = 0; i < 100; i++) {
            x = x + 1;
            x = x - 1;
        }
    }
    public static void main(String[] args) {
         x = 0;
         for (int i = 0; i < 1000; i++){
            new DataRaceDemo().start();
            System.out.println(x);      // x is not always 0!
          }
    }
}
```

7.13 Carefully check the following program to see if deadlock occurs or not. If it occurs, modify the program so that it can be avoided.

```
public class TestDeadlock {
   public static Object a = new Object();
   public static Object b = new Object();

   private static class Thread1 extends Thread {
      public void run() {
         synchronized (a) {
            System.out.println("From a ...");

            try { Thread.sleep(10000); }
            catch (InterruptedException e) {}
            System.out.println("Entering b ...");

            synchronized (b) {
               System.out.println("From b ...");
            }
         }
      }
   }

   private static class Thread2 extends Thread {
      public void run() {
         synchronized (b) {
            System.out.println("From b ...");
```

```
                try { Thread.sleep(500); }
                catch (InterruptedException e) {}
                System.out.println("Entering a ...");

                synchronized (a) {
                   System.out.println("From a ...");
                }
             }
          }
       }

    public static void main(String args[]) {
       Thread1 t1 = new Thread1();
       Thread2 t2 = new Thread2();
       t1.start();
       t2.start();
      }
   }
```

MCQs

7.1 Which of the following is not suitable in a single CPU environment?

(a) Multiprogramming. (b) Multithreading.
(c) Multiprocessing. (d) Multitasking.

7.2 Which class/interface should be considered to create a Java program to define multiple threads?

(a) Thread.
(b) Runnable.
(c) Exception.
(d) No class/interface is required to write a multithread program.

7.3 What is(are) of the following method(s) necessary to be called to start the execution of a thread?

(a) `init()`.
(b) `start()`.
(c) `run( )`.
(d) None of these as a thread program starts it execution automatically.

7.4 Which will contain the body of the thread?

(a) `run();` (b) `start();`
(c) `stop();` (d) `main();`

7.5 Let's consider the following program in Java:

```
class Test extends Thread {
   public void run() {
        System.out.println("I am from Run...");
   }
}

class MyProgram {
   public     static void main(String[] args) {
        Test t = new Test();
        t.start();
   }
}
```

If you run this program, then how many threads will be executed altogether?
(a) One thread only.
(b) Two threads only.
(c) Three threads only.
(d) No thread will run in this case.

7.6 A thread is defined using the `java.lang.Thread` class, which is as follows:

```
public class MyThread extends Thread  {
    public void run()      {
        // Some code here ....
    }
}
```

Which of the following statements will require to create a thread and then start running it?

(a)
```
MyThread t = new MyThread();
t.start();
```

(b)
```
MyThread t = new MyThread();
t.run();
```

(c)
```
MyThread t;
t.start();
```

(d)
```
MyThread t;
t.run();
```

7.7 A thread is defined using the `java.lang.Runnable` interface, which is as follows:

```
public class MyThread implements Runnable  {
    public void run()      {
        // Some code here ....
    }
}
```

Which of the following statements will require to create a thread and then start running it?

(a)
```
MyThread t = new MyThread();
t.start();
```

(b)
```
MyThread t = new MyThread();
t.run();
```

(c)
```
Thread t = new Thread(MyThread);
t.start();
```

(d)
```
Thread t = new Thread(MyThread);
t.run();
```

7.8 What will happen if two threads of different priority values are called to run simultaneously?

(a) The thread for which the `start()` is called first will start its execution first, irrespective of their priority.
(b) The thread with higher priority value will start its execution first, complete its execution, and then the thread with the next lower priority will start.
(c) The thread with lower priority value will start its execution first, complete its execution, and then the thread with the next higher priority will start.
(d) The thread with the higher priority value will start its execution first, and then the thread with the next lower priority will start. Subsequently, both the threads will run simultaneously.

7.9 How many priority values can a thread can be assigned?

(a) 2.
(b) 3.
(c) Any number of values within any range.
(d) Any number of values within the range of 1 to 10 both inclusive.

7.10 What will happen if two threads of the same priority value are called to run simultaneously?

(a) Any one thread can start its execution with 50–50 chance for each.
(b) The thread for which `start()` is called first will start its execution first.
(c) The order of execution is decided by the operating system (OS) of the system where the program is running.
(d) The thread whose `run` method is defined first in the program will be executed first.

7.11 Consider the execution of the following programs:

```
class Thread1 extends Thread {
    public void run()   {
        for(int i = 0; i < 3; i++)   {
            System.out.print("A");
            System.out.print("B");
        }
    }
}
```

```
class Thread2 extends Thread  {
    public void run()     {
        for(int i = 0; i < 3; i++)          {
            System.out.print("C");
            System.out.print("D");
        }
    }
}

class MainThread {
       public static void main(String args[]) {
              Thread1 t1 = new Thread1();
              Thread2 t2 = new Thread2();
              t1.start();
              t2.start();
    }
}
```

What is be the output likely to be?

(a) Will print in this order ABCDABCD ... ABCD.
(b) Will print in this order ACBDACBD ... ACBD.
(c) Will print CDABCDAB ... CDAB.
(d) Will print in any random order of A, B, C, D which is different in different runs.

7.12 Which of the following are the valid constructor(s) of Thread class?

(1) `Thread(Runnable r, String name;)`
(2) `Thread( );`
(3) `Thread(int priority);`
(4) `Thread(Runnable r, ThreadGroup g);`
(5) `Thread(Runnable r, int priority);`

(a) 1 and 2 (b) 2 and 4
(c) 1 and 3 (d) 2 and 5

7.13 Which of the following methods make the thread leave the running state?

(1) `yield()`
(2) `wait()`
(3) `notify()`
(4) `notifyAll()`
(5) `sleep(1000)`
(6) `join()`
(7) `suspend()`

(a) 3, 4 and 7 (b) 1, 2 and 4
(c) 1, 2, 5, 6, 7 (d) 1, 4 and 7

7.14 Consider the execution of the following programs:

```
class Thread1 extends Thread {
  synchronized(this) {
    public void run()   {
        for(int i = 0; i < 3; i++)  {
            System.out.print("A");
            System.out.print("B");
        }
    }
  }
}

class Thread2 extends Thread  {
  synchronized(this) {
    public void run()     {
        for(int i = 0; i < 3; i++)    {
            System.out.print("C");
            System.out.print("D");
        }
    }
  }
}

class MainThread {
        public static void main(String args[]) {
                Thread1 t1 = new Thread1();
                Thread2 t2 = new Thread2();
                t1.start();
                t2.start();
    }
}
```

What is the output likely to be when the we synchronize the execution of the threads?

(a) Will print in this order ABCDABCD ... ABCD
(b) Will print in this order ACBDACBD ... ACBD
(c) Will print CDABCDAB ... CDAB
(d) Will print in any random sequence of AB, CD.

7.15 Let us consider the following program segment:

```
class ThreadDemo implements Runnable {
    String x, y;
    public void run()     {
        for(int i = 0; i < 10; i++)
            synchronized(this)
            {
                x = "Hello";
                y = "Java";
```

```
                System.out.print(x + " " + y + " ");
            }
    }

    public static void main(String args[])      {
        ThreadDemo run = new ThreadDemo ();
        Thread obj1 = new Thread(run);
        Thread obj2 = new Thread(run);
        obj1.start();
        obj2.start();
    }
}
```

(a) There will be an arbitrary order of the two strings Hello and Java 10 times each.
(b) It will print Hello Java … 20 times.
(c) It will print Hello 10 times and then Java 10 times.
(d) This program will not print anything.

7.16 **Which of the following is *not* a method of the `Thread` class in Java?**
(a) `isAlive()`
(b) `getPriority()`
(c) `getNames()`
(d) `sleep()`

7.17 **Which of the following method can be used to know the priority of a thread?**
(a) `getPriority()`
(b) `priority()`
(c) `isRunning()`
(d) `getThreadPriority()`

7.18 **Which of the following can be used to create an instance of `Thread`?**
(a) By implementing the `Runnable` interface.
(b) By extending the `Thread` class.
(c) By creating a new class named `Thread` and calling method `run()`.
(d) By importing the `Thread` class from package.

7.19 **A thread is better defined as:**
(a) a basic unit of CPU utilization.
(b) a control used to manage multiple requests by the same user without having to have multiple copies of the program.
(c) a hardware device like a processor.
(d) multiple copies of the same program.

7.20 **Which of the following statement is *not* true about a thread?**
(a) Thread is a piece of code that runs concurrently with other threads.
(b) Thread is a statically ordered sequence of instructions.
(c) Thread is used to express concurrency on both single and multiprocessor machines.
(d) A thread can be executed independently.

7.21 **Which of the following will contain the body of the thread?**

(a) `run();` (b) `start();` (c) `stop();` (d) `main();`

7.22 **The following is a simple program using the concept of thread:**

```
public class Test extends Thread{
  public void run(){
         System.out.println("Thread started ...");
  }
  public static void main(String args[]){
         Question7 t1 = new Question7();
         t1.start();
  }
}
```

How many threads will be there when this program is in execution?

(a) 0 (b) 1 (c) 2 (d) 3

7.23 **For the following program, what will be the output after its execution?**

```
public class Question8{
    public static void main(String[] args) {
        Thread thread = Thread.currentThread();
        System.out.println(thread.isAlive());
    }
}
```

(a) 0 (b) true (c) 1 (d) false

7.24 **Which of the following is a correct constructor for a thread object?**

(a) `Thread(Runnable a, String str);`
(b) `Thread(Runnable a, int priority);`
(c) `Thread(Runnable a, ThreadGroup t);`
(d) `Thread(int priority);`

7.25 **What does `notifyAll()` method do?**

(a) Wakes up all threads that are waiting on this object's monitor.
(b) Wakes up only one thread among a group of threads that are waiting on this object's monitor.
(c) Wakes up all threads that are not waiting on this object's monitor.
(d) It doesn't wake up any thread that are waiting on this object's monitor.

8

Java IO and File

Input and output are two most important operations in any software system design. This is particularly significant with modern Internet and communication technology where there are many modes of input–output from many sources. This versatility of input–output brings a challenge to software systems developer. Fortunately, Java developer has `java.io`, which provides a brilliant method of managing data in an easy, programmer-friendly, reliable, and robust manner. Today `java.io` API is admired as one of the finest packages which facilitates data manipulation in the best possible way. The addendum `java.nio` offers several features to implement intensive and high-speed IO operations. This chapter gives you an understanding of handling input-output in programs in Java.

8.0 Introduction

Real-world programming requirements

In the previous chapters, you have studied a little about input and output related methods in Java. Chapter 2 mentioned input to programs and output from programs considering the programs are simple and text-based (reading from keyboard), and writing output on the console (display). However, in many real world applications, input–output are more versatile: inputs are from many different sources (such as files, other programs, network channels, etc.); similarly, outputs from a program may go into several destinations like files, external programs, network lines in web, etc. (Figure 8.1).

Java's key to success

While a majority of programming languages are keyboard–console input and output (IO), Java is much ahead of them, supporting efficient, strong, and flexible real-world programming with networking, files, and many more options. Java includes the `java.io` package which contains nearly every class you might ever need to perform IO. As a unique concept, Java introduced *stream* for flow of different forms of data to-and-fro the sources and destinations. There are numerous classes representing different streams for input sources and output destinations. The streams in the `java.io` package support many kinds of data such as primitives, object, localized characters, etc.

The `java.io` package is vast. It defines over seventy classes and interfaces, many of which have a large number of methods. Covering all of them in detail is beyond the scope of this book and often it is not necessary for a programmer to know about them. Only an expert may need to. If you want to learn about any topic of your interest, you should consult Java's documentation available at:

The `java.io` package

https://docs.oracle.com/javase/tutorial/essential/io/index.html

In this book, I shall provide an overall grounding of the concepts involved and to equip you with enough details and knowledge to enable you to perform a number of specific, useful, and practical operations in your programs.

Your learning

This chapter covers the Java platform classes used for basic IO. It first focuses on *IO streams*, a powerful concept that greatly simplifies IO operations. In Java, there are many varieties of IO streams classes which help programmer to read data from several inpute source and write data into several output sources. The chapter also looks at *serialization*, which lets a program write whole objects out to streams and read them back again. Then the chapter looks at file IO and file system operations, including random access files. Further, Java introduces new IO capability in the `java.nio` package. It provide sophisticated ways of reading and write files containing data of primitive data types, as well as data of type String. The new IO capability is much more efficient and in many ways easier to use.

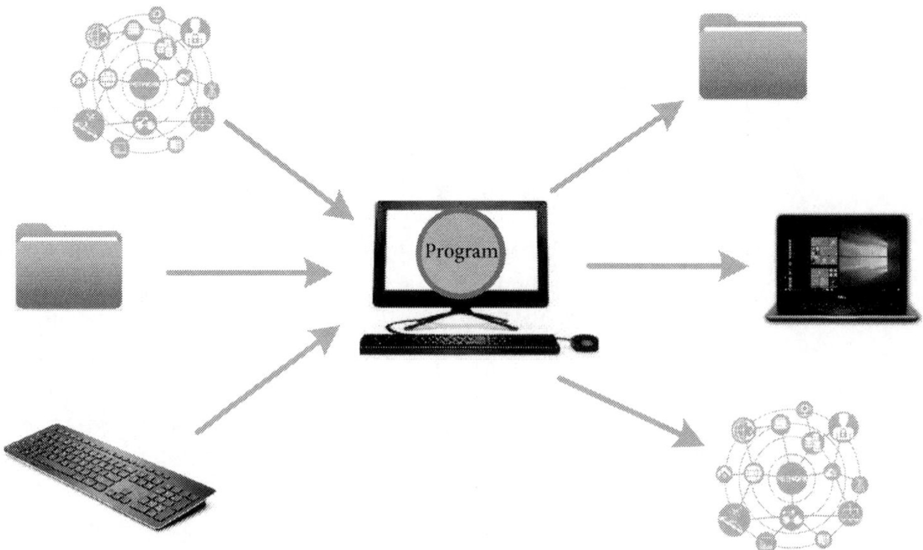

Figure 8.1 IO in Java programming

8.1 About Java IO API

Before discussing the facilities supporting the different forms of input from different sources and output to different destinations, let us have a look at the overall organization of the `java.io` package.

`java.io` class hierarchy

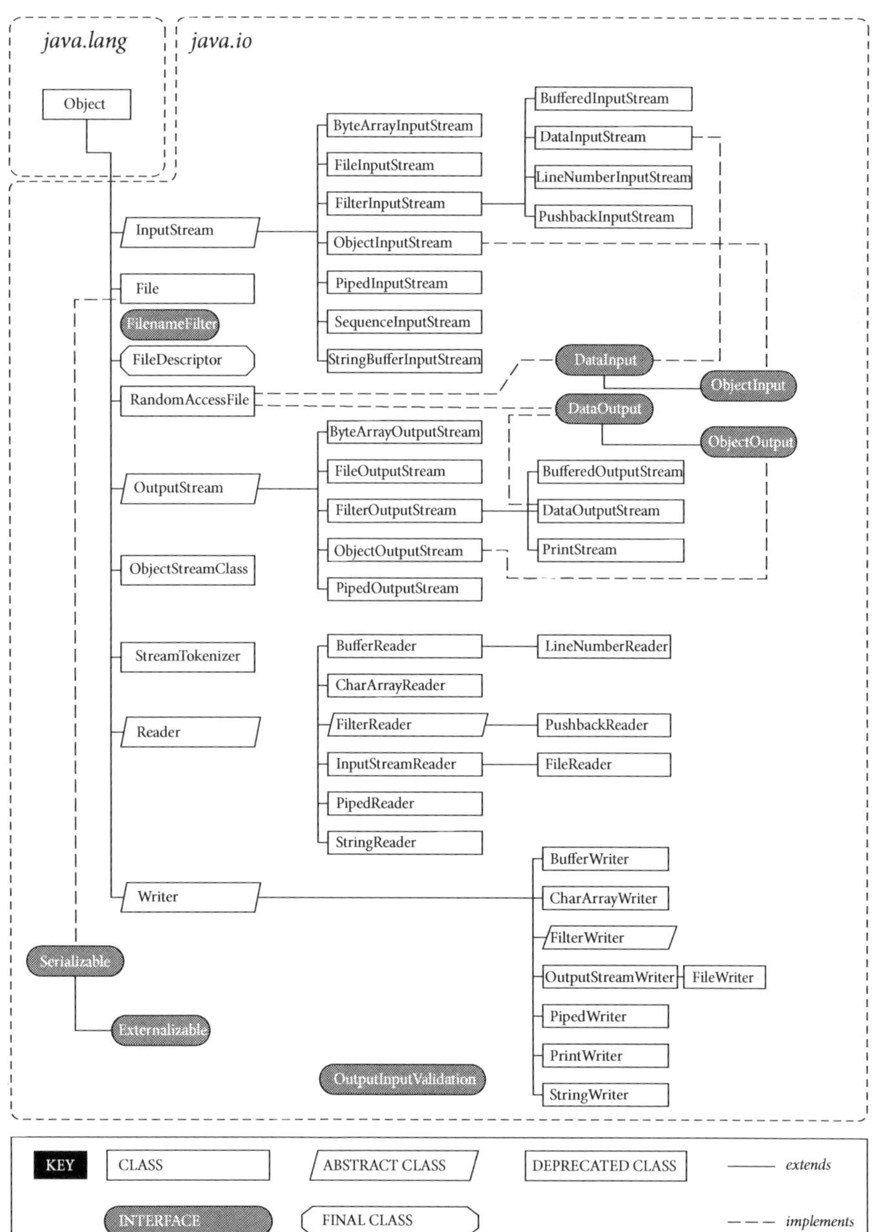

Figure 8.2: The hierarchy of classes and interfaces in `java.io`

Interfaces in `java.io`

Figure 8.2 shows the hierarchy of different classes and interfaces in `java.io`.

The package consists of a number of interfaces and classes. All interfaces in `java.io` package are listed in Table 8.1 with a brief description of each.

Table 8.1 Interface in `java.io`

Interface	Description
`Closeable`	A `Closeable` is a source or destination of data that can be closed.
`DataInput`	This interface provides for reading bytes from a binary stream and reconstructing from them data in any of the Java primitive types.
`DataOutput`	This interface provides for converting data from any of the Java primitive types to a series of bytes and writing these bytes to a binary stream.
`Externalizable`	Only the identity of the class of an `Externalizable` instance is written in the serialization stream and it is the responsibility of the class to save and restore the contents of its instances.
`FileFilter`	A filter for abstract pathnames.
`FilenameFilter`	Instances of classes that implement this interface are used to filter filenames.
`Flushable`	A `Flushable` is a destination of data that can be flushed.
`ObjectInput`	`ObjectInput` extends the `DataInput` interface to include the reading of objects.
`ObjectInputValidation`	This interface is to allow validation of objects within a graph.
`ObjectOutput`	`ObjectOutput` extends the `DataOutput` interface to include writing of objects.
`ObjectStreamConstants`	Constants written into the Object Serialization Stream.
`Serializable`	Serializability of a class is enabled by the class implementing this interface.

Aims of `java.io`

The package `java.io` contains the classes that handle fundamental input and output operations in Java. A list of all the classes is shown in Table 8.2. The IO classes can be grouped as follows.

- Classes for reading input from a source.
- Classes for writing output to a destination.
- Classes that manipulate files on the local filesystem.
- Classes that handle object serialization.

The description of each class is ignored for the time being. We shall discuss about them in the subsequent sections. Two classes `LineNumberInputStream` and `StringBufferInputStream` are now deprecated in the current version and these classes should not be used for new code.

Classes in `java.io`

Table 8.2 The classes in `java.io`

BufferedInputStream	FileWriter	PipedOutputStream
BufferedOutputStream	FilterInputStream	PipedReader
BufferedReader	FilterOutputStream	PipedWriter
BufferedWriter	FilterReader	PrintStream
ByteArrayInputStream	FilterWriter	PrintWriter
ByteArrayOutputStream	InputStream	PushbackInputStream
CharArrayReader	InputStreamReader	PushbackReader
CharArrayWriter	LineNumberReader	RandomAccessFile
Console	ObjectInputStream	Reader
DataInputStream	ObjectInputStream.GetField	SequenceInputStream
DataOutputStream	ObjectOutputStream	SerializablePermission
File	ObjectOutputStream.PutField	StreamTokenizer
FileDescriptor	ObjectStreamClass	StringReader
FileInputStream	ObjectStreamField	StringWriter
FileOutputStream	OutputStream	Writer
FilePermission	OutputStreamWriter	
FileReader	PipedInputStream	

Exception handling

In addition to abstract classes (Figure 8.2) and interfaces, there are some classes called *exception classes* defined in `java.io` package. Basic information about all these exception classes is essential as handling IO usually involves several exceptions and errors. To make the program robust, the methods of

IO classes throw exception objects relevant to exceptions. A class hierarchy of all exception classes relevant to `java.io` classes is shown in Figure 8.3. All the exception classes are listed in Table 8.3 with a brief summary of each.

IO exceptions class hierarchy

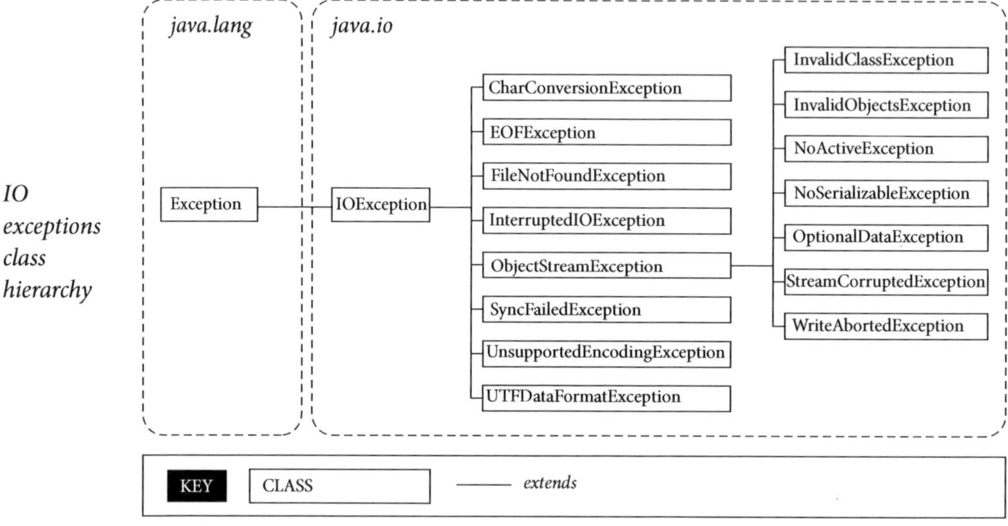

Figure 8.3 A class hierarchy of `java.io` exception classes

8.2 Streams

Concept of stream in `java.io`

IO in `java.io` is based on the concept of *stream*. A stream is an abstract representation of an input device (produces data) or output device (consumes data). A stream is a source of, or destination for, data. Your program can write data to a stream and read data from a stream (Fiure. 8.4). The flow of data from a source stream to a Java program is called *input stream* and the flow of data from a Java program to a destination stream is called *output stream*. We can visualize a stream as a sequence of bytes that flow into or out of a program.

Rationale for stream

The concept of steam is an approach toward unification. The aim is that all streams should behave in the same manner, even if the actual physical devices to which they are linked are different. With this strategy, the same IO methods can be applied to different types of devices. In other words, an input stream can abstract many different kinds of input: from a disk file, a keyboard, or a network socket. Likewise, an output stream may refer to the console, a disk file, or a network connection. Essentially, streams are the simple ways to deal with IO without having underlying mecahanism between a keyboard and a network as two dofferent sources, for example.

IO exceptions classes

Table 8.3 The exception classes defined in `java.io`

Exception	Description
`CharConversionException`	Base class for character conversion exceptions.
`EOFException`	Signals that an end of file or end of stream has been reached unexpectedly during input.
`FileNotFoundException`	Signals that an attempt to open the file denoted by a specified pathname has failed.
`InterruptedIOException`	Signals that an IO operation has been interrupted.
`InvalidClassException`	Thrown when the serialization run-time detects any problem with a class.
`InvalidObjectException`	Indicates that one or more deserialized objects failed validation tests.
`IOException`	Signals that an IO exception of some sort has occurred.
`NotActiveException`	Thrown when serialization or deserialization is not active.
`NotSerializableException`	Thrown when an instance is required to have a serializable interface.
`ObjectStreamException`	Super class of all exceptions specific to `Object` stream classes.
`OptionalDataException`	Exception indicating the failure of an object read operation due to unread primitive data, or the end of data belonging to a serialized object in the stream.
`StreamCorruptedException`	Thrown when control information that was read from an object stream violates internal consistency checks.
`SyncFailedException`	Signals that a sync operation has failed.
`Unsupported EncodingException`	The character encoding is not supported.
`UTFDataFormatException`	Signals that a malformed string in modified UTF-8 format has been read in a data input stream or by any class that implements the data input interface.
`WriteAbortedException`	Signals that one of the `ObjectStreamExceptions` was thrown during a write operation.

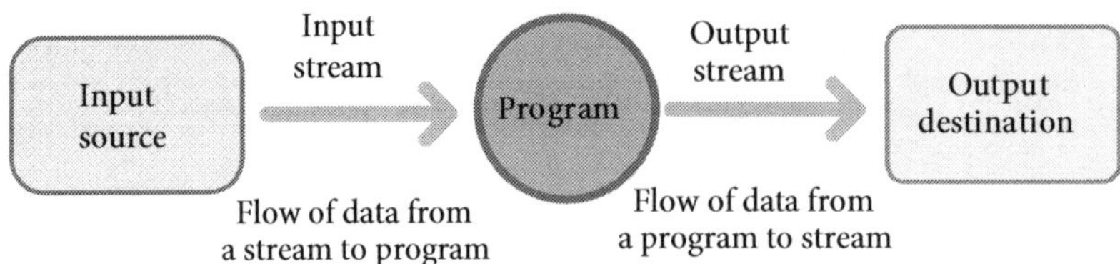

Figure 8.4 Streams in `java.io`

- Java implements streams within class hierarchies defined in the `java.io` package.
- Up to and including Java 1.3, the only way to read and write disk files was to use a stream. The new IO capability in the `java.nio` and `java.nio.channels` packages enables you to read and write files that contain data of the primitive Java types, as well as strings, and completely supersedes the stream IO capability in this context.

- You should not confused Java IO streams (i.e., the stream of `java.io`) with Java 8 `Stream (java.util.stream)`.
- The class `Stream` is one of the major features added to Java 8. The `java.util.stream` API is used to process collections of objects. A stream is a sequence of objects that supports various methods which can be pipelined to produce the desired result.
- The two concepts have very little to do with each other.

8.2.1 Standard IO Streams

Standard IO devices

Each operating system considers three physical entities: default input, output, and errors, when it runs an application program. Such entities are called standard IO devices. To be compatible with the default IO protocol in computing, Java follows three standard IO streams. The concept of standard input and output streams is a C library concept that has been assimilated into the Java environment. There are three standard streams, all of which are managed by the `java.lang.System` class defined in the Java's default `java.lang` package. This package defines a class called `System`, which encapsulates several aspects of the run-time environment. For example, using its methods, you can obtain the current time and the settings of the different properties associated with the system. `System` also contains three predefined stream variables: `in`, `out`, and `err`. These fields are declared as `public`, `static`, and `final` in the class `System`. This means that they can be used by any other part of your program without reference to a specific `System` object.

Java defines three standard streams that are accessible through members of the `System` class (Figure 8.5):

Standard input stream

This is referenced by `System.in`. It is only used for program input and typically reads input entered by the user. The `System.in` is usually corresponding to the keyboard by default. This is encapsulated by the `in` member of the `System` class and is of type `InputStream`.

Standard output stream

This is referenced by `System.out`. It is only used for program output and typically displays information to the user. The `System.out` corresponds to the console (computer's display screen) by default. This is encapsulated by the `out` member of the `System` class and is of type `PrintStream`.

Standard error stream

This is referenced by `System.err`. It is generally used to display error messages to the user. The `System.err` usually maps to the command-line output by default. The `System.err` usually corresponds to the console by default. This is encapsulated by the `err` member of the `System` class and is also of the type `PrintStream`.

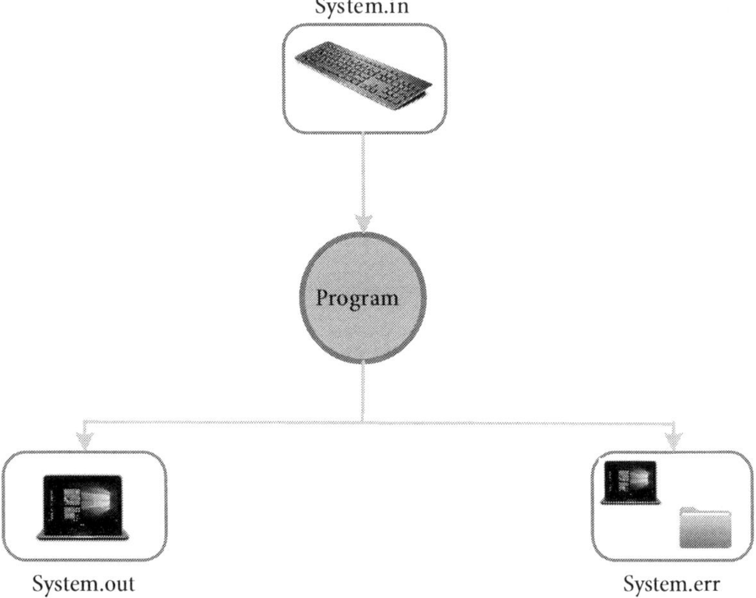

Figure 8.5 Standard IO streams

You can reassign any of the standard IO streams to another stream within a Java application. The `System` class provides the static methods `setIn()`, `setOut()`, and `setErr()` methods for this purpose. The `setIn()` method requires an argument of type `InputStream` that specifies the new source of standard input. The other two methods expect an argument of type `PrintStream`.

Program 8.1 illustrates how to read some data using `System.in` stream.

Program 8.1 *(Use of `System.in` to read from keyboard)*

```
/* This program reads an input from the keyboard. */
Import java.io.*;
class StandardInputDemo {
      public static void main(String args[]) throws
           IOException {
           System.out.println("Enter whatever you
                want...");
           int i = System.in.read();
                //Reading from the keyboard
           System.out.println(i);
           System.out.println((char)i);
                //will print the character
      }
}
```

- The `read()` method is used to read a single character from the stream. You cannot read an integer value say 123 from the keyboard using this method. You can read a byte or an array of bytes using a `read()` method, and that is all. If you want more than that, for example, reading integers, or decimal values, or strings as keyboard input, the `read()` method is not suitable; you should consider something else.
- The second `println()` prints the ASCII value of the first character you have entered.
- The third `println()` prints the first character you have entered.
- There is one class, `java.io.Console`, which you can think for reading a line or multiple lines from the keyboard. Program 8.2 illustrates an example of it.

Program 8.2 *(Reading lines from keyboard)*

```
/* This program illustrates reading line(s) from the
keyboard. */

import java.io.Console;

public class ConsoleDemo {
   public static void main(String[] args) {
      Console console = null;
      String name = null;

      try {
         consol= System.console();
               //Create a path from console to program
         if (consol != null) {
               // If path is successful
            System.out.println("Your name please ");
            name = consol.readLine("Name: ");
               // Read a name
            System.out.println("Hi  " + name + "!");

            System.out.println("Prose a text... ");
            System.out.println(console.readline());
         }
      } catch(Exception ex) {
         ex.printStackTrace();
      }
   }
}
```

- You can use the concept of command-line arguments to read anything from the keyboard and use it in your program (Chapter 2).
- There are many other ways to read from the keyboard with many methods defined in `java.io` which you shall learn in this chapter.

- It is highly recommended to enclose the code within `try-catch` block whenever you are dealing with any sort of streams; otherwise, you may face abnormal termination of the program execution or compile-time error.
- Since `java.io` is not a basic API to be imported automatically, if you use any of the class/method of a package, then you must write the import statement.

Standard output

Now, let us come to the example of standard output `System.out` in Java. You are already familiar to this with `System.out.println()` method (almost in all programs used for illustrations in this book and a brief discussion in Chapter 2). Like `println()`, there are `print()`, `printf()`, and `write()` methods which are used. The `print()`, `println()`, and `printf()` methods belong to `PrintStream` class to give output on a standard output device like a monitor. The `println()` method is to print whatever arguments you provide in string datatype and in unformatted form. The `print()` does the same thing as `println()` except the carriage (that is, the new line) returns to the next line in case of `println()` whereas it remains in the same line in `print()`. The `printf()` method is same as `print()`/ `println()` with a difference that it prints the arguments in its own datatype and this output is in formatted form. A detailed discussion of these methods may be redundant here; instead, for the sake of continuity of the current discussion, Program 8.3 is given for a quick illustration of the methods.

Program 8.3 *(Demonstration of `System.out`)*

```
/* The following program uses println to output data of
various types to the standard output stream. */

class StandardOutputDemo {
    public static void main(String[] args) {
        Thread threadInfo = new Thread();
          // Information about a thread
        String aString = "Joy with Java";
        char[] charArray = { 'a', 'b', 'c' };
        int intVal = 123;
        long longVal = Long.MIN_VALUE;
        float floatData = Float.MAX_VALUE;
        double doubleData = Math.PI;
        boolean booleanData = true;

        System.out.println(threadInfo);
          // Print thread data as string
        System.out.println(aString);
          // Prints the string
        System.out.print(charArrayData);
          // It prints array in one line
        System.out.println();
          //Prints nothing but move to next new line

        System.out.println("i " + + integerData);
          // Print the number
        System.out.printf("x = %x\n min = %2.3f\n"
          longVal, floatData);
```

```
        System.out.println("x=%e\n",floatData/
          doubleData);//OK or Error?
        System.out.write(booleanData);
          // It also prints on the monitor
        System.out.print("\n");  // Same as println()
    }
}
```

- The `print()`, `println()`, `printf()` take variable number of arguments.
- All these methods print anything as a string object only.
- They internally convert all values, whatever be their types, to strings, merge them together to a single string object, and then print on the standard output `System.out`.

- The `print()` method *only* works with argument, otherwise it gives a syntax error.
- Don't use `System.out.write()` at all. It is not intended for writing things to the terminal, but for special handling of streams of bytes with other targets. The following code may not be fruitful if you try to print on the monitor.

```
public class OutWrite {
    public static void main(String[] args) {
      char c = 'X';
       System.out.write(c); // Only this may not work
      /*Trying to print X on monitor you should
      uncomment the following. */
      // System.out.write('\n');
    }
}
```

Finally, let us come to the illustration of messaging error as a standard in a Java program. Program 8.4 is an example to understand where and how to use `System.err`.

Program 8.4 *(Demonstration of `System.err`)*

```
/* The following program demonstrates the use of
System.err in a program. */

class StandardErrorDemo {
    public static void main(String[] args) {
        Thread threadInfo = new Thread();
          // Information about a thread
        String aString = "Joy with Java";
```

```
        char[] charArray = { 'a', 'b', 'c' };
        int a = 5;
        int b = 0;

        try {
            double c = a/b;
            System.out.println("Your result is: " + c);
        } catch (Exception e){
            System.err.println("Arithmetic axcpetion
                occurs...");
            e.printStackTrace();
        }
    }
}
```

A question may arise if there is any difference between `System.out` and `System.err`. There is no difference practically, particularly in the context of Java programming.

Note that both `System.out` and `System.err` are `PrintStream` objects. `System.out` essentally outputs the data which you write to the console. This is often used from console-only programs like command line tools. This is also frequently used to print debug statements of a program. On the other hand, `System.err` works like `System.out` except it is normally only used to output error texts. Some programs (like Eclipse) will show the output to `System.err` in red text, to make it more emphasize that it is an error text. In fact, `System.err` and `System.out` both are the same.

8.2.2 Types of Streams

Byte streams

A stream can be used broadly in two ways: *Byte streams* and *Character streams*. Byte streams considers data in binary representation. Programs use byte streams to perform input and output of 8-bit bytes as illustrated in Figure 8.6(a). For example, when you read (write) data to (from) a byte stream, the data is read (written) from (to) the stream as a series of bytes, exactly as it appears in memory. Binary numerical values are just written as a series of bytes, 4 bytes for each value of type `int`, 8 bytes for each value of type long, 8 bytes for each value of type `double`, and so on.

Character streams

Character streams read data in the form of characters as a unit, as shown in Figure 8.6(b). Java stores its characters internally as Unicode characters (discussed in Chapter 2), which are 16-bit characters. Note that each Unicode character is written to a binary stream as 2 bytes, the higher byte being written first.

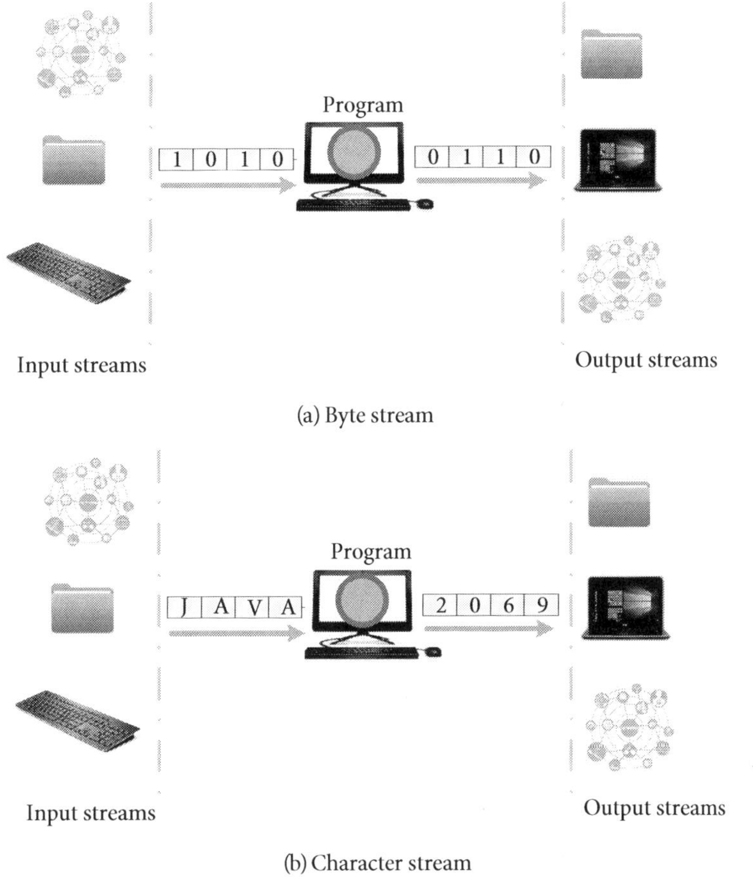

Figure 8.6 Java IO streams

Byte Stream versus Character Streams

Byte stream:

1. No transformation of the data takes place.
2. It is usually faster than its counterpart.

Character stream:

1. It provides a convenient means for handling input and output of characters. It uses Unicode and, therefore, compatible with international standards.
2. Character stream enables platform independency.
3. You may read numeric data as characters. For this, all numeric data has to be converted to a textual representation before being written to a character stream and vice-versa. This involves generating a character representation of the original binary data value.

4. Reading numeric data from a stream that contains text involves much more work than reading binary data. When you read a value of type `int` from a binary stream, you know that it consists of 4 bytes. When you read an integer from a character stream, you have to determine how many characters from the stream make up the value. For each numerical value you read from a character stream, you have to be able to recognize where the value begins and ends and then convert the token, that is, the sequence of characters that represents the value to its binary form.

- Byte streams are used, for example, when reading or writing binary data. Character streams are used for storing and retrieving text.
- The original version of Java (Java 1.0) did not include character streams and, thus, initially all IO was byte-oriented.
- Character streams were added in Java 1.1, and certain byte-oriented classes and methods were deprecated.
- At the lowest level, all IO is still byte-oriented. The character-based streams simply provide a convenient and efficient means for handling characters.

There are many classes defined in `java.io` package to supports the two types of streams. They form a reasonably logical structure which is shown in Figure 8.7. In the following subsections, all these logical entities are discussed in a top-down manner.

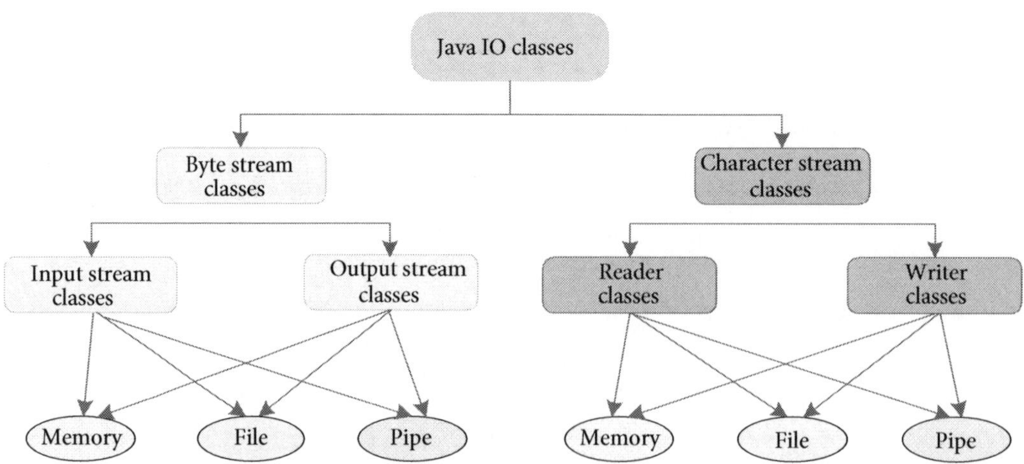

Figure 8.7 `java.io` classes for handling streams

8.2.3 IO with Byte Streams

In `java.io`, byte streams are defined by using two class hierarchies: `InputStream` and `OutputStream`. `InputStream` is the abstract base class for byte stream input operations whereas `OutputStream` is the abstract base class for byte stream output operations. Each of these abstract classes has several sub classes to manage various input/output sources, such as disk files, network connections, memory buffers, etc.

Input Stream Classes

The sub classes of `InputStream` class are shown in Figure 8.8. A brief description of each of the sub class is given in Table 8.4.

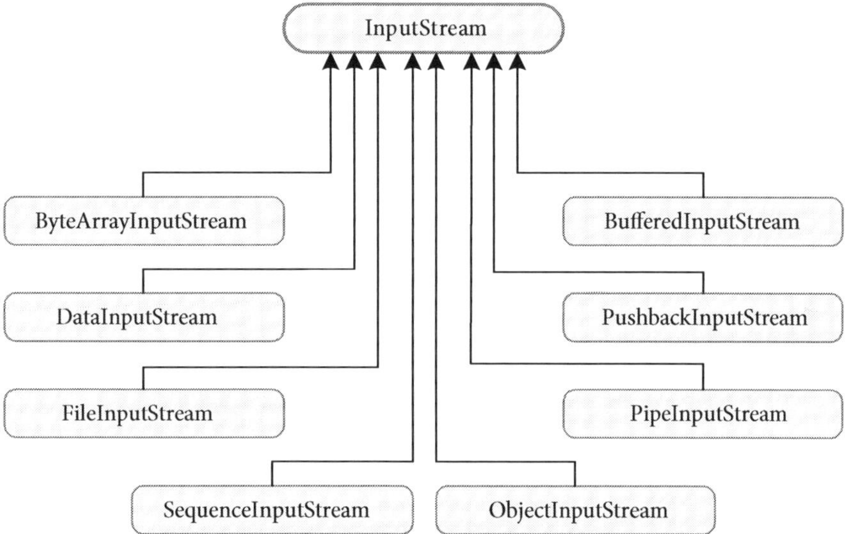

Figure 8.8 Hierarchy of input stream related classes

The `InputStream` class defines a programming interface for reading bytes or arrays of bytes, marking locations in the stream, skipping bytes of input, finding out the number of bytes that are available for reading, and resetting the current position within the stream.

The abstract class `InputStream` defines Java's model of streaming byte input. It implements the `AutoCloseable` and `Closeable` interfaces. All sub classes which extend the `InputStream` class implement many methods for managing input streams. All methods are in polymorphic forms (i.e., have same name but different functionalities). Most of the methods in this class will throw an `IOException` when an IO error occurs. Table 8.5 shows the methods in `InputStream` which are defined in its sub classes.

Table 8.4 `InputStream` sub classes

InputStream sub class	Description
`Buffered InputStream`	Reading a chunk of bytes from an internal buffer associated with a stream. This enables a `FilterInputStream` instance to make use of a buffer for input data.
`ByteArrayInputStream`	Input stream that reads from a byte array. An instance of this class contains an internal buffer to read bytes stream from an array of bytes.
`DataInputStream`	An input stream that contains methods for reading the Java standard data types. An instance of this class enables reading primitive Java data types from an underlying input stream in a machine-independent manner.
`FileInputStream`	Input stream that reads from a file. An instance of this class is used to obtain input bytes from a file in a file system.
`FilterInputStream`	For filtering input from an existing stream. An instance of this class contains some other input stream as a basic source of data for further manipulation.
`ObjectInputStream`	For reading objects from a stream. An instance of this class is used to deserialize an object after it has been serialized by `ObjectOutputStream`.
`PipedInputStream`	For reading from a piped stream like a network socket or port. An instance of this class provides a pipe or buffer for an input byte that works in the FIFO manner.
`PushbackInputStream`	Input stream that supports one-byte "unget," which returns a byte to the input stream. This provides the ability to push back, or "unread," a data byte after reading it.
`SequenceInputStream`	Input stream that is a combination of two or more input streams that will be read sequentially, one after the other. An instance of this class represents a logical concatenation of two or more input streams which are read in sequence, one after another.

An input stream is automatically opened when you create it. You can explicitly close a stream with the `close()` method, or let it be closed implicitly when the object is garbage-collected.

Output Stream Classes

The sub classes of `OutputStream` class are shown in Figure 8.9. A brief description of each of the sub class is given in Table 8.6.

Table 8.5 Methods in `InputStream` sub classes

Method	Description
`int available()`	Returns the number of bytes of input currently available for reading.
`void close()`	Closes the input source. Further read attempts will generate an `IOException`.
`void mark(int numBytes)`	Places a mark at the current point in the input stream that will remain valid until *`numBytes`* bytes are read.
`boolean markSupported()`	Returns true if `mark()` / `reset()` are supported by the invoking stream.
`int read()`	Returns an integer representation of the next available byte of input. –1 is returned when the end of the file is encountered.
`int read(byte buffer[ ])`	Attempts to read up to *`buffer.length`* bytes into *`buffer`* and returns the actual number of bytes that were successfully read. –1 is returned when the end of the file is encountered.
`int read(byte buffer[ ], int offset, int numBytes)`	Attempts to read up to *`numBytes`* bytes into *`buffer`* starting at *`buffer[offset]`*, returning the number of bytes successfully read. –1 is returned when the end of the file is encountered.
`void reset()`	Resets the input pointer to the previously set mark.
`long skip(long numBytes)`	Ignores (or, skips) *`numBytes`* bytes of input, returning the number of bytes actually ignored.

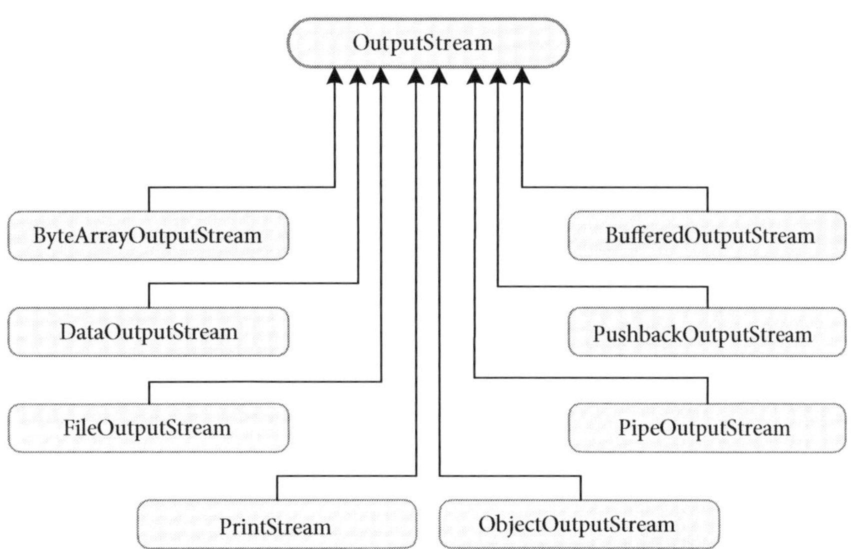

Figure 8.9 Hierarchy of output stream related classes

Table 8.6 Output stream sub classes

OutputStream sub class	Description
`BufferedOutputStream`	Writing a chunk of bytes to an internal buffer associated with a stream. This enables a `FilterOutputStream` instance to make use of a buffer for output data.
`ByteArrayOutputStream`	Output stream that writes to a byte array. An instance of this class contains an internal buffer to write a byte stream.
`DataOutputStream`	An output stream that contains methods for writing the standard Java data types. An instance of this class enables writing primitive Java data types to an underlying output stream in a machine-independent manner.
`FileOutputStream`	Output stream that writes to a file. An instance of this class is used to output a stream for writing data to a file or to a file descriptor.
`FilterOutputStream`	For filtering output to an existing stream. An instance of this class contains some other output stream as a basic source of data for further manipulation.
`ObjectOutputStream`	For writing objects to a stream. An instance of this class is used to serialize an object which can be deserialized with `ObjectInputStream`.
`PipedOutputStream`	For writing to a piped stream like a network socket or port. An instance of this class provides a pipe or buffer for output byte that works in the FIFO manner.
`PushbackOutputStream`	Output stream that supports one-byte "unget," which returns a byte to the output stream.
`SequenceOutputStream`	Output stream that is a combination of two or more output streams that will be written sequentially, one after the other.
`PrintStream`	This empowers the `OutputStream` objects with the ability to print representations of various data values conveniently.

The `OutputStream` class is a sibling to `InputStream` and is used to write data that can then be read by an input stream. The `OutputStream` class defines a programming interface for writing bytes or arrays of bytes to the stream and flushing the stream. Like `InputStream` class and its sub classes, the `OutputStream` class declares several methods which are finally polymorphically defined in their sub classes. The methods which are of importance to manage an output stream are listed in Table 8.7.

Table 8.7 The methods declared by `OutputStream` class

Method	Description
`void close()`	Closes the output stream. Further write attempts will generate an `IOException`.
`void flush()`	Finalizes the output state so that any buffers are cleared. It flushes the output buffers.
`void write(int b)`	Writes a single byte to an output stream. Note that the parameter is an int, which allows you to call `write()` with an expression without having to cast it back to byte.
`void write(byte buffer[ ])`	Writes a complete array of bytes to an output stream.
`void write(byte buffer[ ], int offset, int numBytes)`	Writes a subrange of `numBytes` bytes from the array *`buffer`*, beginning at *`buffer`*`[offset]`.

Like an input stream, an output stream is automatically opened when you create it. You can explicitly close an output stream with the `close()` method, or let it be closed implicitly when the object is garbage collected.

IO programming with byte stream classes

We have learned a little of byte stream classes (Tables 8.4 and 8.6), the methods for input from input streams (Table 8.5), and output to output streams (Table 8.6). In this subsection, we shall discuss and illustrate the following byte stream classes:

I. Byte array streams
II. Buffered byte streams
III. File byte streams
IV. Data streams
V. Print stream
VI. Sequence input stream

To use the streams in your program, you have to create objects of a particular stream. Figure 8.10 illustrates the IO programming concept. For each stream type, there are constructors to create objects. Our objective will be to understand how IO byte stream objects can be created and then how input–output operations can be performed. Note that in the same program, you can create any input stream of any number of times and any output stream of any number of times.

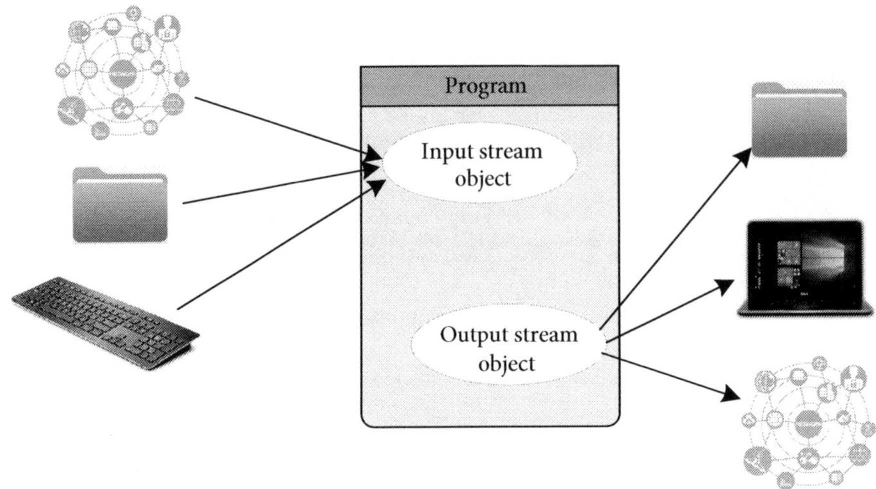

Figure 8.10 IO programming with byte streams

Byte array streams

If you want to read data from an array or write data into an array (to be maintained in memory), you can consider the byte array streams. Two byte array streams: `ByteArrayInputStream` (it is *ByteArray* and *InputStream*) for reading bytes and `ByteArrayOutputStream` (it is *ByteArray* and *OutputStream*) for writing bytes.

`ByteArrayInputStream` class

The `ByteArrayInputStream` class has the following two constructors, each of which requires a byte array to provide the data source:

```
ByteArrayInputStream(byte array [ ])
ByteArrayInputStream(byte array [ ], int start, int len)
```

The first constructor creates a byte array input stream object starting with the array as input source. This array should be of type `byte`. The second constructor creates an input stream object from a subset of the byte array that begins with the character at the index specified by `start` and is `len` long.

Program 8.5 illustrates how a byte array input stream object can be created in a program.

Program 8.5 (Input streams as byte arrays)

```
/* This program illustrates how input streams as arrays
of type byte can be created and the elements in the
array can be read. */

import java.io.*;

public class ByteArrayInputStreamDemo {
  public static void main(String[] args) throws
IOException{
    // Two arrays of data
    byte[] byteArray1 = {11, 22, 33, 44, 55, 66, 77,
          88, 99};
    String s = "Joy with Java";
    byte [] byteArray2 = s.getBytes();
          // Convert data into bytes

    // Create the new byte array input stream with
                                          // byteArray1
    ByteArrayInputStream bin1 = new ByteArrayInput
          Stream(byteArray1);

    // Read data from the input stream
    int k;
    while ((k = bin1.read()) != -1) {
          // Read from the input stream
        //Conversion of a byte into character
        char c = (char) k;
        System.out.println("ASCII of " + k + ": " + c);
    }

    // Create an input streams from byteArray2
    ByteArrayInputStream bin2 = new ByteArrayInput
          Stream(byteArray2);

    // Read data from the input stream bin2
    int c;
    while ((c = bin2.read()) != -1)
        System.out.print(Character.toUpperCase((char) c));

    // Create another input streams from byteArray2
    ByteArrayInputStream bin3=new ByteArrayInputStream
      (byteArray2,0,3);

   bin1.close();    // Closing the input stream
 }
}
```

- The `ByteArrayInputStream` class contains an internal buffer which is used to read byte array as stream.
- The buffer of `ByteArrayInputStream` automatically grows according to data.
- There is no `IOException` in case of `ByteArrayInput Stream` class methods.
- The `close()` method has no effect on a `ByteArrayInputStream`. It is not necessary to call `close()` on a `ByteArrayInputStream`, but doing so is not an error.
- Methods of this class can be called even after closing the stream.

The `ByteArrayInputStream` class inherits all the methods declared in `InputStream` abstract class and implements them. Some of the methods defined for this stream are shown in Program 8.6.

Program 8.6 *(Operations with byte array input stream)*

```
/* This program illustrates the usages of
ByteArrayInputStream methods mark(), read(), skip(),
available() markSupported(), close(), reset() */

import java.io.*;

public class ByteArrayInputStreamMethodDemo{
    public static void main(String[] args) {
        byte[] buffer = {111, 222, 333, 444, 555};

        try {
            ByteArrayInputStream bis =
                new ByteArrayInputStream(buffer);

            // Use of available() method:  Number of
                                // bytes in the input stream
            int number = bis.available();
            System.out.println("Number of bytes
                availabe: " + number);

            // Use of read() method: Read bytes-by-bytes
            int k;
            while ((k = bis.read()) != -1)
                // Read from the input stream
                    System.out.print("Input " + k);
            System.out.println();

            // Use of mark(): Go to 0-th position of
                the stream buffer bis.mark(0);
```

```
            // Use of skip(): It results in skipping
                                                // two bytes
            bis.skip(2);
             // Throws exception if not within the range
            System.out.println("Byte : "+bis.read());
          // Reading 3rd bytes

            // Use of markSupported
            boolean check = bis.markSupported();
            if(check) {
                // Use of reset() method: Repositioning
                                    // to a marked position.
                bis.reset();
                     // Reset to previously set mark
                         // position, i.e., 0th
                System.out.println("Byte : "+bis.read());
            }
            else
                System.out.println("This stream does
                     not support mark resetting");
        }
        catch(Exception e) {
            System.out.println(e);
        }
        finally {
                try{bis.close();}
                catch(IOException e)
                {
                  System.out.print("Error in closing");
                }
        }
    }
}
```

ByteArrayOutputStream class

The `ByteArrayOutputStream` is just the opposite direction of data flow, that is, from a program to an output stream. This class has two constructors as follows:

```
ByteArrayOutputStream()
ByteArrayOutputStream(int size)
```

In the first form, a buffer of 32 bytes is created. In the second, a buffer is created with a size equal to that specified by `size`. The buffer is held in the protected `buf` field of `ByteArrayOutputStream`. The buffer size will get increased automatically, if needed. The number of bytes held by the buffer is contained in the protected `count` field of `ByteArrayOutputStream`. Program 8.7 illustrates how to create output stream in a Java program.

Program 8.7 *(Output stream as byte array)*

```
/* This program illustrates the utility of Byte array
output stream.*/

import java.io.*;

public class ByteArrayOutputStreamDemo {
   public static void main(String args[])throws
      IOException {
         // Creating an output stream of size 12 bytes
         ByteArrayOutputStream bos = new ByteArrayOutput
            Stream(12);

         String s = "Joy with Java!";
         byte b[] = s.getBytes();
         try {
              bos.write(b);
             // Write the array of bytes to output stream
         } catch(IOException e) {
              System.out.println("Error Writing to
                 output stream");
              return;
         }

         // Exercising some methods of
                              // ByteArrayOutputSteam class

         // Write few more into the stream
          bos.write("\n I love Java".getBytes());

          b = bos.toByteArray();
            // Convert stream to byte array
          System.out.println("Print the content");
          for (int i=0; i<b.length; i++)
              System.out.print((char) b[i]);
          System.out.println("    ");
```

```
            // Creating an Byte array input stream
            ByteArrayInputStream bis = new ByteArrayInput
              Stream(b);

            System.out.println("Printing text with upper
              case letters...");
            int c = 0;
            while(( c = bis.read())!= -1) {
               System.out.println(Character.toUpperCase
                   ((char)c));
            }
            bis.reset(); bos.close(); bis.close();
      }
}
```

- The `close()` method has no effect on a `ByteArrayOutputStream`. It automatically closes a `ByteArrayOutputStream`.
- You can write into the stream with three different forms of `write()` as mentioned in Table 8.7.
- There are some other methods explicit to the `ByteArrayOutputStream` class such as `size()`, `reset()`, and `toString()` that can be called for this type of stream.

Buffered byte streams

Another byte-oriented streams in `java.io` is called *buffered byte stream* where a memory buffer is attached to the IO stream. This buffer allows the programmer to perform IO operations on more than a byte at a time, thereby improving performance. There are three buffered byte stream classes known in `java.io`:

```
BufferedInputStream
BufferedOutputStream
PushbackInputStream
```

The three buffered byte stream classes are discussed in the following subsections.

`BufferedInputStream` class

The `BufferedInputStream` class provides reading of chunks of bytes and buffering for an `InputStream` or any of its sub classes. Reading larger chunks of bytes and buffering them can speed up IO quite a lot. When you read a byte from the `BufferedInputStream`, you are actually reading it from its internal buffer. When the buffer is fully read, the `BufferedInputStream` reads another larger block of data into the buffer. This is typically much faster than reading a single byte at a time, especially for disk access and larger data quantities.

The `BufferedInputStream` is defined with the fields (each of with `protected` access specifier) shown in Table 8.8.

Table 8.8 Fields defined by `BufferedArrayInputSream` class

Field	Description
`byte[] buf`	This is the internal buffer array where the data is stored.
`int count`	This is the index, one greater than the index of the last valid byte in the buffer.
`int marklimit`	This is the maximum read ahead allowed after a call to the mark method before subsequent calls to the reset method fail.
`int markpos`	This is the value of the `pos` field at the time the last mark method was called.
`int pos`	This is the current position in the buffer.
`InputStream in`	This is the input stream to be read from.

The `BufferedInputStream` class defines the following two constructors:

`BufferedInputStream(InputStream` *in*`)`: This constructor creates a buffered stream using a default buffer size of 8192 bytes; however, this varies from one system to other. It is, actually, the average size of block to be read from the input device.

`BufferedInputStream(InputStream` *in*`, int` *bufSize*`)`: This is the same as the previous one, with a difference that the size of the buffer is passed in *bufSize*. You should set this value as a multiple of a memory page, a disk block, and so on. Thus this is a system dependent parameter decided by the host operating system, the amount of memory available, and how the machine is configured. Attaching a small buffer to an IO stream is always a good idea.

All methods declared in `InputStream` class (Table 8.5) are defined in the `BufferedInputStream` class. Program 8.8 is a simple illustration showing the uses of `BufferedInputStream` class and some of the methods in it.

Program 8.8 *(Illustration of buffered input byte stream)*

```
/* This program demonstrates the working of
BufferedInputStream class in a program. */
import java.io.*;

class BufferedInputStreamDemo {
    public static void main(String args[]) throws
     IOException {
        // Creating an input stream for this program
         String txt = "The first line of the text\n" +
                      "You can add another lie\n" +
                      "This is the last line in the
                         file.";
         Byte b[] = txt.getBytes();
           // Store the text as a byte array
         // Creating input stream
         ByteArrayInputStream in = new ByteArrayInput
           Stream(b);

         // Creating buffered input stream
         BufferedInputStream bin = new BufferedInput
           Stream(in);

         // Illustrating available method
         System.out.println("Number of bytes:"
           + bin.available());

        // Illustrating markSupported() and mark()
          method
        boolean b=bin.markSupported();
        if (b)
            bin.mark(bin.available());

        // Illustrating skip method
        bin.skip(4);
        System.out.println("Contents after skipping:");

        // Reading the input: use of read()
         int c = 0;
         while ((c = bin.read()) != -1) System.
           outprintln(c);

        // Illustrating reset() method
        bin.reset();
        while ((c=bin.read()) != -1)
            System.out.print((char)c);

        bin.close();  // close the file
    }
}
```

- When the bytes from the stream are skipped or read, the internal buffer automatically gets refilled from the contained input stream, many bytes at a time.
- When a `BufferedInputStream` is created, an internal buffer array is created automatically.
- You can repeat the program reading a large file stored in disk, say, *c:\abc.txt*, just replacing the highlighted part of the code with the following code:

```
FileInputStream in = new FileInputStream("c:\abc.tx");
```

We shall discuss about `FileInputStream` class later in this chapter.

- Buffering an input stream also provides moving backward in the stream of the available buffer. For this you have to use `skip()`, `mark()`, and `reset()` methods in a calibrated manner.
- The `BufferedInputStream` is mark-supported.

BufferedOutputStream class

The `BufferedOutputStream` class is used to capture bytes written to the `BufferedOutputStream` buffer and write the whole buffer in one batch to an underlying output stream. Unlike other output byte stream class, with the `BufferedOutputStream` class, the `flush()` method is used to ensure that data buffers are written to the stream being buffered. Since the point of a `BufferedOutputStream` is to improve performance by reducing the number of times the system actually writes data, you may need to call `flush()` to cause any data in the buffer to be immediately written.

For this class, the following two fields are defined in it:

`byte[] buf`: This is the internal buffer where data is stored.
`int count`: This is the number of valid bytes in the buffer.
`OutputStream out`: This is the underlying output stream to be filtered.

This class includes the following two constructors.
`BufferedOutputStream(OutputStream out)`: This creates a new buffered output stream to write data to the specified underlying output stream.

`BufferedOutputStream(OutputStream out, int size)`: This creates a new buffered output stream to write data to the specified underlying output stream with the specified buffer `size`.

All methods in `OutputStream` (Table 8.7) class are applicable to this class. Let's consider Program 8.9 illustrating the use of `BufferedOutputStream` class in the program.

Program 8.9 *(Illustration of buffered output byte stream)*

```
/* This program demonstrates the application of
BufferedOutputStream class. */

import java.io.*;

class BufferedOutputStreamDemo {
    public static void main(String args[])throws
     Exception {
        ByteArrayOutputStream out = new ByteArrayOutput
          Stream(b);

        //Creating BufferdOutputStream connecting to "out"
        BufferedOutputStream bos new BufferedOutput
          Stream(out);

        // Creating a byte array and Output stream
        // Writing into buffer
        byte[] b = {1, 2, 3, 4, 5, 6, 7, 8, 9);
          // A byte array
        bos.write(b);
          // Write this into the buffer of "bos"


     byte[] c={ 11, 22, 33, 44, 55, 66, 77, 88, 99 };
          // Another byte array
        bos.write(c);
          // Add this into the buffer of "bos"

        //illustrating flush() method
        bos.flush();  //Flushes the data from bos
          buffer to stream out.
        // Finally close the streams
        out.close();
        bos.close();
    }
}
```

- Note how a buffered output stream (`bos`) connects to an output stream (`out`) in Program 8.9. In this program, you have used byte array output stream as the output stream. Instead, you can use some other stream, for example a file, as a destination stream.
- When you write data to a `BufferedOutputStream`, the data is cached internally in a byte buffer until the byte buffer is full, at which time the whole buffer is written to the underlying output stream.

- If you want to make sure that all the written data is written to the destination stream without having to close the `BufferedOutputStream`, you can call its `flush()` method. Calling `flush()` will make sure that all data which has been written to the `BufferedOutputStream` so far is fully written to the underlying output stream.

`PushbackInputStream` class

The `PushbackInputStream` is used on an input stream to allow a byte to be read and then returned (that is, *pushed back*) to the stream. It provides a mechanism to peek ahead a few bytes to see what is coming, before you can determine how to interpret the current byte. Thus, it allows you to push the read bytes back into the stream. These bytes will then be read again the next time you call `read()`.

The following are the fields defined by the `PushbackInput Stream` class:

`byte[] buf`: This is the pushback buffer.
`int pos`: This is the position within the pushback buffer from which the next byte will be read.
`InputStream in`: This is the input stream to be filtered.

`PushbackInputStream` has the following two constructors.

`PushbackInputStream(InputStream in)`: This constructor creates a stream object that allows one byte to be returned to the input stream.
`PushbackInputStream(InputStream in, int len)`: This constructor creates a stream that has a pushback buffer of size *`len`*. This allows multiple bytes to be returned to the input stream.

Beyond the familiar methods of `InputStream`, `PushbackInput Stream` provides methods for pushback, that is, unread. The three methods for this purpose are as follows:

`void unread(int b)`: This method pushes back the low-order byte of `b`. This will be the next byte returned by a subsequent call to `read()`.
`void unread(byte b [])`: This method pushes back the bytes in `b`.
`void unread(byte b[], int offset, int n)`: This method pushes back `n` bytes beginning at `offset` from the buffer `b`.

In all these cases, an IOException will be thrown if there is an attempt to push back a byte when the pushback buffer is full.

Program 8.10 illustrates an application of PushbackInputStream class in a Java program. This program stores the string Joy with Java in an input byte stream buffer, it scans the buffer, when it reads J it will pushback (unread) J and print the remaining string in the buffer.

Program 8.10 *(Illustration of pushback input stream)*

```
/* This program shows an application of PushbackInput
Stream class. */

import java.io.*;

public class PushbackInputStreamDemo {
    public static void main(String[] args)throws
      Exception{
        // Creating a byte array buffered input stream
        String s = "Joy with Java";
        byte b[] = s.getBytes();
        ByteArrayInputStream in = new ByteArrayInput
            Stream(b);

        // Create pushback buffered input stream
        PushbackInputStream pis = new PushbackInput
            Stream(in);

        //  Start scanning the buffer of pis
        int i;
            // Read character to be stored temporarily
        while((i = pis.read())!=-1) {
            //Continue until we reach to the end
           if(i == 'J') {
                System.out.println((char)i);
                  // Print "J" on a line
                pis.unread((char)i);
                  // Pushback the byte into buffer "buf"
                int n = pis.available();
                  // Number of bytes remaining
                // Get the remaining buffer and print on
                                           // the screen
                byte t = new byte[n];
                  // A temporary array of size n
                // Read the buf starting from pos to
                                  // bytes remaining to read
```

```
                if (pis.read() != -1) {
                    System.out.print(new String(t));
                       // Printing bytes t
                    pis.unread(t);  // Unread the block
                }
            }
        }
    }
}
```

- The program would give the following output on the screen:

```
J
Joy with Java
J
Java
```

- On the call of a `read()` operation, it automatically moves to next location to be read.
- `PushbackInputStream` does not support `mark()`/ `reset()` on the input stream.

Byte streams for files

File is treated as one of the most frequently used IO of data. Regarding the file IO, we shall discuss in details later in this chapter. In this section, we shall discuss how a file can be used as a byte stream of raw data such as image, text, audio, video, etc., for input and output, that is, reading/writing as bytes. For IO from files as byte streams, Java defines the following two classes in `java.io` package:

`FileInputStream` (as input stream)
`FileOutputStream` (as output stream)

Let us discuss the composition and working of these two classes.

`FileInputStream` class

The `FileInputStream` class is used to read the contents of a file as a stream of bytes. The class is a sub class of `InputStream`, that is, `FileInputStream` behaves like an `InputStream`. This class defines three constructors, which are listed in Table 8.9.

Table 8.9 Constructors in `FileInputSream` class

Constructor	Description
`FileInputStream(File file)`	Creates a `FileInputStream` object by opening a connection to an actual file by using specified `file` object.
`FileInputStream(File Descriptor fdObj)`	Creates a `FileInputStream` object by using the specified file descriptor `fdObj`, which represents an existing connection to an actual file in the file system.
`FileInputStream(String name)`	Creates a `FileInputStream` object by opening a connection to an actual file named by the specified `name` which represents the path of the file.

The first and third constructors are the most commonly used constructors. All constructors throw a `FileNotFoundException` when they face errors while opening a file. A file can be defined as an object of the class `File`, which we shall discuss later. Following are some examples to understand how to call the constructors:

```
// Declares a name of a file with its path
String fName = "D:/data/abc.txt";

// Create a file object using File
File f1 = new File("D:/data/abc.txt");

// Create a FileInputStream object (using first constructor)
FileInputStteam fis1 = new FileInputStteam(f1);

// Create a FileInputStream object using third constructor)
FileInputStream fis2 = new FileInputStteam(fname);
```

`FileInputStream` is a sub class of the abstract class `InputsStream`, hence all methods declared in `InputStream` class (Table 8.5) are fully defined by `FileInputStream` class. The following additional methods are defined by the `FileInputStteam` class.

`FileChannel getChannel()`: It is used to return the unique `FileChannel` object associated with the file input stream.

`FileDescriptor getFD()`: It returns the `FileDescriptor` object that represents the connection to the actual file in the file system being used by this input stream.

`protected void finalize()`: It is used to ensure that the `close` method is called when there is no more reference to the file input stream.

- `FileInputStream` overrides six of the methods in the abstract class `InputStream` so that the methods can read data in the form of bytes from a file object as input stream.
- The `mark()` and `reset()` methods are not overridden, and any attempt to use `reset()` on a `FileInputStream` object will generate an `IOException`.

Program 8.11 illustrates the use of `FileInputStream` class and the methods used for it. The program shows how to read a single byte, an array of bytes, and a subrange of an array of bytes from a file as input stream. It also illustrates how to use some methods defined in the class `FileInputStream`.

Program 8.11 *(Illustration of file input stream)*

```
/* This program assumes the existence of a file titled
FileInputStreamDemo.java, which is in the current
working directory. */

import java.io.*;

class FileInputStreamDemo
    public static void main(String args[]) throws
      IOException{
            //Creating  file byte input stream
            String fName = "FileInputStreamDemo.java";
            FileInputStream fin = new FileInput
                 Stream(fName);
        try {
            //Illustrating available method
            int size = fin.available();
            System.out.println("File size(in bytes):"+
                 size);

            //Illustrating getChannel() method
            System.out.println("Channel: " + fin.
                 getChannel());

            //Illustrating getFD() method
            System.out.println("File Descriptor: " +
                 fin.getFD());
            //Reading first 40% of the file content and
                                           // display on screen
            int n = (int) 0.4 * size;
            System.out.println("Reading first " + n + "
                 bytes.");
```

```
            for (int i=0; i < n; i++) {
               System.out.print((char) fin.read());
            }

            // Reporting the remaining bytes to read
            size = fin.available();
            n = 0.5* size;
                 // Consider the 50% of the remaining
            byte b[] = new byte[n];

            if (f.read(b) != n)
                System.err.println("Error #1!");
            else
                System.out.println(new String(b, 0,
                       n));//Print the chunk

            // Illustrating the skip() method
             size = fin.available();
             System.out.println("Skipping half of
                 remaining bytes...");
             fin.skip(size/2);
             System.out.println("Bytes after skipping:" +
                 fin.available());

             System.out.println("Reading " + n/2 +
                 "bytes into array");
             if (fin.read(b, n/2, n/2) != n/2)
                  System.err.println("Error #2!");
             else
                 System.out.println(new String
                        (b, 0, b.length)); // Print
         } catch(IOException e) {
              System.out.println("I/O Exception: " + e);
         }
         finally {
                try{fin.close();}
                 // Close the input stream
                catch(IOException e){}
         }
     }
}
```

- On reading from an input stream buffer, the buffer automatically moves to the next byte to be read and the `availability()` method updates the number of unread bytes in the buffer.
- The `finalize()` method ensures that the `close()` method of this file input stream is called when there are no more references to it.
- Java provides `TryWithResource` which is a `try` statement that declares one or more resource. A resource is an object that must be closed after the program is finished with it. For example, in Program 8.11, such a resource is `FileInputStreamDemo.java`. The `TryWithResource` statement ensures that each resource is closed automatically at the end of the statement. Program 8.12 demonstrates the use of `TryWithResource` when you work with a file input stream.

Program 8.12 *(Input stream with* `TryWith Resource`*)*

```
/* This program demonstrates the use of file input
stream with try-with resource(s) construct of exception
handling. */
import java.io.FileInputStream;
class TryWithResourceDemo {
  public static void main(String args[]){
       try (FileInputStream fin=new FileInputStream
           ("test.txt");{
            int i=fin.read();
            System.out.print((char)i);
       } catch(Exception e){
            System.out.println(e);}
       }
  }
}
```

FileDescriptor

`FileInputStream getFD()` returns the `FileDescriptor` object that represents the connection to the actual file in the file system being used by this `FileInputStream`. Program 8.13 illustrates the use of `getFD()` in the context of `FileInputStream` object.

Program 8.13 *(Illustration of* `getFD()`*)*

```
/* This program illustrates the use of getFD()in a
program. */

import java.io.File;
import java.io.FileDescriptor;
import java.io.FileInputStream;
```

```
class FileDescripterDemo {
    public static void main(String[] args) {
        File file = new File("D:/data/test.txt");
        try {
            FileInputStream fis = new FileInputStream
                (file);
            FileDescriptor fd = fis.getFD();
            boolean valid = fd.valid();
            System.out.println("Validity of the
                connection: " + valid);
        } catch (Exception e) {
                e.printStackTrace();
        }
    }
}
```

`FileOutputStream` class

The `FileOutputStream` class is an output byte stream for writing data to an object of type `File` or to a `FileDescriptor`. The following are the important points about the `FileOutputStream` class:

- The class is meant for writing bytes to file object.
- It is a good way to write binary files that cannot be represented as text, such as image, PDFs, etc.

This class defines the following constructors:

`FileOutputStream(File fObj)`
This creates a file output stream to write to the file represented by the specified `File` object `fObj`:

`FileOutputStream(File fObj, boolean append)`
This creates a file output stream to write to the file represented by the specified `File` object `fObj`. If the second argument is true, then bytes will be written to the end of the file rather than the beginning.

`FileOutputStream(String fName)`
This creates an output file stream to write to the file with the specified name `fName`.

`FileOutputStream(String fName, boolean append)`
This creates an output file stream to write to the file with the specified name. If the second argument is true, then bytes will be written to the end of the file rather than the beginning.

`FileOutputStream(FileDescriptor fdObj)`
This creates an output file stream to write to the specified file descriptor, which represents an existing connection to an actual file in the file system.

If the file exists, but is a directory rather than a regular file, or does not exist, cannot be created, or cannot be opened for any other reason, then all the constructors throw `FileNotFoundException` object.

Program 8.14 illustrates the use of `FileOutputStream` class in a program.

Program 8.14 *(Illustration of file output streams)*

```
/* This program demonstrates how a set of number and
strings can be written to files. */

import java.io.File;
import java.io.FileOutputSteam;

class FileOutputStreamDemo {
  public static void main(String args[]){
     String s = "Joy with Java!";
     byte b [] = s.getBytes();

     // Specify the files for output streams
     File f1 = new File("D:\\test1.txt");
     File f2 = new File("test2.txt");
     boolean append = true;
     // Create file output steam object using try-
                                         // with-resources
     Try {
         FileOutputStream fos1 = new FileOutputStream
           (f1);
         FileOutputStream fos2 = new FileOutputStream
           (f2,append);
         FileOutputStream fos3 = new FileOutputStream
           ("test3.txt");){

         // Writing the strings into f1 and f2...
         for (int i=0; i < b.length; i += 2) fos1.
          write(b[i]);
         fos2.write(b); // Write the entire byte array
```

```
            // Writing numbers into f2 and f3...
            for(int i = 0; i < b.length; i++) {
                fos2.write(i);    // Append the numbers
                fos3.write(b[i]);
            }
            fos1.flush(); fos2.flush(); fos3.flush();
        } catch(Exception e){System.out.println
            ("File Error:\n" + e);}
    }
}
```

`FileInputStream getFD()` returns the `FileDescriptor` object that represents the connection to the actual file in the file system being used by this `FileInputStream`.

Data streams

Java supports reading/writing primitive data such as `int`, `long`, `double`, etc. as streams of bytes. This means you can write primitive data as your program declares and store them in bytes form. This is particularly useful to deal with primitive data in a machine-independent way. Java defines following two classes for wrapping data into bytes:

`class DataInputStream`: Allows an application to *read* primitive data from an input stream.

`class DataOutputStream`: Allows an application to *write* primitive data to an output stream.

`DataInputStream` class

`DataInputStream` class extends `FilterInputStream`, which extends `InputStream` (Figure 8.2). In addition to implementing the `DataInput` interface, `DataInputStream` also implements `AutoCloseable` and `Closeable` interfaces.

To create a `DataInputStream` instance, you can use the following constructors, which is the only constructor defined by the class:

`DataInputStream (InputStream in)`: Here, `InputStream in` as parameter is the input stream from which the primitive data types are to be read.

It has the methods listed in Table 8.10 in addition to all methods defined by `InputStream` class (Table 8.5). All these additional methods are to read Java primitive data. All methods throw `IOException` object when an error in reading occurs.

Table 8.10 Additional methods defined by `DataInputStream` class

Methods	Description
`boolean readBoolean()`	This method reads one input byte and returns `true` if that byte is non-zero, `false` if that byte is zero.
`byte readByte()`	This method reads and returns one input byte.
`char readChar()`	This method reads two input bytes and returns a char value.
`double readDouble()`	This method reads eight input bytes and returns a double value.
`float readFloat()`	This method reads four input bytes and returns a float value.
`int readInt()`	This method reads four input bytes and returns an int value.
`long readLong()`	This method reads eight input bytes and returns a long value.
`short readShort()`	This method reads two input bytes and returns a short value.
`int readUnsignedByte()`	This method reads one input byte, zero-extends it to type int, and returns the result, which is therefore in the range 0 through 255.
`int readUnsignedShort()`	This method reads two input bytes and returns an int value in the range 0 through 65535.
`String readUTF()`	This method reads in a string that has been encoded using a modified UTF-8 format.
`static String readUTF(DataInput in)`	This method reads from the stream in a representation of a Unicode character string encoded in modified UTF-8 format; this string of characters is then returned as a String.

Program 8.15 demonstrates reading of data from a keyboard using `DataInputStream` class.

Program 8.15 *(Reading from keyboard with data stream)*

```
/* Reading String, int and double from Keyboard using
DataInputSteam. */
import java.io.*;

public class PrimitiveDataReading{
    public static void main(String args[]) throws
      IOException {
        // Create a connection to keyboard as input
                                                // stream
       DataInputStream dis = new DataInputStream
          (System.in);
        // Reading a string from keyboard
       System.out.println("Enter a String: ");
       String str = dis.readLine();
```

```
        System.out.println("Entered String value is: " +
           str);
         // Reading an integer data from keyboard as a
                                                   // string
        System.out.println("Enter any integer number: ");
        String str = dis.readLine();
        int x = Integer.parseInt(str);

         // Reading an integer data from keyboard as
                                                  // integer
        System.out.println("Enter another integer
           number: ");
        int y = dis.readInt();

         if(x > y)
           System.out.println(x + " is greater than " +
                 y);
         else
             System.out.println(x + " is less than " +
                 y);

         // Reading a floating point value
        System.out.println("Enter any numeric value: ");
        double z = dis.readDouble();
    }
}
```

Program 8.16 is an example illustrating reading of data from a file.

Program 8.16 *(Reading from file with data stream)*

```
/* Program to read primitive data from a file using
DataInputStream. */

import java.io.*;

class DataInputFileReading {
    public static void main(String args[]) {
        try {
            FileInputStream fis = new FileInputStream
             ("D://data.dat");
            DataInputStream dis = new DataInputStream(fis);

            System.out.println("Number of bytes: "+ fis.
             available());
```

```
                System.out.println(dis.readInt());
                System.out.println(dis.readDouble());
                System.out.println(dis.readChar());
                System.out.println(dis.readBoolean());
                System.out.println(dis.readLong());
                System.out.println(dis.readFloat());

                fis.close();
                dis.close();
            }
             catch(IOException e) {
                System.out.println(e);
            }
        }
}
```

- If the data.dat file does not contain the data in the form you are reading, it throws an error. For example, if you want to read data as int (4 bytes), whereas the data is actually stored in the file as double (8 bytes), then it will throw IOException.
- It is better if you create your data file using DataOutput Stream and then read the data from the same file using DatainputStream. In this case, you will avoid such kind of problem.
- One issue to keep in mind when reading primitive data types is that there is no way to distinguish a valid int value of –1 from the normal end-of-stream marker.
- DataInputStream is not recommended where method synchronization is required in multithreaded programming.
- When a DataInputStream is closed by calling close(), the underlying stream specified by InputStream is also closed automatically.

DataOutputStream class

DataOutputStream is the complement of DataInputStream. DataOutputStream class extends FilterOutputStream, which extends OutputStream. In addition to implementing DataOutput, it also implements AutoCloseable, Closeable, and Flushable.

DataOutputStream defines the single constructor stated as follows:

DataOutputStream (OutputStream out): Here, OutputStream out as the parameter is the output stream to which the primitive data types are to be written.

DataOutputStream class has the following methods (Table 8.11) in addition to all methods defined by OutputStream class (Table 8.6). All these additional methods are used to write Java primitive data. All methods throw IOException object when errors in writing occur.

Table 8.11 Additional methods defined by DataOutputStream class

Methods	Description
void writeBoolean()	It is used to write boolean to the output stream as a 1-byte value.
void writeChars()	It is used to write string to the output stream as a sequence of characters.
void writeChar()	It is used to write char to the output stream as a 2-byte value.
void writeDouble()	This method writes eight input bytes and returns a double value.
void writeFloat()	This method writes four input bytes and returns a float value.
void readInt()	It is used to write an int to the output stream.
void writeLong()	It is used to write a long to the output stream.
void writeShort()	It is used to write a short to the output stream.
void writeUnsignedByte()	This method writes one input byte, zero-extends it to type int in the range 0 through 255.
void writeUnsignedShort()	This method writes two input bytes and returns an int value in the range 0 through 65535.
void writeUTF()	This method writes in a string that has been encoded using a modified UTF-8 format.

Program 8.17 illustrates writing data into a file using DataInputStream and then reading the same file using DataInputStream. It is like copying data from one file to another file using data streams.

***Program 8.17** (Writing data into file with data stream, then reading from data input stream)*

```
/* This program copies data from one file to another file
using DataInputStream and DataOutputStream classes. */

import java.io.*;

public class DataInputOutputStreamsDemo {
    public static void main(String[] args) {
        // Create an output stream with file as an output
        try(FileOutputStream fos = new FileOutputStream
           ("data.dat");
            DataOutputStream dos = new DataOutputStream
                (fos)) {
```

```
            // Writing data into data output stream
            dos.writeInt(123);
            dos.writeDouble(6.023E-23);
            dos.writeBollean(true);
        }
        catch(FileNotFoundException e) {
           System.out.println("Cannot open output file");
           return;
        } catch(IOException e) {
              System.out.println("I/O Error: " + e);
        }

        // Create an output stream with file as an output
        try(FileInputputStream fis = new FileInput
           Stresm("data.dat");
            DataInputStream dis = new DataInputStream
                (fis)) {
            // Reading data from the data input stream
            int x = dis.readInt(123);
            double y = dis.readDouble(6.023E-23);
            boolean z = dis.readBoolean(true);
            System.out.println("x = " + x);
            System.out.println("y = " + y);
            System.out.println("z = " + z);

        }
        catch(FileNotFoundException e) {
            System.out.println("Cannot open output
                file");
            return;
        } catch(IOException e) {
              System.out.println("I/O Error: " + e);
        }

    }
}
```

- If the file `data.dat` contains some initial data, then it will be overwritten and data written only will be stored with EOF marking.
- Reading data in different sequence that of writing or with different types will throw `IOException` error.

This byte data streams concept is particularly useful when you want to store objects and read them back in a machine independent way. For this you have to write value of each field of an object and also read accordingly. Program 8.18 demonstrates how a user defined object of type `Student` can be stored and read using `DataOutputStream` and `DataInputStream`, respectively.

Program 8.18 *(Writing and reading objects using byte data streams)*

Define class Student

```
/* This program has three parts:
     Define a class Student
     Writing an object of type Student into a file
          object.
     Reading an object of type Student from the file
          object.
     You are advised to save them as three programs in
          the same directory.
     Run two driver programs one at a time.
*/

// The following is a class definition of Student. Save
                              // this program as Student.java

public class Student {
    private String name;
    private boolean gender;
     // true is male, false is female
    private int age;
    private float mark;

    public Student(String name, boolean gender, int
     age, float grade) {
        this.name = name;
        this.gender = gender;
        this.age = age;
        this.mark = grade;
    }

    public void printData() {
        System.out.println("Name:" +this.name+
          "Gender:" +this.gender);
        System.out.println("Age:" +this.age + "Mark:"
          +this.mark);
    }
}
```

Program for writing objects into file

```
/* The following is the main program which can be used
to write objects into a file student.dat. Save this
program as StudentWriter.java */

import java.util.*;
import java.io.*;

public class StudentWriter {
    public static void main(String args[])
        // Create a list of student objects
        List<Student> list = new ArrayList<Student>();

        list.add(new Student("Joy", true, 21, 88.5f));
        list.add(new Student("Rina", fales, 20,
          94.5f));
        list.add(new Student("Bobby", false, 22, 90.0f)

        // Create data output stream to student.dat file
        try(FileOutputStream fos = new FileOutputStream
           ("student.dat");
            DataOutputStream dos = new DataoutputStream
                (fos)) {

            // Write record into the file
        for (Student student : list) {
                dos.writeUTF(student.name);
                dos.writeBoolean(student.gender);
                dos.writeInt(student.age);
                dos.writeFloat(student.mark);
            }
        }
         catch(FileNotFoundException e) {
            System.out.println("Cannot open file");
            return;
        } catch(IOException e) {
              System.out.println("I/O Error: " + e);
        }
    }
}
```

Program for reading objects from a file

```
/* The following is the main program which can be used
to read objects from a file student.dat. Save this
program as StudentReader.java */

import java.io.*;
```

```
public class StudentReader {
    public static void main(String args[])

        // Create data input stream to student.dat file
        try(FileInputSteam fis = new FileInputStream
          ("student.dat");
           DataInputStream dis = new DataInputStream
          (fis)) {

           // Read records from file and print
           while(true) {
               System.out.println("Name:" + dis.
                    readUTF());
               System.out.print("\t Gender:" + dis.
                    readBoolean();
               System.out.print("\tAge:" + dis.
                    readInt();
               Sysytem.out.print("\tMark:" + dis.
                    readFloat();
               System.out.println();
             }
         }
         catch(FileNotFoundException e) {
            System.out.println("Cannot open file");
            return;
         }
         catch(EOFException e) {
             System.out.println("End of file.");
         }
    }
}
```

`PrintStream` class

About PrintStream class

The `PrintStream` class of the `java.io` package can be used to write output data in commonly readable form (text) instead of bytes. It extends `FilterOutputStream` class, which extends the abstract class `OutputStream`. It implements the `Appendable`, `AutoCloseable`, `Closeable`, and `Flushable` interfaces.

Working of PrintStream

Unlike other output streams, the `PrintStream` converts the primitive data (`int`, `char`, etc.) into text format instead of bytes. It then writes that formatted data to the output stream.

The `PrintStream` class has the constructors defined in Table 8.12.

Constructors

Table 8.12 Constructors defined by `PrintStream` class

Constructor	Description
PrintStream(File file)	Creates a new print stream, without automatic line flushing, with the specified file.
PrintStream(File file, String csn)	Creates a new print stream, without automatic line flushing, with the specified file and charset.
PrintStream(OutputStream out)	Creates a new print stream.
PrintStream(OutputStream out, boolean autoFlush)	Creates a new print stream. A boolean; if true, the output buffer will be flushed whenever a byte array is written, one of the println methods is invoked, or a newline character or byte ('\n') is written.
PrintStream(OutputStream out, boolean autoFlush, String encoding)	Creates a new print stream with auto flash option. It also writes a supported character encoding.
PrintStream(String fileName)	Creates a new print stream, without automatic line flushing, with the specified file name.
PrintStream(String fileName, String csn)	Creates a new print stream, without automatic line flushing, with the specified file name and name of a charset.

The following are some examples which you can consider to create a print stream:

Create a print stream to write formatted data to the file `abc.txt` with auto flush.

```
PrintStream("abc.txt", true);
```

Create a print stream with FileOutputStream to write formatted data to the file `abc.txt`.

```
FileOutputStream fos = new FileOutputStream("abc.txt");
PrintStream out = new PrintStream(fos);
```

Creates a PrintStream using some character encoding, say UTF16.

```
PrintStream out = new PrintStream("abc.txt", true, "UTF16");
```

- The `PrintStream` class does not throw any input/output exception. Instead, we need to use the `checkError()` method to find any error in it.
- The `PrintStream` class has a feature of auto flushing. This means it forces the output stream to write all the data to the destination under one of the following conditions:

   - if newline character `\n` is written in the print stream.
   - if the `println()` method is invoked.
   - if an array of bytes is written in the print stream.
- The `PrintStream` write data to the file using some default character encoding. However, we can specify the character encoding (UTF8 or UTF16) as well.

Since, the `PrintStream` is the child class of `OutputStream` class, it defines all the methods of abstract class. In addition, it also defines methods, which are listed in Table 8.13.

Table 8.13: Methods defined for `PrintStream` class

Method	Description
`PrintStream append(char c)`	This method appends the specified character to this output stream.
`PrintStream append(CharSequence cs)`	Appends the specified character sequence to this output stream.
`PrintStream append(CharSequence cs, int sta, int end)`	Appends the specified character sequence starting from index *sta* to *end* to this output stream.
`boolean checkError()`	This method flushes the stream and checks its error state.
`protected void clearError()`	Clears the internal error state of this stream.
`PrintStream format(String s, Object ...)`	This method writes a formatted string to this output stream using the specified format string and arguments.
`PrintStream format(Locale l, String s, Object ...)`	This method writes a formatted string for a local using the specified format string. Here, the output is tailored to the locale specified by the first argument.
`void print (<primitive type>)`	This method prints data in the format of any primitive type `boolean, int, char, long`, etc. Also, it takes String and Object as arguments.
`void println(<argument>)`	This method prints any data passed as argument and then terminate the line. Here, argument can be nothing or any primitive data type, String, Object.
`printf(String s, Object ...)`	This method writes a formatted string to this output stream using the specified format string and arguments.
`printf(Locale l, String s, Object ...)`	This method writes a formatted string for a local using the specified format string. Here, the output is tailored to the locale specified by the first argument.
`protected void setError()`	This method sets the error state of the stream to true.

Program 8.19 demonstrates the use of `PrintStream` class in a program, where it writes data into a file out.dat.

Program 8.19 *(Illustration of `PrintStream` class)*

```
/* This program illustrates the call of some methods
defined in PrintStream class. */

class PrintStreamDemo{
    public static void main(String args[]) {
        // Create the underlying output stream as a file
        // Create the PrintStream object for outputting
           to output stream
        try{
            FileOutputStream fos = new FileOutputStream
                ("out.dat");
            PrintStream out=new PrintStream(fos, true);
                //Auto flash on
            // Data to be stored are declared
            String s = "It is a string...\n";
            char c[]={'A','E','I','O', 'U', 'M', 'N'};
            int age = 25; float x = 3.141f;
            String j = "Java"; int a = 555;

            // Illustrating print()
            out.print(true); // Writing a boolean value
            out.print(123);  // Writing a consatant
            out.print(x);    // Writing a float value
            out.print(s);    // Writing a float value
            out.print(s+"written.");
                // Concatenated string

            //Illustrating println() which adds newline
                                     // after each print
            out.println(true); // Writing a boolean value
            out.println(123);  // Writing a consatant
            out.println(x);    // Writing a float value
            out.println(s);    // Writing a float value
            out.print(s+"written.");
                                  // Concatenated string
            out.println();     // Print a blank line

            // Illustrating printf(), it is a formatted
                                                // print
            out.printf("Java is %d years old\n!", age);
            out.printf(Locale.PRC, "Welcome to %s
                program: %d", j,a);
            out.printf(s+j);  // Concatenated string
```

```
            // Illustrating some other methods
            out.append(" Applying print stream in
                user's way...");
            out.println(out.checkError());
                //Check if error in stream

            out.flush();
                // Flushing out put to the file...
            System.out.print("Writing \"out.dat\" to
                itself...");
            out.println("\n\n")
            out.print(fos);
            System.out.println("\n\n")

            System.out.print("Printing \"out.dat\" to
                consol...");
            out.print(fos);
            System.out.println("\n\n")
        }
        catch(IOException e){
            System.out.prtintln(e.printStack());
        }
    }
}
```

- You are already familiar with `print(...)`, `println(...)`, and `printf(...)` using the `System.out`. In `java.lang`, the static class `System` is defined with `out` object in it as a field and `out` is the object of the class `PrintStream`. This class outputs data of any of the basic types as a string. For example, an `int` value of `12345` becomes the string `12345` as generated by the `valueOf()` method from the `String` class.
- All the methods can print object of any type. For example, we print `fos` object which is a file. The `toString()` method of `Java.lang.String` class converts any object to a string form and then print it.
- `System.out` and `System.err` are two `PrintStream` objects and they are known as the standard output streams.
- Call of `printf()` method with a constant (e.g., `printf(123)`) or without any argument (e.g., `printf()`) throws `NullPointeException` exception.
- You can output some text tailored to a locale specified by a value defined in `java.util.Local` class. For example, in Program 8.19, we print a string in PRC (the Chinese locale).

- To escape a double quote("), you can use \ as escaping character preceded by ". To print "Welcome to Java" you should use `System.out.print("\"Welcome to Java\" ");`
- When you have finished writing data to the `PrintStream` you should remember to close it. Closing a `PrintStream` will also close the `OutputStream` instance to which the `PrintStream` is writing. Explicitly closing a `PrintStream` can be done by calling its `close()` method.
- There is no explicit `close()` method call if you use `TryWithResources` construct. In Program 8.19, the first `FileOutputStream` instance is not created inside the `TryWithResources` block. This means that the `TryWithResources` block will not automatically close this `FileOutputStream` instance. However, when the `PrintStream` is closed, it will also close the `OutputStream` instance it writes to, so the `FileOutputStream` instance will get closed when the `PrintStream` is closed.
- Unlike other output streams, a `PrintStream` never throws an `IOException`; instead, exceptional situations merely set an internal flag that can be tested via the `checkError()` method.
- Optionally, a `PrintStream` can be created so as to flush automatically.
- All characters printed by a `PrintStream` are converted into bytes using the platform's default character encoding. The `PrintWriter` class (it is discussed later in this chapter) should be used in situations that require writing characters rather than bytes.
- In `printf()` method, you can specify a format to which you want to print a value. This is a single character specifying how the argument is to be presented. The commonly used options for the various formats are listed in Table 8.14.

Table 8.14 Format specifications for `printf()` method

Format	Description
`'d'`, `'o'` and `'x'`	Apply to integer values and specify that the output representation of the value should be decimal, octal, or hexadecimal, respectively.
`'f'`, `'g'`, and `'a'`	Apply to floating-point values and specify that the output representation should be decimal notation, scientific notation (with an exponent), or hexadecimal with an exponent, respectively.
`'c'`	Specifies that the argument value is a character and should be displayed as such.
`'s'`	Specifies that the argument is a string.
`'b'`	Specifies that the argument is a Boolean value, so it will be output as `true` or `false`.
`'h'`	Specifies that the hash code of the argument is to be output in hexadecimal form.
`'n'`	Specifies the platform line separator so `%n` will have the same effect as `\n`.

Filter byte streams

The `java.io` package provides a set of abstract classes that define and partially implement *filter streams*. A filter stream filters data as it is being read from or written to the stream. There are two filter streams classes defined in the `java.io` package (Figure 8.2):

`FileterInputStream`
`FilterOutputStream`

`FilterInputStream` class

The `FilterInputStream` extends the abstract class `InputStream`. The `FilterInputStream` class has the following sub classes (which we have already learned):

- `BufferedInputStream`
- `DataInputStream`
- `LineNumberInputStream` (deprecated now)
- `PushbackInputStream`

Working with filter input streams is as follows:

`FilterInputStream` contains any one of the mentioned input streams, which it uses as its basic source of data, to be used for transforming the data along the way. It also allows the programmer to redefine the methods providing additional functionalities for an underlying input stream. The class `FilterInputStream` itself simply overrides all methods of `InputStream` *with versions that pass all requests to the contained input stream. Sub classes of* `FilterInputStream` *may further override some of these methods and may also provide additional methods and fields.*

For example, consider the following tabular data:

John	789.45	B
Rina	946.23	X
Mini	849.10.	A
...	....	...

The data is stored in a file, say, `student.rec`. Suppose, we want to read the data using `DataInputStream` class. We can use the `read()` method in `DataInputStream` class which reads bytes from the input stream and presents the result in the conventional way (i.e., read as primitive data). If we observe how the data is stored, we find that in each row there are three types of data: `String`, `float`, and `char` and there are `\t` signs between the first and second, and second and third data; also, there is a `\n` sign at the end of the row. Reading such an input stream can be customized and made convenient so that you can filter out the additional ASCII characters hidden in between. This means that you can customize `read()` of the `FilterInputStream` class or add some other method to provide extra functionality.

Program 8.20 is a simple example showing how you can create a filter input stream in your program.

Program 8.20 *(Example of* `Filter Input Stream` *class)*

```
/* This program illustrates the creation of filer input
stream object with a File object as an underlying input
stream. */

import java.io.*;

public class FilterInputStreamDemo {
    public static void main(String[] args) throws
      IOException {
        File data = new File("D:\\test.txt");
        FileInputStream  file = new FileInputStream
           (data);
        FilterInputStream filter = new BufferedInput
           Stream(file);
        int k =0;
        while((k=filter.read())!=-1){
            System.out.print((char)k);
        }
        file.close();
        filter.close();
    }
}
```

`FilterOutputStream` class

The `FilterOutputStream` is the counterpart of the `FilterInputStream`. It extends the `OutputStream` class and it has the following sub classes:

- `BufferedOutputStream`
- `DataOutputStream`
- `PrintStream`

The working of `FilterOutputStream` in the same as `FilterInputStream` except that it works for output.

How to write your own filter streams

Following are the steps to take when you are writing your own filtered input and output streams:

1. Create a sub class of `FilterInputStream` and `FilterOutputStream`. Input and output streams often come in pairs, so it's likely that you will need to create both input and output versions of your filter stream.
2. Override the read and write methods, if you need to.
3. Provide any new methods.
4. Make sure that the input and output streams work together.

Sequence input stream

In many applications, there is a need to merge two or more input streams into a single input stream. The `SequenceInputStream` class allows you to merge multiple input streams.

The `SequenceInputStream` class represents the logical concatenation of multiple input streams. It starts with an ordered collection of input streams and reads from the first one until the end of file is reached, whereupon it reads from the second one, and so on, until the end of file is reached on the last of the contained input streams.

The `SequenceInputStream` class defines the following two constructors for creating an instance:

`SequenceInputStream(InputStream in1, InputStream in2):`

This initializes a newly created `SequenceInputStream` by remembering the two arguments, which will be read in order, first `in1` and then `in2`, to provide the bytes to be read from this `SequenceInputStream`. This constructor is used to create an input stream combining two inputs streams.

`SequenceInputStream(Enumeration<? extends InputStream> e)`

This initializes a newly created `SequenceInputStream` by remembering the argument, which must be an `Enumeration` that produces objects whose run-time type is `InputStream`. This constructor is used to create an input stream combining two or more inputs streams.

The `SequenceInputStream` class extends the `InputStream` class and hence all methods declared in the `InputStream` class are defined by the class.

Program 8.21 demonstrates how to use `SequenceInputStream` to combine two sources of input streams.

Program 8.21 *(Example of* `SequenceInputStream` *class)*

```
/* This program demonstrates comibing two input streams
as a single input streams.*/

import java.io.*;

class TwoInputStreamDemo {
    public static void main(String args[])throws
      Exception {
         InputStream in1 = new FileInputStream
            ("D:\\file1.txt");
         InputStream in2 = new FileInputStream
            ("D:\\file2.txt");
         try(SequenceInputStream in = new SequenceInput
            Stream(in1, in2)){
               int c;
               while((c = in.read())!=-1){
                     System.out.print((char)c);
         }
         } catch(IOException e) {
               System.out.println("I/O Error: " + e);
          }
    }
}
```

- If you do not use `TryWithResources` construct, then you should close the input stream instance calling the `close()` of `SequenceInputStream` class.
- Closing a `SequenceInputStream` will also close all the input streams instances which the `SequenceInputStream` is reading.
- It is not necessary that all input streams are of the same type. For example, one input stream may be of type `BufferedInputStream` while the other may be `ByteArrayInputStream`, etc.

Program 8.22 demonstrates how to use `SequenceInputStream` to combine multiple input streams using enumeration as a collection of input streams.

Program 8.22 *(*`Sequence Input Stream`*)*

```
/* This Java program demonstrates the combining of any
number of input streams. */

import java.io.*;
import java.util.*;
```

```
class MutipleSequenceInputStreamDemo {
    public static void main(String args[])throws
     FileNotFoundException, IOException {
        //Creating the InputStream objects for all the
                                    // following files
        InputStream in1 = new FileInputStream("file1.
          txt");
        InputStream in2 = new FileInputStream("file2.
          txt");
        InputStream in3 = new FileInputStream("file3.
          txt");

        //Creating a collection of input streams
        Vector c = new Vector();

        c.add(in1);
        c.add(in2);
        c.add(in3);

        //Creating enumeration object by calling the
                                    // elements method
        Enumeration e = c.elements();

        //Passing the enumeration object in the
                                        // constructor
        SequenceInputStream in = new SequenceInput
          Stream(e);

        // Determine how many bytes are available in
                                   // the first stream
        System.out.println("" + in.available());

        // Estimating the number of bytes that can be
        // read from the current underlying input stream
        System.out.println( in.available());

        int i = 0;
        while((i = in.read())! = -1) {
            System.out.print((char)i);
        }
        in.close();
          //It closes automatically all the input
                                      // streams used
    }
}
```

Object IO streams

There are two byte stream classes in `java.io` package namely, `ObjectOutptStream` and `ObjectInputStream` used for working with persistent objects (objects which can be retained by any program and later retrieved by any program). The `ObjectInputStream` class enables you to read Java objects from an `InputStream` instead of just raw bytes. The Java `ObjectOutputStream` class enables you to write Java objects to an `OutputStream` instead of just raw bytes.

With an object input (output) stream class, you actually wrap an `InputStream` (`OutputStream`) in an `ObjectInputStream` (`ObjectOutputStream`) and then you can read (write) objects from (to) it. Let us first learn the compositions of the two classes in this category. We shall discuss examples of their usages subsequently.

`ObjectInputStream` class

This class has the following two constructors to create its instance:

`ObjectInputStream(InputStream in)`

This creates an `ObjectInputStream` that reads from the specified `InputStream`.

`protected ObjectInputStream()`

This provides a way for sub classes that are completely reimplementing `ObjectInputStream`.

The `ObjectInputStream` extends `InputStream` and implements `ObjectInput`, `ObjectStreamConstants` and thus it has all the methods of the classes and interfaces it inherits or implements. In addition, it has the methods of its own as listed in Table 8.15.

`ObjectOutputStraem` class

While `ObjectInputStream` reads primitive data types of objects from an input stream, the `ObjectOutputStream` class writes primitive data types and Java objects to an output stream. This class defines following two constructors to create an instance of the `ObjectOutputStream` class:

Table 8.15 Some methods for `ObjectInputStream` class

Methods	Description
`default readObject()`	This method reads the non-static and non-transient fields of the current class from this stream. One cannot use `default readObject()` to read the static fields. This may only be called from the `readObject()` method of the class being desterilized. You cannot use `default readObject()` directly.
`readFields()`	This method reads the persistent fields from the stream and makes them available by name.
`readObject()`	This method is used to read an object from `ObjectInputStream`.
`readObject Override()`	This method is called by the trusted sub classes of `ObjectOutputStream` using the protected default constructor. The sub class is expected to provide an override method with the modifier `final`.
`readUnshared()`	This method reads an "unshared" object from the `ObjectInputStream`.
`enableResolveObject (boolean enable)`	This method enables the stream to do replacement of objects read from the stream. When enabled, the `resolveObject()` method is called for every object being deserialized.
`resolveClass (ObjectStreamClass desc)`	This method loads the local class equivalent of the specified stream class description. Sub classes may implement this method to allow classes to be fetched from an alternate source.
`readStreamHeader()`	This method allows sub classes to read and verify their stream headers. It reads and verifies the version number.

`ObjectOutputStream(OutputStream out)`

This creates an `ObjectOutputStream` that writes to the specified output stream `out`.

`protected ObjectOutputStream()`

This provides a way for sub classes that are completely reimplementing `ObjectOutputStream` to not have to allocate private data just used by this implementation of `ObjectOutputStream`.

The `ObjectOutputStream` extends `OutputStream` and implements `DataOutput`, `ObjectOutput`, `ObjectStream Constants` and thus it has all the methods of the classes and interfaces it inherits or implements. In addition, it has the methods of its own as listed in Table 8.16.

Table 8.16 Some methods for `ObjectOutputStream` class

Methods	Description
protected void annotateClass(class <?> c)	Sub classes may implement this method to allow class data to be stored in the stream.
protected void annotateProxy Class(class<?> c)	Sub classes may implement this method to store custom data in the stream along with descriptors for dynamic proxy classes.
void defaultWriteObject()	This method writes the non-static and non-transient fields of the current class to this stream.
protected void drain()	This method drains any buffered data in ObjectOutputStream.
protected boolean enableReplaceObject(boolean enable)	This method enables the stream to do replacement of objects in the stream.
ObjectOutputStream. PutField putFields()	This method retrieves the object used to buffer persistent fields to be written to the stream.
protected Object replaceObject(Object obj)	This method allows trusted sub classes of ObjectOutputStream to substitute one object for another during serialization.
void reset()	This method disregards the state of any objects already written to the stream.
void useProtocolVersion(int version)	This method specifies stream protocol version to use when writing the stream.
protected void write ClassDescriptor (ObjectStreamClass desc)	This method writes the specified class descriptor to the ObjectOutputStream.
void writeFields()	This method writes the buffered fields to the stream.
void writeObject(Object obj)	This method writes the specified object to the ObjectOutputStream.
protected void writeObjectOverride(Object obj)	This method is used by sub classes to override the default writeObject method.
protected void write StreamHeader()	This method appends or prepends a header to the stream.
void writeUnshared(Object obj)	This method writes an "unshared" object to the ObjectOutputStream.

Let us see how an object can be written into an output stream and read from an input stream. Let us consider the definition of `Person` class, the object of which we shall consider for reading and writing.

Program 8.23 defines the class `Person` so that an object of the class can be stored into an output stream, say file, and be able to retrieve the same from the file later.

Program 8.23 (Declaration of a class to create objects for persistent)

```
/* Definition of a user defined class Person to be used
in Program 8.24 and 8.25. */

public class Person {
    private String name;
    private boolean gender;
    private int age;

    public Employee(String n, boolean g, int a) {
      name = n; gender = g; age = a;
    }

    @Override
    public String toString() {
     return "Name=" +this.name+ "Age=" +this.age+
          "Gender=" +this.gender;
    }
}
```

Program 8.24 used the `Person` class definition, creates object of the class `Person` and then stores the objects in a file named `object.dat`.

Program 8.24 (Writing an object into an output stream)

```
/* This program illustrates how an object of class
Person can be stored in a file. */

import java.io.*;
// import the class Person here

public class ObjectOutputStreamDemo {
   public static void main(String[] args) {
      Person p = new Person("Jay", true, 59);
      System.out.println(p);
           // Object is created successfully

      try(FileOutputStream fos = new FileOutputStream
           ("object.dat");
           ObjectOutputStream oos = new ObjectOutput
                Stream(fos)){
           // Write the object p into the file
           oos.writeObject(p);
      } catch (IOException e) {
         e.printStackTrace();
      }
   }
}
```

Program 8.25 illustrates how the program can read an object stored in the file `object.dat`.

Program 8.25
(Reading an object from an input stream)

```
/* This program illustrates how an object of class
Person can be read from a file. */

import java.io.*;
// import the class Person here

public class ObjectInputStreamDemo {
   public static void main(String[] args) {
      try(FileInputStream fis = new
FileInputStream("object.dat");
          ObjectInputStream ois = new ObjectInputStream
            (fis)){

          // Reading the object p from the file
          Person p = (Person) ois.readObject();
           System.out.println(p);
            // Printing the object

      } catch (IOException e) {
          e.printStackTrace();
      }
   }
}
```

- `ObjectOutputStream` can be used to convert an object to `OutputStream`. In Java, the process of converting object to stream is called *serialization*.
- `ObjectInputStream` can be used to convert an `InputStream` to object. The process of converting the input stream to an object is called *deserialization*.
- For serializing the object, you call the method `writeObject()` of `ObjectOutputStream`, and for deserialization you call the `readObject()` method of `ObjectInputStream` class.
- Other read and write methods defined in these classes also can be used with their respective guiders.
- All objects to be written by `ObjectOutputStream` and read by `ObjectInputStream` should be serializable. That is, you wrap and then you can read objects from it. This is why the bytes read must represent a valid, serialized Java object. Otherwise reading objects may fail.
- Usually, you will use the `ObjectInputStream` to read objects written (serialized) by an `ObjectOutputStream`.

Making serialization objects

Serialization allows you to convert an `Object` to stream so that you can send it over the network or save it as file for later usage. Deserialization is the process of converting `Object` stream to actual object to be used in your program. You have already seen Program 8.23, which gives an example of how you can declare a class compatible for serialization and deserialization. The interface `Serializable` is defined in `java.io`. The interface `Serializable` is a marker interface. It has no data member and method declared in it. It is used to "mark" Java classes so that the objects of these classes may get a certain capability. It must be implemented by the class whose object you want to persist.

Program 8.26 illustrates how an object can be made serializable.

Program 8.26 *(Defining class to create serializable objects)*

```
/* Defining a class Person to be declared as
serializable. This definition is a revised version of
Program 8.23 */

import java.io.Serializable;

public class Person implements Serializable {
    private static final long serialVersionUID =
     19082020L;
    private String name;
    private boolean gender;
    private transient int age;
     // Intended not to be serialized in stream
    // private double salary;

    public Person(String n, boolean g, int a) {
      name = n; gender = g; age = a;
    }

    @Override
    public  String toString() {
     return "Name=" +this.name+ "Age=" +this.age+
          "Gender=" +this.gender;
    }
}
```

- Before you can serialize and deserialize objects the class of the object must implement `java.io.Serializable`.
- Like the interface `Serializable`, `Clonable` and `Remote` are also two marker interfaces.
- The `String` class and all the wrapper classes implement the `java.io.Serializable` interface by default.
- If you don't want some field(s) to be serialized to stream, you have to use the `transient` keyword for that, for example, the field `age` in the class `Person` (Program 8.26). If so, it's value will not be saved to file and hence not retrieved in the new object.
- In Program 8.26, note the declaration of an object property, namely, `versionID` in the class `Person`. It is used by `ObjectOutputStream` and `ObjectInputStream` classes for write and read object operations. Although it is not mandatory to have this field, you should keep it. Otherwise any time you change your class, that don't have effect on the earlier serialized objects and it (i.e., the changed object) will start failing.

Program 8.27 defines two utility methods to accomplish the tasks of serializing and deserializing objects from and to any file object.

Program 8.27 *(Serialization and de-serialization utility methods)*

```
/* This program includes two utility methods, which
can be invoked for de-serialization and serialization
of objects of any type to-and-from any file passed as
arguments. */

import java.io.*;

public class PersistentUtility {
    // Defining the method for object serialization to
                                                // a file
    public static void serialize(Object obj, String
     fileName){
        try(FileOutputStream fos = new FileOutputStream
           (fileName);
           ObjectOutputStream oos = new ObjectOutput
                 Stream(fos)) {
           oos.writeObject(obj);
        }
        catch(IOException e){
           e.printStackTrace();
           return;
        }
     }
```

```
        // Defining the method for object deserialization
                                                // from a file
    public static Object deserialize(String fileName){
        try(FileInputStream fis = new FileInputStream
           (fileName);
           ObjectInputStream ois = new ObjectInputStream
                (fis)) {

           Object obj = ois.readObject()) != -1);
            return(obj);
        }
        catch(IOException e){
           e.printStackTrace();
           return;
        }
    }
}
```

- The method `writeObject()` of `ObjectOutput Stream` class is called for object serialization to an output stream. The method `readObject()` of `ObjectInputStream` class is called for object deserialization from an input stream.
- The serialization and deserialization processes are platform independent. You can serialize an object in one platform and deserialize in a different platform.

Program 8.28 illustrates how the object persistent utility program can be utilized for objects of class `Person`.

Program 8.28 *(Illustration of storing and retrieving object)*

```
/* This program illustrates object serialization
and deserialization by ObjectOutputStream and
ObjectInputStream, respectively. */

import java.io.*;
// The class definition under application, say Person
                                   // should be imported
// The utility program should be accessible to this
                                              // program
public class SerializationDemo {
   public static void main(String[] args) {
      String fileName="abc.dat";
      Person sita = new Person("Sita", false, 35);
```

```
        PersistentUtility x = new PersistentUtility();
        //Serializing (writing) the objects to the file
        x.serialize(sita, fileName);
        //Deserializing (reading) the objects from the
                                                   // file
        Object p = new Person();
        p = x.deserialize(fileName);
        System.out.println(p);
    }
}
```

- Values of all transient variables will not be saved to file and hence not retrieved in the new object.
- Similarly, static variable values are also not serialized since they belong to class and not object.

Deserialization with class refactoring

You should be careful while you do the deserialization (reading an object from an input stream) of objects. This is particularly important if you deserialize an object with class definition, which is majorly different from the class definition used in the serialization of the same object. The objects should be compatible in the process of serialization/deserialization. This implies that, ideally, they should adhere to the same class definition. However, the deserialization of objects permits some changes in the class definitions. Some of the changes in class definition that will affect the deserialization process are:

- Adding new field(s) to the class.
- Changing a field from transient to non-transient.
- Changing a field from static to non-static.
- If you process with a totally different class definition.

For an illustration, refer to the class definition in Program 8.27. You serialize an object with this definition (run Program 8.29). The program will successfully store an object into the file `xyz.dat` as expected.

Program 8.29
(Serialization with class Person)

```
/* This program serializes an object into a file xyz.
dat. */
import java.io.*;
// Import the class definition of Person (Program 8.26).
// Import the utility program (Program 8.27).
public class SerializationPersonDemo {
   public static void main(String[] args) {
      String fileName="xyz.dat";
      Person ram = new Person("Ram", true, 40);
      //Serializing (writing) the objects to the file
      PersistentUtility x = new PersistentUtility();
      x.serialize(ram, fileName);
   }
}
```

Next, modify the definition with the following changes:

Adding a new field:

```
private double salary;
```

Change the field from transient into non-transient:

```
private int age;
```

Now, if you run Program 8.30, it will throw run-time exception objects related to all the changes you have made in the class definition of `Person`.

Program 8.30
(Deserialization with modified class Person)

```
/* This program serializes an object into a file xyz.
dat. */
import java.io.*;
// Import the modified class definition of Person
     (Program 8.26).
// Import the utility program (Program 8.27).

public class DeserializationPerson2Demo {
   public static void main(String[] args) {
      String fileName="xyz.dat";
      Object p = new Person();
      //Deserializing (readting) the objects from the
                                                 // file
      PersistentUtility x = new PersistentUtility();
      p = x.deserialize(fileName);
      System.out.println(p);
   }
}
```

Class refactoring and serialVersionUID field

Let us see how Java run-time manager detects the incompatibility issue while running a deserialization program. Note the field which we defined in Program 8.26:

```
private static final long serialVersionUID = 19082020L;
```

The Java run-time manager verifies if `serialVersionUID` of the previous class and the new class are same; if not, it throws exception objects.

- While defining a class, it is not mandatory to include this field in your class definition. If the class doesn't define `serialVersionUID`, it gets calculated automatically and assigned to the class. Java uses class variables, methods, class name, package, etc., to generate this unique and long number. If you are working with any IDE, you will automatically get a warning like "*The serializable class Person does not declare a static final serialVersionUID field of type long.*"
- Even if you declare the field, it is not necessary to initialize the value of this field. You can use Java utility `serialver` to generate the class `serialVersionUID`, for any class. You can run the following command for the purpose:

```
$serialver -classpath <className>
```

- The same protocol is applied to the inherited class as well. It is allowable that super class may not be defined for implementing the interface `java.io.Serializable`.

Piped IO Stream

Pipes in IO streams provide a connection to reading and writing data simultaneously. The `java.io` package provides two classes, called `PipedInputStream` and `PipedOutputStream`, which facilitate read and write data simultaneously. The two streams can be connected with each other. A `PipedInputStream` needs to be connected to a `PipedOutputStream`. When these two streams are connected to each other they form a pipe. This is particularly relevant when JVM runs two threads such that one thread produces data whereas the other thread consumes data simultaneously.

Let us first understand the composition of the two classes and then we shall discuss writing program using them.

`PipedInputStream` class

The `PipedInputStream` class makes it possible to read the contents of a pipe as a stream of bytes. Following are the three constructors defined in the class `PipedInputStream`:

`PipedInputStream()`

This creates a default piped input stream and is ready to be connected.

`PipedInputStream(int buffSize)`

This creates a piped input stream so that it is not yet connected and uses the specified pipe size for the pipe's buffer.

`PipedInputStream(PipedOutputStream src)`

This creates a piped input stream and is ready to be connected to the piped output stream `src`.

This class inherits `InputStream` class and hence all the methods declared in the class `InputStream` are implemented for this class `PipedInputStream`. Table 8.17 gives the methods in the class `PipedInputStream`.

Table 8.17 Methods in `PipedInputStream` class

Method	Description
`int available()`	This method returns the number of bytes that can be read from this input stream without blocking.
`void close()`	This method closes this piped input stream and releases any system resources associated with the stream.
`void connect(PipedOutputStream src)`	This method causes this piped input stream to be connected to the piped output stream `src`.
`int read()`	This method reads the next byte of data from this piped input stream.
`int read(byte[] b, int off, int len)`	This method reads up to `len` bytes of data from this piped input stream into an array of bytes.
`protected void receive(int b)`	This method receives a byte of data.

`PipedOutputStream` class

The `PipedOutputStream` class is a piped output stream that can be connected to a piped input stream to create a communications pipe. The following constructors are defined for this class to create an instance of the class `PipedOutputStream`:

`PipedOutputStream()`

This creates a piped output stream that is not yet connected to a piped input stream.

`PipedOutputStream(PipedInputStream snk)`

This creates a piped output stream connected to the specified piped input stream *snk*.

This class inherits `OutputStream` class and hence all the methods declared in the class `OutputStream` are implemented for this class `PipedOutputStream`. Following are the methods in the class `PipedOutputStream`.

Table 8.18 Methods in `PipedOutputStream` class

Method	Description
`void close()`	This method closes this piped output stream and releases any system resources associated with this stream.
`void connect(PipedInput Stream snk)`	This method connects this piped output stream to a receiver.
`void flush()`	This method flushes this output stream and forces any buffered output bytes to be written out.
`void write(byte[] b, int off, int len)`	This method writes `len` bytes from the specified byte array starting at offset off to this piped output stream.

Creating a pipe using Java IO

Program 8.31 is a simple example where `PipedInputStream` and `PipedOutputStream` classes communicate with each other while running two threads. One thread writes the data using the `PipedOutputStream` object and the other thread reads the data from that pipe using the `PipedInputStream` object.

Program 8.31 *(Creating pipe using IO byte streams)*

```
/* This program illustrates the piped IO using
PipedInputStream and PipetdOutputStream classes.  Both
the piped stream objects are connected to each other.
*/

import java.io.*;

public class PipedIODemo {
    public static void main(String[] args) {
        // Create piped IO streams
```

```
final PipedOutputStream pipeOut = new Piped
   OutputStream();
final PipedInputStream  pipeIn  = new Piped
   InputStream(output);

// Create pipe connecting pipeOut and pipeIn
pipeIn.connect(pipeOut);
// Alternatively
// pipeOut.connect(pipeIn);

// Thread of writing data to piped output stream
Thread t1 = new Thread(new Runnable() {
    @Override
    public void run() {
        try {
            for(int i = 65, i < 91; i++) {
            pipeOut.write(i);
            Thread.sleep(500L);
                  // Wait for 500 milliseconds
        } catch (IOException e) {
            e.printStackTrace();
        }
    }
}
);

// Thread of reading data from piped input
                                         // stream
Thread t2 = new Thread(new Runnable() {
    @Override
    public void run() {
        try {
            for(int i = 65, i < 91; i++) {
               System.out.print((char)pipeIn.
                 read());
               Thred.sleep(1000L);
                 // Wait for 1000 millisec
        } catch (IOException e) {
            e.printStackTrace();
        }
    }
}
);

// Running the two threads ...
t1.start();    t2.start();
```

```
        // Wait the two threads to finish...
        t1.join();    t2.join();

        // Closing the piped IO streams
        pipeOut.close();  pieIn.close();
    }
}
```

The following are the important points about pipe IO streams.

- Since both streams have their own connect method, any one stream can connect the other stream. Thus, both the piped stream objects are connected with each other.
- `PipedInputStream` is piped with `PipedOutput Stream`. So data can be written using `PipedOutput Stream` (to a source stream) and can be read using `PipedInputStream` (from a sink stream).
- The piped input stream contains a buffer, decoupling read operations from write operations, within limits.
- A pipe is said to be broken if a thread that was providing data bytes to the connected piped output stream is no longer alive.
- Attempting to use both objects from a single thread is not recommended, as it may deadlock the thread. Further, using separate threads for the objects also may create a deadlock condition for the threads.
- Remember, when using the two connected pipe streams, then you should pass one stream to one thread, and the other stream to another thread. Note that the read() and write() calls on the streams are blocking, meaning if you try to use the same thread to both read and write, this may result in the deadlocking of threads.
- The pipe concept in Java is different from the pipe concept in Unix or Linux. In the later cases, two processes running in different address spaces can communicate via a pipe. In contrast, in Java, the communicating parties must be running in the same process but as different threads. In other words, you can not use a pipe to communicate with a thread between different processes (say two JVMs).
- Other than pipes there are many other ways that threads can communicate within the same JVM. In fact, threads more often exchange complete objects rather than raw byte data. But, if you need to exchange raw byte data between threads, you can do that using Java IO's pipes.

Benefits of IO with byte streams

You have learned a lot about different byte stream classes that `java.io` API supports in your program writing. There is another IO with character streams which we shall learn in the next section. In summary, the following points can be highlighted for the input/ output with byte stream classes:

1. Byte streams handle IO of raw binary data.
2. The stream interface to IO in Java provides a clean abstraction for a complex and often critical task.
3. The composition of the filtered stream classes allows you to dynamically build the streaming interface to suit your data transfer requirements.
4. Buffered streams optimize input and output by reducing the number of calls to the native API.
5. Scanning and formatting allows a program to read and write formatted text.
6. Data streams handle binary IO of primitive data type and `String` values.
7. IO from the command Line describes the standard streams and the console object.
8. Java programs are written to adhere to a better abstraction. In the future, the high-level InputStream, OutputStream classes will function properly even when new and improved stream classes are invented.
9. Object streams handle binary IO of objects.
10. Finally, serialization of objects plays an important role in many Java programs. Java's serialization IO classes provide a portable solution in this regard.

8.2.4 IO with Character Streams

Apart from the *byte stream* concept, Java provides another concept which is a convenient means for handling input and output of characters. The byte stream mechanism manages 8-bit bytes of raw binary data, whereas the character stream mechanism manages 16-bit Unicode characters. A Unicode set is essentially a type of character set where each character corresponds to a specific numeric value for the given character set. In general, each programming language adopts a particular character set to represent and manage characters. Apart from Unicode, another commonly used character set is ASCII (American Standard Code for Information Interchange), defined by the International Standard Organization (ISO). At the inception of Java (version 1.0), it did not follow character streams; thus, all IO operations were byte-oriented then. The character streams were introduced later (version 1.1).

In `java.io`, character streams are defined by using two class hierarchies: `Reader` and `Writer`. `Reader` is the abstract base class for character stream input operations whereas `Writer` is the abstract base class for character stream output operations. Each of these abstract classes has several sub classes to manage various input/output sources, such as disk files, network connections, memory buffers, etc.

Reader class

The sub classes of `Reader` class are shown in Figure 8.11. A brief description of each of the sub class is given in Table 8.19.

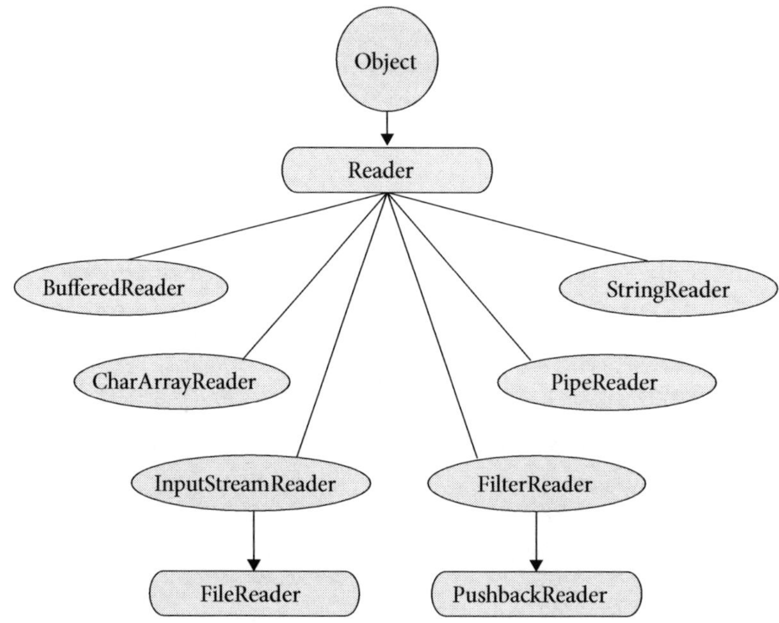

Figure 8.11 Class hierarchy of `Reader` class

Table 8.19 Sub classes of the `Reader` class

Method	Description
`BufferedReader`	Reads text from a character-input stream, buffering characters so as to provide for the efficient reading of characters, arrays, and lines.
`CharArrayReader`	This class implements a character buffer that can be used as a character-input stream.
`InputStreamReader`	An `InputStreamReader` is a bridge from byte streams to character streams: It reads bytes and decodes them into characters using a specified character set.
`PipedReader`	Piped character-input streams. Uses a pipe for character input stream.
`FilterReader`	Abstract class for reading filtered character streams.
`PushbackReader`	A character-stream reader that allows characters to be pushed back into the stream. This enables a character to be pushed back into the stream after reading.
`StringReader`	A character stream whose source is a string.
`FileReader`	Convenience class for reading character files. An instance of this class is used for reading characters from files.

The `Reader` class defines a programming interface for reading characters or arrays of characters, marking locations in the stream, skipping characters of input, finding the number of characters that are available for reading, and resetting the current position within the stream.

The following are the two constructors defined for this class:

`protected Reader()`

Creates a new character-stream reader whose critical sections will synchronize on the reader itself.

`protected Reader(Object lock)`

Creates a new character-stream reader whose critical sections will synchronize on the given object.

The abstract class `Reader` defines Java's model of streaming character input. It implements the `AutoCloseable` and `Closeable` interfaces. All sub classes which extend the `Reader` class implement many methods for managing input streams. All methods are thus in polymorphic forms (i.e., have the same name but different functionalities). Most of the methods in this class will throw an `IOException` when an IO error occurs. Table 8.20 shows the methods in `Reader` which are defined in its sub classes.

Table 8.20 Methods of the `Reader` class

Method	Description
`close()`	Closes the stream and releases any system resources associated with it.
`mark(int readAheadLimit)`	Marks the present position in the stream. Marking is valid until `readAheadLimit` number of characters are read. Subsequent calls to `reset()` will attempt to reposition the stream to this point.
`markSupported()`	Tells whether this stream supports the `mark()` operation.
`read()`	Reads a single character. This method will block until a character is available, an IO error occurs, or the end of the stream is reached.
`read(char[] cbuf)`	Reads characters into an array. This method will block until some input is available, an IO error occurs, or the end of the stream is reached. It returns the number of characters read, or –1 if the end of the stream is reached.
`read(char[] cbuf, int off, int len)`	Reads characters into a portion of an array. This method will block until some input is available, an IO error occurs, or the end of the stream is reached.
`read(CharBuffer target)`	Attempts to read characters into the specified character buffer. The buffer is used as a repository of characters as-is: the only changes made are the results of a put operation. No flipping or rewinding of the buffer is performed. This method returns the number of characters added to the buffer, or –1 if this source of characters is at its end.

`ready()`	Tells whether this stream is ready to be read. This method returns `true` if the next `read()` is guaranteed not to block for input, `false` otherwise.
`reset()`	Resets the stream. If the stream has been marked, then attempt to reposition it at the mark. If the stream has not been marked, then attempt to reset it in some way appropriate to the particular stream, for example, by repositioning it to its starting point. Not all character-input streams support the `reset()` operation, and some support `reset()` without supporting `mark()`.
`skip(long n)`	Skips characters. This method will block until some characters are available, an IO error occurs, or the end of the stream is reached.

- Once the stream has been closed, further `read()`, `ready()`, `mark()`, `reset()`, or `skip()` invocations will throw an `IOException`. Closing a previously closed stream has no effect.
- Not all character-input streams support the `mark()` operation.
- The `read()` reads a character and it returns as an integer in the range 0 to 65535 (0 x 00–0 x ffff), or –1 if it reaches at the end of the stream.

Writer class

`Writer` class is the top level abstract class. It is used to write to character streams. The sub classes of `Writer` class are shown in Figure 8.12. A brief description of each of the sub class is given in Table 8.21.

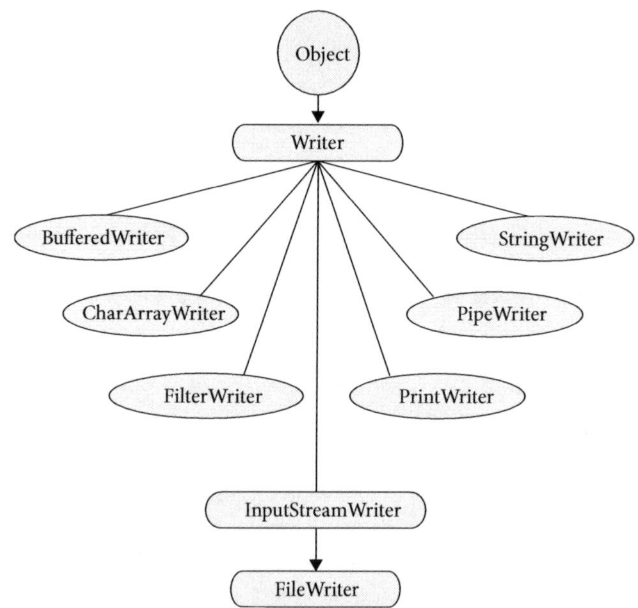

Figure 8.12 Class hierarchy of `Write` class

Table 8.21 Sub classes of the `Writer` class

Class	Description
`BufferedWriter`	Writes text to a character-output stream, buffering characters so as to provide for the efficient writing of single characters, arrays, and strings.
`CharArrayWriter`	This class implements a character buffer that can be used as a writer.
`PipedWriter`	Piped character-output streams.
`StringWriter`	A character stream that collects its output in a string buffer, which can then be used to construct a string.
`FileWriter`	Convenience class for writing character to files.
`FilterWriter`	Abstract class for writing filtered character streams.
`PrintWriter`	Prints formatted representations of objects to a text-output stream.
`OutputStreamWriter`	An instance of this class provides a bridge between character streams and byte streams. Characters are encoded into bytes using a specified character set.

The `Writer` class is a sibling to the `Reader` class and is used to write data that can then be read by an input stream. The `Writer` class defines a programming interface for writing characters or arrays of characters to the stream and flushing the stream.

The following are the two constructors defined for the `Writer` class:

```
protected Writer()
```

Creates a new character stream that can itself synchronize on the writer.

```
protected Writer(Object obj)
```

Creates a new character stream that can itself synchronize on the given object `obj`.

Like the `Reader` class and its sub classes, the `Writer` class declares several methods which are finally polymorphically defined in their sub classes. The methods which are of important to manage an output stream are listed in Table 8.22.

Table 8.22 Methods of the `Writer` class

Method	Description
`append(char c)`	Appends the specified character to this writer.
`append(CharSequence csq)`	Appends the specified character sequence to this writer.
`append(CharSequence csq, int start, int end)`	Appends a subsequence of the specified character sequence to this writer.
`close()`	Closes the stream, flushing it first.
`flush()`	Flushes the stream.
`write(char[] cbuf)`	Writes an array of characters.
`write(char[] cbuf, int off, int len)`	Writes a portion of an array of characters.
`write(int c)`	Writes a single character. Characters being written are contained in 16 lower bits of the `c` integer value, the rest of the 16 higher bits are ignored by the method.
`write(String str)`	Writes a string.
`write(String str, int off, int len)`	Writes a portion of a string.

IO programming with characters streams

We have learned about character stream classes (Tables 8.19 and 8.21), the methods for input from input character streams (Table 8.20), and output to output character streams (Table 8.21). If you compare between `InputStream` classes (Table 8.4) and methods of it (Table 8.5) with `Reader` classes (Table 8.19) and methods in it (Table 8.20), then structurally they are very similar to each other. The same is true between `OutputStream` classes (Tables 8.6 and 8.7) and `Writer` classes (Tables 8.21 and 8.22). They are different as *byte* versus *character*. The two streams' concepts are two different abstractions. Whether byte streams or character streams, they are identical from the logical point of view; they are only functionally different. The following points are pertinent for the two types of streams in Java:

- Character-oriented streams are also known as `Reader` and `Writer` streams. Byte-oriented streams are known as `InputStream` and `OutputStream`.
- Character-oriented streams read character by character while byte-oriented streams read byte by byte.
- Character-oriented streams are tied to data type. Only string type or character type can be read through them while byte-oriented are not tied to any data type; data of any data type can be read.
- Character oriented streams use character encoding scheme (Unicode) while byte oriented do not use any encoding scheme.

The difference is simply for convenience. Some streams are inherently byte-oriented and some are character-oriented. As a result, it is always convenient to handle them with appropriate classes and methods defined java.io stream package. For example, the FileInputStream is meant for reading a raw stream of bytes, such as image data. Similarly, the FileOutputStream object may be used to write a raw byte stream. Similalry, reading and writing files based on character-oriented stream of data are FileReader and FileWrite, respectively. More precisely, `java.io` provide classes with specific methods to manipulate appropriate streams. An analogy between the byte streams and character streams classes are shown in Fig. 8.13.

Character stream classes	Byte stream classes
Reader	InputStream
BufferedReader	BufferedInputStream
CharArrayReader	ByteArrayInputStream
InputStreamReader	(none)
FileReader	FleInputStream
FilterReader	FilterInputReader
PushbackReader	PushbackInputStream
PipedReader	PipedInputStream
StringReader	StringBufferInputStream
(none)	SequenceInputStream
(none)	ObjectInputStream
Writer	OutputStream
BufferedWriter	BufferedOutputStream
CharArrayWriter	ByteArrayOutputStream
FilterWriter	FilterOutputStream
OutputStreamWriter	
FileWriter	FileOutputStream
PrintWriter	PrintStream
PipedWriter	PipedOutputStream
StringWriter	
(none)	ObjectOutputStream

Figure 8.13 Character streams versus byte streams

Now, let us discuss and illustrate the following character stream classes:

I. Character array reader and writer
II. File reader and writer
III. Buffered reader and writer

IV. String reader and writer
V. PrintWriter
VI. InputStreamReader and OutputStreamWriter

Character array reader and writer

The class `CharArrayReader` defined in the `java.io` is used to read characters from an array of characters. The array of characters is the source of the input stream. In order to create a stream reader object of the type `CharArrayRedaer`, any one of the following two constructors can be used:

`CharArrayReader(char[] c)`

Creates a `CharArrayReader` to read from a character array `c` as the input source.

`CharArrayReader(char[] c, int start, int len)`

Creates a `CharArrayReader` to read from a character array `c` a portion of it starting from the index specified by `start` and is `len` the number of characters to be read. It throws `IllegalArgumentException` if `start` is negative or greater than `c.length`, or if `len` is negative, or if the sum of these two values is negative.

The `CharArrayReader` class extends the `Reader` class and hence all methods of the `Reader` class are defined by the `CharArrayReader` class. It does not have any method of its own.

Program 8.32 illustrates the use of different methods to read characters from an array of characters.

Program 8.32 *(Working of `CharArrayReader` class)*

```
/* Java program illustrating the working of
CharArrayReader class. */

import java.io.*;

public class CharArrayReaderDemo {
    public static void main(String[] args) throws
      IOException {
        // Creating an array of characters as a source
                                          // input stream
        String aSet = {0123456789
          ABCDEFGHIJKLMNOPQRSTUVWXYZ aeiou};
```

```
        // Putting the string into the array of
                                          // characters
        int length = aSet.length();
        char c[] = new char[length];
        aSet.getChars(0, length, c, 0);
           // Convert string to an arrays

        // Initializing the reader stream: Constructor 1
        try(CharArrayReader cReader1 = new CharArray
           Reader(c)){
           boolean check=cReader1.ready();
           //Check if the stream is ready
           if(check == true) {
              while((int i = cReader.read()) != -1) {
                  if (i == ' ')  cReader1.skip(1);
                     // Skip the space
                  else
                    System.out.print((char)i);
                System.out.println();  i = cReader1.
                     read();}
            }
            else
               System.out.println("Input array is not
                ready");
          } catch(IOException e) {
              System.out.println("I/O Error:" + e);
          }

        // Initializing the reader stream: Constructor 2
        try(CharArrayReader cReader2 = new CharArray
           Reader(c, 11, 26)){
            while((int i = cReader2.read()) != -1)
                System.out.print((char)i);
            System.out.println();
        }catch(IOException e) {
            System.out.println("I/O Error:" + e);
        }
    }
}
```

- The `read()` method automatically moves to its next location after reading a character from the array.
- The `close()` method implemented by `CharArray Reader` does not throw any exceptions. This is because it cannot fail.
- The `CharArrayReader` is mark-supported.

The class `CharArrayWriter` writes characters to an array of characters as destination. The following two constructors are defined by the class `CharArrayWriter` class:

`CharArrayWriter()`

Creates a buffer of default size. The class maintains an internal buffer of its own to store an array of characters. The buffer is held in the `buf` field of `CharArrayWriter`. The buffer automatically grows when data is written to the stream.

`CharArrayWriter(int len)`

Creates a buffer of size equal to that specified by `len`. The buffer size will be increased automatically, if needed.

The `CharArrayWriter` class extends the `Writer` class and hence all methods of the `Writer` class are defined by the `CharArrayWriter` class. In addition, it defines the methods `toCharArray()` and `toString()` of its own to retrieve the data stored in its buffer.

Program 8.33 illustrates the use of different methods to write characters to a destination array of characters.

Program 8.33 *(Working of `CharArrayWriter` class)*

```
/* This program demonstrates the application of
CharArrayWriter class and some of the methods of it. */

import java.io.*;

class CharArrayWriterDemo {
    public static void main(String args[]) throws
      IOException {
       // Cretaes a default character stream of buffer
       CharArrayWriter cWriter = new CharArrayWriter();

       // Creates a data to be stored
       String s = "Welcome to Jay with Java";
       char c[] = new char[s.length()];
            // An array of characters
       s.getChars(0, s.length(), c, 0);
            // Copy string to array
       try {
            cWriter.write(c);
            // Write data to the writer's buffer
```

```
        } catch(IOException e) {
            System.out.println("Error Writing to
             Buffer");
            return;
        }

        System.out.println("Buffer as a string");
        System.out.println(cWriter.toString());
             //Retrieves data as string

        System.out.println("Into array");
        char a[] = cWriter.toCharArray();
             // Retrieves data as array
        for (int i=0; i<a.length; i++)
            System.out.print(a[i]);

        System.out.println("Doing a reset");
        cWriter.reset();          // Reset its marker
        for (int i=0; i<3; i++)
           cWriter.write('X');     cWriter.append('#');
        System.out.println(cWriter.toString());
    }
}
```

- The number of characters held by the buffer `buf` is contained in the `count` field of `CharArrayWriter`. Both `buf` and `count` are protected fields.
- The `close()` method has no effect on a `CharArray Writer`.
- The `CharArrayReader` and `CharArrayWriter` classes are the counterparts of the `ByteArrayInputStream` and `ByteArray OutputStream` classes.

File reader and writer

File is an important object which acts as a source as well destination of data stream. There are many applications where the file stores text and the text needs to be read. The `FileReader` and `FileWriter` are the two classes defined in `java.io` which support the most convenient ways of reading text from files and writing text into files, respectively.

To create an instance of a file reader, the following three constructors are defined by the class `FileReader`:

`FileReader(File file)`

This constructor creates a new `FileReader`, given the `file` to read from.

`FileReader(FileDescriptor fd)`

This constructor creates a new `FileReader`, given the `FileDescriptor` `fd` to read from.

`FileReader(String fileName)`

This constructor creates a new `FileReader`, given the name of the file to read from.

All methods which are declared in the `Reader` class are inherited to this class and defined for this class (Table 8.20).

Program 8.34 shows how to read lines from a file and display them on a standard output device. It reads its own source file, which must be in the current directory.

Program 8.34 *(Working of `FileReader` class)*

```
/* This program illustrates the reading of a file using
FileReader. */

import java.io.*;

class FileReaderDemo {
    public static void main(String args[]) {
       try ( FileReader fr = new FileReader
           ("FileReaderDemo.java") ) {
           int c;
           // Read and display the file.
           while((c = fr.read()) != -1)
                System.out.print((char) c);
         } catch(IOException e) {
           System.out.println("I/O Error:" + e);
         }

      // Reading a file and coping the content into an
                                                // array
      File f = new File("abc.txt");
          // Let the file be in the working directory
      try (FileReader fr = new FileReader(f)) {
         char[] a = new char[5000];
           //Maximum number of characters in the file
         fr.read(a);
           // Reads the content and store in the array
```

```
            for(char c : a)
               System.out.print(c);
                  // Prints the characters one by one

         } catch(IOException e) {
             System.out.println("I/O Error:" + e);
         }
      }
   }
```

The `FileWriter` class is for writing streams of characters into a file. This class has the following constructors to create required objects:

`FileWriter(File file)`

This constructor creates a `FileWriter` object given a File object.

`FileWriter(File file, boolean append)`

This constructor creates a `FileWriter` object given a File object with a boolean indicating whether or not to append the data written.

`FileWriter(FileDescriptor fd)`

This constructor creates a `FileWriter` object associated with the given file descriptor.

`FileWriter(String fileName)`

This constructor creates a `FileWriter` object, given a file name.

`FileWriter(String fileName, boolean append)`

This constructor creates a `FileWriter` object given a file name with a boolean indicating whether or not to append the data written.

All methods which are declared in the `Writer` class are inherited to this class and defined for this class (Table 8.22).

Program 8.35 *(Working of* `FileWriter` *class)*

```
/* This program illustrates the different ways that you
can write characters into a file. */
import.java.io.*;
public class FileWriterDemo {
    public static void main(String[] args) {
        try {
             FileWriter fw = new FileWriter("abc.txt",
                 true)) {
```

```
            fw.write(65);
            // Writes character with its Unicode value
             fw.write('\n');
            // Writes a newline character
             fw.write("Joy with Java");
            // Writes string into the file

             String s = "This is a line with some text.";
             char b[] = new char[s.length()];
             s.getChars(0, s.length(), b, 0);
             fw.write(b, 10, 19);
                 // Writes a portion of the array of b
             fw.write("Java is nice!", 0,3);
                 // Writes portion of string

             fw.append('#');
                 // Append # at the end of the file

             fw.flush();
                 // Flushes data to the file immediately
             fw.close();
                 // Close the stream now, if it is not
                                              // automatic
        } catch (Exception e) {
            e.printStackTrace();
        }
    }
}
```

Program 8.35 shows how to write to a file using different methods defined in the class `FileWriter`.

- If append is `true`, then the output is appended at the end of the file.
- While writing 65, an integer value as the argument, the `write()` actually writes A into the file; in this case, the `write()` converts the decimal value 65 and stores as A.
- An integer is of 4 bytes, while Java treats a character in Unicode as 16 bits. When you write an integer, the `write()` method stores only the lower two bytes and ignores the higher two bytes.

Buffered reader and writer

When you read from a file or write into a file, because of the speed mismatch between the CPU and secondary device, you have to compromise the throughput in the execution. Such a situation can be avoided if you use a buffer between your program and the IO streams you are working with. The buffered reader and writer simplify reading text from any character input stream and writing text to a character output stream, respectively. They buffer the characters in order to enable efficient reading and writing of text data. They enable you to minimize the number of IO operations by reading or writing chunks of characters and storing them in an internal buffer. While the buffer has data, the reader and writer will read and write from it instead of directly from the underlying streams.

The `java.io` defines `BufferedReader` and `BufferedWriter` as buffered IO streams. Buffered input streams read data from a memory area known as a `buffer`; the `BufferedReader` object is called only when the buffer is empty. Similarly, buffered output streams write data to a buffer, and the `BufferedWriter` object is called only when the buffer is full.

The `BufferedReader` class has the following two constructors to wrap an input stream:

`BufferedReader(Reader rd)`

It is used to create a buffered character input stream that uses the default size for an input buffer.

`BufferedReader(Reader rd, int size)`

It is used to create a buffered character input stream that uses the specified size for an input buffer.

Thus, the two constructors support buffering of any reader. For example, you can wrap a `FileReader` with buffering as follows:

```
File aFile = new File("input.txt");
FileReader fr = new FileReader(aFile);
BufferedReader br = new BufferedReader(fr);
```

The methods which are declared in the `Reader` class (Table 8.20) are defined by the `BufferedReader` class.

Program 8.36 demonstrates how you can read the contents of a file using the `BufferedReader` class.

Program 8.36 *(Working of* `BufferedReader` *class)*

```
/* This program shows how a file can be read through a
buffered reader. */

import java.io.*;
```

```
class BufferedReaderDemo {
    public static void main(String[] args) {
       try (File aFile = new File("BufferedReaderDemo.
           java");
           FileReader fr = new FileReader(aFile);
           BufferedReader br = new BufferedReader(fr)) {

           char[] txt = new char[1000];
           int size = 0;

           System.out.println("Reading the file through
                buffer...");
           size = br.read(txt); // Read in whole file
           System.out.println("File size:" + size);
           for (char c : txt) {
              System.out.print(c);
        }
      } catch (Exception e) {
         e.printStackTrace();
      }
    }
}
```

You can compare Program 8.34 with Program 8.36. The two programs do the same task and the latter is reading through a buffered reader. In general, you can configure `BufferedReader` to take any kind of input stream as an underlying source. You can do it using `InputStreamReader` and wrapping it in the constructor. We shall discuss the `InputStreamReader` class later in this section. Program 8.37 gives an example of how you can read a number of lines of text from a keyboard (`System.in` is the input stream in this case).

Program 8.37 *(Reading lines through* `BufferedReader`*)*

```
/* This program reads lines of text with any character
from console using a BufferedReader. To quit the
program, user should type "Quit" and press ENTER. */

import java.io.*;

class ConsoleReadingDemo {
    public static void main(String args[]) throws
      IOException {
         // create a BufferedReader using System.in
 BufferedReader br=new BufferedReader(new InputStream
      Reader(System.in));
```

```
            String line;
            System.out.println("Enter any lines of text.");
            System.out.println("Enter 'Quit' to quit the
               program.");
            do {
              line = br.readLine();
                   //Read line of any sequence of characters
              System.out.println(line);
            } while(!((line.equals("Quit")
               || (line.equals("quit")))));
       }
}
```

- In Program 8.37, you are reading from `System.in` which typically corresponds to an input from a keyboard.
- `System.in` is line buffered, by default. This means that no input is actually passed to the program until you press enter.
- `System.in` has its own implementation of `InputStreamReader` which acts as a bridge from the byte stream to the character stream.
- Similarly, you could pass an input stream for reading from a socket, file, or any input as a source of text. The only prerequisite is that there should be an appropriate `InputStreamReader` implementation for doing that.
- In addition to buffering, `BufferedReader` also provides helper methods such as `mark()`, `reset()`, etc. for reading a text line-by-line or character-by-character to process the text. This suggests another reason why you should use `BufferedReader` wrapping with say, `FileReader`, other than directly using the `FileReader` only.

The class `BufferedWriter` is defined in `java.io`, which does buffering of an output character stream which is exactly the opposite action of the `BufferedReader`. The `BufferedWriter` class defines the following two constructors which provide the different ways that you can create buffering to output.

`BufferedWriter(Writer wrt)`

It is used to create a buffered character output stream that uses the default size for an output buffer.

`BufferedWriter(Writer wrt, int size)`

It is used to create a buffered character output stream that uses the specified size for an output buffer.

In addition to the methods defined in `Writer` class (Table 8.22), the class also defines `newLine()` method. The `newline()` method uses the platform's own notion of a line separator, calling this method to terminate each output line and thus writing a newline character directly. Program 8.38 writes lines of text into a file.

Program 8.38 *(Writing lines through* `Buffered Writer`*)*

```
/* Write lines of text to a file using BufferedWriter. */

import java.io.*;

class BufferedWriterDemo {
    public static void main(String[] args) throws
      IOException {
        BufferedWriter bw = null;
        String msg1 = "The quick brown fox jumps over
          the lazy dog.";
        String msg2 = "A stitch in time saves nine.";
        String msg3 = "God is good.";
        File myFile  = new File("messages.txt");

        try {
            // Create a BufferedReader wrapped in a
                                    // FileWriter stream
            bw = new BufferedWriter(new FileWriter
                (myFile));
            System.out.println("BufferedWriter bw has
                been opened.");

            // Start writing to the BufferedWriter
                                            // stream
            bw.write(msg1, 0, 10);
            bw.newLine();
                // Write a newline character
            bw.write(msg2, 5, 10);
            bw.newLine();
                // Write another newline character
            bw.write(msg3);
        }
        catch (IOException ex) {
            System.out.println("IO Exception " + ex);
        }
        finally {
            bw.flush();
```

```
                System.out.println("BufferedWriter flushed");
                bw.close();
                System.out.println("BufferedWriter closed");
            }
        }
    }
```

PrintWriter class

The `PrintWriter` class in Java was released in Java 7 as a sub class of the `Writer` class. This class is used for printing the formatted representations of objects to a text-output stream. What the `PrintStream` class does for byte-oriented output streams, `PrintWriter` does the same with the difference that `PrintStream` writes any primitive data of type `int`, `float`, `double`, etc. into raw bytes format, whereas `PrintWriter` writes the same in the form of specified character format, such as Unicode format, as default.

`PrintWriter` class defines the following constructors to create an object for writing data into various possible output streams:

`PrintWriter(String fileName)`

Creates a new `PrintWriter`, without automatic line flushing, with the specified file name. For example:

```
PrintWriter pw = new PrintWriter("abc.txt");
PrintWriter(File file):
```

This allows you to write data into a file as an output stream, without automatic line flushing. For example:

```
File myFile = new File("abc.txt");
PrintWriter pw = new PrintWriter(myFile);
PrintWriter(String fileName, String csn):
```

Creates a new `PrintWriter`, without automatic line flushing, with the specified file name and `charset`. For example:

```
PrintWriter pw = new PrintWriter("abc.txt", "Joy with Java");
```

`PrintWriter(File file, String charSeq)`

This allows to write a sequence of characters `charSeq` into a file as an output stream, without automatic line flushing. For example:

```
String s = "Joy with Java";
File myFile = new File("abc.txt");
PrintWriter pw = new PrintWriter(myFile, s);
```

`PrintWriter(OutputStream out)`

This allows to write data into an `OutputStream` (such as `System.out`, `FileOutputStream`) as an output stream, without automatic line flushing. For example:

```
PrintWriter pw = new PrintWriter(System.out);
```

```
File myFile = new File("abc.txt");
FileOutputStream fos = new FileOutputStream (myFile);
PrintWriter pw = new PrintWriter(fos);
```

`PrintWriter(OutputStream out, boolean autoFlush)`

Creates a new `PrintWriter` from an existing `OutputStream` with automatic line flushing on or off.

`PrintWriter(Writer out)`

Creates a new `PrintWriter`, without automatic line flushing to write data into an output character stream. For example:

```
File myFile = new File("abc.txt");
FileWriter fw = new FileWriter(myFile);
PrintWriter pw = new PrintWriter(fw);
```

`PrintWriter(Writer out, boolean autoFlush) :`

Creates a new `PrintWriter` to write data into an output character stream. For example:

```
File myFile = new File("abc.txt");
FileWriter fw = new FileWriter(myFile);
PrintWriter pw = new PrintWriter(fw, true);
```

The `PrintWriter` class implements all the methods of the `PrintStream` class. However, this class does not have any methods that are used for writing raw bytes.

Program 8.39 illustrates writing of few types of data.

Program 8.39 *(Writing using* `Print Writer`*)*

```
/* This program creates an output stream for writing
characters and primitive data types. */

import java.io.*;
class A {
    int x = 555;
    double y = 4.5e-7;

     public String toString() {
         String s =  "x = " + x + "y = " + y;
         return(s);
     }
}
class PrintWriterDemo {
     public static void main(String args[]){
         A a = new A();    // An object as a data

         try {
             File file = new File("D:\\TextBook.txt");
             PrintWriter pw = new PrintWriter(file);

             pw.println(-7);  // Print integer value -7
             pw.print('A');   // Writes A

             pw.println(23.45f);
             pw.print("Java Rules \n");
             pw.println(a)
                // Writes a's data as a string

             // Use a specified Unicode character set
                                    // to print the text
             pw.printf(Local.PRC, "Dollar is %1$", 123);

             pw.flush();
             pw.close();
         }
         catch(Exception e) {
             System.out.println(e);
         }
     }
}
```

- `PrintWriter` converts the primitive data (`int`, `float`, `char`, etc.) into the text format. It then writes that formatted data to the writer.
- `PrintWriter` supports the `print()` and `println()` methods. Thus, you can use these methods in the same way as you used them with `System.out`. If an argument is not a simple type, the `PrintWriter` methods call the object's `toString()` method and then displays the result.
- `PrintWriter` prints formatted representations of objects to a text-output stream. This class implements all of the print methods found in `PrintStream`. It does not contain methods for writing raw bytes, for which a program should use unencoded byte streams.
- The `PrintWriter` class has some differences when compared to the `PrintStream` class. The `PrintWriter` class has a feature of auto flushing. In the `PrintStream` class, when automatic flushing is enabled, output will be sent when the newline character is the output. But in the `PrintWriter` class, when automatic flushing is enabled, output will be printed when `println()`, `printf()`, etc. methods are invoked. These methods use the platform's notion of a line separator, not a newline character.
- One important thing about the `PrintWriter` class is that it never throws any IO exceptions. However, its constructor does that in case of an error. This class has a method `checkError()`, which can be invoked by the programmer to check whether any error is occurred.
- `PrintWriter` is one of the character-based classes. Using a character-based class for console output makes internationalizing your program easier.
- The `PrintWriter` is useful if you are generating outputs (e.g., reports) where you have to mix text and numbers.

String reader and writer

The `StringReader` class is a character stream with a string as a source. It takes an input string and changes it into a character stream. It inherits `Reader` class. The `StringReader` class enables you to turn a `String` object into a `Reader`. This is useful if you have data as a `String` but need to pass that `String` to a component that only accepts a `Reader`.

`StringReader` defines only one constructor which is as follows:

```
StringReader(String s)
```

This creates `StringReader` to read a string object as a source of character stream. It inherits all the methods defined by the `Reader` class (Table 8.20) and it doesn't have any method of its own.

Program 8.40 demonstrates how you can program with `StringReader` class.

Program 8.40 *(Reading using* `String Reader`*)*

```
/* This program demonstrates the working of some of the
StringReader methods*/

import java.io.*;

class StringReaderDemo {
    public static void main(String[] args) throws
     IOException {
        String msg = "Hello!! \n Welcome to Joy with
          Java";
        StringReader reader = new StringReader(msg);
        int k = 0;
        while((k = reader.read())!=-1)
          // Reading from reader stream
            System.out.print((char)k);

        char c[]=new char[msg.length];

        //illustrating markSupported()
        if(reader.markSupported()) {
            System.out.println("StringRedaer supports
                mark() peration");
            reader.mark(10);
                // Position the mark() at 10th index
        }

        reader.skip(5);
         // Skips 5 characters from the current position

        if(reader.ready()) {
          // If the reader is ready
            System.out.print((char)reader.read());
                // Read the character

        reader.read(c);
          // Copy the String msg to array c

        reader.reset();
          // Return to the marked position
        while((k = reader.read())!=-1)
          // Reading from marked poistion
            System.out.print((char)k);
    }
}
```

- In `StringReader` class, the system resources like network sockets and files are not used, therefore closing the `StringReader` is not necessary.
- `StringReader` does not use any buffer to hold the String object.

If you need to write a string through a buffer, then you should use the `StringWriter` class. This class creates a `String` buffer stream to write as `String` object into it. This class defines the following two constructors to buffer a `String` object:

`StringWriter()`

Creates a new `StringWriter` using the initial or default size of buffer.

`StringWriter(int size)`

Creates a new `StringWriter` using the mentioned size of buffer.

This class inherits all the methods defined in the `Writer` class (Table 8.22). It defines an additional method `StringBuffer getBuffer()` which returns the `StringBuffer` from its buffer.

Program 8.41 exhibits a simple application of `StringWriter` class.

Program 8.41
Writing using *`String Writer`*

```
/* This program shows an application of StringWriter
class. */
import java.io.*;

class StringWriterDemo {
    public static void main(String[] args) throws
     IOException {
       String msg1 = "The quick brown fox jumps over
         the lazy dog.\n";
       String msg2 = "A stitch in time saves nine.\n";
       String msg3 = "God is good.\n";

       // Create with default size of buffer
       StringWriter sw = new StringWriter();
       //Write characters to writer.
       sw.write("This is a sample text to write...");
       sw.write(msg1+msg2+msg3); // Write the messages

       sw.close();  // Close the StringWriter now

       String data = sw.toString();
         // You can use this to read
       StringBuffer db = sw.getBuffer();
         // Read buffer
```

```
            char cArray[] = new char[100];
            db.getChars(0,20,cArray,0);
            System.out.println(cArray);
        }
}
```

- The characters written to the StringWriter are obtained via two methods toString() and getBuffer(). The method toString() returns the characters written to the StringWriter as a String. The method getBuffer() returns the StringBuffer used by the StringWriter to build the string from the written characters. You only need to use one of these two methods.
- Methods of the StringWriter class can also be called after closing the stream as this will raise no IO Exception.

InputStreamReader and OutputStreamWriter

Refer to the program ConsoleReadingDemo (Program 8.37) where the class InputStreamReader is used. You have seen many programs with byte stream classes (in Section 8.3.3 of this chapter). You have learned how you can read bytes from the console using the read() and read(bytes[]) methods of InputStream class. Possibly, they worked fine because we only used characters from the standard 8-bit ASCII character set which has a range of 0 to 127. If you had tried to run the programs with any character outside this range, such as á, you would have got some very strange results! This will return –96131 followed by lots of zeros or the ? character when cast to a char type. The problem arises as you are not reading a character from a 16-bit Unicode character set; rather, you are simply reading a byte to read your input, which has only a limited set of characters. For wider applications and proper internationalization, you indeed need to use the full Unicode character set which has a range 0 to 65,536 and for this we need to use a character input stream.

To read characters from the console we need a class to convert byte streams into character streams. The java.io provides a solution to this problem. Under the character input stream hierarchy (Figure 8.2 and Figure 8.11) you can notice the presence of the class InputStreamReader. The InputStreamReader class acts as a *bridge* for decoding byte streams into character streams. which is exactly what we want. Java recommends that for top efficiency you should *wrap* the InputStreamReader within a reader character stream such as

`System.in`. If you wrap an `InputStreamReader` around an `InputStream` object, the bytes in the byte stream are read and converted to characters using the character encoding scheme specified by the `InputStreamReader` for that `InputStream` object. Every `InputStream` is supposed to have its own implementation how to read and convert a byte stream into character stream. The `InputStreamReader` class defines the following constructors to wrap an `InputStream` source:

`InputStreamReader(InputStream in)`

Creates an `InputStreamReader` that uses the default charset.

`InputStreamReader(InputStream in_strm, Charset cs)`

Creates an `InputStreamReader` that uses the given charset.

`InputStreamReader(InputStream in, CharsetDecoder dec)`

Creates an `InputStreamReader` that uses the given charset decoder.

`InputStreamReader(InputStream in, String charsetName)`

Creates an `InputStreamReader` that uses the named charset.

This class defines all the regular method as in `InputStream` class and, additionally, it defines the method `getEncoding()`, which returns the encoding scheme that the input stream source follows.

Program 8.42 shows a simple example of using the `InputStream Reader` class.

Program 8.42 *(Wraping an input using* `Input Stream Reader`*)*

```
/* This program reads a file abc.txt, checks the
encoding scheme  the source maintains and then displays
the content of the file. You can test the program
with a file that contains some text encoded with UTF-8
standard. */

import java.io.*;

public class InputStreamRederDemo {
    public static void main(String[] args) {
        try {
            FileInputStream fis = new FileInputStream
             ("abc.txt");
            InputStreamReader in = new InputStreamReader
             (fis);
```

```
            // Check the encloding scheme in the file
                                              // content
            System.out.println("Encoding scheme: " +
             in.getEncoding());

            int c = 0;
            while((c = in.read()) != -1)
              System.out.println((char) c);

              fis.close();
              in.close();
          }
          catch (IOException e){ }
          }
     }
}
```

Similarly, you can wrap an `OutputStreamWriter` around any `OutputStream` object so that you can write characters and have them converted to bytes.

`OutputStreamWriter(OutputStream os)`

Creates an `OutputStreamWriter` that uses a default charset for encoding.

`OutputStreamWriter(OutputStream os, Charset cs)`

Creates an `OutputStreamWriter` that uses a `cs` charset for encoding.

`OutputStreamWriter(OutputStream os, CharsetEncoder ce)`

Creates an `OutputStreamWriter` that uses a given encoder.

`OutputStreamWriter(OutputStream os, String setName)`

Creates an `OutputStreamWriter` that uses a named character set.

This class defines all the regular method as in `OutputStream` class and, additionally, it defines the method `getEncoding()`, which returns the encoding scheme that the output stream follows.

Program 8.43 shows a simple example of using the `OutputStream Writer` class.

Program 8.43 *(Wraping an output using* `Output Stream Reader`*)*

```
/* This program demonstrates writing into a file using
a specfic encoding scheme. */

import java.io.*;

class OutputStreamWriterDemo  {
     public static void main(String args[]) throws
           IOException {
          OutputStream os = new FileOutputStream
            ("abc.txt");
          OutputStreamWriter osw = new OutputStream
            Writer(os, "UTF-8");

          char[] cs = {'A','B','C','D','E'};
          osw.write(cs);

          os.close();
          osw.close();
     }
}
```

- The `OutputStreamWriter` is useful if you need to write characters to a file, encoded as, for example, UTF-8 or UTF-16. You can then write the characters (char values) to the `OutputStreamWriter` and it will encode them correctly and write the encoded bytes to the underlying `OutputStream`.
- The `OutputStreamWriter` is a sub class of the `Writer` class. Thus, you can use an `OutputStreamWriter` wherever a `Writer` is required.

8.2.5 Scanner Class

In this chapter, we are mainly discussing `java.io` API. It is worth mentioning another class called `Scanner` which, although not a member of `java.io`, does a fair job while you want to read data from many input sources like keyboard, file, etc. The Scanner class is defined in `java.util`. It is called *formatter* because it reads formatted input and converts it into its binary form and in a user-friendly manner. For example, you can use `Scanner` to read a number from the keyboard and straightway assign its value to a variable.

This class has many constructors to create its instance, which are listed in Table 8.23.

Table 8.23 Constructors of the `Scanner` class

Method	Description
`Scanner(File file)`	Creates a `Scanner` that uses the file specified by `file` as a source of input. It throws `FileNotFoundException`.
`Scanner(File file, String charset)`	Creates a `Scanner` that uses the file specified by `file` with the encoding specified by `charset` as a source of input. It throws `FileNotFoundException`.
`Scanner(InputStream in)`	Creates a `Scanner` that uses the stream specified by `in` as a source of input.
`Scanner(InputStream in, String charset)`	Creates a `Scanner` that uses the stream specified by `in` with the encoding specified by `charset` as a source of input. It throws `IOException`.
`Scanner(Path from)`	Creates a `Scanner` that uses the file specified by `from` as a source of input.
`Scanner(Path from, String charset)`	Creates a `Scanner` that uses the file specified by `from` with the encoding specified by `charset` as a source of input. It throws `IOException`.
`Scanner(Readable from)`	Creates a `Scanner` that uses the `Readable` object specified by `from` as a source of input.
`Scanner (ReadableByte Channel from)`	Creates a `Scanner` that uses the `ReadableByteChannel` specified by `from` as a source of input.
`Scanner(ReadableByte Channel from, String charset)`	Creates a `Scanner` that uses the `ReadableByteChannel` specified by `from` with the encoding specified by `charset` as a source of input.
`Scanner(String str)`	Creates a `Scanner` that uses the string specified by `str` as a source of input.

The `Scanner` class defines a large set of methods. You can check the full list of utility methods from the Oracle documentation in the link:

`https://docs.oracle.com/javase/7/docs/api/java/util/Scanner.html.`

A few methods, which are called `hasNext` and `next` are listed in Table 8.24 and Table 8.25, respectively, and we will refer to them in our subsequent discussions.

Table 8.24 Different `hasNext` methods defined in `Scanner` class

Method	Description
`hasNext()`	Returns true if another token of any type is available to be read. Returns false otherwise.
`hasNext(Pattern pattern)`	Returns true if a token that matches the pattern passed in *pattern* is available to be read. Returns false otherwise.
`hasNext(String pattern)`	Returns true if a token that matches the pattern passed in *pattern* is available to be read. Returns false otherwise.
`hasNextBigDecimal()`	Returns true if a value that can be stored in a `BigDecimal` object is available to be read. Returns false otherwise.
`hasNextBigInteger()`	Returns true if a value that can be stored in a `BigInteger` object is available to be read. Returns false otherwise. The default radix is used (unless changed, the default radix is 10).
`hasNextBigInteger(int radix)`	Returns true if a value in the specified radix that can be stored in a `BigInteger` object is available to be read. Returns false otherwise.
`hasNextBoolean()`	Returns true if a boolean value is available to be read. Returns false otherwise.
`hasNextByte()`	Returns true if a byte value is available to be read. Returns false otherwise. The default radix is used (unless changed, the default radix is 10).
`hasNextByte(int radix)`	Returns true if a byte value in the specified radix is available to be read. Returns false otherwise.
`hasNextDouble()`	Returns true if a double value is available to be read. Returns false otherwise.
`hasNextFloat()`	Returns true if a float value is available to be read. Returns false otherwise.
`hasNextInt()`	Returns true if an int value is available to be read. Returns false otherwise. The default radix is used (unless changed, the default radix is 10).
`hasNextInt(int radix)`	Returns true if an int value in the specified radix is available to be read. Returns false otherwise.
`hasNextLine()`	Returns true if a line of input is available.
`hasNextLong()`	Returns true if a long value is available to be read. Returns false otherwise. The default radix is used (unless changed, the default radix is 10).
`hasNextLong(int radix)`	Returns true if a long value in the specified radix is available to be read. Returns false otherwise.
`hasNextShort()`	Returns true if a short value is available to be read. Returns false otherwise. The default radix is used (unless changed, the default radix is 10).
`hasNextShort(int radix)`	Returns true if a short value in the specified radix is available to be read. Returns false otherwise.

Table 8.25 Different `next` methods defined in `Scanner` class

Method	Description
`String next()`	Returns the next token of any type from the input source.
`String next(Pattern pattern)`	Returns the next token that matches the pattern passed in *`pattern`* from the input source.
`String next(String pattern)`	Returns the next token that matches the pattern passed in *`pattern`* from the input source.
`BigDecimal nextBigDecimal()`	Returns the next token as a `BigDecimal` object.
`BigInteger nextBigInteger()`	Returns the next token as a `BigInteger` object. The default radix is used (unless changed, the default radix is 10).
`BigInteger nextBigInteger(int radix)`	Returns the next token (using the specified radix) as a `BigInteger` object.
`boolean nextBoolean()`	Returns the next token as a boolean value.
`byte nextByte()`	Returns the next token as a byte value. The default radix is used (unless changed, the default radix is 10).
`byte nextByte(int radix)`	Returns the next token (using the specified radix) as a byte value.
`double nextDouble()`	Returns the next token as a double value.
`float nextFloat()`	Returns the next token as a float value.
`int nextInt()`	Returns the next token as an int value. The default radix is used (unless changed, the default radix is 10).
`int nextInt(int radix)`	Returns the next token (using the specified radix) as an int value.
`String nextLine()`	Returns the next line of input as a string.
`long nextLong()`	Returns the next token as a long value. The default radix is used (unless changed, the default radix is 10).
`long nextLong(int radix)`	Returns the next token (using the specified radix) as a long value.
`short nextShort( )`	Returns the next token as a short value. The default radix is used (unless changed, the default radix is 10).
`short nextShort(int radix)`	Returns the next token (using the specified radix) as a short value.

Program 8.44 illustrates how to read different types of data from keyboard.

Program 8.44 (Reading data using `Scanner` *class)*

```
/* This program demonstrates reading data of various
types using Scanner class. */

import java.util.Scanner;

public class ScannerDemo1 {
    public static void main(String[] args) {
        // Create Scanner to connetct keyboard
        Scanner sc = new Scanner(System.in);

        // System.out.println("Enter your name:");
        String name = sc.nextLine();
// Character input
        char gender = sc.next().charAt(0);
        // System.out.println("Enter your age:");
        int age = sc.nextInt();
        // System.out.println("Enter your mobile
           number:");
        long mobileNo = sc.nextLong();
        // System.out.println("Enter your CGPA:");
        double cgpa = sc.nextDouble();

       // Print the values to check if the input was
                                  // correctly obtained.
        System.out.println("Name: "+name);
        System.out.println("Gender: "+gender);
        System.out.println("Age: "+age);
        System.out.println("Mobile Number: "+mobileNo);
        System.out.println("CGPA: "+cgpa);
    }
}
```

- Suppose, you want to read an `int` as an input while you enter a string, then it will throw `IOException`.
- You should check the type before you read. For this purpose, you have to use an appropriate `hasNext` method. Program 8.45 illustrates how you can do that.

Program 8.45 (Reading data using `Scanner` *class)*

```
/This program checks if you have entered the right type
and only then it reads the data from keyboard. */

import java.util.Scanner;
```

```
public class ScannerCheckDemo {
    public static void main(String[] args) {
        Scanner in = new Scanner(System.in);

        // Initialize sum and count of input elements
        int sum = 0, count = 0;

        // Check if an int value is available,
                                 // exit loop, otherwise
        while (in.hasNextInt()) {
            // Read an int value
            int num = in.nextInt();
            sum += num;
            count++;
        }
        int mean = sum / count;
        System.out.println("Mean: " + mean);
    }
}
```

- If you want to check data type XYZ, you should do that with the help of `hasNextXYZ()` method (Table 8.24) where XYZ is the type you are interested in. Then you can read the data with `nextXYZ()` method. The function returns true if the scanner has a token of that type, otherwise false.
- Similarly, to check for a single character, use `hasNext().charAt(0)`.

Reading files using `Scanner`

You have already practiced many programs to read a file object. The `Scanner` class can be used to read any file in the most convenient way. Program 8.46 gives an example of this.

Program 8.46 (Reading data using `Scanner` *class from a file)*

```
/* This program reads different data from a file. This
program assumes that the file abc.txt contains data in
three lines: first line int, seconds line Double, and
the third line a text. */

import java.io.*;

public class FileReadUsingScannerDemo {
  public static void main(String[] args) throws
      IOException {
    File file = new File("abc.txt");
```

```
        Scanner in1 = new Scanner(file);
        String data;
        while (in1.hasNextLine())
          // Print the entire file as text
          System.out.println(in1.nextLine());
          in1.close();

          // Reading data with specific data type
          Scanner in2 = new Scanner(file);
          int x = in2.nextInt();    // Reading as int
          System.out.printf("x = %d", x)

          double y = in2.nextDouble();  // Reading as double
          System.out.printf("y = %f", y).

          data = in2.nextLine();    // Reading as text
          System.out.println(Data);

          file.close();
          in2.close();
    }
}
```

Buffered Reader versus Scanner

You could read a file using `BufferedReader` class or `Scanner` class. There are significant differences between these two classes which can make them either more or less convenient, depending on the use case:

- `BufferedReader` is synchronized (thread-safe) while `Scanner` is not.
- `Scanner` can parse primitive types and strings using regular expressions.
- `BufferedReader` allows for changing the size of the buffer while `Scanner` has a fixed buffer size.
- `Scanner` hides `IOException`, while `BufferedReader` forces us to handle it.
- `BufferedReader` is usually faster than `Scanner` because it only reads the data without parsing it.
- If you are parsing individual tokens in a file, then `Scanner` will feel a bit more natural than `BufferedReader`. But just reading a line at a time is where `BufferedReader` shines.

8.3 Files in Java

The `java.io` package defines many classes to deal with input and output operations with streams. In addition, it also includes the following three classes (Figure 8.2) to deal with files and file systems:

```
class File
class FileDescriptor
class RandomSccessFile
```

Unlike the IO streams classes, these classes do not provide any means to perform input/output operations; rather, they manage files systems such as permission, time, date, directory path, directory hierarchy, file properties, etc. This section devotes discussion to these three classes.

8.3.1 File Class

In computer systems, a file is a central resource and stores information which is sharable among many programs. The class `File` represents a file object, which is uniquely identified by a unique name or a path name. In Java a directory is treated as a `File` object. Naming a file or path is a platform dependent issue, as different platforms follow different formats. With the class `File`, you will be able to create a file, create a new directory, delete a file, list the contents of a directory, determine several common attributes of files and directories, and many more, in a platform independent way. Let us discuss the class `File` and its composition.

This class defines fields, constructors, and methods, which are listed in Table 8.26, Table 8.27, and Table 8.28, respectively, with a brief description to each member.

Table 8.26 Fields of class `File`. All fields are `static` modifier.

Field	Description
`String pathSeparator`	It is system-dependent path-separator character, represented as a string for convenience.
`char pathSeparatorChar`	It is system-dependent path-separator character.
`String separator`	It is system-dependent default name-separator character, represented as a string for convenience.
`char separatorChar`	It is system-dependent default name-separator character.

Table 8.27 Constructors of class `File`. All fields are `static` modifier.

Constructor	Description
`File(String pathname)`	It creates a new `File` instance by converting the given pathname string into an abstract pathname.
`File(String pathName, String fileName)`	It creates a new `File` instance of a file which is under a directory `pathName` and having a filename `fileName`.
`File(File dirObj, String fileName)`	It creates a new `File` instance of a file which is under a directory represented by `dirObj` and having a filename `fileName`.
`File(URI uri)`	It creates a new `File` instance by converting the given file URI into an abstract pathname.

Following are some examples explaining the working of the stated constructors:

```
File myFie = new File("abc.txt");
```

This represents a file object `myFile` which links to the physical file having file name `abc.txt` in the system.

```
File myFile = new File("/java/abc.txt");
```

This represents a file object `myFile` which links to the physical file having the file name `abc.txt` under the directory `java`, which is under the working directory in the system. The pathname `"/java/abc.txt"` is called a relative pathname.

```
File myFile = new File("D:/java/abc.txt");
```

This represents a file object `myFile` which links to the physical file having the file name `abc.txt` stored in the directory `java`. The pathname `"D:/java/abc.txt"` is called an absolute pathname.

```
File myDir = new File("D:/java/tmp");
```

This represents a directory object `myDir` which is the directory named as `tmp` under the directory `java` and physically stored in `D`: drive of a computer system. Note that a directory in Java is treated as a `File` object.

```
File myFile = new File("/java/tmp", "abc.txt");
```

This represents a file object `myFile` which links to the physical file having file name `abc.txt` stored in the directory having relative pathname "/`java/tmp"`.

```
File myDir = new File("D:/java/tmp");
File myFile = new File(myDir, "abc.txt");
```

This represents a file object `myFile` which links to the physical file having file name `abc.txt` stored in the directory having the absolute pathname `"D:/java/tmp"`.

URI uri = URI(`"http://www.java.org/index.htm"`);

```
File myFile = new File(uri);
```

This represents a file object `myFile` which is defined by the URI (Uniform Resource Identifier) object uri. The class URI is defined in `java.net` package.

- Because the file and directory names have different formats on different platforms, a simple string is not adequate to name them. The concept of abstract representations of files and directory pathnames enables platform independency of your application.
- An object of the `File` class is Java's representation of a file or directory path name. For example:

```
File myFile = new File("abc.txt");
File myFile = new File("D:/java/abc.txt");
File myDir = new File ("D:\\tmp\\test\\news");
```

- You can mention absolute pathname, that is, the pathname starting from your home (or you may call root) or you can mention relative pathname with respect to your current working directory.
- Java automatically takes care of path separators on UNIX and Windows as per convention. If you use a forward slash (/) on a Windows version of Java, the path will resolve correctly.

Table 8.28 Methods of class `File`. All fields are `public` modifier.

Method	Description
`String getName()`	Returns the name of the file or directory denoted by this abstract pathname.
`String getParent()`	Returns the pathname string of this abstract pathname's parent, or null if this pathname does not name a parent directory.
`File getParentFile()`	Returns the abstract pathname of this abstract pathname's parent, or null if this pathname does not name a parent directory.
`String getPath()`	Converts this abstract pathname into a pathname string.
`boolean isAbsolute()`	Tests whether this abstract pathname is absolute. Returns true if this abstract pathname is absolute, false otherwise.
`String getAbsolutePath()`	Returns the absolute pathname string of this abstract pathname.
`boolean canRead()`	Tests whether the application can read the file denoted by this abstract pathname. Returns true if and only if the file specified by this abstract pathname exists and can be read by the application; false otherwise.
`boolean canWrite()`	Tests whether the application can modify to the file denoted by this abstract pathname. Returns true if and only if the file system actually contains a file denoted by this abstract pathname and the application is allowed to write to the file; false otherwise.
`boolean exists()`	Tests whether the file or directory denoted by this abstract pathname exists. Returns true if and only if the file or directory denoted by this abstract pathname exists; false otherwise.

`boolean isDirectory()`	Tests whether the file denoted by this abstract pathname is a directory. Returns true if and only if the file denoted by this abstract pathname exists and is a directory; false otherwise.
`boolean isFile()`	Tests whether the file denoted by this abstract pathname is a normal file. A file is normal if it is not a directory and, in addition, satisfies other system-dependent criteria. Any non-directory file created by a Java application is guaranteed to be a normal file. Returns true if and only if the file denoted by this abstract pathname exists and is a normal file; false otherwise.
`long lastModified()`	Returns the time that the file denoted by this abstract pathname was last modified. Returns a long value representing the time the file was last modified, measured in milliseconds since the epoch (00:00:00 GMT, January 1, 1970), or 0L if the file does not exist or if an IO error occurs.
`long length()`	Returns the length of the file denoted by this abstract pathname. The return value is unspecified if this pathname denotes a directory.
`boolean createNewFile()`	Atomically creates a new, empty file named by this abstract pathname if and only if a file with this name does not yet exist. Returns true if the named file does not exist and was successfully created; false if the named file already exists. It throws `IOException`.
`boolean delete()`	Deletes the file or directory denoted by this abstract pathname. If this pathname denotes a directory, then the directory must be empty in order to be deleted. Returns true if and only if the file or directory is successfully deleted; false otherwise.
`void deleteOnExit()`	Requests that the file or directory denoted by this abstract pathname be deleted when the virtual machine terminates.
`String[] list()`	Returns an array of strings naming the files and directories in the directory denoted by this abstract pathname.
`String[] list(FilenameFilter filter)`	Returns an array of strings naming the files and directories in the directory denoted by this abstract pathname that satisfy the specified filter.
`File[] listFiles()`	Returns an array of abstract pathnames denoting the files in the directory denoted by this abstract pathname.
`File[] listFiles(FileFilter filter)`	Returns an array of abstract pathnames denoting the files and directories in the directory denoted by this abstract pathname that satisfy the specified filter.
`boolean mkdir()`	Creates the directory named by this abstract pathname. Returns true if and only if the directory was created; false otherwise.
`boolean mkdirs()`	Creates the directory named by this abstract pathname, including any necessary but nonexistent parent directories. Returns true if and only if the directory was created, along with all necessary parent directories; false otherwise.

`boolean renameTo(File dest)`	Renames the file denoted by this abstract pathname. Returns true if and only if the renaming succeeded; false otherwise.
`boolean setLastModified(long time)`	Sets the last-modified time of the file or directory named by this abstract pathname. Returns true if and only if the operation succeeded; false otherwise.
`boolean setReadOnly()`	Marks the file or directory named by this abstract pathname so that only read operations are allowed. Returns true if and only if the operation succeeded; false otherwise.
`File createTempFile(String prefix, String suffix, File directory)`	Creates a new empty file in the specified directory, using the given prefix and suffix strings to generate its name. Returns an abstract pathname denoting a newly-created empty file. It throws `IOException`.
`File public static createTempFile(String prefix, String suffix)`	Creates an empty file in the default temporary-file directory, using the given prefix and suffix to generate its name. Invoking this method is equivalent to invoking createTempFile(prefix, suffix, null). Returns abstract pathname denoting a newly-created empty file. It throws `IOException`.
`int compareTo(File pathname)`	Compares two abstract pathnames lexicographically. Returns zero if the argument is equal to this abstract pathname, a value less than zero if this abstract pathname is lexicographically less than the argument, or a value greater than zero if this abstract pathname is lexicographically greater than the argument.
`int compareTo(Object o)`	Compares this abstract pathname to another object. Returns zero if the argument is equal to this abstract pathname, a value less than zero if this abstract pathname is lexicographically less than the argument, or a value greater than zero if this abstract pathname is lexicographically greater than the argument.
`boolean equals(Object obj)`	Tests this abstract pathname for equality with the given object. Returns true if and only if the argument is not null and is an abstract pathname that denotes the same file or directory as this abstract pathname.
`String toString()`	Returns the pathname string of this abstract pathname. This is just the string returned by the getPath() method.

It is not possible to comprehensively illustrate all the utilities with `File` class, as the topic is vast. We shall discuss some basic utilities to give some idea about what to do and how to do it. The basic utilities which we will cover include:

- Creating directory and listing
- File related information retrieval
- Read and write operations with files

You can practice writing your own programs while solving many other related problems.

8.3.2 Creating Directory and Listing

A directory is a home of zero or more files or other directory(ies). Every OS follows directory structure (it is like in the form of tree) to organize better to store data. There are two useful file utility methods defined in the class `File` (Table 8.28), which you can use to create a directory:

- The `mkdir()` method
  First, create a path, where you want to create your directory. Next, create an instance of `File` object with the chosen pathname. Finally, call the `mkdir()` for the `File` object. The method returns `true` on success and `false` on failure. Failure indicates that the path specified in the `File` object already exists, or that the directory cannot be created because the entire path does not exist yet.
- The `mkdirs()` method
  With this method, you can create a directory as well as all the parents of the directory.

Program 8.47 demonstrates creating a directory at `/tmp/test/programs`. The program illustrates uses of both the methods.

Program 8.47 *(Creating directory using* `mkidir()`*)*

```
/* This program illustrates how you can create a
directory  under your working directory. */

import java.io.File;

public class CreateDirectoryDemo  {
    public static void main(String args[]) {
        String dirName = "/tmp/test/programs";
        File d = new File(dirName);

        // Create directory when the path exist.
        boolean result = d.mkdir();
        if (result)
           System.out.println("Create directory is
                successful.");
        else {
           result = d.mkdirs();
                // Create directory with parents
           if (result) System.out.println
                ("Path and directory is created.");
        }
    }
}
```

Be careful, while you use black slash (\) while naming a pathname. This is because actually you pass a `String` object and a string with `\n` or `\t` is treated differently. You should use escape sequence (\\) within a string, writing `D:\\news\\test.txt` to represent a file named *test.txt* under *D:\news* directory.

Listing a directory

You can use `list()` method to list down all the files and directories available in a program. For this you call the method for `File` object representing a pathname, that is, a directory as file object. Program 8.48 is an example illustrating this.

Program 8.48 *(Listing a directory using* `list()` *method)*

```
/* This program illustrates the listing of a directory.
The program will list all files and directories under a
directory. */

import java.io.File;

public class DirectoryListingDemo {
    public static void main(String[] args) {
        String[] dList;
        try {
            // Create the file object representing a
                                                  // directory
            File f = new File("/tmp");
                                          // tmp is a directory

            // array of files and directory
            dList = f.list();
                  // Get the list of contents under "/tmp"

            // For each element in dList, print it
            for(String x : dList)
                System.out.println(x);
        } catch (Exception e) {
            e.printStackTrace();
        }
    }
}
```

Listing directory with filter

Sometimes you have to work with a particular type of files inside a directory. In that case, you have to filter the list of files in the directory. Any one of the following methods can be used for the purpose:

```
String [] list(FilenameFilter filter);
File [] listFiles();
File [] listFiles(FilenameFilter filter);
File [] listFiles(FileFilter filter);
```

`FilenameFilter` and `FileFilter` are two interfaces defined in `java.io` package, and they have the following declarations:

```
public interface FilenameFilter {
   public boolean accept(File dirName, String matchName);
}
```

Here, the `accept(...)` method would returns `true` for files in the directory specified by `dirName` that should be included in the list (that is, those that match the `matchName` argument) and returns `false` for those files that should be excluded.

```
public interface FileFilter {
   public boolean accept(File fileName);
}
```

Here, the `accept(...)` method would return `true` for file specified by `fileName` that should be included in the list and returns `false` for those files that should be excluded.

Program 8.40 illustrates how you can define the `accept(...)` method of the interface `FilenameFilter` and write your program to filter a listing of a directory.

Program 8.49 *(Listing a directory using filter)*

```
/* This program illustrates filtering a list which has
the extension .txt. */

import java.io.File;
import java.io.FilenameFilter;

public class MyFileFilter implements FilenameFilter {
    @Override
    public boolean accept(File dirName, String
     matchName) {
        return (matchName.endsWith(".txt"));
    }
}
```

```
public class FilenameFilterDemo {
    private static final String path =
      "D:\\java\\tmp\\test";
    public static void main(String[] args){
        File dirName = new File(path);
        FilenameFilter filter = new MyFileFilter();

    // Getting a filtered list
        File[] files = dirName.listFiles(filter);

        // Display the filtered list
        for(File f : files)
            System.out.println(f.getName());
    }
}
```

8.3.3 Directory and File Related Information Retrieval

You can get a lot of information related to a file or directory, such as whether it is a file or directory, pathname, parent directory, etc. Program 8.50 shows how different information, such as the name, pathname, parent, etc. of a directory and file can be obtained.

Program 8.50 *(Getting directory information)*

```
/* This program obtains name, parent, path, etc. of a
directory or a file. You should pass the name of files
or directories as command-line input. */

import java.io.File;

class DirInfoDemo  {
    public static void main (String args [ ] )
      throws IOException {
        File  f;
        if (args.length > 0 ) {
         for (int i = 0; i < args.length;i++ ) {
            f = new File(args[i]);
            System.out.println("Is File? " +
                f.isFile());
            System.out.println("Directory? " +
                f.isDirectory());
            System.out.println("Name : " +
                f.getName( ) );
```

```
            System.out.println("Path : "
                + f.getPath ( ) );
             System.out.println("Abs Path: "
                + f.getAbsolutePath());
            System.out.println("Parent : "
                + f.getParent ( ) );
        }
        else
            System.out.println
                ("Enter filenames(s)/ pathname(s)");
    }
}
```

Hint: Run the program as follows to test for a file `abc.txt` and directory `tmp`:

`java DirInfoDemo abc.txt tmp \java\tmp\test.txt`

Program 8.51 demonstrates how you can retrieve some information about a file and then delete the file, if it exists.

Program 8.51 *(Creating file, getting information, and deleting file)*

```
/* This program retrieves some information of a file or
directory and then deletes permanently. Enter the name
of the file to be tested as command line. */

import java.io.File;

class FileInfoDemo  {
    public static void main (String args [ ] )
     throws IOException {
        File  f = null;
        f = new File(args[0]);
           // Connect to file, if it exists
        if (f.exists()) {
           System.out.print ("File " + args[0] +
                " exists");
            System.out.println (f.canRead( ) ?
                "and is readable" : "");
            System.out.println ( f.canWrite( ) ?
                "and is writable" : "");
            System.out.println ("Last modified : "+
                f.lastModified( ));
```

```
            System.out.println
                ("File is " + f.length( ) + " bytes" );
            System.out.println ("Deleting file ...");
            f.delete();
        }
        else
            System.err.println ("File does not exist." );
    }
}
```

Hint: Run the program as follows to test for a file `abc.txt` and directory `tmp`.

```
Java FileInfoDemo abc.txt
Java FileInfoDemo tmp
```

8.3.4 Reading and Writing with Files

Ultimately files are for storing data and reading/writing is an obvious requirement so that stored data is sharable across different applications. A file object acts as an input stream source or an output stream destination. In Section 8.2.3 and 8.2.4, you have learned how IO operations can be done considering byte-oriented streams and character-oriented streams, respectively. The following are the classes usully preferred by many programmers for file handling in Java:

For byte-oriented IO operations

```
FileInputStream(File file);     // Reading from a file
FileOutputStream(File file);    // Writing into a file
```

For character-oriented IO operations

```
FileReader(File file);      // Reading from a file
FileWriter(File file);      // Writing into a file
```

- For IO operations with the stream-oriented classes, a file can be opened either in read or write mode.
- If you want to create an instance of any one of these classes for a file, which either does not exist or is not under permissible IO operation, then opening will throw an `IOException` and `FileNotFoundException` if you want to open a file for reading which does not exist.
- You can open a file for writing which may or may not exist. If it is pre-existing, then exiting data will be overwritten if you perform the write operation. If the file does not exist, it will automatically create a file and data will be stored in it.

8.3.5 FileDescriptor Class

The `FileDescriptor` class is used to access a file or any input or output resource such as socket in network, a source or sink of bytes, etc. The class instances serve as a machine-specific structure which represent an open file, socket, another source, or sink of bytes. An application cannot create its file descriptors on its own. The file descriptor is usually used to create a File IO stream.

The `FileDescriptor` class serves as a *handle* to an underlying machine-specific structure of an input source or an output sink. The handle can be `in` (for quality input stream), or `out` (for quality output stream), or `err` (for quality error stream).

The `FileDescriptor` class is defined with the following fields in it:

`static FieDescriptor in`: A handle to the standard input stream.
`static FieDescriptor out`: A handle to the standard output stream.
`Static FieDescriptor err`: A handle to the standard error stream.

This class defines only a default constructor `FileDescriptor()` to create a `FileDescriptor` object, which is initially invalid.

It defines two methods, which are `sync()` and `valid()`.

`public void sync()`: It forces an application's system buffer to synchronize with the underlying device.
`public boolean valid()`: It tests if this file descriptor object is valid or not.

The main application of `FileDescriptor` is when you are sending a file through a network channel to a remote application program or reading network socket to download a file content from a remote machine. Network applications are beyond the scope of this book, so instead, we will discuss a simple program showing an application of `FileDescriptor`. Program 8.52 shows how a data can be stored into a file and then the same can be read utilizing the methods of the class `FileDescriptor`.

Program 8.52 *(An application program with* `File Descriptor`*)*

```
/* This program illustrates writing and reading from a
file in a synchronized manner. */
import java.io.*;

public class FileDescriptorDemo {
    public static void main(String[] args) {
```

```
        FileDescriptor fd = null;
          //Create an instance of FileDescriptor
        String txt = "How old the earth is? It is only
          4.543 billion years as of now!"
        byte[] b = txt.getBytes();
          //Converts String object to byte array

        try {
            // Storing data to a device
            FileOutputStream fos = new FileOutputStream
                ("test.txt");

            // Get the file descriptor associated with
                                            // output stream
            fd = fos.getFD();

            fos.write(b);
                // Writes data to the output stream
            fos.flush();
                // Flushes data to the output sink
            fd.sync();
              // Confirms data to be written to the disk
            fos.close();   // Close the output stream
            // Retrieving data from a device
            FileInputStream fis = new FileInputStream
                ("test.txt");
            // Get the file descriptor associated with
                                            // output stream
            fd = fis.getFD();
            // Check the validity
            System.out.println("Is file descriptor
                valid? " + fd.valid());

            // Printing data on reading from file
            int c = fis.read();
            while (c != -1)  {
                System.out.print((char) c);
                     c = fis.read(); }
            System.out.println("\n Sync() is
                successfully executed!!");

            fis.close();
        } catch (Exception e) {
            e.printStackTrace();
        }
    }
}
```

- The main practical use of `FileDescriptor` is to create a `FileInputStream` or `FileOutputStream` to handle file objects.
- While working with `FileOutputStream`, whatever may be the content present in the file, it will sync your file to the device and overwrite the data. Even if no such file exists, it will create that file on its own, sync the file and will write the content you mention.
- `getFD()` returns the object of `FileDescriptor` that identifies the connection to the actual file in the file system being used by the `FileOutputStream` and `FileInputStream`.

8.4 Random Access File

The `RandomAccessFile` class defined in `java.io` package is a unique class. In many ways it is different from the other classes defined in the same package. Any input stream class (e.g., `FileInputStream`, `FileReader`) as well output stream class (e.g., `FileOutputStream`, `FileWriter`) allows you to perform read and write operations with sequential access to file objects. In contrast, the `RandomAccessFile` class is the only class that does not use a stream for reading or writing data. As its name implies, `RandomAccessFile` provides non-sequential access to a file for both reading and writing purposes. the `RandomAccessFile` class allows you to navigate a file and read from it or write to it as you please. You can replace an existing parts of a file, too. This class allows you to manage a random access file.

A random access file behaves like a large array of bytes. There is a cursor implied to the array called a file pointer. By moving the cursor, we do the read and write operations. If end-of-file is reached before the desired number of byte have been read, then `EOFException` is thrown.

`RandomAccessFile` supports the access modes as depited in Table 8.29.

Table 8.29 Different modes of accessing a random access file

Mode	Description
`r`	Read mode. Calling write methods will result in an `IOException`.
`rw`	Read and write mode.
`rwd`	Read and write mode synchronously. All updates to the file content is written to the disk synchronously.
`rws`	Read and write mode synchronously. All updates to the file content or meta data is written to the disk synchronously.

Let us see how `java.io` defines the `RandomAccessFile` class. This class defines the following two constructors:

`RandomAccessFile(File file, String mode)`

Creates a random access file stream to read from, and optionally to write to, the file specified by the `File` argument.

For example, the following creates an instance of a random access file `myRAF.txt` in read mode:

```
File file = new File("myRAF.txt");
RandomAccessFile(file, "r");
```

`RandomAccessFile(String name, String mode):`
Creates a random access file stream to read from, and optionally to write to, a file with the specified name.
For example, the following creates an instance of a random access file `myRAF.txt` in read-write mode:

```
RandomAccessFile("myFile.txt");, "rw");
```

Methods to manage a random access file are listed in Table 8.30.

Table 8.30 Methods defined by `RandomAccessFile` class

Method	Description
`void close()`	It closes this random access file stream and releases any system resources associated with the stream.
`FileChannel getChannel()`	It returns the unique `FileChannel` object associated with this file.
`int read()`	It reads a byte of data from this file.
`int read(byte[] b)`	Reads up to `b.length` bytes of data from this file into an array of bytes.
`Int read(byte[] b, int off, int len)`	Reads up to `len` bytes of data from this file into an array of bytes.
`void readFully(byte[] b)`	Reads `b.length` bytes from this file into the byte array, starting at the current file pointer.
`XYZ readXYZ()`	This method reads any XYZ numeric data like `int, char, boolean, float, double, long, short, byte, unsigned`, etc.
`String readUTF()`	It reads in a string from this file.
`String readLine()`	Reads the next line of text from this file.
`void seek(long pos)`	It sets the file-pointer offset, measured from the beginning of this file, at which the next read or write occurs.
`void setLength(long newLength)`	Sets the length of this file.

`int skipBytes(int n)`	Attempts to skip over n bytes of input discarding the skipped bytes.
`void writeXYZ(XYZ v)`	It converts the XYZ argument to a `long` using the `XYZToLongBits` method in class XYZ, and then writes that `long` value to the file as an 8-byte quantity, larger byte first. Here, XYZ can be any numeric data type including `int, char, boolean, float, double, long, short, byte, unsigned`, etc.
`void writeUTF(String str)`	Writes a string to the file using modified UTF-8 encoding in a machine-independent manner.
`void write(int b)`	It writes the specified byte to this file.
`void write(byte[] b)`	Writes `b.length` bytes from the specified byte array to this file, starting at the current file pointer.
`void write(byte[] b, int off, int len)`	Writes `len` bytes from the specified byte array starting at offset off to this file.
`void writeBytes(String s)`	Writes the string to the file as a sequence of bytes.
`void writeChars(String s)`	Writes a string to the file as a sequence of characters.
`long length()`	It returns the length of this file.
`FileDescriptor getFD()`	Returns the file descriptor object associated with this stream.
`long getFilePointer()`	Returns the current offset in this file.

Program 8.53 and Program 8.54 illustrates how you can write to and read from a random access file, respectively.

Program 8.53 *(Writing into a random access file)*

```
/* This program illustrates writing to a random access
file. */

import java.io.*;

public class WrireRAFDemo {
    static final String FILEPATH ="myFile.TXT";
    public static void main(String[] args) {
        try {
            writeToFile(FILEPATH, "Joy with Java", 8);
        } catch (IOException e) {
            e.printStackTrace();
        }
    }
```

```
    static void writeToFile(String filePath,
     String data, int position)
        throws IOException {
        RandomAccessFile file = new RandomAccessFile
           (filePath, "rw");
        file.seek(position);
        file.write(data.getBytes());
        file.close();
    }
}
```

Program 8.54 *(Reading from a random access file)*

```
/* This program illustrates reading from a random
access file. */

import java.io.*;

public class ReadRAFDemo {
    static final String FILEPATH ="myFile.txt";
    public static void main(String[] args) {
        try {
            System.out.println(new String(readFromFile
                 (FILEPATH, 0, 18)));
        } catch (IOException e) {
             e.printStackTrace();
        }
    }
    static byte[] readFromFile(String filePath, int
     position, int size)
             throws IOException {
        RandomAccessFile file = new RandomAccessFile
           (filePath, "rw");
        file.seek(position);
        byte[] bytes = new byte[size];
        file.read(bytes);
        file.close();
        return bytes;
    }
}
```

Program 8.55 illustrates how a random access file can be opened both in read and write mode and subsequently read and write operations can be performed.

Program 8.55
(Reading and writing a random access file)

```
/* This program demonstrates how a random access file
can be used in non-sequential manner and also navigated
at random. */

import java.io.*;

class RandomIODemo{
  public static void main (String args[]){
     RandomAccessFile file = null;
try {
        file = new  RandomAccessFile("rand.dat","rw");
        // Writing to the file
        file.writeChar('X');
          // Stores 2 bytes Unicode value of X.
        file.writelnt(555);
          // Write 4 bytes for the integer value.
        file.writeDouble(3.1412);
          // Write 8 bytes of double value

        System.out.printf("Size of the file: %x \n",
          file.length());
        System.out.printf("Current position of file
          pointer: %x \n", file.getFilePointer()
        file.seek (0);
          // Move to beginning of the file

        // Reading from the file from begining
        System.out.println(file.readChar());
        System.out.println(file.readlnt());
        System.out.println(file.readDouble());

        file.seek(2); // Go to the second item
        System.out.println(file.readInt());

        // Go to the end and append false to the file
        file.seek(file.length());
        file.writeBoolean(false);

        file.seek (14) ;
        System.out.println(file.readBoolean());
        file.close();
     }
     catch(IOException e) {
        System.out.println(e);
     }
   }
}
```

8.5 Java New IO

Java 8 introduced different type of streams bundled in the `java.nio` package, which have more interesting uses. Discussion of this is beyond the scope of this book. Java new IO will be discussed in the next volume of this book covering advnaced Java programming features.

Summary

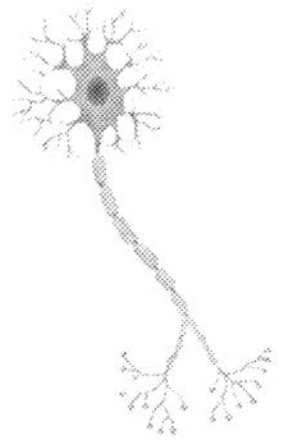

Java supports platform-independent programming. To make the programming platform independent, handling input–output in any application is an important issue. Java developer puts enough effort to resolve all issues related to IO and includes a vast package called `java.io`. This chapter discusses all the facilities available in the `java.io` API. The chapter starts with an overview of `java.io` package constituents followed by a full-length discussion on streams. This is followed by an illustration of standard IO streams. There are two types of streams in Java: byte streams and characters streams. Many classes are known in `java.io` API to work with both type of streams. All such classes are discussed in detail, with simple illustrative program for each of the classes. No discussion is complete without the discussion on file handling. This chapter covers all aspects of files, namely, creating files, file management activities, dealing with files with byte streams as well as character streams, and finally the random access files. Java 8 introduced a new IO as a package `java.nio` API. This is considered as an advanced topic and beyond the scope of this book.

FAQs

8.1 What are the types of IO streams?
8.2 What classes allow you to convert byte streams to character and back?
8.3 What is serialization?
8.4 What are the conditions for "successful" serialization of an object?
8.5 Which class allows reading data from an input byte stream in the format of primitive data types?
8.6 What is the usefulness of buffered input and output for streams?
8.7 What is a random access file and what is its usefulness?
8.8 Which one is more efficient: IO operation with byte stream or IO operation with character stream?
8.9 How you can compare reading a file with `Scanner`, `FileInputStream`, and `FileReader`?
8.10 What is `autoClosable`?
8.11 What are the differences between `File` and `RandomAccessFile`?
8.12 What is a `FileDescriptor`?
8.13 What are the usages of `PrintStream` class and `PrintWriter` class?

The answers to these questions and other problems in this chapter are available at www.cambridge.org/9781009211918. You might have many questions like these. You can post your question in the discussion forum at https://cse.iitkgp.ac.in/~dsamanta/joywithjava/page8.php.

Programs for Practice

8.1 Define a class `Student` with some appropriate fields and methods in it. Create 10 objects of the class `Student`. Store them in an array. For persistent storage of all the objects, using `FileOutputStream` class store them in a file `student.rec`.

8.2 Use the file `student.rec` as created in Problem 8.1. Read all the objects from the file `student.rec` using `FileInputputStream` class and store them in an array, say `student`. Display all the objects stored in the array.

8.3 Repeat Problem 8.1 using `BufferedOutputStream` class to wrap the `FileOutputStrem` class.

8.4 Repeat Problem 8.2 using `BufferedInputStream` class to wrap the `FileInputputStrem` class.

8.5 Repeat Problem 8.1 using `ObjectOutputStream` class.

8.6 Repeat Problem 8.2 using `Object InputStream` class.

8.7 Consider a text file stored with Unicode character set of Chinese language. Read the file and display on the console.

8.8 Repeat Problem 8.7 so that you can convert the text file into another language, say, English. Display the file on the computer console.

8.9 Using a `RandomAccessFile`, take an input text file. Store the content of the file, but in reverse order. For example, if a–b–c is the data in the input file, then it will store c–b–a.

8.10 Consider a data file containing a huge amount of data in it. You can create such a data file using a random number generator. Read the file using (a) `Scanner` class, (b) `DataInputStream` class, (b) `FileReader` class, and (c) `BufferedInputStream` syncing with `FileInputStream` class. In each case, measure the time taken for reading. Compare the results and conclude the efficiency.

8.11 Check the following program and justify the output from its execution:

```
import java.io.IOException;
import java.io.PipedInputStream;
import java.io.PipedOutputStream;

public class PipeExample {
    public static void main(String[] args) throws IOException {
        final PipedOutputStream output = new PipedOutputStream();
        final PipedInputStream  input  = new PipedInputStream
              (output);
```

```
        Thread thread1 = new Thread(new Runnable() {
            @Override
            public void run() {
                try {
                    output.write("Hello world, pipe!".
                            getBytes());
                } catch (IOException e) {
                }
            }
        });

        Thread thread2 = new Thread(new Runnable() {
            @Override
            public void run() {
                try {
                    int data = input.read();
                    while(data != -1){
                        System.out.print((char) data);
                        data = input.read();
                    }
                } catch (IOException e) {
                }
            }
        });

        thread1.start();
        thread2.start();
    }
}
```

MCQs

8.1 In which class, are the method **print()**, **println()**, and **printf()** defined?

(a) `java.lang.System`
(b) `java.io.PrintStream()`
(c) `java.util.Scanner`
(d) `java.awt.Graphics`

8.2 Which statement will work without any error?

(a) `System.out.print();`
(b) `System.out.printf("x = %f", a/b);`
(c) `System.out.println("x = %f", a/b);`
(d) `System.out.print("x = %f", a/b);`

8.3 **Consider the following program segment:**

```
String filename = "C:/myFile.txt";
File aFile = new File(filename);
FileOutputStream fos = null;
  // Place to store the stream reference

if (aFile.isFile()) {
    System.out.println("myFile.txt already exists."); }
else {
     try {
          fos = new FileOutputStream(aFile);
          System.out.println("myFile.txt output stream
              created");
     } catch (FileNotFoundException e) {
           e.printStackTrace(System.err);
     }
  }
```

Which of the following statement(s) is(are) true?

(a) The file will be opened in write mode.
(b) If the file contains old data, writing into the file will overwrite the old data.
(c) Only text will be written into the file.
(d) The file will be closed automatically once the write is over.

8.4 **Check the following program. The purpose of this program is to write some values into a file and then read the file.**

```
import java.io.*;

public class FileReadWrite {
    public static void main(String[] args) {
        File f = new File ("test.dat");
        byte b[] = {11, 22, 33, 44, 55, 66, 77, 88, 99};
        try (FileOutputStream fos = new FileOutputStream(f)
             FileInputStream fis = new FileInputStream("f")) {
             // Storing data to the file
            fos.write(b);  // Writes data to the output stream
            fos.flush();   // Flushes data to the output sink

            // Retrieving data from the same file
            int c = 0;
            while ((value = fis.read()) != -1)
                System.out.print((char) c);
        }
```

```
            catch (Exception e) {
                e.printStackTrace();
            }
            finally {
                fos.close(); fis.close(); f.delete();
            }
        }
    }
```

Which of the following is (are) true about this program?

(a) The same file cannot be simultaneously opened for reading and writing.
(b) `fos` should be closed before `fis` is opened.
(c) Separate `try-catch` block should be there for writing stream and reading stream
(d) The program does not throw any exception, even if the file `test.dat` does not exist at the time of running the program.

8.5 Consider the following program:

```
import java.io.*;
class KeyboardReader {
     public static void main(String args[]) throws IOException {
         char c;
         BufferedReader br = new BufferedReader(new InputStream
              Reader(System.in));
         System.out.println("Enter characters, 'q' to quit.");
         do {
             c = (char) br.read();
             System.out.println(c);
         } while(c != 'q');
     }
   }
```

In this program, which one acts as the bridge between byte stream and character stream?

(a) `System.in` (b) `BufferedReader`
(c) `InputStreamReader` (d) `read()`

8.6 Which of the following is (are) false about the **`RandomAccessFile`** object?

(a) It only reads data as bytes and then converts into an appropriate type.
(b) It can store any primitive data types including `String`.
(c) It stores data as bytes only.
(d) For reading/writing, it acts as a source/sink which can be wrapped by any input/output byte-oriented stream classes.

8.7 Which are the ways to read data from a keyboard?
(a) Using an object of `DataInputStream` class.
(b) Directly from keyboard and using `Scanner` class.
(c) Passing the data as command line input.
(d) All of these.

8.8 Which of the following streams contain the classes which can work on character stream?
(a) `InputStream` (b) `OutputStream`
(c) `FileReader` (d) `FileWriter`

8.9 Which of the following method of **`DataInputStream`** class is used to read multiple characters at once from a file?
(a) `read()` (b) `readChar()`
(c) `readLine()` (d) `readUTF()`

8.10 Which of the following classes can be used to implement the input stream that uses a character array as the source?
(a) `BufferedReader` (b) `FileReader`
(c) `CharArrayReader` (d) `FileArrayReader`

8.11 Which of the following methods help in clearing the contents of the buffer?
(a) `flush()` (b) `clear()` (c) `close()` (d) `exit()`

8.12 In which Java APIs are the classes for handling all IO-streams defined?
(a) `java.lang` (b) `java.util`
(c) `java.io` (d) `java.awt`

8.13 Which of the following statements is (are) ***`not`*** true?
(a) While you are creating an instance of `File` class, and if you do not use the file name according to the convention of the local machine, the constructor will throw an exception of the class `IOException`.
(b) A `File` object can be opened for both reading and writing simultaneously.
(c) When you create an object of `File` class for writing, if the corresponding file does not exist on the local file system, then it will be created.
(d) Closing operation of a `File` object never faces any run-time error and hence need not be placed under `try-catch` block.

8.14 Which of the following code is correct?
(a)
```
FileWriter fileWriter = new FileWriter("../file.txt");
File file = new File(fileWriter );
BufferedWriter bufferedOutputWriter = new
                                BufferedWriter(fileWriter);
```

(b)
```
BufferedWriter bufferedOutputWriter = new
                        BufferedWriter("../file.txt");
File file = new File(bufferedOutputWriter );
FileWriter fileWriter = new FileWriter(file);
```

(c)
```
File file = new File("../file.txt");
FileWriter fileWriter = new FileWriter(file);
BufferedWriter bufferedOutputWriter = new
                        BufferedWriter(fileWriter);
```

(d)
```
File file = new File("../file.txt");
BufferedWriter  bufferedOutputWriter = new
                        BufferedWriter(file);
FileWriter  fileWriter = new
                   FileWriter(bufferedOutputWriter );
```

8.15 Should **`FileReader`** be used to read a Java byte code (e.g, a .class) file? Which of the following is an appropriate answer?
(a) No, byte code files can only be executed, never read.
(b) No, the bytes in byte code files are not intended to be interpreted as characters.
(c) Yes, any file can be read with `FileReader` under byte-stream class.
(d) Maybe, as long as the byte codes were created on the same computer as the program using `FileReader`.

8.16 Which of the following statement is ***not*** true for **`RandomAccessFile`** object?
(a) It can allow to open a file both in read and write mode.
(b) It can allow to store the data fields of any object and then read the same.
(c) The `seek(0)` method of the object places the file pointer at the beginning of the file.
(d) It cannot be used to read a network line.

8.17 Which of the following interface is *not* a member of **`java.io`** package?
(a) `DataInput` (b) `ObjectInput`
(c) `Runnable` (d) `FileFilter`

8.18 Assume that **`Text.txt file`** is already created in the root directory, which is shown here:

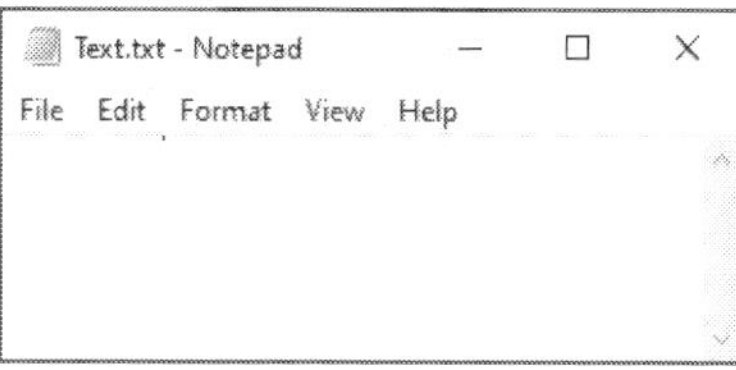

Consider the following program:

```
import java.io.*;

public class Question6{
  public static void main(String[] args) {
    try ( RandomAccessFile rf =
         new RandomAccessFile("Text.txt", "r"); ) {
      int i = rf.readInt();
    }
    catch (FileNotFoundException ex) {
      System.out.println("File not found");
    }
   catch (IOException ex) {
      ex.printStackTrace();
    }
  }
}
```

Choose the correct option.

(a) The program will not be compiled successfully.

(b) The program will be compiled successfully, but will encounter run-time exception

(c) The program produces an output `File not found.`

(d) The program will be executed successfully, but will not produce any output.

8.19 The file `./Text.txt` when opened with the Notepad text editor, shows the content as follows:

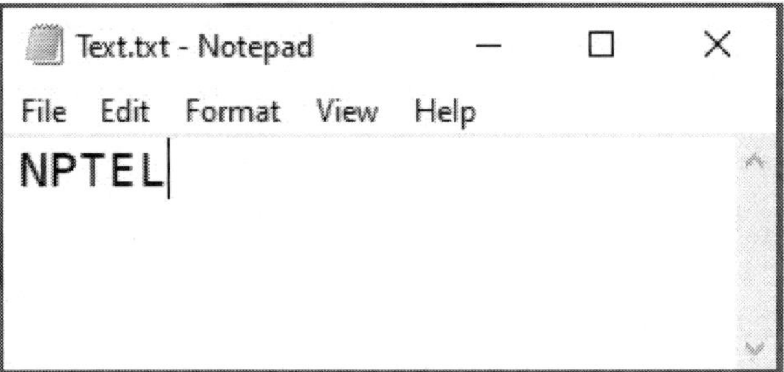

Consider the following program:

```
import java.io.*;

public class Test{
    public static void main(String[] args) {
  try{
          InputStream file = new FileInputStream("./Text.txt");
          System.out.print(file.available());
  }
```

```
  catch(Exception e){
     System.out.print(e);
  }
 }
}
```

Which of the following is (are) the correct output for the `try` portion of the code?

(a) Prints the number of bytes in the file.
(b) Prints the number of characters in the file.
(c) Prints `true`, if the file is present; else prints `false`.
(d) Prints nothing, as an exception will be caught.

8.20 Consider the following program:

```
import java.io.*;
public class Question9{
   public static void main(String[] args) throws IOException  {
       BufferedReader br=new BufferedReader(new FileReader
              (“./Text.txt”));
        String str;
        int c = 0;
        while((str = br.readLine()) != null) {
      c=c+1;
      System.out.println(str.charAt(3));
      }
      System.out.println(c);
   }
}
```

The file **`Text.txt`** when browsed with the Notepad text editor, shows the following content:

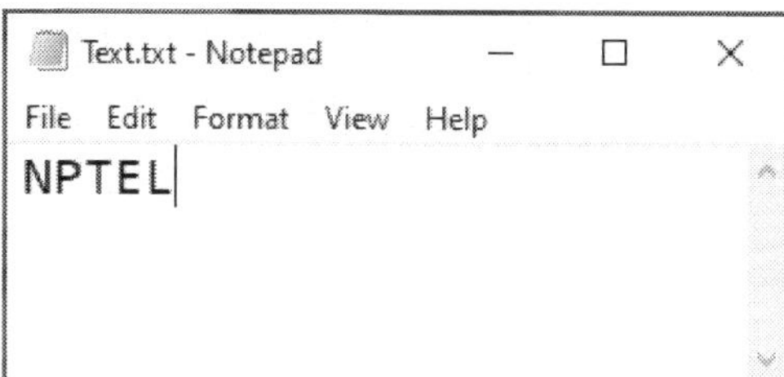

If the program is executed, then what will be the output from the execution?

(a) E
1

(b) E
5

(c) N
1

(d) L
5

8.21 Which of the following cannot be used to read a text file in Java?

(a) `BufferedReader`
(b) `FileReader`
(c) `Scanner`
(d) `System.in`

9

Generic Programming

The task of a programmer is to write a *program* which implements an algorithm. An algorithm specifies operations on data. Data can be of different types and structures. Thus, a program is an amalgamation of algorithm and data structures. Implementing the same algorithm for each different data structure, that is, just code duplication, is cumbersome. The concept of generic programming addresses this issue. With generic programming, a program can be written in terms of *types to-be-specified-later* that are then *instantiated* when needed for specific types provided as parameters. In this way, programs are related to *abstract data types* and such programming helps the programmer to avoid code duplication. Java features generic programming facilities and this chapter will help you to master the subject.

9.0 Introduction

Concept of generic

The dictionary meaning of the word "generic" is "not specific." This word is used as an adjective to imply a characteristic of relating to a class or group of things. For example, a generic drug, which refers to the chemical makeup of a drug and not specific to a brand name under which the drug is sold.

Definition of generic programming

In the world of programming, generic is used to mean an abstraction. The term "generic programming" was coined by David R. Musser and Alexander A. Stepanov in 1989 and defined as follows:

"Generic programming centers around the idea of abstracting from concrete, efficient algorithms to obtain generic algorithms that can be combined with different data representations to produce a wide variety of useful software."

Polymorphism versus generic programming

At an early stage of generic programming (like in LISP, Ada, Smalltalk, etc.) the concept was to write common functions that differ only in the set of types on which they operate when used, thus reducing duplication. Such software entities are known as *generics*. Generic programming can thus be termed broadly as *parametric polymorphism*. The polymorphism concept is an important object-oriented programming paradigm which you are already familiar with in the context of encapsulation and inheritance. Method overloading is parametric polymorphism.

Why generic programming?

With method overloading you can define two or more methods having the same name but with different signatures and different operations. So codes need to be developed for each method. In the sorting problem, for example, what will you do if you want to sort a list of integers, double values, strings of names? You will find it impractical to take care each data type and hence polymorphic method accordingly. At the time of writing the code, you may not even know the type of the data in the list you need to sort. For example, your may have a list of data of class, say Student, Book, Person, and so on. In case of sorting, the same algorithm has to be applied to different data types. For this type of a situation, it would be better if you could write only one instance of code which worked for any type of data. Generic programming facilitates this kind of programming.

JDK 5 introduced the syntactical element called *generics*. Today, generics are an integral part of Java programming, and it is a must-read topic. Using the concept of generics, it is possible to create classes, interfaces, and methods which work in a type-safe manner with various types of data. This is very useful when a particular algorithm is to be followed no matter what type of data is to be manipulated. For example, the mechanism of a sorting technique is same whether it is sorting items of type `Integer`, `Float`, `String`, or `Object`. With generics, you can define a class (it is a program representing an algorithm) independent of the type of data, and then use that class for a wide variety of data types without any additional effort. Indeed, the expressive power of generics when blended to programming fundamentally changes the way software is built.

Applications of generic programming

Your learning

This chapter describes the syntax of defining a method as generic so that it can work on any type data and any number of arguments that you can pass when you call the method. The next topic is how to define a class as generic, which is the core of generic programming. A class, being a program, can work with any data type with which you want to deal. For writing a robust program, there are certain rules and syntaxes to be followed, which also will be covered in this chapter. Finally, some applications will be discussed so that you can get hands-on with some real-life applications.

9.1 Generic Method

A method that can take any parameter is called a generic method. You have already used a generic method in many of the programs in the previous chapter. This is `println()` method which is defined in the `PrintStream` class in `java.io` package. This method prints a value on the computer monitor. Let's see how it takes different type of values as its argument.

```
int i = 123;
System.out.println(i);  // It takes int as an argument

double x = 1.2345;
System.out.println(x); // It takes double as an argument

String s = "Generic method";
System.out.println(s); // It takes String as an argument
```

You are also familiar with a similar method, `printf()`, which is like `println()` and can take a variable number of arguments of any type. For example, the `printf()` method in the following takes three arguments of three different types. You can try with any other number of arguments of any other type as well.

```
int i = 5,; double x = 0.5; String s = "Generic method";
System.out.printf("I am"+s+"printing int %d,double %f", i, x);
```

All of them are fine. Java gives you many such built-in methods. You can define your own generic method in your program. Suppose, in a class we want to define a method which can take any argument to display its content. Program 9.1 illustrates how you can do that.

Program 9.1 *(Defining a generic method)*

```
/* A simple Java program to show how to define a
generic method and call the method with any type of
data you wish. */

// Define a user-defined class
class Student {
    int rollNo;
    String name;
    Student(int r, String n) {
       rollNo = r; name = n;
    }
}

// Define the main class
class GenericMethodDefine<T>  {
    // Defining a generic method to print any data type
     void genericPrint (T t)  {
          // Here, T stands for template type
         System.out.println (t);
    }
```

```
    public static void main(String[] args)    {
        //Creating an object of the class GenericMethod
        GenericMethod aObj;

        // Calling generic method with int argument
        aObj.genericPrint(101);

        // Calling generic method with String argument
        aObj.genericPrint("Joy with Java");

        // Calling generic method with double argument
        aObj.genericPrint(3.1412343);

        // Calling generic method with Student argument
        Student s = new Student(101, "Amir Khan");
        aObj.genericPrint(s);
    }
}
```

- You can readily understand the similarity between method overloading and generic method. Both the concepts have the same objective, but in their own ways. The main difference is that in the case of method overloading, you have to build code for each overloaded method, whereas with generic method, the same code can work for different types of data.
- With the generic method, theoretically, you can pass any type of data as argument; however with method overloading, only a limited number of arguments are allowed and the limitation is according to your defined methods.
- A generic method can be overloaded, and method overriding is also applicable.

9.1.1 Syntax of Defining a Generic Method

Let's learn the syntax to define a generic method in your program.

```
<AccessSpec><ReturnType><methodName>(<ArgumetList>){ //Body }
```

The syntax is very similar to defining a method in a class. It can be specified by `<AccessSpec>` like `public`, `static`, `final`, etc. A generic method can return a value of any type `<ReturnType>` and it can take a list of any number of arguments of any type. To specify any type, you should mention it by a template following a naming convention. Java generic type of naming convention helps you to understand code easily. The naming convention is one of the best practices of Java programming language. Usually, type parameter names are single, uppercase letters to make them easily distinguishable from Java variables. The most commonly used type parameter names are:

- E: Element (used extensively by the Java Collections Framework, for example ArrayList, Set, etc.)
- K: Key (Used in Map)
- N: Number
- T: Type
- V: Value (Used in Map)
- S,U,V, etc.: 2nd, 3rd, 4th types, etc.

Program 9.2 demonstrates a valid declaration of a static generic method.

Program 9.2 *(Defining a static generic method)*

```
/* A simple Java program to show defining of a generic
method with any type. */

class StaticGenericMethod  {
// Defining static generic method to print two data of
                                   // any type T1 and T2
    static<T> void genericPrint (T x, T y )  {
  // The following statement print any type specified
                                   // by the parameter T
         System.out.println (x.getClass().getName()
         ":" + x);
         System.out.println (y.getClass().getName()
         ":" + y);
    }

    public static void main(String[] args)    {
        Integer x = new Integer(101);
          // x is an Integer object
        Double y = new Double(3.1412343);
          // y is a Double object
        String s = "Joy with Java";
          // s is String object
        // Calling generic method with Integer and
                                     // String arguments
        genericPrint(x, s);

        // Calling generic method with String and
                                   // Integer arguments
        genericPrint(s, y);
```

```
// Calling generic method with integer and double
                                                    // arguments
        genericPrint(x, y);

// The following also works, as both arguments are
                                        // treated as String type
        genericPrint(101, 202);

        /* The following, however will give compile-time
                                                         // error!
        int i = 101, double j = 3.1412343;
        genericPrint(i, j);      // This is invalid    */
    }
}
```

- When you call a generic method, the type(s) with which the method is invoked will be resolved at the time of execution.
- You should always pass an object as a type. Any primitive data type cannot be used in template argument.
- Generic method ensures type-safety. Program 9.3 illustrates this feature with a simple example. The program is planned to add an element into a collection of any type.

Program 9.3 *(Type-safety in generic programming)*

```
/* This program creates a collection (see java.util
package to learn about Java collection, if you are not
familiar), add an element into it and then return the
size of the collection after adding the element. */
import java.util.*;
class TypeSafeGenericDemo {
    // Defining a generic method to work with any type
                                               // of collection
    public static<E> int addData(E data, Collection<E>
      list){
        list.addData(element);
           //Add element data into the collection list
        return list.length();
    }
    // The main method having different calls
    public static void main{String args[]) {
        int length;
        String a[] = {"A", "E", "I", "O"};
```

```
        // Creating a collection of Strings and add an
                                          // element into it
        List<String> list1 = new ArrayList<String>
           ("A", "E", "I", "O");
        // Adding a string into list1 and then print
                                         // elements in list1
        length = addData("J", list1);
        System.out.println("Length = "+length+list1);

        // Creating a collection of Integers and add a
                                          // number into it
        List<Integer> list2 = new ArrayList<Integer>
               (Arrays.asList(1, 3, 5, 7, 9));
        // Adding a number into list2 and then print
                                         // elements in list2
        length = addData(0, list2);
        System.out.println("Length = "+length+list2);

        /* The following code however will give
           compile-time error as they are not type-safe,
           i.e., type dies not match.
           addData("K", list2);
               // list2 is of type Integer collection
           Integer i = new Integer(0);
           addData(i, list1);
               // list1 is of type String collection
           addData(list1, "J");
               // Types do not matches
        */
    }
}
```

- In this example, we have used `Collection` and `List` as the two generic interfaces, and `ArrayList` as the generic class. These are defined with a hierarchy of their definitions in `java.util` API.
- The compiler infers the type(s) to be resolved from the call of the generic method.
- A constructors can be declared using generic method concept, which we shall learn when we discuss generic class.
- In Program 9.2 and Program 9.3, we have used Java's class like `Integer`, `String`, etc. You can even define your own generic method with your own class definition. For example, you can modify your program by defining a new user defined class, say `Student`, create a collection of `Student` object and then add a `Student` object.

9.1.2 Generic Method with Variable List of Arguments

In C, there are some standard methods like `printf(...)` and `scanf(...)` which take variable number of arguments. In a C program, you can define a method with variable number of arguments to be passed. Let us see if you can do similar things in Java.

One solution may be to write as many overloading methods as required. Java developer provides an elegant solution. You can write a method so that it will accept an arbitrary number of arguments when it is called. This feature in Java is called *varargs method* or the *variable-arity method*. There are three ways this can be done:

(a) Using an array
(b) Using ellipsis (three dots)
(c) Using `Object` class

Let us look at the syntax and usage of these three ways.

Varargs method using array

This is the simplest method. You can define a varargs method with an argument an array (of any type). Store the values which you want to pass to a method in an array and then pass the array to the method. That's all! This approach is illustrated in Program 9.4.

Program 9.4 *(Varargs method using an array)*

```
/* This program demonstrates a varargs method using
an array to pass a variable number of arguments to a
method.  */
class VarargsMethodArray {
     static void varargsMethod1(int v[])  {
         System.out.print("Number of args: " +
           v.length +" Elements: ");
         for(int x : v)
             System.out.print(x + " ");
         System.out.println();
    }
    public static void main(String args[])  {
        // Following arrays are created for test...
        int x[] = { 1, 3, 5, 7 };
        int y[] = { 2, 4};
        int z[] = { };

        // Calling varargs method
        varargsMethod1 (x);
           // Passed 4 values to the method
```

```
        varargsMethod1 (y);
          // Passed 2 values to the method
        varargsMethod1 (z);
          // Passed no argument to the method
    }
}
```

- This approach needs values to be packed into an array prior to calling.
- Command line arguments is also varargs method for the `main()` in your Java program.
- As an array is to be passed, all values that can be passed are of same type.

Varargs method using ellipsis

The second method is similar to the first but with a different syntax, which is special in Java. A set of three dots (i.e., ...) is called an ellipsis. The syntax to define varargs method using ellipsis is as follows:

```
<AccessSpec><ReturnType><MethodName>(<Type>...<arrayName>){
. . . // Method body
}
```

Here, `<Type>` can be of any type. Program 9.5 illustrates the usage of this syntax.

Program 9.5 *(Varargs method using ellipsis)*

```
/* This program demonstrates varargs method with
ellipsis. */

class VarargsMethodEllipsis {
    //Defining a varargs method
    static void varargsMethod2(int ...v) {
       System.out.println("Number of arguments: " +
          v.length);
        for (int i: v) // For each item i in array v
           System.out.print(i + " ");
        System.out.println();
    }
    public static void main(String args[])      {
        // Calling the varargs method with variable
                                          // arguments
        varargsMethod2 (9);
          // One parameter
        varargsMethod2 (1, -2, 3, -4);
          // Four parameters
```

```
        varargsMethod2 ();
          // no parameter
    }
}
```

- Unlike in the previous method, you can call the method with actual values to be passed. Like the previous method, all parametric values should be of the same type.
- A method can have "conventional" parameters along with a variable-length parameter. However, the variable-length parameter should be the last parameter declared by the method. For example, the following is a valid varargs method declaration using ellipsis:

```
int varMethod(int a, int b, double c, float ... v) { }
```

In this example, in a call to `varMethod()`, the first three arguments used must match to the first three parameters. Then, any number of remaining arguments of type `float` can be matched.

- You can overload a method that takes a variable-length argument. Program 9.6 demonstrates how a varargs method can be overloaded.

Program 9.6 *(Varargs method with overloading)*

```
/* This program demonstrates the overloading of a
varargs method. */
class OverloadingVarargs {
      static void varTest(int ... v) {
           //Overloading method 1
           System.out.print("Arg(int ...): " +
                 "Number of args: " + v.length +
                      " Contents: ");
           for(int x : v)
               System.out.print(x + " ");
           System.out.println();
      }
      static void varTest(boolean ... v) {
           //Overloading method 2
           System.out.print("Arg(boolean ...) " +
                 "Number of args: " + v.length +
                      " Contents: ");
           for(boolean x : v)
               System.out.print(x + " ");
           System.out.println();
      }
```

```
        static void varTest(String msg, int ... v) {
            //Overloading method 3
            System.out.print("Arg(String, int ...): " +
                 msg + v.length + " Contents: ");
            for(int x : v)
                System.out.print(x + " ");
            System.out.println();
        }

       public static void main(String args[])  {
            varTest(1, 2, 3);
            varTest("Testing: ", 10, 20);
            varTest(true, false, false);
       }
}
```

- The varargs parameter must be the last. For example, the following declaration is incorrect.

  ```
  int varMethod(int a, float ... v, double c){}
  ```
- There must be only one varargs parameter. For example, the following declaration is invalid:

  ```
  int varMethod (int ...a, double ...b) { }
  ```

  The attempt to declare the second varargs parameter is illegal.
- When overloading a method that takes a variable length argument, some unexpected errors may result. These errors are due to ambiguity as it is possible to create an ambiguous call to an overloaded varargs method. For example, if you exclude overloaded and change the main() method as follows, then it will give the compilation error:

```
public static void main(String args[])      {
    varTest(1, 2, 3); // Okay
    varTest();        // Compile-time error: Ambiguity
    varTest(1, false, true);//Compile-time error: No match
}
```

Varargs method using class `Object`

Possibly this is the most elegant approach in Java to implement the varargs method. It uses the ellipsis and also the `Object` type. For example, to define a varargs method, your method declaration may take the following form:

```
public static void methodName(Object...obj) {
      // Body of the method
}
```

You may note the restriction that the method can have zero or more parameters preceding this, but this must be the last for reasons you have already learned. Let's consider Program 9.7 to demonstrate the mechanism. This program defines a varargs method which takes any type of values with any count.

Program 9.7 *(Varargs method with class `Object`)*

```
/* This program demonstrates the varargs method taking
any type of arguments as well as any number. */

class VarargsMethodObject  {
       public static void varargsMethod3(Object ...
           obj) {
          for(Object o : obj)
             System.out.print(" "+o);
          System.out.println();
       }
       public static void main(String[] args) {
            varargsMethod3( 1, "String", 2.3, true);
                 // Four arguments
            varargsMethod3 ();
                 // No arguments
            varargsMethod3 (15, 25, 35, 45, 55);
                 // Five arguments
       }
}
```

Note that an array of type `Object` can holds elements of any type. For example, the following is perfectly acceptable in a Java program:

```
float x[] = {1.2, 2.3};
String names[]  = new String[10];
int fib[] = {0, 1, 1, 2, 3, 5, 8, 13};
// Create an arrya of objects of different types
Object[] args = {x, names, fib};
```

In the varargs method, you can declare an array of type `Object` (i.e., the varargs method using an array). For example:

```
public void varArgs(Object o[]);
```

The call of the method `varArgs(args)` will be invoked with 20 arguments of different types. However, you can compare which one is good: using "array of `Object`" or "`Object` with ellipsis."

9.2 Generic Class

A very interesting activity in Java is to work with generic class. Writing a Java program means that you have to define a class. A class implies how the problem is to be solved. Problem solving means manipulating a set of given data. This aspect (manipulation) is called the algorithm to solve the problem. So a class implements an algorithm in Java.

What should be the class definition if you have to follow the same algorithm, but on different types of data? For example, writing a sorting program using `Quick sort algorithm`, which should work to sort a list of integers, double values, `String` of names, or of data of any abstract data type. As the algorithm remains the same and the data is different, overloading, that is, writing as many methods as the different data types, is a possible option. This solution has two drawbacks:

(1) You should know well in advance (that is, while writing your program) what the possible data types are. This information may not be available at the time of writing the program.
(2) Even if this information is available, you have to duplicate the code just to fit with the data type. If the number of data types is large, it will not be a wise solution to duplicate code again and again.

As a case study, let us consider an array of integers to be processed. The tasks are: initializing the array, printing the elements, and reversing the order of elements. Here is the program layout which you should consider to define such a class:

```
class ArrayIntClass {
        // Declare an array of integer values.
        // Constructor to load the array.
        // Method to print the array elements.
        // Method to reverse the array elements.
}
class MainClassInt {
        /* This class create object of the class ArrayIntClass
              and call methods of it to do the tasks. */
}
```

Program 9.8 gives the definition of class and solves the problem as stated with an array of integers.

Program 9.8 *(Working with array of integers)*

```
/* This program works with array of integer numbers. */

class ArrayIntClass {
      // Declaring an array of integer values
      int a[];

      // Constructor to load the array
      ArrayIntClass(int a[]) {
            this.a = a;
      }

      // Method to print the array elements
      void printArray() {
            for(int x : a)
                  System.out.println(x);
      }

      // Method to reverse the array elements
      void reverseArray() {
            int j = a.length; int temp;
            for (int i=0; i<j; i++) {
                  temp = a[i];
                        a[i] = a[j];
                        a[j] = temp;
                        j--;
            }
      }
}

class MainClassIntArray {
      //This class use the class ArrayIntClass to
                                    // manipulate data in it
      public static void main(String args[]) {
            int a[] = {1, 2, 3, 4, 5};
            ArrayIntClass x = new ArrayIntClass(a);
                  // Initialize
            x.printArray();
                  // Prints array
            x.reverseArray();
                  // Reverses array elements
            x.printArray();
                  // Prints updated array
      }
}
```

Now, suppose you have to solve the same problem but with an array of double values with the same objectives. That is:

```
class ArrayDoubleClass {
        //Declare an array of double values
        // Constructor to load the array.
        // Method to print the array elements.
        // Method to reverse the array elements.
}
class MainClassDoubleArray {
    /* This class creates an object of class ArrayDoubleClass
        and call methods of it to do the tasks. */
}
```

Program 9.9 is the same as Program 9.8 with some minor modifications. The modifications are highlighted in bold.

Program 9.9 *(Working with an array of double values)*

```
/* This program works with array of double values. */

class ArrayDoubleClass {
     // Declaring an array of double values
     double a[];

     // Constructor to load the array
     ArrayDoubleClass(double a[]) {
          this.a = a;
     }

     // Method to print the array elements
     void printArray() {
          for(double x : a)
               System.out.println(x);
}

     // Method to reverse the array elements
     void reverseArray() {
          int j = a.length;
          double temp;
          for (int i=0; i<j; i++){
               temp = a[i];
               a[i] = a[j];
```

```
                    a[j] = temp;
                    j--;
               }
          }

 }

class MainClassDoubleArray {
      //This class use the class ArrayDoubleClass to
                                        // manipulate data
      public static void main(String args[]) {
           double a[] = {1.2, 2.3, 3.4, 4.5, 5.6};
           ArrayDoubleClass x = new ArrayDoubleClass(a);
                // Initialize
           x.printArray();      // Prints array
           x.reverseArray();  // Reverses array elements
           x.printArray();    // Prints updated array
      }
}
```

Now, let us consider the case of solving a similar problem with the data stored in array of `Strings`. That is:

```
class ArrayStringClass {
       //Declare an array of String values
       // Constructor to load the array.
       // Method to print the array elements.
       // Method to reverse the array elements.
}

class MainClassStringArray {
       /* This class creates an object of class ArrayString
             Class and call methods of it to do the tasks.
             */
}
```

This time also the programming job is pretty straightforward; just modify any one of them as shown in Program 9.10.

Program 9.10 *(Working with array of* `String` *objects)*

```
/* This program works with array of String objects. */
class ArrayStringClass {
     // Declaring an array of String objects
     String a[];
     // Constructor to load the array
     ArrayStringClass(String a[]) {
         this.a = a;
     }
     // Method to print the array elements
     void printArray() {
        for(String x : a)
           System.out.println(x);
     }
     // Method to reverse the array elements
     void reverseArray() {
         int j = a.length;
         String temp;
         for (int i=0; i<j; i++) {
             temp = a[i];
             a[i] = a[j];
             a[j] = temp;
             j--;
         }
     }
}
class MainClassStringArray {
     //This class use the class ArrayStringClass to
                                                //manipulate data
     public static void main(String args[]) {
          String a[] = {"A", "E", "I", "O", "U"};
          ArrayStringClass x = new ArrayString
               Class(a); // Initialize
          x.printArray();
               // Prints array
          x.reverseArray();
               // Reverses array elements
          x.printArray();
               // Prints updated array
        }
     }
```

Such requirements, with different data type, are common. Although program duplication is simple to do, it is not an acceptable solution. The generic class concept is far better.

9.2.1 Defining Generic Classes

Let's learn how to define a generic class. Then we shall discuss solving the problem in Program 9.8, 9.9 and 9.10 using generic class. A class that can refer to any type is known as a generic class. It is a class whose methods in it can deal with any type of object in it. Like C++, in Java, you should use < > to specify parameter types in creation of generic class. The syntax for declaring a generic class is as follows:

```
[Access] class <ClassName> <<Type1> [, <Type2>, ...]> {
              // body of the class
}
```

Here is the full syntax for declaring a reference to a generic class and instance creation:

```
<ClassName><typeList> objName = new <ClassName><typeList>
([<InputArray>]);
```

Here, `<typeList>` denotes `<<Type1> [, <Type2>, ...]>`. Program 9.11 gives a simple example of how to define a generic class with one type and its use in the main class.

Program 9.11 *(Defining a generic class)*

```
/*A Simple Java program to show working of user defined
generic class.*/

// Defining a simple generic class named GenericClass
class GenericClass<T>  {
     // Use < > to specify class type
    T obj;
     // An object of type T is declared
    GenericClass(T obj) {
     // Constructor of the generic class
       this.obj = obj;
    }

    public T getObject()  {
     // A user-defined method in the class return obj;
    }
}
//Defining a simple class Student
class Student {
    String name;
    int rollNo;
```

```
    Student(String n, int r) {
        name = n; rollNo = r;
    }
}
// Use the defined generic class in a program
class GenericClassDemo  {
     // Main class to test the generic class
    public static void main (String[] args) {
        // Creating Object with Integer type
        GenericClass <Integer> iObj = new GenericClass
           <Integer>(15);
        System.out.println(iObj.getObject());
        // Creating Object with String type
        GenericClass <String> sObj = new GenericClass
           <String>("Java");
        System.out.println(sObj.getObject());
        // Creating Object with Student type
                Student s = new Student("Indu", 123);
        GenericClass <Student> tObj = new GenericClass
           <Student>(s);
        System.out.println(tObj.getObject());
    }
}
```

Addressing code duplication

The generic class definition of a problem can resolve the trouble of writing a program when you want to process different type of data using the same algorithm. Program 9.12 provides a solution with a generic class.

Program 9.12 *(Problem solving with generic class)*

```
/* This program shows how a program can process an
array of any data type.*/

class GenericArray<T> {
     //Declaring an array, which should store any type
                                            // T of data
     T a[];
          // Define that the array a[] can store any
                                          // type of data

     GenericArray(T[] x) {       // Define a constructor
         a = x;
     }
```

```
        // A generic method to print the elements in array
        void printData() {
            for(T x : a)
                System.out.println(x);
        }

        void reverseArray() {
            int j = a.length-1;
            T temp;
        for (int i=0; i<j/2; i++) {
                temp = a[i];
                a[i] = a[j];
                a[j] = temp;
             }
         }
}

Class GenericClassDemo {
        public static void main(String args[]) {
            //Creating an array of integer data
            Integer x[ ] = {10, 20, 30, 40, 50};
             // It is an array of Integers
            // Store the data into generic array
            GenericArray<Integer> arrayInt = new
             GenericArray<Integer>(x);

            // Printing the array
            arrayInt.printData();
             // Printing the array of integer objects

            //Reverse the ordering of array
            arrayInt.reverseArray();

            // Printing the reversed ordering array
            arrayInt.printData();
             // Printing the array of integer objects

            // -------------------------------------------
            // Creating an array of String data
            String y[ ] = {"A", "B", "C"};
             // It is an array of String data

            // Store the data into generic array
            GenericArray<String> arrayString = new Generic
             Array<String>(y);
```

```
            // Printing the data….
            arrayString.printData();
            // Printing the array of strings

            Reverse ordering of data
            arrayString.reverseArray();

            // Printing the data after reverse ordering
            arrayString.printData();
            // Printing the array of strings

            //-----------------------------------------
            // Creating an array of double data
            Double z[ ] = {1.2, 2.3, 3.4, 4.5};
            GenericArray<Double> arrayDouble = new
                  Generic Array<Double>(z);

            // Printing the data….
            arrayDouble.printData();
            // Printing the array of doubles

            //Reverse ordering of data….
            arrayDouble.reverseArray();

            // Printing the data after reverse ordering….
            arrayDouble.printData();
            // Printing the array
      }
}
```

- You cannot instantiate an array whose element type is a type parameter. The following is invalid:

  ```
  T a = new T[5];
  ```

  The reason you cannot create an array of `T` is that there is no way for the compiler to know what type of array to actually create.
- In parameter type, you cannot use primitives type like `int`, `char`, or `double`. Only class can be referred as the template data. This is why the wrapper class for `int`, `float` and `String` are used as `Integer`, `Double`, and `String`, respectively.
- You can also pass multiple parameters in type specification to design your generic classes. This aspect is discussed in the next subsection.

9.2.2 Generic Classes with Multiple Type Parameters

You can create a generic class with more than one type parameters so that more than one data types can be manipulated in a generic program. Program 9.13 is an example of defining a generic class with two parameters.

Program 9.13 *(Generic class with multiple type parameters)*

```
/* This program illustrates a generic class with
multiple parameters. */

class GenericClass2<T1, T2>  {
    T1 obj1;      // An object of type T1
    T2 obj2;      // An object of type T2

    GenericClass2 (T1 obj1, T2 obj2) {    // Constructor
        this.obj1 = obj1;
        this.obj2 = obj2;
    }

    public void print()       {     // A local method
        System.out.println(obj1);
        System.out.println(obj2);
    }
}

class MutiTypeGenericClassDemo {
     // Main class using generic class
    public static void main (String[] args)  {
        GenericClass2 <String, Integer>
           p1 = new GenericClass2<String,
                Integer>("Generic2", 9);
        p1.print();
        GenericClass2 <Double, Integer>
           p2 = new GenericClass2<Double,
                Integer>(1.2345, 999);
        p2.print();
    }
}
```

- Generic methods may introduce their own type parameters. This is similar to declaring a generic type, but the type parameter's scope is limited to the method where it is declared.
- Static and non-static generic methods are allowed, as well as generic class constructors.

If your generic method has template parameter(s), while you call such a method, you can explicitly specify the actual parameter(s) enclosed within angular brackets <   > with which the method will be called. Also, Java has a feature known as *type inference*, which allows you to invoke a generic method as an ordinary method, without specifying a type between angle brackets. Generally, this can be left out and the compiler will infer the type that is needed. Program 9.14 illustrates the features of type inference in generic programming.

Program 9.14 *(Type inference)*

```
/* This program shows the type inference in generic
programming. */

// A user-defined generic class with two parameters
public class Pair<K, V> {
    private K key;
    private V value;
    public Pair(K key, V value) {
        this.key = key;
        this.value = value;
    }
    public void setKey(K key) {
        this.key = key;
    }
    public void setValue(V value) {
        this.value = value;
    }
    public K getKey(){
        return key;
    }
    public V getValue() {
        return value;
    }
}
// A class to demonstrate type inference features
public class TypeInfer {
    // Defining a generic method: which compares two
                                                // Pair objects
  public static<K,V) boolean compare(Pair<K, V> p1,
     Pair<K, V> p2) {
        return (p1.getKey().equals(p2.getKey()) &&
                p1.getValue().equals(p2.getValue()));
    }
```

```
    public static void main(String args[]) {
         // Explicit type specification
         Pair<Integer, String> p1 = new Pair<>
           (1, "apple");
         Pair<Integer, String> p2 = new Pair<>
           (2, "pear");
         // The call when type is explicitly provided
         boolean same = TypeInfer.<Integer, String>
           compare(p1, p2);
         System.out.println(same);
         // Implicit type inferencing
         Pair<Double, Double> p3 = new Pair<>
           (1.11, 2.22);
         Pair<Double, Double> p4 = new Pair<>
           (1.11, 2.22);
         // The call when type is NOT explicitly provided
         same = TypeInfer.compare(p3, p4);
         System.out.println(same);
    }
}
```

9.2.3 Bounded Types in Generic Class Definition

If a class `A` is declared as generic with type parameter `<T>`, then the object of the class can be created of any type. This is fine, but, in several situations, it may cause error during execution. Program 9.15 illustrates this problem.

Program 9.15 *(Error in generic class definition)*

```
class GenericError<T> {
     T[] array;              // An array of type T
     // Pass the constructor a reference to an array
                                                // of type T
     GenericError (T[ ] t) {
          array = t;
     }

     double average() {    // Return type double in all
          cases
        double sum = 0.0;
        for(int i=0; i < array.length; i++)
            sum += array[i].doubleValue();
                // Here is compiler error!
        return sum / array.length;
     }
}
```

Here, you will note that the method doubleValue( ) is well defined for all numeric classes, such as Integer, Float and Double, which are sub classes of the class Number (defined in java.lang API), and this class Number defines the doubleValue( ) method. All numeric wrapper classes thus inherit this method. This implies that the defined class GenericError<T> will work only if the type parameter T is limited to Number and any of its sub classes.

However, the generic class is free to create object of any type parameter, and it will be a problem if that type does not have the method doubleValue() defined. For example, if you want to create an instance of GenericError<String>, then the compiler will not be able to resolve the doubleValue() for String as the class String has not defined such a method in it. The compiler does not have any knowledge that you are only interested in creating objects of numeric types. Thus, the program reports compile-time error showing that the doubleValue() method is unknown.

To solve this problem, you need some way to tell the compiler that you intend to pass only numeric types to T. In addition, you need some way to ensure that only numeric types are actually passed.

To do this, Java provides the concept of bounded type. When specifying a type parameter, you can create an upper bound that declares the super class from which all type arguments must be derived. In Java, this is accomplished through the use of the clause extends. The syntax would like the following:

```
<T extends super className>
```

This specifies that T can only be replaced by super class, or sub classes of super class. Thus, here, super class superclassName defines an inclusive upper limit.

An example of generic class definition with bounded type parameter is shown in Program 9.16. This program considers the type to be bounded to Number or any of its sub class. In this case, T is called *parametrized type* instead of simple T as in the earlier discussion.

Program 9.16 *(Generic class with bounded type parameter)*

```
/* This program demonstrates how a generic class with a
parameterized type can be defined. */

class GenericBound<T extends Numbers > {
     T[] array;
     // An array to store any numeric data

        // Pass the constructor a reference to an
                                          // array of type T.
```

```
        GenericBound (T[] t) {
            array = t;
        }

        double average() {
        // Return type double in all cases
            double sum = 0.0;
            for(int i=0; i < array.length; i++)
                sum += array[i].doubleValue();
                    // Now, it is okay
            return sum / array.length;
        }
}

// The main class is as follows.
class GenericBoundDemo {
    public static void main(String args[]) {
        Integer intArray[] = { 1, 2, 3, 4, 5 };
        GenericBound <Integer> intData = new Generic
            Bound <Integer>(intArray);

        double avgInt = intData.average();
        System.out.println("Average is " + avgInt);

        Double doubleArray[] = { 1.1, 2.2, 3.3, 4.4,
            5.5 };
        GenericBound <Double> doubleData = new
            GenericBound <Double>(doubleArray);
        double avgDouble = doubleData.average();
        System.out.println("Average is " + avgDouble);
        String strArray[] = { "1", "2", "3", "4", "5" };
            // This is Okay
        /*
        // The folowing won't compile because String is
                              // not a subclass of Number.
        GenericBound <String> strData = new
            GenericBound <String>(strArray);
        double avgStr = strData.average();    // ERROR!
        // average() calls doubleValue(), which is not
                                   // defined for String
        System.out.println("Average is " + avgStr);
        */
    }
}
```

- Bounded type parameters allow you to invoke methods defined in the bounds. For example, `doubleValue()` for `Short`, when you create an instance of `GenericBound<Short>`.
- The bounding of a parameterized type guarantees type safety of a generic class definition. You can limit the scope of the defined generic class.
- An argument of a generic method can be parametrized. Program 9.17 illustrates how a generic method can be defined with a bounded type parameter. This program also include an example how an interface can be included in a bounded parameter.

Program 9.17 *(Generic method with bounded type parameter)*

```
/* This program demonstrates how a generic method can
be bounded with a parameterized type. In this program,
a generic method is defined to count some elements
stored in an array of elements of a parameterized type.
*/

public class BoundedGenericMethod {
     public static <T extends Comparable<T>> int
           countGreaterThan(T[] anArray, T t) {
          int count = 0;
          for (T e : anArray)
              if (e.compareTo(t) > 0)
                  ++count;
          return count;
     }

    public static void main(String args[]) {
          Integer intArray[] = {55, 35, 65, 25, 85, 95,
                75, 15, 45};
          Double doubleArray[] = {9.1,6.7,2.5, 4.6, 8.2,
                7.3, 5.5, 3.7};
          String strArray[] = {"a", "e", "i", "o", "u",
                "UOIEA", "X"};
          int x = 50;
          System.out.printf("Counting integer list for
                %d ", x);
          System.out.println(countGreaterThan
                (intArray, x);
          double y = 5.5;
          System.out.printf("Counting list of doubles
                for %f ", y);
          System.out.println(countGreaterThan
                (doubleArray, y);
```

```
            String z = "String";
            System.out.print("Counting list of strings
                  for " + z);
            System.out.println(countGreaterThan
                  (strArray, z);
      }
}
```

- The syntax for defining a parameterized method should be noted. The bounding of parameter should be defined before the return type. In Program 9.17, the bounded parameter `<T extends Comparable<T>>` is defined before `int`.
- The parametrized type `<T extends Comparable<T>>` uses `Comparable<T>`. Here, `Comparable` is a generic interface defined in `java.lang` package. This also shows how an interface can be used to define a parameterized generic method. The same can be applied to define a generic class as well.
- Note that, `extends` is used in a general sense to mean either `extends` (as in classes) or `implements` (as in interfaces).
- The interface `Comparable<T>` declares the method `compareTo()`. If you want to define a class and if you want to compare any two objects of this class, then that class should implement `Comparable<T>` interface and define (i.e., overwrite the `compareTo()` method) how to do that. If you compare between two objects `x` and `y`, then the method can be called as `x.compareTo(y)`. It returns a positive value if `x` is greater than `y`, zero if `x` is equals to `y`, and a negative value if `x` is less than `y`.
- This method is already defined for the class `Number` and all of its sub classes. Also, the class `String` defines this method. In case of `String` objects, a string is compared in accordance with the collating sequence; thus, `A` is less than `a`, `P` is greater than `M`, etc.

Program 9.18 shows how you can define your own class so that any two objects of this class are comparable, like numbers and strings.

Program 9.18 *(Generic class comparable for ordering)*

```
/* This program demonstrates how a generic class will
be defined to sort objects of user defined type Book by
their titles. */

import java.util.*;

// Defining the user-defined class Book with Comparable
public class Book implements Comparable<Book> {
```

```
      String author;
      String title;
      double price;

      Book(String a, String t, int n){
          author = a;
          title = t;
          cost = n;
      }

      // Define how to find ordering of two books: Sort
                                        // books by titles.
      @Override
      public int compareTo(Book b){
           // Compare the current (this) with b
           int result = this.title.compareTo(b.title);
            // Defined for String
           return result;
     }
}

// The main class defines a generic class with Book as
                                      // parameterized type
class SortList<T extends Book> {
       public static void main(String args[]) {
           // Declare a collection of books
           ArrayList<Book> books = new ArrayList<Books>();
           // Create a list of books
           books.add(new Book("John", "Python", 25.5));
           books.add(new Book("Tom", "C"));
           books.add(new Book("Fox","C++"));
           books.add(new Book("Herbert", "Java"));
           books.add(new Book("Debasis",
            "Data Structures", 50.5));

           /*
            * Sorting the list using Collections.sort()
                method; you
            * can use this method because you have
                implemented the
            * Comparable interface in your user defined
                class Book
           */
      Collections.sort(books);
```

```
        // Print the sorted list...
            for(Book b : books)
             // For each book in the sorted list
              System.out.println(b.title + " "+
                  b.author + "  " + b.price);
        }
}
```

- `SortList` class sorts a list of books.
- It also sorts a list of numbers (such as integers, floating point values, char, etc.) and Strings. Because, the class Numbers and String implements the interface Comparable.
- You can modify Program 9.16 to sort books by their cost. You need a little modification in the overriding of `compareTo()` method. For example, you can write:

  `int result = this.cost.comapreTo(b.cost);`
- You can define a generic class with multiple bounded parameters. This topic is discussed in the next subsection.

The bounding of a type parameter is applicable to user-defined class and class hierarchy. Program 9.19 shows how a generic class can be defined with user-defined class as a bound.

Program 9.19 *(Generic class with any class as bound)*

```
/* This program defines a generic class whose type
parameter is bound to class A or any of its sub class.
Passing any other type will cause compiler time error.
*/

// Defining a user-defined class
class A {
     public void whoAmI() {
          System.out.println("I am A");
     }
}

class B extends A {
     public void whoAmI() {
          System.out.println("I am B");
     }
}
```

```
class C extends B {
     public void whoAmI() {
         System.out.println("I am C");
     }
}

// Defining a generic class with bounded type to class A
public class GenericClass<T extends A> {
      private T t;

      public GenericClass(T t){
         this.t = t;
      }

      public void whoAreU() {
           this.t.whoAmI();
      }

      public static void main(String[] args) {
            // Creating an instance of with sub class C
                                    // as type parameter
            GenericClass<C> c = new GenericClass<C>
                (new C());
            c.whoAreU();
           // Creating an instance of with sub class B
                                    // as type parameter
            GenericClass<B> b = new GenericClass<B>
                (new B());
            b.whoAreU();

            // Creating an instance of with class A as
                                       // type parameter
            GenericClass<A> a = new GenericClass<A>
                (new A());
            a.whoAreU();
            /*
            *  Following instantiantion is not valid,
                as type parameter
            *  is not class A or any of its sub class.
            GenericClass<String> x = new GenericClass
                <String>("Test");
                                 // Compile-time error
            x.whoAreU();        // Compile-time error*/
     }
}
```

Multiple bounds

Program 9.16 and Program 9.17 illustrate the use of a type parameter with a single bound. But a type parameter can have *multiple bounds* also. The syntax for defining a generic class, for example, if you want to include `B1`, `B2`, and `B3` as bounds is as follows:

```
<T extends B1 & B2 & B3>
```

This mechanism is subjected to the following restrictions:

(a) A type variable with multiple bounds is a sub type of all the types listed in the bound.
(b) If one of the bounds is a class, it must be specified first. If the class is not specified first, you will get a compile-time error.
(c) You can have any number of interfaces.
(d) Only one class is allowed to be used as type parameter and that class must be first, followed by interface(s).

For example, suppose you have the following definitions:

```
interface B { /* ... */ }
interface C { /* ... */ }
interface D { /* ... */ }
class A implements B, C, D { /* ... */ }
```

Assume that then you can verify the following:

```
class X <T extends A & B & C> { /* ... */ }
   // Correct
class Y <T extends B & C & D> { /* ... */ }
   // Compile-time error
class Z <T extends B & A & C> { /* ... */ }.
   // Compile-time error
```

The concept of the multiple bound generic class is that the generic class can access any methods declared in the class and interface(s). Program 9.20 demonstrates the usage of multiple bound generic class.

Program 9.20 *(Multiple bound generic class)*

```
/* This program illustrates how a generic class can be
defined with multiple bounds. */

interface WarmBlooded {
      void printMe();
}
interface ColdBlooded (
      void printMe();
}
```

```
class Vertebrate {
      whoAmI("I am vertebrate.");
}
class Bird extends Vertebrate implements WarmBlooded {
      public void printMe() {
           System.out.println("I am a bird.");
      }
}
class Reptile extends Vertebrate implements ColdBlooded{
      public void printMe() {
           System.out.println("I am a snake.");
      }
}

class AnimalDemo <T extends Vertebrate & WarmBlooded &
     ColdBlooded> {
    public static void main(String args[]) {
       AnimalDemo<Bird> bird = new AnimalDemo<Bird>();
       bird.whoAmI(); bird.printMe();

       AnimalDemo<Reptile> snake = new AnimalDemo
           <Reptile>();
       snake.whoAmI(); snake.printMe();
    }
}
```

9.3 Wildcard in Generic Programming

In Java, the question mark symbol (`?`) is known as the wildcard in generic programming. Whenever you need to represent an unknown type, you can do that using the `?` symbol. The wildcard is a mechanism to cast a collection of a certain class. To understand the usefulness of this, let us consider an example first.

The following class definition in Program 9.21 is to make a program so that a student's marks can be stored in any kind format like, `Integer`, `Short`, `Double`, `Float`, `Long`, etc.

Program 9.21 *(Defining a generic class)*

```
/* This class defines a class Student and a method in
it to compare marks of two objects of it. */

class Student <T extends Number> {
     String name;
```

```
    T [ ] marks;
         // To store the marks obtained by a student

    // The usual constructor for the generic class
                                               // Student
    Student (T [ ] m) {
         marks = m;
    }

    // This method to calculate the total of marks by
                                             // a student
    double total( ) {
         double sum = 0.0;
         for(int i = 0; i < marks.length; i++)
              sum += marks[i].doubleValue();
         return (sum);
    }

    // Method compares marks obtained by this student
                                  // with another student
    boolean compareMarks(Student<T>  otherS) {
        if ( total() == otherS.total() )
             return true;
        return false;
    }
}     // End of the generic class definition
```

This program will compile successfully. Now, let us execute the program with different instances of `Student` objects, whose marks are stored in their own number format. The driver class of using the generic class is given in Program 9.22.

Program 9.22 *(Need of type casting for parameterized type)*

```
/* The following class demonstrates the problem while
instantiating the Student generic class with different
number formats.   */

class GenericLimitationDemo {
     public static void main(String args[]) {
          // Marks stored in integer for s1
          Integer intMarks1[] = { 44, 55, 33, 66, 77 };
          Student<Integer> s1 = new Student<Integer>
           (intMarks1);
          System.out.println("Total marks " +
           s1.total());
```

```
            // Marks stored in integer for s2
            Integer intMarks2[] = { 49, 39, 53, 69 };
            Student<Integer> s2 = new Student<Integer>
             (intMarks2);
           System.out.println("Total marks " + s2.total());

            // Compare marks between s1 and s2
            if (s1.compareMarks (s2))
                  System.out.println("Same marks");
            else
                  System.out.println("Different marks.");

            // Marks stored in double for s3
            Double doubleMarks[] = { 43.5, 55.5, 32.5,
                   66.5, 77.0 };
            Student<Double> s3 = new Student<Double>
                   (doubleMarks);
           System.out.println("Total marks " + s3.total());

            // Marks stored in float for s4
            Float floatMarks[] = { 50.0F, 40.0F, 60.0F,
                   65.0F };
            Student<Float> s4 = new Student<Float>
                   (floatMarks);
           System.out.println("Total marks " +
                   s4.total());

            // Compare marks between s2 and s3
            // if(s.compareMarks(s3)) // Run-time error!
            //       System.out.println("Same marks");
            //else
            //       System.out.println("Different marks.");

            // Compare marks between s3 and s4
            // if (s3.compareMarks(s4))
                                // Here also Run-time error!!
            //    System.out.println("Same marks");
            // else
            //     System.out.println("Different marks.");
      }
}
```

There is no error when `s1` is compared with `s2`; however, the same is not true for `s2` and `s3` or `s3` and `s4`. The reason is that the `si.compareMarks (sj)` method works only when the type of the object `sj` is same as the invoking object `si`.

Such a problem can be solved by using another feature of Java generics called the *wildcard argument*. The wildcard argument is specified by the ? symbol. The generic class A<T> and A<?> both specify the class with parameterized type. T conveys to create an object of *any type*; in contrast ? conveys to create an instance of A of *an unknown type*. The specification of T works in a narrow context, whereas ? is in wider context; the latter gives a more generic solution.

Thus, with reference to Program 9.21, you have to change the boolean compareMarks (Student <T> t) method to wildcard as boolean compareMarks(Student<?> t) to avoid type mismatch that you have faced while running the program. To understand this let us rewrite Program 9.21 with wildcard. Program 9.23 gives this modified version of Program 9.21.

Program 9.23 *(Modified version of Program 9.21)*

```
class Student <T extends Number> {
     String name;
     T [ ] marks;
           // To store the marks obtained by a student

     // The usual constructor for the generic class
                                                  // Student
     Student (T [ ] m) {
         marks = m;
     }

     // This method to calculate the total of marks by
                                                // a student
     double total( ) {
          double sum = 0.0;
          for(int i = 0; i < marks.length; i++)
              sum += marks[i].doubleValue();
          return (sum);
     }

     /* This method compares the marks obtained by this
          student with another student, so that types
          of the two should not matter. */
     boolean compareMarks(Student<?>  otherS) {
          if ( total() == otherS.total() )
                return true;
          return false;
     }
}      // End of the generic class definition
```

The driver code will remain same as in Program 9.22. The program will run without any error in this case.

- Question mark (`?`) is the wildcard in generics and represents an unknown type. The wildcard can be used as the type of a parameter, field, or local variable, and sometimes as a return type.
- You can't use wildcards while invoking a generic method or instantiating a generic class.

9.3.1 Bounded Wildcard Arguments

We have learnt how Java's wildcard feature helps in generic programming. Wildcard features are useful in other ways too. This is about scope of accessing a method defined in a class which belongs to a hierarchy of classes. There are three bounds known in Java. These are:

- Upper bound wildcard
- Lower bound wildcard
- Unbound wildcard

Let's discuss these three ways of bounding a type parameter in generic programming.

Upper bound wildcard

This wildcard can be used when you want to write a method that works on *the class where it is defined or any of its sub class.* Figure 9.1 illustrates the concept. Suppose, a method `gm()` is defined using the wildcard with upper bound of class `C`. Thus, the calls of method `gm()` are valid with an argument of object of class `C` or any of its sub classes: `Z`, `D`, and `E`. Therefore:

```
D d;  gm(d);        // Valid
B b;  gm(b);        // Invalid
Z z;  gm(z);        // Valid
```

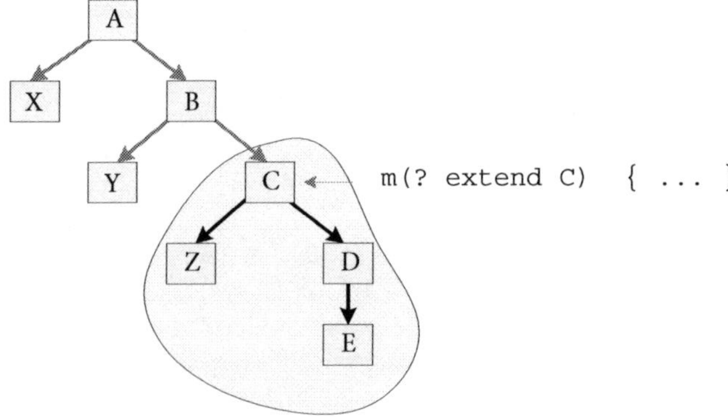

Figure 9.1 Upper bound wildcard

Syntax

To declare an upper-bounded wildcard, use the wildcard character `?` followed by the `extends` keyword, followed by its upper bound class name. For example, say, `C` denotes the upper bound. Here, `C` can be a class or interface. Then the wildcard for the generic method `gm()` bounded up to `C` is:

```
<type> gm(GC<? extends C> gc) {
        /* Body of the method */
}
```

Here, `GC` is a generic class. The call of this method is valid with any object of the class `C` or any of its child class as argument. Program 9.24 illustrates a use of upper bound wildcard.

Program 9.24 *(Upper bound wildcard)*

```
/* This program uses a class hierarchy with an
inheritance chain. A generic method is defined with
upper bound wildcard of type class B as upper bound
and the method is called through different objects of
classes in the chain. */

// Defining a user-defined class
class A {
     public void whoAmI() {
         System.out.println("I am A");
     }
}

class B extends A {
     public void whoAmI() {
         System.out.println("I am B");
     }
}

class C extends B {
     public void whoAmI() {
         System.out.println("I am C");
     }
}

// Defining a generic class to work with
class GC<T> {
    T t;
    GC(T t) {
```

```
        this.t = t;
    }
    T me() { return t; }
}
// Main class showing working with upper bound type
public class UpperBoundWildcardDemo {
      // Defining a generic method with upper bound
                                                  // wildcard
      public static void whoAreU(GC<? extends B> t) {
           t.me.whoAmI();
      }

      public static void main(String[] args) {
         // Creating an instance of class C
         C c = new C(); GC<C> x = new GC<C>(c);
         whoAreU(x);   // Okay: C is the sub class of B

         // Creating an instance of class B
         B b = new B();  GC<B> y = new GC<B>(b);
         whoAreU(y);  // Okay: Upper bound is B
         /*
       *  Following instantiantion is not valid, as the
       *  object is not class B or its sub class C.*/
            // Creating an instance of class A
            // A a = new A(); GC<A> z = new GC<A>(a);
            // whoAreU(z);        // Compile-time error
      }
}
```

Lower bound wildcard

If you want to limit the call of a method for the object of a class or any of its parent classes only, then you can use lower bound wildcard. Figure 9.2 illustrates the concept. Suppose, a method `gm()` is defined using the wildcard with lower bound of class `C`. Thus, the method `gm()` is accessible to any of its sub classes `A`, `B`, and `C`. Therefore:

```
A a;  gm(a);   // Valid
B b;  gm(b);   // Valid
C c;  gm(c);   // Valid
D d;  gm(d);   // Invalid
E e;  gm(e);   // Invalid
X x;  gm(x);   // Invalid
Y y;  gm(y);   // Invalid
```

Syntax

A generic class `GC` is expressed using the wildcard character `?`, followed by the `super` keyword, followed by its class name.

```
<type> gm(GC<? super C> gc) {
/* Body of the method */
}
```

The call of this method is valid for any object of the class `C` or any of its parent class. Program 9.25 illustrates a use of upper bound wildcard.

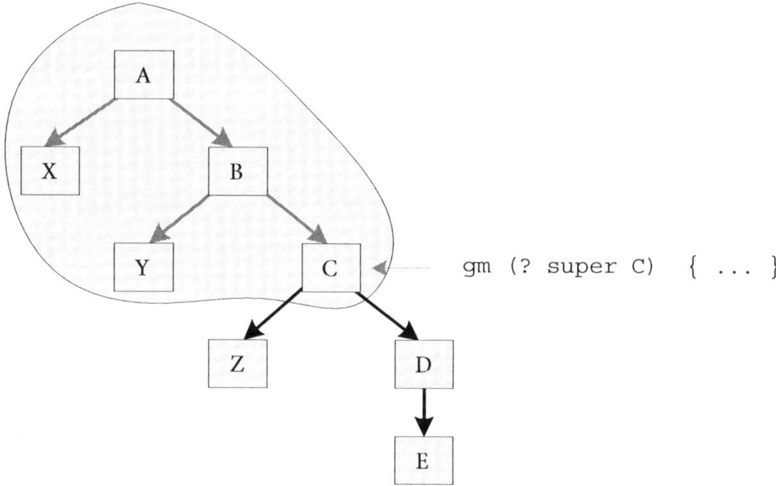

Figure 9.2 Lower bound wildcard

Program 9.25
(Lower bound wildcard)

```
/* This program uses a class hierarchy with an
inheritance chain. A generic method is defined with
lower bound wildcard with class B as the lower bound of
type and the method is called through different objects
of classes in the chain. */

// Defining a user-defined class
class A {
     public void whoAmI() {
         System.out.println("I am A");
     }
}

class B extends A {
     public void whoAmI() {
```

```
        System.out.println("I am B");
    }
}

class C extends B {
    public void whoAmI() {
        System.out.println("I am C");
    }
}

// Defining a generic class to work with
class GC<T> {
    T t;
    GC(T t) {
      this.t = t;
    }
    T me() { return t; }
}
// Main class showing working with upper bound type
public class LowerBoundWildcardDemo {
      // Defining a generic method with lower bound
                                                    // wildcard
      public static void whoAreU(GC<? super B> t) {
            t.whoAmI();
      }

      public static void main(String[] args) {
            // Creating an instance of class B
            B x = new B();   GC<B> b = new GC<B>(x);
            whoAreU(b);   // Okay: B is the class itseslf

            // Creating an instance of class A
            A y = new A(); GC<A> a = new GC<A>(y);
            whoAreU(a);  // Okay: Lower bound is A
            /*
        *  Following instantiantion is not valid, as the
        *  object is not class B or its parent class A.
            // Creating an instance of class C */
            // C z = new C(); GC<C> c = new GC<C>(z);
            // whoAreU(z);        // Compile-time error
    }
}
```

Unbounded wildcard

An unbounded wildcard in generic can represent any type. This is useful in the following cases:

- When writing a method which can be employed using functionality provided in `Object` class.
- When the code is using methods in the generic class that don't depend on the type parameter.

Syntax

A single `<?>` is used to represent a method with unbounded wildcard. For example, given a generic class `GC`, it is expressed as:

```
<type> gm(GC<?> gc) {
      /* Body of the method */
}
```

The call of this method is valid for any object of any type. It provides the highest level of flexibility on passing method argument. Program 9.26 illustrates a use of the unbounded wildcard.

Program 9.26 *(Unbounded wildcard)*

```
/* This program uses a class hierarchy with an
inheritance chain. A generic method is defined with
unbound wildcard and the method is called through
different objects of classes in the chain. */

// Defining a user-defined class
class A {
     public void whoAmI() {
         System.out.println("I am A");
     }
}

class B extends A {
     public void whoAmI() {
         System.out.println("I am B");
     }
}

class C extends B {
     public void whoAmI() {
         System.out.println("I am C");
     }
}
```

```
// Defining a generic class to work with
class GC<T> {
    T t;
    GC(T t) {
      this.t = t;
    }
    T me() { return t; }
}

// Main class showing working with upper bound type
public class LowerBoundWildcardDemo {
      // Defining a generic method with lower bound
                                                // wildcard
      public static void whoAreU(GC<? super B> t) {
            t.whoAmI();
      }

      public static void main(String[] args) {
            // Creating an instance of class A
            A a = new B(); GC<A> x = new GC<A>(a);
            whoAreU(x);    // Okay

            // Creating an instance of class B
            B b = new B();   GC<B> y = new GC<B>(b);
            whoAreU(y);  // Okay

            // Creating an instance of class C
            C c = new C();   GC<C> z = new GC<C>(c);
            whoAreU(z);  // Okay
     }
}
```

9.3.2 Illustration of Bounded Wildcard Arguments

Let's look at a real-life application, where all the concepts we have discussed can be illustrated better. Our program will be a little long. This is against the policy of the book, but this is the minimum-sized program which can meet the current learning objective. A simple class hierarchy is given in Figure 9.3 which will be referred to in the subsequent discussions. Figure 9.3 shows taxonomy of animals. Our objective is to have a better hands-on experience of the different ways to pass an argument to methods using bounded wildcards in generic programming.

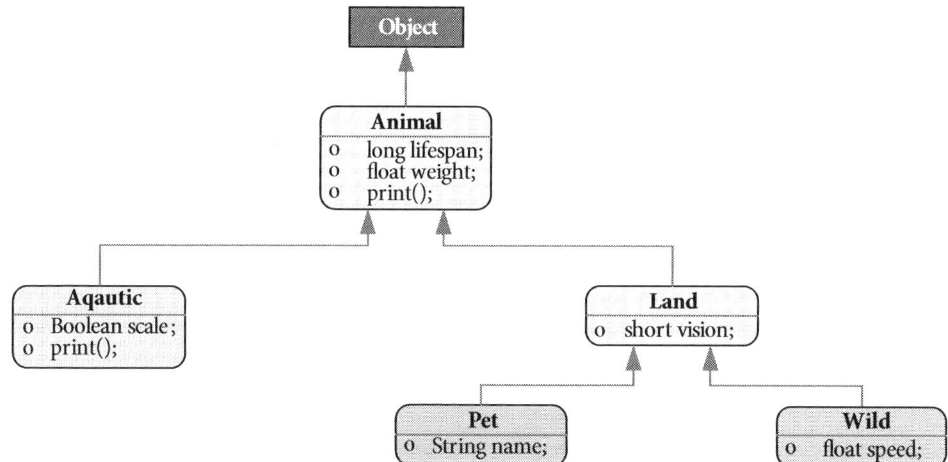

Figure 9.3 Animal class hierarchy

Our program should include different methods in different classes with their respective bounded wildcard arguments and then call the methods for different objects of the class in the animal class hierarchy. Our program will consist of the following codes:

1. Definition of all the classes as shown in Figure 9.3 (Program 9.27).
2. Declaration of the generic class, which can be used to store lists of animals of different types (Program 9.28).
3. Definitions of different methods to handle objects of different classes in the class hierarchy (Program 9.29).
4. Driver class to test the invocation of methods of different objects (Program 9.30).

Codes given here and all of them have been written in a structured form, so that you can learn the code very easily. You can archive all codes in a single program file, say `BoundedWildcardArgumentsDemo.java`, in your working directory.

Program 9.27 *(Java wildcard in generic programming: Definition of classes of animal hierarchy)*

```
/* This program includes the definitions of all the
classes of the animal class hierarchy. */

class Animal {
    long lifespan;
    float weight;
    Animal(long years, float kg) {
        lifespan = years;
        weight = kg;
    }
```

```
    public void print( ) {
        System.out.println("Maximum longevity: " +
          lifespan + " in years");
        System.out.println("Maximum weight: "    +
          weight + " in kgs");
   }
}   // End of class Animal

class Aquatic extends Animal {
      boolean scale;
          // true: has scale, false: no scale
      Aquatic(long years, float kg, boolean skin) {
            super(years, kg);
                // Super class constructor
             scale = skin;
        }

        public void print( ) {
             super.print();
                // Call the super class method
            System.out.println("Has scale?" + scale);
       }
}   // End of class Aquatic

class Land extends Animal {
      short vision;
          //0 = nocturnal, 1 = only day light, 2 = both
      Land(long years, float kg, short vision) {
           super(years, kg);
                // Super class constructor
           this.vision = vision;
     }
}   // End of class Land

class Pet extends Land {
      String name;
      Pet(long years, float kg, short vision, String
          name) {
          super(years, kg, vision, name);
          // Super class constructor
             this.name = name;
       }
}   // End of class Pet
```

```
class Wild extends Land {
      float speed;  // Maximum running speed in mph
      Wild(long years, float kg, short vision, float
           speed) {
          super(years, kg, vision, name);
           // Super class constructor
          this.speed = speed;
      }
}   // End of class Wild
```

***Program 9.28** (Java wildcard in generic programming: Definition of generic class)*

```
/* Defining the Generic class to maintain lists of
different animals. */

class AnimalWorld<T extends Animal> {
            //Type parameter is limited to Animal and
                                         // its sub classes
        T [ ] listOfAnimals;

        AnimalWorld(T [ ] list) {
            // Generic constructor to create a list of
                                                  // type T
            listOfAnimals = list;
        }
}   // End of the generic class AnimalWorld
```

***Program 9.29** (Java wildcard in generic programming: Definition of methods with different bounds of wildcard)*

```
/* Defining different methods with different bounds of
     arguments .*/

class BoundedWildcards {

//Case 1: Unbound wildcard: Any object can be passed as
                                          // its argument.
   static void vitality(AnimalWorld<?> animals) {
      //To print the vitality of animals in the list of
                                                // animals
      for(Animal a : animals.listOfAnimals)
          a.print();
      System.out.println();
   }

// Case 2: Lower bounded wildcard: Any object of
      //Aquatic or Animal can be passed as its argument.
```

```
    static void showSea(AnimalWorld<?  super Aquatic>
          animals) {
          //For aquatic or unknown animals
          for(Object obj : animals.listOfAnimals)
              obj.print();
                   // Call the method defined in
                                  // Animal/ Aquatic class
          System.out.println();
    }

// Case 3a: Upper bounded wildcard: Any object of Land/
             // Pet/ Wild can be passed as its argument.
    static void showLand(AnimalWorld<?  extends Land>
          animals) {
         //For Land or any of its subclasses
         for(int i = 0; i < animals.listOfAnimals.
          length++)  {
             animals.listOfAnimals[i].print();
                 // Call the method defined in Animal
                                              // class
             System.out.println("Vision : " +
                       animals.listOfAnimals[i].vision);
          }
          System.out.println();
    }

// Case 3b: Upper bounded wildcard: Any object of only
             // Pet class can be passed as its argument.
       static void showPet(AnimalWorld<?  extends Pet>
          animals) {
            //For lists of Pet objects only
            for(int i = 0; i < animals.listOfAnimals.
                length)  {
                  System.out.println("Pet's name: " +
                         animals.listOfAnimals[i].name);
                  animals.listOfAnimals[i].print();
                     // Call the method defined in
                                         // Animal class
                  System.out.println("Vision : " +
                       animals.listOfAnimals[i].vision);
            }
            System.out.println();
       }
```

```
// Case 3c: Upper bounded wildcard: Any object of only
            // Wild class can be passed as its argument.
        static void showWild(AnimalWorld<?
            extends Wild> animals) {
              //For objects of Wild class only
              for(int i = 0; i < animals.listOfAnimals.
                  length++)  {
                  animals.listOfAnimals[i].print();
                        // Call the method defined in
                                                // Animal class
                  System.out.println("Maximum running
                        speed: " +
                        animals.listOfAnimals[i].speed +
                                              " in mph");
                  System.out.println("Vision : " +
                          animals.listOfAnimals[i].vision);
              }
              System.out.println();
        }
}  // End of the method definitions in class
                                          // BoundedWildcards
```

Program 9.30 *(Java wildcard in generic programming: The main program demonstrating the calls of different methods of different objects)*

```
/* Main Java program utilizing the above-defined
classes. */

class BoundedWildcardArgumentsDemo {
    public static void main(String args[]) {

        // Create a list of unknown animals of class
                                                // Animal
        Animal unknown = new Animal(40, 720);
                  // An unknown animal object is created
        Animal u [] = {unknown};
           // Array of unknown animals
        AnimalWorld<Animal> uList = new
           AnimalWorld<Animal>(u);
                         // Place the unknown into a list

        // Create a list of aquatic animals
        Aquatic whale = new Aquatic(90, 150000);
                             // A whale object is created
        Aquatic shark = new Aquatic(400, 2150);
                             // A shark object is created
        Aquatic q [] = { whale, shark };
                              // Array of aquatic animals
```

```
AnimalWorld<Aquatic> qList = new
  AnimalWorld<Aquatic>(q);
            // Place the aquatics into a list

// Create a list of land animals
Land owl = new Land(3, 1, (short)0);
               // A land owl object is created
Land l[] = { owl };
  // An array of land objects is created
AnimalWorld<Land> lList = new AnimalWorld
  <Land>(l);
          // Place the land animals into a list

// Create a list of pet animals
Pet dog = new Pet(15, 75, 2, "Prince");
                // A pet dog object is created
Pet p [] = { new Pet(15, 75, (short)2,
  "Prince") };
          // An array of pet objects is created
AnimalWorld<Pet> pList = new AnimalWorld
  <Pet>(p);
                 // Place the pets into a list

// Create a list of wild animals
Wild cheetah = new Land(15L, 75.0f, (short)2,
  1.5f);
                // A cheetah object is created
Wild deer = new Land(10, 50, 1);
                   // A deer object is created
Wild w [] = { cheetah, deer };
               // Array of non-aquatic animals
AnimalWorld<Wild> wList = new AnimalWorld
  <Wild>(w);
                // Place the wilds into a list

// Call the methods and see the outcomes
// vitality(…) is with unlimited wildcard
// argument and hence we can pass argument
                               // of any type
    a.vitality (uList);      // OK
    a.vitality (qList);     // OK
    a.vitality (lList);    // OK
    a.vitality (pList);   // OK
    a.vitality (wList);  // OK
```

```
        // showSea(...) is with lower bound wildcard
        // argument with class Aquatic and its super
                                                  // classes
            a.showSea (uList);       // OK
            a.showSea (qList);      // OK
            a.showSea (lList);     // Compile-time error
            a.showSea (pList);    // Compile-time error
            a.showSea (wList);   // Compile-time error

        // showLand(...) is with upper bound wildcard
        // argument with class Land and its subclasses
            showLand (uList);       // Compile-time error
            showLand (qList);      // Compile-time error
            showLand (lList);     // OK
            showLand (pList);    // OK
            showLand  (wList); // OK

        // showPet(...) is with upper bound wildcard
        // argument with class Pet and its subclasses
            a.showPet (uList);       // Compile-time error
            a.showPet (qList);      // Compile-time error
            a.showPet (lList);     // Compile-time error
            a.showPet (pList);    // OK
            a.showPet (wList);   // Compile-time error

        // showWild(...) is with upper bound wildcard
           argument with class Wild and its sub classes
            a.showWild (uList);       // Compile-time error
            a.showWild (qList);      // Compile-time error
            a.showWild (lList);     // Compile-time error
            a.showWild (pList);    // Compile-time error
            a.showWild (wList);   // OK
      }
}
```

- You can specify an upper bound for a wildcard, or you can specify a lower bound, but you cannot specify both.
- Use `extend` wildcard when you want to get values out of a structure and super wildcard when you put values in a structure. Don't use a wildcard when you get and put values in a structure.
- Bounded wildcard argument ensure type safety.

- We can use a wildcard as a type of a parameter, field, return type, or local variable. However, it is not allowed to use a wildcard as a type argument for a generic method invocation, a generic class instance creation, or a supertype.

9.3.3 When to Use Which Wildcard

There is a need to decide which type of wildcard best suits a condition. To understand this, let us first classify the type of parameters passed to a method as `in` and `out` parameter. They are defined as follows:

- `in` variable: An `in` variable provides data to the code. For example, `copy(src,dest)`. Here `src` acts as the `in` variable, being data to be copied.
- `out` variable: An `out` variable holds data updated by the code. For example, `copy(src,dest)`. Here `dest` acts as the `out` variable having copied data.

Guidelines for Using Wildcards

- Upper bound wildcard: If a variable is of `in` category, use `extends` keyword with the wildcard. This is called an upper bound wildcard.
- Lower bound wildcard: If a variable is of `out` category, use `super` keyword with the wildcard. This is called a lower bound wildcard.
- Unbounded wildcard: In this case a variable can be accessed using `Object` class metho. This is called an unbound wildcard.
- No wildcard: If code is accessing variables in both `in` and `out` category, do not use a wildcard.

9.4 Applications of Generic Programming

To complete your understanding, you should practice solving some problems. Since programming implies implementation of algorithms, and an algorithm means dealing with data structures, you can consider writing sorting programs to sort any type of list or search an element in a list of any type. If you are skilled in Computer Science, then you can think of implementing many other algorithms and data structures, like `stack`, `queue`, `binary tree`, `set`, `graph`, etc. In `java.util` API, readymade solutions for some of the data structures are already available as a Java Collection framework. But you can still build your own. This endeavor will enhance your programming skills. In this section, we will discuss two examples related to the following:

- Implementation of stack data structures using an array.
- Implementation of linked list structures.
- Implementation of stack data structures using linked list.

9.4.1 Generic Programming for Stack Using an Array

A *stack* is a linear data structure. It is very useful in various applications of Computer Science such as evaluation of an arithmetic expression, traversing a graph, etc. The implementation of a majority of systems programs such as recursion implementation, code compilation, etc., is simplified using this data structure. Before discussing this data structure, let us first consider a few examples of the stack phenomenon (Figure 9.4).

Shunting of trains in a railway yard

Suppose there is a railway yard with a single track. Trains enter the railway yard for parking, and when they exit, it is in opposite order to what they followed when they had entered, that is, the last train comes out first.

Shipment of cargo

For shipment, goods are loaded into a cargo compartment. At the destination, they are unloaded exactly in the opposite sequence to that in which they were loaded. That is, the goods loaded last get unloaded first.

Plates on a tray

Suppose a chef places the dishes on a tray one above the other. The waiter serves the dishes to the customers in the opposite order to what the chef had placed them, that is, the dish at the top which was placed last by the chef is served first. The first dish placed by the chef on the tray is served last by the waiter.

From these examples, it is clear that a *stack* is something which follows the last-in first-out strategy. This is why a stack is also called LIFO (Last-In-First-Out) structure.

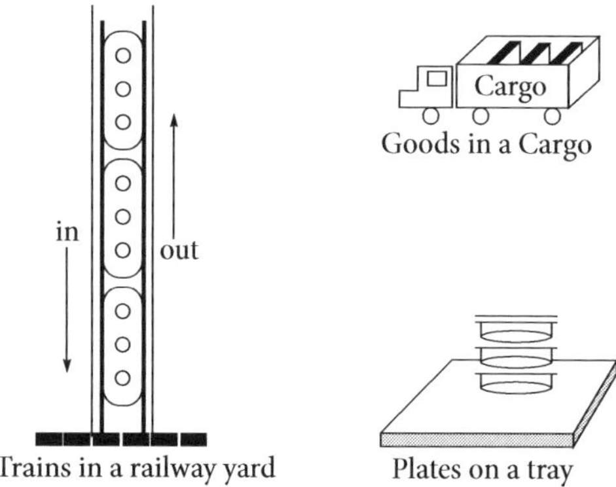

Figure 9.4 Some examples of stacks

The concept of stack is used to manipulate data in the required manner. This implies that a stack can hold data, like a railway yard stores coaches of trains. If you use a stack to store data, then you have to follow the following rules:

- A stack can store any type of data.
- A particular stack should store only one type of data in it.
- It should be considered as an ordered collection. Neither you can insert data into a stack nor can you delete data from a stack. The insertion and deletion must take place at one end only. The end is called the "top of a stack."

In Figure 9.5, `push()` is the operation to add an item into stack at top and `pop()` is an operation to remove an item from the top.

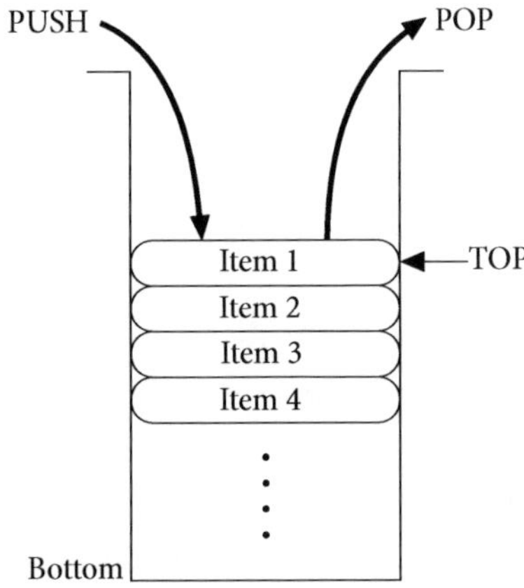

Figure 9.5 Stack data structure

Programming for stack data structure using an array

As an implementation of stack, you can use an array to store data of a stack. This means that a stack is an array but an array is not a stack. Like an array, stack stores homogeneous data and unlike an array, you can insert/delete at or from the top of the stack only.

While programming a stack, you need to define a generic class so that it can store any type of data (numeric, characters, string, object of any type) and define the methods for managing the data. Following operations are usually important:

`Push` : This operation adds an element into the stack.

`Pop` : This operation returns and removes the element from stack.

`Peek` : This operation returns the element at the top.

`Status` : This operation checks if an array is empty or full.

`Print` : This operation prints all items in the stack.

A generic program implementing a stack data structure using an array is shown in Program 9.31.

Program 9.31 *(Generic program for stack using array)*

```
/* This program shows how a stack can be defined using
an array. */

// Defining generic class
class StackA<T> {
    T[] data;              // Array to store data
    int length;           // Maximum capacity of the array
    int top;             // Points to the top of the stack

    // Constructor to create and initialize a stack
    StackA(T[] a) {
        data = a;
        length = a.length;
        if (a.length == 0)
           // If the array is not pre-loaded
            top = -1;
                // This means that stack is empty
        else
            top = 0;
              // The first element is the element at top
    }
   // Defining the push operation
    void push(T e) {
        if(top < length-1) {
            top++;
            data[top] = e;
        }
        else {
            System.out.println("Stack is full. Push is
                failed.");
        }
    }
```

```
    // Defining the pop operation
    T pop() {
        T e = null;
        if(top == -1) {
            System.out.println("Stack is empty. Pop is
                not possible.");
        }
        else {
            e = data[top];
                // Get the element at top
            top--;
                // Update top and logically remove
        }
        return e;
    }

    // Defining an operation to print an entire stack
                                                // content
    boolean isEmpty() {
        if(top == -1)  {
            return true;            // Stack is empty
        }
        else  {
            return false;           // Stack is non-empty
        }
    }

    // Defining an operation to print all elements
                                    // present in the stack
    void printStack() {
        if(top == -1) {
            System.out.println("Stack is empty");
        }
        else {
            for(int i = top; i>=0 ; i--) {
                // Print from top to bottom
                System.out.print(data[i] + " ");
            }
            System.out.println();
        }
    }
} // End of generic class definition
```

Program 9.32 shows how the class definition `StackA` can be used to test a stack.

Program 9.32 *(Illustration of application of* `StackA`*)*

```
/* This program illustrates the usage of the class
StackA. You should include the class definition here.
Let it be in myStack package */
import myStack;
class StackADemo {
    public static void main(String[] args) {
        Integer a[] = new Integer[2];
          //Define an Integer array of size 2
        // Create a stack: Initially empty
        StackA<Integer> st = new StackA<Integer>(a);
        st.push(5);
        st.printStack();
        st.push(6);        // Stack is full
        st.push(7);        // Push operation is failed
        st.printStack();
        st.pop();
        st.printStack();
        st.pop();         // Stack is now empty
        st.printStack();
        st.pop();         // Pop operation is failed
       System.out.println(" Is empty? " + st.isEmpty();
    }
 } // End of the demo class
```

- You can run Program 9.32, with stack of any other type, for example, `Double`, `String`, `Student` (e.g., a user defined class), etc. and then check the working of the program.
- You cannot create a stack of integer data with the following:

```
// Declare an array of integer of size 2
int a[] = new Integer[2];
// Create a stack
StackA<int> st = new StackA<int>(a);
```

- Program 9.32 work even if you do the following in the program:

```
// Declare an array of Strings elments
String vow s = {"a", "e", "i", "o", "u");
// Create a stack
StackA<String> st = new StackA<String>(vow);
```

- You can use your `StackA` class to solve any problem. For details of applications of stack data structures, you can read the book *Classic Data Structures* by Debasis Samanta, second edition, published by Prentice Hall of India.

9.4.2 Generic Programming for Linked List

An array is a data structure where elements are stored in consecutive memory locations. In order to occupy the adjacent space, the block of memory required for the array should be allocated beforehand. Once the memory is allocated, it cannot be extended any more. This is why the array is known as a *static data structure.* In contrast to this, the linked list is called a *dynamic data structure* where the amount of memory required can be varied during its use. In the linked list, the adjacency between the elements is maintained by means of *links* or *pointers.* A link or pointer actually is the address (that is, reference, or memory location) of the subsequent element. Thus, in a linked list, data (actual content) and link (to point to the next data) both are required to be maintained.

An element in a linked list is a specially termed *node*, which can be viewed as shown in Figure 9.6. A node consists of two fields: *Data* (to store the actual information) and *Link* (to point to the next node).

A *linked list* is an ordered collection of finite, homogeneous data elements called *nodes* where the linear order is maintained by means of links or pointers. The pointers are maintained depending on the requirements, and accordingly the linked list can be classified into three major groups: single linked list, circular linked list, and double linked list. We shall limit our discussion here to the single linked list structure.

A linked list can store data of any type like an array. However, unlike an array, data is stored in a dispersed manner across the memory space. A typical view of a linked list structure with some data stored in it is shown in Figure 9.7. There is a specially designated node called "header" from which you can start traversing the linked list. Note that you cannot jump to any node (and hence access data in it) at random; rather, you have to start from "header" and sequentially move from one node to the next node. Also, note that the last node does not point to any node. The null value of "header" implies that the list is empty.

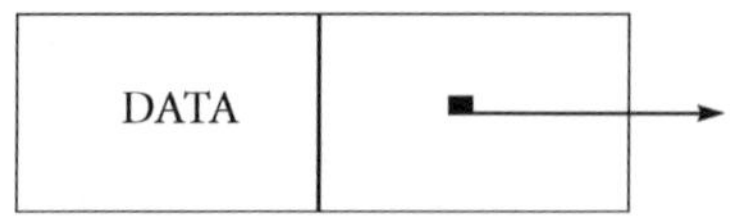

Figure 9.6 Node of linked list

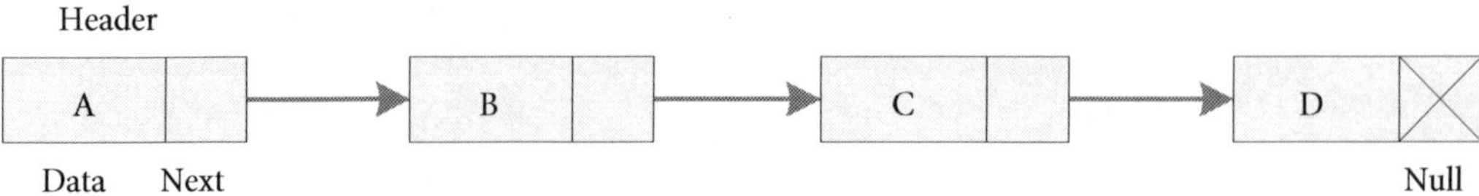

Figure 9.7 Logical view of a single linked list structure

Operations with linked list

In order to manage and maintain data in a linked list structure, the following operations are necessary:

Traversing: Visiting (e.g., printing data) nodes or reaching a node.

Inserting : Inserting a node in the list.

Deleting : Deleting a node from the list.

Merging : Merging a linked list with another linked list to make a larger list.

Searching : Finding a node containing a particular data in it.

Sorting : Ordering of data in a list in a particular arrangement.

Reversing : Ordering the data in a reverse order.

Among these operations, the insertion, deletion, and merging operations are discussed further.

Insertion operations

If you want to insert data into a linked list, then there can be three situations:

- Insertion in the front, that is, insert as header.
- Insertion at the end, that is, insert as the last element.
- Insertion at any position, for example, insert after the node containing some specified data in it.

These three operations are a manipulation of the link fields of some nodes. How you should manipulate the link fields, is shown in Figure 9.8. You should note the order in which you should change the link fields; otherwise, the operations lead to an inappropriate list.

Deletion operations

Like insertion operations, the deletion operations face three different situations:

- Deletion in the front, that is, insert as header.
- Deletion at end, that is, insert as the last element.
- Deletion at any position, for example, insert after the node contacting a specified data in it.

Again, like the insertion operations, the deletion operations are the manipulation of link fields of some nodes. The order of manipulation of the the link fields is shown in Figure 9.9.

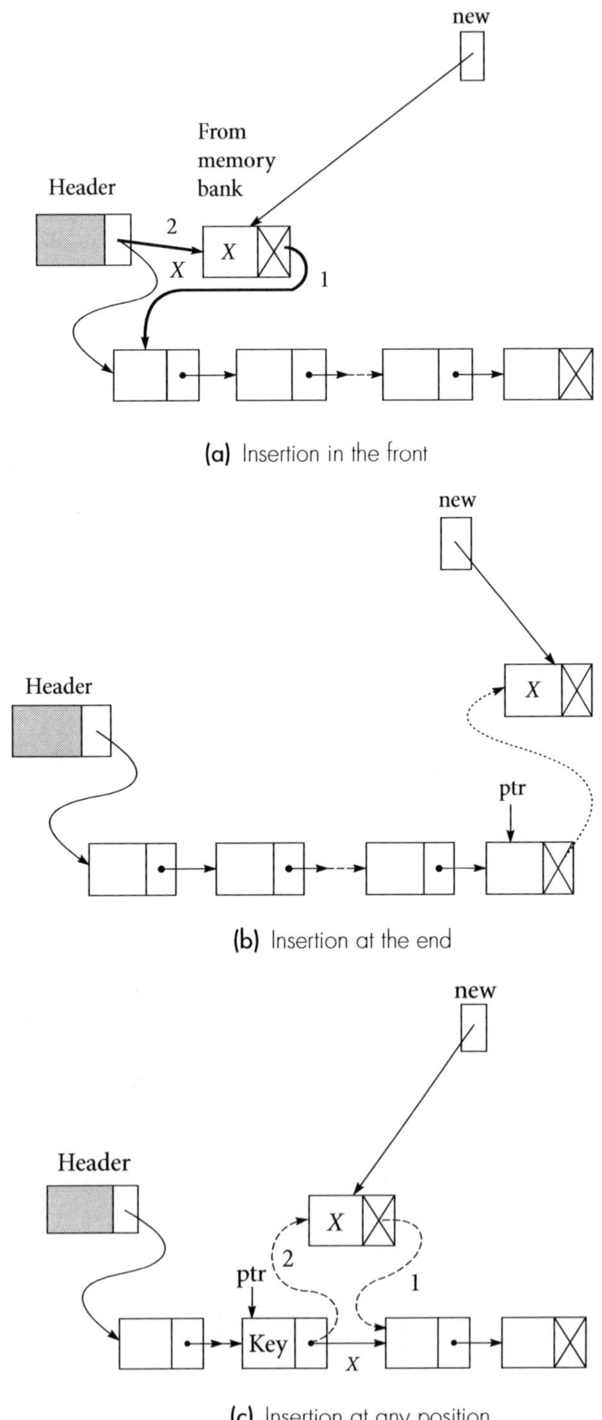

(a) Insertion in the front

(b) Insertion at the end

(c) Insertion at any position

Figure 9.8 Insertion operation on a single linked list

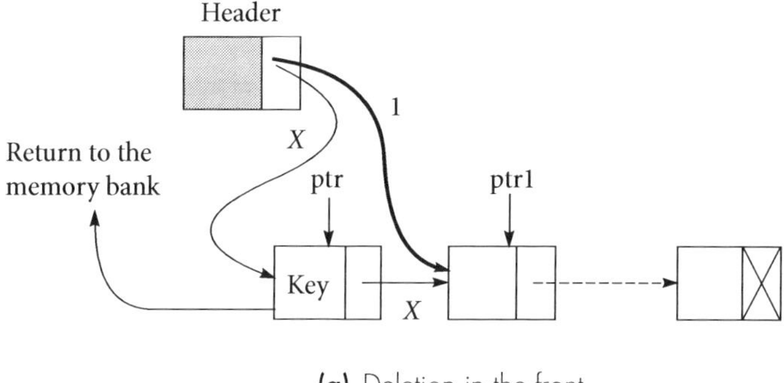

(a) Deletion in the front

Header

Return to the memory bank

ptr1

ptr

X

(b) Deletion at the end

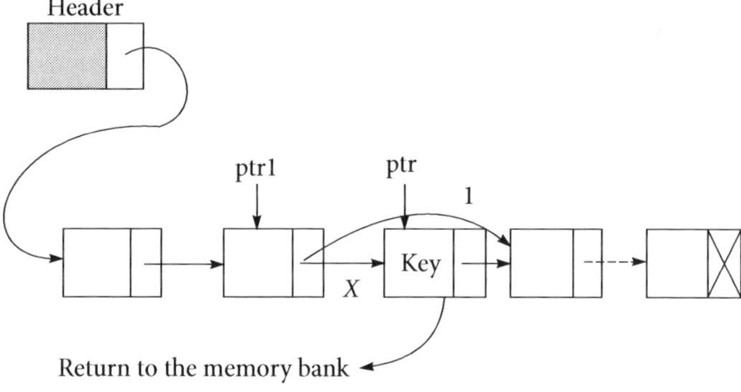

(c) Deletion at any position

Figure 9.9 Deletion operations on a single linked list

Merging operation

The merging of two lists is a relatively straightforward operation. Figure 9.10 shows how you can change the link fields of the two input lists to merge them.

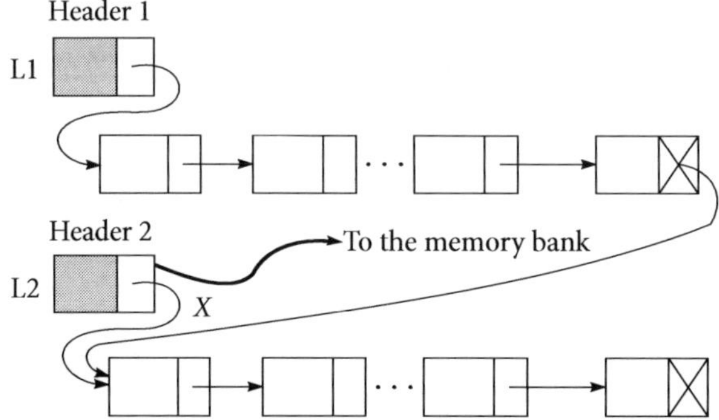

Figure 9.10 Merging of two linked lists

Programming for single linked list

Now, you are in a position to implement a linked list structure with generic programming. Program 9.33 demonstrates how you can implement a single linked list structure.

Program 9.33 *(Generic program for single linked list)*

```
/* This program shows how to define a single linked
list data structure to manage data of any type,. */
class JLinkedList<T> {
    // Define the node structure for single linked list
    class Node {
         T data;
         Node next;
         // Constructor
         Node (){
             data = null;
             next = null;
         }
         Node(T d){
             data = d;
             next = null;
         }
     } // End of node definition
     Node header; // header of the of list
     // Constructor to create a single linked list
```

```
JLinkedList(){     //LinkedList Header Node
      header = new Node();
       // Initially, header is empty
}
public boolean isEmpty(){
        if(header.next == null)return true;
        return false;
}
/* In the next, the different operations on single
       linked list are defined. */
// Defining the method to insert at the front
public void insertFront(T data){
     // Create a new node with given data
     Node newNode = new Node(data);
       // Allocate a new node
     newNode.next = this.header.next;
     // Make the new node as the first node
     this.header.next = newNode;
}

// Defining the method to insert at the end
public void insertEnd(T data){
     Node newNode = new Node(data);
       // Allocate a new node
     newNode.next = null;
     // Move to end, that is, the last node
     Node temp = this.header;
     while(temp.next != null) {
          temp = temp.next;
     }
     temp.next = newNode;
       // Add the node as the last node
}

// Defining the method to insert at any position
public void insertAny(T data , T key) {
     Node newNode = new Node(data);
       // Allocate for a new node
     newNode.next = null;
     // Move to the node, which contains key
     Node temp = this.header;
     boolean status = false;
     while(temp != null){
          if(temp.data == key) {
               status = true;
                    // Node is reached
```

```
                break;
            }
            temp = temp.next;
        }
         if(status) {
          // If the node with key is found
               newNode.next = temp.next;
                    // Insert new node after temp
               temp.next = newNode;
         }
    }
    // Defining the method to delete a node at the
                                                // front
    public T deleteFront() {
         T x = null;
         Node temp = this.header;
         if(temp != null) {
          // Check if the list is non-empty
              x = temp.data;
              this.header = temp.next;
               // Changed header
              // Display the message
              System.out.println("Element is deleted");
              free(temp);
               // Return the node to free memory
         }
         return x; // Return the deleted data
   }
   // Defining the method to delete a node from the end
   public T deleteEnd() {
        T x = null;
        Node temp = this.header, prev = null;
        if(temp != null) {
          // If the list is not empty
             while(temp != null) {
               // Move to the last node
                prev = temp;
                temp = temp.next;
             }
             x = temp.data;
             prev.next = null;     // Delete the node
             free(temp);
               // Return the node to free memory
         }
         return x;
   }
```

```
// Defining the method to delete a node from any
                                        // position
 public void deleteKey(T key){
     Node temp = this.header, prev = null;
     while(temp != null) {
        // Move to the target node or to end
         if(temp.data == key) {
              prev.next = temp.next;
                   // Node is deleted
              // Display the message
              System.out.println(key + " is deleted");
               break;          // Done: Break the loop
         }
         else {
              prev = temp;
             temp = temp.next;
         }
     }
}

// Defining the method to merge two lists into a
                                       // single list
public void merge(JLinkedList<T> l2) {
 //l2 is the list to be merged
      Node l1Node = this.header;
        // The current list
      Node l2Node = l2.header;
      while(l1Node.next != null ) {
        // Move to the last node
           l1Node = l1Node.next;
      }
      l1Node.next = l2Node;
 }

 // Linked list traversal: Defining the method to
                                     // print the list
 public void printList(){
     Node currNode = this.header;
        // Start from the header
     System.out.print("LinkedList: ");
     // Traverse through the LinkedList
     while(currNode != null) {
          // Print the data at current node
          System.out.print(currNode.data + " ");
```

```
                currNode = currNode.next;
                  // Move to next node
            }
            System.out.println();
        }
    }  // End of the definition of the generic class
```

The main class to demonstrate the working of the generic class `JLinkedList<T>` is shown in Program 9.34.

***Program 9.34** (Illustration of application of `JLinkedList`)*

```
/* This program illustrates the usage of the class
JLinkedList<T>. You should include the class definition
here. Let it be in myList package */
import myList;

class LinkedListDeletionDemo  {
     public static void main(String[] args) {
         // Create a linked list of Integer type
         JLinkedList<Integer> list = new
           JLinkedList<Integer>();
         // Insert the data into the list
         list.insertFront(1);
         list.insertFront(2);
         list.insertFront(3);
         list.insertFront(4);
         list.insertFront(5);
         list.insertFront(7);
         list.insertFront(8);
         list.insertFront(9);
         list.insertEnd (0);
         list.insertAny(6, 5);

         // Print the LinkedList
         list.printList();
         // Perform a few more operations
         list.deleteKey(1);
         list.printList();

         list.deleteFront( );
         list.printList();

         list.deleteEnd();
         list.printList();
```

```
        // Demonstrate merge operation
        // Create anoter linked list of Integer type
        JLinkedList<Integer> list2 = new JLinkedList
          <Integer>();
        // Insert the data into the list
        list2.insertFront(11);
        list2.insertFront(12);
        list2.insertFront(13);
        list2.insertFront(14);
        list2.insertFront(15);

        list.merge(list2);
        list.printList();
    }
}
```

9.4.3 Generic Programming for Stack Using Linked List

In Section 9.4.1, you learned how a stack can be implemented using an array. It was simple. However, the implementation has a problem: it can face *Stack overflow* error as the implementation is limited to the size of the array it uses. The linked list structure that you have implemented in Section 9.4.2 can be used to implement a stack which does not suffer from stack overflow error, until the computer memory overflows. This is the implementation of a dynamic stack in contrast to the static stack implementation using an array.

The dynamic stack implementation using an array is simple. You need to import your `JLinkedList.class` file into your next implementation. Program 9.35 shows how you can implement stack using a linked list.

Program 9.35 *(Implementation of Stack using* `JLinkedList`*)*

```
/* This program shows how a stack can be defined using
a linked list. */

// This program uses linked list related implementation.
// So, include the package, where all those programs
          // are defined. Assume the package is myList

import myList;

// Defining the generic class for stack using linked list
class StackL<T> {
   JLinkedList<T> list;          // Header to the list
   int length;                   // Length of the list
```

```
    StackL() {
         list = new JLinkedList<T>();
         length = 0;
     }

     // Defining the push operation
     void push(T data) {
         length += 1;
         this.list.insertFront(data);
     }

// Defining an operation to know the status of the stack
        boolean isEmpty(){
            if(this.list.isEmpty()) {
                  return true;
            }
         else {
             return false;
        }
     }

     // Defining the pop operation
     T pop() {
         T data = null;
         if(!isEmpty()){
             length -= 1;
             this.list.deleteFront();
         }
         else {
             System.out.print("Stack is empty");
         }
         return data;
     }

     // Defining an operation to print an entire stack
                                                      // content
     void printStack() {
         if(this.list.isEmpty()) {
              System.out.print("Stack is empty");
         }
         else {
              this.list.printList();
         }
     }
}
```

Note the defined `push()` and `pop()` operations in the class `StackL<T>`. The two operations take place at the front of the linked list. The working of the new implementation is demonstrated in Program 9.36.

***Program* 9.36** *(Demonstration of working of `StackL`)*

```
/* This program illustrates the usage of the class
StackL. You should include the class definition here.
Let it be in myStack package */

import myStack;

class StackLinkedListDemo {
     public static void main(String[] args) {
        StackL<String> st = new StackL<String>();
        st.push("J");
        st.push("A");
        st.push("V");
        st.push("A");
        st.printStack();

        st.pop();
        st.pop();
        st.pop();
        st.pop();      // Now stack becomes empty
        System.out.Printl("Is Stack empty? " +st.
           isEmpty());
        st.pop();
     }
}  // End of the demo class
```

9.5 Some Facts of Generic Programming

You have learned a few basic features of generic programming and you will be able to write generic methods, write generic methods with variable number of arguments, define generic classes, define generic classes with bounded type parameters, write wildcards and their bounds in generic programming, and understand applications of generic programming.

Apart from this, the following are important facts about Java generics which we shall discuss in this section:

- Type inference
- Code compatibility with generic programming
- Java type erasure
- Generic constructors
- Generic interfaces
- Generic inheritance
- Type casting
- Generic restrictions

9.5.1 Type Inference

Suppose, you have defined a generic class, say `GC`, which is as follows:

```
class GC<T, U, V> {
      /* Body of the class… */
}
```

Now, in your program, you want to create an object of the class `GC`. You can do this in the following manner:

```
GC<String, Integer, Double> obj = new GC<String, Double,
                                Integer>("Java", 2020, 2.1);
```

The type arguments `<String, Integer, Double>` have to be specified twice: once on the left-hand side and once on the right-hand side after `new`. You should take care to mention both in their proper order. This is now an old practice. JDK 7 onwards, Java allows a shortened form of doing the same. You can use the following instead of the old format:

```
GC<String, Integer, Double> obj = new GC<>("Java", 2020, 2.1);
```

Such a feature is called *type inference* in Java generic programming. The syntax of type inference is generalized as follows:

```
className<typeArgList> objRef = new className <>(valueList);
```

Note the instance creation portion simply uses `<>`, which is an empty type argument list. This is referred to as the *diamond* operator. It tells the compiler to infer the type arguments needed by the constructor in the `new` expression. The principal advantage of this type-inference syntax is that it shortens what are sometimes quite long declaration statements.

Type inference can also be applied to parameter passing. For example, suppose, there is a method `genMeth()` defined as:

```
static void genMeth(GenClass<T, V> o)  {
     /* Body of the method... */
}
```

With the type inference feature, the following call is valid:

```
genMeth(new GenClass<>("Java", 2020));
```

In this case, the type arguments passed to `genMeth()` can be inferred from the parameter's type, that is, `String` and `Integer` in this case.

- The type-inference syntax does not work with older compilers prior to JDK 7 release.
- Most of the examples in this book use the full syntax when declaring instances of generic classes. In this way, the examples work with any Java compiler that supports generics.
- I recommend the full-length syntax in your programming practice. The full-length syntax makes it very clear precisely what is being created and improves readability and code debugging.

9.5.2 Code Compatibility with Generic Programming

Often software engineers have to work with pre-existing code, also called legacy programs. You may have to combine old code (e.g., without generic implementation) with your new code (e.g., with generic programming). This may bring a code compatibility issue. What will happen if you mix the legacy code developed with JDK 4 compiler to the code with JDK 7 compiler (the generic programming features were added in JDK 5)? Java developer take care of this so that old, pre-generics codes, are compatible with generic codes.

For this reason, Java allows a generic class to be used without any type arguments. This creates a *raw type* for the class. This raw type is compatible with legacy code, which has no knowledge of generics. Program 9.37 illustrates how you can use raw type in your program.

Program 9.37 *(Raw type in generic programming)*

```
/* This program demonstrates how you can define an
instance of an object of a generic class without any
type specification. */

// Let's have a generic class with a single type
                                             // parameter
class GenClass<T> {
     T t;
     GenClass(T t) {
```

```
        this.t = t;
    }
    T getob() {
        return t;
    }
}

// This program illustrates how objects can be created
                                        // in different ways
class RawTypeDemo {
    public static void main(String args[]) {
        // Create an object for Integers with generics
        GenClass<Integer> gObj = new GenClass
          <Integer>(123);

        // Create another object for Strings with
                                                // generics.
        GenClass<String> strOb = new GenClass<String>
          ("Generics");

        // Create an object of GenClass without any
                                        // type specification
        GenClass rawObj = new GenClass(new Double
          (123.456));//This is raw type

        double d = (Double) rawObj.getob();
          // Cast is necessary because type is unknown.
        System.out.println("value: " + d);
    }
}
```

- The main drawback of using the raw type is that the type safety of generics is lost. A raw type is not type safe. This is because a variable of a raw type can be assigned a reference to any type of an object of a generic class. The reverse is also allowed; a variable of a specific generic class type can be assigned a reference to a raw generic class object. However, both operations are potentially unsafe because the type checking mechanism of generics is circumvented.
- The use of a raw type can lead to run-time exceptions.

Here are some examples (with reference to the object `rawObj` created in Program 9.27.

```
int i = (Integer) rawObj.getob(); // Run-time error
```

The following assignments overrides type safety and leads to run-time error:

```
strObj = rawObj; // Valid
```

`strObj` so obtained leads to run-time error for the following:

```
String str = strOb.getob(); // Run-time error
```

The following assignment also overrides type safety:

```
rawObj = gObj; // Valid, but potentially wrong
d = (Double) raw.getob(); // Run-time error
```

- Because of the potential for danger inherent in raw types, the Java compiler displays *unchecked warnings* when a raw type is used.
- You should limit the use of raw types to those cases in which you need to combine pre-existing legacy code with newer generic code. Raw types are simply a transitional feature and not something that should be used for new code.

9.5.3 Java Type Erasure

It is interesting to know how the Java compiler transforms your source code with generic features into object code. Generics in Java was added to provide type-checking at compile-time and it has no use at run-time. The way Java implements generics while satisfying this type-checking is called the *Java type erasure*. Let us learn how erasure works. At the time of Java code is compilation, all generic type information are removed (i.e., erased). This is done by replacing type parameters with their bound type, which is `Object`. Thus, there are no explicit bound specified. Following this, the appropriate casts (determined by the type arguments) are applied to maintain type compatibility with the types specified by the type arguments. The compiler finally enforces this type compatibility. For example, if you have a generic class like the following:

```
public class Node<T extends A> {
    private T data;
    private Node<T> next;

    Test(T d, Test<T> n) {
        this.data = d;
        this.next = n;
    }

    public T getData() {
        return this.data;
    }
}
```

The Java compiler replaces the bounded type parameter T with the first bound class, as per the following code:

```
public class Node {
    private A data;
    private Node next;

    public Node(A d, Node n) {
        this.data = d;
        this.next = n;
    }

    public A getData() {
        return data;
    }
}
```

This approach to generics means that no type parameters exist at run-time. They are simply a source-code to object-code mechanism. Type erasure ensures that no new classes are created for parameterized types; consequently, generics incur no run-time overhead.

9.5.4 Generic Constructor

It is possible for constructors to be generic, even if their class is not. For example, consider Program 9.38 which shows how you can define a generic constructor in a non-generic class.

Program 9.38 *(Generic constructor)*

```
/* This program demonstrates a generic constructor. */

class GenericConstructor {
     private double d;
     <T extends Number> GenericConstructor(T t) {
         d = t.doubleValue();
     }
     void print() {
         System.out.println("Value: " + d);
     }
}

class GenericConstructorDemo {
     public static void main(String args[]) {
          GenericConstructor obj1 = new Generic
               Constructor(123);
```

```
            GenericConstructor obj2 = new Generic
                  Constructor(123.456F);
            obj1.print();
            obj2.print();
      }
}
```

In this program, `GenericConstructor()` specifies a parameter of a generic type, which must be a sub class of `Number`. Thus, `GenericConstructor()` can be called with any numeric type, including `Integer`, `Float`, or `Double`. Therefore, even though `GenericConstructor()` class is not a generic class, its constructor is generic.

9.5.5 Generic Interface

You have learned how to define generic methods and generic classes. You can also define generic interfaces. Generic interfaces are specified just like generic classes. Program 9.39 is an example of how you can define a generic interface. Program 9.39 defines a generic interface called `MinMax` which includes the declaration of methods `min()` and `max()`, which return the minimum and maximum value of some set of objects.

Program 9.39 *(Generic interface)*

```
/* This program illustrates how you can define a
generic interface and implement the same in a class. */

// Definging an interface
interface MinMax<T extends Comparable<T>> {
     T min();
     T max();
}
// The following class definition implements the MinMax
                                             // interface
class A<T extends Comparable<T>> implements MinMax<T> {
     T[] array;

     A(T[] a) {
        array = a;
     }

     // Defining the min()
     public T min() {
         T result = array[0];
         for(int i=1; i < array.length; i++)
```

```
            if(array[i].compareTo(result < 0) result =
               array[i];
        return result;
    }

    // Defining the max()
    public T max() {
        T result = array[0];
        for(int i=1; i < array.length; i++)
            if(array[i].compareTo(result > 0)
               result = array[i];
        return result;
    }
}

class GenericIinterfaceDemo {
    public static void main(String args[]) {
        Integer x[] = {9, 5, 2, 4, 6, 3, 1, 7, 8};
        Character y[] = {'a', 'e', 'i', 'o', 'u' 'm'};
        A<Integer> a = new A<Integer>(x);
        System.out.println("Max value in inums: " +
              a.max());
        System.out.println("Min value in inums: " +
              a.min());

        A<Character> b = new A<Character>(y);
        System.out.println("Max value in chs: " +
              b.max());
        System.out.println("Min value in chs: " +
              b.min());
    }
}
```

- All rules and syntax for generic class are also applicable to generic interface.
- You can define a class to implement one or more generic interface(s) including non-generic interface(s) as well.
- If a class implements a generic interface, that class must also be a generic class.
- Once the bound is specified in the class clause, there is no need to specify it again in the implements clause. It is incorrect to do so. For example, the following declaration is incorrect and gives a compile-time error:

```
class A<T extends Comparable<T>>  implements MinMax<T
extends Comparable<T>> {
/* Body of the class...
}
```

- The following is also not a valid declaration of a class:

```
class A implements MinMax<T> { {
/* Body of the class...
}
```

- The following is a valid declaration though the declared class is non-generic:

```
class A implements MinMax<String> { {
/* Body of the class...
}
```

9.5.6 Generic Inheritances

Class inheritance formalism is equally applicable to generic programming as to the inheritance of non-generic classes. A generic class can act as a super class or be a sub class. Only one thing in generic class hierarchy needs to be ensured: that any type arguments needed by a generic super class must be passed up the hierarchy by all sub classes. This is similar to the way that constructor arguments must be passed up a hierarchy.

Generic sub class of a generic super class

Program 9.40 illustrates how you can derive a generic sub class from a generic super class.

Program 9.40 *(Inheritance in generic programming: Defining a sub class)*

```
/* This program illustrates the definition of a sub
class from a generic super class. */

class GenericSuper<T extends Number> {
    T[] array;
    GenericSuper(T[] a)  {
        array = a;
    }

  public void print()  {
       for(T t: array)
           System.out.print(t + " ");
       System.out.println();
   }
}
```

```
// Defining a generic sub class of GenericSuper.
class GenericSub<T extends Number> extends
  GenericSuper<T> {
     GenericSub(T a) {
          super(a);
     }
     public void average() {
         double sum = 0; double val = 0.0;
         for(int i = 0; i < array.length; i++)
             sum += array[i].doubleVlaue();
         try {
            val = sum/array.length;
         } catch(Exception e) {
            System.out.println(e);
         }
         System.out.println("Result: " + val);
    }
}

public class GenericInheritanceDemo1 {
     public static void main (String args[]) {
       // Create an array of integer numbers
       Integer a[] = {1, 9,  2, 8, 3, 7, 4, 6, 5};
       GenericSuper<Integer> s = new GenericSuper
           <Integer>(a);
       s.print();
       s.average();

       // Create an array of double values
       Double b[] = {1.9,  2.8, 3.7, 4.6, 5.5};
       GenericSub<Double> u = new GenericSub<Double>(b);
       u.print();
       u.average();
   }
}
```

- Generic classes in the inheritance chain can use a simple type parameter as well as type parameter with bound.
- Generic sub class declaration must use the same declaration as in the super class. For example, the following sub class definition is valid:

```
GenericSuper<T> {
    ...
  }
```

```
GenericSub <T> extends GenericSuper<T> {
        ...
}
```

This implies that the type parameter `T` is specified by `GenericSuper` and should also be mentioned for `GenericSub` in the `extends` clause. Thus, the following sub class definition is not valid:

```
GenericSuper<T> {
        ...
 }

 GenericSub <U> extends GenericSuper<T> {
        ...
 }
```

- The `GenericSub` does not use the type parameter `T` except to support the `GenericSuper` class. Thus, even if a sub class of a generic super class would otherwise not need to be generic, it must still specify the type parameter(s) required by its generic super class.
- A sub class definition is free to add its own type parameters, if needed. For example, Program 9.41 shows a slight modification of Program 9.40 in which `GenericSub` adds a type parameter of its own. This program also shows that usual concept of method overriding is valid in the generic sub class definition.

Program 9.41 *(Inheritance in generic programming: Defining a sub class with its own type parameter)*

```
/* This program illustrates the definition of a sub
class from a generic super class with its own type
parameter(s). */

class GenericSuper<T> {
    T a;
    GenericSuper(T a)  {
        this.a = a;
    }

  public void print()  {
       System.out.println(a);
   }
}

// Defining a generic sub class of GenericSuper with an
                                       // additional type
class GenericSub<T, U> extends GenericSuper<T> {
```

```
        U b;
        GenericSub(T a, U b) {
              super(a);
              this.b = b;
        }
        // Overriding method
        public void print()  {
          System.out.println("From parent: " + a);
          System.out.println("From child: " + b);
      }
}
public class GenericInheritanceDemo2 {
   public static void main (String args[]) {
        // Create an object of parent class

        GenericSuper<String> p = new GenericSuper
            <String>("C++");
        p.print();

        // Create an object of child class
        GenericSub<Integer, String> c1 =
            new GenericSub<Integer,String>(1995, "Java");
        c1.print();

        GenericSub<String, Integer> c2 =
           new GenericSub<String, Integer>("Java", 1995);
        c2.print();
   }
}
```

Generic sub class of a non-generic super class

The Java generic programming allows you to define a generic sub class deriving from a non-generic super class. Program 9.42 illustrates this aspect.

***Program 9.42** (Inheritance in generic programming: Defining a sub class of a non-generic super class)*

```
/* This program illustrates the definition of a generic
sub class from a non-generic super class. */

class NonGenericSuper {
    int a;
    NonGenericSuper(int a)  {
        this.a = a;
    }
    public void print()  {
       System.out.println(a);
```

```
    }
}

// Defining a generic sub class of NonGenericSuper
class GenericSub<T> extends NonGenericSuper {
     T b;
     GenericSub(int a, T b) {
          super(a);
          this.b = b;
     }
     public void print()  {
       System.out.println("From parent: " + a);
       System.out.println("From child: " + b);
   }
}
public class GenericInheritanceDemo3 {
   public static void main (String args[]) {
       // Create an object of parent class
       NonGenericSuper p = new NonGenericSuper(2020);
       p.print();

       // Create an object of child class
       GenericSub<String> c1 =
                   new GenericSub<String>(1995, "Java");
       c1.print();

       GenericSub<Integer> c2 =
                    new GenericSub<Integer>(1995, 2020);
       c2.print();
   }
}
```

9.5.7 Type Casting in Generics

In generic programming you can create different objects from the same generic class with varying parameterized type(s). This may lead to a compatibility issue and hence reliable program execution. It is advisable to check if an object is an instance of a particular class with which you are working. Java provides the `instanceof` operator for the purpose. The `instanceof` is a keyword used for checking whether a reference variable contains a given type of object reference or not. It returns `true` if an object is of the specified type and if it can be casted to the specified type. The `instanceof` operator can be applied to objects of generic classes as well.

Program 9.43 demonstrates the use of the `instanceof` operator in a Java program.

Program 9.43
(Illustration of `instanceof` operator)

```
/* This program demonstrates the working of instanceof
operator. */

// Creating a sample class
class Person {
    String name;
    Person (String name) {
       this.name = name;
    }
}

// Creating a sample class hierarchy
class Animal {
     String category;
     int age = 0;
     Animal (String c) {
       this.category = c;
    }
}

class Dog extends Animal {
     String name;
     int age = 15;
     Dog (String category, String name) {
         super(category);
         this.name = name;
     }
}

class InstanceOfDemo  {
    public static void main(String[] args)  {
        // Creating some instances of different classes
        Person p = new Person("John");
        Animal a = new Animal("Aquatic");
        Dog d = new Dog("Land", "Tom");
        Animal c = new Dog("Pet", "Jim");
        Person x = null;
        Boolean test;

        // A simple case

        test = p instanceof Person;     // Return true
        System.out.println("Is p instance of Person?" +
          test);
```

```
        test = d instanceof Dog;          // Return true
        System.out.println("Is d instance of Dog?" +
          test);

        test = a instanceof Animal;       // Return true
        System.out.println("Is d instance of Animal?" +
          test);
        test = c instanceof Animal;       // Return true
        System.out.println("Is c instance of Dog?" +
          test);

        test = x instanceof Person;
          //Return false: Null object cannot be
        System.out.println("Is x instance of Person?" +
          test);

        test = d instanceof Object;  // Return true:
          Object is super class
        System.out.println("Is d instance of Object?" +
          test);
    }
}
```

- Any object of any class is an instance of the class `Object`.
- The method `instanceof()` returns false for an object with null reference.
- A parent object is not an instance of any of its sub class.
- A parent object referring to a child class is an instance of the child class's object.

The reference variable of a super class is capable of holding its own object's reference as well as its child object's reference. Thus:

```
Animal a1, a2;
a1 = a2;
Dog d;
a1 = d;
```

You can access a reference of parent type element through an object reference to a child object. Thus, the following is valid:

```
Animal a;        // Reference to a parent class
Dog d = new Dog("Land", "Tom");   // An instance of type Dog
a = d;
System.out.println(a.m);    // Access parent's member's m
System.out.println(d.m);  // Access child's member's m
```

You can access a child data member through the reference of parent's object if you do the type casting:

```
Animal a;        // Reference to a parent class
Dog d = new Dog("Land", "Tom");   // An instance of type Dog
a = (Dog) d;
System.out.println(a.m);    // Access child's member's m
```

When we do type casting, it is always a good idea to check if the typecasting is valid or not. The `instanceof` operator helps you here. You should always first check for validity using `instanceof`, then do type casting. The syntax for type casting is as follows:

```
<parentRef>  = (<ChildClass>)<childRef>;
```

This is also called *down* type casting. Such a type casting ensures that you access the members (both non-method and method) of the child class.

Program 9.44 illustrates an example of type casting in a simple program.

Program 9.44 *(Illustration of* `instanceof` *operator)*

```
/* This program shoes how you can do type casting in a
program. */

interface I{
    public void iMethod();
}

class A implements I {
  public void iMethod(){
       System.out.println("Hi A!");}
  }
class B implements I{
  public void iMethod(){
       System.out.println("Hi B!");}
  }

class CallClass {
  void call(I i) {      // Call with upper type
```

```
        if(i instanceof A){
             A a =(A)i;        // Down type casting I to B
             a.iMethod();
                  // Access the method defined class A
        }

        if(i instanceof B){
             B b =(B)i;        // Down type casting
             b.iMethod();
                  // Access the method defined in class B
        }
  }
} //End of Call class

class TypeCastingDemo{
  public static void main(String args[]){
          CallClass c = new CallClass();
          I i = new A();
          c.call(i);

          I j = new B();
          c.call(j);
  }
}
```

Run-time type compatibility testing in generic programming

Now, let us understand how type casting matters in generic programming. Program 9.45 shows some type compatibility implications in generic programming.

Program 9.45 *(Illustration of type compatibility in generic programming)*

```
/* This program inspects how different objects are
compatible to each other when they are instantiated
with different classes in a generic class hierarchy. */

class GenericSuper<T> {
    T t;
    String iAm = "Parent";
    GenericSupet(T t) {
        this.t  = t;
    }
    public void print()  {
       System.out.println(iAm + t);
```

```
    }
}

// Defining a sub class of GenericSuper<T>.
class GenericSub<T> extends GenericSuper<T> {
    String iAm = "Child";
    GenericSub(T t) {
        super(t);
    }
public void print()  {
        System.out.println(t + " from " + iAm);
    }
}

// The main class demonstrating instance of checking of
                                              // objects
class GenericInstanceOfDemo {
  public static void main(String args[]) {
    // Create objects for parent and child classes.
    GenericSuper<Integer> intP = new GenericSuper
          <Integer>(1985);
    GenericSuper<String> strP = new GenericSuer
          <String>("Ada");
    GenericSub<Integer> intC = new GenericSub
          <Integer>(2020);
    GenericSub<String> strC = new GenericSub
          <String>("Java");

    Boolean test;

    // Checking Upward compatibility...
    // Testing if intC is some form of GenericSuper and
                                              // GenericSub
    test = intC instanceof GenericSuper<?>;
    System.out.println("Is intC is instance of
          GenericSuper? " + test);
    test = intC instanceof GenericSub<?>;
    System.out.println("Is intC is instance of
          GenericSub? " + test);
    System.out.println();

    // Testing if strC is some form of GenericSuper and
                                              // GenericSub
    test = strC instanceof GenericSuper<?>;
    System.out.println("Is strC is instance of
     GenericSuper? " + test);
```

```
    test = strC instanceof GenericSub<?>;
    System.out.println("Is strC is instance of
          GenericSub? " + test);
    System.out.println();

    // Checking Downward compatibility...
    // Testing if intP is some form of GenericSuper and
                                          // GenericSub
    test = intP instanceof GenericSuper<?>;
    System.out.println("Is intP is instance of
          GenericSuper? " + test);
    test = intP instanceof GenericSub<?>;
    System.out.println("Is intP is instance of
          GenericSub? " + test);
    System.out.println();

    // Testing if strP is some form of GenericSuper and
                                          // GenericSub
    test = strP instanceof GenericSuper<?>;
    System.out.println("Is strP is instance of
          GenericSuper? " + test);
    test = strP instanceof GenericSub<?>;
    System.out.println("Is strP is instance of
          GenericSub? " + test);
    System.out.println();

    /*
     * The following code cannot be compiled as generic
     * type information does not exist at run time.
    // test = intC instanceof GenericSub<Integer>);
     */
    }
}
```

- The use of the wildcard enables `instanceof` to determine if an object is compatible with an object of any type of a given class.
- The results show that `intC` (a child object) is an instance of both super and child classes. The same is true for `strC`.
    - *A child class object is always compatible with an object of its parent class of any type as well as objects of any type of its own class.*
- The results show that `intP` (a child object) is not an instance of its sub class. The same is true for `strP`.

- *A parent class object is **not** compatible with an object of any type of its child class and for obvious reasons a parent class object is compatible with objects of any type of its own class.*

- You can cast one instance of a generic class into another only if the two are otherwise compatible and their type arguments are the same. For example:

```
GenericSuper<Integer> x = <GenericSub<Integer>)intC;
     // Legal
GenericSuper<Integer> y = <GenericSub<Long>)intC;
     // Illegal
```

9.5.8 Some Restrictions in Generic Programming

There are some restrictions you should keep in mind while you work with generic programming. A few important restrictions are listed here and discussed in the subsequent subsections:

- Instantiation of type parameters
- Use of static members
- Use of generic arrays
- Generic exceptions
- Ambiguity errors

Instantiation of type parameters

You cannot create an instance of a type parameter. If you do so, it will result in compile-time error. For example:

```
    T x = new T();          // Illegal:  Compile-time error
```

In a program the instantiation of an object with a type parameter is illegal, because the compiler does not know what type of object to create. In a generic program, a type parameter like `T` acts like a simple placeholder, not an actual type. To create an object, you should specify an actual type or class.

```
ClassName<Integer> x = new ClassName<Number>;      // Legal
```

Use of static members in generic class definition

In your definition of a generic class, you cannot declare a member (non-method and method) with static keyword. For example:

```
class GenericClass<T> {
        static T t;   // Illegal: Static variable of type T
                         // cannot be declared
```

```
        static T getob() {                    // Illegal!
              // Body of the method
        }
        static int aMethod() {                // Legal
              // Body of the method
        }
}
```

You cannot declare a method with `static` keyword if it uses a type parameter in its declaration (i.e., return type, argument). However, you can declare methods with `static` keyword without any type parameter involved. This is because a static member is sharable among all instances of that generic class, and it is impossible to share a static member among different instances of different types, for example, `GenericClass<Integer>`, `GenericClass<String>`, etc. This will not be an issue if it is without any type parameter.

Use of generic arrays

When you want to use arrays in your generic program, you should keep restrictions in their uses. Some of these restrictions are:

```
T array[];          // Okay
```

Here, `array` is a reference to an object of type `T`. Java knows at compile-time with the Java `erasure` the type of reference to an array.

However, the following is not valid:

```
array = new T[10];   // Wrong!
```

This is wrong because you cannot create an array of `T` as there is no way for the compiler to know what type of array actually to create.

The following are invalid declarations for an array in generic programming:

```
List<Integer> list[] = new ArrayList<Integer[10];
GC<Strings> names[] = new GC<String>[20];
                           // Here, GC<T> is a generic class
```

You are not allowed to create generic arrays because array carry type information of its elements at run-time. If elements type does not match to the defined type then it throws `ArrayStoreException` at run-time. Since generics type information gets erased at compile-time by type `erasure`, the array store check would have been passed where it should have failed.

In contrast, you *can* create an array of references to a generic type if you use a wildcard, as shown here:

```
GC<?> array[] = new GC<?>[10];   // Okay
```

This approach is better than using an array of raw types, because at least some type checking will still be enforced.

Generic sub-typing

Generics doesn't support sub-typing, so the following will not compile:

```
List<Number> numbers = new ArrayList<Integer>();
```

Generics does not support sub-typing. This is because sub-typing causes issues in achieving type safety. That is why `List<T>` is not considered as a sub type of `List<S>`, where `S` is the super type of `T`. To understanding why it is not allowed, let us see what could have happened if it has been supported:

```
List<Long> list1 = new ArrayList<Long>();
list.add(Long.valueOf(10));
List<Number> list2 = list1;// Assume no compiler-error
List2.add(Double.valueOf(1.23));
```

From this code, you can see that if generics would have been supporting sub-typing, we could have easily added a `Double` to the list of `Long`; that would have caused `ClassCastException` at run-time while traversing the list of `Long`.

Generic exceptions

A generic class cannot extend `Throwable`. This means that you cannot create generic exception classes.

Java ambiguity errors

There are some peculiar situations which even the compiler cannot detect. To understand such a situation, let us consider the following definition of a generic class:

```
class GenericClass<T, V> {
     T t;
     V v;
     GenericClass(T t, V v) {
          this.t = t;
          this.v = v;
     }
```

```
        void print(T t) {
            System.out.println(t);
        }

        void print(V v) {
            System.out.println(v);
        }
}
```

In this generic class definition, two overloaded methods have been defined. This seems acceptable as `T` and `V` appear to be different types. However, there are two ambiguity problems here:

Ambiguity 1

The `GenericClass <T, V>` definition can be used to create many instances, for example:

```
GenericClass<Integer, String> x = new ...
GenericClass<String, String> z = new ...
GenericClass<Integer, Integer> y = new ...
```

The last two are ambiguous. This is because these two make both version of `print()` identical, causing an error.

Ambiguity 2

Ambiguity errors occur when erasure causes two seemingly distinct generic declarations to resolve to the same erased type, causing a conflict. In the previous example, the type erasure of `print()` reduces both versions to the following:

```
void print(Object o) {
            System.out.println(o);
        }

        void print(Object o) {
            System.out.println(o);
        }
```

Thus, the overloading of `print()` as done in `GenericClass` is ambiguous.

Such an ambiguity error is tedious to fix. This ambiguity error is a kind of conceptual error, and even the compiler cannot find it.

Summary

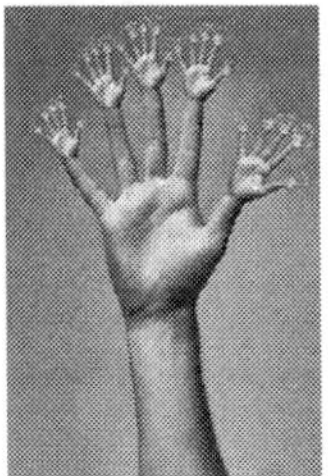

Generic programming is an interesting topic in Java. This chapter covers the different features of generic programming in Java. To make the discussion appealing, how a method can be made generic is discussed first. Next, how a generic method that takes variable number of arguments can be declared is covered. Then the concept of generic class and its importance is illustrated. The syntax of declaring a class generic is discussed with an illustration. How a generic class can be defined with multiple number of type parameters is also covered. There are certain issues while working with generic classes. One important issue is bounding type parameter. The mechanisms of bounding a type parameter with a single bound as well as multiple bounds are discussed. Wildcard is an advanced feature of generic programming. The concepts of wildcard in generic programming, bounded wildcard arguments, and applications of wildcards are discussed with a number of illustrations. Some applications like implementations of generic arrays, linked lists, and stack data structures are given. These applications give practical examples of applying generic programming to real-life applications. Some intricate things in generic facility, such as type inference, code compatibility, type erasure, type casting, generic constructors, generic interfaces, generic inheritance, etc., are covered in detail. Some restrictions that a programmer should be aware of when working with generic programming are included at the end of the chapter.

FAQs

9.1 What is a generic type parameter?
9.2 Why do we use generics in Java?
9.3 What is `T` in generics?
9.4 How does generics work in Java?
9.5 What is type erasure?
9.6 What is type inference?
9.7 What is a bounded type parameter?
9.8 What is a wildcard type?
9.9 What is the difference between `List<? extends T>` *and* `List <? super T>`?
9.10 How are the generic class and simple class the same or different?

The answers to these questions and other problems in this chapter are available at www.cambridge.org/9781009211918. You might have many questions like these. You can post your question in the discussion forum at https://cse.iitkgp.ac.in/~dsamanta/joywithjava/page8.php.

Programs for Practice

9.1 Define a class hierarchy as shown in the following figure. For each class define methods for measuring different items like, length, area, perimeter, volume, etc. Implement the class with generic programming. Use different classes to solve applications, like for a collection of geometric objects, to calculate total area occupied, the volume of the collection of objects, sorting object according to some measurement(s), starching an object in the collection of objects, etc.

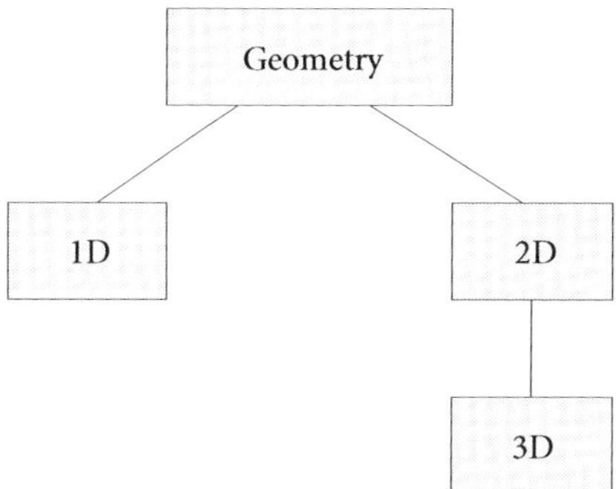

Figure Problem 9.1

9.2 Consider the following method that counts the number of elements in an array `T[]` that are greater than a specified element x, x is given as input.

```
public static <T> int countGreaterThan(T[] anArray, T elem) {
    int count = 0;
    for (T e : anArray)
        if (e > x)
            ++count;
    return count;
}
```

What is wrong with this program?
Hint: The program does not compile because the greater than operator (>) applies only to primitive types such as `short`, `int`, `double`, `long`, `float`, `byte`, and `char`. You cannot use the > operator to compare objects. To fix the problem, use a type parameter bounded by the `Comparable<T>` interface.

9.3 Define a generic class, say `GenericSort<T>`, which will sort objects of any type in an order. For example, you can sort a collection of user defined objects of type Book, Person, Circles, etc. Also, this class with sort numbers of type integer, float, double, and String objects.

9.4 Extend the program in the Problem 9.3 with a generic class, say `GenericSearch<T>`, which will search an object from a collection of objects of any type.

9.5 Define a generic class to realize a double linked list which can store any type of data in it and perform operations like insert, delete, traverse, search, sort, reverse, merge, etc.

9.6 Extend the problem in Program 9.5 to implement a queue data structure which allows to insert at one end and delete at the other end of a double linked list.

9.7 A binary search tree is tree data structure which can store data of any type. Define a generic class to implement a binary search tree. Your generic class definition should include all operations on the binary search tree such as insert, delete, traverse, search, sort, etc.

9.8 A graph is another data structures used in many real-life applications, such as transportation network, airline connectivity, etc. Define a generic class for graph data structures and implement some graph to solve algorithms like the shortest path from a source node to a destination node, traversing a graph, insertion/ deletion of a node, minimum spanning tree calculation, etc.

Hint: You can use a single linked list structure to define your graph structure.

9.9 What will happen to the following program?

```
public class Box<T> {
    private T t;
    public void set(T t) {
        this.t = t;
    }
    public T get() {
        return t;
    }
    public <U extends Number> void inspect(U u){
        System.out.println("T: " + t.getClass().getName());
        System.out.println("U: " + u.getClass().getName());
    }
    public static void main(String[] args) {
        Box<Integer> integerBox = new Box<Integer>();
        integerBox.set(new Integer(10));
        integerBox.inspect("Some text");
    }
}
```

If program does not compile/run, make the necessary modifications to make it executable.

9.10 What is the following program doing?

```
import java.util.*;
abstract class Shape{          // Defining an abstract class
      abstract void draw();
}
class Rectangle extends Shape{
    void draw(){System.out.println("The shape is rectangle.");}
}
class Circle extends Shape{
     void draw(){System.out.println("The shape is circle");}
}
class WildcardTest {
   public static void drawShapes(List<? extends Shape> lists){
     for(Shape s:lists){
          s.draw();
     }
   }
```

```
    public static void main(String args[]){
          List<Rectangle> list1=new ArrayList<Rectangle>();
          list1.add(new Rectangle());

          List<Circle> list2=new ArrayList<Circle>();
          list2.add(new Circle());
          list2.add(new Circle());

          drawShapes(list1);
          drawShapes(list2);
    }
  }
```

9.11 What is the following program doing?

```
import java.util.ArrayList;
import java.util.List;

public class GenericsTester {

class Animal {                          // Super class
   String name;
   Animal(String name) {
      this.name = name;
   }
   public String toString() {
      return name;
   }
}

class Cat extends Animal {               // Child class of Animal
   Cat(String name) {
      super(name);
   }
}

class RedCat extends Cat {
   RedCat(String name) {
      super(name);
   }
}

class Dog extends Animal {
   Dog(String name) {
      super(name);
   }
}

   //Upper bound wildcard
   public static void deleteCat(List<? extends Cat> catList,
        Cat cat) {
```

```
        catList.remove(cat);
        System.out.println("Cat Removed");
    }

    //Lower bound wildcard
    public static void addCat(List<? super RedCat> catList) {
        catList.add(new RedCat("Red Cat"));
        System.out.println("Cat Added");
    }

    //Unbounded wildcard
    //Using Object method toString()
    public static void printAll(List<?> list) {
        for (Object item : list)
            System.out.println(item + " ");
    }

    public static void main(String[] args) {

        List<Animal> animalList= new ArrayList<Animal>();
        List<RedCat> redCatList= new ArrayList<RedCat>();

        //add list of super class Animal of Cat class
        addCat(animalList);
        //add list of Cat class
        addCat(redCatList);
        addCat(redCatList);

        //print all animals
        printAll(animalList);
        printAll(redCatList);

        Cat cat = redCatList.get(0);
        //delete cat
        deleteCat(redCatList, cat);
        printAll(redCatList);
    }
}
```

MCQs

9.1 Suppose, there are *n* different types of data to be processed for which *m* different algorithms are known. Then the number of programs which may be implemented with simple programming (i.e., an individual program for a specific type of data) versus generic programming (that is, one program for any type of data) are:

(a) Simple programming = n*m, generic programming = m
(b) Simple programming = n + m, generic programming = n
(c) Simple programming = m, generic programming = n*m
(d) Simple programming = n*m, generic programming = n + m

9.2 **Which of the following statement is true?**
(a) Generic method can neither be overloaded nor overridden.
(b) Both generic method and method overloading are parameterized polymorphism.
(c) Generic method does not require code duplication.
(d) Method overloading does not require code duplication.

9.3 **Which of the following methods is (are) NOT varargs generic method?**
(a) `println()` (b) `printf()` (c) `scanf()` (d) `main()`

9.4 **Which of the following statement(s) is (are) *not* true?**
(a) Bounded type parameters can be used in the context of defining a generic method as well as a generic class.
(b) Bounded type parameters can be used to define a generic interface.
(c) If you want to specify an interface `A` to parameterize a type, say `T`, then you should use `T extends A`.
(d) If you want to specify an interface `A` to parameterize a type, say `T`, then you should use `T implements A`.

9.5 **Check the following program, whose objective is to find the largest among three elements:**

```
public class MaximumTest {
   public static <T extends Comparable<T>> T maximum(T x, T y, T
         z) {
         T max = x;    // Assume x is initially the largest
         if(y.compareTo(max) > 0) {
              max = y;    // y is the largest so far
      }
      if(z.compareTo(max) > 0) {
         max = z;    // z is the largest now
      }
      return max;    // returns the largest object
   }

   public static void main(String args[]) {
      // Test #1:
      System.out.printf("Max of %d, %d and %d is %d\n\n", 3, 4, 5,
                                                maximum( 3, 4, 5 ));
      //Test #2:
      System.out.printf("Max of %.1f,%.1f and %.1f is %.
        1f\n\n", 6.6,
                                   8.8, 7.7, maximum( 6.6, 8.8, 7.7 ));
      //Test #3:

      System.out.printf("Max of %s, %s and %s is %s\n","Apple",
         "Onion", "Potato", maximum("Apple", "Onion", "Orange"));
   }
}
```

Which of the following is true for this program?

(a) The program will give correct results for all three test cases.
(b) The program will give a compile-time error for the Test Case #3.
(c) The `compareTo()` method is undefined for the defined parameterized generic method.
(d) The same program can be used to compare any three objects of user-defined class.

9.6 Which of the following is valid to create an object of a generic class, say **`GenericClass<T>`**?

(a) `GenericClass<int> = new GenericClass<int>(123);`
(b) `GenericClass<String> = new GenericClass<String>(123);`
(c) `GenericClass<Integer> = new GenericClass<Integer>("Welcome");`
(d) `GenericClass<String> = new GenericClass<>("Welcome");`

9.7 Consider the program:

```
class A {
    int value = 1000;
    A()
    {
        System.out.print("Super class A >> ");
    }
}

class B extends A {
    int value = 10;
    B() {
        System.out.print("Sub class B >> ");
    }
}

class TestResult {
    public static void main(String[] args) {
        B b = new B();
        System.out.println("Value :" + b.value);

        A a1 = new B();
        System.out.println("Value :" + a1.value);

        A a2 = b;
        System.out.println("Value :" + a2.value);

        A a3 = (B) b;   // Down type casting
        System.out.println("Value :" + a3.value);
    }
}
```

What will the following program print?

(a) Sub class B >> Value 10
Sub class B >> Value 10
Super class A >> Value 1000
Super class A >> Value 10

(b) Sub class B >> Value 10
Sub class B >> Value 1000
Super class A >> Value 10
Super class A >> Value 1000

(c) Sub class B >> Value 10
Sub class B >> Value 10
Super class A >> Value 1000
Super class A >> Value 1000

(d) Sub class B >> Value 10
Sub class B >> Value 10
Super class A >> Value 10
Super class A >> Value 10

9.8 Consider the following declaration:

```
class A { }
class B extends A { }
...
A a = new A();
B b = new B();
```

Which of the following is true?

(a) A = (B) b; // Down type casting
(b) B = (A) a; // Up type casting
(c) a = b;
(d) b = a;

9.9 Which of the following statement(s) is(are) valid?

(a) Generic methods allow programmers to declare a single method for a set of related methods and related data types
(b) Function overloading allows programmers to declare a single method for a set of related methods and related data types.
(c) In function overloading, we have to build code for each overloaded method.
(d) In generic methods, we have to build code for each related method.

9.10 What will be the output of the following code snippet?

```
public class DemoClass {
    static void DemoMethod(int ...v) {
       for (int i: v)
            System.out.print(i + &quot; &quot;);
       }
    public static void main(String args[]) {
          DemoMethod(9, 5, 4);
```

```
                DemoMethod();
        }
}
```

(a) Compile-time error (b) 9 5 4
(c) Run-time error (d) 0

9.11 Which of these is wildcard symbol?
(a) ? (b) ! (c) & (d) %

9.12 Which of these keywords is used to declare upper bounded wildcard?
(a) bound (b) extends (c) implement (d) super

9.13 Which of the following keywords are used for lower bounding a wild card?
(a) bound (b) extends (c) implement (d) super

9.14 Which of the following is true?
(a) You can specify both an upper bound and a lower bound for a wild card.
(b) Bounded wildcard argument ensures type safety.
(c) It is allowed to use a wildcard as a type argument for a generic method invocation.
(d) We cannot use a wildcard as a type of a parameter, field, return type, or local variable.

9.15 Consider the following program:

```
public final class Question {
      public static <T>  min(T x, T y) {
           return x < y ? y : x;
      }
}
```

Which of the following statement(s) is(are) true?
(a) Compiler error.
(b) Run-time error.
(c) It will return the minimum of x and y.
(d) It will return the maximum of x and y.

9.16 Which of the following statement(s) is(are) *not* correct?
(a) You cannot instantiate an array whose element type is a type parameter.
(b) In parameter type you can use primitives type like `int`, `char`, `double`, etc.
(c) A class that can refer to any type is known as a generic class.
(d) In parameter type you can use the wrapper class for primitive data types.

9.17 Which of the following syntax(s) is(are) correct for "Bounded wildcard arguments"?
(a) `<type> method2(? extends A) { ... }`
(b) `<type> method1(? super A) { ... }`
(c) `<type>  method3(?) { ... }`
(d) `<type>  method4(A extends A) { ... }`

9.18 **What will be the output of the following Java code?**

```
public class AnyData <T extends Number> {
        // Two field of generic type T is defined below
        private T x;
        // Constructor
        public AnyData(T t) {
        x = t;
        }
        // Print the T-type value for an object
        public void printData() {
              System.out.println (x);
        }
}

class SimpleGenericClassTest {
        public static void main( String args[] ) {
              // A data with the member as String
              AnyData<String> a = new AnyData<String> ("Java");
              a.printData();
              // A data with the member as integer value
              AnyData<Integer> b = new AnyData<Integer> (123);
              b.printData();
              // A data with the member as float value
              AnyData<Double> c = new AnyData<Double> (3.142);
              c.printData();
        }
  }
```

(a) Java
123
3.142
(b) 123
(c) 3.142
(d) Error

9.19 **Which of the following statement(s) is(are) true?**
(a) No class can inherit a generic class.
(b) If a class inherits a generic class, then the sub class is also a generic class.
(c) A generic class cannot be abstract.
(d) It is not possible to define a generic interface.

9.20 **For which of the following reason(s) can you use wildcard in generic programming?**
(a) When you want to specify any class you can use `?` as wildcard just like a template class `T`.
(b) If you want to type cast a template class, then you should use wildcard `?`.
(c) Wildcards can be used when you want to write a method that works on the class where it is defined or any of its sub class.
(d) When you want to limit the call of a method defined in class `A` and its parent classes only, then you can use a lower bound wildcard.

9.21 What will be the output of the following Java code?

```
class VarargsMethod1 {
        static void varargsMethod1(int v[]) {
        System.out.print("Number of args: " + v.length +"
        Elements: ");
        for(int x : v)
        System.out.print(x + " ");
        System.out.println();
        }
        public static void main(String args[]) {
              int x[] = { 1, 3, 5, 7 };
              varargsMethod1 (x);
        }
}
```

(a) Number of args: 4 Elements: 1 3 5 7
(b) Number of args:
(c) Run-time error
(d) Compile-time error

INDEX

Printed in Great Britain
by Amazon